Eastern European Nationalism in the Twentieth Century

Eastern European Nationalism in the Twentieth Century

Peter F. Sugar, Editor

The American University Press

The American University Press
4400 Massachusetts Avenue, NW
Washington, DC 20016

Distributed by arrangement with
University Publishing Associates

4720 Boston Way
Lanham, Maryland 20706

3 Henrietta Street
London, WC2E 8LU England

Printed in the United States of America
British Cataloging in Publication Information Available

Library of Congress Cataloging-in-Publication Data
Eastern European nationalism in the twentieth century / edited by
Peter F. Sugar.
p. cm.
Includes bibliographical references and index.
1. Europe, Eastern—Politics and government—20th century. 2.
Nationalism—Europe, Eastern. I. Sugar, Peter F.
DJK49.E17 1995 320.5'4—dc20 95–4255 CIP

ISBN 1-879383-39-X (cloth: alk: ppr.)
ISBN 1-879383-40-3 (pbk: alk: ppr.)

™The paper used in this publication meets the minimum
requirements of American National Standard for Information
Sciences—Permanence of Paper for Printed Library Materials,
ANSI Z39.48—1984

Contents

1

Introduction

by Peter F. Sugar

Eastern Europe, a label applied to the lands situated between the German- and Italian-speaking region in the west and the Russian-Ukrainian-Belarus region in the east, is a term that is not accepted and is even resented by those who live there. They consider themselves to live geographically in Central Europe or Southeastern Europe and culturally to belong to the West. Yet in the West, they are considered to be Eastern Europeans. As such, they are neglected by scholars and even more by the media and the general public except when events in their lands are sensational or historic enough to warrant coverage on the front page or the network news. This interest in Eastern Europe never lasts very long, and the great majority of those presenting the news and an even larger percentage of those reading or listening to it have great difficulty placing the people involved in a geographic or historical context. During the cold war, this neglect of the more than 130 million people who live in the region became even worse: they were considered nothing more than satellites of the Soviet Union, incapable of deciding their own fate just as they had been in the earlier part of the century when they followed Germany's lead.

The end of the cold war, the collapse both of the Soviet Union and of Communist parties around the globe, and the end of Communist rule in Eastern Europe and the former Soviet empire spurred a deeper and more prolonged interest in these people and countries, and it was this interest that prompted this volume. This book is not designed for experts, but for those who would like to know why the people of this region behave as they do since gaining their independence, and why nationalism has replaced communism as the major force dictating their behavior.

As editor, in trying to organize this volume in order to best serve the intended audience, I had to make a few basic decisions. The first concerned at what time in history the volume should begin. The focus is on nationalism, an ideology which in its "modern" form first appeared in Eastern Europe in the late eighteenth and nineteenth centuries and acquired an important and often dominant role by the second half of the nineteenth century. On one hand, covering roughly two centuries would have made the tome much too long and unwieldy, and developments during much of the previous two centuries could be omitted. On the other hand, dealing only with the last few years—say, since 1980 when Marshal Tito died and Mikhail Gorbachev came to power—would have tackled the issues *in medias res,* defeating the purpose of the work. What had to be shown was the constant role nationalism played in the self-identification of people in the region and in how they were viewed by others, even under Communist rule. These considerations led me to decide to deal only with the twentieth century.

The second decision that had to be made was how best to show the constant role of nationalism in dictating the behavior of a great variety of different people during a period of roughly a hundred years. Having "country experts" say so seemed insufficient; the people of Eastern Europe had to be allowed to speak for themselves. Fortunately, they had done that in various forms and at great length, and it was decided to share these self-expressions in the form of "documents." To give these—and the entire work—a certain unity, the documents had to cover roughly equal and historically distinct periods. These were not difficult to determine: the years before World War I, the "long armistice" between the two World Wars, the long decades of Communist domination, and finally the post-Communist period.

The final decision that had to be made concerned the length of the work. If it included documents as well as essays that explained the documents and did not shortchange the voices of the people of Eastern Europe, then the volume would have to be longer than most. Fortunately, from the beginning we were able to work with a publisher that understood what was needed. It was decided to deal with nations not with countries, and to give each nation the same coverage as far as possible, which is why the multi-nation chapters are longer than those that deal with only one people.

I have always been interested in Eastern Europe but have never specialized in the history of a given people or country, and so having answered all the basic questions, my next task was to find country specialists to write the various chapters. I was fortunate to secure the collaboration of a group comprised of both well-established and younger scholars. Within the framework of the agreed length for each chapter, the authors were given a free hand: they selected the documents and decided how much emphasis to give to these and to their essays. Some documents are short because they clearly illustrate the point for which the author selected them. Others are longer either to make their meaning clear or because of their historical importance (a good example is the 1986 memorandum by the Serbian Academy of Science and Arts on "The Situation of Serbia and the Serb Nation" reproduced in chapter 9).

What follows is a short and consequently sketchy history of the development of Eastern European nationalism prior to the present century, designed to serve as background for the story to be told in the following pages.

Historical Background

Historians of the peoples of Eastern Europe commonly stress that these peoples historically have been unified, self-conscious of their identity, and always striving to achieve self-determination and self-rule within their ethnic and historical borders. These historians do this by endowing their recent and not-so-recent forebears with nationalistic actions and thoughts roughly a millennium before nationalism actually made its appearance. Over roughly the last two centuries, this approach had its political utility, even if it was historically incorrect. Human beings always have differentiated between *we* and *they* for a variety of reasons. "We" could mean a small unit such as the family, or a large group such as a clan or tribe which, according to Hugh Seton-Watson, could and should be called a nation.[1] These peoples might have comprised nations, but they were not nationalists.[2] The terms "homeland" and "borders" were not clear or well-defined concepts until fairly recently, and for long periods their meanings were changeable. The "we" group has been defined and kept together by numerous factors, including a deity or cluster of them, a belief in a common ancestor (often fictitious), a leading family of special status, dietary habits, or a common language, among many others.

For example, when the people of the Balkans first inhabited the peninsula, their major loyalties were directed either to a leading family or to deities. This was also true of other European people, for whom language, while important, was not basic. The Bulgarians became speakers of a Slavic tongue, and the

---

1 Hugh Seton-Watson, *Nations and States* (Boulder, CO: Westview Press, 1977), 4–5.

2 See, among others, John A. Armstrong, *Nations before Nationalism* (Chapel Hill: University of North Carolina Press, 1982); Ernest Gellner, *Nations and Nationalism* (Ithaca, NY: Cornell University Press, 1983); and Anthony D. Smith, *The Ethnic Origin of Nations* (New York: Basil Blackwell, 1986).

Dacians became Romanians speaking a Latin language. The leaders of these groups often were multilingual. As an example, members of one family considered to be national heroes by Hungarians and Croatians alike signed their names interchangeably as Zrinski (Croatian), Zrínyi (Hungarian), or Zrinius (Latin).

Present-day national claims and pretensions find little justification in either territorial or historical continuity. For example, neither Račka and Zeta, the early Serb states, was located in the bounds of present-day Serbia. One theory that describes the Romanian people as descendants of both the people of Dacia and the Romans leaves a gap of several centuries in Romanian history, from the year 270, when the Romans gave up the province of Dacia, until 1330, when Besarab established Wallachia, and 1359, when Bogdan established Moldavia.

The Albanians claim that they are direct descendants of the classical Illyrians. If this is correct, they are the only original inhabitants of Eastern Europe who still live there. The territory and affiliation of most other peoples of the region have shifted over time. "The original home of the Greeks was probably in the Danube region. They...gradually filtered into the Greek Peninsula from about 2000 B.C. on...."[3] Despite their different dialects, they were one people who differentiated themselves from the "barbarians" around them, but it was not until the Macedonian conquest in 338 B.C. that there was a united Greek state. The first Slavs in the region, the Slovenes, came in the sixth century A.D., with the Serbs and Croats coming roughly 100 years later.[4] Turkish-speaking Bulgarians date their arrival at 681 A.D. The Slovene area was conquered by Charlemagne at the turn of the eighth century and thus became part of Western Christianity. The Croat state, which was on the border between Western and Eastern Christianity, ultimately joined the Western church, but other inhabitants of the Balkans became Orthodox Christians, living either in independent states or under Byzantine rule until the Ottoman conquest of their lands, which began in 1354 and was completed in 1453. Ottoman rule lasted some five centuries, during which the Romanian Principalities became a vassal state of the sultans, while certain regions in the Morea and some of the Aegean islands retained self-rule. (During the last two centuries of Ottoman rule, the

---

3 Albert A. Trevel, *History of Ancient Civilization* (New York: Harcourt, Brace & Co., 1936), 146.

4 Francis Dvornik, *Slavs in European History and Civilization* (New Brunswick, NJ: Rutgers University Press, 1962), 2ff; John V. A. Fine, Jr., *The Early Medieval Balkans* (Ann Arbor: University of Michigan Press, 1983), chapter 2.

Greek Phanariotes practically became co-rulers with the masters of the Sublime Porte.[5]

The Finno-Ugric Hungarians (Magyars) date their conquest of present-day Hungary at 896. In establishing their new homeland, they destroyed the Greater Moravian state where a Western Slav people lived in what is now Slovakia and Southern Moravia. Under their first king, St. Steven (997–1038), the Hungarians conquered and annexed Transylvania (1003). The Hungarian conquest of Greater Moravia shifted the center of what remained of this state to Prague, where a native Czech dynasty, the Přemyslids (1197–1306), established their rule. The Hungarians, Moravians, and Czechs accepted Western Christianity. With the marriage of a Czech princess to Mieszko I, the first ruler of the Polish Piast dynasty (960–1370), and his acceptance of Western Christianity, Hungary, the Czech and Slovak lands, and Poland—in what we have called the "northern tier" of Eastern Europe—became solidly oriented toward Western Europe. The religious division between Western and Eastern Christianity that had occurred in the Balkans became a problem when Poland expanded, both peacefully and by conquest, to areas inhabited by Lithuanians, Ukrainians, and White Russians.[6]

No definition of "nationalism" covers all aspects of its manifestation, nor has any gained general acceptance.[7] Nationalism developed first in the most rapidly progressing area of the modern world, Western Europe, where in the eighteenth century, after various wars of religion and dynastic struggles—the prime loyalties capable of mobilizing the masses—a new force began to claim people's allegiance. Without going into detail, a number of historical developments combined to produce nationalism: the improvement of short- and long-distance communications; the voyages of discovery and the resulting economic revolutions and competitions which led to mercantilism; the demand of rapidly expanding and economically more dominant urban populations for political rights commensurate with their wealth and status; the scientific revolution which weakened the power of the conservative clergy; and, finally, the

---

[5] Barbara Jelavich, *History of the Balkans: Eighteenth and Nineteenth Centuries* (New York: Cambridge University Press, 1984), 53–57, 102–105, 106–110.

[6] Dvornik, *Slavs in European History and Civilization,* chapters 1 and 2; and Peter F. Sugar, Peter Hanak, and Tibor Frank, eds., *A History of Hungary* (Bloomington: Indiana University Press, 1990), chapters 2–3.

[7] In *Encyclopedia of Nationalism* (New York: Paragon House, 1990), Louis L. Snyder spends several pages and uses several headings trying to define nationalism (pp. 240–51).

new political theories of Locke, Rousseau, Montesquieu, and other Enlightenment thinkers. The result of these dramatic changes was a new emphasis on the value of the individual and on the community to which the individual voluntarily transferred some of his rights, the nation. This, in turn, produced nationalism, an expression of the claims and demands made in the name of the nation. Before the advent of nationalism, society had been organized according to estate, class, profession, language, and religion; these were superseded by a new distinction, the nation. Membership in a nation was defined primarily on political rather than ethnic lines, which allowed the formation of multi-ethnic states, but also opened the possibility of ethnic conflict in some political entities that had not faced such problems previously.

The Balkans

Friendly cohabitation among various ethnic groups was not typical of the Balkans before the Ottoman conquest of the fourteenth century. Local lords opposed Byzantine rule and fought against Venice and Hungary when these states tried to extend their rule into the Balkans over nearly 1,000 years. When a local lord managed to create a state of his own, free from foreign rule, he too was resisted. The Balkans also were home to a number of religious witch-hunts and wide persecution of alleged heretics. The arrival of the Ottomans after 1354 put an end to these local conflicts and brought roughly 200 years of peace. Looking to the clashes that predated the Ottomans' arrival for the roots of "historic hatreds" among the people is a patently invalid exercise, regardless of how many people may try to convince us otherwise. When Ottoman rule became corrupt and inefficient, the people of the Balkans revolted, and those who did are presented by Balkan historians as heroes who rewaked the various nations and charted the course to independence. This too is incorrect. So-called *âyans,* who were able to establish short-lived states within the state, were almost always Muslims willing to work with and arm anybody ready to follow them. *Hajduks, Klephts, Martalose, Morlaks, Uskoks,* and others roamed rather limited and often inaccessible regions, acting like so many Robin Hoods, and while they were indeed members of the local population and spoke the language of their regions, to think of these illiterates as nationalistic freedom fighters is patently ridiculous, despite the fact that they are often presented in this light.[8]

---

[8] Peter F. Sugar, *Southeastern Europe under Ottoman Rule, 1354–1804* (Seattle: University of Washington Press, 1977), chapter 11.

The "Northern Tier"

The Ottoman advance into the "northern tier" of Eastern Europe affected only the Hungarians and Transylvanians. The Ottomans defeated the Hungarian forces at Mohács in 1526, and the subsequent division of the country into three parts—a division that stood for 150 years—had lasting results. The western part of the country was ruled by the Habsburg dynasty, which extended its rule over the rest of Hungary-Transylvania in 1699, an area that served as a buffer between the Habsburgs' other possessions and the Ottomans and suffered under constant warfare. The central plains fell under Ottoman rule and underwent heavy ethnographic and ecological damage. After 1699 the Habsburgs tried to repopulate this central region basically by making the state multi-ethnic for the first time. The ecological damage was only slowly redressed, with some of the damage lingering into the present. Transylvania, in the east, was nominally a vassal state subject to the sultan. In fact, however, it was ruled independently from 1526 to 1699 by princes. These rulers were Hungarian magnates who ruled with the help of people who retained the privileges they had acquired from Hungary's kings: the nobility, the German settlers, and the Székelys (people used as borderguards). These people belonged to the various Western Christian churches and gave no political or religious rights to the Romanian-speaking, Orthodox Christian peasant masses. In this respect, Transylvania resembled the Balkans. Also like the Balkans, Transylvania suffered repeated Ottoman raids.[9]

Unlike the Balkans, the northern tier was dominated by a nobility. This was true of the "Lands of St. Wenceslas's Crown"—Bohemia, Moravia, Silesia, and Poland-Lithuania—as well as the "Lands of St. Steven's Crown"—Hungary, Transylvania, and Croatia. Nobles—rich or poor, Catholic or Protestant—were the "nation" in the latter three major political units. They were free individuals and the only group with political rights. This is extremely important to a discussion of the origin of nationalism: while the rights and privileges of the nobility were basically the same as those enjoyed by the "estates" in Western Europe, when they had to be defended it was not against the actions of "national" rulers, but rather against those of "foreign princes." The national *we,* limited as it was to the political nation, fought the foreign *they* who ruled or tried to rule over the nation. In Hungary and the Czech lands the "foreign" rulers were the Habsburgs; in Poland-Lithuania they included the rulers of Prussia/ Germany, Russia, Saxony, and Sweden. This explains why Hungarian Catholic

---

9 John F. Cadzon, Andrew Ludanyi, Louis J. Elteto, eds., *Transylvania: The Root of Ethnic Conflict* (Kent, OH: Kent State University, 1983), part I; and Sugar, Hanak, and Frank, *A History of Hungary,* chapter 7.

nobles fought for the religious rights of their Protestant brethren and why German-speaking nobles, who were originally foreigners in Czech lands, became champions of Bohemian State Rights *(Böhmisches Staatsrecht)*. The noble families in these predominantly Roman Catholic lands controlled most of the wealth of their own and of the church's landed estates, which represented the overwhelming proportion of the national wealth because cities were small and economically insignificant. It is easy to understand, therefore, why the role of the nobility became paramount in transforming medieval states into modern nations.

The Arrival of Nationalism

The roots of today's problems—the inability of the various nations living in the Balkans to cooperate and the so-called historical hatred that separates them—can be found in the arrival of nationalism and in modern interpretations of historical events. In Central and Eastern Europe the character of nationalism changed according to local conditions: the farther an area was from the lands in which nationalism developed, the less its nationalism resembled the original model. Even basic expressions of nationalism such as a constitution, freedom, or republic acquired different meanings in more eastern areas of Europe. This is anything but surprising. People who grew up in the Orthodox world and were not affected by the major cultural, religious, and political movements that transformed the Western Christian world—such as the scientific revolution, Renaissance, Reformation, or Enlightenment—or by the drastic economic and societal changes that accompanied them, were bound to attach different meanings to the concepts of nationalism. This was particularly the case for people in the Balkans who had lived under Muslim rule for centuries.

New concepts and ideas could be discovered and transmitted only by literate people. Most people in the Balkans read neither French nor English, and they got their new knowledge secondhand through German or Russian translations. This fact makes the accomplishment of Father Paiisi (1722–1798), namely, his writing of *Slavo-Bulgarian History* in 1762, even more remarkable. He worked in a monastery on Mount Athos with no access to the major Western authors of the eighteenth century, yet his work shows him to be a nationalist in the modern sense. Clergymen were important everywhere because they were literate. Equally important were businessmen, who were not only literate, but who came into contact with a great variety of people through their work. This gave the Greeks a double advantage: Greek was the language of the Orthodox Church under Ottoman rule; and Greek Phanariotes not only controlled the most successful international business network but also occupied important ecclesiastical positions, conducted foreign affairs at the Sublime Porte, and after 1711, served as hospodars in Moldavia and Wallachia. These same Phanariotes, who also served some foreign courts, were the first truly well-educated people in the contemporary European sense.

Clergymen and businessmen were the first in the Balkans to speak of nations and nationalism in the modern sense. For example, the first anti-Ottoman revolt, by the Serbs, was led by illiterate *knezes,* who were leaders of their communities and almost always were also successful businessmen. This is true of the leaders of the first phase (1804–1813) and second phase (1814–1815) of this revolt, George Karadjordje (1752–1817) and Miloš Obrenović, respectively. The intellectual and diplomatic leaders of these revolts were Serbs who had come from the north (today's Vojvodina), crossing into territory that later became part of Serbia. There, the Serb Metropolitanate of Karlovci maintained schools and seminaries, and in 1792 Serb leaders, who were then living under Habsburg rule, held an important political meeting to voice relatively modern political ideas.[10]

The Slovenes and parts of Dalmatia and Croatia received a large dose of Western influence at about the time the Serbs were fighting the Ottomans: from 1809 until the defeat of Napoleon, these lands were united into the province of Illyria and integrated into France. The introduction of French institutions and laws had lasting effects. This, along with the rather localized nature of the Serb revolt, increased the existing differences between these two regions. Miloš Obrenović, the first ruler of modern Serbia, earned the sobriquet of the Christian pasha because he ruled like one (as did some of his successors). In the Illyrian province, the so-called Illyrian movement emerged, which was the first movement to consider all Southern Slavs to be part of one nation and to push for their unification into a single state. Its main theoretician, Ljudevit Gaj (1809–1872), spoke of a realm stretching from Villlach to Varna. Gaj was a Slovene, but most of his followers were Croats. The Illyrian movement died as a result of the events of 1848.[11]

As important as the development of nationalism in the Balkans prior to 1848 were events that occurred north of the Danube and Sava rivers. The Poles developed a modern nationalism and stressed their ethnic identity fairly early in response to being under attack for a long time and to the disappearance of their state after its third partition in 1795. Poles who lived under Russian rule revolted

---

[10] On the Serb war of independence, see Wayne S. Vucinich, ed., *The First Serbian Uprising* (New York: Columbia University Press, 1982).

[11] The best work on this subject is Elinor Murray Despalatovic, *Ljudevit Gaj and the Illyrian Movement* (New York: Columbia University Press, 1975).

in November 1830, and those under Habsburg rule did so in 1846. The feeling shared by Poles in all three regions of the partitioned country was well expressed by the first line of what was to become Poland's national anthem, first sung by the Polish Legion recruited by Napoleon in Northern Italy: "Poland is not yet lost as long as we live." The aim of Poles after 1848 was the rebirth of Poland, irrespective of the means. Many of the events that followed—the revolt against Russian overlordship in January 1864; Triple Loyalism which preached collaboration as a path toward strength; and even the socialism of men like Piłsudsky—were simply different approaches to the same final goal.[12]

While the Poles continued to rely for leadership on the nobility and clergy even after the Partitions, the Czechs and Slovaks were without such leadership, which explains the rather belated emergence of nationalism among these peoples. The Czechs, who were nominally Roman Catholics since the Counter-Reformation, still harbored their doubts about the Church, making the clergy unfit for leadership. Nor was the nobility looked toward for leadership. It had been replaced by the Habsburgs with a foreign nobility after the Battle on the White Mountain in 1620. After having lived in Bohemia and Moravia for some 200 years under the centralizing influences of Vienna, however, the nobles of the Czech lands did become champions of Bohemian State Law *(Böhmisches Staatsrecht),* which opened the door to nationalism in these lands. Only slowly did the nobility's fight for protection of a regional, estate-based right transform into a modern Czech nationalism. Even František Palacký's *History of the Czech Nation,* considered by many to represent the beginning of this nationalism, appeared first in German between 1836 and 1845.[13] It was only during the second half of the nineteenth century that Czech nationalism developed, in part as a reaction to the growing and intransigent nationalism of the Habsburg monarchy's Germans.[14]

During their many years under Hungarian rule, the Slovak nobility became "Magyarized." The hierarchy of the Roman Catholic Church, to which the great majority of the Slovaks belonged, was also Hungarian. The population of most cities was primarily German or Hungarian, and what schools existed taught in these languages. Among the early champions of Slovak nationalism

---

12 For details, see Piotr S. Wandycz, *The Lands of Partitioned Poland, 1795–1918* (Seattle: University of Washington Press, 1974).

13 On the beginnings of modern Czech nationalism, see Joseph F. Zacek, *Palacký: The Historian as Scholar and Nationalist* (Paris: Mouton, 1970).

14 On the further development of Czech nationalism, see Peter Brock and H. Gordon Skilling, eds., *The Czech Renaissance in the Nineteenth Century* (Toronto: University of Toronto Press, 1970).

were Lutherans who had been educated in German schools, but they were considered "heretics" by the uneducated Slovak masses. For these reasons, Slovak nationalism did not emerge until the last decades of the century, when village priests became champions of the Slovak People's Party. Just as German intransigence helped the emergence of Czech nationalism, the Hungarians propelled a Slovak national awakening by their resistance to reform.[15]

Nationalism developed early among the Hungarians for the same reason as it did among the Poles—foreign domination—although the Magyars faced this problem 250 years before the Poles. After the battle of Mohács in 1526, about half of Hungary and the Slavonian part of Croatia-Slavonia became provinces of the Ottoman Empire, and the area west of the occupied lands was ruled by the Habsburgs, who looked at this part of Hungary as a defense zone for their Austrian possessions. From this point on, the Hungarian nobility, led first by those in Transylvania, fought for its traditional, "constitutional" rights. After the Ottomans were forced out of the country in 1699, this fight spread to the liberated areas. The struggle was transformed into a virulent nationalism when the Hungarians discovered the modern ideology of nationalism and when they realized they had become an ethnic minority in lands they had ruled for close to 1,000 years. This realization and the fear of nationalism among the other inhabitants of the state led the country's leaders in 1848 to adopt shortsighted, ethnocentric policies. At that time, a democratic revolution led not only to a war of independence, but also to a civil war in which Hungary's minorities turned into adversaries—if not enemies—of the Hungarians. This, along with the widespread belief among the Hungarians that the *Ausgleich* of 1867 that created the Austro-Hungarian Empire did not fully restore the country's independence, had the effect of turning most Hungarian patriots into chauvinists.[16]

The Croats had been ruled by the same monarch who sat on the Hungarian throne since 1102, and they reacted to the growing nationalism of the Magyars—and their claims that the Croat lands were part of Hungary—by

---

[15] The beginning of Slovak nationalism is sympathetically presented by Peter Brock in *The Slovak National Awakening* (Toronto: University of Toronto Press, 1976). A good English language history of the Slovak is badly needed.

[16] The events in Hungary in 1848–49 are well presented in Istvan Deak, *The Lawful Revolution: Louis Kossuth and the Hungarians, 1848–1849* (New York: Columbia University Press, 1979). On Hungarian politics during the dualist period, see Andrew C. Janos, *The Politics of Backwardness in Hungary, 1825–1945* (Princeton, NJ: Princeton University Press, 1982), chapters 3 and 4; and Péter Hanák, *Ungarn in der Donau-Monarchie* (Budapest: Akadémiai Kiadó, 1984).

using the newly minted terms of modern nationalism to fight for their rights and independence. The main battleground was Vienna and the imperial court.

Clearly, the three major nations that would later comprise Yugoslavia had moved in different political directions before 1848; the differences between them continued to grow sharper and sharper. During 1848, the great revolutionary year, the Slovenes remained rather passive, while the Serbs in what was then south-central Hungary revolted against the revolutionary Hungarian Republic, receiving some aid from Serbia. Croatians joined the Habsburgs in the battle to regain the throne of Hungary. The battles between Hungary and the Habsburgs also included the civil war in Hungary, as already indicated. The Serbs and Croats, as well as the Romanians and Slovaks, fought a Hungarian government that distinguished itself by rapidly alienating all non-Hungarians by their incredibly shortsighted, chauvinistic policies. Nationalism, in its extreme form, envenomed the relationships among all these peoples in 1848, and set the tone for their relationships since.

A self-centered supreme nationalism made relations among the future Yugoslavs very difficult. The Serbs were very proud that they fought and won a war of independence. In their eyes, they had become the legitimate leaders of all Southern Slavs, because they alone had military genius and leadership potential, while others were weak—able to trade and make speeches, but not to achieve anything. This was not a view shared by their western neighbors, who considered the Serbs to be troublesome cutthroats and bullies who lacked education and refinement. These nationalistic differentations compounded the great and real differences that had historically separated the Southern Slavs.

It was Ilija Garašanin (1812–1874) "who laid the foundation of the Great Serbia policy of [Southern Slav] unification, [which remained axiomatic among] the conservative circles and individuals in Serbia...until 1914."[17] Under this policy, Serbia was to be the "Balkan Piedmont" that would unify all Southern Slavs by making them part of a Greater Serbia. It was this policy that Nikola Pašić (1845–1926), then prime minister of Serbia, seemingly gave up when he signed the Korfu agreement on 20 July 1917 that created Yugoslavia. (He and his successors continued to act as partisans for a Greater Serbia, which created problems that are discussed by Dennison Rusinow in chapter 9.) It was this belief in the "justified" supremacy of the Serbs that reappeared after the breakup of Yugoslavia at the end of 1990 and fueled the subsequent wars.

---

[17] Ivo Banac, *The National Question in Yugoslavia: Origins, History, Politics* (Ithaca, NY: Cornell University Press, 1984), 82–83.

After the Austro-Hungarian Compromise of 1867 the Croats were forced into a new relationship with Hungary. When the Hungarian parliament and the Croatian Sabor ratified the *Nagodba* in September 1868, Croatia was basically subordinated to Hungary because the Sabor's jurisdiction was limited and the Hungarian prime minister was given the right—previously exercised by the ruler—to nominate the *banus,* Croatia's head of state. Croatian politicians subsequently fought Budapest to regain the rights given up under this agreement, while the *banuses* cleverly played the Serbs in Eastern Slavonia (where most of the fighting of the 1990s occurred) against the Croat majority in the Sabor. Two Croats, Bishop Josip Juraj Strossmayer (1815–1905) and Canon Franjo Rački (1828–1894), revived the Illyrian movement to unite all Southern Slavs into a single nation in the form of Yugoslavism.

As already mentioned, the Greeks were better placed than any other people of Eastern Europe to act on the basis of new ideas because of their literacy, the widespread use of the Greek language throughout the Orthodox world, and their far-flung business networks. Their attempt to gain independence began in 1820, with a military expedition from Russia into Moldavia under the leadership of a Phanariote in Russian service, Alexander Ypsilanti (1792–1828). He had hoped that religious motives remained strong enough to spur all Balkan Christians to join him in a crusade against the Ottomans. His movement quickly died in Moldavia, but it spurred two other revolts. The first, in Wallachia, was led by Tudor Vladimireşcu (1780–1821) and quickly turned into a peasant revolt that was suppressed by the Romanian boyars. The second began in the Morea, where local Greeks remained dominant in some localities even under Ottoman rule. This uprising evolved into a Greek war of independence, which later involved the Great Powers. It ended with the Treaty of London, signed in February 1830, which created a small, indepdendent Greek state. From this time until the defeat of Greek forces in Asia Minor in 1922, the idea of a *Megale Idea* (Great Greece) dominated Greek thinking and foreign policy. The idea, simply stated, was that all lands in which Greeks lived must become part of Greece. In its extreme form, this idea would have meant the recreation of the Byzantine Empire, but even in more modest forms, it clashed with the idea of a Greater Serbia and with several other nationalistic concepts to be discussed below. It involved Greece in further wars with the Ottomans and in the two Balkan wars, and finally, it led to the Greek expedition into Asia Minor, which ended tragically for Greece.

Bulgaria gained her independence from the Ottomans much later than Serbia and Greece. It was easier for the Ottoman authorities to retain control over Bulgarian lands because they were closer to Istanbul. Also helping the Ottomans to retain control was the existence of a group of relatively affluent merchants and tradesmen who worked for the Istanbul market and of a group of Bulgarians, the *çorbacis,* who held administrative offices—all people who profited from Ottoman rule. To a considerable extent, those who worked for Bulgarian independence lived in the large Bulgarian colonies outside the country, in cities such as Istanbul, Odessa, Bucharest, and Beograd. When the famed Bulgarian revolutionaries, Vasil Levsky (1837–1873), Georgi Rakovski (1821–1867), Hristo Botev (1848–1875), and Lyuben Karavelov (1837–1879), crossed the borders into what would become the Bulgarian state, they found little support for their movements and most of them were easily defeated, paying for their actions with their lives.

Bulgaria ultimately gained independence as a result of the Russo-Ottoman war of 1877–78). Planning to use Bulgaria as a base for further forays into the Balkans, Russia created a large Bulgarian state by forcing the Ottomans to sign the Treaty of San Stefano (today's Yeşilköy) on 3 March 1878. In the same year, Great Britain and Austria-Hungary, with the help of Germany, forced Russia to accept different borders under the Treaty of Berlin of 13 July. A considerably truncated Bulgaria was further split into Bulgaria proper and Eastern Rumelia, the latter being a Christian-governed province of the Ottoman Empire. Even after these two provinces were reunited in 1885, the dream of regaining the territory defined under the Treaty of San Stefano remained the Bulgarian equivalent of the Greek *Megale Idea.*

By 1885, the "Macedonian question" was already fifteen years old.[18] The problem was born in 1870, when the Ottoman government created the Bulgarian Exarchate, an independent Bulgarian church. Numerous parishes were placed into the newly created ecclesiastical unit, but even more were left unassigned to any church because the nationality of the faithful was under question. Some of these unassigned parishes, which were given the right to vote on the issue of where to belong, were in an area roughly coincident with the part of the Ottoman Empire left intact by the Treaty of Berlin, which stretched from Istanbul to the Adriatic Sea in present-day Albania and which separated Greece, Serbia, and a soon-to-be-established Bulgaria from each other. The irredentist claims of a Greater Serbia, a Great Greece, and a "San Stefano Bulgaria" were all directed toward this region. In advance of the votes, churchmen as well as

---

[18] The best work on the origins of the Macedonian question is Fikret Adanir, *Die Makedonische Frage. Ihre Entstehung und Entwicklung bis 1908* (Wiesbaden: Franz Steiner Verlag, 1979). Another good study is Duncan M. Perry, *The Politics of Terror: The Macedonian Revolutionary Movement, 1893–1903* (Durham, NC: Duke University Press, 1988).

various revolutionary organizations and filibustering expeditions representing all three groups entered these areas.

Which claims were more justified? Leften Stavrianos writes:

> Those inhabitants of Macedonia who lived close to the Greek, Bulgarian and Serbian frontiers could be classified as being mostly Greek, Bulgarian and Serbian, respectively. The remainder of the population, with the exception of such distinct minorities as Turks, Vlachs, Jews and Albanians, may be considered as being distinctively Macedonian. These Macedonians had a dialect and certain cultural characteristics which justify their being classified as a distinct South Slav group.[19]

Nobody was willing to recognize the existence of this distinct group, the Macedonians. The Serbians and Bulgarians claimed that the language spoken by this group was a dialect of their respective tongues, while the Greeks called them "Slavophone Greeks." What resulted was an undeclared guerilla war that claimed numerous victims. The Ottoman sultan stationed those officers whom he suspected of being oppositionists in the area, hoping that the locals would get rid of them for him. It is of some interest to note that as in 1993, when a United Nations force attempted to end a local Balkan war, in 1903 the so-called Mürzsteg Agreement tried to quell the Macedonian disorders by placing the local security forces under international command. This proved to be no solution. In the end, the three irredentist Balkan states fought two Balkan wars and divided among themselves what was left of the European provinces of the Ottoman Empire west of present-day Turkey. To keep Serbia from gaining an outlet to the sea, the Great Powers, on Austria-Hungary's request, created the new state of Albania at the end of these wars.

The Albanians were, indeed, a distinct people, and some of the small number of educated people among them had begun calling for an Albanian state. The majority of the Albanians, however, still lived in a rather backward, tribal society. Following the establishment of Albania, the Serbs claimed that northern Albania, where some people followed Orthodox Christianity, should have been included in their country. Nobody claimed the large Muslim Albanian majority, but the Greeks claimed a segment of the new country, which they called Northern Epirus, where a Greek minority lived. The Albanians themselves

---

19 Leften S. Stavrianos, *The Balkans Since 1453* (New York: Holt, Rinehart, and Winston, 1977).

felt that they should have been given more territory. In other words, nobody was satisfied and further hostilities could be expected.

In addition to these conflicting territorial claims in the Balkans were several irredentist claims that included the lands of the Habsburg Dual Monarchy. The apostles of a Greater Serbia were claiming Bosnia-Hercegovina, which was then under Austro-Hungarian rule, and were in close touch with individuals in Croatia who advocated a Yugoslav solution. The Romanians also held a number of varied claims.

The Romanians begin their national history with the Dacians, whose well-organized state (in, roughly, modern-day Transylvania) was conquered by the Romans in A.D. 106. The Romans gave up their Dacian province in 271, and relatively little is known of what happened in the following centuries, except that wave after wave of various people overran the lands of modern-day Romania. There is no doubt that the remnants of the Dacians survived these critical centuries. When the last conquerors, the Hungarians, entered Transylvania, the forefathers of today's Romanians were there, and they lived under Hungarian rule until the end of World War I.

Romanians also lived on the eastern and southern slopes of the Carpathians, subject first to Byzantines and later to Polish and Hungarian rulers. Two principalities emerged in these areas in the fourteenth century: Wallachia, created by Besarab I (1310–1352), and Moldavia, created by Bogdan I (1359–1365). South of these the once-strong Balkan states had disappeared and, in the resulting confusion, the Ottomans appeared. The successors of Besarab and Bogdan not only were able to keep their states intact in these troubled times, but they also kept them from being subjugated by the strong Anjou rulers of Hungary to the west. They ruled with the help of a nobility which grew stronger and stronger as time passed and which totally and thoroughly subjugated the peasantry. In Transylvania, the upper-class Romanians were assimilated by one of the other three nationalities that ruled this Hungarian province (Hungarian, German, and Székely), while the majority became serfs on the estates of the landed nobility. Their situation did not improve under the rule of independent Transylvanian princes during 1526–1699, nor subsequently under Hungary's Habsburg rulers.

Unlike the other rulers whose lands were endangered by the advance of the Ottomans, the rulers of Moldavia and Wallachia recognized that resistance was futile and concluded vassalage agreements with them (Wallachia in 1476, Moldavia in 1512). These agreements, while involving heavy and often arbitrary taxes, kept the principalities free from Ottoman troops and protected the priviliged positions of the rulers and nobility. Beginning with the rule of Peter the Great in Russia (1672–1725), the rulers of the Romanians found themselves wedged between their old overlords and a new Russian power moving down from the north. Obviously, they preferred the Russians, the enemy of their by now very corrupt and capricious masters. The native rulers lost the confidence of Istanbul, and beginning in 1711 in Moldavia and four years later in Wallachia, they were replaced with Phanariote hospodars appointed by the sultans. These hospodars moved in with large retinues, whose members took over the most lucrative offices and who stayed when their masters were replaced. They intermarried with the local nobility and brought them the benefit of their superior education and culture. While the peasantry lived very badly, this new, cosmopolitan ruling class lived well and was rather content.[20]

The same could not be said of the Transylvanians. Here discontent was rife. In 1699 an Imperial Patent created a Uniate Church in Transylvania in an attempt to break the Romanians' contact with the Orthodox world, to which the other two principalities (Wallachia and Moldavia) belonged. This turned out to be a very important move. While most of the Orthodox clergy in Transylvania were practically illiterate, the Uniate clergy, originally under the tutelage of the Jesuits, received a good education and therefore were the first group that could effectively speak for the Transylvanian Romanians. The most famous early Uniate clergyman was the church's second bishop, Ioan Inocentiu Micu, later known as Baron Klein (1692–1768), who can be considered to be the first Romanian nationalist. It was he who first stressed the Latinity of the Romanians and who sent numerous petitions to the Transylvanian Diet and to the emperor-king to try to improve the lot of the Romanians. His example was followed by other clergymen, both Uniate and Orthodox, and later by an intelligentsia trained in the schools run by these churches. By 1848, people in all three Romanian principalities, which were undergoing revolutions, felt they were one nation and began to work for unification. In 1878, the country of Romania was created from Moldavia and Wallachia and was freed from all dependence on the Ottomans. It was at this time that the Romanian irredentists began to make their claims for Transylvania and parts of the Bánát of Temesvár, which were ruled by Hungary; the Bukovina, which had been ruled by Austria since 1775; and Bessarabia, originally part of Moldavia and the site of the Moldavian Republic of the former Soviet Union. The question of the Dobrudja separated the

---

[20] Sugar, *Southeastern Europe under Ottoman Rule,* chapter 6; and R. W. Seton-Watson, *A History of the Roumanians* (Cambridge, England: Cambridge University Press, 1934), chapter 5.

Romanians from the Bulgarians. In other words, by 1914 there was not a single border beyond which Romania had no irredentist claims.[21]

Although Turkey is not included in this study, a few words must be said about the Turks. The Ottoman Empire, while Turkish in language, was not based on nationality—everyone who satisfied certain preconditions could become part of the ruling elite irrespective of nationality. The professional Ottomans, as this ruling elite is known today, was predominantly but not exclusively Muslim, as the history of the Phanariotes shows, and all thought in imperialist terms, even those who, beginning with the rule of Sultan Selim III (1807–1808), realized that the empire could not survive long in its current form and who introduced a great many reforms during the nineteenth century. Even the young officers whom Abdülhamid II (1876–1909) sent to die in Macedonia and their friends in the Union and Progress movement—who are better known as the Young Turks—advocated Ottomanism or Turanism, a form of supernational nationalism, rather than Turkish nationalism. As a matter of fact, the term "Turk" meant something like "stupid country bumpkin" to those who ran the state's business in Istanbul. It took World War I, the destruction of the Ottoman Empire, the creation of the Turkish Republic by Mustafa Kemal Atatürk (1881–1938), and his teaching and propaganda to make the Turks aware of their "Turkishness" and to make them proud of their history.[22]

World War I and Its Aftermath

World War I drastically changed the map of Eastern Europe. In the Balkans, Turkey retained the European lands left to the Ottoman Empire after the second Balkan war; Albania retained the 1913 borders; and Bulgaria lost 8.1 percent of its territory and its outlet to the Aegean Sea. The victors were Greece, whose territory increased by 11.9 percent; Romania, whose size increased by 128.6 percent, more than doubling its territory; and Serbia, which was replaced by the state of Yugoslavia, which was 183.6 percent larger than Serbia had been in 1914. Already at the peace conference in Paris, problems were surfacing in the new Yugoslavia. The Yugoslavs had trouble with the Italians over Dalmatia, but

---

[21] Seton-Watson, *A History of the Roumanians,* chapters 15–17. A good, objective modern history of Romania in English is badly needed.

[22] There still is no first-rate biography of Atatürk. The best available in English are H. C. Armstrong, *Grey Wolf: Mustafa Kemal. An Intimate Study of a Dictator* (London: Arthur Baker, 1932); and Lord Kinross, *Ataturk: A Biography of Mustafa Kemal, Father of Modern Turkey* (New York: William Morrow, 1965).

they spoke with two voices: Nikola Pašić, the prime minister, was ready to give up part of Croatia in order to realize further Serb expansion on Yugoslavia's sourthern and eastern borders. His Croat minister of foreign affiars, Ante Trumbić (1864–1938), favored making concessions in the east and defended every inch of Croat or Slovene soil.[23] Their differences ran deep on their concept of the kind of state Yugoslavia should be.

> While Pašić stood for a centralized system as Serbia already had, Trumbić announced that although he was for state unity, he was not for a united state. "This is not a fine point," he assured... "but a conception."[24]

Pašić wanted a centralized state that left little for the regional governments to do, while Trumbić wanted a weak central power in a confederated state. Here began the problems of Yugoslavia, which ultimately led to its dissolution in late 1990.

North of the Balkans, changes were even more drastic after World War I. Hungary was the major loser, giving up 70 percent of its territory and 60 percent of its total population, including 28 percent of those who spoke Hungarian.[25] A new state, Czechoslovakia, was born, and Poland regained independence. That the losers were unhappy goes without saying; what is important to note is that the victors also were dissatisfied. Some were aggrieved that they had not received more land, and all resented that the peacemakers in Paris forced them to sign a declaration protecting the numerous minorities within their borders and giving these minorities the right to appeal to the League of Nations when they felt abused. The only country that was satisfied was Turkey, which took the place of the Ottoman Empire. Led by Mustafa Kemal, the Turks rejected the peace treaty presented to them in Paris, fought for what they considered to be theirs by right, and finally signed a treaty that gave them the borders they considered just.

---

23 For the beginnings of the Serb-Croat controversy at the Paris Peace Conference, see Ivo J. Lederer, *Yugoslavia at the Paris Peace Conference: A Study in Frontiermaking* (New Haven: Yale University Press, 1963).

24 Michael Boro Petrovich, *A History of Modern Serbia*, II (New York: Harcourt, Brace, Jovanovich, 1976), 647.

25 Hungary's territory shrunk from 282,000 square miles to 93,000, and its population fell from 18 million to 8 million.

Conclusion

Nationalism in its modern form was imported into Eastern Europe slowly at first and with growing speed and strength beginning in the late eighteenth century. The process by which various individuals or groups brought this new idea to their conationals and made them aware of their national identities differed from nation to nation. The Western concept of nationalism emerged in many variations, as it was adapted by the people living in Eastern Europe, and the manifestations of nationalism varied from country to country, nation to nation, and sometimes even from locality to locality.[26] As the nineteenth century progressed, these differences began to diminish, and Eastern European nationalism began to take on the features of the most aggressive and chauvinistic variants evident in Western Europe. The original differences disappeared, and irredentist claims of some nations were refuted with equal vehemence by those whose lands were claimed. This left all the variations of nationalism in Eastern Europe as "integral nationalism," in accordance with the following definition:

> Integral nationalism rejected sympathy for and cooperation with other nations, promoted jingoism..., militarism, and imperialism, and opposed all personal liberties when they interfered with the aims of the State. Loyalty to the nation state...came before all other loyalties, and even religious considerations were subordinated to the ends of nationalism.[27]

It was with this unfortunate baggage of nationalism that Eastern Europe entered the twentieth century, which is the subject of the rest of this volume.

---

[26] Peter F. Sugar and Ivo J. Lederer, eds., *Nationalism in Eastern Europe* (Seattle: University of Washington Press, 1969), 3–54.

[27] Snyder, *Encyclopedia of Nationalism,* 132, following Carlton J. H. Hayes's classification.

2

Albanian Nationalism in the Twentieth Century

by Bernd J. Fischer

Document 1

from *The Memoirs of Ismail Kemal Bey* (1920).[1]

Dwelling in a sort of isolation, they were variously grouped under the generic name of Macedonians or Illyrians, according to the caprice of different conquerors. But they themselves, profoundly indifferent to these arbitrary arrangements, which did not interfere with their race, their language or their national character, seemed hardly to be aware of the fall of Empires or the changes of frontiers. Proudly they preserved the independence of which no power could deprive them. On the fall of the Roman Empire, they reappeared on the world's stage to prove that they were of a race whose solidity time could not effect [sic], and whose national genius custom could not pervert. Since those days, whenever an attack has been made upon their liberties, they have been found as intrepid as in the far-off times when they followed Alexander the Great or Pyrrhus; and to-day they display the singular and interesting spectacle of a nationality preserved pure and undefiled through the centuries, in spite of so many successive conquests by Romans, Byzantines, Normans, Bulgarians, Serbs, Italians, and Turks.

In spite of the religious and other consequences of the Turkish domination, the Albanians have remained faithful to the customs and habits of their

---

1 Somerville Story, ed., *The Memoirs of Ismail Kemal Bey* (London: Constable and Company, Ltd., 1920), 356–60.

ancestors. The three principal objects of an Albanian's devotion are his honour, his family and his country... [T]wo virtues preside over the public life of my compatriots, not only in their domestic arrangements, but also in their history and their demeanour towards peoples and sovereigns with whom they have had relations of friendship or hostility. These two virtues—fidelity to their word of honour and the religion of patriotism, with which goes the love of independence—have never ceased to guide them through all the reverses their country has suffered.

Document 2

from an interview by the *Daily Telegraph* with King Zog of the Albanians (12 October 1928).[2]

First and foremost, let me say that we have no aggressive intentions towards the Jugoslavs, and we wish to remain on the best of terms with them. Secondly, we have no intention of surrendering our independence to any other nation. I can only point to history. Albania is the only country in the Balkans which has always maintained her independence in spite of many invasions. The character of the Albanian race is based on a love of freedom under their own chiefs. We will never allow ourselves to be ruled by Italy. The people would never submit to Italian domination.

But we have to consider our position. We are centuries behind the rest of Europe in civilization. The people can neither read nor write; there are few written laws which are obeyed, and blood feuds are still prevalent in many parts of the country. It is my determination to civilise my people and make them as far as possible adopt Western habits and customs. Now we cannot do this without assistance. Is there really any nation that can stand by itself, independent of all others? We have had to make a start and adopt any methods which appeared most convenient. We needed money more than anything else. How could we get it? Only by borrowing from another power. We tried to raise a loan through Geneva, but this failed. We tried in several other countries, including England, but were unsuccessful.

---

2 E. Ashmead-Bartlett, C.B.E., "Special Interview with Albanian King," *Daily Telegraph* (London), 12 October 1928.

Then Italy came to our assistance, and lent us 2,000,000 pounds sterling on conditions highly favorable to ourselves. The loan was approved by the official of the League of Nations who was sent out here to look into the matter. The money is now being utilised for various public works: roads, bridges, drainage, and on the new harbour works at Durazzo. Then we wanted expert assistance, such as trained financiers, officers to organize our army and navy, engineers, doctors etc. Naturally, as Italy lent us the money she has a prior right to superintend the spending of it. That is why we now have so many Italians working with us. But this does not mean that we have lost our political independence. We are still a nation, and our own master, and will never allow ourselves to be dictated to or exploited in the interests of others...

I regard the army as an educational factor of the highest value. The country's crying need is education, and the men who are called up under the conscription will return to their homes with very enlarged ideas. You must understand that the average Albanian knows nothing about nationality. He had always looked up to the head of his tribe, or his Bey, as the supreme authority. He has got to be taught gradually to transfer this local allegiance, admirable in itself, to the central government. He must learn in fact that while remaining the member of the tribe, he is also a citizen of the State.

Document 3

from the introduction to *Laying the Foundations of the New Albania*, by Enver Hoxha (1984).[3]

In the many centuries of Albanian history, our people's state power and the monolithic unity of our people, embodied in the organization of the Democratic Front, are two of the greatest and most brilliant achievements, two of the most monumental works of the epoch of the Party.

These two immortal monumental works, like the Party itself, which was and remains for ever their powerful brain and heart, were not born in marble halls, were not the product of "great minds," lolling in the easy chairs of cafes or parliamentary seats. No, they were born from the barrel of the partisan rifle, in the

[3] Enver Hoxha, *Laying the Foundations of the New Albania* (Tirana: "8 Nëntori" Publishing House, 1984), 5–7.

fire of the war for freedom, were nurtured in the bosom of the people, and the humble homes of the people became their place of residence.

Today, looking back over more than four decades, we Albanian communists feel proud that ever since the days of their creation, the Democratic Front of Albania and our people's state power, under the leadership of our glorious Party, have performed their tasks and mission for the people and the Homeland with honour, have been tempered in the sternest battles and tests, have withstood and defeated the plans of all internal and external enemies and have been turned into impregnable fortresses of triumphant socialism and the fine new life which is flourishing in Albania...

These two colossal achievements of ours will continue to exist and function through the ages, but the earliest times, the moments when we laid the foundations, when in the heat of the war we created the National Liberation Front and our people's state power, shall never be forgotten. We have looked back over that unforgettable period again and again, not from nostalgia, but in order to illuminate the problem from all aspects and to make as clear and concrete as possible to the younger generations how we, their parents, managed to overthrow the old and set up the new.

Document 4

from a speech by Albanian President Ramiz Alia to the General Assembly of the United Nations (28 September 1990).[4]

Mine is a small country. The Albanian people, however, are among the most ancient inhabitants of the European continent. During the thousands of years of their existence, they have never attacked anyone, never provoked any aggressive war, never threatened or encroached upon the security of their neighbours. On the contrary, they have gone through fire and flames to preserve their existence and assist others. George Kastrioti-Skanderbeg, our National Hero of the 15th century, has been and remains the symbol of the brilliant fighter for the defence not only of his own people, but also the first champion of European humanism and civilization.

History has not caressed the Albanian people, either in ancient or in modern times. But it has also taught them that, for their freedom, independence,

---

[4] *Albania Report,* Bulletin no. 69 (October 1990).

national sovereignty, originality and identity to be protected, they must boldly fight and oppose any attempt at their infringement, just as it has taught them to support and back up all international actions and initiatives that contribute to the strengthening of peace and general security.

Introduction

The four documents presented here reflect the four stages of the formation of Albanian nationalism in the twentieth century, and they help to illustrate the central role played by nationalism in all aspects of Albanian development. These four authors, who have commented on the struggle to instill nationalism in the Albanians—because politics in Albania has always been highly personal—also have been leaders in bringing this about. They worked against tribalism, regionalism, and a myriad of other obstacles in order to construct a viable nation-state held together by modern nationalism.

The first document is an excerpt from the memoirs of Ismail Kemal Bey, an urbane, westernized politician and diplomat of Albanian origin who served the Ottoman Empire in various capacities over sixty years. Ismail Kemal distinguished himself by presiding over the declaration of Albanian independence in Vlorë on 28 November 1912, and is, as a result, recognized as the father of modern Albania. He also was responsible for laying the cornerstone of Albanian nationalism.

The second document is an interview with Ahmed Zog—who dominated Albania during the interwar period—given shortly after he became king. Despite being roundly condemned both by his contemporaries and by subsequent generations of Albanians, Zog did much to lay the foundation of Albanian nationalism upon which the postwar regime was built.

The last two documents reflect the continued growth of nationalism in the post–World War II period. They lend credence to the argument that despite the radical Stalinist orientation of Enver Hoxha and the Albanian Party of Labor, nationalism continued to be the principal focal point of Albanian politics. The third document, an introduction to one of Hoxha's numerous books, demonstrates this point. The final document is an excerpt from a speech by Hoxha's successor, Ramiz Alia, that reflects nationalism unmasked and hints at the forms that such nationalism might take. Under Alia, the government of Albania began to participate, however unwillingly, in the rapid reforms of the late 1980s and early 1990s. Many of Hoxha's political themes were stripped away, exposing a new nationalism refined to reflect the new situation of Albania in a world with far fewer enemies. With Alia's resignation in April 1992, it fell to his democratic successors to direct this new nationalism along a more constructive path, emphasizing cooperation in the international arena and replacing Hoxha's state-of-siege nationalism.

These four documents in many ways represent the history of Albanian nationalism, which essentially is a twentieth-century phenomenon. Although it had its roots in the late nineteenth century, Albanian nationalism was neither a popular movement nor a distinctly Albanian movement. The question, then, is why the Albanians were so late in developing what the rest of the Balkan peoples had begun to construct in the eighteenth and early nineteenth centuries. The answer to this question, while complex, in general lies in both conscious Ottoman policy and the nature of the Albanian people themselves.

Ottoman Rule

The Ottomans, who ruled the Albanians for some four centuries, instituted policies that adversely affected the development of a national Albanian consciousness. Some of these policies were applied to the Balkan peoples in general, while others were developed particularly with the Albanians in mind. An example of the former is the Ottoman's division of their subjects into administrative units which cut across national lines. The Albanians found themselves divided into four separate *vilayets*. As an example of the latter, following the rise of Serbian and Greek nationalism at the beginning of the nineteenth century, the Ottomans began to place obstacles in the way of the development of similar nationalistic sentiments in Albania. Since religion was not associated with nationality in Albania (as it was in much of the rest of the Balkans), the Ottomans correctly concluded that language, education, and culture were at the heart of the Albanian national identity. Normally, these were of little concern to the Ottomans, but in the case of the Albanians, severe restrictions were placed on teaching of the Albanian language because it was feared that a common written language could lead to a common literature, the discovery of a common past, and the growth of nationalism. This had been the pattern by which nationalism was awakened among other Balkan peoples, and the Ottomans were determined that Albania would be "spared."[5]

The Ottomans were supported in their efforts by the Orthodox Patriarch in Constantinople, who enforced similar restrictions on the Orthodox Albanians in the southern part of the country. If they wished to become literate, they would have to learn Greek. The Porte (the government of the Ottoman Empire) had less

---

[5] Leften Stavrianos, *The Balkans Since 1453* (New York: Holt and Rinehart and Winston, 1958), 501.

control over the Catholics who lived in the north, and so the first schools to teach the Albanian language were in the Catholic community. But even here, the circumstances were far from ideal: by 1878 the Albanian language was taught in only two Roman Catholic schools in Shkodër, where the primary language was Italian.[6] The success of the Ottoman language policy is evidenced by the fact that the Albanians could not agree on a single alphabet for written Albanian until 1908.

Not all the obstacles that the Ottomans placed in the way of the development of Albanian nationalism were oppressive. In fact, the Albanians found themselves in a favored position within the Ottoman Empire. For many Albanians, the Ottoman Empire provided favors and a career in the army or in administration, where they served in disproportionate numbers. Sultan Abdul Hamid II often commented that his empire depended on the Albanians and the Arabs.[7] Therefore, they did not share the discontent with foreign rule felt by most of the other Balkan peoples. Quite the contrary, the Albanians saw the Turks as protectors against the often hostile Greeks and Serbs.

The Turks, Greeks, and Serbs were not responsible for all of the obstacles in the way of the growth of Albanian nationalism, however. The nature of Albanian civilization and heritage also contributed significantly to the problem. The various divisions and various levels of development within the Albanian community encouraged localism and inhibited the development of a national frame of reference. The existence of three religious groups prevented churches from playing the unifying role they played in many other areas of Eastern Europe. Much more important, the nature of Albanian society provided a powerful block to unity: apart from their religious differences, the Albanians also were divided linguistically, culturally, socially, and economically. This disunity was fostered by the coexistence of three groups within the population, each of which was characterized by a distinct and conflicting stage of civilization: the primitive, fiercely independent mountain clans in the north; the feudal Beys in the south, who ruled over a generally docile Muslim Tosk peasantry; and the more educated and urbanized population of the Hellenic and Catholic fringes.[8] The Turks took advantage of the disunity and the lack of development by

---

6 Stefanaq Pollo and Arben Puto, *The History of Albania* (London: Routledge and Kegan Paul, 1981), 115.

7 T. Karajowow, "Albanien, Ein Politischer und Wirtschaftlicher Überblick," *Südostliche Warte* (1929), 157.

8 Great Britain, Public Record Office, Foreign Office 371/10654 (C217/52/90): Durazzo (5 January 1925).

instigating discord between and within these groups, often assuming the role of arbiter.

Albania therefore was at something of a disadvantage when the nineteenth century brought the revival of Balkan nationalism, lacking all of the necessary preconditions for the growth of nationalism, as identified by Albanian scholar T. Zavalani.[9] It had no state, no religious unity, no leadership by a self-conscious class. Albania had no foreign intellectual stimulus and no linguistic unity. Albania did not even have a population discontented with foreign rule.

Ismail Kemal Bey and the Birth of Albanian Nationalism

When nationalism did finally appear among the Albanians, it was late, rather weak, and certainly unique. Of course, nationalism has proved to be unique wherever it developed. Albania is no exception. Still, while other Eastern European variants were generated from abroad—often from Western Europe through Germany—in its infancy Albanian nationalism was actually developed abroad, beyond the reach of Greek and Ottoman officials. The first real spark of Albanian nationalism, a cultural awakening, took place in the 1860s among the Italo-Albanians in southern Italy, where many Albanians had fled after the defeat of Skënderbeg, the fifteenth-century Albanian national hero. Since these nationalists wrote in Italian, and the illiteracy rate in Albania was then virtually 100 percent, their influence naturally was limited.

Many historians have suggested that the true beginning of Albanian political nationalism was the League of Prizren, a hastily organized group whose purpose was to prevent the occupation and annexation of Albanian territory following the Eastern Crisis of 1875–78, which led to the Treaties of San Stefano and Berlin. The League's activities certainly were nationalist. It began to break down the religious, territorial, and cultural divisions by providing the first clear call for administrative autonomy, which was articulated by a group headed by the southern Muslim patriot Abdul Frashëri. Further, the League directly prevented the foreign annexation of some Albanian territory and, for the first time, brought the existence of an Albanian nationality to the attention of the powers of Europe.

---

[9] T. Zavalani, "Albanian Nationalism," in *Nationalism in Eastern Europe,* Peter F. Sugar and Ivo J. Lederer, eds. (Seattle: University of Washington Press, 1969), 56.

On the other hand, the significance of the League should not be overemphasized. Northern leaders supported the call for autonomy in order to exempt themselves from taxes and the military draft, not as a step toward unity and eventual independence. Central Albania, which faced no threat of foreign invasion, continued to identify with the Turks. The League represented the highest levels of modern nationalist development only among southern leaders, primarily Muslims, who could conceive of a nation in intellectual terms. The vast majority of Albanians were simple peasants and tribespeople who had a traditional love of the land that was not expressed in terms of either a nation or a state. They fought mainly because foreign armies were attempting to rob them of their land, not because they were dedicated to creation of an autonomous or independent Albania.[10]

The Turks crushed the League in 1880, although, as the prominent Albanian scholar Stavro Skendi suggests, a certain spirit remained.[11] The roots of nationalism certainly were there, but its further development, let alone its maturity, would have to wait.

While Albanians undertook occasional insurrections against the Porte during the last decades of the nineteenth century, the primary cause of these was local grievance. With the turn of the century, however, such insurrections began to produce demands that were more national in character. A French consul suggested at the time that "There are no longer those periodical gatherings where many chiefs of clans come together to treat of questions which divide them without speaking about an independent Albania, without fixing the frontiers of the future state, without even being concerned about the form of government which will best fit it."[12] Much of the talk among these clan chiefs certainly referred to regional, rather than national, independence and was motivated by foreign intervention. Still, a change had taken place.

Compared to the situation at this time in Western Europe, this might not be thought to represent nationalism, but in Albanian terms this change was significant. Clearly, a feeling that individuals belonged to a group larger than a tribe was slowly taking hold, and the differences between the north and the south were slowly breaking down. There are a number of possible explanations. For one, the aggressive policy of the Young Turks led to an increase in the number of often spontaneous insurrections against the Turks. Until the turn of

---

[10] Stavrianos, *The Balkans Since 1453*, 504.

[11] Stavro Skendi, *The Albanian National Awakening, 1878-1912* (Princeton, NJ: Princeton University Press, 1967), 108.

[12] Skendi, *The Albanian National Awakening*, 467.

the century, the Albanians had most often fought for, rather than against, the Turks. In return, the Albanians had been promised constitutional government, the protection of all of their privileges, the opening of Albanian schools, and the right to retain their weapons.[13] With the victory of the Young Turks in 1908, there was a flurry of nationalistic activity in Albania, including the founding of schools, newspapers, cultural and political organizations, and—perhaps of primary significance—the meeting of the Monastir congress in November which was called to decide on a common alphabet for the Albanian language.

Even though but a handful of Albanian intellectuals were responsible for much of this activity (many of whom like Ismail Kemal Bey were now allowed to return from exile), the Young Turks were unprepared for the magnitude of the response. They recognized that their repressive policies had been a mistake and were determined to reverse the process first by persuasion and then by force. When persuasion failed, clubs and societies, printing presses, and schools were abruptly closed. In June 1909 the Young Turks, pursuing active centralization, called for a census as a basis for taxation and for the confiscation of Albanian weapons, thus countervening two of the last standing privileges enjoyed by the Albanian mountaineers. The response—contrary to the advice of most Albanian nationalist leaders—was a revolt in Kosovë, the first of a series of sporadic revolts which, by 1912, had engulfed all of Albania.

By 1912 the Young Turks had managed to alienate most of the divergent groups in Albania, which forced them to cooperate with each other. For the first time, the revolts were general, although there was still no generally recognized Albanian authority to coordinate and direct these insurrections and despite that the participants pursued highly divergent goals. These revolts included the central Albanians, who had not yet participated in any national uprisings because they were peasants who had been completely dominated by their feudal lords and because they had never been threatened by foreign powers. Now the feudal lords of central Albania themselves wanted the restoration of the old regime and were opposed to the Young Turks, and they revolted against the central authority. Ismail Kemal writes that the aggressive policy of the Young Turks was "the leaven that caused their national sentiments to revive and flourish afresh."[14]

The second significant factor, in addition to the reaction against the Porte, that helps to explain the rise of Albanian national consciousness around the turn of the century was an increased interest in Albania on the part of foreign powers,

---

13 Skendi, *The Albanian National Awakening*, 343.

14 *The Memoirs of Ismail Kemal Bay*, 367.

particularly Italy and Austria-Hungary. While the Albanians did not have "benefactors" as did the peoples of the rest of the Balkans, they found that these two powers were intent on preventing the expansion of Greece and Serbia at the expense of Albanian territory. Italy and Austria-Hungary, which also distrusted each other, therefore had developed a strategic interest in Albania.

To secure a foothold in Albania, the Italians founded schools, consulates, and commercial agencies at a pace that alienated and divided many Albanian nationalists, with some in support of the Italians and others, such as Ismail Kemal Bey, against them. In an area already so divided, these additional sources of divisiveness were unwelcome. On the other hand, the Italian government did help to facilitate the growth of an Albanian national consciousness through its efforts in shipping, trade, and education, which exposed many Albanians to Western ideas and culture.[15]

While these external factors were important, considerable credit for the first steps toward the construction of an Albanian national consciousness must go to a handful of patriots (primarily in southern Albania and abroad) who, removed from the still largely illiterate population of Albania, often served to link the various parts of the country. Although very much divided in terms of goals, most of these patriots, like Abdul Frashëri and his brothers, were involved in an unarmed struggle to achieve cultural autonomy which they perceived as the necessary first step toward the creation of national sentiments. Most opposed armed struggle, fearing foreign intervention, and saw Albania's future to be closely linked with a strengthened, more modern Ottoman Empire.

Ismail Kemal Bey, the father of Albanian independence, can be counted among this group. The privileged son of a wealthy Muslim feudal lord from Vlorë, Ismail Kemal studied at the Greek gymnasium in Janina and graduated from the Turkish law school in Istanbul. Despite his liberal and reformist political orientation, he was appointed to important posts under the sultans. In 1900, however, he was sent to Tripoli, which he perceived as virtual exile. In response, he fled the empire for Western Europe and turned his attention, essentially for the first time, to Albanian problems.

Ismail Kemal had no illusions about the level of Albanian development. While he believed that the Albanians had maintained a certain independence and "the religion of patriotism," it is clear from his programs and policies that his comments were meant in a very general sense; he was describing a nationalism still in its infancy. To him, an independent Albania not only would be free of

---

[15] For more on the Italian role in Albania, see Bernd J. Fischer, "Italian Policy in Albania, 1894-1943," *Balkan Studies* 26 (1985), 101–12.

foreign rule, but also would end the isolation of various groups of Albanians from each other. Such isolation, particularly among the Ghegs of the north, had encouraged the recognition of common blood ties as well as common enemies. This recognition did much to tie some, but not all, Albanians together, but it remained true that when they were not fighting outsiders, they were fighting each other. Ismail Kemal also, to some extent, overestimated the unity among Albanians, or at least focused on the unifying factors, in an effort to gain needed foreign support for Albania. He was a pragmatist who was conscious of foreign opinion, and he believed that without foreign involvement nothing would come of the efforts of the handful of Albanian patriots who struggled to instill in their fellow Albanians a sense of national consciousness. Recognizing that this process would take some time, Ismail believed that to struggle for Albania, one had to struggle for a strengthened Ottoman Empire. His policy was simple and remained constant until just before the declaration of Albanian independence: along with most educated Albanian patriots, he supported the unification of the four *vilayets* inhabited by Albanians and the attainment of administrative autonomy, to be achieved not through armed insurrection but through collaboration between all the oppressed nationalities of the empire, which included the Turks themselves.[16]

Toward this end, Ismail Kemal vigorously involved himself with reform movements. He participated in the Young Turk congress in Paris in 1902, and after the victory of their revolution in 1908, he became the leader of the Albanians in the new Turkish parliament. It soon became clear to Ismail Kemal, however, that the only thing he had in common with the Young Turks was their mutual distaste for Hamidian despotism. Their initial cooperation quickly degenerated to mutual tolerance and finally to mutual hostility. In April 1909, following the Bosnian crisis, the Young Turks concluded that they had let Albanian nationalism go too far and were determined to stop the process. The relationship deteriorated further as the Young Turks became more repressive. Still, neither Ismail Kemal nor the patriotic societies would give up on the Turkish connection and continued to express confidence in the Turkish state.[17]

By the end of 1911, the situation had become more complex. By then, Italy had attacked Turkey, and the Balkan states were in the process of plotting the dismemberment of Ottoman Europe, including Albania. Ismail Kemal, who must be considered the most farsighted of the Albanian patriots at this time, left for Europe. He had come to the conclusion that to prevent Albanian lands from

---

[16] Pollo and Puto, *The History of Albania*, 137.

[17] Skendi, *The Albanian National Awakening*, 402.

being swallowed, direct European support was necessary, and although he was initially hesitant, he finally concluded that Austria-Hungary was Albania's last best hope. He called for the creation of an Austro-Hungarian protectorate.[18]

The rapid defeat of Ottoman troops in the first Balkan war once again changed the situation for Albania. Much Albanian territory was occupied by Serbia and Greece, who saw the area as legitimate spoils. In the face of this crisis, Albanian historiography suggests that in Trieste, on his was back to Albania from Vienna, where he had secured Austrian support, Ismail Kemal decided that independence—regardless of how unprepared the Albanians might be—was the only way to save Albania from being dismembered.[19] With the support of Austria-Hungary and Italy, success was at least possible.

Ismail Kemal arrived in Vlorë, which was still unoccupied by foreign troops, on a ship provided by Austria. He convened a small assembly of eighty-three Albanian notables, which proclaimed the independence of Albania on 28 November 1912. Albania's Balkan neighbors ignored the declaration, which caused Ismail Kemal, who had been elected president, to hurry off to Europe to gain material and moral support for his besieged government and to plead for equitable frontiers. It was not to be. While it suited Europe's purpose to preserve an independent Albania, the Conference of Ambassadors in London (which met to redraw the borders of Southeastern Europe following the first Balkan war) awarded Kosovë, with its predominantly Albanian population, to Serbia and determined that the new government in Albania would be led by a European prince. Ismail Kemal and his national government were overlooked both because he had begun to demonstrate his independence from Austria-Hungary and Italy and because he seemed to have been involved in a plot against Serbia and Greece.[20]

Ismail Kemal Bey had been forced along by events and then overrun by them. Despite his assertions about the deeply entrenched "religion of patriotism," he knew Albania was unprepared for independence at least partially because modern nationalism had yet to develop. He hoped for time and support to consolidate his gains and to build the institutions necessary to further the spread of nationalism, but he had been disappointed. The European powers found a young, inexperienced, and basically ignorant prince to rule Albania—Prince William of Wied—who served a scant six months before leaving Albania in September 1914, never to return. Ismail Kemal was never to return

---

18 Skendi, *The Albanian National Awakening*, 444.

19 Pollo and Puto, *The History of Albania*, 148.

20 Pollo and Puto, *The History of Albania*, 156.

either. He and his new fledgling state were soon overwhelmed by events and by the armies of six different powers. The struggle to construct a national consciousness had to be restarted, essentially from the beginning, following World War I, which had allowed the Albanians to resurrect tribalism and localism.

The contributions made by Ismail Kemal and his generation were very important to the growth of nationalism in Albania. Ismail Kemal had helped to lay the groundwork, leaving it to others to build the foundations. His task was complex, and his achievements were more remarkable as a result. While King Zog, Enver Hoxha, and Ramiz Alia would have the power of the state behind them as they struggled for an Albania, Ismail Kemal had the power of the state against him. Yet, despite the obstacles, he had succeeded in making Albania a factor in international relations, and his stature as the father of the nation (although certainly not immediately recognized by Albania's divergent groups) helped to bridge some of the deep divisions in Albanian society. The status of Albanian nationalism following World War I was perhaps best summed up by the Italian political figure Count Francesco Guicciardini, who wrote in 1901, after an extensive trip through Albania: "As far as the Albanian sentiment of nationality, one may say that it is in its latent state and manifests itself in jerky movement and with indeterminate objectives, but the smallest educative work would make it conscious in movement and aims."[21] Future Albanian leaders tried to awaken the sentiment by such educative work, as well as by other means.

Zog and the Foundation of Albanian Nationalism

Albania emerged from World War I battered, with much of its territory occupied and its marginal prewar state infrastructure destroyed. Ismail Kemal and his colleagues had too little time to engrain any strong nationalist feelings into the people of Albania, and much of what they had achieved had evaporated in the chaos of war. The war, however, did further their work in one sense: the extended foreign occupation helped reinforce Albanians' sense of distinctiveness. But the process of constructing a widespread national consciousness and the process of constructing a state apparatus had to begin anew under Ahmet Zogu, who controlled Albania during the interwar years.

---

[21] Quoted in Skendi, "Albanian Political Thought and Revolutionary Activity," 195.

Zogu began his political career as a minor Muslim Gheg chieftain from the northern district of Mati. Although he had a truncated education, his cunning, energy, willingness to use violence, and sheer audacity enabled him to seize control of the state in 1922. He ruled first as prime minister, then as president, and from 1928 until his overthrow in 1939 by Benito Mussolini, as King Zog. As indicated by his interview with the *Daily Telegraph* excerpted above, he was aware that his task was to lay the foundation for national unity and a national consciousness, which he could not achieve without a stable political system and a functioning economy. Since these also would support his own position, Zog's personal motives coincided with national goals. But attaining these goals was a Herculean task, and though Zog's ambition was limitless, his abilities were somewhat limited. The obstacles to national unity, discussed above, had not changed significantly by the 1920s. Perhaps the only natural advantage that Zog had was the absence of any large and vocal minorities (although the Greek minority in the south often became an issue).

Zog's first priority was to create a political structure that would be strong enough to withstand the inevitable strains of rapid modernization. He first came to power as prime minister of a highly unstable parliamentary government, which was ill-suited to Albania's primitive state of political development and its heritage of Ottoman beys and tribal chieftains. Following Zog's overthrow in early 1924 and his hasty return in late 1924 as the head of a motley invasion force, Zog overthrew not only the regime in power but the entire system of government as well. He replaced the principality structure with a semiauthoritarian republic.

After several years, the political turmoil that brought Zog to power had been slowed, although it had not been entirely eradicated. The political structure needed further adjusting. As soon as Zog felt his position was strong enough, he created a monarchy with himself as king. The new 1928 monarchical constitution consolidated most power in the hands of the king, and Zog was thereby able to break the remaining opposition and end much of the remaining political turmoil simply by putting an end to participatory politics. The system Zog finally created was a reasonably stable, traditional, nonideological, authoritarian government in which limited political and social reform was permitted, provided that Zog's own position was not threatened.

Having stabilized his own political position as much as possible, Zog turned his attention to Albania's desperate economic situation. Four centuries of Ottoman domination had not created any of the bases for modern economic development and in fact had retarded such development. In 1922, over 90 percent of the population was engaged in either agriculture or animal husbandry, although only 9 percent of the land was arable.[22] Industry was either nonexistent or comprised of handicrafts. Mineral resources were undeveloped, and transportation facilities were primitive. On the few roads that did exist, wheeled traffic was possible only during the summer months. In the early 1920s the country's entire rolling stock consisted of three old Fords left behind by an American relief mission.[23] There were no railroads, and imports outnumbered exports by nearly nine to one.[24]

Zog was fully aware that without economic reform, national unity and the creation of a modern nation-state would be impossible, and yet his options were limited. Not the least of his problems was his genuine lack of understanding of modern economics and his inability to attract effective advisers. Zog was one of those Balkan politicians who showed remarkable energy and ingenuity in coming to power but once there seemed to be unable to formulate and carry out effective policies.

Much of the difficulty, however, had little to do with Zog's ignorance of economics; Albania's major developmental problem was a lack of capital. Given the country's agrarian economy, indigenous capital accumulation depended on modernizing the agricultural sector, which was controlled by feudal Muslim landowners. Since these people constituted an important part of Zog's principal political support, the king did not feel comfortable pressuring them. An agrarian reform program was drawn up in the 1930s, but it was never implemented and remained little more than a sop to the few Albanian liberals.

The only other option open to Zog was to appeal for foreign aid. When the League of Nations refused to grant Albania a loan, that left fascist Italy as the only foreign power with enough strategic interest and financial resources to provide the "uneconomic" loans needed to bolster the Albanian economy. Zog asked for aid and Mussolini's government obliged—on the assumption that economic aid would lead to economic and political control and would provide Italy with a foothold in the Balkans. The first loan came in the form of an Italian-sponsored company to develop Albania's resources. The company loaned the Albanian government a significant sum to be guaranteed by Albanian customs receipts. The company also dictated how the money was to be spent.[25]

---

22 Stavro Skendi, *Albania* (New York: Praeger, 1956), 152.

23 Marcel W. Fodor, *Plot and Counterplot in Central Europe* (Boston: Houghton Mifflin, 1937), 95.

24 Bernd J. Fischer, *King Zog and the Struggle for Stability in Albania* (Boulder, CO: East European Monographs, 1984), 48.

25 Fischer, *King Zog and the Struggle for Stability in Albania,* 89–92.

The cost of this loan included an onerous pact of friendship and security with Italy which restricted Zog in terms of foreign policy and virtually allowed for Italian intervention in Albania's internal affairs as well.[26]

Zog felt that he could take the Italian money and use it to strengthen the Albanian economy to create unity and yet, through subversion, deny the Italians the type of political control they coveted. It can be argued that Zog succeeded: he got the money and he kept control of the state. But if it was a victory, it was certainly a pyrrhic one. First, the money was used unwisely. The roads and bridges constructed from the funds were built primarily for Italian military purposes. The buildings constructed were principally nonessential, including ostentatious fascist government buildings and a palace for Zog. Albania's pressing needs, including drainage and canalization and the development of indigenous industry, generally were ignored.[27] Finally, Zog's refusal to allow a complete Italian takeover helped convince Mussolini that effective control of Albania could only be achieved by invasion. Zog's successful defense of Albania's political independence ultimately cost Albania its freedom.

There was an ironic byproduct of this struggle: it facilitated the growth of nationalism. Some of the Italian money was used to send Albanian students abroad for higher education, and upon their return, these students conducted prolonged, though unorganized, agitation against Italian encroachment. Zog could not ignore this movement, and in response he stepped up his own resistance to the Italians.

Zog's religious and social policies also contributed to the growth of nationalism, but in a more direct way. Once again, the principal motivation for his policies was seeking political survival through uniting and stabilizing the country. Zog recognized that while most Albanians were not religious fanatics, their adherence to three different religions whose clergy were answerable to hierarchies outside of Albania not only presented a block to unity but allowed for considerable foreign interference in Albanian affairs. Zog sought, therefore, through the construction of autocephalous churches, to bring as many indigenous church leaders as possible under his control. Partly as a result of Zog's efforts, Albanian Muslims officially separated themselves from outside control in 1923. Following considerable intrigue and pressure, Zog succeeded in 1937 in securing the acquiescence of the Orthodox patriarch in Istanbul for the establishment of an autocephalous Albanian Orthodox church.

---

26 League of Nations, *League of Nations Treaty Series* LX (1927), 16–21.

27 Giovanni Zamboni, *Mussolini Expansionspolitik auf dem Balkan* (Hamburg: Helmut Buske Verlag, 1970), lxxi.

The greatest resistance came from Albania's smallest religious community, the Roman Catholics, who were considered the most dangerous because of their obvious connections to Italy. Recognizing that total separation was impossible, Zog hoped to remove as much of the influence of the Roman church from the Albanian Catholic community as seemed feasible. In 1925, in the hope of eliminating the custom of shooting faithless wives, along with decreasing the influence of the church, Zog instituted a new civil code which, among other things, called for civil marriages and divorces. The archbishop of Shkodër and the papal nuncio objected strenuously. However, they were told in no uncertain terms that any priest who took his objections too far would soon be provided "a tree with adequate strength to support his weight."[28] Zog underscored the threat by occasionally hanging a priest involved in rebellious activity.

While his religious policies enjoyed considerable success, Zog was clever enough to realize that the key to both modernism and nationalism was an aggressive education policy. When Albania gained its independence, it had no state educational system because of the centuries-long Ottoman ban on Albanian schools. When Zog came to power, the Albanian language was inadequate for literary and educational purposes—its vocabulary was limited, and the different dialects spoken in the north and south had not yet been merged into a single national language.[29]

By 1930 Zog had made some progress by establishing some 580 primary schools and thirteen secondary schools, which served 33,000 students out of a total population of just over one million.[30] Although there was no institution of higher learning, many Albanians were sent abroad on scholarships. In the mid–1930s, Albania took a step backward in terms of education by closing all foreign schools in the country. The move served the cause of nationalism, but it handicapped the cause of education, which was slow to recover. Nonetheless, by the time of the Italian invasion of 1939 there were 633 elementary schools and nineteen intermediate schools serving 62,000 pupils. In the main, however, these measures proved to be a modest start. When the Italians invaded, Albania still had an illiteracy rate of 85 percent.[31]

---

28 Great Britain, Public Record Office, Foreign Office 371/12847 (C2557/2557/90): Durazzo (27 March 1929); and Public Record Office, Foreign Office 371/12844 (C1351/146/90): Durazzo (3 February 1928).

29 Stavrianos, *The Balkans Since 1453*, 715.

30 Great Britain, Public Record Office, Foreign Office 371/15148 (R1412/1412/90): Durazzo (24 February 1931); and Skendi, *Albania*, 51.

31 Stavrianos, *The Balkans Since 1453*, 730.

Zog also hoped that the military would aid the spread of nationalism. First, as he mentioned in his interview with the *Daily Telegraph*, he hoped that the military would serve an educational purpose, that it would help soldiers transfer their allegiance from the tribe to the central government—a step that would turn them into modern citizens. He also hoped that the military would reduce brigandage and blood feuds, which were both rampant in Albania in the 1920s.[32] Because he relied on Italians as military advisers and instructors, his first goal eluded Zog. These Italians, rather than furthering Albanian nationalism, effectively served as agents of Italian influence, creating pro-Italian cells within the military. The Albanian military was infiltrated to the extent that when Mussolini invaded, the army was of little use to either side. However, Zog was able to reduce blood-feud killings and, in the process, broke down some regional barriers to national unity. His program to disarm the population was partially successful, although his application of the policy was selective—he allowed his own tribe, as well as those who pledged their support, to keep their weapons. Still, by 1939 the security situation had improved significantly, and this allowed for greater contact between the various parts of Albania.

Modern Albanian historiography dismisses Zog as a completely negative force.[33] While his achievements were limited, this verdict is overly harsh. Despite Zog's many failures, by the 1930s the central government was recognized in all parts of the country. The political stability which resulted, though relative, created the environment necessary for the growth of a national consciousness. Zog's resistance to the Italians provided a focus, if negative, for this growing consciousness. His contribution, then, was considerable. Those who succeeded him as rulers and who continued the construction of a modern state found their task somewhat less arduous as a result of the foundation of nationalism laid by Zog.

Enver Hoxha and State-of-Siege Nationalism

The experience of World War II in Albania, like that of World War I, served both to reinforce and to undermine the growing nationalist sentiment. Once again, the ordeal of foreign occupation did much to reinforce Albanian distinctiveness. The divisive effect of the war, however, was more profound.

---

32 In the 1920s blood-feud deaths in some areas of Albania accounted for up to 40 percent of all deaths.

33 Michael Schmidt-Neke, *Entstehung und Ausbau der Königsdiktatur in Albanien, 1912-1939* (München: R. Oldenbourg Verlag, 1985), 302.

Following their invasion and occupation, the Italians sought to integrate the traditional Albanian elite into Mussolini's new Roman Empire. Some of their efforts failed, particularly the creation of the Albanian Fascist Party. Still, many elements of the prewar political and social hierarchy compromised themselves by cooperating with the fascists and thereby contributed to what has been called the process of denationalization.[34] The success of this fascist policy fostered class division, with many middle-class Albanians—a relatively small group—and many peasants resentful of Italian and, after 1943, German occupation. The divisions between north and south were accentuated by the formation of resistance groups with regional agendas. Even the limited stability that Zog had created was jeopardized and to some extent undermined. For example, blood-feud murders increased dramatically during the war.

Following the liberation of Albania in November 1944, a bitter civil war ensued between the Communists and the nationalists. A fledgling Communist movement came to power under the leadership of Enver Hoxha. Hoxha is best described first as a nationalist, then as a Stalinist Communist, and finally as an intellectual.[35] He was a Muslim Tosk from the south and relates that the most important early influence on his life was his atheist and devotedly nationalistic uncle.[36] Since his family was reasonably prosperous, Hoxha received a good education (part of it abroad on one of Zog's scholarships) and began his career as a school teacher, a position he lost as a result of his radical politics. A brilliant organizer and politician, Hoxha is primarily responsible for turning a small faction-ridden Communist movement into the only political power in Albania in 1944. This was a remarkable achievement given Albanian's agrarian economy and the limited support a Communist movement therefore could theoretically expect.

Hoxha's greatest challenges, however, presented themselves only after his movement proved victorious in war. Hoxha was faced with not only the same problems that had confronted Zog but with the additional problem of Kosovë. The region of Kosovë, with its overwhelmingly Albanian population, had served as the cradle of Albanian nationalism in the nineteenth century but, following World War I, had become a part of Yugoslavia. Zog, although he titled himself "King of the Albanians" in order to help establish his nationalist credentials, had

---

[34] Arshi Pipa, *Albanian Stalinism: Ideo-Political Aspects* (Boulder, CO: East European Monographs, 1990), 3.

[35] Peter Prifti, "The Labor Party of Albania," in *The Communist Parties of Eastern Europe*, Stephen Fischer-Galati, ed. (New York: Columbia University Press, 1979), 17.

[36] Elez Biberaj, *Albania: A Socialist Maverick* (Boulder, CO: Westview Press, 1990), 16.

not pursued an irredentist policy for a number of reasons, and Kosovë chieftains were among his most dangerous rivals. It is also possible that Zog concluded an agreement with the Yugoslavs to leave Kosovë to them in return for the support they gave him in 1924. Finally, Zog may have come to the sensible conclusion that the rest of his problems precluded expansion. Maintaining power was far more important to Zog than a dangerous foreign policy which could lead to war with a much stronger neighbor and to internal conflict.

With the destruction of Yugoslavia in 1941, Germany awarded Kosovë to Italian Albania. Since this move proved popular both in Kosovë and in Albania proper, the nationalist resistance groups called for the incorporation of Kosovë into postwar Albania. The Communists, however, were in a very awkward position: Hoxha, whose party was formed with extensive help from Tito's emissaries, found himself caught between popular opinion, which called for enlarged frontiers, and his Yugoslav mentors, who discouraged the notion.[37] The Kosovë question remained a serious problem for Hoxha, with his domestic opponents criticizing him for failing adequately to pursue the issue, while his foreign critics, particularly those in Yugoslavia, accused him of trying to stir revolution in the region. Hoxha did not pursue actively the question for many of the same reasons that Zog had not pressed the issue. In the end, Hoxha's reluctance to move on Kosovë forced him to become extreme on other nationalist issues in order to deflect criticism and to flaunt his nationalist credentials.

Despite facing the same problems that stood in the way of Zog and despite the dangerous issue of Kosovë, in many respects Hoxha was in a better position than Zog to pursue his policies. When Hoxha came to power he had a relatively free hand as a result of his military victory in the civil war between the Communist and royalist resistance forces and by virtue of the partisan army, which Albanian sources maintain had reached 70,000 by late 1944.[38] Equally important, however, World War II had destroyed or at least completely discredited the traditional ruling classes in Albania, which had either collaborated outright or had done nothing for the resistance. Hoxha benefited from a number of other advantages as well. He had the example of Zog, which occasionally allowed him to avoid mistakes. More important, he had the legacy of fascism and the

[37] See Reginald Hibbert, *Albania's National Liberation Struggle: The Bitter Victory* (London: Pinter, 1991), 25–26. The question of what role the Yugoslavs played in the formation of the Albanian party and what position the Yugoslav party took on Kosovë during the war has caused considerable debate among historians.

[38] Prifti, "The Labor Party of Albania," 15.

sometimes manufactured but frequently real specter of capitalist encirclement to help shape his policies.

Hoxha, then, was faced with the task of rebuilding Albania on the foundation—or what was left of it—laid by Zog. Like Zog, his main goal was predetermined and was, in the simplest sense, the creation of a viable independent nation-state and what he colorfully described as "the monolithic unity...of the Albanian people."[39] Since his goals were similar in many areas to those of Zog, it is perhaps not surprising that his policy priorities often were similar as well. Despite the violent rhetoric of Stalinism, Hoxha really had no choice but to become as ardent a nationalist as Zog had been. Indeed, given the narrow base of support the Communist movement had and given Hoxha's need to downplay the Kosovë issue, extreme nationalism was the best means (added, of course, to maintaining the army and other security forces) by which Hoxha could remain in power and progress toward a modern socialist state. Nationalism proved to be the principal element in all of his policies.

Given the limited support for communism in Albania, Hoxha recognized that to gain legitimacy, he had to rapidly construct an adequate political system. This proved to be less arduous a task for him than it had been for Zog, primarily because of Hoxha's military power and the postwar political vacuum in Albania. Following the example of the Yugoslavs, in May 1944 Hoxha arranged for the establishment of the Anti-fascist Committee of National Liberation, which invested itself with all the power of a temporary government.[40] In October 1944 the committee was transformed into Albania's first postwar government with Hoxha, who had already been named commander-in-chief, as prime minister. Once in power, Hoxha hoped to stabilize his position, and he employed both intelligence and savage brutality to achieve this goal.

Hoxha's first moves toward this end included the physical removal of those forces he considered dangerous to the construction of the new socialist state. These forces were initially identified only by the somewhat generic term "war criminals," but the term soon became synonymous with "noncommunist."[41] At the same time, the term "fascism" became synonymous with "U.S.–British imperialism." Hoxha was creating the state of siege with which he would rule Albania for over forty years.

---

39 Hoxha, *Laying the Foundations of the New Albania,* introduction.

40 Pollo and Puto, *The History of Albania,* 239.

41 Great Britain, Public Record Office, Foreign Office 371/66898 (R8707/945/90): Belgrade (19 June 1947).

By 1946 the party had held its first elections, garnering 90 percent of the vote. The new national assembly abolished the monarchy, proclaimed Albania to be a people's republic, and approved a new constitution along Stalinist lines, similar to the one that had been adopted in Yugoslavia.[42] Although much of Albania's Ottoman tradition still remained, in a very short time Hoxha had succeeded in constructing a highly personal and reasonably stable regime as totalitarian as any regime to be found in 1946. Hoxha used the legacy of fascism, Albania's wartime experiences, and the fear of foreign intervention—in other words, he appealed to nationalist sentiment—to pursue more quickly and effectively the political policies that Zog had attempted in the late 1920s. The new authoritarian governmental structure allowed Hoxha to turn quickly to Albania's pressing economic and social problems.

Albania's postwar economic condition was little changed from that of the mid–1920s. The country was still overwhelmingly agricultural, and industry (in 1938) accounted for only 4.4 percent of the national income.[43] Agriculture and stock-breeding methods remained primitive. Transportation and communication still were arduous. In 1939 there were still no railroads and only 500 miles of roads, most of which were in a state of disrepair. Albania found it necessary to import all its manufactured goods as well as significant quantities of wheat, corn, and rice.[44] The war and the Axis occupation had not substantially altered Albania's economic condition.

When Hoxha came to power, then, he faced an economic situation that was similar to that faced by Zog in 1925 and which was clearly the most difficult internal economic situation in Eastern Europe. It should not be surprising, therefore, that his policies were similar to Zog's, although they were carried out with the speed and ruthless determination that was so characteristic of Hoxha. Hoxha's government obtained its initial operating expenses by confiscating the property of its "enemies," by levying a crippling war-profits tax on the bigger merchants, and by forcing subscription to internal loans.[45] This was followed by a policy of extreme centralization, which included nationalization of all industry, mobilization of all trained people, and a ban on the exportation of anything of

---

42 Anton Logoreci, *The Albanians, Europe's Forgotten Survivors* (Boulder, CO: Westview Press, 1977), 86.

43 Nicholas Pano, *The People's Republic of Albania* (Baltimore: Johns Hopkins University Press, 1968), 13.

44 Stavrianos, *The Balkans Since 1453*, 729.

45 Great Britain, Public Record Office, Foreign Office 371/48081 (R9255/46/90): Tirana (29 May 1945).

value (gold, jewelry, etc.). By 1944, industrial production had been nearly totally nationalized, which dispersed the archaic prewar economy and ultimately destroyed the small prewar middle class.[46] Socialization of agriculture, another priority, proceeded somewhat more slowly because of peasant objections, but by 1967 it had been fully achieved.[47]

Albania experienced considerable economic growth during the first years of Hoxha's regime. Despite this progress, the costs of government remained high—particularly those associated with security—and the sacrifices demanded of the people were extreme. The armed forces absorbed 10 percent or 11 percent of GNP. Added to this were the direct costs of maintaining the virtual state-of-siege, in particular the construction of tens of thousands of variably sized pillboxes, which, in their peculiar and rather eery fashion, still dot the Albanian landscape today.

Hoxha was aware, as Zog had been, that in the face of these expenses Albania could neither hold its own nor progress toward modernism without outside financial aid. Like Zog, Hoxha had few options at the outset. Tito's Yugoslavia had played a significant role in the formation of not only the Albanian Communist Party but also Hoxha's tactics and the structure of his government. Yugoslavia became the first state officially to recognize the Hoxha regime, giving it needed international legitimacy, and soon became Albania's economic model and first postwar "benefactor." The sequence of events proved to be frighteningly parallel to Zog's experience with the Italians. Working with powerful pro-Yugoslav members of the Albanian politburo, Belgrade intended to shape the Albanian economy, to take control of it, and then to swallow Albania outright. In March 1948 Hoxha came precariously close to suffering the same fate as Zog; had it not been for the break between Stalin and Tito in the summer of 1948, it is likely that Hoxha would have been arrested and shot by his pro-Yugoslav opposition on the politburo. Hoxha took advantage of the Soviet-Yugoslav break to sever all ties with Yugoslavia.

Albania, of course, was still far from ready for economic independence. Hoxha, more wary as a result of his Yugoslav experience, nevertheless turned for economic aid first to the Soviets and then to the Chinese, both far enough removed geographically to suit his purposes. While not as dangerous as the

---

46 Great Britain, Public Record Office, Foreign Office 371/43561 (R1471/1471/90): London (24 November 1944); and Peter Prifti, *Socialist Albania Since 1944* (Cambridge, MA: MIT Press, 1978), 53.

47 Richard F. Staar, *Communist Regimes in Eastern Europe* (Stanford, CA: Hoover Institution Press, 1967), 19.

Yugoslav connection, these relationships also proved unsatisfactory. Hoxha was therefore forced to initiate a policy of self-reliance, which involved limited commercial contact with selected European states. This policy proved modestly successful, at least for a time.[48] These shifts from "benefactor" to "benefactor" were officially justified on the basis of retaining Albania's ideological purity. In reality, they were motivated by pure nationalism, as Hoxha countered perceived and real threats to Albania's national sovereignty. When he could, Hoxha used these threats to his advantage. He was able to identify every setback, foreign or domestic, as the result of coordinated, aggressive activity by the Greek monarcho-fascists, Italian neo-fascists, or Yugoslav and Soviet revisionists supported by U.S. and British imperialists.[49] Hoxha hoped to convince the Albanians that they were still—to use one of his more colorful and favored phrases—hacking their way through history, sword in hand. But Hoxha's narrow nationalist approach, which led to economic isolation, was bound to fail and it did, which led directly to Albania's current desperate economic predicament.

As with politics and economics, Hoxha was forced to contend with many of the same religious and social problems that had plagued Zog. Once again, his policies and goals were similar to Zog's while his methods and results were different. His religious policies not only went further than Zog's but also went further than those of any other socialist leader. Hoxha, like Zog, saw religion as a divisive factor in Albanian society, and more important, he saw religion as perpetuating foreign control in Albania. Once again, nationalism was the primary motivating factor behind Hoxha's actions.

Hoxha began with the Catholics, who were singled out because many Catholics had either collaborated with the Italians during World War II or at least had vigorously opposed the postwar Communist takeover. Hoxha subsequently determined that the Catholic Church was controlled by—as he defined them—reactionaries, subversives, and antinationalists who represented foreign interests. The church leadership was either executed or imprisoned, with

---

48 Prifti, *Socialist Albania Since 1944*, 257; and Jan Halliday, *The Artful Albanian* (London: Chatto Press, 1986), 15.

49 For example, see Institute of Marxist-Leninist Studies, Central Committee of the Party of Labor of Albania, *History of the Party of Labor* (Tirana: The Naim Frashëri Publishing House, 1971), 350.

the rank and file clergy pensioned off or retained as civil servants.[50] In July 1951 the Catholic Church in Albania was required to sever its links with Rome.

The Orthodox and Muslim communities also were brought under state control. Those who resisted were arrested, including the entire leadership of the Orthodox Church. With the appointment of new leaders, the Orthodox Church was in effect nationalized.[51] What Hoxha hoped would be the final blow occurred in 1967, when he issued special decrees revoking the charters of all three major religions and closed—or transformed into community centers—all churches. The government proudly proclaimed Albania to be the first atheist state in the world.

Hoxha recognized that these measures alone could not eradicate religion from the minds of the people. For this, education and culture became his most useful tools. Education was, of course, a priority in any case, in light of the 85 percent illiteracy rate (as of 1939). He used education as the principal means by which to wean Albanians from their archaic social system and to encourage them onward in the struggle for the creation of "monolithic unity" and a socialist state. Once again, Hoxha began his crusade during the war. When they were not fighting, the men and women of the partisan movement received basic instruction in reading and writing, as well as in politics. Instructors maintained that all people who were not in the movement were connected with fascism, and they blamed capitalism for the failed prewar economic system.

Once the war ended, education and culture received more serious attention, and the major themes indicate the depth of Hoxha's nationalism. Extreme reverence was paid to the heroes of Albanian nationalism, whether or not they were "politically correct." Skënderbeg was, of course, one central focus, with his statue sharing a place of honor in Tirana's central square with statues of Lenin and Stalin and his castle at Krujë turned into a national shrine, with—what must be an archeologist's nightmare—a large museum constructed squarely in the center of the ruins. As important national anniversaries of the late nineteenth and early twentieth centuries Hoxha selected and designated the meeting of the League of Prizren in 1878, the linguistic congress at Monastir in 1908, and an event in which Zog played a major role, the removal of the Italians from Vlorë in 1920.[52] Particular homage was paid to Ismail Kemal Bey, despite the fact that he was the head of one of Albania's great feudal families which was

---

50 Ramadan Marmullaku, *Albania and the Albanians* (London: C. Hurst and Company, 1975), 76; and Logoreci, *The Albanians,* 154.

51 Prifti, *Socialist Albania Since 1944,* 151.

52 Prifti, "The Labor Party of Albania," 8.

later credited with producing many reactionaries and collaborators.[53] Much care was extended to the preservation of national monuments, historic towns, and cities—with the exception perhaps of Skenderbëg's castle at Krujë—many of which have been designated as museum cities. Hoxha insisted that Albania's cultural heritage, folk costumes, folk songs, and dances be preserved.[54]

Despite this emphasis on history, the central focal point for education and culture continued to be—at least until Hoxha's death in 1985—the liberation struggle of the Albanians against the invader.[55] Textbooks, traditional histories, literature for children, general literature, drama, and film—all were limited to variations on this same theme. Even Albanian coins depict a successful armed struggle against foreign invasion.

Although the content of Albanian education remained static under Hoxha, there were significant achievements. The illiteracy rate was reduced to 30 percent by 1950. Five years later, the regime proudly proclaimed that illiteracy among adults under the age of 40 had been completely eradicated.[56] Not only could most Albanians now read and write, but Hoxha had insured that they did so in a uniform way; in order to achieve integration and to further reduce internal divisions, Hoxha decreed that the Tosk dialect, with some Gheg additions to enrich the vocabulary, would be Albania's official language.[57] His action takes on more meaning in light of the fact that the Communist movement originated and was much stronger among the Tosks and that Hoxha himself was a Tosk. Although he was motivated by nationalism and the desire to construct a modern nation-state, he justified the move on the basis of Stalinist doctrine. Albanian scholar Arshi Pipa summarizes this policy by suggesting,

> Hoxha was decisive in producing a cultural atmosphere totally dominated by a doctrinaire propaganda exalting nationalism. Linguistics, literature, history, geography, folklore, and ethnology have been cultivated, not only to give the people a sense of their own past, but also to spread and inculcate

---

[53] Schmidt-Neke, *Entstehung und Ausbau der Königsdiktatur in Albanien,* 302.

[54] Prifti, "The Labor Party of Albania," 9.

[55] As an example see Ismail Kadare, *Doruntine* (New York: New Amsterdam, 1988), the major theme of which is the danger of foreign entanglements.

[56] Logoreci, *The Albanians,* 112.

[57] Pipa, *Albanian Stalinism,* 254 n30.

xenophobia, slavophobia, isolationism, ethnic compactness, and linguistic uniformity.[58]

Ramiz Alia and the New Nationalism

When Enver Hoxha died in 1985, he was succeeded by his longtime associate Ramiz Alia, a Muslim Gheg from Shkodër, who was born to parents who fled Kosovë during the Balkan wars of 1912–13. As a child, Alia had joined the fascist Youth of the Lictor but then joined the Communist Party in 1943.[59] Demonstrating considerable administrative talent and loyalty, he worked his way up to become a close associate of Hoxha, a politburo member, and Albania's chief ideologue, responsible for much of Hoxha's traditional and nationalistic cultural policy. When Alia came to power in 1985, he did not need to focus his attention on beginning to instill nationalism, as did Ismail Kemal, or restarting the process, as did Zog and Hoxha. Still, Alia's task was no less difficult. He soon found it necessary to redefine completely Albanian nationalism because of the rapid changes then underway in Eastern Europe.

Alia's challenges included the need to function under the cult of personality that still surrounded Hoxha, who lived on as the father of the socialist nation and as its chief theorist and intellectual. Hoxha's widow Nexhmije served as the guardian of ideological purity. Far more serious, however, were the economic difficulties that faced Alia almost immediately. Hoxha's extreme centrism and his emphasis on heavy industry, as well as the economic isolation that was the result of his policies, soon led to dislocation, stagnation, and shortages. By the late 1980s, following two bad harvests, Albania, which since the mid–1970s had declared itself to be agriculturally self-sufficient in bread grains, found itself unable to provide for the basic needs of its people. Simultaneously, the determination with which the conservatives maintained Hoxha's state-of-siege nationalism at the core of Albanian society led to social and cultural stagnation. Internal disenchantment was further enhanced by the introduction in the Soviet Union under Gorbachev of *glasnost* and *perestroika*, developments generally reported accurately by the Albanian press.

Alia found himself driven by events. His support for Stalinism and for the ideas of Hoxha, although loudly proclaimed, became little more than hollow

---

58 Pipa, *Albanian Stalinism,* 121.

59 Skendi, *Albania,* 322.

rhetoric. While he roundly condemned *glasnost* and *perestroika* as counterrevolutionary and as precursors to capitalism, Alia began to implement the very tenets he denounced. Alia called for backing away from Albania's rigid nationalist themes. He declared that "Socialist society must support individual creativity... Art in particular is not made with patterns and prefabricated materials."[60] This was a significant shift from the cultural policy he had set in 1965 when he stated that the chief function of literature and art was to provide young people with the necessary immunity against the poisons of both bourgeois and revisionist ideologies.[61] In 1965 he intended Albania's youth to be exposed to nothing other than Hoxha's siege nationalism. By 1990, as demonstrated by his speech excerpted above, Alia was concentrating on less hostile nationalist themes—emphasizing the need for progress and traditional nationalism more than the achievements of socialism, and for regional and international cooperation rather than embattled encirclement.

Once the process of reform had been given official sanction, it could not be stopped. By 1989 the collapse of Eastern European regimes as well as continuing economic deterioration at home forced Alia to broaden his cultural reforms to include economics and politics. In attempting to stimulate the economy, Alia took another page from *perestroika*. Enterprises and agricultural cooperatives were granted more independence in wage incentives, planning, production, and investment, and elements of economic accountability were introduced.[62] This decentralization was accompanied by a degree of *glasnost*, with the press beginning regularly to criticize the conservative mentality of those who stood in the way of reform.

During the summer of 1990 unrest reached new heights, when thousands of Albanians stormed foreign embassies in the hope of getting out of the country. Alia responded with an appeal to nationalism, labeling those who participated in these actions as "anti-national."[63] But he accompanied his criticism with reform: he called for democratization, liberalization, and further reforms which would not endanger socialism. He introduced liberalization in personal relations and personal conduct. He began to release political prisoners in

---

60 Pipa, *Albanian Stalinism,* 171.

61 Logoreci, *The Albanians,* 160.

62 Louis Zanga, "Albania Moving Along, But Slowly," *Report on Eastern Europe,* vol. 1, no. 1 (RFE/RL Research Institute, January 1990), 5.

63 Speech by Ramiz Alia to the 11th Plenum of the CC of the PLA, The Institute of Marxist-Leninist Studies at the CC of the PLA (Tirana: "8 Nëntori" Publishing House, 1990), 16.

1986 and continued in 1987, and by March of 1991 the government maintained that all political prisoners had been freed. The powers of the Sigurimi, the state security service, including arbitrary internment and internal deportation, were curtailed. In a major step in early 1990, Alia revoked the restrictions on religious worship in the home and travel abroad. At about the same time, he extended economic freedom to peasants, allowing them to sell not only vegetables but also fresh poultry and meat on the free market.

Political reform inevitably followed the economic reforms, albeit more slowly. Alia was more resistant to reform in this area, fearing the reappearance of internal divisions. He argued, "As a small country, we need to have strong unity. We cannot accept divisions as it may be the case with a big country."[64] But once the reform started, it moved beyond his control. Following student riots and demonstrations in Albania's major cities, Alia liberalized the local election process by allowing voters to choose from among more than one Communist candidate. Ultimately, Alia agreed to allow the formation of opposition parties and called for multiparty elections. The strongest of these opposition parties, the Democratic Party, put together a vague platform calling for private property, economic shock therapy, and respect for human rights.[65] With little time to organize and little access to the electorate—and given Albania's lack of democratic tradition—it is perhaps not surprising that the Communists won a comfortable majority in the first multiparty election held in March 1991. Perhaps seeing the writing on the wall, the Party of Labor—what the Communists had called themselves since 1948—was renamed the Socialist Party. Alia, who was reelected as president by the last assembly to be dominated by the Party of Labor, did not become a member of the new Socialist Party.

Equally as dramatic were the changes in Albania's foreign relations. Motivated by continuing economic problems, Alia began drifting from Hoxha's isolationism soon after he came to power. He clearly decided that from a strictly economic standpoint, state-of-siege nationalism was a disaster. Albania's relations with its Balkan neighbors became a top priority for commercial reasons and also because this represented Albania's most pressing foreign policy problem. Despite the continuation of national and territorial disputes, in 1987 Alia was able to end the technical state of war that had existed between Albania and Greece since World War II.

---

64 David Binder, "Albanian Leader Says the Country Will Be Democratized but Will Retain Socialism," *New York Times*, 14 May 1990.

65 Kenneth Roth, "Democracy's Race Against Fear," *Nation*, 6 May 1991.

On the other hand, relations with Yugoslavia, Albania's chief trading partner, remained strained because of the growing problem of Kosovë. Slobodan Milošević, the Serbian president, had increased both repression and Serbian chauvinism. This, and the corresponding easing of Stalinism in Albania, led Kosovë's two-and-a-half million Albanians to think more positively about the possibility of reuniting with Albania.[66] Alia recognized that Hoxha's policy of simple vitriolic verbal abuse needed to be changed, yet he seemed unsure of how to proceed. He therefore initiated what might be described as a dual or contradictory policy. On one hand, in the interest of normalizing relations with Yugoslavia and in the name of Balkan cooperation, Alia toned down the nationalistic rhetoric and on occasion suggested that Kosovë was primarily a Yugoslav problem. In November 1986 Alia announced, "We do not want the situation in Kosovë to grow worse. In no instance and in no way have we sought to destabilize Yugoslavia."[67] At a 1988 Balkan conference held in Belgrade, Alia's foreign minister declared that the question of minorities was a domestic concern.[68]

On the other hand, Alia, whose parents were Kosovars, recognized that he could ignore Kosovë irredentism only at his peril. As a result, Kosovë remained an important issue in the Albanian press, and the Alia government strongly supported the goal of republic status (within Yugoslavia) for Kosovë. (The language used was considerably more gentle, however, with the terms "mistaken policy" and Serbian "anti-constitutional action" replacing Hoxha's traditional venom against Yugoslavia.)[69] To further demonstrate his nationalist credentials, Alia took the problem to the United Nations on 28 September 1990, an event made all the more noteworthy because it marked the first time Alia had traveled abroad as president and the first time an Albanian head of state had addressed the United Nations. Perhaps even more important, it was the first time the Albanian government had made a major statement regarding Kosovë before the United Nations, which brought international attention to the issue.

Motivated primarily by economic factors, Alia also hoped to integrate Albania into the international community. In a dramatic reversal of Hoxha's

---

66 Christopher Cviic, *Remaking the Balkans* (New York: Council on Foreign Relations Press, 1991), 104.

67 Biberaj, *Albania, A Socialist Maverick*, 95.

68 Pipa, *Albanian Stalinism*, 161.

69 "The Constitution of the Republic of Kosovo, a Legal Historical Act," *Zëri i Popullit*, reproduced in *Albania Today* 114, no. 5 (1990), 60.

isolationist policy, Alia supported multinational regional cooperation in the Balkans and even applied for membership in the European Community, something that will not be granted for decades. Alia's rejection of Hoxha's state-of-siege mentality and narrow nationalism was perhaps capped by Albania's resumption of relations with both the Soviet Union and the United States.

Alia's new policies, while undoubtedly positive, were too little too late. They failed to arrest Albania's slide into economic despair and chaos. As of May 1992, Albania remained in a desperate situation. The economy had essentially collapsed. Unemployment hovered at 50 percent; inflation was reported to be out of control; and wages, although on the increase, had failed to keep pace with rapidly rising costs.[70] The government's principal remaining source of revenue seemed to be the sale of relief goods, most of which had come from Italy. Albanian politicians estimated that as many as 200,000 Albanians—mostly young and able-bodied—had fled the country. The immediate economic future remained bleak.

By 1992 the head of Albania's national police had reported an explosion of crime. The once-secured streets had been overrun by thieves, black marketeers, money-changers, and aggressive beggars. Armed mobs attacked trains and convoys carrying relief supplies. The police complained that they were powerless against this type of mob action. The statues of Stalin and Hoxha had been pulled down, but so were trees from public parks to be used for fuel, and public walls to be used for building material.

Political freedom had not yet engendered many positive results. Many Albanians, who lacked even the idea of a democratic tradition, saw democracy as a license to act in any manner they choose. This notion contributed significantly to the chaos. The initial elections of 1991 did much to emphasize social fragmentation—the opposition did well in the towns, while the Communists held the countryside, where more than 70 percent of the population is concentrated.[71] Whether the relaxation of restrictions on religious expression will serve to emphasize further the religious divisions remains to be seen. In any case, Alia's fears that Albanian society would fragment were realized. Hoxha's forced monolithic unity has proved to be quite fragile.

---

70 Brenda Fowler, "Albania Searches for Stable Future," *New York Times*, 16 February 1992; and Henry Kamm, "No Food or Jobs or Spirit: Albania Prepares to Vote," *New York Times*, 15 March 1992.

71 David Binder, "A Bitter Split for Albania," *New York Times*, 4 April 1991.

Although Alia presented himself as a longtime supporter of democratization and the free market, the inability of his government to deal with Albania's economic problems ultimately overwhelmed him. In the March 1992 elections, the Democrats surged to power with about 65 percent of the vote. On 3 April, after the Democrats made it clear that they would not submit their cabinet nominees to Alia, he resigned. Alia noted that he had governed for the sake "of people's unity, political progress of the country and the consolidation of democracy" and that he was resigning for the same reason.[72] Still, Albania's best hope for the future may be Alia's new nationalism, redefined, less rigid, and operating in a world with fewer enemies. Albanians must now develop a post-Hoxha national self-definition. To stem the tide of emigration by the most productive members of Albanian society, Albania must, like many of its neighbors, rediscover its identity and reevaluate the shared responsibilities of its citizens. Of course, this process is dangerous. Significant nationality problems clearly still exist, and since the new nationalism is less rigid and controlled, there is the possibility of a different variety of extremism. For example, extreme nationalists may oppose the reformers' efforts to grant economic and political rights to Albania's Greek minority. While Hoxha's treatment of the Greek minority was never warm, he never considered it in his best interest to dictate severe repression. Modern extremists may not be as circumspect. They may look for new enemies in order to garnish popular support in an infant democracy. There also is the perennial problem of Kosovë, which some observers have identified as the most potentially dangerous problem in the Balkans today.[73] Still, no state is actively pursuing the destruction of Albania; indeed, no state even covets Albanian territory. The dearth of foreign foes allows Albania to undertake regional and international cooperation, which it sorely needs in order to begin the process of recovery. The Democrats have committed themselves to a complete break with the past. This pledge should include further distancing of Albania from Hoxha's state-of-siege nationalism and acceleration of the process of redefining nationalism, which Alia began.

Conclusion

The four Albanian nationalists considered here had a similar goal: to instill modern nationalism through the creation of a viable nation-state in Albania, where both had been lacking for much of the twentieth century. They achieved

---

72 "Communist Quits as Albania Chief," *New York Times*, 4 April 1992.

73 Cviic, *Remaking the Balkans*, 105.

varying degrees of success. Ismail Kemal had the most difficult task. Despite the myriad obstacles he faced, his main achievement—the declaration of Albanian independence—is recognized as significant and lasting. If Ismail Kemal helped to prepare the ground for nationalism and creation of an Albanian nation-state, then Zog laid the foundation. His opportunities were greater, as were his achievements. By 1939 Albanians, for the first time, were beginning to think of themselves in broader terms than their tribal and regional affiliations.

Much of Zog's hard-won progress, however, was reversed during World War II. Enver Hoxha, therefore, like his predecessors, found it necessary to begin again. Hoxha had more time and was both more ruthless and more determined. He was also more successful, forcibly obliterating tribal, regional, linguistic, religious, and economic divisions and replacing them with a rigid, narrow nationalism supported by a state-of-siege mentality.

Alia, when he came to power in 1985, discovered that, despite Hoxha's success, significant divisions remained below the surface. To bridge them, he hoped to reconstruct Albanian nationalism in a more progressive, less doctrinaire form, but because he also hoped to save socialism, he was soon swept away. Albania's new democratic leaders have pledged themselves to construct a new open Albania based on cooperative, nonaggressive nationalism. If economic factors do not overwhelm them, the Democrats may succeed in inaugurating the first truly progressive period in the brief history of independent Albania.

3

The Course and Discourses of Bulgarian Nationalism

by Maria Todorova

Document 1

from the preface to *The Bulgarians in Their Historical, Ethnograhical and Political Frontiers,* by D. Rizoff (1917).[1]

For many years the Balkan peninsula has been the principal source of strife between the Great Powers of Europe....And after the Balkan states commenced to live their own political lives, the Balkans became a new arena of discord among these nations themselves. This became particularly the case after Bulgaria was liberated (in 1878) and, through an unfortunate decision of the Congress of

[1] D. Rizov, *Die Bulgaren in ihren historischen, ethnographischen und politischen Grenzen (Atlas mit 40 Landkarten)* (Berlin: Königliche Hoflithographie, Hof-Buch- und Steindruckerei Wilhelm Greve, 1917). The author was Bulgarian minister plenipotentiary in Berlin during World War I. The long tetralingual preface (German, French, English, and Bulgarian) is, in fact, an independent pamphlet which summarizes the national aspirations of the Bulgarians until the catastrophic outcome of the war. Although as a whole all three translations from the Bulgarian into German, English, and French are professional and of high quality, there are some discrepancies and mistakes. The present text is a revised English translation (by M. Todorova) compared against and corrected with the original Bulgarian text of the author, so as to meticulously reflect all possible nuances.

Berlin, whole provinces were torn away and handed around to its neighbors: Macedonia to Turkey, the Nish province to Serbia, and the Dobrudja to Romania....

Wronged and rent asunder at the Congress of Berlin, the Bulgarians perceived early the danger which threatened not only their national unity but even their political existence. They made haste to declare, in September 1885, the union of the two severed Bulgarias—north and south—in order also to be better able to defend their frontiers towards Romania and Serbia, and to occupy themselves more seriously with the fate of Macedonia. But so natural a union as this, which did not make even Turkey, whose interests were infringed by it, indignant, was not to the liking of Serbia and, in the name of the "equilibrium in the Balkans," it attempted to frustrate it by attacking Bulgaria in the night of 1/13 November of the same year. To its misfortune, it was defeated in thirteen days and compelled to seek peace. But the Bulgarians were not intoxicated with their victory over Serbia. In their constant striving to live in peace with other nations—particularly with their neighbors—they made peace with Serbia "without annexations and indemnities." And soon afterward they brought forward the most equitable and practical solution for an agreement regarding Macedonia among the Balkan states interested in it. That solution was the autonomy of Macedonia, guaranteed and applied under the protectorate of the Great Powers. But Serbia and Greece declared themselves opposed to autonomy. They did this because they knew that Macedonia is populated by a Bulgarian majority which, under an autonomous government, would give the whole of Macedonia a Bulgarian physiognomy, and would not wait long before it united into the Bulgarian Principality—as occurred with Southern Bulgaria in 1885. In the face of this opposition of Serbs and Greeks to the autonomy of Macedonia, the Macedonian Bulgarians decided to achieve it themselves, arms in hand....

From this instructive history, narrated here in its chief episodes, I think that I can deduce the following propositions and conclusions:

That the Balkan peninsula has been for many years the principal hearth wherefrom have come the sparks which have kindled most of the wars in Europe, and which kindled the present Great War.

That the Balkan peninsula could have been such a hearth because it has not been crystallized nationally, politically, and economically. Turkey, to whom it belonged for more than five centuries, ruled it only thanks to military force, while, after the liberation of Serbia, Greece, and Bulgaria, a large part of the Balkan peninsula remained in Turkish hands and became an object of conquest for the Balkan states and of rivalry among the Great Powers.

That all attempts at the pacification of the Balkans during the last forty years have been made by Bulgaria alone—the only Balkan state which has striven for an agreement with its neighbors (preferably with Serbia), and which has made three formal attempts [in 1897, 1904, and 1911] to bring about this agreement.

That for the realization of this aim, Bulgaria has been ready even to sacrifice union with Macedonia, consenting to have an autonomous state formed out of it, which would serve as a unifying link between the Balkan states, and as an independent political unit would enter into a future Balkan confederation.

That for the same purpose Bulgaria even consented, in 1912, to suffer a living member of its national organism to be severed by agreeing to have a part of the Bulgarian lands in Northern Macedonia ceded to Serbia.

That, all for the same purpose, Bulgaria has never raised any question regarding its lands in the Dobrudja and the Nish province....

That Bulgaria has always nourished aspirations only for lands that have belonged to it in the past, with which it has shared the Turkish yoke for centuries and which have been recognized as Bulgarian by all authoritative travelers in European Turkey, as well as by Turkey itself and the Great Powers at their Constantinople Conference in 1876–77.[2]

And finally, that the legend regarding some sort of ambition on the part of Bulgaria to impose its hegemony upon the Balkan peninsula—a legend concocted by the Greeks and the Serbs in 1913—is one of the most groundless and perfidious libels ever cast on a nation....

The pacification of the Balkan peninsula is possible only if the Balkan states crystallize nationally, politically, and economically. Such a crystallization is possible only when these states settle their final frontiers. The fixing of these frontiers has to be based upon the following fundamental principles: that they be as natural as possible; that they enclose the respective nations in their national constitutive parts; that they safeguard the economic independence of these nations; that they correspond to their historical traditions and do not conflict with the right of each nation to self-determination....

A crystallization of the Balkan peninsula on the basis on the enunciated principles will result in the following political frontiers for the Balkan states:

Turkey will have to retain in Europe its present frontier with Bulgaria fixed by the Turko-Bulgarian Boundary Convention of 24 August–6 September....

Romania shall have to renounce formally and irrevocably possession of the old Dobrudja presented to it in 1878 as well as of the new Dobrudja seized by it in 1913, and to withdraw to its old frontier behind the Danube. This must be

---

[2] Note: At the Constantinople conference, which convened in December 1876, an agreement was reached between the European powers that Bulgaria should be divided into an eastern and a western autonomous province (whose overall territory anticipated the future frontiers of San Stefano Bulgaria). The conference failed, as the sultan rejected its provisions and promulgated the first Ottoman constitution. —Ed.

done not only because Dobrudja is the cradle of the Bulgarian people[3] and for twelve whole centuries has been a Bulgarian province; not only because Romania in 1878 considered Dobrudja a Bulgarian province and was indignant that Russia should deprive it of Bessarabia in exchange; not only because the whole of Dobrudja has already been taken from Romania by force of arms; but also because Romania has never belonged to the Balkan peninsula and must not encroach on it any further if peace with Bulgaria be desired and, in general, if the peace of the Balkans should not be disturbed. Romania must quit Dobrudja also for another reason: the mouth of an international river such as the Danube should not be held by any one state alone....

Bulgaria would have to reunite to itself all provinces that were torn away by force in 1878 and distributed to its neighbors, namely Macedonia, Dobrudja, and the Nish province. Bulgaria has national, moral, historical, and geographical rights to them, acknowledged by the former rulers of these provinces themselves, by nearly all the authoritative geographers and travelers to the Balkans, and by all the Great Powers. It is true that in the course of the forty years' possession of Dobrudja by Romania and of the Nish province by Serbia, these two states succeeded in imposing upon them, by the power of their rule, their national imprint. But it is no less true that the Bulgarian rights to these provinces are so inalterable and incontestable that they can be defended both by the French formula of *désannexion* enunciated by French Prime Minister Ribot, and by the German formula of *réannexion*, advanced by German professor and economist Adolf Wagner....

It is scarcely necessary to prove that Bulgaria must also take back Macedonia, which even its enemies have recognized in the past as Bulgarian, and to reunite all parts that have a Bulgarian majority. As for the capital, Thessalonika, its only port, it must either be neutralized as a free city, or else become a joint possession ("condominium") of Greece and Bulgaria, as it was between the two Balkan wars (1912–13)....

Serbia must be restored in the boundaries which remain (after the restitution to Bulgaria of the provinces taken in the past), annexing, on the other hand, the whole of Montenegro and the whole of northeastern Albania, e.g., Metohia and—famous for its history and fertility—Kossovo Pole. In this manner, Serbia will obtain an outlet to the sea, so much dreamt of and so necessary, on the Adriatic [which]...will ensure the economic independence of

[3] Note: The proto-Bulgars of the seventh century settled in the Danube delta, and the newly created Bulgarian state, which was recognized by the Byzantines in 681 (considered the birthdate of Bulgaria), was centered in northeast Bulgaria (the Dobrudja included). —Ed.

the Serbian people. One indispensable condition for guaranteeing the peace is that Serbia once and for all renounce Macedonia.

Montenegro, as said, must be annexed to Serbia: because it is a purely Serbian country; because the entire Montenegrin people ardently desires this union with Serbia; because Montenegro does not possess the necessary conditions for a modern independent state....

Albania, like all other Balkan countries, has a right to an independent political existence. But the experiment with independence during 1913–15 showed that it does not possess the qualification required for a politically sovereign state. It would be even less viable after Metohia and Kossovo Pole are given to Serbia—for without them the union of Serbia and Montenegro is virtually impossible. Albania might still be set up as an autonomous state under the protectorate of one of the great Adriatic powers, Austria or Italy. But in such a case, it would only be a foreign colony and, what is worse, would become a new source of rivalries and dissensions in the Balkans. Therefore, for all the sympathy one should feel for the political independence of this original nation..., I think that it would be preferable for both the Albanians themselves and the pacification of the peninsula if Albania were to enter as a component part of the neighboring Balkan states—with a guarantee, by an international act, of course, for religious and national-educational liberties for the Albanian nation....

Greece, so generously expanded by the accession of the upper Epirus and of southern Albania, should restore to Bulgariose Macedonian segments seized in 1913, and to whose cession to Bulgaria Venizelos himself had consented before the second Balkan war....

When the above frontiers of the Balkan states crystallize at an international congress, and the great humanitarian principle of international arbitration becomes compulsory for them, no further doubt could arise about the attainment of a pacification of the Balkan peninsula....

Bulgaria is a small country. It can neither afford to dream of any imperialism or hegemony in the Balkan peninsula, nor to strive to achieve national political unification merely by force. Neither can it cover its war aims with the lofty phrase of fighting "for the liberty and civilization of the whole world." For Bulgaria, the moral element in policy is obligatory. Therefore, Bulgaria must bring proof of its inalienable rights over the provinces it considers Bulgarian and, in this manner, gain the moral sanction of the whole world for unification.

Document 2

from "The Psychology of the Bulgarian," by Constantine Gîlîbov (1934).[4]

The psychology of today's Bulgarian is to a considerable degree the psychology of a person in a transition period, when his life very rapidly changes from one set of structures to another. There are many dislocated elements in his psyche. Our quick uprooting from the rural and semi-rural life, our fast integration into the culture of Western Europe, made us turn 180 degrees around on our own axis, with the result that we are disoriented.

To what extent we are confused is evident, for example, from the fact that we held it necessary to build one of the most modern and expensive theaters in Europe before providing Plovdiv with a drainage system; to boast of one of the most luxurious university halls in the world, of which even Herriot was astonished and, at the same time, to locate our faculty of physics and mathematics in a building that we are ashamed to show to foreigners; to build prisons more hygienic than sanatoria but to keep our peasant children and a good part of our urban children in schools that stink worse than stables. Our individual and social lives seem to be obsessed by a practical spirit; yet, we are extremely unpractical: we tend to satisfy the less pressing needs first, putting aside the urgent ones.

To what extent we are confused is evident further from our politics. Reared in the spirit of freedom which rages in our revolutionary songs and which exploded like a volcano during the great April uprising and later during two revolts of Macedonians and Thracians, we managed to drive away the centuries-old and much stronger enemy during the Balkan war with our indomitable zeal to win. Immediately, however, we became victims of our own proclivity towards disorientation: we imagined that we could achieve the reunification of the Bulgarian people at once, instead of at separate stages. We were given a lot, but we wanted all, and therefore we received nothing. It is a great delusion to claim that the Bulgarians have a practical spirit. After all, is it practical to believe that after having fought for months on end, while your allies have been resting behind your back, you would be able to defeat them all at one time, assuming

---

[4] Excerpts from Konstantin Gîlîbov, *Ornamenti (Filosofski i literaturni eseta)* (Sofia, 1934). Reprinted in M. Draganov, ed., *Narodopsikhologiya na bulgarite. Antologiya* (Sofia: Otechestven front, 1984), 567–69. The author was a literary critic and writer. Translation by M. Todorova.

at the same time that Turks and Romanians would let the grass grow under their feet? This is much more than being impractical—it is sheer stupidity. Our individual and social lives seem to be obsessed by a practical spirit; yet, we are extremely unpractical: in 1913 we lost our self-assessment, we lost our sense of reality, we took on for ourselves a task far beyond our powers and unattainable at the time, only to become even more confused in 1915! The reunification of the Bulgarians is a complicated political task of a European order and our politicians recognized this well, but in their attempts to come closer to its solution they became confused even before the Balkan war, and were twice as confused once they got down to solving it. Our politicians did what they could because they were not fit to do any more. May God forgive their sins; the people will never forgive them...

The psychology of today's Bulgarian is determined to a great extent by his way of life. What is this way of life? It is the way of life of a country that is under the continuous influence of the closely located and closely related civilized states of Europe; of a country gripped with the desire to catch up with their development; of a country that is swiftly incorporating the cultural requirements of these states; but, at the same time, of a country that is poor, with limited opportunities for economic development and, therefore, impotent to satisfy these needs. The Bulgarian wants to have everything that people in the civilized European states have—proper dress, electricity, radio, etc.—but his means are few, and what follows is a ferocious struggle of each against everybody to accumulate money and an ensuing roughening of the souls. And since the europeanization of our poor country will continue to be difficult, the struggle of each against everybody and the roughening of the souls will continue for a long time. What the Bulgarian is today has its deep roots in the peculiar cultural-historical stage in which our people are living, and it is impossible to eliminate these roots. The Bulgarian will be tomorrow what he is today—as long as his will for cultural progress is alive and as long as he continues to be so poor.

Document 3

from a speech by Todor Zhivkov, "Address on Bulgaria," delivered on the occasion of the 1300th anniversary of the Bulgarian state (20 October 1981).[5]

What are the qualities and traditions that characterize our people?

First and foremost, there is the fighting spirit, and *democratic and revolutionary traditions*. Our history is a sequence of countless protest movements, rebellions, conspiracies, and uprisings, a perpetual struggle by the people against foreign and domestic plunderers and oppressors, for justice and liberty, for a decent human life, for social progress. The revolutionary traditions found a logical continuation in the struggle of the working class against capitalism. They have been one of the main motivating forces of our progress, of our struggle to construct a mature socialist society and to build communism.

A striking characteristic of our people is their *thirst for knowledge, for education,* their receptivity to all which is good and progressive in other peoples and, at the same time, their readiness to share with others their own cultural achievements, their social experience....

Another valuable feature that we, as a people, should continue to foster and cultivate within ourselves is *industry.* Our people hate plunderers and despise idlers. Our ideal of man is the laborer, the creator and producer of material and spiritual values....

Ardent patriotism is one of our people's outstanding qualities. For centuries, forced to defend the freedom and independence of the fatherland, our people

---

[5] Todor Zhivkov (b. 1911) was First (General) Secretary of the Bulgarian Communist Party from 1954 to 1989. Excerpts from Todor Zhivkov, "Address on Bulgaria," delivered at the ceremonial assembly dedicated to the 1300th anniversary of the Bulgarian state (20 October 1981). *Slovo za Bulgariya, proizneseno na turzhestvenoto zasedanie na CK na Bulgarskata Komunisticheska Partiya, Narodnoto subranie, Durzhavniya i ministerskiya suvet na NR Bulgariya, US na Bulgarskiya Zemedelski Naroden Suyuz, NS na Otechestveniya Front, CK na Bulgarskite Profesionalni Suyuzi, CK na Dimitrovskiya komunisticheski mladezhki suyuz i Obshtonarodniya yubileen komitet, posveteno na 1300-godishninata ot osnovavaneto na bulgarskata durzhava. 20 oktomvri 1981* (Sofia: Partizdat, 1981). Reprinted in Todor Zhivkov, *Izbrani suchineniya* 32 (Sofia: Partizdat, 1984), 223–46. There has been an English translation in *Todor Zhivkov: Statesman and Builder of New Bulgaria,* second rev. ed. (White Plains, NY: Pergamon Press, 1985). The above is a translation from the Bulgarian original by M. Todorova.

have known how to love and sacrifice themselves for it. But love of the fatherland is typical of every people. *A distinctive feature of the Bulgarian people is the combination of patriotism and internationalism.* Good and bad people do not exist. What exists are evil oppressors—both foreign and domestic....

In fighting against the Ottoman oppressors, our haiduts and insurgents were not at war with the Turkish people. Hundreds of Bulgaria's sons fought valiantly for the freedom and independence of neighboring peoples just as they fought for the freedom and independence of their own people. Thousands of Armenians found refuge, home, and motherland in Bulgaria. When the German fascists and their Bulgarian puppets committed outrages throughout the country, the Bulgarian Jews escaped the fate of the Jews in most other European states thanks to the struggle of our people. No other than the great Lenin himself called the Bulgarian "narrow socialists" internationalists in deed.[6] No other than the first party secretary and state leader of the Soviet Union, Leonid Brezhnev, defined Bulgarian-Soviet friendship as a model of socialist internationalism in action....

Respect for the rights and freedoms of other peoples, friendliness, love of peace, an inner conviction that there is nothing more precious than peace, mutual understanding and good neighboring relations is another characteristic feature of our people, directly linked to internationalism....

Filled with respect toward Bulgaria's past, we do not forget that our history is the history of class societies, of class struggle. The past also has had dark periods of reactionary domination; there have been harrowing tragedies for the people and for the nation.

But no single oppressor, whether foreigner or domestic, has ever been able to boast of having subdued the Bulgarian people. History remembers the powerful movement of the Bogomils; the vanquishing sword of the peasant king Ivailo glows in it. For five long centuries of slavery, the clattering hooves of King Ivan Shishman's legendary cavalry resounded across the Bulgarian lands. Ceaseless class battles also have marked the century since the country's liberation from foreign yoke. If one word is to express the quintessence of our history, that word would be *struggle.* And always, in the front ranks of this struggle were Mother Bulgaria's dearest children, her brightest minds: men of letters and enlighteners, haiduts and voevods, rebels and revolutionaries, and, during the last nine decades, our own Communist Party.

This is what we glorify. This is what gives us legitimate right to high national self-esteem.

---

6 Note: Following the congress of 1903, the Bulgarian Social Democratic Party split into "narrows" and "broads," similar to the division in Russia between Bolsheviks and Mensheviks. —Ed.

Our people have respect for themselves, for their achievements and history. We are proud of having been able also to "contribute something to the world." However, national conceit, national arrogance are alien to us. We respect the order of other households; we are grateful to everyone from whom we have received something. We have no need to appropriate other peoples' merits and history; we are satisfied with our own. As for those who attempt to humiliate and slander us, to distort and rob us of our past, to them we shall repeat the words of the passionate Father Paisii: "Read the history!"...

The lasting grandeur of the accomplishments of our ancestors lies in the fact that the Bulgarian state—unlike other states then existing on our continent—was built on the principle of nationality [*narodnost*], as a state of one people—the Bulgarian people. It originated from three main components—Protobulgarians, Slavs, and Thracians—that together formed one nationality, the Bulgarians. This was the first Slav state, heralding the political and spiritual awakening of millions of Slavs, which helped them to join the civilization of the day and propelled them to take their place in the vanguard of that civilization.

Glory be to the great prime builders, under whose leadership the Bulgarian people created their own centralized state: the khans Asparukh, Krum, and Omurtag; prince Boris I; the tsars Simeon, Samuil, Assen, and Peter, Kaloyan, and Ivan-Assen II!...

Bulgaria is the home of the Slavic alphabet, of the Slavic script and culture.... Glory be to the brothers Cyril and Methodius, who in the darkness of the early Middle Ages gave our people and all of Slavdom the inextinguishable torch of education and progress!...

Our people survived under two yokes which lasted for centuries and slowed down their natural development. They were deprived of a state, of land, of rights, of their Orthodox faith; they were deprived of everything, except hope. They were denied all, but obedience. One could say that these were sorrowful, disgraceful centuries in our history, but they were illuminated by the continuous struggle for freedom and independence.

The legendary haiduts never left the enslavers in peace, and the people began singing songs to their valor... Uprisings broke out. Then came our resurrection—the National Revival. Great ideologists and leaders of the national-democratic revolution emerged: Georgi Rakovski, Lyuben Karavelov, Vassil Levski, Hristo Botev, Georgi Benkovski, Gotse Deltchev, Yane Sandanski. Hundreds of clandestine revolutionary committees laid the beginning of an original, popular organization for struggle, of a type unknown at the time anywhere else in the world....

Let us give homage to the shining memory and the exalted deeds of the enlighteners, martyrs, and heroes, known and unknown, of our National Revival and our national-democratic revolution! Eternal glory be to them!...

After the Liberation, the Bulgarian bourgeoisie betrayed the ideals of our National Revival, the ideals of our revolutionary democrats, the ideal of a pure and sacred republic [the ideal for the future liberated state formulated by Vassil Levski].

However, only thirteen years after the liberation of Bulgaria, which was centuries behind in its social and economic development, it was there again, in the proud Balkans on Mount Buzludzha, that the foundations were laid of a revolutionary Marxist party of the young Bulgarian proletariat, of our working people. Our people nurtured great revolutionaries during the past hundred years....

And then came the great day One, the ninth of September 1944. With the decisive assistance of the Soviet Army, our people accomplished the socialist revolution that opened a new page in the immortal book of Bulgarian history....

Today we can declare proudly that the people of socialist Bulgaria have proven worthy of their glorious past, both distant and more recent.

Document 4

from a speech by Lyudmila Zhivkova, "Unity of the Past, the Present, and the Future," delivered prior to the 1300th anniversary of the Bulgarian state (13 October 1978).[7]

Every single nation, every single country has its own historical past, its own cultural and spiritual destiny.... And we must find the place of the Bulgarian nation in this vast human, international, planetary cultural, spiritual, and historical process. We must find the place of Bulgaria not only with respect to the past but also in order to outline the role the Bulgarian nation plays in the contemporary international process, its participation in the construction of the future historical, cultural, and spiritual destiny of mankind....

I should like to reflect on the magnificent national prospects presented to the Bulgarian people through the idea of aesthetic education, of incorporating the human individual into the Realm of Beauty. For the first time in the

[7] 11Lyudmila Zhivkova (1942–1981), the daughter of Todor Zhivkov, held the post of minister of culture beginning in 1975 and was a member of the Politburo beginning in 1979. Excerpts from Lyudmila Zhivkova's speech to the National Coordination Commission "1300 Years Bulgaria," printed in the daily *Otechestven front* (13 October 1978). Translation by M. Todorova. For an English translation of the whole speech, see *Lyudmila Zhivkova, Perfecting Man and Society* (Sofia: Sofia Press, 1980), 309–16.

historical development of Bulgaria the great aim of the complete and harmonious development of the human individual has been promoted to the status of party and state policy. The ideal of developing man according to the laws of Beauty has become a high social ideal. We ourselves must defend this idea, the high perspective and aim which man has now before him, by creating the public and social atmosphere essential for the continual discovery and development of the creative abilities inherent in each human individual, by creating the conditions that allow each person to be able to defend his sacred evolutionary right to form himself as a complete personality, to perfect himself and to harmonize his relations with other human individuals and with the reality he lives in, to globalize and universalize his consciousness. This idea is directed toward the future, it is built on the evolutionary basis of the unlimited utilization of creative and spiritual abilities. May the preparations for the celebration of the 1300th anniversary focus on these great national ideas, purposes, and tasks, and may they mobilize the efforts of every citizen of our socialist society, of every Bulgarian, so that he should take a worthy part in the struggle to raise the material, cultural, and spiritual level of our nation!

Document 5

from "Alarm for the Nation's Unity," by Ilcho Dimitrov (1990).[8]

The Bulgarian nation is dangerously divided. Mistrust is becoming the predominant state of social relations. Personal ambitions hide behind common ideals. Authoritarian personalities raise the banner of democracy. Violence is being promoted as a remedy against violence. Narrow partisan interests are prevailing over the national ones. Never has the state authority been so powerless.

What is most disturbing and frightening in today's overly emotional atmosphere is that, completely engrossed in the drive to power, public feeling does not pay attention to events that are indicating dark prospects for our future as a nation, for the future of our state.

---

[8] Published in the daily *Duma,* no. 74 (16 June 1990). Translation by M. Todorova. The author, a university professor of history, was a cabinet minister in the govern-ment of Georgi Atanasov (1986–89).

For the first time since 1886, foreign intervention in our nation's sovereign rights to elect its supreme legislative body is quite overt.[9] At that time, the Third Grand National Assembly was being elected. The emissary of Alexander III, the Russian general with the German name Kaulbars, had launched a propaganda campaign to threaten the Bulgarians that their country would be lost if they did not elect Russophiles.[10] Now foreigners are speaking at rallies, and a Western diplomat with a Slavic name seems to have been lured into assuming Kaulbars's role.[11] We shouldn't wonder at the foreigners; after all, even while raising the most humane slogans, they are following their own interests. But have Bulgarian politicians learned nothing from history?

Both before and after 1944, our troubles were caused by, among other things, the violation of national sovereignty. Are we going to miss this opportunity to restore fully our independence, to raise our national dignity? I am neither an Anglophile, a pro-American, nor a Russophobe, but I am a son of Bulgaria, and it hurts to see how resigned we are to the idea that our existence is impossible unless we are somebody's satellite—some time ago of Germany, yesterday of the Soviet Union, tomorrow of the United States.

Our history, recent and past, has been rich in deplorable incidents. We have gone through a lot of disgrace; let us stand no more of it. Our land has been mutilated, living in parts of our nation's body have been torn away....

I would not hesitate to qualify as a crime the registration, under the pressure of the street, of the Movement for Rights and Freedoms [MRF] as a political party. It already has borne its first bitter fruits: in the Grand National Assembly the illegal party comes in third according to the number of its deputies.[12] The assertion that the registration is only for the electoral period, and

---

[9] Note: The first post-Communist democratic elections were held on 10 and 17 June 1990, seven months after the overthrow of the Zhivkov regime. —Ed.

[10] Note: General Nikolai Kaulbars was the emperor's special commissioner to Bulgaria. His heavy-handed treatment caused the rupture of relations between the two countries for nearly a decade (1886–96). —Ed.

[11] Note: This is an allusion to the emotional U.S. ambassador, Saul Polanski, who passionately declared his *parti pris* in the election campaign. The fact that he was Jewish was irrelevant given the absence of a tradition of anti-Semitism in Bulgaria, as distinct from Poland or other East European states. On U.S. policies toward Bulgaria in 1989–90, see among others Misha Glenny, *The Rebirth of History: Eastern Europe in the Age of Democracy* (New York: Penguin, 1990), 175–77.—Ed.

[12] Note: Of the 400 deputies in the Grand National Assembly, 211 were socialists (52.75 percent), 144 (36 percent) represented the Union of Democratic Forces, 23 (5.75 percent) were from the MRF, 16 (4 percent) from the Agrarian Union, and 6 (1.5 percent) from four other tiny parties. The MRF was founded on 4 January 1990, at the height of the nationalist demonstrations organized against the government's decision

that following that period the Movement would again become a social and cultural organization, is meant to mislead the public. This is an unworthy play upon words. As if the label can cover up the essence. During the 1930s the fascist party of Professor Alexander Tsankov bore the name "National Social Movement."

We have all grounds to accuse the main political parties (the BSP, the UDF, and the BANU)[13] of putting up with the creation of a pro-Turkish and pro-Muslim party, moreover, of facilitating it. Thus, following an ancient tradition of ours, short-term partisan interests have prevailed over our common national interests. These are all reasons to believe that the Grand National Assembly will not resist the temptation to collaborate with the movement-party, again pursuing narrow, partisan interests and underestimating and neglecting the common national ones.

Public opinion, preoccupied with the pre-election contest for power, does not recognize the growing danger to our nation's future. The erosion of the Bulgarian nation by Islam and Macedonism is being renewed without opposition.[14] What is being propagated is the setting apart, against the majority, of a part of the nation. This propaganda is covering up separatist tendencies. We Bulgarians have the habit of failing to see the consequences in time and then of bewailing our lot after things get out of hand. Fairly or not, we accuse our predecessors of having betrayed our national ideals. But do we realize the responsibility we ourselves are now assuming? Future generations might curse us for failing to preserve even what we inherited.

We listened to the first radio and TV appearance of Mr. Doganov as a party leader.[15] How cunningly he avoided any critical word on Turkish politics—the pan-Turkic ambitions, the attempts at interfering in our internal affairs, the Armenian genocide, the aggression against the Republic of Cyprus, the

---

at the end of December 1989 to revoke the assimilation policies of the previous years. It claimed to be a supra-party organization dedicated to human and ethno-religious rights and not to be confined to representing any given minority, despite its mostly Muslim membership. According to the constitution, there were to be no parties based on ethnic or religious criteria.—Ed.

13 Note: BSP, Bulgarian Socialist Party; UDF, Union of Democratic Forces; BANU, Bulgarian Agrarian National Union.—Ed.

14 Note: This is a reference to the curbed attempt by a Macedonian organization, "Ilinden," whose goal was the recognition of a Macedonian minority in Bulgaria, to register as a political party. —Ed.

15 Note: The author insists on calling Ahmed Dogan, leader of the MRF, Doganov, as he was known before 1989 and under which name he was first registered in the electoral lists. —Ed.

war of extermination against the Kurds... How are we to believe that his movement is based on international agreements on individual and community rights? I have examined the platforms of some of the candidates for deputies from the Movement, and I have wondered which parliament they wish to enter—the Sofia or the Ankara national assembly?

Mr. Doganov declares himself a guarantor for Bulgaria before Europe. According to him, the road to Europe passes through the Bosphorus, Turkey, and the Muslim world.[16] He should know that Bulgaria appeared thirteen centuries ago in this part of the continent—the cradle of European civilization—that our centuries-old state is Bulgarian in its history, language, and tradition. Europe has geographic boundaries: the Urals to the east, the Straits to the southeast. Beyond the Straits is Asia. We have already tried the route through Turkey, and we have paid for it with a lot of blood and centuries of backwardness.

History offers a tragic example of a party created on an ethnic basis: the Sudetendeutsche in Czechoslovakia during the interwar period. Its contribution to the dismemberment of the Czechoslovak state and also to the fate of the very Sudeten Germans was tragic.

I appeal to the Bulgarian Turks themselves: the Movement for Rights and Freedoms is not your defender; it is a threat to your interests. Ambitious would-be leaders are deceiving you by pushing you down the road of separation and opposition, of animosity and conflict. Your legal interests can be safeguarded only by a united national policy, in confidence, mutual understanding, and unity with the majority of the nation.

I would remind the entire Bulgarian people that democracy does not mean that we should entrust all our hopes to the parliament, the parties, and the government. We, the people, are the main force for democracy. We always have to be on the alert, to react, to articulate our will, to compel the political forces and authorities to follow our common national interest in all their activities.

Let us insist that the national assembly take a stand against the deputies elected on an ethnic and religious basis. The three parties represented in parliament should pledge not to seek parliamentary support from such deputies.

---

16 Note: This ill-suited metaphor was used by Ahmed Dogan in a speech in which he tried to point out that in the future Bulgaria's economy would be oriented to a great extent to the markets of the Middle East. His unfortunate and rather tactless wording, which was taken out of context, produced a predictable outcry. —Ed.

Introduction

This chapter traces the articulation of Bulgarian nationalism during the twentieth century—its main ideas, its goals, its style, its code words. The aim here is not merely to expose the nationalist discourse—this task is far too easy. It is rather, to analyze, by looking at its typical, moderate, and, as far as possible, more sophisticated proponents, the problems of continuity and discontinuity in ideas, language, and conceptual apparatus.[17] Of course, even a cautious replacement of the term "nationalism" with "national discourse" is not sufficient. After all, just as no nation is monolithic or homogeneous, nationalism as such does not exist; national discourse is the interplay of competing views of nationalism. The five texts excerpted above are representative of the dominant, but by no means the sole or universally accepted, views on Bulgarian nationalism during this period. I have purposely abstained from offering crass examples of extreme and vituperative nationalism, which can be found in all periods but in particular between the two world wars.

Nationalism has not and, I believe, cannot produce a sophisticated national discourse. Even at its best, such as nineteenth-century emancipatory ideology, it offers honest and emotional but intellectually one-dimensional constructs. This obviously raises questions about the creators of this discourse. In the documents excerpted here, they were either politicians or intellectuals, or most often that hybrid so typical of Eastern Europe, the politician-intellectual. These are not articulations of mass nationalism, a phenomenon that merits separate research. In these particular cases, the masses are the object of the discourse, which is meant to influence and to shape a definite national identity, as well as to mobilize public opinion (domestic and foreign) behind a particular program or standing. Thus, the texts chosen are as much a reflection of the dominant views of the political and intellectual elites of the times, as they are a representation of national political propaganda.

Although all five texts can be characterized simply as prose, there was an attempt to provide examples of different elements of what constitutes national discourse. The first document is the preface to a historical-geographical atlas comprised of some forty maps. The use of maps, and especially national atlases, as political propaganda tools in modern Europe has a long tradition, but maps

---

[17] It is only proper to note the complementary nature of this chapter to Marin Pundeff, "Bulgarian Nationalism," in *Nationalism in Eastern Europe*, Peter Sugar and Ivo Lederer, eds. (Seattle: University of Washington Press, 1969). I regard Pundeff's study to be an excellent and thorough *histoire evenementielle* and consider this more analytical piece to be a complementary, rather than substitutive, work—mine is an attempt to give a somewhat different reading, in a different style, to the same events.

also have served as much more than that: they have been political icons, "symbols of power, authority, and national unity"—indeed, "the perfect symbol of the state."[18] The first text, therefore, is the verbal concomitant of the map. The other documents—a literary essay, two public speeches, and a newspaper article—are, as will be argued below, particularly representative of the character of the national discourse at the times they were written.

As used here, the concepts of ethnicity and nationalism are both considered to be essentially byproducts of (although in some circumstances they can act as catalysts for) such developments as the crisis of religion and secularization, the revolution in and intensification of communication and mass education, economic growth and industrialization, and the rise of the modern secular state and bureaucracy. Whether the authors of the documents analyzed here give precedence to social, economic, political, or cultural factors, they all treat the rise of nations and nationalism as phenomena that essentially spring from the forces of modernization (regardless of whether these forces are treated as contingent or deterministic).

I define ethnicity as one side of the self-definition and self-designation of a person—a commitment, ideology, or faith (often secular) based on a sense of (most often invented) kinship and common historical experience and, as a rule, on a community of language, religion, and custom. One important element of this definition is that unlike language, territory, religion, race, etc., which are essentially "dividers" along one criterion (although this does not imply that they cannot be very complex or ambiguous dividers), ethnicity is a complicated sum-total, a particular combination or aggregation of different qualities that are used to demarcate ethnic boundaries. Although this particular sum-total can be recognized and analyzed in concrete historical cases, and despite the fact that we can both describe a process by which ethnicity is constructed and analytically define its components, we *cannot* "discover" the ethnicity of a person or group by examining the synthesis of its components. That is, ethnicity is a conscious act of self-definition, and does not exist in the absence of this act. In such a context, the crucial criterion is not the potential presence in an individual of the characteristics that identify ethnicity, but the proof that the combination of these characteristics is dominant in the form of one type of group identification—ethnicity—over other forms of group identification, such as religion, caste,

---

[18] Mark Monmonier, *How to Lie with Maps* (Chicago: University of Chicago Press, 1991), 88.

kin, localism, etc. It seems that we do not possess enough historical evidence to claim this for any period before the modern era.[19]

On the other hand, I define nationalism as the merger of ethnicity and statehood. There have been two distinct, although sometimes parallel or coincident, processes by which nationalism was established throughout modern Europe. One was the gradual formation of a distinct group consciousness defined variously as national revival, as cultural revival or rebirth, and, here, as ethnicity, and linked explicitly with modernity. This process has been uneven chronologically, paralleling the uneven process of modernization, but as a whole the process flowered in Europe during the eighteenth and nineteenth centuries, although there were some earlier and some later manifestations.

The other process by which nationalism was established was through the merger of this consciousness with statehood, which created a new consciousness and ideology—nationalism. Ethnicity and nationalism are not coterminous, although at least in the European experience, nationalism seems to have evolved around an ethnic nucleus. In parts of Western Europe, these processes were blurred and for practical purposes indistinguishable because of the continuous existence of dynastic states and later absolutist monarchies and because they ran parallel to each other. In large parts of Central, Southern, and Eastern Europe, on the other hand, this "construction" of ethnicity and nationalism, as understood and defined here, can be traced as distinct historical processes. In what follows, an attempt will be made to apply these theoretical observations to the Bulgarian case.

The Development of Ethnicity in Bulgaria

The development of the Bulgarian national idea can be seen as having undergone two general phases, both of which had internal sub-phases: the formation and manifestation of a *Kulturnation*, from approximately the middle of the eighteenth century until 1878, and the formation and manifestation of a *Staatsnation* after 1878. In an influential work on the social preconditions of national revival in Europe, Miroslaw Hroch distinguished between three phases of national development: 1) the "scholarly phase," in which a small elite begins the study of language, culture, and history; 2) the "national agitation phase,"

---

[19] For an expanded treatment of these theoretical problems, see Maria Todorova, "Ethnicity, Nationalism and the Communist Legacy in Eastern Europe," paper presented at a conference on The Social Legacy of Communism, held in Washington, DC (February 1992). The papers from this conference will be published by the Institute for Sino-Soviet Studies.

during which patriots outside the elites are mobilized; and 3) the "era of mass national movements."[20] This applies to the Bulgarian case as follows.

The Scholarly Phase

Between approximately the middle of the eighteenth century and the 1820s (with some manifestations during the earlier part of the eighteenth century), there appeared several histories of the Bulgarian people, the most famous and influential being by Father Paisii. This period also witnessed the appearance of the first printed works in the Bulgarian vernacular. By the 1820s, there had developed a distinct impulse to establish Bulgarian secular schools instead of the existing Helleno-Bulgarian schools, which offered a bilingual Greek and Bulgarian education and which dated from the beginning of the century.

The National Agitation Phase

The second phase, during which patriots beyond the elites were mobilized, coincides with a distinct period of national awakening and revolutionary struggle which had the following three traditional characteristics: a movement for educational emancipation; a movement for religious independence or church autonomy; and a movement for political or national independence.[21] The movement for educational emancipation and the beginning of the church conflict lasted approximately until the Crimean War (1853–56).

The Era of Mass National Movements

During the 1860s and 1870s there was the gradual formation of a mass movement in two spheres: the church struggle and the struggle for political emancipation. The church struggle did not spring from doctrinal issues but was essentially a political movement for a separate church following the conflict between Greeks and Bulgarians, which itself was triggered by the contradictions between a developing ethnic consciousness among the Bulgarians and the policies of the emerging Bulgarian nation-state. The struggle ended with the official recognition in 1870 by the Ottoman Porte of the Bulgarian exarchate as

---

[20] Miroslav Hroch, *Social Preconditions of National Revival in Europe: A Comparative Analysis of the Social Composition of Patriotic Groups among the Smaller European Nations* (Cambridge, England: Cambridge University Press, 1985).

[21] For a detailed factological survey of this period, see the three-volume *Istoriya na Bîlgariya*, vol. 1 (Sofia: BAN, 1961), as well as the multivolume *Istoriya na Bîlgariya* (Sofia: BAN), vol. 4 (1983), vol. 5 (1985), and vol. 6 (1989). For an English-language account see Richard Crampton, *A Short History of Bulgaria* (Cambridge, England: Cambridge University Press, 1987).

separate from the Constantinople patriarchate. This added a religious divider as an important, though not dominant, constitutive element of Bulgarian ethnicity.

As for the political movement, there were two main views and programs for the political future of the Bulgarians. The first, which was conservative or moderate and was centered in Constantinople, stressed enlightenment and education, which were considered to be the means to achieve a gradual emancipation. The second, which was revolutionary or radical and was centered in Bucharest, envisaged the achievement of political independence by means of a revolutionary organization and network that would bring revolution and eventually a war that would involve some of the Great Powers. Bulgarian autonomy and later independence were achieved as the result of the outbreak of the April uprising of 1876, the subsequent Russo-Turkish war, and the treaties of San Stefano and Berlin in March and June/July of 1878, respectively. The San Stefano Treaty was perceived by the Bulgarians to have called for the true and just recreation of the entire Bulgarian nation-state along the frontiers of the Bulgarian exarchate. The Berlin Treaty, which, following European Great Power considerations, divided the country, has been viewed ever since as a predatory arrangement and has incited Bulgarian irredentist feelings.

The Emergence of Nationalism

This short account of the development of Bulgarian nationalism indicates that the construction of Bulgarian ethnicity was underway until 1878. This does not mean that there were no nationalists prior to this time. In fact, the political struggle for independence and for creation of a nation-state, promoted above all by revolutionary circles, embodied more than just the raw elements of nationalism. However, the building of a nation and the development of nationalism as a full-fledged movement and ideology can be traced only after the late 1870s.

Still, several elements of the pre-state legacy left a permanent mark on the character of nationalism in the post–1878 period. One was the essentially defensive quality of the Bulgarian national idea. Defensiveness vis-à-vis Europe is a common trait of all Balkan nationalisms, but in the Bulgarian case it was particularly acute because the Bulgarians were defining themselves in opposition against the earlier nationalisms and previously articulated irredentist programs of its neighbors. This defensiveness is evident in the first articulation of Bulgarian nationalism by Paisii, in what has since become the bible of Bulgarian nationalism (or, I would argue, of Bulgarian ethnicity):

> So I wrote down for you what was known about your race and language. Read and know so that you would not be ridiculed and reproached by other tribes and peoples... I wrote it for you

> who love your people and Bulgarian fatherland, and who like to know about your people and language... But there are those who do not care to know about their own Bulgarian people and turn to foreign ways and foreign tongue; and they do not care for their own Bulgarian language but learn to read and speak Greek and are ashamed to call themselves Bulgarians. O, you senseless fool! Why are you ashamed to call yourself Bulgarian and do not read and speak your own language? Or had the Bulgarians no kingdom and state?... In the entire Slavic race the Bulgarians have had the greatest glory, they first called themselves tsars, they first had a patriarch, they first became Christians, and they ruled over the largest territory... But why, stupid, should you be ashamed of your people and linger after a foreign tongue? Here, you say, the Greeks are wiser and more cultivated, and the Bulgarians are simple and stupid, and have no refined speech; therefore, it is better to become part of the Greeks. But look, you senseless, there are many more people wiser and more glorious than the Greeks. Has any Greek abandoned his tongue and learning and people?... You, Bulgarian, do not be fooled, but know your people and language, and learn your language![22]

There is an intensive defensiveness, a feeling of humiliation, and a struggle against an inferiority complex. At the same time, there is also an acute counter-offensiveness, based on intensive pride in the glories of the past.

The other fundamental characteristic of Bulgarian nationalism that had its roots in the pre-state period, and which also can be found in the above passage, was the centrality of language. The crucial role of language as an agent of unification has been recognized by practically all European cultural and national figures, to be elevated in the Herderian vision to the status of ethno-linguistic sanctity. Because of Bulgarians' opposition against both the Greeks and the Turks, the linguistic divider was evoked earlier and remained stronger than the religious one. With the emergence of an educational movement in the second quarter of the nineteenth century, there developed three schools of thought, each with a distinct vision of how to create a literary national language: the Modern Bulgarian school, which stressed the vernacular; the Slavo-Bulgarian school, which insisted on the medieval linguistic legacy; and the Church Slavonic school, which was based on the language used by the church. By the middle of the nineteenth century, the Modern Bulgarian school

---

[22] *Istoriya slavenobolgarskaya,* pod. red. na Petîr Dinekov (Sofia, 1972), 41–44.

had gained unconditional preponderance. This can be explained by the major influence of the merchant and artisan circles in the organization of the modern Bulgarian educational network, as well as by the passionate interest of Bulgarians in folklore, which was especially intensive during the 1840s, and by developments in both Germany and Russia. However, until 1878 when an autonomous Bulgarian principality was created, despite the obvious aspirations of Bulgarian writers toward a united literary practice, linguistic diversity was retained, primarily because of the absence of a single political and cultural center, as well as of common and obligatory norms.[23]

The growth of nationalism in Bulgaria after 1878 can be divided into four distinct phases:

1. the program of state nationalism: unification (1878–1918)
2. nationalism in crisis: revisionism (1918–44)
3. communism and "communist" nationalism (1944–89)
4. post-totalitarian nationalism (1989–present)

This can be further refined by dividing the first phase into two, split roughly by the turn of the century, and by carving out about a decade of the fourth phase (1944–56) to represent the relatively brief caesura of a nonnational Communist experiment in what was otherwise a nationalist continuum throughout the nineteenth and twentieth centuries.

The Program of State Nationalism: Unification (1878–1918)

In the popular perception, the twentieth century is considered the nadir of Bulgarian nationalism, just as the nineteenth century is considered its zenith. Yet, twentieth-century Bulgarian nationalism actually began in 1878, the year of its greatest triumph and its greatest defeat. With the Treaty of San Stefano, signed by the Russian and Ottoman armies on 3 March 1878, a great autonomous Bulgarian principality was created, extending from the Black Sea to Lake Okhrid and from the Danube to the Aegean. It followed the frontiers of the dioceses of the Bulgarian exarchate and was considered, therefore, to conform most closely to the natural ethnic (e.g., linguistic and religious) boundaries of the Bulgarian nation. Opposition on the part of the Great Powers and the other Balkan countries against the creation of this huge Balkan state, which was perceived to be a future Russian satellite, led to revision of the San Stefano Treaty at the Congress of Berlin where, on 13 July 1878, the recently established principality was divided: Bulgaria proper, with a territory of one-third of the

---

[23] Maria Todorova, "Language as Cultural Unifier in a Multilingual Setting: The Bulgarian Case during the Nineteenth Century," *East European Politics and Societies* 4:3 (Fall 1990).

former state, was to be an autonomous principality squeezed between the Danube and the Balkan range; Eastern Rumelia was handed back to the Ottoman Empire but with a Christian governor; and Macedonia was returned to Constantinople altogether. The San Stefano Treaty became the sui generis metahistorical event in the development of Bulgarian nationalism, a dream almost come true, and an *idée fixe* for decades to come.[24]

The first decisive moment in the evolution of Bulgarian nationalism after 1878 was the unification of the Bulgarian principality with Eastern Rumelia in 1885 and the subsequent Serbo-Bulgarian war. The mass recruitment of volunteers and the formation and unexpected victory of the national army were an enormous catalyst in the construction of a unified national loyalty. However, undoubtedly the single most important factor in the construction of a national consciousness was the creation of a standard and obligatory national language and education. The lack of a normative language system was overcome only after Bulgaria's liberation, with the gradual elaboration of orthographical, grammatical, and phonetic norms. This process was completed with the introduction of the Drinov-Ivanchev orthography in 1899.[25]

What is important to emphasize is the decisive role of the different institutions of the state in achieving the final formation and acceptance of the literary language.[26] In particular, the introduction of a secularized, centralized, uniform education proved to be instrumental in the final elaboration of a normative standard language. No less important was the role of the army, which proved to be an equally powerful instrument for socializing the masses into their new role as citizens. The Bulgarian case provides a particularly favorable illustration of the idea that the presence of the state is crucial to the formation of

---

[24] For a good English-language treatment of Bulgarian history in this first period of Bulgarian nationalism, see Richard Crampton, *Bulgaria 1878–1918: A History* (Boulder, CO: East European Monographs, 1983).

[25] Rusin Rusinov, *Bîlgarskiyat knizhoven ezik sled Osvobozhdenieto (1878–1944)* (Veliko Tîrnovo, 1985), 2.

[26] On the role of the ministry of education, see Roy E. Heath, "The Establishment of the Bulgarian Ministry of Public Instruction and Its Role in the Development of Modern Bulgaria, 1878–1885" (Madison: University of Wisconsin, unpublished dissertation, 1979). Heath reaches the interesting conclusion that in the effort to rebuild the destroyed school network of the former period, and with the shortage of qualified personnel (as intellectuals tended to fill the newly opened political and bureaucratic jobs), in this initial period until the reunification with Eastern Rumelia the ministry did not take as its priority the definition and creation of a Bulgarian national identity (pp. 427–29).

a national consciousness and for the strengthening (or sometimes creation) of an ethnic consciousness.

Thus, after the turn of the century, the process of turning "peasants into Bulgarians" had been accomplished. When Stamboliiski, faced with a mass movement in favor of war against Turkey, complained in 1912 that the whole nation seemed to have lost its mind,[27] he was recognizing precisely this fact: nationalism had become the dominant form of group consciousness.

Rizoff, Bulgarian minister plenipotentiary in Berlin, wrote the piece excerpted above (Document 1) in the aftermath of the Balkan wars and while World War I was still raging, in the twilight of the first period, which had brought Bulgaria two of the three "national catastrophes" of the first half of the twentieth century. Despite the timing, his essay had not yet internalized these defeats or any resignation to them, which would be so typical of the subsequent period. Instead, Rizoff reflects the prevailing optimism of the Bulgarian irredenta, which was full of resentment against the Treaty of Berlin, but in a spirit of defiance not despair. In fact, Rizoff's preface is a succinct summary of the program of Bulgarian state nationalism as it was formulated and pursued in the four decades after 1878. Because of this, it merits closer analysis.

Already, the opening statement focuses unambiguously on the pivotal problem in the Bulgarian national question: the correlation between nation and territory, or, in other terms, between ethnicity and the state. "Bulgaria" is used both as a synonym for the Bulgarian people and to designate the territory of the state. The national ideal held that a nation could develop fully and adequately only within independent national borders which would encompass all members of the nation, as did other nineteenth-century European nationalisms.

In Rizoff's language, this desirable equilibrium was called national, political, and economic "crystallization," which he unhesitatingly linked with the process by which "states settle in their final frontiers." The crux of the matter was defining the "finality" of these frontiers, which was to rest on four fundamental principles: "naturalness" as far as possible in terms of geographic unity; economic viability; correspondence with ethnic frontiers; and conformity to historical tradition and the principle of self-determination.

All of these principles are ambiguous in themselves, let alone in combination. This is most obvious in the case of the fourth criterion, that frontiers "correspond to their historical traditions and do not conflict with the right of each nation to self-determination." Historical tradition was evoked because it had been the dominant criterion in legitimizing the claims of the "historic nations" of Europe and was based on the existence of dynastic states. As for the

---

[27] V. A. Zhebokritskii, *Bolgariya nakanune balkanskih voin 1912–1913 gg.* (Kiev, 1960), cited in Pundeff, "Bulgarian Nationalism," 134.

Balkans, each of the medieval Balkan states (Byzantium, Bulgaria, and Serbia) had at one time or other, and to a greater or lesser extent, incorporated a significant part (or all) of the territory of the Balkan peninsula. Logically, each newly created nation-state in the Balkans, as it sought its medieval or ancient state-precedent, evoked a period of grandeur and maximal territorial extension, which rendered the coexistence of the different historical traditions of these states virtually impossible. As an accomplished diplomat whose atlas was aimed primarily at a foreign audience, Rizoff was careful and cautious to spell out only a moderate and realistic version of the historical claims of the Bulgarian state. However, the maps in the atlas, together with his additional comments, very clearly defined the whole Bulgarian "historical tradition," giving pictorial proof of all possible territorial claims, even as they avoided possible accusations of expansionism and aggressiveness and conveyed an impression of modesty and moderation.

The first fourteen maps cover the period from the seventh to the fourteenth century—the two medieval Bulgarian kingdoms. As is to be expected, they fix moments of greatest political expansion of the Bulgarian state, when it incorporated Dobrudja and Macedonia, and at various times part or all of Serbia, Wallachia, Albania, Bessarabia, and even Transylvania and considerable parts of Greece. There is no doubt that the whole historical argument was focused on Dobrudja and Macedonia, and particularly on the latter, the perpetual wound in the Bulgarian national psyche. The only map showing the Byzantine domination, which had lasted nearly two centuries during which Bulgaria had disappeared from the political map of the Balkans, outlines the extent of the Okhrid Patriarchate and is supposed to evidence the unity of Bulgaria and Macedonia (notwithstanding the obvious counterargument that the presence of Serbia within the bounds of the patriarchate could be interpreted as evidence of the unity of Serbia and Macedonia).

The interesting point is that, although at least four maps support strong "historical" claims on the territories north of the Danube River, those claims were never raised against Romania (except concerning Dobrudja). Rather, they are implicitly neutralized by the first two criteria—that frontiers be "as natural as possible," and that they should "safeguard the economic independence" of the nations. As the Danube is taken to be the natural frontier of the Balkans—in a revealing twist of the argument—Romania is deemed never to have belonged to the Balkan peninsula, despite the historical record. Therefore, the frontiers of Romania were held to be entirely behind the Danube. The claim on the Dobrudja thus appears very strong in that it meets all the criteria: it is the cradle of the Bulgarian nation; it always has been part of the medieval Bulgarian state (as the maps show); it is within the Balkan peninsula; and returning it to Bulgaria would prevent the mouth of the Danube, an international river, from being under the control of a single state.

It is obvious that the historical claim argument could rest on the boundaries of only the medieval Bulgarian state. Nearly five centuries of Ottoman rule in fact denied this claim, or more precisely, shifted this claim to the Ottomans. It is for this reason that the bulk of the material in the atlas (the next sixteen maps) are nineteenth-century ethnographic maps designed by different European authorities—French, Austrian, German, English, Russian, Serbian, and Greek geographers and ethnographers—and that among them there are only two Bulgarian maps. These sixteen maps were offered in support of the second part of the fourth criterion, the right to self-determination. The main purpose of these maps was to prove, on the basis of unbiased evidence, the Bulgarian character of the population that inhabited the regions severed from Bulgaria proper after 1878. The chief focus, however, was on Macedonia, and the accompanying comments argued strongly against the existing Greek and especially Serbian claims to this region. Since all these maps (along with a map of the Bulgarian exarchate and of Bulgaria according to the Constantinople conference of 1876) chronologically preceded 1878, they quite successfully argued the case for the objective foundations of Bulgaria, as defined under the San Stefano Treaty, and against the artificial division following Berlin. The final group of eight political maps, dating from between 1878 and 1915, chronicle the attempts to rectify the unjust provisions of the Berlin Treaty.

At first glance, it would seem strange that historical claims and self-determination are invoked in combination. After all, European history has shown (and is showing) only too well that these two principles are basically incompatible. It was precisely the conflict between the new idea of national self-determination and the older historical claims of the imperial idea that produced the proliferation of small nation-states in the Balkans, as well as in Central and Eastern Europe.[28] Why, then, summon a contradictory argument, of which Rizoff could not help but be well aware?

The explanation seems to lie in what has been identified as one of the main characteristics of Bulgarian nationalism: its defensiveness. Operating in a Balkan and larger European context, the relative lateness of their nationalism forced the Bulgarians to mobilize all possible arguments in its defense. As the great debate over "historical" and "unhistorical" nations was raging in Europe, with the Balkan peoples (with the exception of the Greeks) ranged at the bottom of the hierarchical order of nations, the Bulgarians were at great pains to show that they qualified, even according to this expansive criterion. The historical

---

[28] As already indicated, the fact that Western Europe had renounced the imperial idea much earlier, and had developed in the framework of smaller dynastic states which "created" nations within their frontiers, blurred this implicit conflict and gave the superficial impression that both processes were essentially complementary.

claim argument was without doubt targeted primarily to the attention of the European governments, who were expected to arbitrate future arrangements in the Balkans. In his essay, Rizoff portrays the Balkans as an inextricable part of Europe, but he does not hint that they might or could manage their own affairs. That Great Power interests actively shaped the fate of the region was recognized (and often manipulated) even if it was no less actively resented. The lessons of Berlin and of the decades until the outbreak of World War I clearly had demonstrated that the small states of the Balkans were objects rather than subjects of international politics, and that they had to live within a system of patronage-cliental relations. This explains, not least, Rizoff's opening, the aim of which was to draw the favorable attention of Europe even at the expense of Balkan "reputation." Whenever he discussed European affairs at large, European relations with the Balkans in particular, Rizoff entirely, but consciously and uncritically, employed the then orthodox European discourse with all its mythology: that the Balkans were the powder keg of Europe; that the reason for this was their backwardness, underdevelopment, or immaturity (in Rizoff's euphemism the lack of national, political, and economic "crystallization"); and that international arbitration undoubtedly would be beneficial to the Balkans and would pacify them.

Aside from this, for all practical purposes, Bulgarian nationalism had followed principally the line of self-determination. All pre–1878 revolutionary propaganda, which had as its ideal the political independence of the Bulgarians, was based almost exclusively on national, not on historical, rights. Even when Rizoff clearly defined the territorial aspirations of Bulgaria by invoking historical rights ("lands that have belonged to it in the past"), he was not concerned with *all* lands that had belonged to Bulgaria in the past but only the ones that "have been recognized as Bulgarian by all authoritative travelers in European Turkey, as well as by Turkey itself and the Great Powers at their Constantinople Conference."

For Rizoff, as for all Bulgarians, there was no question of how to determine what was meant by the Bulgarian "nation." It was, first and foremost, the linguistic unity that defined it. It was the official recognition of a separate Bulgarian *millet*, under the jurisdiction of the Bulgarian exarchate in 1870 that specified the extent of the Bulgarian nation and which became a significant step toward further political independence. However, this traditional division along religious lines only conformed to existing practice in the Ottoman Empire. In fact, the group it recognized (the Bulgarians) was within the same religious entity (Orthodoxy) but had developed an ethnic consciousness in opposition to the Greeks that primarily revolved around linguistic unity. The primacy of linguistic identity remained dominant in subsequent periods, as witnessed, for example, by the claims after 1878 that the *Pomaks* (Bulgarian Muslims) were Bulgarian because of their linguistic identity with the Orthodox population, or by the obstinacy with which, in the Communist and the post-Communist period, the existence of a separate Macedonian nation was denied because it allegedly did not have its own separate language.

Having insisted on the sanctity of the "inalterable and incontestable" national, moral, historical, and geographical rights of the Bulgarians, Rizoff stresses that, in practice, the Bulgarians were pursuing a realistic and even minimalist policy, to the point of sacrificing their union with Macedonia for the sake of a future Balkan confederation, in which Macedonia as an independent political unit would serve as a unifying link. Of course, in this particular case, Rizoff presented only one of the existing alternatives under Bulgarian foreign policy as the sole and uncontested one. In reality, the Bulgarian cabinet entered the Balkan wars having renounced the "autonomy" principle for Macedonia and having opted for partition, as attested by the secret annex of the Bulgarian-Serbian treaty of February/March 1912.[29]

The appeal to the moral element in policy was not merely a propaganda device. Rizoff and his contemporaries were acutely aware of the limitations of power politics for a small country, and this awareness was handed down as a permanent feature of Bulgarian nationalism. This made all the more necessary a reliance upon legalisms "necessary to ward off the brute pressures of the great powers and also to have a case for the record in the event of a catastrophe,"[30] as well as upon other arguments that were based on sheer military strength.

In the face of this insistence on the moral criterion, Rizoff's lengthy arguments against an independent Albania and in favor of partitioning the lands inhabited by Albanians was all the more flagrant. These arguments rested on realpolitik, and neither Rizoff nor practically any other Bulgarian or other Bulgarian politician of the time seem to have been bothered by the double standard. It was, of course, precisely the revenge of real power politics, if not realpolitik, that sealed the defeat of the program of Bulgarian state nationalism in the aftermath of World War I.

Rizoff's text is by no means a unique document but is typical of a genre that has always been utilized in the Balkans but which proliferated at an incredible rate in the first decades of the twentieth century. These were for the most part historical-political pamphlets, lavishly illustrated with historical and ethnographic maps, that implicitly and, most often, explicitly, argued the case of the Bulgarian irredenta. The authors of these books and brochures were almost exclusively university professors and scholars of repute or diplomats (like Rizoff). Their works were published in Bulgaria (in Bulgarian) and also abroad, as part of

---

29 *Istoriya na Bîlgariya*, vol. 2 (Sofia: BAN, 1962), 250–52.

30 Henry L. Roberts, *Eastern Europe: Politics, Revolution and Diplomacy* (New York: Alfred Knopf, 1970), 188.

a virtual propaganda industry, mostly in France and Switzerland (in French, the diplomatic language of Europe).[31]

Rizoff's preface, as already noted, presented a summary of the unification program of San Stefano Bulgaria, as it was formulated and pursued in the four decades between 1878 and World War I. This program, whether it was used as a blueprint for practical political action or merely as an unattainable but justified ideal, continued to be the main inspiration of Bulgarian nationalism throughout the next period, until World War II.

Nationalism in Crisis: Revisionism (1918–1944)

The two national catastrophes alluded to above followed each other within the short span of five years (in 1913 and 1918): the second Balkan war and World

---

[31] The following is an inexhaustive list of publications of this genre, arranged alphabetically with books published abroad listed first and books published in Bulgaria listed thereafter: D. M. Brancoff, *La Macédoine et sa population chrétienne. (Avec 2 carte ethnographiques)* (Paris, 1905); I. E. Guéchoff, *L'Alliance Balcanique* (Paris, 1915); A. Ischirkoff, *La Macédoine et la constitution de l'Exarchat bulgare (1830 à 1897) avec une carte hors texte* (Lausanne, 1918); A. Ischirkoff, *Le nom de la Bulgarie; éclaircissement d'histoire et d'ethnographie* (Lausanne, 1918); A. Ischirkoff, *Les Bulgares en Dobrudja; aperçu historique et ethnographique* (Berne, 1919); A. Ischirkoff, *Les confines occidetaux des terres bulgares; notes et documents; onze cartes* (Lausanne, 1915); I. Ivanoff, *Les bulgares et leurs manifestations nationales: documents historiques, ethnographiques et diplomatiques, avec trois cartes en couleurs* (Berne, 1919); D. Mikoff, *Pour le droit et la paix dans les Balkans* (Geneva, 1919); I. Mintschew, *La Serbie et le mouvement national bulgare* (Lausanne, 1918); D. Mishew, *America and Bulgaria and Their Moral Bonds* (Berne, 1918); C. Stephanove, *The Bulgarians and Anglo-Saxondom* (Berne, 1919); St. Tchilingirov, *Le pays de la Morava, suivant des témognages serbes; études d'histoire de d'ethnographie, avec une carte hors texte* (Berne, 1917); R. A. Tsanoff, *Bulgaria's case* (s.l., 1918); *Ethnographie de la Macédoine* (Philippopoli, 1881); S. Chilingirov, *Pomoraviya po srîbski svidetelstva* (Sofia, 1917); S. Chilingirov, *Dobrodzha i nasheto vîzrazhdane* (Sofia, 1917); A. Ishirkov, *Prinos kîm etnografiyata na makedonskite slavyani* (Sofia, 1907); A. Ishirkov, *Zapadnite kraishta na bîlgarskata zemya. Belezhki i materiali. S 11 karti* (Sofia, 1915); Y. Ivanov, *Severna Makedoniya* (Sofia, 1902); Y. Ivanov, *Bîlgarski starini iz Makedoniya* (Sofia, 1908); Y. Ivanov, *Bîlgarite v Makedoniya. Izdirvaniya i dokumenti za tyakhnoto poteklo, ezik i narodnost. S etnografska karts i statistika* (Sofia, 1917); V. Kînchov, *Makedoniya. Etnografiya i statistika. 11 karti* (Sofia, 1911); M. Markov, *Istoricheskite prava na Bîlgariya vîrkhu Dobrodzha* (Sofia, 1917); M. Mavrodiev, *Dobrodzha* (Sofia, 1917); D. Mishev, *Bîlgariya v minaloto* (Sofia, 1916); Ofeicoff, *La Macédoine au point de vue ethnographique, historique et littéraire* (Sofia, 1889); *La verité sur les accusations contre la Bulgarie* (Sofia, 1919); G. Zanetov, *Zapadnite bîlgarski zemi i Sîrbiya. Istoriya i etnografiya* (Sofia, 1917).

War I. These produced a profound public frustration which has been carefully handed down from generation to generation and the effects of which can be felt even today. The refugee problem, which in the long run contracted the Bulgarian-claimed territories and, thus, limited the span of the Bulgarian irredenta, in the short run intensified to an unprecedented degree the tensions in Bulgaria proper. This, coupled with a severe economic crisis and raging social problems, could not but make the Neuilly Treaty of 1919 into the counterpart of Versailles for Germany. The response was an outcry of bitter and humiliated nationalism.

Unlike the period immediately preceding the Balkan wars, however, nationalism had lost its mass appeal, surviving "in numerically small pockets such as the officers' corps, segments of the intelligentsia and the bourgeoisie and, of course, the refugees' organizations."[32] Even more telling, nationalism had lost its almost unanimous voice and was being articulated in different pitches and with varying degrees of intensity. Ranging from moderate to extreme right-wing, small nationalist organizations proliferated, and they voiced resentment against the postwar arrangements and propagandized the program of revisionism.[33]

Some of these organizations espoused radical ideologies with unmistakably racist, fascist, and even Nazi overtones. It is from these quarters that the most virulent examples of the extreme type of exclusive Bulgarian nationalism

---

[32] Pundeff, "Bulgarian Nationalism," 145.

[33] The most notorious of these were *Narodno sotstialno dvizhenie* (National Social Movement) of Professor Tsankov; *Sîyuz na bîlgarskite natsionalni legioni* (Union of Bulgarian Legions) of Ivan Dochev—the "Legionnaires"; *Vsebîlgarski sîyuz "Otets Paisii"* (Father Paisii's All-Bulgarian Union); its more radical and activist offspring *Bîlgarski mladezhki sîyuz "Otets Paisii"* (Father Paisii's Union of the Bulgarian Youth); *Ratnitsi za na predîka na bîlgarshtinata* (Champions for the Advancement of Bulgariandom) of Assen Kantardzhiev—the "Ratniks"; *Sîyuz na Bîlgarska rodna zashtita* (Union of Bulgarian National Defense); *Bîlgarska natsionalsotsialisticheska rabotnicheska partiya* (Bulgarian National-Socialist Workers Party); *Natsionalna zadruga—fashisti* (National Union—Fascists); *Bîlgarski fashist* (Bulgarian Fascists); *Bîlgarska orda* (Bulgarian Horde) of D. Sîsîlov; *Mlada Bîlgariya* (Young Bulgaria), and the "Union of Bulgarian Scholars, Writers, and Artists." For an overview of the political scene in the interwar period, see Velichko Georgiev, "Razvitieto na politicheskata sistema v Bîlgariya, 1918–1944," *Bîlgariya 1300 Institutsii i dîrzhavna traditsiya* 1 (Sofia, 1981); Velichko Georgiev, *Burzhoaznite i drebnoburzhoznite partii v Bîlgariya, 1934–1939* (Sofia, 1971); Plamen Tsvetkov and Nikolay Poppetrov, "Kîm tipologiyata na politicheskoto razvitie na Bîlgariya prez 30-te godini," *Istoricheski pregled 46:2* (1990); and Nikolay Poppetrov, "Organizatsiite *Otets Paisii* i *Bîlgarska orda* prez vtorata svetovna voina," *Istoricheski pregled* 43:9 (1987).

stemmed. These were based on a reassessment of Bulgarian history, in which the proto-Bulgarian element was emphasized, with its state-organizing potentialities, its military element, strong kin (tribal) relations, and centralized leadership (all a perfect legitimation of authoritarian rule). At the same time, this so-called Hunnic theory was in vehement opposition to the Slavic theory of Bulgarian ethnogenesis and clearly served the foreign political orientation of Bulgaria on the eve of World War II. All this was garnished with an overdose of social Darwinism and racism.[34] Although they were undoubtedly the most vociferous and some of the most active in generating nationalist propaganda, proponents of these views are not representative of the overall scene of Bulgarian nationalism in this period. After all, only one or two of the above-mentioned nationalistic organizations had more than a few thousand members, and the one that produced the most vituperative texts never had even 100 members.[35]

The predominant genre of this period, which had claims as a separate and legitimate academic pursuit, was what can be termed "folk psychology." There had been early attempts to construct a psychological self-portrait of the Bulgarians dating as far back as the second half of the eighteenth and first half of the nineteenth centuries, but they were always marginal to the main theme of the nationalist discourse, which was focused on the educational, religious, and political emancipation of Bulgaria. There was a certain shift in the development of folk psychology after the liberation of the country in 1878 until the first decade of the twentieth century. In place of the revolutionaries, journalists, poets, and public figures of the previous period, folk psychology became the domain chiefly of ethnographers. However, it was only later (during the interwar period) that the discipline became an independent area of research with its own particular subjects and methods.

The period between 1918 and 1944 brought not only the most profuse outpouring of folk psychology writings, but also its greatest achievements.[36]

---

[34] D. D. Sîsîlov, *Pîtyat na Bîlgariya* (Sofia, 1936). See also *Bîlgarska orda: osnovni nachala* (Sofia, 1938); and *Izvestiya na bîlgarska orda.*

[35] Poppetrov, "Organizatsiite," 42 n.52.

[36] Anton Strashimirov, *Kniga za bîlgarite* ("On the Bulgarians") (Sofia, 1918); Anton Strashimirov, *Narod i poet* ("The People and the Poet") (Sofia, 1922); Anton Strashimirov, *Nashiyat narod* ("Our People") (Sofia, 1923); Nikola Krîstnikov, *Opit za psikhologicheski analiz na nashiya obshtestven zhivot* ("An Attempt at Psychological Analysis of Our Social Life") (Sofia, 1922); Boyan Penev, *Istoriya na novata bîlgarska literatura* ("History of the Modern Bulgarian Literature"), vols. 1–4 (Sofia, 1976, reprint 1978); Boyan Penev, *Izkustvoto e nashata pamet* ("Art Is Our Memory") (Varna, 1978), a collection of essays published during the interwar period; Konstantin Petkanov, "Kharakterni cherti na bîlgarina" ("Characteristic Traits of the Bulgarian"), *Filosofski*

Clearly, the fiasco of the national unification program produced a social and political climate that led to the type of introspective mood that infected the intelligentsia en masse and which is reflected in these writings. An apt illustration of the change in spirit evident in this period is the work of the military historian Petîr Dîrvingov, who exerted a powerful influence over generations of Bulgarian officers. His first book, published in 1903, was essentially a comparative study of the psychology of the Bulgarian and Turkish armed forces and, in broader terms, of the two nations.[37] His second important work (alongside a number of widely read military treatises) was likewise an example of the intimate link between the military institution and the construction of Bulgarian nationalism in its "optimistic" period.[38] After the war, Dîrvingov turned to more speculative philosophical themes and published his major work of folk psychology, in which he espoused the ideas of geographical

---

Bulgarian"), *Filosofski pregled* 4 (1930), Konstantin Petkanov, "Dushata na bîlgarkata" ("The Soul of the Bulgarian Woman"), *Filosofski pregled* 5 (1933); Konstantin Gîlîbov, *Zovît na rodinata (Kulturniyat pît na bîlgarina. Literaturni opiti)* ("The Call of the Fatherland: The Cultural Course of the Bulgarian—Literary Endeavors") (Sofia, 1930); Konstantin Gîlîbov, *Ornamenti (Filosofski i literaturni eseta)* (Sofia, 1934); Stefan Gidikov, "Polovata svitost na bîlgarina kato osnova na negoviya kharakter" ("The Sexual Reticence of the Bulgarian as the Basis of His Character"), *Filosofski pregled* 2 (1934); Spiridon Kazandzhiev, *Pred izvora na zhivota* ("At the Source of Life") (Sofia, 1937); Ivan Khadzhiiski, "Optimistichna teoriya za nashiya narod" ("An Optimistic Theory of Our Nation"), in *Sîchineniya* ("Selected Works"), vol. 1 (Sofia, 1974); and Ivan Khadzhiiski, "Bit i dushevnost na nashiya narod" ("Life and Ethos of Our People"), in *Sîchineniya* ("Selected Works"), vol. 2 (Sofia, 1974). Khadzhiiski, who was killed during World War II, wrote most of his works in the latter half of the 1930s and the early 1940s. Although published immediately outside the strict chronological boundaries of the second period (1918–1944), the following two influential works belong to the same intellectual tradition: Todo Panov, *Psikhologiya na bîlgarskiya narod* ("Psychology of the Bulgarian Nation") (Sofia, 1914); and Stoyan Kosturkov, *Vîrkhu psikhologiyata na bîlgarina* ("On the Psychology of the Bulgarian") (Sofia, 1949).

37 Petîr Dîrvingov, *Ot Plovdiv i Sofia kîm Tsarigrad i Skopie (Paralel na voennite sili)* ("From Plovdiv and Sofia to Constantinople and Skopye: A Comparison of the Armed Forces") (Sofia, 1903).

38 Petîr Dîrvingov, *Voenna Bîlgariya. Sotsiologicheski etyud na bîlgarskata deystvitelnost* ("Military Bulgaria: A Sociological Essay of Bulgarian Realities") (Sofia, 1911).

determinism in order to legitimize the territorial claims of the Bulgarian state.[39] This work secured him election to the Bulgarian Academy of Sciences.[40]

The self-image of the Bulgarian, as portrayed in practically all works on folk psychology (with the exception of Dîrvingov, who even in the 1930s retained some of the disciplined uptight military spirit), was martyrological—part of a victimized nation, isolated and on the sidelines of world attention, but with a peculiar combination of inert collectivism and anarchic individualism; a social egalitarianism that fosters democratism; and, at the same time, a lack of civic discipline and responsibility, which negates the tendency toward democracy. The interesting question, of course, is how much this self-image affected Bulgarian society beyond the Bulgarian intelligentsia that produced it. The intelligentsia was only a small part of Bulgarian society, which was comprised of an overwhelmingly egalitarian peasant majority with a growing but still weak urban middle class, but without a nobility. In general, this accounted for the immense and disproportionate influence of the educated class—which, for its part, had direct social roots in the mass of the population. Although it is difficult to prove the extent to which these ideas diffused through society, their continuing appeal to large segments of following generations of intelligentsia is undisputed, which adds yet another distinctive feature to the complicated character of Bulgarian nationalism.

Constantine Gîlîbov in many ways captures and exemplifies the typical introspective temper of the times in Document 2. Yet, with its depth of vision and crisp analytical prose, this essay clearly surpasses intellectually the average example of the genre. In fact, of all the documents reprinted here to illustrate the history of Bulgarian nationalism in the twentieth century, Gîlîbov's is undoubtedly the most sophisticated. It might be even argued that, with its subdued passions and cultivated language, it is not so typical of the nationalism of the period. Yet, the text is not a denunciation of the national idea; on the contrary, there is no question that the national idea is justified and worth fighting for. What is attacked are the ways and manner of achieving the national idea: "we imagined that we could achieve the reunification of the Bulgarian people at once, instead of at separate stages." It is the unpractical maximalism that is the object of scorn, not the aim itself. Without doubt, here is a person and a discourse that lies within the framework of the national idea, but which has the realism and wisdom borne of the lessons of defeat and which has a sobriety of manner quite distinct from the elevated prose of the previous period. Without explicitly defining it in detail, Gîlîbov obviously embraces the goal of unification as

[39] Petîr Dîrvingov, *Dukhît na istoriyata na bîlgarskiya narod* ("The Spirit of the History of the Bulgarian Nation") (Sofia, 1932).

[40] Pundeff, "Bulgarian Nationalism," 146 n81.

formulated in the prewar era. The very fact that he employs the word "reunification" instead of "unification" clearly indicates the looming presence of the San Stefano Treaty. He, like Rizoff, accepts as a condition sine qua non the European tutelage, although he words this recognition very cautiously: "the reunification of the Bulgarians is a complicated political task of a European order."

The real value of this piece, however, lies in the broader approach it takes to the Bulgarian problem. Not only does Gîlîbov place the Bulgarian case not only within the more general political context of Europe, but he focuses primarily on the social and economic aspects of the country's integration into the larger framework of the continent. It is not merely and, more important, not primarily Bulgaria's defeat in the wars that is seen as the cause of the frustration and disorientation of Bulgarian society, but the rapid structural shifts in the society (chiefly the urbanization process), accompanied by a quick adaptation to the new cultural patterns brought from Europe. The disparity between the quick cultural reorientation and internalization of European values and expectations, on one hand, and the limited material resources of the country, on the other, made and would continue to make, according to Gîlîbov, the process of europeanization extremely tortuous. Gîlîbov's concluding remark sounds today like a prophecy fulfilled: "The Bulgarian will be tomorrow what he is today—as long as his will for cultural progress is alive and as long as he continues to be so poor."

Communism and "Communist" Nationalism (1944–1989)

World War II was a watershed in the development of Bulgarian nationalism. At first glance, this is usually attributed to the fact that a Communist dictatorship was imposed that espoused an ideology that was anti- or supra-nationalist. During the interwar period, communism was indeed the only serious adversary and alternative to nationalism. However, the hegemony of the classical Marxist doctrine in the immediate post–World War II period in Bulgaria (and in Eastern Europe in general) was only a brief, and certainly not uncontested, caesura that was quickly replaced by the practice of state communism and which left its mark only on the articulation of the national idea.

In discussing communism, it is important to make a distinction between the ideology of pre-state communism or classical Marxism and the communist state praxis, which had its own discourse. The crucial distinction between communism as ideology and as practice is the attitude toward the state, which indeed serves almost as a litmus test. Whereas the state is the raison d'être as well as the modus vivendi of both nationalism and practical communism, classical Marxism embodies an ambiguous attitude toward the state (although it is not always explicitly anti-state). The Bolshevik Revolution and the building of "real socialism" or communism included the appropriation of some elements of the Marxist doctrine, namely, its ideas of social equality and justice, but primarily its modernizing potential, especially in the drive for industrialization. From the outset, the variety of communism practiced in and exported from Russia, especially after World War II, was, among other things, an ideology of modernization, an attempt to produce a unique way to meet the challenge of a hegemonic West. Both nationalism and state communism responded to the same challenge, becoming tools of modernization. Just as the nation-state was imposed as the gold standard of "civilized" international organization in the nineteenth and twentieth centuries, so also did industrialization become the standard for economic progress.

Like liberalism, Marxism can be faulted for underestimating, indeed for discounting, the political significance of ethnicity and nationalism. The huge blow dealt to the central idea of Marxism by the rejection of proletarian solidarity in favor of ethnonationalism during World War I prompted Lenin and other Communist leaders to attempt to adapt communism by favoring the principle of self-determination, including the right to secession. This principle was endorsed by the Communist International, and after 1924 all Communist parties had to adopt it.[41] It became one of the important strategies for appealing to broad segments of the population, but it remained only a strategy. In the end, Lenin failed to develop a general theory of nationalism and "left open the question of the nature and role of nationalism in its relationship with socialism."[42] That Marxism failed to develop an adequate theory of nationalism has become a truism, but it should also be recognized that the reason that "Marxists have failed in their efforts at incorporating the reality of nationalism into their theoretical understanding...is deeply rooted in the nature of Marxist thought itself."[43] The incompatibility between a cosmopolitan, universalist ideology and a particularist romantic creed precludes their theoretical syncretism.[44]

---

41 John F. Stack, Jr., "Ethnic Mobilization in World Politics: The Primordial Perspective," in *The Primordial Challenge: Ethnicity in the Contemporary World,* John F. Stacj, ed. (Westport, CT: Greenwood Press, 1986), 6–7.

42 Shlomo Avineri, "Toward a Socialist Theory of Nationalism," *Dissent* (Fall 1990), 451.

43 John Ehrenreich, "Socialism, Nationalism and Capitalist Development," *Review of Radical Political Economists* 15:1 (1983); and Ephraim Nimni, *Marxism and Nationalism: Origins of a Political Crisis* (Concord, MA: Pluto Press, 1991).

44 For a more extensive argument against the theory of an ideological symbiosis between communism and nationalism, see Todorova, "Ethnicity, Nationalism and the Communist Legacy in Eastern Europe."

In Bulgaria, only the "narrow" social-democrats who later became Communists, along with some of the agrarians, distanced themselves from the widespread popular support of the political parties for World War I. The interesting ideas of the social-democrats for solving the national problem centered around the concept of a Balkan federation. These ideas (especially concerning Macedonia) underwent dramatic evolution and vacillations and conformed as a whole to the general policy of the Moscow-based Communist International, although there was significant dissent and discussion within the party.[45] However, during the interwar period, these views were not seriously considered outside the narrow group of their followers. The considerable attention that these ideas received in the postwar period is certainly disproportionate to their real social impact; rather, it is a direct product of the power monopoly and dictatorship of the Communist Party. Likewise, attempts to depict the standing of the Communist Party as a national treachery that proved decisive and fatal in the final loss of Macedonia are naive and overstated.

The decade-long Communist caesura cannot be analyzed exclusively in the context of the dominant ideology, with its supranational stance and its variety of doctrinal considerations—primacy of class struggle over national issues, subordination of national interests to the cause of the global proletarian revolution, adherence to the proletarian international discipline, etc.[46] Of much more immediate importance were various foreign policy considerations, specifically the shift of Stalin's support from the Bulgarian to the Yugoslav Communists during and immediately after the war and the general treatment of the country in the international arena as an ally of Germany and a loser in the war, a legacy that ironically was handed over to the Communists.[47] The proverbial servility of the Bulgarian Communists toward Moscow can be seen as

---

[45] On the different positions within the Communist Party in the interwar and immediate postwar period, see Marin Pundeff, "Nationalism and Communism in Bulgaria," *Südost-Forschungen* XXIX (1970); Vasil Vasilev, "The Bulgarian Communist Party and the Macedonian Question between the Two World Wars," *Bulgarian Historical Review* XVII:1 (1989); and Dimitîr Sirkov, "Bulgaria's National Territorial Problem during the Second World War," *Bulgarian Historical Review* XIX:3 (1991).

[46] The only attempt at a local transposition of Lenin's theory of self-determination seems to be the "affirmative action" toward the Turkish population in the late 1940s and early 1950s, when the Turks enjoyed rights and privileges they never had before or since.

[47] See, in this respect, the "undoctrinal" stand the Bulgarian Communists took toward Western Thrace. As Pundeff has pointed out, "it took the personal intervention of Churchill to reverse the first nationalist move of the Bulgarian Communists" (Pundeff, "Nationalism and Communism in Bulgaria," 152).

a consciously (although not always well) calculated price for acquiring a Great Power patron—one of the persistent characteristics of Bulgarian nationalism.

By the time of Stalin's death, and especially after the famous April Plenum of the Bulgarian Communist Party in 1956, Bulgarian communism had acquired all the characteristics of etatist communism.[48] As already stated, etatist communism appropriated important elements of Marxist doctrine, above all its self-designation, and thus legitimized its claims on the basis of the Marxist discourse (a perfect example of ideological nominalism used for legitimation). The so-called communist nationalism was nothing but a transvestite, ordinary nationalism.

The domination of the communist discourse, or the language of Marxism-Leninism, primarily reflected power politics and was a tribute to the Cold War. The "genuine" Marxist discourse was very soon replaced by the imagery of nationalism, translated into an idiosyncratic Marxist slang. It was the nation-state that had subverted earlier short-lived utopian attempts to build society around the priority of class-consciousness. The ongoing conflict between the two discourses, as well as between different articulations of the nationalist discourse, reflected a power struggle within the intellectual elite. It was in this period that a renewed interest in the interwar heritage emerged. In this particular case, it took about two decades after World War II for proponents of the procrustean vulgar variety of Marxism that was thriving in the country to begin to acknowledge and accept this different discourse. This was true even for prewar Marxists such as Ivan Khadzhiiski, whose collected works were reissued only in the 1970s. The 1970s and 1980s saw a wide effort at reissuing many of the prewar works of the folk psychology genre.[49] This period also saw some original works of contemporary authors published, which were for the most part emulations of past models.[50]

---

48 For pre–1956 manifestations of state considerations submerging the doctrinal ideological approach, see Pundeff, "Nationalism and Communism in Bulgaria," 153–59.

49 See Mincho Draganov, ed., *Narodopsikhologiya na bîlgarite. Antologiya* ("Folk Psychology of the Bulgarians: An Anthology) (Sofia, 1984). This lengthy anthology encompasses texts from the ninth to the twentieth centuries and offers excepts of practically all the works of folk psychology cited in note 36 above, many of which underwent new editions in the 1970s.

50 Marko Semov, *Dushevnost i otselyavane* ("Ethos and Survival") (Plovdiv, 1982); Mincho Draganov, "Za izuchavaneto na natsionalniya kharakter" ("About the Study of the National Character"), *Filosofska misîl* 11 (1982); Mincho Draganov, *Sotsialnata psikhologiya v Bîlgariya* ("Social Psychology in Bulgaria") (Sofia, 1971); and Efrem Karanfilov, *Nai-bîlgarskoto vreme* ("The Most Bulgarian Time") (Sofia, 1979).

As for "communist nationalism" per se, the widely accepted view is that the national ideology was adopted in order to be overcome.[51] Instead, it was the national ideology that adopted the language of Marxism in order to gain legitimacy. In Bulgaria, where the official policy was (or was given to be) one of complete consent with the center (Moscow), the majority of the Party leadership and the ruling elite shared the national ideology but articulated it in a more cautious way, using the hegemonic Marxist discourse clearly for purposes of gaining legitimacy.

In this context, Todor Zhivkov's "Address on Bulgaria" (Document 3) is a wonderful example of nationalist discourse that employs Communist clichés. In addition, it is a remarkable symbiosis between a typical genre of the Communist period—the political speech or address—and a typical nationalist ritual—anniversaries of historical events. For example, after the 1960s the anniversary of the San Stefano Treaty (3 March) was increasingly commemorated in public meetings, concerts, and other ceremonies, yet only the first non-Communist government after 1990 dared to make it an official national holiday.

For all its unsophisticated plainness, Zhivkov's speech displays an ingenious combination of the elements of two completely different discourses. On one hand, there is the tribute to the constitutive elements of the Communist doctrine; on the other, these are given an interpretation that clearly indicates another intellectual foundation. For example, the class struggle of the proletariat is subsumed into the much more important "perpetual struggle by the people against foreign and domestic plunderers," and the order in which these are enumerated ("foreign" before "domestic") is not by chance.

Central to this discussion is the interpretation of "the combination between patriotism and internationalism." Under internationalism fall such events as the Bulgarians' restraint while fighting their Ottoman oppressors, namely that they did not go to war with the Turkish people; their solidarity and help to the Armenian refugees after the massacres in the Ottoman Empire; their saving the Bulgarian Jews during World War II; and, above all, of course, the friendship between Bulgaria and the Soviet Union. A key phrase of the text is "that there is nothing more precious than peace, mutual understanding, and good neighboring relations...directly linked to internationalism." In one respect, at least, World War II indeed was a watershed in the development of Bulgarian nationalism: passive or active, the nationalism of the prewar period can be generally defined as irredentist, while the nationalism of the postwar period is unambiguously a status quo nationalism.

---

[51] Katherine Verdery, *National Ideology under Socialism: Identity and Cultural Politics in Ceausescu's Romania* (Berkeley: University of California Press, 1991), 314.

This can be illustrated also by comparing two poems known by heart by practically every Bulgarian.[52] One was written by the patriarch of Bulgarian literature, Ivan Vazov, in 1872, before the liberation of the country, and gives a poetic expression of the territorial program of Bulgarian unification.

If men ask me where the sunrise
Warmed me first when I was small,
If men ask me where the land is
That I cherish most of all,

This will be my simple answer:
Where the mighty Danube flows,
Where the Black Sea brightly dances
In the East and stormy grows;

Where the Balkan raises nobly
To the sky its mountain chain,
Where the broad Maritsa slowly
Wanders through the Thracian plain;

Where the turbid river Vardar
Through green fields and meadows roars,
Where mount Rila's summit sparkles
Where lake waves lap Okhrid's shores;

Where the people suffer anguish
And in bondage pine today,
Who in one and the same language
Voice their sorrow, weep, and pray.[53]

The other poem was written some hundred years later by Georgi Dzhagarov, an undoubtedly talented poet, who was one of a number of "court" poets, a member of the immediate Zhivkov entourage, and a fierce nationalist who was personally implicated in the anti-Turkish propaganda at the time of the

---

[52] Both of these poems were part of the obligatory school curricula of the postwar period and were also often chanted, as they were musically arranged to popular melodies. Vazov's poem, in particular, was sung on all occasions, official or unofficial, and was perhaps more popular than the national anthem.

[53] *Anthology of Bulgarian Poetry*, Peter Tempest, transl. (Sofia, 1980), 93–94.

"renaming" process during the 1980s. His poem displays the same intensity of feeling, but alongside it is a deeply internalized recognition of reality:

A land just like a human palm...
A bigger land I don't require.
I'm glad your mountains are flint-hard
And that your blood has Southern fire.

A land just like a human palm...
But tougher, able to withstand
The poison of Byzantium,
The bloody Turkish yatagan.

Traders in blood and in tobacco
Who parcelled out your earth for sale
Fell to the ground with broken backs
For you, though small, were never frail.

A land just like a human palm...
To me you are the world entire.
I measure you not by the yard
But by the love that you inspire.[54]

The other side of the "indissoluble combination" of socialist patriotism and proletarian internationalism is patriotism. Its legitimacy should rest not on historical, geopolitical, linguistic, or other rights, but on "high national esteem," on a healthy respect for one's historical achievements, and the pride "of having been able also to contribute something to the world." It is quite symptomatic that in this latter phrase, which had become somewhat of a *Stichwort* in Bulgarian, Zhivkov in fact was reviving the title of a popular book on folk psychology which collected the most fantastic claims of greatness that Bulgarian nationalism had invented.[55] At the same time, Zhivkov emphasizes that this

---

[54] *Anthology of Bulgarian Poetry*, 443.

[55] Stilyan Chilingirov, *Kakvo e dal bîlgarinît na drugite narodi* ("What the Bulgarian Has Given to the Other Nations") (Sofia, 1941). Among the many contributions are the Bogomil heresy which, via the Hussites and Protestantism, brought the Enlightenment and the French Revolution to Europe; that Princess Olga, who converted Russia to Christianity in the tenth century was, in fact, the granddaughter of King Boris I who converted Bulgaria a century earlier; that Russian was only an offshoot of medieval Bulgarian; that a variety of great figures in European history had Bulgarian blood

patriotism had nothing to do with the exclusive and aggressive nationalism of the prewar era. In the only passage that was obviously aimed at Macedonia (although it does not explicitly mention it), Zhivkov refers to the longlasting, virulent dispute between Bulgarian and Macedonian historians over the same history: "We have no need to appropriate other people's merits and history; we are satisfied with our own."[56] This is a long way from the prewar irredenta: clearly, at least abroad, Bulgarian nationalism was being pursued only as cultural nationalism.

At the same time, the intensity of nationalism was turned to the internal scene. For at least two decades, in the 1960s and especially in the 1970s, there was a continuous escalation in the national feelings of all groups within the intelligentsia, but primarily among those in the liberal arts, and this was particularly acute among historians and writers. Given the significant degree of symbiosis between the intelligentsia and the Party in Bulgaria, compared to some of the other East European countries where the "divorce" had occurred earlier,[57] it would be unfair to say that these feelings were only well monitored and manipulated by the Party authorities; in fact, they were sometimes cautiously and most often overtly supported and directly inspired by the political elites.

The professional historians in particular took it upon themselves voluntarily to protect and promote the "national interests" and the "national cause," espousing the false, but self-satisfying, illusion that they were taking a dissident position. The rehabilitation and glorification of the great leadership figures of the medieval past—the scores of khans and tsars, who had created a strong Bulgarian state—was seen by the historians and writers as a way to counter the pernicious effects of what was considered to be "national nihilism," and to overcome what seemed to them to be the anonymous, anti-individual, deterministic, and overly schematic methodological approach of socioeconomic Marxist history.

flowing their veins, the most notorious of whom was Napoleon.

56 The other instance where the text touches on the Macedonian question (again only implicitly) is when seven of the leaders of the Bulgarian national-democratic revolution are called by name, among them two active in the Macedonian movement, Gotse Delchev and Yane Sandanski, who are hotly claimed by both Bulgarian and Macedonian historians as belonging exclusively to their respective nation's pantheon.

57 On the peculiar position of the Bulgarian intelligentsia within the political context, see Maria Todorova, "Improbable Maverick or Typical Conformist? Seven Thoughts on the New Bulgaria," in *Eastern Europe in Revolution*, Ivo Banac, ed. (Ithaca, NY: Cornell University Press, 1992), 148–67.

The political leadership not only found this acceptable, but saw in it the ideal legitimation of its authoritarian, and often totalitarian, ambitions. It was the centralized state of the past, with its strong individual leadership, that appealed to them as a model to emulate, and Zhivkov explicitly states this: "Glory be to the great prime builders, under whose leadership the Bulgarian people created their own centralized state: the khans Asparukh, Krum, and Omurtag; prince Boris I; the tsars Simeon, Samuil, Assen, and Peter, Kaloyan, and Ivan-Assen II!"[58]

The triunine theory of Bulgarian ethnogenesis (Thracian, Protobulgarian, and Slavic), which postulates that the Bulgarian nationality had assumed its final shape and unity by the ninth century, was warmly welcomed and officially endorsed. In Zhivkov's speech, this assumed the absolutely fantastic assertion that the Bulgarian state has followed a unique course in European history, "unlike other states then existing on our continent," in being built on the "principle of nationality as a state of one people." That this was scholarly insupportable and logically untenable was of no importance. Given the genre—an oral speech that was to be broadcast by the media to the entire nation—and given the political culture, which was looking for the blueprint of the current political course between the lines, the assertion meant that the principle of the unitary state was being endorsed with no accommodations for ethnic or other minorities.

Such a reading of Zhivkov's speech obviously gives priority to its nationalistic contents over its careful (although not very successful) attempts to conform to the orthodox Communist clichés.[59] In many ways, the nationalist policies of the Zhivkov administration culminated in the esoteric and messianic patriotic frenzies of his irrational daughter, Lyudmila Zhivkova, who became a

---

[58] It was widely circulated by what can be termed the "oral culture" of the intelligentsia that in Lyudmila Zhivkova's spiritualist soirees her father was considered to be the incarnation of the early ninth-century khan Krum, who strove to establish the absolute power of the ruler.

[59] One of the "sensations" of the post–1989 era was the discovery that in the 1960s Zhivkov had offered Moscow to turn Bulgaria into a sixteenth republic of the Soviet Union. This has been widely interpreted as a proof of the treacherous, anti-national nature of communism, which is willing to sacrifice national interests for the sake of Communist imperialism, etc. This particular move of Zhivkov still awaits a careful historian to meticulously weigh motivations versus reception, but my preliminary guess is that it was a very well-calculated personal affidavit of political loyalty that was not expected to produce any practical results. The last thing Moscow would have wanted to do in the 1960s was to change the territorial status quo, especially at the expense of its most loyal satellite—which would anyway have caused international pandemonium and accusations of Soviet expansionism.

Politburo member and headed cultural policies until her early death in 1981—the year of the lavishly and expensively prepared festivities commemorating the 1300th anniversary of the Bulgarian state, which was supposed to be the consummation of her long efforts to raise Bulgaria's self-esteem and international reputation.

Although she was precisely the embodiment of a rising nationalism, there occurred an important shift in the articulation of the discourse, which shed almost all but an obligatory minimum of Communist formulae. This can be seen in one of the tamer examples of Zhivkova's idiosyncratic prose (Document 4), which on a single page focuses on concepts such as "spiritual destiny," "spiritual tasks," "spiritual abilities," "spiritual level," "spiritual processes," "the Realm of Beauty," "the laws of Beauty," "sacred evolutionary rights" of the human individual, "the place of the Bulgarian nation," "the role of the Bulgarian nation," "national prospects," and "great national ideas." "Socialist" is used once, as an attribute *inter alia* of contemporary Bulgarian society. It was apparently this shift of discourse, and not a thorough analysis of the underlying ideas, that prompted an almost unanimous appraisal in the West of her policies as a manifestation of independence and as a window to the West.[60] On the other hand, the resistance that she and her entourage incurred among the so-called hard-liners, although clad in accusations of deviation from the orthodoxy, displayed simply the reluctance of the old entrenched Party functionaries to yield to a new generation of Party bureaucrats, a natural process.

Undoubtedly, the policy to "rename" the Turks in Bulgaria, which was launched in late 1984 and which reached its crisis in the summer of 1989, can be assessed as the culmination (and biggest miscalculation) of a long-term nationalist line of the Zhivkov regime.[61] It had an important cumulative effect on

---

[60] Given the nature of her thought, an in-depth analysis would find kindred intellectual analogs in astrology, numerology, a variety of esoteric schools of thought, and specifically in the teachings of the founder of an original Bulgarian esoteric movement in the interwar period, Petîr Dînov (Beinsa Duno). On the other hand, given the Ceauşescu precedent, the acclaim she was given in the West was hardly surprising. See, among others, the assessment of her in Crampton, *A Short History of Bulgaria*, and Joseph Rothschild, *Return to Diversity: A Political History of East Central Europe since World War II* (New York, 1989).

[61] On the Communist Party policies toward the "Turkish question" and the change of course after 1956, see Stefan Troebst, "Zum Verhältnis von Partei, Staat und türkischer Minderheit in Bulgarien 1956-1958," in *Nationalitätenprobleme in Südosteuropa*, Hrsg. R. Schönfeld (Munich, 1987), 231–56; Wolfgang Höpken, "Türkische Minderheiten in Südosteuropa. Aspekte ihrer politischen und sozialen Entwicklung in Bulgarien und Jugoslawien," in *Die Staaten Südosteuropas und die*

the whole range of international and domestic events that led to the series of "velvet" revolutions in Eastern Europe, which in Bulgaria was called much more soberly and modestly "the changes of 10 November."

Post-Totalitarianism (1989–Present)

What happened after 1989 in Eastern Europe did not result from the release of the genie of nationalism out of a tightly capped bottle but was essentially the result of three things. First, to elaborate on my earlier description of "communist nationalism" as being ordinary transvestite nationalism: after 1989, it gloated in its newly acquired nudity—it no longer had to pay lip service to the formerly dominant jargon. Second, and much more important, the international status quo had drastically changed, and under the new great power vacuum in the region, attempts can be made (or, at least, are perceived to carry few grave risks) to realize the nationalist claims articulated in the national discourse. Third, and perhaps most significant, nationalism (and ethnicity) have proved to have strong psychological appeal in times of frustration and deep economic, social, and cultural transformation.

As for Bulgaria, all signs indicate that there is no reversal in the status quo nature of nationalism, no matter how and by whom it is articulated. The two potentially sensitive spots of Bulgarian nationalism are the Macedonian question and the Turkish problem. As far as the first is concerned, despite the creation of several "Macedonian" organizations, the issue seems to be likely to remain within the confines of cultural nationalism—even in its most outspoken, and even shrill, articulations, the irredenta is absent.[62]

The "Turkish problem," on the other hand, presents a much more serious challenge. It cannot be reduced to a problem within the context of Bulgarian nationalism; it involves many independent issues outside its scope—problems of regional security, global security, ethnic minority status, the right to protect ethnic minorities, and the right to intervene in the domestic affairs of a neighboring nation, among others. These are all tantalizing issues that have not yet received a uniform and unanimous interpretation in global international law and

---

Osmanen, Hrsg. Hans Georg Majer (Südosteuropa Jahrbuch 19) (Munich, 1989); and Todorova, "Improbable Maverick or Typical Conformist?" 148–67.

62 The hasty recognition of Macedonian and Bosnian state independence (but not of the Macedonian nation) by Bulgaria, before any other entity, including the European Community and the United States, should be seen precisely in these terms—as a public statement that Bulgaria has no territorial claims.

politics, let alone in the Balkans.[63] Still, it can be safely argued that in many respects the national discourse now revolves around the Turkish problem. Questions about the study of Turkish at school and about the scope and character of the Turkish and Muslim propaganda are often discussed in terms reminiscent of the debate over multiculturalism in the United States.

The central issue, however, is the existence of the Movement for Rights and Freedoms (known as the "Turkish Party"). The Bulgarian Socialist Party (the former Communist Party) argues that the presence of the Movement (the third political force) in Parliament is unconstitutional, since the constitution forbids parties based on religious or ethnic principle. Ironically, the Socialist Party has dropped any ideological arguments, resorting exclusively to legalistic considerations. This particular position of the BSP reflects (but not exclusively) the expediency of playing the nationalist card in the power struggle (the usually advanced explanation or accusation). There is, however, also the legacy of the period when the party was identical with the state and when considerations of raison d'état were paramount. Conversely, the former democratic opposition, now in power, increasingly appropriates ideological arguments. Until now, in the overall euphoria, the anti-communist card has worked, but with the inevitable fading of this as an issue, the government finds its electoral alliance with the Turkish Party increasingly uncomfortable in the pervading atmosphere of openly expressed nationalism.

The open expression of the national idea has taken shape, as mentioned, in the formation of several groups defending the "national cause," but primarily in the press. One of the few and greatest achievements on Bulgaria's thorny road to pluralism and the creation of civil society is the creation of a free press. In this respect, the media have been the principal beneficiaries not only of the great power vacuum but also of the "authority vacuum,"[64] although there are already unmistakable signs that this period might be remembered in the near future as the sweet, short honeymoon of a free press. The newspaper article has become, for the first time in many decades, a powerful and effective tool and the dominant genre of *any* discourse, including the national discourse.

In this respect, Ilcho Dimitrov's article (Document 5) should be interpreted not merely as an example of the discourse of nationalism within the

---

63 As overblown as it might sometimes appear to the outside observer, in Bulgaria there is a real concern over the often aggressive standing of a strong (50 million), highly militarized Turkey, which has open U.S. support. This concern is further fed by the precedent of Cyprus and the character of the Greek-Turkish relations. Additional anxieties include the spread of Islamic fundamentalism, the Albanian Kosovë problem, and the example of the tragedy in Bosnia.

64 Susan L. Woodward, "The Tyranny of Time," *Brookings Review* (Winter 1992).

context of the Socialist Party, but as quite representative of the overall considerations of Bulgarian nationalism(s). As a journalistic piece, it employs some effective, apt, and well-phrased remarks. As an intellectual essay, it offers nothing new but functions essentially in the framework of past national discourses. The central idea of the article, as reflected in the title, is the importance of the "nation's unity," based on the central notion of nationalism in general that there exist "common national interests," "common national ideals," and "united national policy." The only interesting difference from past discourse is the appeal for political independence from great power tutelage, the call that Bulgaria not be "resigned...to the idea that our existence is impossible unless we are somebody's satellite." As noted, the articulation of this sentiment is possible only because of the unprecedented great power vacuum in the Balkans.

In a manner much less sophisticated than the discourse of the East Central European ideologues, this article also advances the argument that Bulgaria is a natural and inalienable part of European civilization. At the same time, just as the proponents of the East Central European idea attempted to sub-ghettoize Southeastern Europe (the Balkans) within Eastern Europe and to oust Russia from the region altogether, Dimitrov performs the same operation on Turkey: "Europe has geographic boundaries...Beyond the Straits is Asia."

Finally, as a recipe for political action, the article is a manifest example of authoritarian power politics. Characterizing the registration of the Turkish Party as a crime that should be rectified by banning and isolating the party is not surprising, given that the author was a cabinet minister in the Zhivkov regime at the time of the most virulent campaign against the Turks. What is surprising and very interesting is the subtle shift in the discourse. Instead of employing the usual (long used and abused) formula "in the name of the people," the author deftly accommodates his language to Jeffersonian democracy and, in appealing to public opinion to counter parliament, the political parties, and the government, utilizes the powerful phrase, "We, the people." It is one of the earliest examples of what I believe will be widespread in the future—appropriating the clichés of the democratic discourse for the purposes of nationalism.

Conclusion

This analysis of the different discourses of Bulgarian nationalism throughout the past century essentially shows a continuum, with some significant differences between the separate sub-periods. Until World War II, Bulgarian nationalism can be generally characterized as an irredentist nationalism, although the strong and dominant optimism of the period before World War I was transformed into a gloomy introspection during the interwar period. After 1945, the irredenta basically was dropped from the political agenda, and Bulgarian nationalism adjusted to reality, turning into a status quo nationalism. The defense of the "national cause" outside the country's borders was relegated to academia and to different public educational/cultural societies, whose passionate and sometimes overblown discourse is for all practical purposes harmless because it has no serious influence on government policy. Thus, the greatest discontinuity in the development of Bulgarian nationalism is in the realm of political aims, with World War II being the watershed.

This brought about an additional tension in the interpretation of "nation," which has not been addressed explicitly but is clearly present in the postwar texts. This is, on one hand, continued discussion of the nation as a historical entity centered around linguistic, religious, and cultural unity. On the other hand, it is the increased acceptance of the nation as a formation of the citizens of the state (a direct illustration being Dimitrov's statement that Islam and Macedonism are "setting apart, against the majority, of a part of the nation"). That these two claims—i.e., that the Turks in Bulgaria are part of the Bulgarian nation (according to the second criterion), and that the Macedonians and others are outside Bulgaria (according to the first criterion)—are logically incompatible is an issue that is carefully avoided.

In all other aspects, the articulation of Bulgarian nationalism has demonstrated a remarkable continuity of ideas and feelings. To the fierce defensiveness and the centrality of the linguistic criterion as a legacy from the pre–1878 period was added in subsequent periods an almost fatalistic resignation to great power interference. Another important addition, which has persisted unchanged since World War I, is the self-image of the Bulgarian which, to paraphrase Lacan, displays an "imaginary rape" syndrome. The greatest continuity, however, can be traced in the language of the discourses.

Anthropomorphism is a basic attribute of nationalism in general, which treats the nation as a living organism. The sacred formula "living parts/members of the nation's body/organism are torn away" can be traced unchanged from Rizoff to Dimitrov. This presupposes the undifferentiated treatment of the nation as one, with common ideals and interests, and therefore makes divisions along any lines aberrant. The same is true about the nation's evolution in time: it is treated as a perennial (or, at least, very ancient) entity to which, seemingly, no changes have occurred in character or ideals. There is a whole series of code words and phrases that have been employed uninterruptedly through all periods. In this respect, only the language of Gîlîbov stands outside this simplistic imagery. By locating Bulgaria in a relational European framework, he instead evokes at present feelings of déjà vu.

At the same time, there have been important additions to and shifts in the discourse. National ideology, which is a fundamental product and indispensable attribute of the nation-state, has included more than one discourse and has displayed a remarkable ability to appropriate the discourses of often opposing ideologies for legitimizing purposes. This was the case during the period of Communist rule, and this seems already to be occurring in attempts to adapt the language of the hegemonic discourse of democracy to the needs of the national ideology in the post-Communist period.

4

Czech and Slovak Nationalism in the Twentieth Century

by Carol Skalnik Leff

Document 1

from a letter from Milan Štefánik to Professor Antonín Vavro (1905).[1]

My Dear Professor,

...A year ago a Slovak monthly *Hlas* began to appear, a journal calling for the rebirth of our [Slovak] intelligentsia and our entire national life. Its trenchant articles evoked vehement polemics and spurred political crystallization. It created two camps: "the old nationalists," and those of *Hlas*. *Narodnie noviny,* headed by Vajanský, saw their conservative clericalist ultranationalist outlook as the heritage of their fathers; they therefore felt justified in

---

[1] Letter from Milan Štefánik to Professor Antonín Vavro, 11 February 1905, reprinted in *"Z korespondencie predstavitel'ov českeho a slovenského národného hnutia na prelome 19. a 20. storocia (II Čast')," Historický časopis* 17:3 (1969), 436–37. Translation by C. S. Leff. This letter, from the most prominent of the Slovak exile leaders (later minister of defense of the new state) encapsulates several important elements of the pre-independence national struggle, above all the divisions in outlook within the Slovak nationalist movement and the alignment of a younger, struggling "progressive" camp with the Czechs. The Hlasisti were an important core of the "Czechoslovaks" in Slovakia after independence.

condemning anything foreign, western and thereby modern, and opted for passivity, believing that only God and the czar could bring our truth to victory.

In opposition to this, the progressive group emphasized in *Hlas* that we must seek our salvation in ourselves with 1) a bold active policy, 2) democracy, 3) persevering, small scale cultural work *(drobna praca)*, 4) economic emancipation from hostile elements, and 5) instead of practicing russophilism, cultural unity with the Czechs, and above all freedom of word and conviction.

No one doubts the sincere, honorable effort of the elders, their honesty and sacrifice; however...the popular progressive approach of the Hlasist program is more...efficacious. It captured the enthusiasm of all Slovakia and created a new current in politics and social-cultural work. I cannot write at length, because my eyes are burning and my head aches... Now only some brief comments. Dr. Srobar, editor of *Hlas* and a physician in Ružomberok (I was with him and young Slavušek this summer) writes me that the small number of subscribers, although demand is sufficient, caused a deficit substantial enough to halt publication. This is a sad testimonial for Slovak society, that it can't sustain a single progressive periodical, whose editor and contributors don't require remuneration for their work, but rather themselves sacrifice financially for it.

It would mean immeasurable damage to our national affairs should *Hlas* cease to publish, and we should do everything to prevent that. Among others we thought of those in Prague, who might contribute something, when poor students and similar young adherents make sacrifices.

Before we take any other step, I wanted to ask you, dear professor, in confidence—1) Do you think that our endeavor is fruitless? 2) In case it is not, kindly advise me to whom we should turn, in what form? (I'm not speaking of thousands [of crowns] but hundreds). The least support would be welcome.

I wouldn't trouble you were it not a matter of national importance—and you are so good and concerned about my Slovak nation.

If health permits, I will write in more detail, but I must stop now; I'm quite tired. My best wishes.... asking you to remember me, dear professor, devotedly,

Milan Štefánik

Document 2

Editorial in *Nástup* (1934).[2]

In the first post-revolutionary years, the further development of Czechoslovak power was glibly thought about and discussed. At national and political meetings, it was approvingly asserted in empty phrases that in ten or fifteen years there would be no misunderstandings, we would be one nation speaking and writing the same language, fused into one because it was so determined by history.

It seems that for our politicians it was only a matter of time, that after the passage of a certain more or less vague period, the realization of some kind of ideal coexistence in the form of the fusion of Czechs and Slovaks would occur automatically to the detriment of the Slovaks, of course. Now, after fifteen years have passed, it is undeniable that distrust has not only failed to vanish, or at least to lessen, but precisely the opposite has occurred; today the gulf separating Czechs and Slovaks is greater than it was at any previous time.

The old leaders who built the republic pushed affairs to this point with the thesis of mutuality and have, thereby, created a certain paradox: Czechoslovak mutuality was wrecked precisely by its forcible imposition. These elders, when they became aware of their mistakes and failure, began to entrust the task of coming to an agreement to the young. And what happened?...

Today the public is less informed mutually about each other than was the case before 1918. We can mention expeditions of Czechs to Slovakia and also the reverse. The study and acclimatizing travels of distinctive individuals...[we can mention, and] finally, the significance of Detvan [the Slovak Student Association in the Czech lands] and the studies of young Slovaks in Prague. Interest was great, and we can unhesitatingly state that in those days the Czech public was more precisely and objectively informed about Slovakia than [it is now] when everything is presented through a political prism and even with incomprehensible hatred. The young Czech generation in schools is inculcated with prejudice towards all things Slovak; Czech children learn from infancy to look at Slovak affairs as less valuable, less worthy. It is no wonder,

---

2 This essay, published in the radical Slovak nationalist journal *Nástup* (1 January 1934, pp. 205–206), is representative of the Slovak nationalist challenge to Czechoslovakism that emerged in the younger Slovak generation of the 1930s. It is a highly charged rebuttal to core "Czechoslovak" expectations about compatible coexistence and the advent of national fusion in the younger generation socialized in a common state. Translation by C. S. Leff.

then, that this generation, when grown up, comes to Slovakia feeling and acting like an Englishman arriving in India.

Document 3

"Report on Slovakia?" (*"Zpráva o Slovensku?"*) (1981).[3]

The relationship of Czechs to Slovaks in the past ten or fifteen years developed or rather (to put it simply) became worse. These days, at least in unofficial publications, which reflect the position of most aware citizens, there has long been an "inertial state." It is, unfortunately, a state of disappointed, injured disinterest, not always dressed convincingly in the virtuous garb of "noninterference" in Slovak affairs.

In 1968, and possibly still more explicitly in the first years of normalization, it was acknowledged that many people in the Czech lands refused to believe that despite the justifiably contested concept of "administrative" federal pluralism, there existed in reality a pluralism of lacks of identity between the Czech and Slovak parts of the republic. At first and even after an appraising glance, the results of the differences always seemed to point to the disadvantage of the Czechs: Alas! Slovaks are better off. And [are better off] to our detriment!

Unreflective and unconfirmed impressions ultimately elicited a mass mood that can be characterized only as wretched. Czech nationalism, which had been gradually and in spite of grave protest deprived of anything positive, found its substitute object, its almost officially approved lightning rod [in this anti-Slovakism, as] (anti-Sovietism and anti-Russianism are risky in the pub). Several good jokes and a long list of painfully malicious ones about Slovaks did understandably not touch the essence of the differences.

---

[3] This essay was published in the exile periodical *Listy* (9:1, 8 January 1981, 15–16) as an introductory gloss on the contributions of two dissident writers based in Slovakia, the Czech Milan Šimečka and the Slovak Miroslav Kusy. It is a valuable reflection of mutual Czech-Slovak attitudes in the "normalization" era after the Soviet invasion, a commentary on the state of Czech national sentiment at that time, and, finally, a reflection of outward-looking Europeanism prevalent among much of the dissident intellectual community. (The question mark in the title refers to the fact that the report from Slovakia is not *about* Slovakia.) Translation by C. S. Leff.

The unofficial publicists do not acknowledge that nationalism is in decline and, therefore, fail to spread it. By failing to come to terms with it, they are, of course, deprived of the possibility of using even the smallest chance for self-analysis: a better understanding of the Slovaks and the metamorphosis of Czech-Slovak (and vice versa) relations would mean precisely the possibility of understanding more objectively the Czech problem!

Recently, it is possible to discern among these publicists in the approach to writing about Slovakia (or more accurately, in the manner of alluding to Slovakia) a peculiar Czech noblemindedness: if one writes something exclusively about Czech economics, Czech history, and so forth, then the writer will be certain to point out explicitly that he is writing only about Czech economics, Czech history, and so forth. For long decades, the Czech outlook was promulgated as "Czechoslovak," and Slovaks felt justly wounded by that pontifical paternalism. But not today: more often, as an obligatory flourish, there appears, unnecessarily, the disclaimer: "insofar as Slovakia, Slovaks, and Slovak relations are concerned, we maintain the standpoint that that is a Slovak affair, let them speak about it themselves..." Of course, if they or anyone has something to say without official permission, that anticipates the silent rebuke. Good, everyone for themselves, you had always wanted that—but can you accomplish it without us? There is in all that precept from the past, in that injury, a bit of envy, even foolish pride, from the inertial feeling of superiority. What is worse, there is resignation in it as well: we know nothing about you, and won't try too hard to find anything out, we will be silent, so that you can't reproach us with speaking for you... At the same time, it is clear that, for many reasons (which would stand for more careful analysis!), practically no Slovaks speak in dissident forums, thus only strengthening the superficial "pro-Czech" impression that Slovakia is entirely silent and bought off.

Slovakia simply speaks in other ways, and we must finally take that calmly into account. We in the Czech lands should long since have followed Slovak publicists and Slovak culture more closely, and tried to understand other things than dissident speech because we otherwise don't hear that Slovakia is simply Slovakia and not the Czech lands, and we thus only vaguely apprehend what it all means! Interest in Slovakia is insubstantial and a tone of resignation about a common future resonates....

Here we have a "double book" by Slovak-based authors with the title *Big Brother and Big Sister,* which came out in a Petlice edition [the samizdat press]. Chapters are excerpted without the knowledge of the authors, which must be introduced with a brief comment drawing on what was said above.

The Czech reader, surprised by the ostentatious silence of domestic authors in explanation of the Slovak spectrum, impatiently expecting perhaps a Slovak self-defense (in the style of a typical Slovak "exculpation complex" going back to the time of linguistic separation) will be disappointed and annoyed. He should instead, however, be aroused to thoughtfulness, because in a book by practically the only publishing Slovak dissidents, there is absolutely nothing about Slovakia and Slovak affairs.

One need not doubt whether both authors have anything to say about Slovakia. Obviously, they considered it more important, when giving voice, to think and write above all about what weighs on us, not only as Czechs and Slovaks, or as citizens of the ČSSR, but as people living in that great empire of real socialism, and, in the last analysis, in Europe. Both authors—each in an entirely different way—tries above all to transcend singularities and exceptions, but also to include and thus to explain them in a broad and still broader context—ultimately in the European context. It is really a book about how only distance—in time and space, but also distance from personal errors, disappointments, losses, and inflicted scars—makes it possible, in the complex social reality of today's world, to really understand, and how only that broader understanding can give more practical meaning to a concrete national self-knowledge.

Document 4

Ludvík Vaculík, "Our Slovak Question" *("Naše slovenská otázka")* (1990).[4]

By nationality I am a Czech of Moravian stripe; by education, civic outlook and working aspiration a Czechoslovak. I thought a bit about the Czechoslovak state; to think additionally about the Czech lands with Moravia had no justification for me except in a poetic or humorous sense. My frame of reference was the whole Czechoslovak territory; all Slovaks were Czechoslovaks to me; I set great store by the Czechoslovak state course for the long run, as well as the Czechoslovak flag and the two-part anthem, which they sang here in Prague last year as one song. The Czech state did not exist for me, Czech symbols and circumscribed Czech interests receded. I think that the majority

---

4 This article, by one of the most famous Czech intellectual dissidents, appeared in a Czech intellectual daily *(Literární noviny,* 3 May 1990) early in the transition period and proved highly controversial. It is equally important for capturing some of the sense of an emerging Czech awareness of national needs, separate from those of the common Czechoslovak state, and for its critical portrait of the Slovak outlook. Translation by C. S. Leff.

of us are this kind of "bad" Czech. Petr Pithart long criticized us for that under Husák, and when, as head of the Czech government, he recently proclaimed a program of Czech statehood, it struck me as a bad prognosis. To develop an exclusively Czech state would be a step backward.

We Czechs are much indebted to Slovaks, but it is a debt of a different sort than is generally argued. It is a debt so heavy, that the weaker Czech doesn't even understand it, and so complexly subtle that to acknowledge it now to the Slovak while fighting over the name of the state is superfluous... Our debt, roughly speaking, is that we gladly took physical and spiritual possession of the Slovak lands, but did not so evidently assimilate Slovak perceptions, feelings and thoughts. We didn't enter into their Slovak consciousness. For the most part, we acknowledge the individuality of Slovak language and culture, but stand apart from it, rather than enter into it, unlike the Slovak approach to our Czechness... (But who among us feels the need to read at least one Slovak cultural/political journal, in order to absorb more Slovak material than is forced on us?)

Slovaks today unintentionally defer our understanding of this our debt, presenting us with a primitive termination of the problem for immediate superficial resolution. We removed the word "socialist" from the title of the republic, because one doesn't obtain an attribute with a word, but we were forced to accept the word "federative" as if that desirable attribute could be acquired with a word. If there are substantive problems, they must be legally and organizationally resolved. With their curse on the name Czechoslovakia, the Slovaks insulted precisely our supranational aspect, the more tolerant and ambitious side, precisely what had previously made us able to make sacrifices for the Slovaks. To be a Czechoslovak—that is a seemly task. To be only a Czech will make each of us foolish in front of the Slovaks.

The Slovak grievance against us has deeper roots that cannot be removed by any administrative adjustment. It is of an individual and psychological nature. I think that Slovaks aren't sufficiently prepared for free and equal relations to another nation. They never had their own state; the state of 1938–45 cannot honestly be considered as such; it was a wartime accident. It was useful however in subsequent efforts to conceptualize a genuine state. A nation either affirms its independence, or subsides into a social group in a greater whole. We experienced this mainly vis-à-vis the Germans, they with regard to the Hungarians; this however was soon overthrown by other forces and the Slovaks were almost inevitably led again into a common state with someone else.... We gradually built industry, educated the teachers and intelligentsia, and they accepted this from us at a time of sudden emergency, and ever thereafter complained of the quality of our contribution. After the defeat of fascism, it would have been wise to make a critical accounting of the fascist experience; instead, with the renewal of their adherence to the "good"

Czechoslovakia, they effaced their defeat without self-appraisal. Furthermore, after the war, communists in Slovakia were much weaker, but under the influence of central Prague authority, the Slovaks fell under the same regime as we did. Again, there was no crisis of awareness, because Czech communism gave them more in material terms than it did to the Czechs. Furthermore, when we tried in 1968 to free ourselves from dictatorship, the Slovaks regarded that as our concern and went for autonomy. The Slovaks seemed to be saying, "You, the Czechs, imported communism into Slovakia, so you will have too remove it." ...Misled by their history, spoiled by Czech intervention on their behalf, the Slovaks don't know how an autonomous and proud nation should behave. In the future, they will continue to seek excuses for their own shortcomings, blaming them on the Czechs.

...With us, every Catholic is unconsciously a bit of a Hussite, and vice versa. Each of us [Czechs] is a little German and a little Slovak. All of us new democrats and liberals will be also a bit socialist. Our dough is kneaded with euphoria and depression. In contrast to that, Slovaks have neither reason nor time to suffer through something deeply and settle it; it sufficed for them to wait, and something else would come along. Not even the uprising against the Nazis for its shortness of duration and territorial limits was sufficient to confront each Slovak with the basic existential and moral question: who are you and what do you want? We can't be sure today that the uprising, with its anti-German character, was automatically pro-Czechoslovak; a third party seized its fruit. Not having anyone on whom to demonstrate their maturity, the Slovaks mistakenly used us for this purpose. While we know that we get only what we earn, they know that they can always exact something from us. Therefore, this year when things got a little freer, and they looked around for the nearest harmless enemy, they saw us. Do we need this?

Recently I went to Bratislava, and all my friends asked me why we are so disturbed, that the nationalist outcry comes from careerists or fools or intriguers. I heard that gladly. I would have expected, however, that the wiser majority would have disciplined or voted down the worse minority. No, instead of that the wise ones say to us that it is wiser to stand aside, when the matter isn't important; and thus, in our and their wisdom, that unimportant thing can pass into law. I know that my Slovak friends will find what I write here painful, those who until recently we had to meet secretly to talk about literature, politics and life and its purpose. I know, that even now they would almost fully agree. We prepared for and looked forward to today, even when we didn't believe that it would overtake us yet. We also knew, however, that this day would divide us a little and give more impetus to that which differentiated us personally. But the day is here, fortunately, and I must say publicly what could only be said privately and secretly before: that this is possibly the propitious occasion, when the best people of the Slovak nation turn their dissatisfaction inward. Finally and without external threat, the Slovak nation can turn to the quest for its happiness, in order to function again at a higher level. Let tension in the nation refine its thought and force. It is harmful and mistaken to debase it with the venting of diversionary spleen on the Czechs.

Milan Šimečka, my Czech friend in Bratislava, wrote to us that the Slovak younger brother had grown up, wanted his own bed, and the Czech older brother ought to give it to him. But we know this younger brother—he will want his bed by the window in summer and by the stove in winter. No bed for you, brother, you have your own house.

After the first embitterment, regret, or anger, however, one must soberly assess the situation: what it means, what it takes and gives to us. Why do the Slovaks try to obtain everything from us by centimeters, when they could have everything at once? By severance from the Slovaks, which is solely at our will, we will forfeit—judging by previous experience—economic losses. Politically we will forfeit the Hungarian and Ruthenian problems. We will place yet another boundary between ourselves and the Soviet Union. We will have only one government. All matters will finally be resolvable quickly and pertinently, without special regard for the Slovaks. Without the occasion for the eruption of national disputes, we can perhaps introduce democratic forms and methods more quickly. By ourselves we can undoubtedly catch up faster with the more developed states. We will have more peace in the search for a life-style resistant to aggressive commerce and consumption. When the same twenty years lost in federation with Slovakia are devoted to cooperation and contact with Austria, we will approach a possible workable federation or union, the functioning of which wise members won't burden with their depressions, complexes and recriminations. And our relation to Slovakia? Economic and other questions can be resolved through contractual relations such as exist between Denmark and Sweden. No?

Let us consider whether we can't gain from the Slovak stimulus our own favorable opportunity to start a new life. After three centuries of Habsburg subjection and seventy years of oppressing another nation [we would] live with a clean conscience and new horizons. As a matter of fact, everything would be different! The prospects are favorable because they come now: even last year such considerations would have been suspect of the intention to offer Slovakia to the Soviet Union. After seventy years, that would have been to refuse help to the younger brother... Security in contemporary Europe is an entirely different question than when we Czechs were Czechoslovaks. How everything is changed all at once, only if one acknowledges it!

Introduction

Czech and Slovak nationalisms shaped and were shaped by a series of political regimes in the twentieth century, with each successive political environment posing a different problem for national identity and with each successive regime transmitting an ambiguous legacy to the next. The Czech lands and Slovakia began the century within the confines of the Austro-Hungarian empire, the former a distinct, historically recognized territory within Austria and Slovakia integrally incorporated into the territory of Hungary as Felvidék, or northern Hungary. The collapse of the Habsburg regime following World War I facilitated a joint experiment in national self-determination and independence; this common state was temporarily abrogated by the German intervention of 1938–39. During a brief but telling period of separation, the Czech lands fell under a German protectorate, and Slovakia was detached to pursue a circumscribed independence within the Axis camp. The postwar communization of a reunited state was not a politically undifferentiated period; for twenty years, Slovak distinctiveness received a very modest tribute in the form of "asymmetrical" Slovak political organs subordinate to the central government in Prague, a peculiar arrangement which gave way to the formal federalization of the state in the aftermath of the Prague Spring reform period of 1968. Since 1989, democratization efforts stalemated over the ultimately unresolvable question of the balance of national interests within a common Czech and Slovak state. Czechoslovakia, in many ways distinctive in its successes—the sole interwar regime in the region that maintained a parliamentary democracy, a developed economic base, and a tradition of peaceful politics—is now distinctive in the character of its failure, disintegration not by violence but by deadlock and acquiescence.

Over this era of highly varied political experiences—monarchy, parliamentary democracy, authoritarian occupation, and Communist rule—the circumstances of national expression changed with relentless frequency. The impact of these changes on Czech and Slovak national aspirations, and the eventual failure to reconcile them, will be the central focus of this analysis. First it will be useful, however, to set a broader context for this examination of two nationalisms bound together by an experiment in statehood, to look at some of the basic distinctions that demarcate the boundaries of two societies that have been politically and economically integrated without having achieved a clear vision of mutual destiny.

National Identities of the Czechs and Slovaks

National identity itself is not a constant, static bond. It does not "emerge," "go into hibernation," and then "resurge," if by that we are assuming a fixed quality with fixed reference points, much less a fixed agenda. The question "who are we?" and the nature of the action, remedy, or resolution that identification requires, evolves over time in response to shifting political and economic circumstances, as well as to changing elite perceptions of threat and opportunity.

By and large, the relevant national elites *did* recognize national identity as a dynamic factor, subject to change and redefinition. The political evolution of national identity in the twentieth century, in fact, was shaped not only by successive efforts to redefine political structures, but also by conscious social engineering of the national fabric. The most striking of these efforts at social engineering include the "magyarization" policies of the Hungarian state through World War I, through which it sought to turn Slovaks into Hungarians; the identification of the interwar state with an elusive "Czechoslovakism"; the national ideology of the Slovak state; and the postwar Communist efforts to resolve the national question. In each case, the architects of national policy assumed that national identity was malleable, susceptible to redefinition in consonance with state purposes. In each case, the result was less than satisfactory, and the national question remained unresolved.

Part of the problem lay with differences in the focus and core values of the two nations—Czech and Slovak—that were to be harnessed in a joint undertaking. A sense of identity with a national group is a widespread building block of modern politics. Although the phenomenon of nationalism by definition contains an integral political component, there is no inherent or "natural" ideological content to its expression. It is common, but not inevitable, for nationalism to carry religious cargo; religious identity is often one of the core values that differentiates the national group, with the church serving as "custodian of cultural identity."[5] Moreover, national leaders may appeal to common religious identity in order to demarcate and mobilize a national constituency.

Religion was clearly an important politicizing factor in the Slovak pursuit of national goals. From the beginning of the twentieth century through the First Republic (1918–38), this centrality was evident in the prominence of religious figures in the national movement, above all Father Hlinka, revitalizer of the pre- independence movement that was reconstituted as the HSLS (Hlinka Slovak People's Party) under his personal leadership and which he led until his death in 1938. Priests forged multiple and enduring links with the local populations in a context where the parish remained a central element in village life and where control of education also resided to a significant extent

[5] Raymond Pearson, *National Minorities in Eastern Europe: 1848–1945* (London: Macmillan, 1983), 22.

with the clergy. In a politically constrained environment, where Slovak elites in traditional political niches tended to be magyarized, the priesthood as well as the free professions formed an alternative political recruiting ground that clearly differentiated the Slovak political elite from the Czech well into the early years of the common state—as evidenced by the particularly high proportion of priests in the moderate core of the HSLS.[6] The striking preeminence of religious leaders among Slovak politicians was not destined to persist indefinitely. Even during the First Republic, the progress of elite diversification eroded the dominance of the "premodern" religious and professional representatives in favor of more workers and business people, for example. Moreover, the high religious profile of the World War II Slovak state provoked a postwar backlash against priestly engagement in politics (a particularly troubling problem for the Vatican), which of course only accelerated as Communist influence drove the clergy from politics altogether.

However, the direct participation of religious leaders in nationalist politics was in some sense only a marker denoting the strong salience of religion for Slovak national identity; the larger relevance of religion to nationalism is a continuing thread throughout the century. In the First Republic, confessional issues were a constant factor in the nationalist agenda for an HSLS Party that sought to protect both the Catholic Church as an institution and the integrity of religious values—"For God and Country"—against a more secularly oriented central government and against Czech "atheism/agnosticism." The association of the Czech historical tradition with the Hussite rebellion and the Reformation impulse was, of course, part of the problem. The Slovak "Parish Republic"[7] of World War II was a delicate balancing act for a leadership imbued with

---

6 Sixteen percent of the Slovak parliamentary delegates (but only 1 percent of the Czechs) in the interwar period were ministers or priests, rising to 32 percent of the leaders of the identifiably nationalist parties. See Carol Skalnik Leff, *National Conflict in Czechoslovakia: The Making and Remaking of a State, 1918–1987* (Princeton, NJ: Princeton University Press, 1988), 189–90. See also James Felak, *Andrej Hlinka and the Slovak People's Party, 1929–1938* (Pittsburgh: University of Pittsburgh Press, forthcoming); and Jorg K. Hoensch, "Slovakia: 'One God, One People, One Party!' The Development, Aim and Failure of Political Catholicism," in *Catholics, the State and the European Radical Right,* Jorg K. Hoensch and Richard J. Wolff, eds. (New York: Social Science Monographs, Columbia University Press, 1987), 159–81.

7 Yesahayu Jelinek, *The Parish Republic: Hlinka's Slovak People's Party, 1939–1945* (New York: Columbia University Press, 1976).

Catholic faith but confronted with the profound moral ambiguity of dependence on the Third Reich.

In the postwar period, under a hostile Communist regime, the submergence of the religious component of Slovak national identity failed to extirpate the durable core of avowed believers. In the census of 1991, the proportion of religious believers of all faiths in the Czech lands was 44 percent (39 percent Roman Catholic), while Slovakia recorded almost 73 percent of its population as adherents of a religious faith (60 percent Roman Catholic).[8] Moreover, religious concerns—for religious instruction, the training and practice of priesthood, and the dissemination of religious materials—had been clearly visible in the reform period of 1968, and the revival of dissident activity in the 1970s had reconfirmed the centrality of religion as a focus of Slovak concern. Prosecutions of Slovak priests for illegally celebrating Mass or hearing confession triggered local demonstrations, while religious pilgrimages and petition drives demanding religious rights had become commonplace in the 1980s.[9] After 1989, the reclamation and rebuilding of church institutions and the rehabilitation of Father Hlinka as both nationalist and son of Czechoslovakia has been part of a broader national restoration.

The religiosity of the Slovaks meshed poorly with the more secular Czech evolution. The seeming Catholic predominance in the Czech lands eroded steadily in the twentieth century, complicated by a strong anticlerical tradition that had nationalist roots in the Hussite rebellion and that was a reaction against the thoroughgoing Counter-Reformation that accompanied the seventeenth-century eradication of the Czech state. The clear Catholic presence in the national renaissance was crosscut with the perception that the church hierarchy served Austrian interests.[10] Although Moravia remained a firmer religious bastion, the number of Czech nonbelievers already neared 10 percent in the 1920 census and climbed to almost 40 percent in 1991 after decades of

---

8 See *"Obyvatelstvo ČSFR podle národností a náboženského vyznání," Dokumentační přehled ČTK* 32 (1991), H1–3.

9 "Religion: The Repression Behind the Rhetoric," *RFE Czechoslovak Situation Report* 7 (12 June 1987), 9–13; and Helsinki Watch, *Toward Civil Society: Independent Initiatives in Czechoslovakia* (August 1989), 37–38.

10 See Jonathan Luxmoore and Jolanta Babiuch, "Truth Prevails: The Catholic Contribution to Czech Thought and Culture," *Religion, State and Society* 20:1 (1982), 103–19.

communism. By contrast, Slovakia's nonbelievers reached the 10 percent mark only in 1991.[11]

This demographic differential had powerful political import that underpinned overt tensions between the two national groups. Even before statehood, Father Hlinka claimed to worry less about language than about Czech "atheism."[12] Czech politicians found it easier to cooperate with the influential Slovak Protestant minority, who shared their concern over the "exorbitant religiosity" of the Slovak population as an impediment to rational governance—a posture that inevitably promoted intense resentment at home.[13] Following World War II, the execution of Msgr. Tiso for his actions as head of the Slovak state triggered intense Slovak anger over the greater leniency shown his Czech counterpart, Emil Hacha, an outrage intensified by the seeming Czech disregard for his priestly calling.[14] Thus, differences in religious outlook often poisoned Czech-Slovak understanding during the first half of the century, and subterranean differences simmered under communism, as the discrepancy in religious attachment persisted.

Nationalism also can carry distinctive political orientation. It certainly can be integrated with authoritarian political institutions, with one-party rule, and with strong personal leadership, as was the case in the wartime Slovak state. Yet this linkage is hardly automatic. It is, after all, possible to speak of a "democratization" of nationalism in the national revivals of the nineteenth century, at least insofar as the "people" rather than a narrow elite was increasingly perceived as the proper repository of national sovereignty.[15] Elite

---

[11] See L'Office de Statistique d'état, *Manuel statistique de la Republique tchécoslovaque, 1921* (Prague: Státní úřad statistický, 1921), 380; and *"Obyvatelstvo ČSFR podle národností a náboženského vyznání,"* H–3.

[12] Cited in Leff, *National Conflict in Czechoslovakia,* 23.

[13] From the brochure *Co hatí Slováky,* reprinted in Albert Pražák, *T. G. Masaryk a Slovensko* (Prague: Edice corona, 1937), 74. For a recent review of the religious components of interwar national tension, see Michal Dzvoník, *"Sme dedičmi dobrého i zlého: Andrej Hlinka a česko-slovenské vzt'ahy," Národná obroda* (26 October 1991).

[14] For a detailed acccounting of the political maneuvering surrounding the Tiso trial, see Vladimír Huml, *Slovensko před rozhodnutím* (Prague: Naše vojsko, 1972), 125–51.

[15] See Jozef Chlebowczyk, *On Small and Young Nations in Europe: Nation-Forming Processes in Ethnic Borderlands in East Central Europe* (Wroclaw: Polskiej Akademii

competition to mobilize co-nationals gave concrete form to this conception. The process, of course, represented a twofold challenge to traditional government, for the nationalist challenge to a multinational state could readily attach itself to demands for more representative government, alarming both officials and the dominant German and Hungarian nations as well. Even when the nation became a concept inclusive of the mass public, however, popular connection to politics still ran across a spectrum from demagogic populism to autonomous citizen initiative. Tensions between Czechs and Slovaks rest in part on a controversy over the democratic tendencies of each side.

Notwithstanding support for the Communist transformation of the 1940s, it is not a distortion to make the argument that the most dominant tendency of Czech national political expression has been liberal democratic in the tradition of Tomáš G. Masaryk. The architects of the Czechoslovak state of 1918 were nationalists/internationalists; Masaryk himself clearly hoped that the successor states of East Central Europe would be part of a larger pan-European democratization process, perhaps even within a Euro-federalist framework, that would supplant power politics with a more just and humane vision of national self-development infused with universal human values.[16] Although his vision failed in the international arena, and often fell afoul of domestic political intrigues, the broad spectrum of interwar Czech electoral politics remained responsive to the liberal parliamentary ideal and largely unreceptive to fascism.[17] The reconstruction efforts of 1918, 1945, 1968, and after 1989 were closely tied to the practice of free elections, parliamentary politics, and individual (as opposed to collective) rights, and even the Communist revolution of 1948 spoke to the humanitarian tradition in ways that proved highly problematic in practice.

The Czech orientation, however, found itself at odds with the Slovak in ways that marked long-standing controversies over the character of democracy and the authenticity of each nation's democratic credentials—in which regard the Czechs periodically accused the Slovaks of forgery. From the outset, Czechs discerned in Slovak nationalist politics a "demagogic" slant that delegitimated Slovak nationalist demands. The intemperate character of some of Hlinka's pronouncements and the radicalism of the younger HSLS faction tended to discredit the movement—and the electorate naive enough to vote for them—as

---

Nauk, 1980).

16 Zděnek Šolle, "Masaryk's Voyage to the New Europe," *Czechoslovak and Central European Journal* 10:2 (Winter 1991), 56–57.

17 See Joseph Zacek, "Czechoslovak Fascisms," in *Native Fascism in the Successor States*, Peter F. Sugar, ed. (Santa Barbara, CA: ABC-Clio, 1971).

"politically immature" in Czech eyes. This diagnosis of Slovak political immaturity, both in the interwar period and later, tended to cast doubt on the capacity of Slovaks to govern themselves, insofar as Czechs and many Slovaks refused to believe that strong electoral support for the HSLS and later nationalist groups mirrored true Slovak interests, or that free speech defined those interests responsibly in the marketplace of ideas.[18] In 1991, Czech analysts were still speculating that nationalist electoral support in Slovakia was the product of insufficient public understanding of the motivations of their leaders. To some extent, this perception became a self-fulfilling prophecy, as it impeded responsiveness to Slovak demands, further radicalized the Slovak opposition, and left it unable to resolve its grievances in the context of politics as usual. This in turn was a contributing factor to the dismemberment of the state in the late 1930s.

Later scholars and politicians would pick up the interwar democracy debate and reinterpret it. If "Czechoslovak" Slovaks of the First Republic bemoaned the retrograde tendencies of its electorate, seeing the young voters as having been sidetracked from democratic liberalism by demagogic nationalists, later analysts questioned whether the ideological coloration of the HSLS was an inherent component of Slovak nationalism or the product of elite choices and impaired vision. Reform Marxist scholars identified an unnatural "alignment in which the progressives were bound to an artificial Czechoslovakism, leaving the field free to more reactionary forces to dominate the symbols of national legitimacy."[19] Still later, post-Communist discussion challenged the dismissal of the HSLS as undemocratic and reactionary. But the issue of democratic credentials remained very central to the historical understanding of the stakes of national politics.

Evaluations of the democratic propensities of Slovak nationalism underwent several shifts in focus during the Communist period. The message of the bourgeois nationalist trials that sent several highly placed Slovak leaders, including Gustav Husák, to jail in the 1950s was clearly that nationalism was inherently undemocratic in the classic Marxist sense.[20] Efforts for their rehabilitation fed directly into the reform impulse that sustained the Prague

---

[18] Leff, *National Conflict in Czechoslovakia,* 196–97).

[19] Samo Falt'an, *Slovenská otázka v Československu* (Bratislava: VPL, 1968), 95–96.

[20] The best general coverage of the trial and purge years, available in Czech and English, is edited by Jiri Pelikan, *The Czechoslovak Political Trials, 1950–1954,* 2 vols. (Stanford, CA: Stanford University Press, 1971). See also Karel Kaplan, *Dans les archives du Comité Central: Trente ans de secrets du Bloc soviétique* (Paris: Albin Michel, 1978).

Spring in Bratislava. In 1968, however, the debate over the content of Slovak national identity raged once again, this time over the priority to be attached to the federalization of the state on the one hand, and its democratization on the other. Czechs and a recognizable segment of the Slovak elite urgently warned of the "tragic mistake" looming if "we separated federation from democratization, if we saw in it some kind of end in itself, the attainment of which would in itself resolve the nation's problems and ensure its unobstructed development."[21] After the Velvet Revolution of 1989, this argument was to resurface, with Czechs and Slovaks sympathetic to the federal solution accusing those who favored independence or confederation of being less committed to democratic values and more prone to authoritarianism—a continued linkage of Slovak nationalism with the "threat of the onset of undemocratic forces" embodied in the memory of a clerico-fascist wartime Slovak state. Even those who sympathized with Slovak aspirations warned that a "democratic and legal state, led by realistic political forces, is the clear barrier to nationalist, romantic-reactionary and isolationist forces, which always seek to use the national-emancipatory process to bad ends."[22]

At stake here, above all, is a discrepancy in the definition of the prerequisites of democracy. Slovak parties with nationalist grievances, from the HSLS to the HZDS (Movement for a Democratic Slovakia) of current Prime Minister Vladimir Mečiar, have tended to focus on the extent to which true democracy is inseparable from the safeguarding of a channel for the collective expression of national interests. A constitutionally liberal state, with full protection of basic individual rights, may nonetheless be undemocratic if the core power resides in a central authority that can govern by majority rule without the braking power of institutions to protect minority interests, collectively defined. Whether the formula is regional autonomy, "authentic" federalism, or independence, the democratic logic of Slovak nationalism has focused on the marginalization of Slovak interests whenever *majorizácia* (majority rule) by Czech numerical preponderance determines political outcomes. The controversy thus pits liberal democracy against the collective rights of nations to institutional protection.

Czech and Slovak nationalism, therefore, has displayed some profound historical incompatibilities. Nationalisms with "compatible" political content may of course fight to the death, and incompatibility may be a result of differences in power and influence. Nonetheless, the divergent ideological

---

21 Julius Strinka, *"Federalizácia a demokratizácia," Kultúrny život* (5 April 1968), 1.

22 Boris Zala, *"Česká zodpovednosť za česko-slovenské vyrovnanie," Literárny týždenník* (29 February 1992).

content of the two national currents, bound together in a single state but unable to reach a mutually acceptable constitutional equilibrium, is a significant contextual element in the long-term political conflict.

With these enduring tensions in national self-definition in mind, this analysis views the central issues in the evolution of Czech and Slovak nationalism through a series of lenses but, above all, in the context of the multinational framework within which the two nationalisms have played out their conflicting aspirations. It is the task of the subsequent sections to bring that multinational context into historical focus in order to facilitate a more intensive examination of Czech and Slovak interactions with their historical German and Hungarian antagonists and neighbors and with each other. A final section zeroes in on an important subtheme of all of these interactions: the extent to which national politics tends to redefine the political agenda as a whole, using the critical question of economic policy as a case study.

The Context of Conflict and Collaboration: Nineteenth-Century National Revivals and the Experience of Habsburg Rule

Although both Czechs and Slovaks forged a distinct national identity in the national awakenings of the nineteenth century, there were profound differences in context. Neither nation started from a politically auspicious baseline. In the period preceding the nineteenth-century national revival, the Czechs have been described by one scholar as having been "reduced to an ethnic group unable to organize higher forms of national existence" in the wake of the seventeenth-century destruction of national elites.[23] Those who have examined the subsequent resurgence of Czech national identity root it, in part, in the diversification of the socioeconomic base that accompanied industrialization. The national renaissance itself is beyond the temporal scope of this study,[24] but its consequences clearly are not. By the early part of the twentieth century, Czech national sentiment was embedded in a political and socioeconomic matrix that provided significant support for the protection of some basic

---

[23] Aleksander Gella, *Development of Class Structure in Eastern Europe* (Albany, NY: SUNY Press, 1989), 32.

[24] See, for example, Peter Brock and H. Gordon Skilling, eds. *The Czech Renascence of the Nineteenth Century* (Toronto: University of Toronto Press, 1970).

interests: education, bureaucratic and political representation, and cultural activity. The contrast with Slovakia was quite marked.

Both Czechs and Slovaks were stateless peoples at the onset of the twentieth century, each subsumed within the architecture of the peculiar dual monarchy of Austria-Hungary. Each people occupied territory that was comparatively more industrially advanced than that of the empire as a whole. For example, Bohemia and Moravia harbored nearly three-quarters of Austria's industry, and Slovakia was the most industrially advanced sector of the weaker Hungarian economy. But this parallelism is misleading. In occupational structure, Slovakia still was overwhelmingly agricultural, with 60 percent of its people engaged in largely subsistence agriculture centered on village markets, in contrast with only around 30 percent in the Czech lands, where a strong cooperative movement gave impetus to commercialization. Nearly 40 percent of the population in the Czech lands worked in the industrial sector, as opposed to some 18 percent in Slovakia.[25]

Moreover, to the extent that elites are important carriers of national traditions and elite competition is the "basic dynamic which precipitates ethnic conflict,"[26] Czech and Slovaks lived in quite different environments. Whereas Slovakia had lost its territorial identity in its eleventh-century absorption into Hungary, the Czech lands had retained a geographical and political/administrative distinctiveness under the Habsburgs.

The decapitation of elites common to both nations also took different forms. To some extent, industrial growth and urbanization generated tendencies toward "spontaneous assimilation" throughout the region; linguistic and cultural adaptations to a larger, ethnically distinctive society were a necessary by-product of the integration into a new economic niche. This process reinforced and overlapped with more conscious assimilationist policies to intensify the challenge to national identity. Assimiliationist pressures of both kinds were more fully operative in Slovakia.[27] Long subordinate to a Magyar nobility and landholding class, Slovaks were largely a peasant, or "plebeian" nation; the accelerated magyarization drive after the Ausgleich of 1867 which engulfed fledgling secondary education only reinforced and accentuated the class boundaries between nations. Upward mobility in Slovakia meant

---

[25] For a more extensive discussion see Leff, *National Conflict in Czechoslovakia,* 12–16; and L'Office de Statistique d'état, *Manuel statistique de la Republique tchécoslovaque, 1920* (Prague: Státní úřad statistický, 1922), 19–22.

[26] Paul R. Brass, *Ethnicity and Nationalism: Theory and Comparison* (Beverly Hills, CA: Sage Publications, 1991), 13.

[27] Chlebowczyk, *On Small and Young Nations in Europe,* 86–87.

deracination—education and further advancement all within Hungarian Magyar-speaking institutions imbued with a Magyar ethos. The Czech loss of its national elite after 1620 through exile, religious conversion, and germanization proved more temporary. Through the nineteenth century, it was increasingly possible to mobilize national sentiment institutionally—this in fact was a distinguishing feature of the Czech national revival, which grew from cultural and journalistic roots to recapture political and economic space. As Czech nationalism reasserted itself in the founding of cultural vehicles—a Czech wing of venerable Charles University, a Czech national theater and museum—Slovaks were losing the circumscribed educational and cultural institutions that their revival had fostered.

Czech political organization and Czech representation in the bureaucracy grew apace with economic development. At the same time, a restricted suffrage and a notoriously corrupt Hungarian electoral system held Slovak parliamentary representation to a prewar maximum of seven deputies.[28] Czech parties held more than 80 of the Reichsrat's 400 seats by the turn of the century.

These differentials shaped both the manifestations of early twentieth-century nationalism in politics and the character of the statehood bargain after 1918. Slovak nationalism was the defensive elite nationalism of a nation at risk from magyarization. The threat of national extinction is a frequent theme in the rhetorical arsenal of nationalist politics. It is very clear that in the early twentieth century there was cause for considerable alarm about the consequences of the prolonged magyarization drive. The constricted scope of political activity was the concrete expression of an absence of political leverage, and Hungarian dominance seemed sufficiently complete to generate dire predictions of national demise for the Slovaks. Contemporary Western scholars accepted the reality of this threat. Carlile Macartney foresaw the complete triumph of magyarization had not World War I intervened, while R. W. Seton-Watson thought the Slovaks a mere generation from national obliteration.[29] They echo the fears of Slovak awakeners. The fear of annihilation is

---

[28] *Dejiny státu a právy na území Československa v období kapitalismu* (Bratislava: SAV, 1973), 732; and *Slovensko I: Dejiny* (Bratislava: Obzor, 1971), 575. On the corruption of the Hungarian electoral system, see R. W. Seton-Watson, *Corruption and Reform in Hungary* (London: Constable, 1911); and Andrew Janos and William Slottman, eds., *Revolution in Perspective: Essays on the Hungarian Soviet Republic of 1919* (Berkeley: University of California Press, 1971), 10–11.

[29] Carlile Macartney, *National States and National Minorities* (London: Oxford University Press, 1934), 94; and R. W. Seton-Watson, ed., *Slovakia Then and Now* (London: Allen & Unwin; Prague: Orbis, 1931), 30.

vividly captured in the wartime letter of Masaryk's prime Slovak loyalist, Vavro Šrobár, to Czech party leader Švehla:

> We have no teachers...we have no secondary schools and no professors, the number of Slovak intelligentsia is so low that in several years the cities and then the towns will succumb to the pressure of magyarization. The wave of magyarization washes over us with such force, that it only halts in the Tatras and then there will no longer be a Slovak nation. In ten to fifteen years the cities will be fully magyarized, in twenty to thirty years, Slovak towns will constitute only small islands in the Magyar sea.[30]

More recent scholars, however, marshal countervailing evidence to paint a less dismal picture. David W. Paul points to a diversification of the Slovak elite in the industrializing decades preceding independence, and Owen V. Johnson investigates a range of indicators to make a persuasive case for continuing national vitality.[31] It is in fact unlikely that Slovaks, profoundly touched by the nineteenth-century national revival, were about to share the fate of the Sorbs and the Wends, who were almost fully absorbed by the Germans. This should not, however, understate the task of the architects and builders of the Slovak national identity.

Despite a more favorable environment for Czech national assertion, Czech opinion, however diverse in other respects, was united around the view that its fundamental goals had hardly been realized. To fight, and even to win, certain political and economic battles was not tantamount to achieving an institutionalized recognition of the political integrity of the Czech lands, which would represent the guarantee of secure national rights on a historically defined territory—a guarantee, in short, independent of the tilt of central Viennese institutions, the power of local Germans, and the monarchy itself. Prior to World War I, the favored option was the federalization of the empire rather

---

[30] Vavro Šrobár, *Osvobodené Slovensko,* vol 1: *Pamäti z rokov 1918-1920* (Bratislava: Čin, 1928), 159–83; and Šrobár, cited in František Soukup, *Revoluce Práce: Dejinný Vývoj Socialismu a československé socialně demokratické strany delnické,* vol. 2 (Prague: Usteřdní dělnické knihkupectví, 1938), 954–55.

[31] David Warren Paul, "Slovak Nationalism and the Hungarian State, 1870–1910," in *Ethnic Groups and the State,* Paul Brass, ed. (London: Croom Helm, 1985), 115–59; and Owen V. Johnson, *Slovakia, 1918–1938: Education and the Making of a Nation* (New York: Columbia University Press, 1985), 15–49.

than its dissolution. This would grant to the component nations of Austria-Hungary space to maneuver and a sphere of autonomy that would amount to institutionalized recognition of the multinational character of the state. It is notable, but hardly surprising, that the prevalent premise was *not* independence—a treasonous proposition. It is also notable, but perhaps superficially more surprising given the eventual composition of the state, that the inclusion of Slovakia in national aspirations was hardly the mainstream view. In fact, for many Czechs, the extension of national self-definition to include Slovakia was seen to carry the risk of seriously diluting claims to self-government rooted in the "historical lands" of Bohemia and Moravia.[32] The rationale for a federalist orientation did not hinge entirely on the political reality of Habsburg control. Small nations must find some solution to their security and survival needs; integration into a larger and more powerful state entity is clearly one solution, and current adherents of closer regional collaboration continue to press the logic of this position.[33]

The peculiarity of these two nations harnessed together as a state is their substantial lack of previous common historical experience. Yet the separation had never been complete. The bridge of similar languages left its mark in the liturgy of Slovak Protestantism. More broadly, the linguistic kinship facilitated communication and interaction in several important, though not always constructive, ways. A defining moment in the relationship was the resolution of the nineteenth-century debate over the codification of Slovak in the form championed by L'udevít Štúr, on the basis of the central Slovak dialect. This decision ensured orthographic and lexigraphical difference between the two literary languages, erecting walls against the melding of the two tongues in a

---

[32] On the Czech identification of national interest with claims on the "historic lands," see Jan Galandauer, "Jak se slovenská otázka prosazovala do českého politického programu v období příprav samostatného československého statu (1916–1918)," *Historický časopis* 19:2 (1971), 177–97; and Leff, *National Conflict in Czechoslovakia*, 33–37. On the difficulty of melding "Czechslovak" reciprocity and Czech historic claims, see Zdĕnek Šolle and Alena Gajanová, eds., *Po stopĕ dĕjin: Češi a Slováci v letech 1848–1938* (Prague: Orbis, 1969), 141.

[33] The Habsburg model also survives in the debate over Czech-Slovak relations, with analysts such as historian Jan Rychlík presenting the dual monarchy as a useful prototype for a reconfigured Czech and Slovak state. See *"Vzorem Benelux či Rakousko-Uhersko?" Rudé právo* (20 December 1991); "Nedomyslené súvislosti Rakusko-uhorské vyrovnanie ako vzor pre Česko-Slovensko?" *Národná obroda* (6 April 1992); and Jan Rychlík, "Rakousko-uherské vyrovnání—inspirace?" *Lidové noviny* (5 February 1992).

way that some subsequent "Czechoslovaks" would rue. In turn, linguistic distinctiveness became a rallying cry for interwar nationalists.[34]

Czech "reciprocity" with Slovaks was a delicate matter, for the cultural and political differences between the two nations could trigger significant misgivings, particularly insofar as Czech "progressivism" generated suspicion among the more religious Slovaks. The primary architect of the state and its president-liberator, Tomáš G. Masaryk, himself embodied this problem: despite the central place religion occupied in his writings on moral values and national identity, he was more a moral philosopher than a supporter of established religious institutions. In fact, the more conservative wing of the Slovak national movement feared the influence of his "agnosticism." Other Czech activists in the Slovak cause, such as Karel Kalal, also found themselves embroiled in polemics over the form and content of Slovak politics.[35]

The imperfect fit between the two sets of national aspirations may not have been a significant impediment to the engineering of joint statehood in 1918, a feat that was more heavily contingent on winning international approval than on building a firm consensus at home. However, that politically antiseptic birth—a state won in crisis amidst the collapse of the Austro-Hungarian Empire, and confirmed at the conference tables of Paris—meant that national liberation efforts at home never came to terms in a systematic way with mutual expectations. Wartime communications were so truncated that a hastily assembled congress of Slovak notables would proclaim adherence to a new Czech-Slovak state, without joint conferral over the character of the union and its meaning for national identity—indeed, without even being aware of the parallel Czech action two days earlier. The absence of preparation would be a breeding ground for future mistrust in the arranged marriage between these two nations.

---

[34] See, for example, *"O sloven'čine," Nástup* (1 January 1934), 202–203; and O. Vočadlo, "Jazykový Dualismus v cizině a u nás," *Nové Čechy* 18 (1935), 141–45.

[35] Thomas D. Marzik, "The Slovakophile Relationship of T. G. Masaryk and Karel Kalal prior to 1914," in *T. G. Masaryk: 1850–1937*, vol. 1, Stanley B. Winters, ed. (New York: Macmillan, 1990), 191–209; and H. Gordon Skilling, "T. G. Masaryk and Slovakia," *Czechoslovak and East European Journal* 10:2 (Winter 1991), 20–44.

Founding of the State: The Dilemmas of National Identity

The arithmetic of national diversity decisively shaped the character of the state at its genesis. Masaryk argued during World War I that a Czechoslovak alliance "would raise the Slav majority of the population to almost nine million, and be so much the stronger vis-à-vis the minority"—particularly in counter-balancing some three million Germans with an approximately equal number of Slovaks.[36] Although Foreign Minister Edward Beneš spoke of multinational Switzerland as a model at the postwar peace conference, the power equation generated by amateur political mathematicians produced quite a different constitutional formula. To organize the state according to the logic of regional autonomy (except belatedly in the treaty-governed case of Subcarpathian Ruthene) seemed a recipe for disintegration in light of the substantial German and Hungarian minorities. Thus constitutional arrangements that might allow Slovakia greater autonomy would, according to Beneš "mean for this state the slogan Slovakia to the Slovaks, German regions to the Germans, Magyar regions to the Magyars." "Czechoslovak"-oriented Slovaks agreed that decentralization would be a "suicidal policy."[37] A unitary state rooted in the presumed existence of a constituent *(státotvorný)* Czechoslovak nation seemed the surest safeguard of cohesion and survival. "Czechoslovakism"—the declaration of what the interwar Communists derisively but not inaccurately described as "an immediate a priori Czechoslovak nation...created by decree"[38]—was at once the affirmation of a "will to unity," demonstrated by the very decision to form a common state, and a prescription for political and cultural uplift that would raise Slovakia to a developmental level at which its distinctiveness from the Czech lands would form no obstacle to future cooperation.

---

36 Masaryk cited in Karel Pichlík, *Zahraniční odboj 1914–1918 bez legend* (Prague: Svoboda, 1968), 214.

37 Foreign Minister Eduard Beneš, quoted in František Janáček, "Poznámky k hodnocena Čechoslovakismu v odboji," in *Československá revoluce 1944–1948,* Jaroslav Cesár and Zděnek Snítil, eds. (Prague: Academia, 1979), 79; and letter from Pavol Blaho to Vavro Šrobár (30 November 1918), cited in Ferdinand Peroutka, *Budování státi,* vol. 1: *Československá politika v letech popřevratových* (Prague: Fr. Borovy, 1936), 41.

38 Karl Kreibich, "The National Question in Czechoslovakia," *Communist International* 2 (1924), 59.

The Masaryk prescription for consolidating a Czechoslovak identity was preeminently cultural and envisaged socialization through education of a new generation of Slovaks within the context of the new state. This cultural engineering of unity, however, produced startlingly contradictory results in the national radicalism of the young Slovak generation of the 1930s. The controversial meeting of Slovak youth in 1933 shocked Czechs, above all, with the recognition that "it was possible that Czechoslovak schools *educated* such opposition to Czechs and against Czechoslovak unity."[39] The first experiment in Czechoslovak statehood thus failed to produce the necessary "Czechoslovaks" to sustain it.

Czech and Slovak Nationalism: Responses to Hungarian and German Influence

This exploration of the construction of the state suggests that a central factor in the contours of national identity for both Czechs and Slovaks was reactive—reactive to the relationships of power and culture forged by countervailing German and Hungarian national forces in the region. It is therefore important to explore the extent to which the concept of "us" requires a "them," that is, the problem of national threat and coexistence. In this section, I will sketch German-Czech and Hungarian-Slovak relations over time, relations that gave impetus, as we have seen, to the genesis of a Czech-Slovak state, as well as to a broader process of national self-definition.

For the Czechs, the nineteenth-century national revival would be largely unintelligible without the German presence, unintelligible first because of the influence of German scholars, thinkers and nobles such as Johann Gottfried von Herder, who in the early phases variously encouraged the exploration of Slavic identity and even the consolidation of a Bohemian *Landespatriotismus* that initially transcended ethnicity. The German presence, of course, also contributed to intensifying competition as bilingual and binational institutions became increasingly self-consciously Czech in language and orientation. Czech penetration of politics and the economy eventually prompted a sense of threat among the Germans residents in Bohemia and Moravia, a backlash nationalism that only sharpened the Czech national question.[40] This Czech self-definition

[39] Jiří Sújan, "Devis otázky Československi," *Nové Čechy* 16 (1933), 227–36.

[40] For richly detailed studies of the individual facets of these issues, see Barbara K. Reinfeld, *Karel Havlíček (1821–1856): National Liberation Leader of the Czech*

found its practical expression in socioeconomic and political rivalry with Germans, who had hitherto been more dominant in urban areas, and its philosophical expression in the effort to differentiate Czech identity and peaceful democratic values from the aggressive authoritarian German ethos.

Later evaluations of the Czech-German nexus were not uniformly negative, however. There were those, with prominent historian Josef Pekař among them, who cast Germandom not as chief villain in a national morality play, but as the mediator of Western culture to the Czechs, an inspiration to emulation and competition that not only activated Czech nationalism but also disrupted a more backward-looking linkage with Eastern influences. Under this view, Germans had, as both threat and influence, made Czechs more European.[41]

"Us versus them" defines a threat, internal or external, and it often defines a strategy as well. The decision to form the Czechoslovak state in 1918 was just such a strategy, as Czechs barricaded themselves against German influence in this constitutional arrangement. Slovaks, of course, sought the partnership as a bulwark against Hungary, although the baldly stated arithmetic in which Slovaks were to balance Germans generated Slovak suspicion that Czech ties to them were largely pragmatic and instrumental, a mere convenience or antidote to "the threat of spiritual germanization." "Slovakia was to sacrifice itself in the interest of the spiritual preservation of the Czechs."[42]

In any case, the joint state hardly represented a resolution of the predicament. A divorce from empire left a flock of minority stepchildren who had interested and irredentist relatives next door. Czechoslovakia became, with the enactment of a constitution in 1920, a unitary state to discourage those who might find it easier to carve along the dotted lines of a federation. However, at the same time, the parliamentary liberal principles of governance were permissive of an electoral voice for minorities. Interwar politicians of the Czech and Slovak nations did try to accommodate the representation of minorities from those minority parties willing to accept the system. After 1926,

---

Renascence (New York: East European Monograph Series, Columbia University Press, 1982). Joseph Zacek offers a succinct summary of the entire period in "Nationalism in Czechoslovakia," in *Nationalism in Eastern Europe,* Peter F. Sugar and Ivo J. Lederer, eds. (Seattle: University of Washington Press, 1969), 175–85.

41 See Milan Hauner, "Josef Pekař: Interpreter of Czech History," *Czechoslovak and Central European Journal* 10:1 (Summer 1991), 1–12.

42 *"Slováci—material pre česky národ?" Slovenské spravy* (29 January 1992).

German Social Democrats or Christian Democrats—"activist" parties prepared to cooperate in the new state—held ministerial portfolios in all peacetime governments. A viable multiethnic state could not behave entirely as a single nation-state, and most historians based in the West have been kinder to Czech concessions in this regard than were the Western political leaders of the late 1930s, whose censorious views of German beleaguerment in the interwar state helped assuage the consciences of those who participated in the Munich accords.[43]

The failure of this multinational undertaking lies in the international arena, with the rise of Adolf Hitler, who could indulge minority resentment and use it as a fulcrum for dislodging a state. Historians may disagree about the degree of Sudeten German attachment to the Czechoslovak state, in which they had been the dispossessed masters,[44] but the consequence was unequivocal: some six years of German rule that was marked by the bisection of the state, the subordination of the Czech economy, and a cultural catastrophe symbolized in the closing of Czech universities for the duration of the war. Goaded by the loss of statehood and the crushing of the resistance, Czech exile and underground movements began to plan for the rectification of the disaster as early as 1940, seeking international support for the massive population transfers of German collaborators, broadly defined, after the war.

The landmark event in postwar Czech-German relations was thus the forced population transfers for which the exile government of Edward Beneš had painstakingly negotiated Allied approval. The most direct effect of the transfer, of course, was to produce, for the first time, an essentially ethnically homogeneous Czech national territory, through the eviction of some three million Germans with ancestral roots in the area that dated back more than half a millennium. The thrust of the action was both punitive and practical: an assessment of collective guilt on Sudeten Germans for their collaboration with Hitler, and a safeguard against any future undermining of the state from within. The decision was widely popular and largely uncontested at the time,

---

43 See in particular J. W. Bruegel, *Czechoslovakia before Munich: The German Minority Problem and British Appeasement Policy* (Cambridge, England: Cambridge University Press, 1973); and Radomír Luža, *The Transfer of the Sudeten Germans: A Study of Czech and German Relations, 1933–1962* (New York: New York University Press, 1964).

44 Ronald Smelser, *The Sudeten Problem, 1933–1938* (Middletown, CT: Wesleyan University Press, 1975) and Luža, *The Transfer of the Sudeten Germans*, in particular, offer contrasting assessments.

and its essential justice remains an article of faith for much of the contemporary population.

With the deportation of the country's German minorities, the German-Czech relationship took on a more abstract character, initially defined by the schizophrenia of socialist brotherhood with East Germany and the depiction of West Germany as a revanchist successor to Hitler's Third Reich. This formulation, tempered by the modulation of relations in the era of *Ostpolitik*, left the German question in political limbo, largely denuded of its catastrophic threat to identity and sovereignty by the disappearance of the German minority, but still vivid in public rhetoric.

In a sense, the great "virtue" of Communist hegemony was the stasis it imposed on regional reordering in Czechoslovakia and elsewhere. The collapse of Soviet control after 1989 reanimated fears of a more complex threat to sovereignty amid a welter of distinct and potentially compromising assertions of power and interest by Czechoslovakia's neighbors. It was a new world order, in which rumors could circulate of a secret decoded fax that unveiled a German-Soviet plot to divide Czechoslovakia and link the Czech lands with Germany and Slovakia with the USSR![45]

The demise of the Soviet Union, far from quieting such fears, reinvigorated older historical tensions with Germans and Hungarians. Resurgent German influence in the ČSFR has been a special source of stress for the Czech lands. The signing of the German-ČSFR treaty of neighborliness and friendly cooperation in February 1992 evoked demonstrations of some 2,000 opponents, who chanted "Hanba Hradu" ("shame on the castle"), while the parliament's Initiative and Petition Committee received 100,000 signatures opposing the treaty.[46] The phraseology of the treaty generated anxious media discussion of German intent: should the ČSFR government tolerate imprecise language designating state borders or the description of the postwar evacuation of the Sudeten Germans as an expulsion?

At the core of this debate was a collision between two views: on the one hand was the governmental Europeanist/universalist perspective that had sought in dissident years to acknowledge Czech national failures as well as to champion national liberation, and on the other was the hypernationalist view about the collective guilt of the postwar German population. Long before

---

45 *"Čechy Němcom a Slovensko Rusom," Práca* (8 November 1991). The ČSSR (Czechoslovak Socialist Republic) was renamed the ČSFR (Czech and Slovak Federative Republic) in 1990 after heated controversy.

46 *"Co děje s peticemi," Zěmedělské noviny* (31 March 1992).

public debate on the decision reopened in the course of the treaty negotiations, there had been serious questioning of the deportations within dissident circles.

Contemporary scholars ponder the brutalizing effects of war that could produce such an "incredibly violent act" of hypernationalism—its target "not strangers, but our fellow countrymen who for some seven centuries had shared our land."[47] Exile publications such as Svědectví canvassed the decision repeatedly,[48] and some of them were very harsh in their judgment of a Czech nation that had descended to the level of their enemies. These underground controversies found a direct line of continuity in the Havel-Dienstbier axis that shaped the ČSFR's foreign policy after 1989. Hence, the government adopted a posture of moral condemnation of the Beneš approach, without, however, challenging the legality of the action.[49]

On the other hand, strong public revulsion against rebalancing the wartime moral equation found journalistic expression in an explosion of articles recapitulating Nazi crimes and Sudeten German complicity. Critics of the German treaty placed the deportations in the context of Hitler's policy in Central Europe, decried the fallacy of establishing an equivalency between Czech and German nationalism, and cited Nazi support among Sudeten Germans and their widespread participation in the bureaucracy of the protectorate.[50] The vividness with which this issue reemerged after fifty years demonstrates that Czech nationalism is hardly dormant when core sensitivities are involved.

---

47 Heda Kovaly and Erazim Kohak, *The Victors and the Vanquished* (New York: Horizon Press, 1973), 192.

48 See, for example, *"Tak já vám řeknu, co si opravdu myslím... Výsledky nezávislého průzkumu současného smýšlení v Československu," Svědectví* 22:78 (1986), 258–334.

49 *"Vláda ČSFR nyní jednoznačně: odsun vyhnáním nebyl," Rudé právo* (26 March 1992). The government position is encapsulated in the Civic Forum's uncomfortable formulation of the issue in November 1990: "We are not and will not be able to redress all wrongs in our history. Easing the effect of wrongs or compensation for losses cannot go beyond the date of the Communist coup on February 25, 1948... This all does not change our opinion that the principle of collective guilt is inadmissible in a democratic society." *CTK* (6 November 1990), cited in *Foreign Broadcast Information Service* (hereafter FBIS), FBIS-EEU-90-217 (8 November 1990), 16.

50 *"Německo—a my," Právo lidu* (30 January 1992). For a survey of the treaty controversy, see Jan Obrman, "Czechoslovak Assembly Affirms German Friendship Treaty," *RFE/RL Research Report* (22 May 1992), 18–23.

Germany's current economic might has aroused equal concern. While the government might stoutly argue that capital investment knows no nationality, and that the real concern was the paucity of foreign investment,[51] there were many doubters who shuddered at the existing level of German dominance: 86 percent of foreign investment came from Germany as of the spring of 1992.

If the specter of the small nation in the shadow of resurgent German power once again punctuated political dialogue on the viability of the Czech nation, the Slovak rendezvous with its historical links to the Hungarians has loomed equally large in Slovakia's search for security. The sense of facing a siege by an aggressively nationalist Hungarian state was of course the central legacy of the period preceding statehood; the watchword was "one thousand years of the Magyar yoke."[52]

The "Magyar" problem shifted focus with the emergence of Czechoslovakia as a state in 1918. The former hegemon now resided next door, but this internationalization of the relationship was no more a final resolution for Slovakia than it was for the Czechs and Germans. Tensions persisted under the irredentist pressure of a Hungarian state that had suffered immense territorial, population, and economic losses as a result of the Treaty of Trianon.

Hungarian influence politics was highly visible at the time and was enthusiastically documented by later Marxist scholars, but it was also a whipping boy in Slovak politics. Certain figures in the nationalist camp, such as Béla Tuka, retained Hungarian sympathies and financial connections that tainted Slovak nationalism as the cat's-paw of Hungarian interests. Czechoslovaks were always quick to decry Slovak demonstrations and demands for autonomy as a stratagem that played into the hands of Hungarian territorial ambitions, whether intentionally or innocently.[53]

---

[51] See, for example, "Kapitál neznamená germanizáci," *Mladá fronta dnes* (6 February 1992); "Chceme do Evropy ne do Německa," *Rudé právo* (6 February 1992); "Bude Československo kolonii Západu?" *Lidové noviny* (4 February 1992); "Sousedy Německa naveky: Ideálem diversifikovaný kapitál," *Respekt* 6 (1992); and "Německa kapitál a my," *Svobodné slovo* (28 January 1992).

[52] Július Mésároš has explored this legacy in "Deformácie vo vedomí slovenskej a maďarskej národnej pospolitosti o spoločných dejinách a ich zdroje," *Historický časopis* 39:3 (1991), 316–22.

[53] See, for example, Albert Pražák, *"Souběžnost autonomistů s maďarskými irredentisty," Nové Čechy* 14 (1934), 1–4. This perception of Slovak collaboration with foreign power is a recurrent theme in Czech-Slovak relations, for Slovak

Hungarian territorial acquisitions in satisfaction of the irredentist agenda after Munich promoted a nationalist backlash in Slovakia comparable to the Czech reaction to its German minority. However, the resultant population transfers, billed as exchanges with Hungary, were less thoroughgoing.[54]

The Communist period incubated a series of persistent, though less cataclysmic, tensions centered on the debate over rights of minorities and the institutional support of their cultural identity.[55] A spirited debate on these issues in 1968 presaged the open controversy of the 1990s, but it was, in fact, only after the Velvet Revolution, in an environment of free discussion bolstered by popular electoral clout, that the relationship could be fully, and painfully, explored. History thus became a weapon in the settling of current accounts. If Hungarians challenged the postwar assumption of collective Hungarian guilt, Slovaks counterattacked to recall the effects of magyarization, or the treatment of Slovaks under the terms of the Vienna award of Slovak territory to Hungary in 1938.[56]

The 1992 elections further polarized Hungarian-Slovak relations. The Hungarian Independent Initiative (MNI), which after service in the VPN (Public Against Violence) governing coalition reconstituted itself as the Hungarian Civic Party, was unable to form an electoral alliance requisite to surmount the 5 percent hurdle for parliamentary representation. The successful Hungarian parties, now entirely in opposition, faced a more overtly nationalist Slovak government whose leaders had been strongly critical of minority political spokespeople and hostile to the concept of collective rights.[57] This tense alignment reflects a deeper dilemma: Hungarians in Slovakia and abroad have since 1989 favored a federal solution to the problem of Slovakia's identity,

---

nationalism would subsequently be linked to the realization of Nazi designs in World War II and to the restoration of Soviet hegemony after the Warsaw Pact invasion of 1968.

54 See H. G. Skilling, "Revolution and Continuity in Czechoslovakia, 1945-1946," *Journal of Central European Affairs* 20 (January 1961), 363–64; Robert R. King, *Minorities under Communism* (Cambridge, MA: Harvard University Press, 1973), 52–57; and Kalman Janics, *Czechoslovak Policy and the Hungarian Minority, 1945-1948,* vol. 9 of *War and Society in East Central Europe* (New York: Social Science Monographs, Columbia University Press, 1982).

55 See especially King, *Minorities under Communism*, chapter 8.

56 *"Felvidék znie divne," Práca* (5 March 1992).

57 See the comments of Slovak Prime Minister Vladimir Mečiar on Bratislava Radio, 1 July 1992, cited in FBIS-EEU-92-128 (2 July 1992), 15.

in order to set minority relations in the larger framework of a Czech-Slovak state rather than a Slovak-Hungarian tête-à-tête in an independent Slovakia. Slovak independence, therefore, carries with it the specter of intensified conflict with its Hungarian minority and of the escalation of Hungarian state concerns.[58]

Czech Nationalism: Satisfied or Sublimated?

How did the achievement of statehood redefine the national question? In this section, I will canvass the revised "Czech question" as it evolved after the seeming attainment of its most ambitious national goal, statehood, and will set the context for a further development of the corollary "Slovak question," which will come into clearer focus in subsequent sections.

The fate of Czech nationalism after the achievement of statehood in 1918 remained a "Czech question," albeit a vexed and problematic one. One of the most striking features of Czech nationalism was its urgency and vibrancy at the beginning of the twentieth century and its seeming elusiveness at the close. Echoing the query of the national anthem ("where is my home?"), many commentators question the very existence of a conscious, purposive nationalism, if not as a sense of identity, then as an active force driving politics and policy.

This perception of a missing national focus is rooted in several discrete but overlapping circumstances and perspectives, which, taken collectively, form a reality somewhat more complex than mere self-abnegation. At the same time, examining these circumstances sheds light on the ways in which Czech nationalism has indeed been muted.

The first of these circumstances is the character of the state constructed in 1918—a multinational state primarily directed by Czechs, but always conditioned by its multiethnic nature. To preserve identity did not mean to celebrate Czech nationalism as such, but rather to give at least rhetorical primacy to the Czechoslovak amalgam, construed in the interwar period as a numerically dominant counterweight to minorities. The exact meaning of "Czechoslovakism"—which was simultaneously a ritually proclaimed actuality and a prescription for engineering deeper unity through Slovak cultural uplift—was the subject of diverse interpretation. However, its practical import was to fuse (or confuse) Czech interests with "Czechoslovak" interests. As one

---

58 See Juraj Kramer, *Iredenta a separatizmus v slovenskej politike 1919-1938* (Bratislava: VPL, 1957).

scholar later put it in defining the post–1968 political context: "Prague is simultaneously Czech and federal," the core of a nation and of a larger state.[59]

Many analysts thus saw the interests of the multinational state to be wedded to the interests of the Czech nation in such a way as to obscure the overt and distinct expression of a uniquely Czech nationalism. Although many Slovaks have seen this extension of Czech identity as a masked hegemonic impulse, and although its practical import may at times have had that effect, there is no reason to oversimplify Czech attitudes in this manner.

A second element in the muting of Czech nationalism also was rooted in the architecture of Europe since 1918, where the disappearance of Austria-Hungary left "a huge gap in the conceptual geography of the continent,"[60] and in the failure of successor states to find a stable guarantee of security in the face of larger, predatory neighbors. To the extent that German and later Soviet hegemony squelched the autonomous expression of national identity, one clear response was to safeguard values by seeking a broader, European or universal context as a repository of core meanings.

The quest to return to the European fold after 1989 was both an immediate response to the need for decommunization and a larger recognition that fragmented East European states were relatively powerless to define their own separate destinies. This led to a consuming interest in the concept of a Central European cultural and political basin that looked back to the Habsburg era of cosmopolitan interaction and forward to a more democratic manifestation of shared history and interest. The pursuit of this vision in Central European dissident communities beyond Czechoslovakia itself before 1989—a vision of Central Europe as a "community of destiny" that embraced Germans, Slavs, and others[61]—was also marked, but as Melvin Croan notes, in all cases, elite consciousness of this larger community of reference went hand in hand with a

---

59 Vladimír Kušín, "O novém pojetí česko-slovenské vzajemnosti," *Listy* 2 (1992). Postwar constitutional arrangements providing first for the asymmetry of a subordinate Slovak government and later for federalization came to appear as an "expression of the fact that Slovakia indeed belonged to the Slovaks, but Czechoslovakia—to the Czechs." Petr Pithart, *Osmašedesátý* (Prague: Rozmluvy, 1990), 192.

60 Tony Judt, "The Rediscovery of Central Europe," *Daedalus* 119:1 (Winter 1990), 25.

61 Jacques Rupnik, "Central Europe or MittelEuropa?" *Daedalus* 119:1 (Winter 1990), 255.

sense that this orientation was somehow higher and "morally superior to national parochialism."[62]

During the years of Communist rule, therefore, the primary oppositional currents did not focus exclusively on a Czech question, but rather set on a larger framework, an orientation that carried over into the opposition's responses once in power. Many Czech dissidents would sympathize with the way future president Václav Havel defined himself in the extended interviews he gave in the mid–1980s:

> Personally, I don't bother myself with such questions [as, what is the role of our nation?]. To me, my Czechness is a given, along with the fact that I am a man, or that I have fair hair.... And the main worry is one common to all people everywhere: how to deal with one's life.... The fact that I happen to have these dilemmas as a Czech living in Bohemia...is obviously related to the fact that—as Svejk says—we are all from somewhere.... In other words, I do not feel our Czechness is a burning or acute problem, and it seems to me that, if our national fate depends on anything, then it chiefly depends on how we acquit ourselves in our human tasks.[63]

After the Velvet Revolution, the question of a stable national identity took pragmatic form in aspirations to rejoin Europe, a staple campaign slogan for most major parties in the 1990 elections. This powerful impulse, to be realized through organizational affiliation with prosperous Western European transnational institutions such as the European Union (the ČSFR became an associate member in late 1991) met with broad popular response in the Czech lands, but complicated the negotiation process with Slovakia. In the interests of the broader quest for integration into Europe, Slovaks were urged to have patience and to moderate their national claims so as not to endanger the state's international prospects and drive Czechoslovakia out of step with Europe. It would be absurd, argued Alexander Dubček in May 1990, "to establish our

[62] Melvin Croan, "Lands In-Between: The Politics of Cultural Identity in Contemporary Eastern Europe," *East European Politics and Societies* 3:2 (Spring 1989), 185.

[63] Later published as Václav Havel, *Disturbing the Peace* (New York: Random House, 1990), 178–79.

interior disintegration nowadays when we strive to integrate into Europe."[64] Aspirations for a larger identity, then, marked Czech national sentiment and separated it from those in Slovakia who argued that "Europe can wait."

A third factor that has shaped the articulation of Czech identity is the legacy of self-doubt that flowed from Czech responses as a small nation to unfavorable geopolitical realities. The ultimate threat to the small nation is defeat, subjugation, and even annihilation. The political, economic, and moral damage inflicted by this experience is universal, though its specific manifestations may be highly diverse. Twentieth-century Czechoslovakia experienced three such defeats: Hitler's conquest of 1938–39, the assertion of Soviet dominance after 1948, and the crushing of the Prague Spring by the Warsaw Pact invasion in 1968. The impact of these traumas on national identity is, of course, complicated by their differential meaning for Czechs and Slovaks.

For the international community, the Munich syndrome became shorthand for the unwisdom of appeasement. For Czechoslovakia, victim of the Munich Diktat, the message was even more resonant. This was no heroic defeat, but a capitulation in the face of seemingly insurmountable odds and international isolation. Was Beneš, and through him the Czech nation as a whole, a realist whose calculation of the forces arrayed against him foreordained only one sensible course of action? Or was there something morally corrosive in being sensible at such a time, an admission of the failure of the interwar experiment? As elsewhere in Europe, the questioning would only be enhanced by the war experience itself, with its moral ambiguities, divisive pressures for collaboration and resistance, and personal betrayals spurred by fear and greed.[65]

The Munich complex had tangible consequences. In particular, perceptions of Western treachery impelled Beneš eastward toward closer collaboration with the Soviet Union[66] and a sense of domestic frailty gave impetus to the postwar deportation of minorities. However, the psychological effect of passivity in crisis on national identity was also profound and enduring.

---

64 *ČTK,* 11 May 1990, in FBIS-EEU-90-094 (15 May 1990), 35. See also the address of Slovak Prime Minister Čič, Bratislava *Pravda* (12 March 1990); and *ČTK,* 31 March 1990, in FBIS-EEU-90-064 (3 April 1990), 19.

65 See, for example, Heda Margolius Kovaly, *Under a Cruel Star* (New York: Viking Penguin, 1986), 22, 56–57; and Kovaly and Kohak, *The Victors and the Vanquished.*

66 See Eduard Taborský, "President Edvard Beneš and the Czechoslovak Crisis of 1938 and 1948," in *Czechoslovakia: Crossroads and Crises, 1918-1988,* Norman Stone and Eduard Strouhal, eds. (New York: St. Martin's Press, 1989), 120–44.

To be sure, one perspective saw the Munich surrender as an affirmation of Czech national reasonableness, the only feasible choice given the limited options Beneš faced and the certainty of "defeat and prostration" in the face of superior German forces.[67]

The postwar Marxist perspective, of course, highlighted the theme of capitalist betrayal and the bourgeois government's unwillingness to turn to the proferred support of the Soviet Union, though the more critical historians of the 1960s pointedly noted the absence of hard evidence of Soviet readiness to extend assistance.[68] Other practical arguments critical of the decision not to resist focused on the miliary capabilities of the Czechoslovak army, and its capacity to mount a credible defense.[69]

The submission to Soviet invasion in 1968 raised many similar questions about national will. Again, the leadership issued calls for nonresistance to superior force, and heroism became an individual decision rather than an official, collective act. Despite well-documented spontaneous nonviolent resistance, the epitaph of the Prague Spring is encapsulated in the sad epigram, "Czechoslovakia is the most peace-loving country in the world; it does not even intervene in its own internal affairs." What would a futile resistance have accomplished? And yet, for many, the sensible response of 1968 left its mark. The search for a more effective, somehow more honorable, alternative to capitulation continued underground. Illustrative of the issues raised is the standpoint of Václav Havel, who rejected as "naive" the idea that an army "riddled with Soviet agents," and organized for entirely different mobilization strategies, could have responded effectively in the national defense. Yet he also speculated that invasion might have been forestalled by political means if a note of uncertainty had been injected into Soviet calculations about the

---

67 Pavel Tigrid, cited in Karel Bartošek, "Could We Have Fought—The `Munich' Complex in Czech Policies and Czech Thinking," in *Czechoslovakia: Crossroads and Crises, 1918-1988*, Norman Stone and Eduard Strouhal, eds. (New York: St. Martin's Press, 1989), 117; and Eduard Beneš, *Paměti: Od Mnichová k nové válce a novému vitězstvu* (Prague: Svoboda, 1968).

68 František Lukeš, *"Poznámky k Československo-sovetským vztahům v září 1938," Československý časopis historický* 5 (1968).

69 Bartošek, in "Could We Have Fought—The 'Munich' Complex in Czech Policies and Czech Thinking," 110–14, gives extensive coverage to the analysis offered in a then unpublished manuscript by Václav Kural, *"Vojenský moment v česko-německém vztahu roku 1938,"* which investigates this and other international considerations in building the case for resistance rather than submission.

Czechoslovak response by a display of national pride and confidence, and an earlier effort to mobilize a home guard—in short, by a display of autonomy rather than the demeanor of a "guilty servant." Havel and his dissident colleagues linked the incapacity to respond on 20 August to the internal contradictions of the Communist reform movement itself. But by 21 August it was too late.[70]

Like Beneš, however, the leaders of the Prague Spring, with the eventual exception of Smrkovský, saw no choice but the one they took. Much of the public agreed with them. But just as the catastrophe of 1938 had helped to crystallize doubts about the efficacy of the complex interwar parliamentary government, so leadership behavior in 1968—the failure to stand firm, the coerced signing of the Moscow protocols validating the invasion—form part of the rethinking that accentuated the inadequacies of the Prague Spring's socialism with a human face. In both cases, defeat cast into question the linkage between the nation and the state, attenuating the worthiness and viability of the state as a vehicle of national self-determination.[71]

The pattern of pragmatic accommodation with superior force manifest in Munich and in 1968 thus reinvigorated the question for a new, post-Munich generation. "Why did we not fight then? Why do we never defend ourselves?... What sort of people are we?"[72]

Was a "habit of surrender" an integral part of being Czech? Is there something ethically and nationally deficient in a policy of mere "biosocial survival" *(Schweikism)?* For those whose soul-searching led to the rejection of a Munich-style submission to superior force, the locus of blame varied. Some saw it as a broad national failure that implicated each citizen. Others, with the logic of Catholic philosopher Václav Benda, saw the "fumbled" opportunities to assert the nation's claim to destiny as a "catastrophic failure on the part of our political leaders."[73]

---

70 Havel, *Disturbing the Peace,* 103–104.

71 See Pithart, *Osmašedesátý;* Milan Hauner, "The Prague Spring—Twenty Years After," in *Czechoslovakia: Crossroads and Crisis, 1918-1988,* Norman Stone and Eduard Strouhal, eds. (New York: St. Martin's Press, 1989), 217–24; *Svědectví,* vols. 37 (1969) and 42 (1971); and *Listy* (March 1975).

72 Bartošek, "Could We Have Fought—The `Munich' Complex in Czech Policies and Czech Thinking," 107.

73 Benda, cited in the samizdat publication *Informace o Charte,* in Bartošek, "Could We Have Fought—The `Munich' Complex in Czech Policies and Czech Thinking," 118.

The final challenge to a coherent Czech national identity stems from the emergence of an internal schism, the self-conscious assertion of a separate Moravian identity with its own political agenda and aspirations. Shunted aside in 1968, the Moravian question resurfaced, with an electoral base to lend it political weight, after 1989.

Zděnek Tichý, chair of SMS *(Společnost pro Moravu a Slezsko)* argues that "the political and social discrimination against the population of Moravia and Silesia objectively evoked a process of national consciousness-raising, the result of which is 1.4 million ethnic Moravians and some tens of thousands of Silesians who thus comprise the largest national minority in the ČSFR," but who lack the legal standing to satisfy their distinctive social needs. Proponents of a distinctively Moravian identity seek not only a political expression of regional clout, but also the educational propagation of regional patriotism, imbued with "a modern interpretation of the history of Central Europe from the standpoint of...Moravia and Silesia." The cultivation of a nationally conscious elite remains an important bulwark of identity.[74]

Moravian and Silesian aspirations, however, met with damaging resistance elsewhere. There has been little popular resonance outside their own territory; an October 1991 survey, for example, showed only 2.6 percent of the public in Slovakia expressing interest in a tripartite federation with a Moravian component.[75] Multipartite federation, however, did speak to the frustrations of bipolar politics. Czech Prime Minister Petr Pithart lamented, "One or four or five—anything is better than two national governments, I can assure you...It is a relationship in which you cannot take a vote, because when a stance is taken by one it is in fact a veto of the other's stance."[76] Slovak Marian Čalfa, federal prime minister from 1990 until June 1992, made a similar point in arguing that a federation of two was "the worst type of federation imaginable. There is no majority in a binational federation, the two simply have to come to

---

74 "Manévry na Moravském poli," *Lidové noviny* (3 March 1992).

75 "Malé referendum Práce," Práca (2 November 1991). The popular Slovak nationalist leader Mečiar did profess a willingness to deal with Moravia "if relations with the Czechs end in crisis." However, this was a tricky offer to accept without alienating Bohemia, and Mečiar's listeners found his political intentions suspect. See *Svobodné slovo* (4 November 1991).

76 Interview with Prague Television Service, cited in FBIS-EEU-90-7 (10 December 1990), 28.

an agreement... [T]he decision of one immediately predetermines the situation of the other."[77]

This frustration with bilateralism in federal politics, however, never figured in serious negotiations over the future of the state. In March 1992, President Havel deemed it "too early" to consider the inclusion of Moravia in a federal scheme. Moravian cultural and economic distinctiveness, however, still takes political form in a party alignment decidedly weighted to religious and regional interests, and certainly has influenced debate on the future organization of the Czech state.[78]

All of these otherwise diverse factors work in the same direction—to complicate the process of defining a Czech identity comfortable with its own nationalism and centered on an agenda that incorporates a consciously Czech dimension. This need not, in general, be a disadvantage; some regard it as a sign of political maturity. However, it may well have been a handicap in understanding and responding effectively to the countervailing Slovak demands and grievances that historically have challenged the state's flexibility. In fact, Slovaks found it infuriating to meet with such incomprehension of the basic nationalist premises of their argument for self-governance, making Czechs appear, as Havel would recurrently remind them, arrogant and superior. Ultimately, divergent perceptions of national interest destroyed the state, a dynamic which is the focus of the final sections.

Tension in Czech-Slovak Relations: Slovak Nationalism and the Common State

Karel Kosík once argued, "The Czech question is a universal question, but the practical test of that universality is the Slovak question. In a certain sense we could even say that the Slovak question constitutes the essence of the Czech question."[79] While other forces and relationships certainly have shaped each nation's sense of identity and security, Kosík nonetheless defined a primary arena for twentieth-century national assertion, as each nation has been bound

---

[77] Čalfa, interviewed on Prague Domestic Service, 6 November 1990, reprinted in FBIS-EEU-90-217 (8 November 1990), 17.

[78] *"Havel o federaci," Mladá fronta dnes* (27 March 1992); and *"Moravané 'cítí' Moravu," Telegraf* (10 August 1992).

[79] Pithart, *Osmašedesátý*, 83.

to the other, not always happily, since 1918. Czechoslovakia since 1918 has been in the throes of multiple—and conflicting—political quests. The resolution of the most basic of national questions, the organization of the state, never has been clearly legitimate to a significant minority of the population. The biggest political challenge, from the inception of the republic in 1918 to the Velvet Revolution, was to try to reconcile state and nation in such a manner that the institutional consequences would be durable and widely accepted.

I cannot offer a complete survey of the evolution of Slovak nationalism here, but it is important to try briefly to encapsulate its distinctive contextual perspective, the perspective of a chronically dissatisfied nationalism that lacked the political clout to surmount its minority status within the state. Hustled by the pace of events in 1918, the Slovak cause was at a tactical disadvantage in the early years because of undeniable deficiencies in the nation's economic and political preparedness for independence—deficiencies that even autonomists acknowledged by voting at the outset for a centralist constitution. Father Hlinka and his HSLS Party demanded autonomy "as soon as our nation is capable of it," and proferred support for a unitary state in 1920 only with the proviso that this concurrence was not an abandonment of legislative autonomy, but a deferral until Slovakia was better prepared."[80] The commitment of HSLS to a common state was a message that, as James Felak cogently establishes,[81] was continually undercut by the activities of the factionalized party's radical wing and the quixotic behavior of Hlinka himself. Despite a brief HSLS stint in the governing coalition (1927–29) and despite growing national assertiveness and repeated negotiations, the interwar state retained its unitary character until Munich forced eleventh-hour concessions. Lacking leverage to reorient the political priorities of the central government, whose complex coalitional politics raised the specter of immobilism or constant renegotiation of other issues, the Slovak nationalist impulse assumed the character of a perennial opposition, with a ready parliamentary platform to enunciate grievances.

Following World War II, the ethnically based logic of unitarism and "Czechoslovakism" eroded significantly with the deportation of the Sudeten Germans, which transformed the Czech lands from a national amalgam that was only two-thirds Czech before the war to one that had a 94 percent Czech population in 1950. The spasm of postwar Czech nationalism that produced this ethnic purification might logically have cleared the way for a Czech-Slovak

---

[80] Jorg Hoensch, *Dokumente zur Autonomie politik der Slowakischen Volkspartei Hlinkas* (Munich, 1984), 130.

[81] Felak, *Andrej Hlinka and the Slovak People's Party.*

federation.[82] Instead, a partial solution was adopted, an "asymmetry" according to which Slovakia had its own Slovak National Council (SNR), party, and bureaucratic institutions, without a comparable differentiation among Czech political organizations. Czech representation remained vested in the central government.

The Communist era had important consequences for the search for constitutional order. National identity had always been a vexing question for Marxist theory, and the enshrinement of Marxist orthodoxy during the Communist era had an undeniably chilling effect both on the evaluation of prior efforts to realize national objectives and on contemporary expressions of national identity. Ideologues shrilly reviled both "Czechoslovakism" and Slovak "clerico-fascist" nationalism with its avowed hostility to "Judeo-bolshevism."

The intent was to start from a tabula rasa, on which would be imprinted a paradigm of national theory that bore a striking resemblance to Soviet elaborations of the problem. Under socialism, the "epiphenomenon" of nationalism would gradually be submerged in state patriotism; nations themselves would undergo a process of growing together that would culminate in a "merging" of identities and culture. The vocabulary of the argument was incorporated, in very direct translation, into orthodox Czech and Slovak understandings that the national question would be resolved by economic development, climaxing in the fusion of state and national interests. The 1960s brought a revision of the classical orthodox view and an acknowledgment that because the "ethnic structure of society is historically older than the class structure," the mere "uprooting of a given form of class structure will not automatically result in the fusion of nations."[83] Although this less reductionist approach heralded the federalization of the state that accompanied the unleashing of a broad reform movement in 1968, the post-invasion normalization sharply curtailed the intellectual and political gains generated by uncensored speech and reform politics.

---

82 Generally speaking, postwar population statistics from the ČSSR continue to be utilized in the period after 1989. The most common critique of these statistics concerns the figures published in statistical yearbooks on emigration, which apparently understated emigration volume by discounting illegal emigration. See, for example, Jan Vachel, "Česko-slovenské vztahy ve světle demografických údajů," *Hospodářské noviny* (25 October 1991).

83 Jan Šindelka, "Národnostní vztahy a sociální struktura socialismu v ČSSR," in *Sociální struktura socialistické společnosti*, Pavol Machonin, ed. (Prague: Svoboda, 1966), 622–24.

The consequence was the jettisoning of substantial parts of the specifically Czech and Slovak historical understanding. Class analysis again colored the interpretation of national assertion of the past, and the major figures of the national revivals, as well as the carriers of national traditions in the twentieth century, were subject to an intensive redesignation that reframed the historical legacy in an orthodox "progressive" context. As Marxist historian Jaroslav Purš put it, "We shall not take from the past all we know about it. We take up only what is pure, progressive and revolutionary."[84]

Thus, the Hussite period could retain its luster as a struggle against established religion and foreign power. A central figure such as Masaryk, however, could not stand as president-liberator, for what did the title mean divorced from class context? Soviet-oriented ideologists found "Masarykism" especially threatening in the wake of the Prague Spring, and accused the reformers of 1968 of "trying to substitute Masarykism for Marxism."[85] What David Warren Paul aptly labeled the "loss of a usable national past" was a continuing concern of historians in the normalization period of the 1970s and 1980s.[86] Dissident historians saw the normalization purges of the intellectual community as a "warrant for the arrest of the entire culture." Their concern was not merely with the restoration of a hagiography of past national heroism; indeed, many were highly critical of the Czech and Slovak past. Rather, the need to confront unresolved, and temporarily undebatable, issues in the national legacy and to preserve a broad understanding of historical experience fueled a lasting conflict with the regime over taboos and professionalism.[87]

The years of Communist rule apparently did not efface the broad popular resonance of national heritage. Polls conducted in the Czech lands in 1946 and

---

[84] Cited in Vilém Prečan, "Pogrom of Historians," *Index on Censorship* 4 (1986), 26.

[85] See David Warren Paul, *The Cultural Limits of Revolutionary Politics* (New York: East European Monograph Series, Columbia University Press, 1979), 66–67. For a normalization period critique of Masaryk's outlook, see M. Silin, *A Critique of Masarykism* (Moscow: Progress Publishers, 1975).

[86] See Petr Pithart, "Let Us Be Gentle to Our History!" *Kosmas* (1983), 7–22; Milan Šimečka, "Black Holes: Concerning the Metamorphoses of Historical Memory," *Kosmas* (1983), 23–28; and Miroslav Kusý, "Slovak som a Slovak budem...," *Listy* 12 (December 1982), 46–49.

[87] Vilém Prečan, Letter to the Participants of the World Congress of Historians, San Francisco (August 1975), reprinted in Hans Peter Riese, ed., *Since the Prague Spring* (New York: Vintage, 1979), 123.

in late 1968 reflected public concurrence in both years on four of the five most glorious periods in Czech history: the Hussite period, the nineteenth-century national revival, the reign of Charles IV, and the First Republic (1968 replaced St. Václav's reign in the later survey). Yet this still-valued legacy, as Paul argues, was at odds with the official presentation of a history denuded of sources of national pride, which widened the distance between regime and public. This was a history shorn of triumphs and deprived even of tragedies, for even the loss of independence is devalued if independence itself is seen as a class conspiracy.

The Slovak historical legacy was still more constrained. Differing from Czech historical memory in its de-emphasis of the First Republic as a rallying point,[88] the Slovak legacy was further haunted by the political incorrectness of virtually its entire twentieth-century nationalist tradition, a nationalism dubbed "clerico-fascist"—even the gravesites of the major figures of that heritage were unknown. Prior Czech failures to resolve the Slovak question were a legitimate subject of Slovak historical inquiry, but this was a historiographic landscape without positive reference points, without acceptable nationalist heroes. The officially sanctioned nationalism of the 1970s and 1980s, therefore, had a certain rootless quality that was further hampered by the political stasis of the centralized Communist regime. In the political silence, Czechs would feel that Slovaks were prime beneficiaries of the normalization led by Slovak Gustav Husák: "Slovaks retained at least formal federation, while the Czechs, disillusioned, abused and abandoned, were left with empty hands." Slovaks, strongly aware of the Pragocentric character of the Husák regime, felt that the Czechs still called the shots.[89]

Expectations of the need for rectification of the national bargain were codified in the term "authentic federalism," which cropped up with particular frequency in the discussions of the Slovak partner to the Czech Civic Forum, the Public Against Violence (VPN). Authenticity encompassed two basic ideas. The first approximated the reformism slogan of 1968, "no federalization without democratization." The silence of the intervening decades on this issue covered an awareness that an organizational blueprint for federalism was no

---

88 Historical surveys show different sets of national heroes and national periods of glory and shame, differences that apply even to the recent shared history. For a discussion of these patterns, see Archie Brown and Gordon Wightman, "Czechoslovak Revival and Retreat," in *Political Culture and Political Change in Communist States,* Archie Brown and Jack Gray, eds. (New York: Holmes & Meier, 1971), 159–96.

89 Pithart, *Osmaředesátý,* 93.

protection against the inherent centralizing forces that operate in an unfree society. Electoral politics and public scrutiny must protect any functional version of federalism.

A related but quite different element of authentic federalism was more controversial: authenticity meant a federal bargain built from the regional base upward, and not from the center down. "In contrast with the past," asserted Dušan Nikodým for the VPN—who was himself active in the federalist debates of 1968—"the basis of sovereignty is the sovereignty of each of the two national republics, to which the sovereignty of the federation is delegated."[90] This reorientation centered the constitutional bargain not on individual civil rights but on the nationalist criterion of collective group self-determination.

It was clearly the resulting jurisdictional question that drove the constitutional debate through more than a dozen trilateral meetings of the Czech Republic, the Slovak Republic, and the Czech and Slovak Federal Republic (ČSFR) from 1990 to 1992; plainly differentiated concepts of national interest divided the camps. From the early period of his presidency, Václav Havel, along with other federal officials, resisted the "transfer from a federative principle to a confederative one" espoused by a number of leading Slovak politicians who warned of the evils of "incorrigible Pragocentrism,"[91] and sought maximal competence for Bratislava. For some, *no* form of federation could secure national identity; with a sovereign center, federation would remain merely a "continuation of the traditional, and only slightly modified, Czechoslovakism," which could not safeguard national equality. To them, only two sovereign republics met the test of an adequate constitutional bargain.[92] However, an assertion of sovereignty for the Slovaks seemed the deathblow for the state to many Czechs, tantamount to a declaration of independence, to whom loose confederation expressed no common national ideal and was scarcely worth maintaining the fiction of statehood for. When, after repeated earlier

---

90 *"Bez suverenity niet národa," Verejnosť* (2 June 1990); and *"Šanca pre Slovensko," Verejnosť* (29 May 1990).

91 *Mladá fronta,* 26 May 1990, in FBIS-EEU-90-106 (1 June 1990), 18.

92 *"Šanca pre Slovensko (Sprievodca programom hnutia Verejnosť proti nasiliu)," Verejnosť* (4 May 1990); *"Čo bude presadzovat VPN," Verejnosť* (26 May 1990); *"Silná národná republika," Verejnosť* (23 May 1990); and *"S Václavom Havlom o jedenástej večer," Verejnosť* (19 May 1990); Anton Hrnko, *"Prečo Nie Federácia!" Slovenský národ* (14 January 1992). For a useful overview of Slovak party positions on the constitutional question, see *"Federácia, a či samostatnosť?" Pravda* (6 May 1992).

failures, the 1992 election results cleared the path for the Slovak sovereignty declaration of July 1992, it proved the proverbial last straw that drove Havel to resign his transitional presidency and to abandon his official efforts to preserve the state.[93]

The reasons for repeated historical failure to achieve a decisive constitutional resolution were partly structural. It is important to realize that not until 1990 were there authorized bargaining agents for both nations, validated by the electoral process, who could deal with each other. There *was* no Czech government before federalization of the state in 1969, and no real chance to bargain before 1989. The pattern of national interaction shifted almost immediately, as landmark "summits" of the Czech and Slovak governments soon became a routinized component of the decision-making process.

In the event, the new framework for decision foundered on the volatility of the transitional partisan coalitions, which proved fissiparous and schismatic, as general principles gave way to concrete policymaking. The disintegration of the ruling OF/VPN coalitions in early 1991 left the country without a clear governing majority to make durable decisions. This development—perhaps inevitable in a fledgling system burdened with a triple democratic, economic, and national transition—presented a major structural barrier to resolution of the national question.

Underlying the practical complexities of the transitional party system were long-standing, historically intractable issues. An enduring dilemma was the persistent illegitimacy of the Slovak nationalist outlook in Prague, where throughout both the First Republic and the Communist regime, the "real interests" of Slovakia were entrusted to "Prague Slovaks" who spoke the same political language and accepted the existing contours of the state. Slovak nationalists, in turn, came to identify a broad range of difficulties with the policies of the center, and beyond that with the Czech leadership who

---

93 Czechs were more initially favorable to a federal solution by a margin of 63 percent to 45 percent (*Hospodářské noviny*, 26 June 1990, in FBIS-EEU-90-126, 29 June 1990, 26). Over time the support for centralized solutions steadily diminished. The hotly contested declaration of Slovak sovereignty finally won a 53 percent majority at the SNR's 7 May 1992 session, but failed to cross the needed 60 percent threshold. A core of Slovak leaders centered in the old VPN hesitated to pursue a sovereignty crusade that they deemed legally irrelevant but politically dynamite. "Politický dynamit alebo samozrejnosť?"*Smena* (13 April 1992); and "Koniec jednej parlamentnej ery: SNR reprjala navrh na vyhlasenie zvrchovanosti," *Národná obroda* (8 May 1992). For the text of the approved sovereignty declaration, see "Deklarácia Slovenskej Národnej Rady of zvrchovanosti Slovenskej Republiky" (18 July 1992).

predominated therein. Conflating Czech-based Pragocentrism with the totalitarian centralism of any Communist regime, or economic hardship with Czech colonial designs, were political simplifications easy to transmit and easier still to mold into a conspiracy theory that Czechs never made it a priority to disprove by accommodation of the political demands for autonomy. The result was a continuing sense on the part of Slovaks that they were under siege, and a pattern in which they seized in crisis what the political system failed to deliver under conditions of political normalcy.

Therefore, the Czech and Slovak experience of the fundamental crises of the state's short history—crises that destroyed it in World War II and subjugated it to a foreign power thereafter—was not entirely a shared experience. The external pressures that generated crisis acted on Slovakia differently because the national stakes were different; Slovak nationalist goals had become firmly wedded to the search for a constitutional formula that protected identity. The continuing discontent of the Slovaks with their status within the state and the fact that their aspirations were stymied by Slovakia's minority position in statewide politics as usual, allowed international crisis to be seen as an opportunity to renegotiate the national bargain. This pattern is clear throughout the period of joint statehood, from the exile bargain embodied in the Pittsburgh Pact of World War I; to the Žilina Accords ceding significant Slovak autonomy following Munich and the emergence of a contingently independent Slovak state under Nazi tutelage in 1939; to the programmatic formula of the Košice Agreement of 1945 which was to reconstitute the joint state on the basis of equality *(rovný s rovným);* to the realization of federalization in the wake of the Soviet invasion of 1968. The more positive and hopeful international crisis within Soviet communism in the late 1980s had a similar effect; the opportunity this opened to restructure a democratic state inevitably reopened the Slovak question and triggered the search for "authentic federalism." In short, crisis always did what politics as usual on the national question persistently failed to do: provide an opportunity to redefine the terms of the Czech and Slovak bargain. Slovakia became both a "catalyst of crisis" and a potential beneficiary of it.[94]

Historically, this linkage has had an inconclusive effect—Slovakia never realized permanent and unequivocal national gains from these interludes—as well as a frequently deleterious impact on Czech-Slovak relations. In a more extensive analysis elsewhere, I have written of a political ethos of mutual

---

94 Stanley Riveles, "Slovakia: Catalyst of Crisis," *Problems of Communism* 17 (May 1968), 1–9.

betrayal.[95] On the one hand, there has been an undercurrent of Slovak grievance over subordinate status within the state and over the absence of institutional guarantees to consolidate national identity in political form and to prevent the erosion of commitments made in crisis. Where was the autonomous diet promised in the Pittsburgh Pact? Or the realization of the Košice ideal of equality? On the other hand, Czechs saw a Slovakia so obsessed with the search for national affirmation as to be willing to indenture honor and the very survival of the state to external enemies. The continuing resonance of each crisis was evident in the subsequent one, as old grievances resurfaced and served as cautionary tales, burdening the renewed effort to redefine national relations. This pattern of recrimination, the continued exhumation of the negative messages of the past, is a chronicle of residual and revived mutual suspicion that colored serious efforts to do better "this time," with each nation reminding the other of past betrayals. Slovaks evoke broken promises, and Czechs resent perceived ingratitude for their past efforts and what seems a heedless and primitive Slovak priority to national interests to the detriment of larger issues. Was not Slovak independence in World War II a morally culpable bargain with Nazi Germany? Was federation more important than democracy to the Slovaks in 1968? These motifs date back to the turn of the century, but their perpetuation in the framing of the debate in each successive period poisoned interaction and impeded constructive problem-solving.[96]

The recycled historical controversies of the early 1990s were part of this pattern. As in prior reckonings, old misunderstandings were exhumed, reviewed, and sometimes rekindled in the search for a historical anchor for contemporary identity. In this context, the World War II Slovak experiment with a circumscribed but recognized independence was a crucial reference point, and a very divisive one. Czechs were repeatedly and vocally uneasy about the degree to which Slovaks had come to terms with this nationalist past. Slovaks, to be sure, display a spectrum of responses to that heritage—the heritage of Hlinka and of Tiso. Hlinka, the politician and priest, is defined now even by many Czechs as a loyalist to the First Republic whose grievances against the state had a measure of validity and whose prescriptions for constitutional reconstruction to recognize Slovak interests must be respected.

---

[95] Leff, *National Conflict in Czechoslovakia,* 148–78.

[96] In a roundtable discussion of the Czech-Slovak relationship in 1967, L'ubomír Lipták noted of the historical debate that "not one argument has surfaced which a historian would not recognize from the pre-Munich period." Lipták quoted in Karel Bartošek, *"Co si myslí Češi o Slovensku," Reporter* (22–29 May 1968), 6.

The Tiso heritage—the heritage of the independent state of World War II—was another matter. Here the characteristic Czech view was hostile:

> Slovakia attained autonomy in 1938 as a consequence of the Munich disaster and the breakup of Czechoslovakia.... If a justified demand is carried through in the shadow of injustice and violence, its justification is automatically in doubt.[97]

Even in Slovakia, the response to Tiso ranges from those who install commemorative tablets to this martyred national leader; to those who look for middle ground, focusing on his ambiguous struggle to compromise with Nazi power in defense of national interests; to those who indict him and the Slovak state itself for its implication in Nazi war crimes and who vigorously reject his legacy.[98] Slovaks, tired of hearing that "the post-Munich betrayal by the Slovaks was a stab in the back of Czechs which cannot be forgotten," resurrected earlier meditations on the inability of Czechs to rid themselves of interwar "Czechoslovak" attitudes and "Beneš stereotypes."[99]

Some in the Czech media have darkly pondered the parallel between 1938 and the renegotiations of the 1990s. Was the hard Slovak bargaining over true federation a genuine commitment to forging a durable common state, or merely the prelude to its disintegration, as Žilina was prelude to the Slovak declaration of independence in 1939? "If one makes a concession to (Slovak Prime Minister Mečiar) today, the next demand is already confederation. Next will come a customs union. And what will come then?"[100]

As the negotiating stalemate continued, a supplementary Czech concern, also rooted in historical parallelism, was that the Slovaks might again sacrifice democracy to a demagogic, authoritarian nationalism. The Slovaks, in turn,

---

[97] Jan Petr, *"Česko(-)slovensko není samozřejmosti: Triasedmdesát let oproti tisici leté odlišnosti," Respekt* (27 October 1991), 4.

[98] *"Pôjdesi v Hlinkových šl'apjách?" Nový čas* (23 October 1991); interview with SAV historian Ivan Kamenec, *"V histórii, áno, na tabuli nie: Historik o sebe a činnosti Jozefa Tisu," Práca* (17 October 1991); and Boris Zala, *"Česká zodpovednosť," Literárny týždenník* (29 February 1992).

[99] *"Slovensko na svuj obraz," Národná obroda* (13 April 1992); and Igor Cibula in *Národná obroda* (4 December 1990). Beneš initially invoked the "stab in the back" phraseology during the war (cited in Jan Křen, *"Hodža a slovenská otázka v zahraničním odboji," Československý časopis historický* 16:2 (1968), 199.

[100] Jiří Hanak in *Lidové noviny* (10 December 1990).

questioned Czech willingness to build a really equal constitutional relationship. Just as the "scarecrow of Czechoslovakism" hovered over the debates of 1968, so did that debased term echo through the protracted negotiations of the 1990s. "Pragocentrism," which Czechs defined as a reflection of Communist authoritarian control from the center, is received in Slovakia as that and more—as a *Czech* phenomenon underpinned with a Czech nationalism all the more deleterious for being unacknowledged. Politicians, such as Czech Prime Minister Pithart and moderates of the Slovak VPN, who tried to bridge this perceptual gap and work for the resolution of practical differences, risked the fate of all compromisers—to be attacked as insufficiently stalwart in the defense of national interests.[101]

Inevitably, mutual elite perceptions tend to degenerate, under the pressure of bargaining, into the conviction that political ambition governs the policy thrust of rivals. Father Hlinka was seen by many Czech politicians in the interwar period as a "disappointed office seeker" whose early rebuff generated a movement designed to restore his prestige. Eventually, Beneš would even see his own Slovak allies as "chasing after money and careers," to the neglect of tangible interests that could be seized upon by the nationalists.[102] In 1968, there were few who did not see Gustav Husák, rehabilitated Slovak "bourgeois nationalist," as a turncoat reformer willing to play the federalist card in the furtherance of his own power. Again in the 1990s, Czech commentators would see the nationalist controversy as a political-electoral ploy: "Although they claim that they want justice for the Slovaks, they are playing for (political) posts."[103] Ultimately, by the spring of 1992, significant forces within both the Czech and Slovak elites came to believe that their opposite numbers were negotiating in bad faith. "Let Czech political representatives finally say publicly that they want an independent Czech republic closely tied to Germany (!) and we will obviously respect that," taunted Slovak nationalists. In April 1992, in the shadow of a heated election campaign, the largest single group in the public attributed current tensions to the activities of politicians.

Certainly, elite political ambition is an integral part of the dynamics of the confrontation over national identity. However, to debase the debate to the level of cynical manipulation also tends to devalue the national issue itself, a damaging misperception that stymied the definitive resolution of the problem within a common territory.

---

[101] *Lidové noviny* (15 December 1990), 3.

[102] Beneš cited in Libuše Otahalová and Milada Červinková, eds., *Dokumenty z historie československy politiký* (Prague: Academia, 1966), 719.

[103] Vladimír Kučera in *Práca* (1 December 1990), 2.

The deepest irony of the historical tensions between Czechs and Slovaks is the extent to which the conflicts *have* been elite-driven. We have no definitive evidence of Slovak popular attitudes toward the state in earlier periods; these were measurable only indirectly (in the electoral preferences of the First Republic) or temporarily (during the Prague Spring era). The existence of impatience with Prague's definition of national status within the First Republic is evident enough in the electoral support granted the autonomist party HSLS in the 1920s and 1930s. Consistent public enthusiasm for reordering the Czech-Slovak relationship reemerged in 1968. Likewise, there is a record of considerably less urgent Czech public response to the necessity of reconfiguring the alignment of national power within the state. However, this difference in priorities did not carry with it a sense of national grievance sufficient to fuel a clear majority-based secessionist movement.

Oddly enough, even on the eve of a "velvet divorce," it was hard to argue that there was a broad, popularly based secessionist impulse. Popular support for independence failed to surmount the 20 percent threshold even after the 1992 elections.[104] This is not a signal of polarization and irreconcilable national differences. Yet the constitutional confrontation continued; Slovak voters opted for parties whose stances on the national question were most assertive and even inclined to the disintegration of the state. How to interpret this murky picture?

One Czech publicist tackled the paradox with the supposition that Slovak voters were too inclined to take rhetorical expressions of commitment to the state at face value, and that when these voters grasped true partisan intentions, they would realign. This interpretation, comforting to adherents of joint statehood, seems oversimplified and rather condescending. It is reminiscent of First Republic assessments of a Slovak electorate that showed its immaturity by voting for the autonomist party in naive defiance of its own interests. Moreover, it should be remembered that both the existence of a common state and its character are at issue; Slovak voters shopped for those

---

[104] See, for example, the opinion data published in *"Jak stát si přejí občani," Rudé právo* (21 January 1992). Moreover, the personal linkages beneath the surface of political argumentation are not inconsiderable. A sociological survey conducted in 1990 by the *Ustav pre socialni analyzu* of Komenius University in Bratislava reported the following findings: 23 percent of Czech Republic citizens had relatives of Slovak origin, 45 percent had Slovak friends, and 33 percent had Slovak contacts through work. Slovak citizens re-ported that 31 percent had Czech relatives, 57 percent had Czech friends, and 30 per-cent had contact with Czech colleagues. "Samostatné a demokratické?" *Kultúrny život* (10 December 1991). See also "Vztahy Čechů a Slováků," *Rudé právo* (7 April 1992).

who would drive a hard and durable bargain protective of Slovak interests. The result may indeed have been more drastic than voters anticipated.

Beyond this, the apparent misfit between public attitudes and political consequences says something significant about politics itself, and the decisive role of political elites in defining the agenda, particularly in a multi-tiered, multiparty state where no one actor can decisively determine outcomes. Political maneuvering during negotiations, the delicacy of justifying compromise, and the temptation to grandstand unleashed competitive political forces that left parties prone to charging their rivals with grandstanding demagoguery, ulterior motives, and hidden agendas. This political dynamic overlay the core negotiations.

The record of Czech-Slovak interaction finally compels one to conclude that the common state has not left a common history—or rather, to paraphrase Winston Churchill, that the Czechs and Slovaks are two nations divided by a common state. It is perhaps evocative of these disparate perspectives that in 1938, on the eve of crisis, when Czechoslovakia was celebrating a twentieth-anniversary jubilee, the presidium of the Slovak nationalist HSLS led by Hlinka met to resolve that the jubilee year of the republic would be celebrated as the jubilee of the as yet unfulfilled Pittsburgh Pact.[105] Without resolution of the constitutional question, there can be no resolution of the national questions.

The common state thus has foundered on an institutional and political incapacity to negotiate national differences. The most recent and perhaps final chapter in the failure was the postelection confrontation of 1992. The polarization of Czech and Slovak parties after the elections produced particularly unlikely political bedfellows. Victorious in the Czech lands was a Civic Democratic Party (ODS) led by radical economic reformer Václav Klaus, whose empathy for shock therapy met with serious apprehension in Slovakia. The victorious Movement for a Democratic Slovakia (HZDS), led by formerly ousted but now triumphant Vladimír Mečiar, espoused a leftist economic agenda and a program of national sovereignty compatible with confederation or independence. The shifting partisan fortunes swept away most of the federal cabinet, including the highly popular Foreign Minister Jiří Dienstbier.[106] With

---

[105] *"Rozhledy," Naše doba* 45:5 (February 1938), 294.

[106] For an election analysis, see Jan Obrman, "Czechoslovak Elections," *RFE/RL Research Report* (26 June 1992), 12–19. The Republican Party, a nationalist right-wing group that plays upon fears of foreigners, garnered 6 percent of the vote in the Czech lands, with strongholds in north and west Bohemia and consistent levels of support outside Prague; it will be a voice for intolerant nationalism in the CNR and federal assembly.

the silencing of more moderate voices on national and economic politics, the election results only confirmed the divergent perspectives of the two republics.

The elections, however, did not resolve the fate of the state; elite negotiations and referenda ultimately will do that. Two unlikely coalition partners, presiding both over their republic governments and over a caretaker federal government, set a provisional deadline of 1 January 1993 for dissolution.

By summer 1992, then, as the Czech leadership appeared increasingly to have given up on federation and after the Slovaks had declared sovereignty, the interaction between the two frequently took on the appearance of maneuvering to affix the blame for dissolution on the other. Mečiar disavowed the ulterior purpose of independence, asserting that he was being pressured into it by a Czech leadership now bent on separation. Indeed, Klaus spoke repeatedly of the normalization and stabilization of politics that could occur in two smaller states divested of the radicalizing effect of the vexatious national question, even as he accelerated contingency planning for Czech independence.[107] Each national leadership left the door open rhetorically for continued statehood; but both embraced mutually unacceptable preferred options, federation for the Czechs and confederation for the Slovaks. Each side's unwillingness to relinquish its first choice has produced a deadlock apparently broken only by the public's last choice, dissolution.

Case Study: The Economic Dimension of Nationalism

One of the defining features of the politics of nationalism is that it tends not only to expand the political agenda quantitatively, but also to complicate it, by redefining the existing agenda. Disputes over language of instruction suffuse the educational agenda. Jurisdictional disputes take on a national coloration that supersedes technical questions of administrative practicality. And economic problems endemic to any state gain a new dimension when controversies over national equity are conjoined to class divisions to redefine the classic political question of who gets what. Thus, nationalism not only shapes arguments over the *structure* of the state, it also permeates the *content* of politics insofar as the individual national groups measure policy effectiveness and equity against the yardstick of collective group benefit.

---

[107] Václav Klaus interviewed in *Respekt* (29 June–2 July 1990).

This essential feature of multinational politics has marked political discourse in Czechoslovakia since 1918; economic discrimination has been a standard charge ever since. The geographic contours of the Czech regions of the First Republic had been justified in part by the value of maintaining the integrity of a complex industrial economy so as "not to disrupt existing economic life."[108] Economic policy would not be static, however, for it impinged on the national standing of all parties to the new state. Land reform was widely deemed essential, yet Germans would soon question the fairness of a distribution policy that favored Czechs over Germans and shifted the regional ethnic balance in the process. The "Czechization"—in ethnic terms—of industry and finance, launched well before independence, accelerated thereafter, and was a further sore point.

No scholar now argues that perfect equity reigned in these policy decisions, although Bruegel notes the salutary presence of German ministers in the cabinet in defining policy and concludes that the interwar republic was "neither heaven nor hell" for Germans.[109] Politically, however, electoral politics was a ready forum for charges of malfeasance, and it is less important to the emerging pattern of nationalist conflict whether the charges were valid than that the nationalist perspective was an integral component of policy disputes.

This was equally true of the Slovak-Czech relationship. A fledgling Slovak economy suffered clear de-industrialization in the 1920s, even before the depredations of the global depression, as it met a superior competitive economy to the west and lost its Hungarian markets to the south. Although both Czechs and Slovaks inherited a valuable industrial sector from the dual monarchy, the more competitive Czech lands clearly outperformed Slovakia. The Slovak share of national income skidded from a prewar 18.2 percent on the two territories to 15 percent in 1929, to recover and then fall back by 1937; per capita income responded in similar fashion. Free competition has been stigmatized as unhealthy for Slovakia ever since.[110] Likewise, suspicion of the economic

---

[108] Foreign Minister Beneš, at the Commission for the Czechoslak Question at the Paris Peace Conference, cited by J. W. Bruegel, "The Germans in Pre-war Czechoslovakia," in *A History of the Czechoslovak Republic, 1918–1948,* Victor S. Mamatey and Radomír Luža, eds. (Princeton, NJ: Princeton University Press, 1973), 171.

[109] Bruegel, "The Germans in Pre-War Czechoslovakia," 167–87.

[110] Zora Pryor, "Czechoslovak Economic Development in the Interwar Period," in *A History of the Czechoslovak Republic, 1918–1948,* Victor S. Mamatey and Radomír Luža, eds. (Princeton, NJ: Princeton University Press, 1973), 188–215; and "Slovensko na svuj obraz," *Národná obroda* (13 April 1992).

consequences of taxation without adequate collective representation has marked political discourse.

Slovaks saw the interwar economic stress as reflecting, at best, an indifference to regional hardship and, at worst, a calculated policy of colonizing Slovakia, an impression solidified by the flow of "missionary" Czech bureaucrats to Slovakia. This contingent, initially deployed to staff positions vacated by Hungarian officials, was at first seen as a necessary evil. Their continued presence, as Slovak educational levels and administrative skills rose, became a focus of active resentment and a symbol of Czech overlordship.[111] The political certitude that centralist fiscal policy drained resources from Slovakia, that Prague decision-makers inevitably favored Prague, and that Czech bureaucrats battened off the region reverberated through the autonomist debates of the interwar Republic. Slovakia, it was argued, had no political protection against predatory financial and industrial incursions from the Czech lands, no support in Slovakia's painful severance from the Hungarian economy after 1918, no recourse for disparities in law and economic practice that distorted economic relations within the First Republic and penalized the less developed east, and no power to purge the Slovak administrative bureaucracy of Czechs who had outstayed necessity and welcome by the 1930s. Autonomy was a path to the redress of economic grievances. "We're paying for Slovakia," retorted the Czech media, summarizing Prime Minister Malypetr's argument that the internal transfer of resources amounted to a subsidy of Slovakia.

The postwar state, it might be presumed, should have escaped such a focus of nationalist grievance. The Communist regime, decrying the First Republic's insufficient attention to Slovak economic development, made economic investment in Slovakia a major budgetary and programmatic priority.[112] Where Masaryk and the governments of the interwar period had started with the presumption of the primacy of sociocultural advancement in resolving the Slovak question, Marxist policy engineering, of course, highlighted the centrality of economic restructuring as the key to assuaging nationalist grievances. As Communist regimes discovered elsewhere as well, however, there was no economic key to lock the door on nationalist tensions. Though Slovakia's share of national production gradually rose, and was

---

[111] The burgeoning Czech colony grew by more than 100 percent in each decade between 1910 and 1940. See Ján Svetoň, *Vývoj obyvateľstva na Slovensku* (Bratislava: Epocha, 1969), 227.

[112] An orthodox articulation of the argument may be found in Jan Pasiak, *Riešenie slovenskej národnostnej otázky* (Bratislava: VPL, 1962).

triumphantly declared to be proportional to its population share in 1986,[113] Czech and Slovak perceptions of national equity remained divergent throughout the Communist era, even when submerged under a veneer of controlled and optimistic rhetoric of achievement.

The reemergence of interwar arguments in postwar Czechoslovakia again reflected Slovak perceptions of regional powerlessness and pitted against Czech perceptions of the central government's fundamental commitment to Slovak economic development. When public discussion opened in the 1960s, the issue of economic equity immediately reemerged as part of the political debate over what was then described as "asymmetry" because there were no Czech political and administrative organs corresponding to the Slovak National Council (SNR). In 1968, an uncensored press strikingly echoed the interwar conflict over who was subsidizing whom, as Czech media recorded a sense of Slovak ingratitude "that what had been invested...was disparaged and abused."[114]

Federation of the country as of January 1969 did not resolve the underlying tension about who benefited from the joint Czech-Slovak state, not least because federation itself was politically operative only in a fairly circumscribed sense. Economic decision-making powers first allotted to the republics were reabsorbed into the center by the early 1970s.[115] Greater Slovak representation in Prague ministries after federation could convince Czechs that an ethnic takeover of sorts had occurred, while Slovaks could feel that Prague still called the shots economically. While these issues were not discussed bluntly in the official media, the dissident press began to treat them—gingerly—by the 1980s.[116]

In 1990 the old tension over budgetary allocations and preferential economic treatment reemerged—this time, however, in trilateral fashion, with pronounced complaints from Moravia about the need for "a just distribution of national income" and investment in consonance with higher Moravian productivity.[117] Slovaks and Czechs also sparred over equity in the distribution of economic resources and the problem of federal policy jurisdiction. Ministers of the Czech National Council, working from the Czech premise that past

[113] *"Vzroste podíl Slovenska na jednotný ekonomice," Rudé právo* (17 March 1986).

[114] Štefan Gronský, "Jsme nevděční?" *Kulturni tvorba* (25 April 1968), 8–9.

[115] For a discussion of the rationale behind the 1970 recentralization of economic coordination, see Jan Šindelka, *Národnostní otázka* (Prague: SPN, 1972), 92.

[116] *"Bez suverenity niet národa," Verejnosť* (2 June 1990); and *"Šanca pre Slovensko," Verejnosť* (29 May 1990).

[117] Prague, *ČTK,* 11 February 1990, in FBIS (12 February 1990), 27.

budgetary outlays had subsidized Slovak development, pledged in the spring 1990 that each republic would subsequently decide upon the disposition of the resources created on its own territory, living "mainly off resources generated" at home.[118] Each national grouping expressed the belief, often belligerently or peevishly in fact, that such a division of jurisdiction would benefit its own population.[119]

The argument over who subsidizes whom is not a dispute that can be resolved for the political arena through scholarly argumentation. Its importance lies in its repeated recurrence since 1918 and in the relevance of national interest to the process of negotiating economic benefits between two—or more—clearly defined subgroups each acutely sensitive about its own collective well-being.

The massive overhaul planned for the country's economy in consonance with democratization and re-federalization raised new points of contention, over military conversion and privatization, in particular. The question of who controlled the economic levers was not a purely legalist one, for Czech and Slovak opinion profiles showed a pronounced difference in attitudes toward economic change, not only since the Velvet Revolution, but as far back as 1968. Respondents in the Slovak Republic consistently registered a 10 to 15 percentage point difference from those in the Czech Republic on commitment to rapid economic reform. Those polled in Slovakia, for example, were less willing to accept major price increases, more committed to state welfare

---

118 Prague, *ČTK,* 23 April 1990, in FBIS-EEU-90-079 (24 April 1990), 20; and *Svobodné slovo,* 25 May 1990, in FBIS-EEU-90-105 (31 May 1990), 25.

119 The Czechoslovak Socialist Party, for example, challenged the "constantly repeated views that within the framework of the Czechoslovak Republic, Slovakia has been economically and politically hindered." Affirming the need to derive federal competence only from the republics, the party stoutly maintained that this step should not be construed as a remedy for the neglect of Slovakia but rather as "first and foremost, in the interest of the Czech Republic." *Svobodné slovo,* 15 May 1990, in FBIS-EEU-90-096 (17 May 1990), 15. Late in the 1990 election campaign, the Czech National Council reviewed an "interesting study" purporting to show that a territorial review of revenues generated and budgetary expenditures would put the Czech treasury in budgetary surplus, and the Slovak treasury in deficit two billion koruny. The clear implication that the federal budget did indeed subsidize Slovakia elicited a prompt and detailed rebuttal from the Slovak Ministry of Finance. See *Svobodné slovo,* 25 May 1990, in FBIS-EEU-90-105 (31 May 1990), 25; and Bratislava *Pravda* (7 June 1990).

responsibilities, less committed to accepting austerity measures, and more worried about a declining standard of living and unemployment.

The disagreement is rooted in the differential levels of development and competitiveness that ensure that change will have equally different impacts. Just as the Slovaks suffered in the First Republic in competition with the more advanced Czech economy, so did Slovaks later fear that the free market augured greater harm to them. These fears are not misplaced, for transitional disruptions were indeed far greater in Slovakia, generating three times the level of unemployment there by the spring of 1992 than in the Czech lands. Proponents of a federal solution hoped for coordinating mechanisms that would ensure the close synchronization of Czech and Slovak economic transformations. This was precisely what the mainstream Slovak public opinion most feared: a radical transformation that would further ravage a Slovak economy already disproportionately burdened by the initial transition.

From the outset, Slovak officials were far from comfortable with this idea. In December 1990, after the provisional division of competence agreement finally passed the Federal Assembly, then Slovak Prime Minister Mečiar made it clear that there was a strong economic component to his government's perception of distinguishably Slovak national interests. Dismissing the "incomplete" federal economic program as "merely monetaristic," Mečiar promised "different concepts," and above all "a different social net," "tailored to Slovakia's needs."[120] The formula articulated by the schismatic Klepáč Christian Democrats in the spring of 1992 was: "where the responsibility for the economy lies, there should be the economic instruments for its direction and guidance as well"—in short, Bratislava, not Prague, should regulate the economic activity of Slovakia. Mečiar HZDS, ultimately triumphant in the June 1992 elections, also resisted the application of Czech "shock therapy" to the Slovak economy.[121]

Ultimately, then, the national issue worked to differentiate the interests of two components of a long-integrated joint economy. Once the specter of disintegration loomed, the economic debates became even more divisive. Czechs began to insist on the restriction of budgetary outlays for a Slovakia that might soon depart from the state; Slovaks questioned the expenditure of

---

[120] *Národná obroda*, 13 December 1990, 11–12, in FBIS-EEU-90-244 (19 December 1990).

[121] "*Nič viac, ale ani menej,*" *Nové slovo* (6 April 1992). *"Je žiaduce, aby podobne postupovali Česi?" Národná obroda* (25 March 1992).

funding on a "largely useless" federal bureaucracy.[122] The Slovaks devoted increasing attention to the economic effects of the "catastrophic scenario"—the separation of the two republics—arguing alternatively for its inevitability or its unthinkability.[123] Historically, economics has been pivotal in the definition of national interests and, ultimately, a barometer of the prospects for common statehood.

Conclusion

Several enduring factors have conditioned Czech and Slovak nationalism in the twentieth century. The first is the geopolitical dilemma of nations embedded in the heart of Central Europe—Zacek defines geography as *the* ultimate determinant of Czech nationalism[124]—which generated strong defensive responses to German and Hungarian political hegemony at the outset of the century, and to the continuing, sometimes catastrophic, international resonance of German and Hungarian interest in their minorities within the Czechoslovak state.

The second factor was the fateful decision to neutralize the influence of foreign masters by seeking national self-determination within the framework of a joint Czech-Slovak state. This choice, in turn, created a new dilemma—solidifying a sense of common destiny in the face of clashing Czech and Slovak perceptions of the effective institutional form for national guarantees. The appropriate link between nation and state was thus a contentious issue from the

---

[122] *"Doplácí se na Slovensko?"Zemedělské noviny* (3 March 1992); *"Rozpad federáce?! Nastane-li 'čas' nemela by česká vlada s menovou a hospodářkou odlukou váhat," Lidové noviny* (5 March 1992); and *"Doplácáme na federálnu byrokraciu," Nový Slovák* (9 April 1992).

[123] See, for example, Ivan Horsky, *"Samostatnosť, a čo potom?" Národná obroda* (21 April 1992). Notable were three official 1991 reports pessimistically assessing Czech and Slovak economic viability in the event of the breakup of the state: the Czech National Council's analysis and two reports from the Slovak Academy of Sciences (SAV) and Slovak National Council. For a discussion of the specific assumptions and projections of these reports, see Peter Martin, "Calculating the Cost of Independence," *RFE/RL Research Report* (20 March 1992), 33–38.

[124] Zacek, "Nationalism in Czechoslovakia," 169.

establishment of the unitary state in 1920 to the tormented negotiations for a mutually acceptable division of authority in the 1990s. The complex political decision-making structures of successive regimes proved too cumbersome to manage the problem of two interrelated national questions, and the policy agendas of successive regimes remained burdened with unresolved issues that inevitably took on a nationalist coloration.

A corollary factor was the historically persistent difference in socioeconomic development and political position, which facilitated Slovak perceptions of a misfit between the interests of Prague and Bratislava and engendered Czech resentment of Slovak ingratitude for decades of Czech efforts to promote Slovak development.

The durability of the initial bargain of 1918 underwent its ultimate test in 1992. Czechs and Slovaks were bound by a lengthening common past, with its attendant history of economic integration, and by the very complexities of divorce, which threatens the international credibility of polities bent on rejoining Europe even as it augurs the escalation of historical tensions between small Slavic states and their German and Hungarian neighbors. All this in the shadow of the disintegrating Soviet giant. The common state faces the prospect of a final collapse of attempts to adapt the federal order to post-Communist political realities, attempts that have been impeded by a crisis in the linkage of popular sentiment to politically negotiated outcomes and by a crisis of confidence in the intentions of leadership and the meaning and value of a shared existence. Even had the state survived in attenuated confederal form, core decisions would have devolved to the republics. And even as it crumbles, economic and diplomatic collaboration may yet persist. In either case, the current period will see the inauguration of yet another experiment in the harnessing of national identity to the organization of the state.

5

Hellenism and the Modern Greeks

by Gerasimos Augustinos

There is always an intermediate step between a nation and the outside world. The mediating context is also a dilemma for Greece, which is simultaneously part of the Eastern European sphere (Byzantium, Orthodox Christianity, Russophilia) and of the western European world (Greco-Latin, strong links with the Renaissance, modernity).

Milan Kundera[1]

Document 1

from Ion Dragoumis, *"Stratos Kai Alla"* ("The Army and Other Things") (1909).[2]

A ruin this state, small Greece with its frontiers brought down to the plains of Thessaly either must grow or it will be lost. One thing I am certain of; this state is a temporary one and we must consider it only in this way.

---

1 Milan Kundera, "The Umbrella, the Night World, and the 'Lonely Moon,' " *The New York Review of Books* 38:21 (19 December 1991), 48.

2 Ion Dragoumis, *"Stratos Kai Alla,"* in *Deka Arthra Sto "Nouma"* (Athens, n.d.). This first appeared in the periodical *O Noumas* (27 December 1909). Translated by G. Augustinos.

That is why the state must grow, create new frontiers, widen and take in within its new borders at the least most of the Greeks without. The more of the outside Greeks who can become inside Greeks, so much the better will they be able to take care of the economic needs of the state....

The Great Idea

So, therefore, if the state must be enlarged, why is the Great Idea a lie? Is it not the same thing when we say that the state must create wider frontiers and take within its borders the majority of the outside [Greeks]? No.

The great idea is a memory which remained, burrowed deeply and nested in the soul of the Romios, from the time that the Turks, in 1453, took the City. It is the remembrance that the Romios, with the City as capital, possessed the East in bygone years, the Eastern state with many peoples, which he inherited little by little from the ancient Romans.

Ideas must correspond to reality, and to agree they must spring from that reality. Present-day conditions tell us that the Byzantine Empire with its complex and dynamic mechanism, cannot be resurrected; it cannot be reborn. The Greeks must seek their ideals elsewhere, and concentrate all of their energies elsewhere.

A New Ideal

And if we remove the City and the Byzantine state from our memory forever...what will remain in the heart of the Nation? What idea will take the place of the Great Idea?

If therefore the Great Idea has foundered and is gone, because it cannot be realized by us, here is a realistic ideal for us Greeks; the unification of the larger portion of Greek lands in one respected Greek state.

Therefore, the problem for Hellenism is not that the Little Greece shall be completely justified nor that the Great Idea be attained. The problem is something else. The issue is that the Greek race be united one hour sooner into one strong state, in order to live better and enable the race to show its strength.

And now everyone's obligations are clear:

1) The Greeks of the [Hellenic] state must try to govern themselves in as natural a manner as possible, if for no other reason than to build an army, which will help unite the race. The most natural government for the Greeks is local self-government, which will relieve the state from many burdens and lots of headaches, leaving it free to look after the army and its foreign policy.

2) The Greeks outside *{exomerites}* must organize their communities so that they will be able to sustain their schools by themselves and to be ever ready in order to defend themselves from those who conspire against them and to rise against the Turk (in Europe and the islands).

3) Parallel with all these obligations, the Greeks altogether have a responsibility to reform their educational system. And education will be reformed above all by employing their natural language....

The struggle for the unification of the race, undertaken by all the Greeks, will make right our human personality. The same struggle, along with local self-rule, will put in order, as much as possible, our political personality.

We commend to the whole nation, therefore, clearly and openly, the following program:

a) An organized, revolutionary struggle to unify the race in one Greek state, different from the current small and transient state, which is a wreck.

b) To support everywhere, in all the Greek lands, but especially in the Helladic [Greek] state, where it is trampled on, local self-rule.

c) To speak and write the language of its mother, and to have only this as its national language, and to require teachers to instruct their students in this tongue.

O, benumbed nation, where is your pride? Do not place your trust in anyone, neither the Great foreign [powers] of the earth, nor in your Great ancestors, but only in yourself.

Document 2

from Georgos Theotokas, *Elefthero Pneuma (Free Spirit)* (1929).[3]

The question of the neohellenic character greatly concerns the Greek intellectuals. It is one of the great issues which demoticism put forward. Before the demoticist movement our intellectuals, devoted to our ancient progenitors, paid little interest to contemporary Greek life. However, when they discovered their living language, they discovered the living reality of their country, and they attempted to discern the characteristics that constituted it. Certainly the issue had to be dealt with. This tendency of the Greek intellectuals to recognize the neohellenic reality and the neohellenic character is similar to the attempt of a young person to come to know himself, his physical inclinations, his strengths, his chances before he begins his life. I am afraid, however, that this issue has been considered very badly and that the debate, as it is being conducted today, circumscribes our opportunities instead of developing them.

---

3 Georgos Theotokas, *Elefthero Pneuma,* edited by K. Th Dimaris (Athens, 1973 [1929]), 14–28. Translated by G. Augustinos.

I will confine myself to the examination of one theory of the neohellenic character that has been supported with unusual strength in the last ten years and has exercised, I believe, a significant influence. It is the only one of the theories about which we can say that it created a "following."

The theory can be summarized, I believe, as follows:

Outside of our national tradition and our national character we are lost. We have no support and we will never be able to develop our spiritual strengths. Whatever we create outside our "reality" is a farfetched, artificial, false, and sterile imitation of foreign ways.

I believe that I discern some misconceptions of the issues in the theory....

The first misunderstanding is the belief that the character of living people can be separated, measured, and weighed just like the production of raisins and tobacco.

The second misconception...a fateful result of the first, is a fixation on the past and the ignoring of the present.

The neohellenic character...is the totality of the feelings and the "ideals" which are contained in the monuments of the popular (demotic) tradition.... In other words, it is something that took final form in certain tests, something immovable, unyielding, and finished.

The adolescence of our nation, tempered by the hardship of the last two decades and by the impulse of the century, is our greatest worth and the most significant guarantee of our future. The beauty of our present-day capital is to be found precisely in those things that enrage the protectors of tradition and provoke their anathemas: in the pulse of a new life which struggles to open new directions....

All those who write about Athens deplore and weep over it, longing for the small, quiet capital of the good old days. This pandemonium of neighborhoods that are being torn down and neighborhoods being built...of the dirty refugee towns...of the great human masses strains their weak nerves. The first steps, disorderly but daring, of the dawning capital of the eastern Mediterranean makes them dizzy. No one knows where they stand. But we, however, like this disorderliness that rules our spiritual and social life because it is a *crisis of development* [emphasis in original]. We feel that something is coming, and instead of trying to choke it because it overturns established customs and shakes up our serenity, we will try to understand it.

Document 3

from an article by Andreas Papandreou (1965).[4]

The Rules of Foreign Policy

The translation of Greek ideals to positions of foreign policy demand the setting of rules. The rules noted below constitute an irreversible foundation of our foreign policy.

1. Greece is a peace-loving country, and it is a rule of the first order that we always endeavor to solve every national problem through peaceful means. But if our territorial integrity should ever be threatened, or our independence, or our freedom, we are ready, we must be ready, to defend it with all means and with all sacrifices.

2. The short-term foreign policy problems must be examined through the prism of a long-term inspired strategy, which will determine the long-term position of Greece as a Mediterranean and European power.

The foreign policy of the country must cease to be determined behind the scenes. It must become the property and living experience of the ruling body of the people.

3. We must apply the realistic principle of European diplomacy, whatever the purpose of our foreign policy, if we are to have results and not just to win at debates. The basic rule that we desire is the strengthening of our national interest—not some foreign interest—with regard to whatever is of concern. We must become the masters of our destiny.

4. We must recognize our alliances as instruments to promote our national interests. As a counterweight to the faithful execution of our responsibilities to our allies—and Greece always carries them out faithfully—must be the loyal vindication of our national interests. We observe our alliances and we carry out our responsibilities with integrity. Concurrently, we undertake—as we have a responsibility to our people to act with integrity—our rights. For example, Turkey never has had any difficulty in exercising pressure toward the promotion of its national interests and thus has become more respected.

5. We must protect the freedom of our decisions in the event of an international crisis. We must make it clear to our allies that a treaty of alliance only binds us in case of an unprovoked attack.

---

4 Andreas Papandreou, *"Exoteriki Politiki kai Ethniki Anagenisi,"* in *Dimokratia kai Ethniki Anagenisi* (Athens, 1966), 72–79. This first appeared as an article in *To Vima* (23 and 24 August 1965). Translated by G. Augustinos.

6. We must maintain complete freedom to develop political and economic relations with all the countries that really wish to peacefully cooperate with us.

7. We must have complete supervision over decisions that relate to the basic sectors of our society. It is antithetical to our overall planning if decisions are taken by autonomous centers, foreign states, or foreign private companies, such as Litton.

8. We must develop a comprehensive outlook for the defense of the country. In the military sector this demands the development of our defenses not only in the case of a world war, within the framework of our alliance, but also in the case of a local war—the threat of which, with the development of the Cyprus issue in the hands of the foreign-serving government—constantly remains alive.

9. In the economic sector, the comprehensive outlook for the defense of our country demands complete vigilance and preparedness for the difficult competition in the Common Market. And it demands, furthermore, the responsible reexamination of the conditions of our participation.

10. In the political sector it is necessary for us to establish respect for the state among foreigners. The public services must be unhooked from dubious ties with foreign embassies and agents. National secrets must be protected—and not to be given to foreigners before the Greek Government can even learn of them. Also, it is necessary that foreigners be taught that no Greek Government or other Greek authority accepts their intervention in the domestic affairs of the country. And, finally, it is an unbreakable rule that the responsible bearer of Greek foreign policy is the lawful government—the government that proceeds from the free expression of the will of the governing Greek nation. No other agent has the right to intervene in the shaping of foreign policy.

National Dangers

There exists something called a Greek character and Greek ideals and which expresses our common origin in the Greek earth. Also, there exists a way of being and thinking which is clearly Greek. This "Greekness," this "Romiosini" of ours, is the starting point of our tradition as well as of our goals and our common ideals. If we lose it, we cease being Greeks. We will be diffused into broader entities. Our history forbids such a catastrophe.

In summary, we may say that we wish the following for Greece:

Unity: So that the declarations of national schism and selling out will cease, so that all the sources of strength will work for a national rebirth.

Strength: That it will consciously seek to become a Mediterranean and a European power, which other countries will take seriously.

Pride: That it project itself worldwide not only for what we have inherited, but for what we can create. Greece must not be identified only with ruins and statues, but with creativity and people who are alive.

Independence: With full national sovereignty. Greece for the Greeks.

Document 4

from an editorial in *Anti* (1992).[5]

Two years after the assumption of the governance of the country by the New Democracy Party, the situation regarding the serious domestic as well as the external problems is anything but pleasing.

The serious economic problem...does not seem to find solutions which do not shake [public] confidence and social cohesion. Only the sacrifices are visible and tangible. But the future is indiscernible and unforeseeable. The way out announced by those who rule is uncertain and unproven—spasmodic measures, social injustices, vacillations, the lack of self-confidence, of planning, and of a serious policy with goals.

National issues have reached a critical turning point. Economically weakened, with a nonexistent national strategy, with a wavering and uncertain government, the country is unable to defend vigorously its national interests. The government is deeply divided over the Skopje issue, and that thorny problem is only the tip of the iceberg. The opposition parties are playing a game of hide-and-seek either with inflammatory nationalism or with half-truths. No one explicitly assumes his responsibilities before the Greek people.

Introduction

As with all political ideologies, nationalism contains both purpose and function.[6] In the case of the Greeks, two broadly conceived purposes can be

---

5 *Anti* no. 490 (3 April 1992), 4. Translated by G. Augustinos.

6 In Greek there are two expressions that can be used to mean nationalism: *ethnikismos* and *ethnismos*. The first term best approximates the meaning in

discerned. Political and cultural leaders have focused on the nation as the instrument to create favorable opportunities for social and economic progress. If a nation has validity as the most beneficial community for human development, then the primary effort must be directed toward this goal. Another, equally persistent and powerful view has been the concern with the physical continuity of the nation (as *fyli*). The purpose of the state and its institutions, therefore, is to guarantee the survival of the people as a unique entity.

The multifarious forms of Hellenism make any consideration of Greek nationalism an elusive undertaking, unless we take account of the few basic factors that have shaped it. To begin with, the development of Hellenism, in its political, cultural, and social forms, in the modern world has turned on a dynamic relationship different from that of earlier eras of Hellenism in the classical and Byzantine civilizations. The appearance of the ethnically defined Greek state challenged the Greek confessional and communal world, enlivening as well as complicating the meaning of the identity and the destiny that nationalism presumably embodies for a people.

While the focus here must of necessity be on the Greek nation-state, the larger world of Hellenism cannot be ignored. Though physically scattered and politically weaker, its human, cultural, and economic significance made it a fundamental issue in the political considerations of Greece's leaders into the twentieth century. Most of all, we must not assume a common purpose of intent between the two ethnic realms—state and community.

A second determining factor in Greek nationalism has been the intertwined and problematic relations between the small state and the Great Powers. From its creation as the offspring of the efforts by three "Protecting Powers"—Great Britain, France, and Russia—to balance their interests in the Near East, Greece has had to reckon with the consequences of its strategic location in the context of the historical dynamics of diplomacy. Encounters with larger and more powerful states have shaped and been shaped by the Greeks' nationalism. More properly, we need to consider the great power factor in Greek nationalism in terms of the political culture of the country, its regional interests vis-à-vis neighboring states and the Greek communities, and how these concerns have influenced the country's statecraft.

If the *Megali Idea* ("Great Idea") was assertive in emotional appeal and expectations among the Greek people, its realization was nevertheless clearly

---

which nationalism is discussed here. *Ethnismos,* translated as "nationism," has found favor with scholars in literature, sociology, and anthropology. It is more readily associated with cultural than political issues. Among some Greek intellectuals, it is considered a more positive expression of a phenomenon often viewed negatively.

circumscribed by the reality of the capabilities of a small, unaided state. Attainable territorial objectives vied with romantic historical visions in the calculations of government leaders. These contradictory views produced a good deal of tension in the country's national political life down to the end of World War I. In the aftermath of that enormous conflict, however, territorial ambitions were reined in and frontiers solidified through conflict and compromise. Subsequently, Greek nationalism was shaped by a third demand: balancing the need to maintain the territorial inviolability of the state with the desire to continue a mutually beneficial relationship with the Hellenic world beyond the frontiers of the nation-state.

Perhaps the most significant factor affecting Greek nationalism in the twentieth century has been the demographic transformations and attendant social changes that the country has experienced. The exchange of populations and the absorption of refugees from Asia Minor after World War I; the outward migrations, involuntary and voluntary, in the aftermath of the civil war of 1946–49; the rural to urban movement that swelled in the 1960s; and the subsequent return from *xenitia* of many Greeks have challenged the social stability of the nation. With these fundamental social and demographic shifts, traditions perceived as being rooted in rural values have confronted urban-driven modernizing tendencies. And this societal sea change has raised questions regarding the identity and thus the values of the people as a nation.

By taking these various factors into account, Greek nationalism can then be placed in its proper setting—the geographic, historical, and human environment in which it has developed. To trace its development requires examining the two main expressions of nationalism: political, in national issues, and cultural, in intellectual pronouncements. At times, these two forms of expression have melded in the voice and actions of a particular person. At others, a critical opposition has formed between the two realms. This dynamic remains at the heart of the ongoing development of the nationalist ethos.

From the "Great Idea" to the Ionian Tragedy

That the Greek kingdom was territorially a fragment of the Hellenic nation was immediately apparent to the country's first generation of political leaders. The Greeks spent almost a century wrestling with the meaning of state and nation. One had only to mention the names of towns and regions such as Ioannina, Trebizond, Constantinople, Serres, Thessaly, and Crete, as the Epirote physician and party leader Ioannis Kolettis did in the 1840s, and vivid images associated with Hellenism from the days of antiquity readily came to mind for a people now being schooled in their nation's past.

Associating Hellenism with the Greek communities in the various towns and regions of the Balkans, Asia Minor, and the islands in between meant that these places had to be considered as national lands. This left open the issue of how to deal with the non-Greek Orthodox Christians who also lived in these areas. There was not a uniformity of views between the secular leaders of the kingdom and the spiritual hierarchs of the Greek, or *Rum-i millet,* in the Ottoman Empire on how to resolve this matter. By the third quarter of the nineteenth century, the debate had come to a head and both *enosis,* the union of the unredeemed lands, and the cultural defense of the outposts of Hellenism through education were championed by the country's political overseers.[7]

To implement nationalist visions through statecraft required economic power and military strength, as Prussian success in unifying the German lands had clearly shown. But in the last decade of the nineteenth century, Greece revealed its weakness in both areas, which triggered a nationalist reaction against the country's political leadership.

The connection between economic growth and national progress was not lost on Harilaos Trikoupis, who served as prime minister on several occasions in the 1880s and 1890s. His development strategy was to upgrade the country's economic infrastructure by seeking foreign loans and by better handling domestic tax sources. However, competition from his leading opponent, Theodore Deligiannis, and the need for moderation in reforms so as not to put off potential investors, including Greeks in other countries, left Trikoupis's domestic program only partially successful.

Deligiannis succeeded Trikoupis as premier, and in a few years the country paid the price for weakness in the other area of needed strength—military capability. Seeking to promote the nationalist ideal, the *Megali Idea,* Deligiannis took up the cause of *enosis* with Greece of Ottoman-ruled Crete. The hoary politician spurned offers by the sultan's government for autonomy for the Great Island and mobilized troops in March 1897. Conflict flared in the recently acquired territory of Thessaly, as Greek irregulars took to arms. Fighting lasted but a month before Greece was soundly defeated by the better-prepared Ottoman army.[8]

---

7 Elli Skopetea, *To 'Protypo Vasileo' kai i Megali Idea* (Athens, 1988), chapters 1 and 3; Evangelos Kofos, "Attempts at Mending the Greek-Bulgarian Ecclesiastical Schism (1875-1902)," *Balkan Studies* 25:2 (1984), 1–29; and Skopetea, "Dilemmas and Orientations of Greek Policy in Macedonia: 1878-1886," *Balkan Studies* 21:1 (1980), 45–55.

8 Theodore G. Tatsios, *The Megali Idea and the Greek-Turkish War of 1897* (Boulder, CO, 1984), chapters 4–6.

Military defeat and economic weakness were joined in this humiliating episode in the nation's history. Greece got off rather lightly in the peace that followed the cessation of hostilities, but the Great Powers imposed an International Financial Control Commission on the country to manage payments on its sizable foreign debt. The result was a mounting sense of national frustration and an outcry from the younger generation of intellectuals and those of the middle class who sided with them.[9]

Without doubt, the clearest and most striking voice to be raised over matters national in the following years was that of Ion Dragoumis (see Document 1). Scion of a family well established in the country's political elite, Ion Dragoumis (1878–1920) came of age during the political and intellectual ferment that stirred the nation in the aftermath of the 1897 conflict. As a devotee of Nietzsche, Dragoumis sought to combine both thought and action in his life.

A member of a family that benefited from the politics of personality and patronage, which by now had become entrenched in Greece, Dragoumis leveled broadsides in books and essays at what he believed was a political establishment consumed by and feeding off nationalist rhetoric. Dragoumis railed against a political establishment that seemed to him to have grown comfortable and timid. Following Nietzsche's philosophy of strength-through-will, Dragoumis placed the blame on the smothering of the people's spirit of independence and liveliness, as exemplified in the popular Eastern "Romaic" culture of Greek folk society, by a political and cultural establishment that preferred the civilized ways of classical Greece and its spiritual descendant, the modern West.[10]

Dragoumis epitomized both the tensions and the contradictions that assailed the consciousness of Greek society. Since the creation of the state, culture had slowly become centralized and standardized through the establishment of *katharevousa* as the language of the state and high culture. Hence, the national voice was really that of a small social stratum, and the official tradition emphasized the high culture of classical Athens and the Orthodox Church while downplaying the continuously evolving popular folk culture.

Posted to Macedonia, Istanbul, Bulgaria, and Thrace as a consular official, Dragoumis worked with local ecclesiastics and leaders of the Greek communities in these areas to further the nation's cause. He belabored these community leaders for endeavoring to promote what he saw as the artificial high culture rather than the natural folk, or *demotic,* traditions that

---

9 Gerasimos Augustinos, *Consciousness and History: Nationalist Critics of Greek Society, 1897-1914* (Boulder, CO, 1977), chapter 2.

10 Augustinos, *Consciousness and History,* 89–96.

represented the very essence of the nation. But while Dragoumis claimed to despise the weakling state, he did serve the purposes of the Greek national center in his dealings with the Greeks in the Ottoman Empire.

Dragoumis's neo-romantic conservative nationalism reflected the frustration then common in Athenian political and intellectual circles. In fact, he was a member of the social stratum that dominated political life in the Greek capital. This frustration with national affairs among elements of the political order and their call for new ways is evidenced in the political activities of Dimitrios Gounaris. Capable and eager to see economic reform that would strengthen the country, Gounaris later founded the People's Party *(Laiko Komma)* and during World War I became the leading political opponent of Eleftherios Venizelos. Therein lay the seeds of eventual national catastrophe.

The pressing national issues, including the need for economic reform and strengthening of military capability, as well as concerns about the future of the Greeks in the Ottoman Empire, soon were bound up with a new leader. Eleftherios Venizelos, already seasoned in politics on Crete, came to power in 1910 on the heels of a military revolt that ousted the government in 1909. Quick to appreciate the need for a mass-based movement, he built a following that coalesced around him as the Liberal Party *(Komma Fileleftheron)*.

Though welcomed by many as an alternative to "old party politics" *(palaiokommatismos)*, Venizelos's success as a national leader was built on an eloquent personal style of politics, shrewd diplomacy, and a moderate domestic reform program. New equipment and better training made the military more sound. There was social legislation to aid agriculture, provide incentives to industry, and ensure the state's recognition of the rights of the working class. As for the initial demands for political change that had brought Venizelos to Athens, the Cretan statesman worked out a series of constitutional amendments in conjunction with the king. Thus the bourgeois movement guided by Venizelos ensured that social stability and political moderation would prevail under an emerging liberal economic order.[11]

Such progress enabled Venizelos to proceed with efforts to cooperate with Serbia and Bulgaria with regard to the remaining Balkan territories of the Ottoman Empire. The first Balkan war was a great success for Greece, but the wrangling over the distribution of territory between Bulgaria on the one hand and Greece and Serbia on the other led to further conflict. From Greece's perspective, the outcome of these regional struggles was a vindication

---

11 See Nikos Mouzelis, *"Oikonomia kai kratos tin epochi tou Venizelou,"* in *Meletimata Gyro Apo Ton Venizelo Kai Tin Epoche Tou* (Athens, 1980); and Georgios Leontaritis, *"To elliniko ergatiko kinima kai to astiko kratos 1910-20,"* in *Meletimata Gyro Apo Ton Venizelo Kai Tin Epoche Tou* (Athens, 1980).

of the new leadership of the country and the growing realization of the nationalist vision, the *Megali Idea*.

Nevertheless, the victories in the Balkans also fed a simmering problem and growing dilemma—Greek-Turkish tension over the fate of the Hellenic communities in Asia Minor. In the aftermath of the Balkan wars, the pressure mounted against the Greek Orthodox by the increasingly nationalist Young Turk government.[12]

How best to secure both Greece's national interests and those of the Greeks in Asia Minor? Once the Ottoman Empire entered World War I in early November 1914 on the side of the Central Powers, Venizelos believed an unparalleled opportunity was at hand. An alliance with the Entente states would bring Great Britain and France to Greece's side and ultimately help to realize the long-held promise of the *Megali Idea*—the union with Greece of the Asia Minor Greeks and the two most important areas of their settlement, Ionia and the Pontos. Staying out of the war and remaining neutral, in Venizelos's view, would benefit neither Greece nor Hellenism in Asia Minor. Though the Asia Minor Greeks might suffer in the short run, Greece's entry into the war against the Ottoman Empire was the only way to secure Hellenism in the lands bordering the Aegean Sea.

Opponents of Venizelos, who remained premier until March 1915, lined up with King Constantine. Men such as General Ioannis Metaxas believed that only under the most favorable of political and military circumstances could Greece hope to protect Hellenism in Asia Minor through its presence there. They advocated, and King Constantine supported, a policy of neutrality in the war. An unbridgeable chasm soon opened between the two political camps over how best to promote national interests. It was a division that pitted supporters of the state (the anti-Venizelists) against the nation (the Venizelists).[13]

Venizelos believed the king's stance was untenable once Bulgaria entered the conflict on the side of the Central Powers in September 1915. Relations between Venizelos, who had once again become premier in the summer of 1915, and Constantine rapidly deteriorated in the ensuing months, as did those between the monarchy and the Entente Powers. In August 1916, officers sympathetic to Venizelos rose against the royal government. Venizelos, who

---

12 See Carnegie Endowment for International Peace, *Report of the International Commission to Inquire into the Causes and Conduct of the Balkan Wars* (Washington, DC, 1912), chapter 6; and Dimitri Pentzopoulos, *The Balkan Exchange of Minorities and Its Impact upon Greece* (Paris: Mouton, 1962), 53–57.

13 George Mavrogordatos, *Stillborn Republic: Social Coalitions and Party Strategies in Greece 1922-1936* (Berkeley, CA, 1983), 282–88.

had resigned in October 1915, joined them and formed in Thessaloniki a countergovernment to the one in Athens. Under pressure from the Entente, which eventually recognized Venizelos's government, King Constantine abdicated in favor of his son in June 1917. Venizelos was soon in Athens and, once in power there, his supporters took their revenge on their opponents. This included exiling Dragoumis and Metaxas to Corsica, which deepened the political wounds the country was already suffering. Greece entered the war in 1917, and with victory the next year, Venizelos prepared to secure the nation's interests at the peace conference in Paris.[14]

Greek territorial claims on behalf of Hellenism that were put forward in Paris amounted to the culmination of the Great Idea. The desired areas, containing substantial Greek Orthodox populations, included: northern Epiros, part now of a recently created Albania; Thrace, the remnant of Ottoman territory in southeastern Europe of which part had gone to Bulgaria in 1912; the imperial capital of Istanbul (Constantinople); the Pontos and Smyrna regions in Asia Minor; the Dodecanese islands off the western coast of Asia Minor; and Cyprus, Ottoman territory controlled by Great Britain since 1878. With the signing of the Treaty of Sèvres in August 1920, Venizelos could return home rightly claiming that he had fulfilled much of the Great Idea. Cyprus, northern Epiros, Constantinople, and the Pontos were not to be "redeemed" according to the treaty, but much of Thrace and Smyrna and the surrounding countryside were secured for Greece.[15]

Greece's success abroad in the war and the peacemaking that followed was marred by domestic political feuding. The magnitude of the bitterness between supporters and opponents of Venizelos and the strain of the war effort had taken a toll on the nation which was reflected in the elections held in November 1920. Venizelos's supporters lost control of parliament. Deeply disappointed, the charismatic Cretan went into exile, while Constantine returned to the throne. Savoring the scent of revenge, the anti-Venizelists, led by Gounaris and his People's Party, took power in Athens. In foreign matters the new government was not about to abandon the fruits of the peace. Greek troops had been stationed in Smyrna since May 1919 to secure the region. Thousands more came as Greece prepared to protect its national interests on the Aegean littoral of Asia Minor against the growing threat of the nationalist movement led from the interior by Mustafa Kemal.

---

[14] N. Petsalis-Diomidis, *Greece at the Paris Peace Conference 1919* (Thessaloniki, 1978), chapter 2.

[15] Petsalis-Diomidis, *Greece at the Paris Peace Conference,* chapters 4–5.

Some, such as Venizelos and eventually Metaxas, while supportive of the gains for Hellenism in Paris, believed that Greece must of necessity take a defensive posture and maintain a protective stance around only the Smyrna enclave assigned by the treaty. Others, representing the royalist government, claimed that they were working for the allies' interests in carrying out the peace settlement, and they argued for a military policy of sending Greek troops into the interior of Asia Minor against the Kemalist forces. With the approval of King Constantine, the Greek army advanced into the heart of the Anatolian plateau in the spring of 1921.

Success ultimately eluded the Greeks as the Turkish nationalists turned back the attack. On the diplomatic front, Greece was left to its own devices by its erstwhile allies. By September 1922 the Greek forces had been defeated and pushed back to the edge of Asia Minor. As the Greek military and civilians departed the shores of Asia Minor, the Greek Orthodox Christians bore the brunt of the Turkish nationalists' wrath. Smyrna was burned, and the Greek Christians tried their best to save themselves by fleeing when possible. When peace was agreed between Greeks and Turks at Lausanne in July 1923, Hellenism in Asia Minor was no more. A required exchange of populations ultimately uprooted from their ancestral homes 1.25 million Greek Orthodox and brought them to Greece as refugees. As the national vision of redeeming Hellenism across the sea, the Great Idea was now irrevocably shattered.[16]

Greece Between the Wars: The Search for Meaning and Stability

In the years immediately following the Asia Minor disaster, nationalism as an ideology did not trouble Greek political life. All the political parties had supported the Great Idea in the past. The "national schism" *(ethnikos dihasmos)* that developed during World War I involved the eruption of fractious political rivalries. In November 1922, the political denouement to the military defeat was the peremptory trial and execution by a revolutionary committee of military men of five leading government officials, including Gounaris and the commanding general held responsible for the national defeat. The legacy of bitterness kept Venizelists and anti-Venizelists feuding. Neither side had anything really new to say in terms of nationalism; national politics during the interwar era for the party leaders involved fending off the military to keep hold

---

16 Michael Llewellyn-Smith, *Ionian Vision* (New York, 1973), chapters 10–13.

of their domains while contesting with each other for control of the state apparatus. In the maneuvering that resulted, the real national issues remained unresolved or, at best, only indirectly addressed.[17]

The country faced an unprecedented combination of newly acquired lands and newly arrived fellow Greeks. All of these problems stirred a political atmosphere already turgid with the inexplicable reversal of political fortune. Political leaders struggled with the vast social and economic challenges facing the country, while the intellectuals tried to delineate the features in Greek society and culture that defined its distinctive character. Ought Greece to adhere to the political and economic parameters within which it had developed up until that time? And could the cultural canons formed over the preceding century continue to serve the nation?

Georgos Theotokas provided the manifesto for the intellectual debate over the content of national culture during the interwar years. His *Free Spirit (Elefthero Pneuma),* which appeared in the fall of 1929, defined the concerns of the 1930s generation (see Document 2).

Born an Ottoman subject in 1905, Theotokas spent his youth in Constantinople (Istanbul). An avid interest in Greek literature during these early years led him to espouse the cause of the demoticist movement as the exponent of the living, creative spirit in Hellenic culture. In 1922 he arrived in Athens to study law at the university. Rejecting all narrow and dogmatic approaches to defining national character and purpose, including even some in the demoticist literary camp, in his writings Theotokas encompassed the wider meaning of Hellenic culture, as exemplified by his own life. Theotokas championed a Hellenism that went beyond physical frontiers and an immutable cultural complexion. As a new Greek from outside the country, he represented the Hellenic world beyond the state's frontiers. Theotokas personally had experienced the physical uprooting from its cultural and geographical homeland that had befallen inhabitants of that world. To make sense of this great upheaval in his own life, he wrote poignantly about his youth while welcoming the new challenges to his nation. To him, the generative forces within the nation could not be pinned to any one moment nor

---

17 Thanos Veremis, "The Officer Corps in Greece, 1912-1936," *Byzantine and Modern Greek Studies* 2 (1976), 113–34; Mavrogordatos, *Stillborn Republic,* 304–309; and Veremis, *Oikonomia kai Diktatoria* (Athens, 1982), chapters 3–4, pp. 124–30.

physically confined within the state frontiers. The creative impulse in Hellenic culture was a continuous force that could only thrive through outside influences.[18]

A "dialogue" between two creative talents, Constantine Tsatsos and George Seferis, at the end of the 1930s succinctly pointed up the issues arising over the nature and development of Hellenism. Tsatsos, a university professor of philosophy, later became the president of the Hellenic Republic created after the demise of the colonels' regime in 1974. In an article published in 1938, he sought to provide the youth of his time with a stabilizing intellectual focus against the currents of cultural iconoclasm that were flowing from many European capitals. Seferis, a Greek from Asia Minor who served in the Greek diplomatic corps and later became a Nobel prize winner for poetry, responded. The manner in which his nation's culture had been formed was as significant as its content to Seferis, a Greek from the shores of Asia Minor:

> Since the time of Alexander the Great we have scattered our Hellenism far and wide. We have sown it throughout the world.... And this vast diaspora was to have a significant result. Hellenism was worked up, reformed and revived, right down to the time of the Renaissance, by personalities who were sometimes Greek and sometimes not. And after that time, which marks the enslavement of the Greek race, it was shaped by personalities who were not Greek at all and who worked outside the Greek area.[19]

Amid a rising tide of nation-centered visions that divided the peoples of the continent, including those in his own country, Seferis sought out the historically developed diversity in culture that instilled confidence, promoted creativity, and ultimately ensured the survival of his people. His was a vision that emphasized the embodiment of Hellenism by all the Greek people and not by those only within certain geographic frontiers.

---

18 Theotokas, *Eleftbero Pneuma (Free Spirit),* 13–36; and Theotokas, *Pneumatiki Poreia* (Athens, 1961), 54–77. See also Kl. Paraschos, *"Neoellinikos Ethnikismos," Eleftheros Logos* (20 January 1927), and the discussion in Dimitrios Tziovas, *The Nationism of the Demoticists and Its Impact on Their Literary Theory (1830-1930)* (Amsterdam, 1986), 316–20.

19 George Seferis, "Dialogue on Poetry: What Is Meant by Hellenism," in *On the Greek Style: Selected Essays in Poetry and Hellenism,* Rex Warner and Th D. Frangopoulos, translators (Boston, 1966), 92.

For Seferis, as for Dragoumis, cultural Hellenism was a living presence imbued with a creative spirit that drew upon past Greek civilizations rather than just appropriating them as a national treasure. Again, like Dragoumis, Seferis believed that the national spirit in his people emanated from the individual's personal identification with his or her culture. He espoused the demoticist cause, still an anti-establishment movement, as a rejection of the nationalization of culture. Seferis's vision of Hellenism, unlike that of Dragoumis, however, was a reflection of his broader sense of national identity.

The content of national character that concerned many interwar intellectuals necessarily turned on the issue of the character of national society. That Greece's problems required not only new responses but new ways of looking at society had already been proclaimed at the close of World War I by G. Skliros. Skliros, a pseudonym for Giorgios Konstantinidis, came from southern Russia. He had studied in Germany and early on espoused the causes of Marx and demoticism. Skliros pointed out societal problems that adversely affected the nation's development. He castigated the Greeks' penchant for individualism and atomism rather than for cooperation in their social ethos. Equally detrimental were the historically derived grandiose visions of past greatness. The Greeks needed to reject anachronistic perceptions of themselves and to embrace the living tradition in a modern popular culture. This needed to be done, however, without rejecting the dynamism found in modern European civilization. Most important, Skliros saw new social dynamics developing in Greece with the enlargement of the state frontiers and the growth of industry. This was a productive development and need not be feared. His concern was that political life would remain the same, with governments promoting social uniformity in order to maintain society as it had been.[20]

Greece did face a new era in the 1920s as Skliros discerned, but without a significant industrial base and with an inefficient agricultural sector, the country had to struggle with the enormous task of providing housing and land to the refugees. Rural settlement, primarily in the new lands to the north, proved more successful for the refugees than dealing with them in the urban centers, where jobs were few and existence was precarious for those without skills or property. Remarkably, the country managed to cope with the strain of war and the new Greeks. Large estates were divided up, loans were obtained to undertake large-scale public projects to bolster the country's infrastructure, agricultural wealth grew, particularly through the energetic

---

[20] G. Skliros, *Ta Sychrona Provlimata tou Ellinismou* (Alexandria, 1919), 24–39, 152–56. See also the views of Dimosthenis Daniilidis, a socialist concerned with the role of geoeconomic factors on Greek society, in *I Neoelliniki Koinonia kai Oikonomia* (Athens, 1934), 1–22, 142–80, 254–65.

efforts of the newcomers in growing tobacco, and there were government measures to stabilize the currency and to promote new industries.[21]

The new circumstances, especially the presence of the refugees, no doubt figured into the political changes that marked the interwar era. In 1924 the monarchy was abolished through a plebiscite, and a republic was declared. As a result, the Venizelists formed a series of governments, although their nominal leader participated only briefly in 1924 before going abroad. Republicanism, born of political antagonism, fared poorly, however. Aggravated by the seeming political instability which they blamed on party factionalism, military men who had backed the formation of the republic charged onto the political stage by orchestrating coups. In 1928 Venizelos returned from abroad to seize the day and establish a measure of political stability by winning an overwhelming vote with his Liberal Party. He held office as premier until 1932.

Even before the onset of the Depression and its attendant difficulties for the nation, the Greece that Venizelos governed—some said ruled—was a visibly changed society that demanded new direction. But the middle-class politicians who sparred in parliament, whether they belonged to the Liberal Party, the People's Party, or the far smaller parties across the political spectrum, preferred to follow tried and temperate policies. As George Papandreou, who served as education minister in the Liberal government, confidently asserted:

> The Great Idea remains immortal. It simply changed its content. Instead of the increase of territory it aims at the increase and elevation of civilization.... The nation united strives for its economic, intellectual, and moral development.[22]

If improvement was the national ideal, national unity was the necessary prerequisite to attain that ideal, and social stability was the primary element needed to attain that unity. This is why Venizelos's government passed the *Idionymnon* law that sought to protect the "established social order" as well as "the whole of the State's territory" by prosecuting anyone who might

---

[21] Gerasimos Augustinos, "Development through the Market in Greece: The State, Entrepreneurs, and Society," in *Diverse Paths to Modernity in Southeastern Europe,* Gerasimos Augustinos, ed. (New York, 1991), 92–96.

[22] G. Papandreou, *Politika Keimena,* quoted in Mark Mazower, *Greece and the Inter-War Economic Crisis* (Oxford, England, 1991), 34.

conceivably challenge such notions.[23] The law addressed a touchstone of Greek nationalism, the territorial integrity of the state. The new lands to the north that were so recently "redeemed" had been coveted by neighboring states. They also contained a Slavic-speaking element as well as Muslims. Athens would not tolerate any attempt to alter what were considered integral territories of the nation.

Social issues and the integrity of the nation became embroiled in postwar politics with the emergence of the Socialist Labor Party in 1918, which later became the Greek Communist Party (KKE). Under pressure from the Communist International and the Bulgarian Communists, the KKE in 1924 accepted the notion that an independent Macedonian state be created. Their position changed in 1935, when they instead supported equality for all minorities in Greece in light of Moscow's policy of encouraging popular fronts in Europe against fascism. But the impression stuck among conservative politicians such as Ioannis Metaxas that the Communists in Greece would support neither the social nor the national unity of the country.[24]

Greece's national and social stability, as well as the confidence of Venizelos's government, were seriously tested with the international financial crisis of the early 1930s. Surprisingly, the economy of the country survived the crisis, as the nation increasingly relied on its own resources, but the health of the political culture, the guiding force in social and national development, declined. Republican institutions did not hold up as political life became hostage to contests of party will in parliament that paralyzed the country's leadership.

Venizelos stood by past domestic policies and political tactics that he believed would continue to work, but the electorate believed that reforms were needed given the difficult times, and the Liberal Party suffered defeat in elections held in 1932 and 1933. Worse still, republican officers saw these setbacks for Venizelos's party as a sign of resurgent monarchist feelings. Acting on their fears, they twice attempted to overthrow the government, in 1933 and 1935. Venizelos, in a move that damaged his reputation and the country's political institutions, supported the second revolt. Its failure brought the People's Party, now led by Panagis Tsaldaris, to power in the election that followed. Through a plebiscite engineered in November 1935 by General Georgios Kondylis, a Venizelist republican turned royalist, the monarch, George II, returned.

---

23 Mavrogordatos, *Stillborn Republic*, 99.

24 Evangelos Kofos, *Nationalism and Communism in Macedonia* (Thessaloniki, 1964), 66–92.

Once the king was back, he ousted Kondylis and tried to return the country to regular parliamentary life. He called for new elections in January 1936, the outcome of which indicated that the electorate supported the two major parties, the Liberals and the People's Party. But it also produced parliamentary gridlock—the Liberals had recovered, but neither party had a clear majority. This left the Communists, who had received less than 6 percent of the vote, holding the crucial balance. King George would not accept a coalition government that included the Communists in such a critical role. A caretaker government was created, with the king naming as premier General Metaxas, who had even less popular appeal than the far left.

As the two major parties tried to form a new coalition government, the political ground was swept from under them. Social ferment had erupted in strikes by workers in several cities during the first half of 1936. Metaxas, with the approval of the king, already had responded with force to stifle the unrest. On 4 August, Metaxas took the ultimate step by persuading the king to dissolve parliament and allow him to institute martial law. Constitutional government, the representation of civic society, and the expression of the national will, had collapsed.[25]

With the king warily considering the developments, Metaxas proceeded to emasculate political life. He attempted to promote a new era in the nation's history, but the elderly general had not come to power at the head of any mass-based nationalist movement, nor had he brought the military along with him. His self-defined cause was the renewal of the nation through emotional appeals, especially to the youth. His instruments were the state institutions and those in the technical, academic, and administrative professions who were willing to collaborate with him in building the "New State."

The "Fourth of August" regime initiated by Metaxas was an amalgam of authoritarian rule and populist rhetoric. It was inspired by a dislike of parliamentary politics and the individualism and freedom inherent in a capitalist economy. The new order was to be grounded on a hierarchy of authority proceeding from the monarchy, which appointed the "leader" *(Arhigos)* who would promulgate and implement policies in consultation with advisory councils. The people would be asked for their approval through plebiscites, avoiding any need for political parties. Authoritarian rule was justified by a nationalist ideology that appealed to history: the nation was to

---

[25] Mazower, *Greece and the Inter-War Economic Crisis,* chapter 10; and John S. Koliopoulos, *Greece and the British Connection 1935-1941* (Oxford, England, 1977), 38–50.

embark on a mission to create a third Greek civilization greater than that of classical Greece or Christian Byzantium.[26]

The "Fourth of August" regime placed its hopes in the nation, but the nation did not reciprocate. Despite organized demonstrations of support and a flood of propaganda, Metaxas's rule never generated the widespread national support it claimed to have. While national defense was a priority, the regime's nationalist focus was inward-looking rather than outward-directed.

Metaxas's redeeming moment came with Mussolini's attack on Greece in October 1940. The propaganda and personal vanities were put aside as the elderly general struggled to spur on his people and the military. His death at the end of January 1941 came during Greece's gravest hour. King George tried to maintain the country's political and military determination, but operation Maritsa, the German offensive in the Balkans, engendered despair among some political and military figures. Greece's defenses were overwhelmed, and the country was occupied by the end of April.

War, Civil War, and Cold War: The Nation Divided Against Itself

Once the initial shock of defeat passed and the grim reality of occupation settled on the nation, scattered signs of resistance appeared. By the spring of 1942 a number of organized resistance movements had been formed and were preparing to send men into the mountains. Of the prewar political leaders who remained in the country, however, most were only minimally involved in the resistance efforts. A striking exception was the Communist Party (KKE). Though the party had been infiltrated and its leaders imprisoned by Metaxas's police, the movement survived through discipline and some good luck. In the turmoil of war and occupation, some Communists managed to become free. Following the German attack on the Soviet Union, they began organizing a resistance movement in the towns and the countryside.

Instead of criticizing an imperialist war, the Greek Communists now came out for a policy of struggle against the forces of fascism. By January 1942, at the eighth plenum of the party's Central Committee, the tactics and policies

---

[26] *Tessera Hronia Diakyverniseos I. Metaxa* (Athens, 1940?), 185–216; Koliopoulos, *Greece and the British Connection,* 51–58; Nikos Alivizatios, *Oi Politikoi Thesmoi se Krisi 1922-1974,* 2nd ed. (Athens, 1986), 108–34; and Sp. Lindardatos, *I 4i Avgoustou* (Athens, 1966), 83–109.

already were clearly formed. In the fall of 1941 the party had created the National Liberation Front (EAM), intended to bring together "all the political parties, all of the people, without distinction by ideology, race, religion, and nationality...." The objectives of EAM were: "the struggle for the liberation of the country from the foreign yoke, the struggle for the protection of the daily necessities of life of our people, and the struggle to attain popular freedoms and the solution of all internal problems according to the free will of the majority of the people."[27] Class struggle had given way to the struggle for the nation.

In line with these patriotic proclamations, the KKE asserted that it supported "popular democracy" to be established by a popularly elected assembly once the country was free of foreign forces. Greece's Slavic-speaking minority was encouraged to resist the blandishments of the Bulgarians who occupied areas of northern Greece and to "unite their struggle with the national liberation struggle of the Greek, Serbian, and Bulgarian people." The KKE leadership also affirmed its belief that there were elements among the country's political and military circles who were preparing to establish an "antipopular dictatorship" once the occupying forces were gone.[28]

With the legal government of the nation far removed in London, the National Liberation Front and its sister organizations, which targeted workers (EEAM) and youth (EPON), proceeded to gather recruits into a fighting force (ELAS) and to organize for action. The resistance effort became more complicated and politically problematic as non-leftist movements were formed. The British also were involved through the activities of SOE, the Special Operations Executive, aimed at promoting armed resistance. However, British efforts to coordinate the operations of the various resistance organizations were only partly successful.

By the spring of 1944 the Communists were working to strengthen their position politically and militarily. They established the Political Committee of National Liberation (PEEA) in March to oversee the areas under EAM control in Greece and to bargain with the government-in-exile. During the previous winter ELAS units had clashed with noncommunist resistance bands in an attempt to secure military superiority.

The only real counter the government-in-exile had to the leftists' growing power was British support. Anticommunist Security Battalions that had been created by the collaborationist government in Greece only increased

---

27 Alekos Papapanagiotou, ed., *To Kommounistiko Komma Elladas Ston Polemo kai Stin Antistasi. Episima Keimena. Tomos Pemptos: 1940-1945* (Athens, 1974), 95.

28 Papapanagiotou, *To Kommounistiko Komma Elladas Ston Polemo kai Stin Antistasi*, 95–96.

tension between the left and the royal government. Political maneuvering continued during 1944 with the appointment of the Venizelist George Papandreou as prime minister. From May to September, the voluble Papandreou negotiated with EAM to build a government of national unity and to place the left's military forces under its authority.

The withdrawal of the Germans from the country in October allowed Papandreou to return to Athens. He immediately tackled the sensitive issue of negotiating with the left, seeking to get them to lay down their arms and integrate their forces with a national army under the government's control. Relations between Papandreou and EAM leaders grew ever more strained as the left denounced what it feared was the growing force of anticommunists in the country. An EAM–sponsored demonstration in Athens in early December led to violence as the crowd was fired upon by the police. Feeling betrayed, the ELAS forces attacked government outposts. All-out war was averted, and the presence of British troops, rushed to Athens, helped save the government. A wary political truce was established in February 1945.

The Varkiza agreement that followed the cessation of hostilities offered some hope for peace to a nation shattered by war and political antagonism. ELAS agreed to turn in quantities of weapons. For its part, the government offered political amnesty, a purge of collaborationists from its ranks, and a referendum on the future of the monarchy. Distrust continued, however, and the larger national issues resulting from the effects of the war were not addressed.

Political life returned to the capital during 1945 and the spring of 1946, when the first elections were held since the Metaxas regime. The Liberals and the People's Party reemerged but in a climate of fractionalization among the non-leftist parties, who were in turn distrusted by the left. The left refused to participate in the March election, and the right, led by the People's Party, won a majority. Once in power, the People's Party called for a plebiscite on the monarchy. Held in September 1946, the vote went in favor of the king's return by a comfortable majority, and George II was back in Athens later that month. The plebiscite was not an indication of growing political stability but rather of a markedly divided nation at a historical crossroads. As Great Britain and eventually the United States anxiously sought the emergence of a stable, effective government in Athens, the left endeavored to maintain its appeal through organizational strengthening and the promise of a better future for the nation.

To achieve that brighter future the left argued that Greece needed to break with its past politically and economically. How this might be possible was cogently argued by a leftist, Dimitrios Batsis. He wrote in 1947 that Greece was not a naturally poor country whose salvation could come only from without by linking its economy to foreign interests. For that matter, Batsis believed that the century-long nationalist vision, the *Megali Idea,* was a misconceived policy for economic benefits, although he accepted the need for the unification of the various parts of the nation. Batsis asserted that the country's economic and therefore its national viability was not a matter of physical or demographic factors, but a question of social policy. The productive strata in society—workers, agriculturalists, craftsmen, professionals, and intellectuals—needed to take political power. Over time, as short-term problems were solved, the economy could be reorganized through nationalization and then turned toward heavy industry. This was the left's vision of self-sufficiency, which would enable the nation to become independent of foreign financial and economic markets while accumulating needed wealth domestically.[29]

As appealing as such nationally focused ideas might have been to a society in dire straits, the Communists were caught up in the politics of other national issues and ideologically driven great power competition in Europe. Constantine Tsaldaris, who had become leader of the People's Party upon the death of his uncle, Panagis, headed the government in 1946 and showed little inclination for any conciliatory moves in his domestic politics. He was interested, however, in pursuing the country's concerns abroad. Tsaldaris demanded reparations from Bulgaria and made territorial claims against that country for the improvement of Greece's defenses. Claims also were presented against Albania for the province of Northern Epiros and against Italy for the Dodecanese islands—all as lands that were ethnically Greek.

In formulating its policies on domestic national issues the KKE had to deal with circumstances that militated against effective action. On one hand, it had to take into consideration the interests of the Soviet Union, even when conditions in Greece were not compatible with the party line from Moscow. On the other, the party itself was divided over tactics and strategy.[30]

Elaborating and maintaining a policy regarding Greece's northern border that would satisfy several interested parties, always difficult, became a real dilemma by 1946. Marshal Tito, whose political visions encompassed much of the Balkans, had promoted the Macedonian cause during the war. Now in power in Yugoslavia, he was in a position to press the unification of Greek Macedonia with the Yugoslav Macedonian territory. The KKE needed Tito's support and therefore acquiesced in some of his ideas on Macedonia. Yet

---

[29] Dimitrios Batsis, *I vareia viomihania stin Ellada,* 2nd ed. (Athens, 1977), 27–29, 194–205, 375–77.

[30] Peter J. Stravrakis, *Moscow and Greek Communism, 1944-1949* (Ithaca, NY, 1989), 66–69, 99–126.

the Greek Communists could not afford to alienate popular opinion on this issue, and they had to consider the interests of the Slavic speakers in Greek Macedonia as well. Thus, as the Greek left prepared for military action with the creation of the Democratic Army (DSE) in October 1946, it had to keep the support of Tito and Stalin. Trying to satisfy Tito's desire for a Macedonian state without betraying Greece's national interests eventually put the KKE in an impossible situation.[31]

By the end of 1946 full-scale civil war had commenced. Controlling much of the mountainous area near Greece's northern frontier, the Communists hoped for political recognition of their cause from the Communist states in Eastern Europe. Though they received material aid, the Greek leftists never legitimized their cause internationally even among countries in the Soviet bloc. In 1947 the government in Athens countered with foreign diplomatic and material support from the United States through the Truman Doctrine and the Marshall Plan. When the Communist Party was outlawed in December of that year, the DSE appealed to the "People" *(o Laos)* for support. It was an appeal couched in apocalyptic terms as the struggle of two antithetical forces. Greece was a battleground (a "jungle") with a foreign-dominated government in Athens ready to give away the "territorial integrity, the national independence, the national honor" of the country. It had to choose between two paths: "National Honor" or "National Betrayal." In a bid for support, the Communists announced the creation of a Provisional Democratic Government (PDK).[32]

The struggle continued for the next year and a half, until the fall of 1949, when the hostilities ended and what remained of the Democratic Army retreated into Albania. In human and material terms, the cost of the war and the civil war that had followed was enormous. There was not only the outright destruction of human life and dwellings, but a mass of people who had been forced from their homes and who were completely dependent on the state for support. The political consequences for the nation were also severe, and the price could not yet be fully calculated.[33]

---

31 Stavrakis, *Moscow and Greek Communism,* 133–46. For the Macedonian problem, see John O. Iatrides, *Revolt in Athens* (Princeton, NJ, 1972), 269–75; and Stephen G. Xydis, *Greece and the Great Powers 1944-1947* (Thessaloniki, 1963), 329–32.

32 *To Kommounistiko Komma tis Elladas, Episima Keimena. Tomos Ektos: 1945-1949* (Athens, 1987), 447–51.

33 For the material and human destruction in the 1940s, see Augustinos, "Development through the Market in Greece," 100–104; and John Iatrides, ed., *Greece in the 1940s* (Hanover, VT, 1981), 61–80, 220–28, 319–41.

Recovery and reconstruction using aid from the United States and under U.S. oversight began in earnest once the civil war ended. It did so within the confines of an ideologically and militarily polarized world and an exclusionary and proscriptive political culture. The external parameters of that world remained until the late 1980s; the internal political ethos continued until the mid–1970s.

There was no room for doubt or discourse in the new national society. Reflecting the Manichean outlook manifested in cold war ideology, the right reduced Greek nationalism to bare essesntials. The territorial integrity of the country and its national unity were weapons in the struggle against the enemies of the nation, deftly denominated as the "Slavo-communist" menace. The police, secret and public, became the guarantors of political correctness and order. The military defined its mission in unambiguous terms as "defenders of the nation." It carried out its mission as much inside the country as without, through political rehabilitation camps and control of one of the two broadcasting systems (which applied to television once this medium began operating). The pervasiveness of nationalist order extended to basic aspects of public life. Before any license, permit, or passport could be issued or if public employment was sought, an individual was required to obtain a certificate of national loyalty *(pistopoiitikon ethnikon fronimaton)*.[34]

The tenor of intellectual and educational life in the decade after the civil war reflected the prevailing theme in domestic and foreign affairs—the emphasis on security and stability. Greek academic and intellectual life was imbued with a defensive nationalist tenor. This is apparent in the work of Dionysios Zakythinos. A scholar in medieval and modern Greek history who was educated abroad, Zakythinos held professorial posts beginning in 1939 and served as director of the country's national archives for a number of years. In the midst of the civil war, Zakythinos defended the nation against a perceived depreciation of Greek cultural influence in the Balkans. He staunchly defended the Hellenic cultural realm in the Balkans.[35] Over the next two decades, in wide-ranging essays Zakythinos sought to define the meaning of "modern Hellenism." He concluded that modern Greek history had to be understood through three basic "concepts": that of the *"Genos"* (race), the *Ethnos* (nation), and the "Great Idea." Together, these concepts expressed the meaning of

---

[34] Constantine Tsoucalas, "The Ideological Impact of the Civil War," in *Greece in the 1940s,* John O. Iatrides, ed. (Hanover, VT, 1981), 328–30.

[35] Zakythinos was reacting to the views expressed in *Balkan Federation: A History of the Movement toward Balkan Unity in Modern Times,* by L. S. Stavrianos. Dionysios A. Zakythinos, *La Grèce et les Balkans* (Athens, 1947), 18–27.

modern political life as well as the three eras that comprised Greek history. Zakythinos's writings reinforced the nationalist view of history conceived as a proud and continuous lineage that went back to the ancient Greeks but that conveniently stopped at 1940, a moment that was unambiguous in national history—the determination to resist foreign aggression.[36]

It was not until the fall of 1952 that political stability was achieved. It was accomplished by the victory of the right, which called itself the Greek Rally and was headed by Marshal Papagos who had led the government forces in the civil war. The power of the state over its citizens was strengthened, and the national character of society affirmed in a new constitution introduced in January 1952. The constitution stated that the purpose of education was the "development of the national consciousness of the youth on the basis of the ideological directions of Hellenochristian civilization."[37]

In the matter of foreign affairs, rightist governments in the 1950s sought stability through security in a world divided into "two camps" by improving relations with other states in the region along with seeking military and political support from the United States, now the predominant great power influence in Greece. Stalin's power perturbed security-conscious leaders in southeastern Europe and stimulated Greece, Yugoslavia, and Turkey to improve relations among themselves and even to create an alliance reminiscent of the "Balkan entente" in the interwar era. Cooperation across ideological frontiers proved ephemeral, however. In 1952 Greece joined NATO, the military alliance of one camp, while Tito pursued nonalignment in response to a bipolar world.

The contradictory relationship between national interests and international commitments became readily apparent in the early 1950s over the question of the fate of Cyprus. With a population that was 80 percent Greek, Cyprus became a touchstone of national rights and justice for Greece. In the debates and negotiations over the island's fate among Great Britain, Greece, and eventually Turkey, the argument was made that the population could not possibly have a distinct ethnic identity after so many centuries of foreign invasion and rule. For the Greek government it was absolutely clear "that the

---

36 Dionysios A. Zakythinos, *I Politiki Istoria tis Neoteras Ellados,* 2nd ed. (Athens, 1965), 38–56. An English translation of the relevant passage can be found in Zakythinos, *The Making of Modern Greece* (Totowa, NJ, 1976), chapter 9.

37 Alexandrou Svolou, *Ta Ellinika Syntagmata 1822-1952,* 3rd ed. (Athens, 1972), 213.

overwhelming majority of the population was Hellenic in race, language, religion, mores, culture, and feelings."[38]

Greece took up the cause of *enosis,* or union, in the early 1950s, fortified with the principle of ethnic justice and the freely proclaimed desire of the Greek Cypriots as expressed in a plebiscite held on the island early in 1950. Initially, Greece sought to resolve the question by direct negotiations with Great Britain. When this approach elicited no favorable response, Greece turned to the United Nations, where it hoped world opinion and the influence of the United States, its powerful patron, would bring the desired result.[39]

The Cyprus question became both an international problem and a potent issue in Greek domestic affairs. Diplomatic discussion was soon followed by violence as Colonel George Grivas, a Cypriot of far-right sympathies, mounted a resistance campaign in Cyprus against British rule through his National Organization of Cypriot Fighters (EOKA). The Greek Cypriots now had their own spokesman, Archbishop Makarios. As *ethnarch,* or leader of the Greek Orthodox community, Makarios pressed the cause of *enosis* in Athens and with other states, following his own tactical line.

Dealing with the Cyprus question fell to Constantine Karamanlis, who succeeded Papagos as head of the government. Karamanlis, a member of the Greek Rally, reformed the rightist party as the National Radical Union (ERE). His foreign minister, Evangelos Averoff, sought to have the question dealt with as a colonial issue between the Greek Cypriots and Great Britain and not as a nationalist cause for territory which would involve the Turkish government.[40]

The British were only willing to concede limited self-rule and took a hard line with Makarios's politics and Grivas's armed tactics. Turkey also injected itself into the problem on behalf of the interests of the Turkish Cypriots. With Makarios easing his demand for *enosis* as the only solution, Karamanlis and his Turkish counterpart worked out an agreement in 1959, acceptable to the British, that called for an independent Cyprus guaranteed by all three states. Although Karamanlis and Makarios both would have liked to see union, the Greek premier had to surmount sharp questioning in parliament and the press over his commitment to the nation in his handling of this problem.[41]

---

[38] Stephen G. Xydis, *Cyprus, Conflict and Conciliation, 1954-1958* (Columbus, OH, 1967), 313.

[39] Nancy Crawshaw, *The Cyprus Conflict* (London, 1978).

[40] Xydis, *Cyprus, Conflict and Conciliation,* 46, 312–29.

[41] C. M. Woodhouse, *Karamanlis: The Restorer of Greek Democracy* (Oxford, 1982), 61–94. For a critical view of the role of Greece as spokesman for the nation

Karamanlis had plenty of incentive to find a "settlement" to the Cyprus issue. Though his party had done well against the center-left parties, which were fractionalized, the banned Communists had found a legal voice as the United Democratic Left (EDA). They used the Cyprus issue and a proposal to base nuclear weapons at U.S. installations in the country to portray the government party as serving foreign interests, particularly those of the United States. EDA favored a neutralist policy for Greece, a position that was reinforced by proposals from the Communist bloc for a nuclear-free zone in the Balkans. Relations with Yugoslavia were satisfactory, although Tito did not wish to renew the Balkan Pact. Bulgaria desired to restore diplomatic relations, but the Greek government insisted that its northern neighbor pay what it owed in wartime reparations. As Karamanlis noted to President Eisenhower on the latter's visit to Athens in late 1959, Greece "belongs ideologically to the West, but she is isolated geographically and racially."[42] It was on this matter of national direction that developments in the decade that followed pivoted.

By the early 1960s people began to question the system of social control imposed by the rightists in the aftermath of the civil war. George Papandreou, whose political life had been formed under dictatorship, war, and civil war, brought various political factions together to form the Center Union Party (EK). Rallying his supporters to oppose the right-wing extralegal tactics in politics, Papandreou won an absolute majority of the popular vote and control of parliament in the spring of 1964.

There was not time to rest on that accomplishment, however. During the previous winter Greeks and Turks in Cyprus had clashed as Archbishop Makarios, president of the republic, attempted to revise the country's unworkable constitution. Papandreou, leader of Greece, the "national center," set out a strategy that was aligned with popular national feeling in the country. Unwilling, as Karamanlis had done, to stay within the family fold of NATO in dealing with the problem, the Greek premier turned to the world forum—the United Nations—for support. Greek forces were built up on the

---

with regard to Cyprus, see Paschalis Kitromilides, *"To Elliniko Kratos os Ethniko Kentro,"* in *Ellinismos Ellinikotita,* D. G. Tsaousi, ed. (Athens, 1983), 159–63. Van Coufoudakis provides a good overview of the period after 1974 in "Greece and the Problem of Cyprus 1974-1986," in *Greece on the Road to Democracy: From the Junta to PASOK 1974-1986,* Speros Vryonis, Jr., ed. (New Rochelle, NY, 1991).

42 Quoted in Woodhouse, *Karamanlis,* 90–91. For the impact of foreign issues on national affairs, see Theodore A. Couloumbis, *Greek Political Reaction to American and NATO Influences* (New Haven, CT, 1966), 93–132.

island, and Grivas was allowed to return to Cyprus to see that Makarios lined up with Athens on policy. Papandreou mounted an independent stand vis-à-vis the United States by rejecting a plan by former Secretary of State Dean Acheson that would have brought *enosis* with Greece but at the cost of partition *(taksim)* of the island to mollify Turkey. Cyprus was now a continuing national issue.[43]

If the elder Papandreou was seen as troublesome by opponents in Greece and by the administration in Washington, his son's political beliefs were even more suspect. Andreas Papandreou, who knew the United States well, attracted the leftists in the party. Charges that there was a conspiracy of leftists in the army who looked to Andreas for support embroiled the elder Papandreou with the army and the monarchy. King Constantine, certainly not gifted in the ways of politics, sought to create a government more to his liking. Out of office in 1965, George Papandreou prepared for elections the following spring, feeling that he would easily return to power.[44]

For his part Andreas made clear his desire to make a different path from the past in domestic and foreign policy (see Document 3). In an appeal to national pride, the younger Papandreou asserted that Greece must have the final say in its affairs. The nation had to be treated with respect and not as a dependency by foreign powers. Reacting to cries that the country was an instrument of outside interests that had penetrated the administrative and military institutions, Papandreou called for the "nationalization" of those state instruments to cleanse them of foreign influence. Greece faced a great challenge in seeking to become part of the Common Market. It needed to develop its productive capabilities so that it would be more than a playground

---

[43] Theodore A. Couloumbis, *The United States, Greece, and Turkey* (New York, 1983), 44–48.

[44] B. S. Markesinis, *The Theory and Practice of Dissolution of Parliament* (Cambridge, England, 1972), 217–23. The crisis stirred the Athenian press and induced a flurry of partisan commentary. Worth noting in the context of this work are the series of articles by Georgos Theotokas in the Athens daily *To Vima,* which were collected and published in book form as *I Ethniki Krisi* (Athens, 1966). Theotokas believed that the country was in the grip of a "national crisis." The cause was deeper than the maneuvering of political leaders. Greece was a semi-developed nation, in his view, that had made progress in a haphazard manner which had produced stark social inequalities. When the center government sought to address the problem, it triggered a fear-motivated reaction from the right (see pp. 35–41).

for foreigners. It was time for "national change" to bring about a "national rebirth."

Such ideas and the strident tone in the ensuing debate led many in high military and political circles to conclude that the stability of the country was in jeopardy, but the outcome of the crisis was unexpected. Fearing that a return to power of the Center Union would be to their personal detriment, a far-right conspiratorial group of army officers seized control of the country on 21 April 1967. The colonels' coup, led by military intelligence officer George Papadopoulos, superficially seemed to confirm the idea that history repeats itself. Much as Metaxas had done, the conspirators claimed that they were saving the nation from a communist threat. They also tried to elaborate a legitimizing ideology with the slogan "a Greece of Helleno-Christians." And, like the "Fourth of August" regime, there was a populist tone to the junta's appeal for support in the country, as well as the use of the secret police to silence opposition. But the "Twenty-first of April" regime was dominated by a generation of military men who were in the unique position of being both "haves" and "have-nots." As junior officers, they benefited from the military aid the country received from the United States. Also, their profession brought appropriate perquisites. However, the colonels felt that their careers were being blocked by an older generation of more senior officers. And, for them, the monarchy was as much a hindrance as a help.

During its years in power the junta tried to generate and secure a new political culture. It gave short shrift to all politicians and parties. Through a flood of propaganda, both in the country and among Greek communities abroad, the Papadopoulos regime sought to associate itself with the national past as its successor and guarantor. There was also a cathartic streak among the junta leaders as they vowed to fight moral decadence among the youth, which stemmed from foreign (Western) influences.

The colonels heralded their regime as a "revolution"—it was an accomplished fact for Papadopoulos and there was no reversing what the colonels had begun. To gain support and credence, the military rulers used the instruments of the state to make grants for public works projects to benefit small contractors, to extend favorable terms for investors in tourist facilities, to encourage industrialists to seek foreign investment for use by Greek businesses, and to entice Greeks abroad, particularly shipowners, to invest in the country by creating legislation favorable to them. While the rhetoric was for the many (helping the workers), in reality few benefited.[45]

---

[45] Augustinos, "Development though the Market in Greece," 114–17; and George Papadopoulos, *To Pistevo Mas,* vol. 4 (1969), 134–41, and vol. 6 (1970), 156–60.

To reinforce the notion of the military as the "defender of the nation" and itself as a worthy successor in that role, the junta mounted an exhibit on the "military history of the Greeks" in Athens a year after seizing power.[46] But when it came to securing national interests in the region, the "Twenty-first of April" regime was ineffective and ultimately was undone by its handling of those interests.

At the beginning, the junta's dealings with some of the country's neighbors seemed to take a promising direction. Relations with Communist states such as Albania, Bulgaria, and Romania, which had been cool in the past, improved. It was a different matter, however, when it came to Greece's NATO ally, Turkey. Papadopoulos tried to pursue the idea of Cypriot *enosis* with the Turks while employing the instruments of Greek policy that had been put in place on the island during the Papandreou government—a large contingent of Greek troops and Colonel Grivas. The junta actually suffered a reversal of fortune: Turkey became even more resistant to the idea of *enosis* between Greece and Cyprus in response to Grivas's attacks on Turkish Cypriot communities and the close cooperation between the Greek officers and the Cyprus National Guard. The upshot was that Greece was forced to withdraw both Grivas and its soldiers from the island.[47]

Papadopoulos now tried to take the high road. To a Turkish reporter, he stated in the spring of 1971 that the source of friction between Greece and Turkey over Cyprus was "psychological." Each state, he argued, regarded the other's moves with doubt and wariness. Greece and Turkey, however, as "parents" had to show the way to their "children"—the Greek and Turkish communities in Cyprus. Such effusive statements could hide neither the setback the regime had suffered in pursuing the nationalist goal of *enosis* nor the equally deleterious downturn in relations between Athens and the archbishop's government in Nicosia.[48]

The situation for Greece and Cyprus only worsened when Papadopoulos was removed from power in late November 1973 by officers who were unhappy over his handling of student protests and distrustful of his political strategy. Relations with Turkey became more difficult when oil was discovered in the Aegean, and Greece claimed that its islands marked the country's continental

---

46 A lavishly illustrated two-volume work based on the exhibition was issued at the same time. The work was still available two decades later—minus the last chapter on the contributions of the "Twenty-first of April" regime.

47 Crawshaw, *The Cyprus Conflict,* 376–79; and Kyriakos C. Markides, *The Rise and Fall of the Cyprus Republic* (New Haven, CT, 1977), 132–40.

48 Papadopoulos, *To Pistevo Mas,* vol. 7 (1972), 92–95.

shelf, thus limiting what waters Ankara could explore for natural resources. To cap things off, the enmity between the Greek and Cypriot governments had climbed to an unbridgeable level. In mid–July 1974, the Cyprus National Guard turned against Makarios with the backing of the Athens regime. The archbishop survived the attack, but Turkey sent troops onto the island, eventually controlling almost 40 percent of it. In Athens the junta called for a general mobilization, but the result was only a muddle and a refusal by the armed forces to go to war. The military regime collapsed, and a civilian government was restored with Karamanlis returning from self-imposed exile to lead the country.

After the tragic civil war in the 1940s, Hellenism, the identity and character of the Greek nation, had been appropriated by one segment of political society. Narrowed in focus and controlled in content, Hellenism as intellectual and political culture had become entwined with the international ideological conflict and the determination of those in power to create progress through stability. Eventually, it deteriorated to unthinking rhetoric embodied in the phrase "a Greece of Helleno-Christians" and outright dictatorship in the hands of the junta. Greece as the national center remained. However, from the point of view of the Greeks in Cyprus, the actions of the center had brought only tragedy.

The Great Challenge: Democracy, Progress, and National Integrity

Seven years of military rule had set back the country's domestic affairs as well as its foreign relations. Greece was clearly at a crossroads in its development. Broadly stated, the nation needed to define its position in the modern world and the development path it would follow. The choices made would be an indicator of how the nation perceived itself as a society and what role the state should have in that society. Domestic issues inevitably were linked to the question of Greece's political and economical position in the international system. Specifically, this meant the nature of Greece's political and military ties with the United States, its association with the European Community, and its relations with the other states in the region. All of these issues ultimately reflected what Hellenism as national self-identify meant to the Greeks.

Rather than trying to take a position on all these issues, Karamanlis seized the moment to call for popular support for his role as the restorer and best guarantor of democracy. Karamanlis had reformed the moderate elements of his old rightist party, the National Radical Union, into the New Democracy

Party. His was a gamble on moderation and linkage with the West as the best way to bring Greece out of a traditional, patriarchal world, beloved of the political right, to a modern nation with an open society. To accomplish this, Karamanlis declared that Greece no longer would be compliant and unquestioning in its dealings with the United States, a condition that the right itself had allowed to develop. National defense interests were to be strengthened by closer military ties with Western European states.

Greece "belonged to the West," and to Karamanlis this meant it should rapidly meet the requirements for full membership in the European Community. The goal was attained in January 1981, with Karamanlis proudly supporting the move in his new position as president of the republic, to which he had recently been elected by parliament. Also, the government accepted demotic Greek, the popular idiom, as the language of the nation, thus realizing an ideal that had been espoused by a number of intellectuals over the past century, including Dragoumis and Theotokas. Finally, the New Democracy leadership sought to improve interstate relations in the region by building an opening with the Communist East. Through bilateral talks, Greece steadily created better relations with its northern neighbors, although this did not extend to its dealings with Turkey.

On all these issues there was now a vigorous opposition political view. At the time of the 1974 election, Andreas Papandreou had formed a new party, the Panhellenic Socialist Movement (PASOK). Under a banner emblazoned with a rising green sun, Andreas crafted a political program that was appealing in its nationalist fervor and populist calls for "change" *(Allagi)*. The slogan, shortened from his phrase of "national change" of the 1960s, offered a vision of a better national future built on a reorganized national economy, social benefits, national independence in foreign relations, and government by the popular will of the people.[49]

With regard to foreign matters, Papandreou was adamant that U.S. bases in Greece be closed, and he stridently attacked the United States for tilting toward Turkey, as exemplified by the events of the summer of 1974. Greece, therefore, needed to renegotiate its position in NATO in order to maintain its national, territorial rights in the Aegean. A range of issues in addition to the Cyprus problem had arisen to bedevil relations with Turkey,

---

[49] Andreas Papandreou, *Edafiki Akeraiotita kai Ethniki Exoteriki Politiki,* 3rd ed. (Athens, 1978), 3–20, 37–70. PASOK put forward four goals in its program: national independence, the sovereignty of the people, social liberation, and democratic processes. Cited in Dimitri C. Constas, "Greek Foreign Policy Objectives: 1974-1986," in *Greece on the Road to Democracy: From the Junta to PASOK 1974-1986,* Speros Vryonis, Jr., ed. (New Rochelle, NY, 1991), 43.

including the limits of territorial waters and the Aegean continental shelf, command and control over air space between the two countries, defense fortifications on Greek islands in the eastern Aegean, and the treatment of respective minorities in each other's country. On these matters, Papandreou was militant in his defense of national interests, and he summed up his views in the phrase, "All Together for a New Greece, a Greece that belongs to the Greeks."[50]

Papandreou tempered his stand on all these issues when he was elected Greece's first socialist premier in the fall of 1981. Greece remained part of NATO, and Papandreou accepted agreements worked out with the commander of the alliance.[51]

During the 1980s the great breach that had opened within the nation as a result of the civil war gradually was closed. Greek Communists, who had spent decades in the Soviet bloc countries, returned to their homeland under a repatriation program proclaimed by Papandreou in the spring of 1983 which continued a process begun after the fall of the junta. After three decades of silence, the left now could openly give its version of the events in the 1940s. No longer labeled *andartes* (guerillas) who had fought against the nation as bandits *(symmorites)*, the Communists declared that they had been part of the resistance *(antistasi)*. In a dramatic break with a dark legacy of the post–civil war era, millions of files that had been created by the police on tens of thousands of citizens were to be destroyed in 1989.

After 1974 and into the 1980s, control of the government went from the center-right to the left of center, yet Greek foreign policy reflected a continuity in national concerns as well as the reality of the cold war and its shifting dynamics. With regard to national interests, all the heads of the government, from Karamanlis on, recognized that Greece had to adjust its foreign policy in light of the Turkish intervention in Cyprus in the summer of 1974. On the other hand, the development of détente with the Helsinki accords and the eurocommunist movement provided new opportunities for Greece in the context of the cold war. The convergence of the two sets of foreign policy

---

50 Andreas Papandreou, *Poreia Pros tin Allagi,* 2nd ed. (Athens, 1980), 3–23; Augustinos, "Development though the Market in Greece," 122–23; and Couloumbis, *United States, Greece, and Turkey,* 117–24.

51 Augustinos, "Development though the Market in Greece," 122–25; Constas, "Greek Foreign Policy Objectives," 48; and Thanos Veremis, "Greece and NATO," in *Greece on the Road to Democracy: From the Junta to PASOK 1974-1986,* Speros Vryonis, Jr., ed. (New Rochelle, NY, 1991), 71–78.

considerations determined Greek policies and the country's position vis-à-vis neighboring states.

As the issues that divided Greece and Turkey multiplied, it was only logical to seek a bettering of relations with the other states in the Balkans. The New Democracy governments of Karamanlis and his successor George Rallis stepped up efforts at rapprochement with Greece's northern neighbors. Rather than to try for a breakthrough in relations, the goal was to improve understanding and promote greater cooperation by seeking to overcome the ethnic and nationalist-related problems that had created difficulties in the past.

Contradictory though it seems, issues related to nationality and ethnicity could both hasten and hinder accommodation between the Greek government and those in the other Balkan countries. Athens and Sofia, for example, shared a concern over the Muslim minorities in their respective states, though each government approached the problem in a significantly different manner. Similarly, Greece appreciated Belgrade's position on the question of the Albanians in Kosovo province. Consequently, Greece's political contacts with Yugoslavia and Bulgaria grew, as did bilateral agreements for economic cooperation in the late 1970s.

During the 1980s the leftist PASOK government of Papandreou sought to increase and strengthen those ties, especially by appealing to its neighbors to support the creation of a nuclear-free zone in the Balkans. It sought to expand a series of meetings on matters of common interest including trade, transport, tourism, terrorism, commerce, industry, and agriculture that were held in the various Balkan capitals starting in 1976. However, the potential for interstate tension over nationality issues limited the degree of cooperation between Greece and its Balkan neighbors. Athens remained sensitive to the status under atheistic communism of the Greek-speaking minority in Albania, the northern Epirotes *(Voreioepirotes),* and to Belgrade's promotion of a Macedonian republic with a distinct ethnic identity in Yugoslavia. Likewise, the Greek government took note of the nationalist overtones in Bulgarian educational culture that Todor Zhivkov's daughter, Lyudmila, encouraged.[52]

Turning to national interests relating to Turkey, one must recognize the prime importance of the Cyprus problem. In the aftermath of the Turkish invasion of the island in July 1974, the problem became synonymous for the Greek public with foreign meddling in the nation's affairs and became a

---

[52] Evangelos Kofos, "Greece and the Balkans 1974-1986," in *Greece on the Road to Democracy: From the Junta to PASOK 1974-1986,* Speros Vryonis, Jr., ed. (New Rochelle, NY, 1991), 98–117; and Demetres Michalopoulos, "PASOK and the Eastern Bloc: A Growing Relationship," in *Greece under Socialism,* Nikolaos A. Stavrou, ed. (New Rochelle, NY, 1988), 346–62.

question of the very survival of Greek integrity and sovereignty. Among political leaders, including Karamanlis and Andreas Papandreou, Turkey's actions in Cyprus brought a new and harsh reality. The Anatolian state was revealed to have foresworn Atatürk's policy of not seeking territorial aggrandizement; the advance into Cyprus signalled to the Greeks a Turkish willingness to pursue the politics of expansionism not only on that island but in the Aegean and in Thrace as well.

This assessment of Turkish tactics raised the question of an appropriate national response. It was a problematic issue for it required reconciling nationalist sentiment with political reality, the very problem that had bedeviled the realization of the *Megali Idea* in the nineteenth century. Not only was Greece unable to project its national will through power, as the fate of Cyprus in 1974 made painfully clear, but it perceived its superpower patron, the United States, to favor a settlement of the problem that was potentially injurious to Greek national interests. Moreover, there was the matter of Greece's relation to the state of Cyprus. Was Athens the arbiter of national purpose and Nicosia the faithful extension of the center's will? Or were Greece and Cyprus two distinct states, each with its own but congruent political program? The government in Athens decided that in order to best defend the interests of Cyprus, Greece must show its support for the island without trying to decide what policies it should follow.

Karamanlis implemented this view by letting the government of Cyprus take the lead in trying to deal with the divided condition of the island. The Cyprus problem was not to be seen as a Greek-Turkish issue; Greece was an interested supporter, not the patron of Cyprus. Resolving the problem meant backing the government of Cyprus in the international arena, namely, in the United Nations and the European Community, where third parties could promote a solution. On the island, Athens urged that the two communities initiate talks that might end the presence of occupying troops and the de facto partition.[53]

By the time PASOK came to power in 1981, little progress had been made toward resolving the problem. Before becoming premier, Papandreou had sharply criticized the New Democracy government for working within the Western political alliance, which included the United States and Turkey, to seek a solution. PASOK agreed with New Democracy that the Cyprus problem ought to be resolved through recourse to intercommunal talks and to international bodies, but the leftist party was more explicit in associating Cyprus with the Hellenic nation and more vocal in its call for greater efforts among states, aligned and nonaligned, to settle the problem.

---

[53] Coufoudakis, "Greece and the Problem of Cyprus 1974-1986," 123–31.

Once in power, PASOK's foreign policy initiatives followed its declared position. However, despite seeking out new support from abroad and urging the Cyprus government to pursue actively intercommunal talks, it was unable to effect a resolution of the issue. Indeed, in November 1983, the Turkish-Cypriot leader, Rauf Denktash, organized a separate Turkish state on the island. Greece worked assiduously to see that it went unrecognized internationally except by Turkey. Papandreou was firm and forthright in associating Cyprus with Greek national interests and in warning Turkey to cease any efforts to change the status of any recognized territory, Greek and Cypriot, in the Aegean. "We have repeatedly warned our partners in the EEC and our allies in NATO that any Turkish attack on Greek-Cypriot positions would be a first step to the progressive shrinking of Greek national territory."[54]

The last decade of the twentieth century began ambivalently for Greece. Undoubtedly, the country had made significant progress in its social and national advancement—the standard of living had risen, as had the nation's international standing as a member of the increasingly prominent European Community—but there was also an economic and political reckoning to come. Inflation was eating away at consumer confidence as the inflated state service sector held down productive efficiency while keeping up the public sector debt. The country found itself in the worst economic straits since the early 1950s.

In foreign affairs the demise of communism throughout Eastern Europe seemed to presage an era of better relations between the states in the Western alliance and their neighbors. Paradoxically, the dawn of political pluralism in the former one-party states was a catalyst for increasing state instability in the Balkans after years of a stable, cold war status quo. Altogether, it was a time of both promise and some peril for Greece, which led to pointed questions about the ability of the country's leaders to define and implement an effective national policy (see Document 4).

In April 1990, Constantine Mitsotakis, leader of the New Democracy Party and a member of George Papandreou's Center Union Party in the 1960s, became prime minister. After three elections in less than a year, Mitsotakis managed to gain a majority in parliament.

Foreign issues remained for many Greeks the real challenge to national integrity and a sense of identity. While disputes with Turkey over Aegean questions remained and the Cyprus problem had yet to be resolved, and despite some renewed interest by the administration of President George Bush

---

54 Quoted in Constas, "Greek Foreign Policy Objectives," 53. See Coufoudakis, "Greece and the Problem of Cyprus 1974-1986," 131–37; Yannis Kapsis, "The Philosophy and Goals of PASOK's Foreign Policy," in *Greece under Socialism,* Nikolaos A. Stavrou, ed. (New Rochelle, NY, 1988), 44–57.

in Washington, highly charged and potentially serious issues rose up between Greece and the states on its northern frontier.

In Albania the abysmal failure of communism as a socioeconomic system was compounded by the unwillingness of many Albanians to remain in their country now that it was disintegrating. Greece, seeing itself as the protector of the *Voreioepirotes,* spoke out for the rights of the Greek minority in Albania and tried to secure their interests in negotiations with the Communists, who still clung to power during late 1990 and early 1991. The problem quickly turned from one of protecting the Greek minority in Albania to coping with them in Greece. As thousands of Albanians, mostly ethnic Greeks at first, poured into Greece as refugees, the Mitsotakis government was forced into the uncomfortable position of working with the Albanian government to try to stem the exodus. The government in Athens was not prepared to absorb the inflow, even if they were the Greek minority.[55]

The events that led to the disintegration of Yugoslavia were perceived in Athens as a far more serious threat to the country's national interests than the Albanian refugee problem. With declarations of independence by the former Yugoslav republics of Slovenia, Croatia, Bosnia, and Macedonia, Greece feared the development of a twofold danger. On one hand, concern mounted over the potential for religiously based nationalism among Muslims in southeastern Europe. There was talk of an "Islamic arc" on Greece's borders stretching from Albania through southern Yugoslavia, including the Muslims in Bulgaria and Greece and even across Asia, which could become a destabilizing element in the nation-state system if appeals were made to religious loyalties.[56]

The second danger—far more threatening in Greek national thinking—was the effort by the leaders of the former Yugoslav republic of Macedonia to seek international recognition as an independent nation-state bearing that name. To the Greeks, this was nothing less than an illegitimate appropriation of their national past. A massive rally was organized in February 1992 in Thessaloniki, the country's second largest city and capital of the province of Macedonia, in support of the government's stand on this issue. The Greek government's campaign to block international recognition of the Southern Slav state as long as the name Macedonia was involved was not simply the response of nationalist sentiment. The attempt to establish a state called Macedonia conjured up the memory of events at the turn of the century

---

[55] *New York Times* (2 January 1991), 3; (14 January 1991), 4; and (22 January 1991), 9.

[56] *Athena Magazine* 51 (November 1991), 345–47.

when nationalist campaigns were waged over the same territory. Though diplomats in other European countries saw little for Greece to fear from a small, landlocked state, the issue went to the heart of what was perhaps a more basic question for many Greeks—whether or not the Greeks were a nation united and able to maintain their collective identity.

With its entry into the European Community in 1981, Greece was poised to play a role in the increasingly dynamic and vigorous culture and economy of the West. At the end of 1991 it was invited to join the Western European Union.[57] Yet with troubled conditions in the Balkans and the persistence of outstanding issues with Turkey, as Constantine Karamanlis had noted in 1959, Greece might be part of the West, but it still felt the need for security because of its geographical position.

Conclusion

Examining the vicissitudes of Hellenism, embodied in the development of the Greek nation-state and the culture of its people over more than a century, one can discern a few fundamental points. Since its inception as an independent state, Greece has had to cope with the twin limitations of small state status and a strategic location. Recognizing those limitations and trying to offset them, Greece has turned to great power patronage. In the first half of the twentieth century Great Britain filled this role, which was later taken over by the United States. While Greece benefited at times from this relationship, it also was forced by it to rein in or even to abandon nationalist interests, especially with regard to territory. Despite its small power status, the Greek state took it upon itself to embody Hellenism and to defend the interests of the Greek nation wherever there were communities of compatriots. This meant, however, as in the case of Cyprus, the development of tensions between the

---

57 *Athena Magazine* 52 (December 1991), 362–72. A few Greek intellectuals saw their nation losing its identity by becoming more closely linked with Europe. A leading exponent of this view is Stelios Ramfos, whose writings began to appear in the mid–1970s. He gained a small following in the succeeding decade. Philosophically akin to Aleksandr Solzhenitsyn, Ramfos believes that the Orthodox faith and the demotic Greek language are the main supports of the "living tradition" that is Hellenism. See Ramfos, *I Glossa kai i Paradosi,* 2nd ed. (Athens, 1984), 25–40; and Ramfos, *Topos Iperouranios,* 2nd ed. (Athens, 1983), 32–46.

pole and the periphery whose views did not necessarily coincide. For much of the twentieth century, Greece was a nation divided by politics, but those politics only reflected the social, regional, and historical divisions that belied its seeming homogeneity.

In essence, Hellenism for the Greeks has been the imperative to maintain their country's territorial integrity and cultural uniqueness. That is to say, it has been the means to guarantee the physical survival of the people. That uniqueness in cultural matters, paradoxically, has been best served by remaining open to varied influences from abroad and within, as writers such as Theotokas and Seferis argued. Otherwise, the national character could become noncreative, repeating formulaic slogans, as it did in the wake of the civil war.

Nationalism has served the Greeks in their effort to maintain themselves as a distinct people, but it has also created tensions in interstate relations and complicated issues between members of the nation within and without the state frontiers. Hellenism at its best has been the creative synthesis between a people and the culture they have used as a mediating context with the rest of the world through history.

6

Nation, National Minorities, and Nationalism in Twentieth-Century Hungary

by Tibor Frank

Document 1

from Oszkár Jászi on Forcible Magyarization (1912).[1]

The politics of forced assimilation differs sharply in its means and result from state to state because it is undertaken under different economic, cultural, religious, and moral...circumstances. Yet, in its essence it is everywhere the same...

If we do not forget that these events are not the basic factors of national movements, but the necessary results of specific historical and economic development, then we will learn very much by establishing the laws of forced assimilation irrespective of where they occur...

The patriotism of an oppressed nation will have the characteristics of a democratic movement even if it follows clerical or nationalistic flags because the protection of the mother tongue and self-government represent the minimal preconditions for each nation's cultural life... The national movement of an oppressed nationality is a mass movement of this kind. Opposing

1 Oszkár Jászi, *A nemzeti államok kialakulása és a nemzeti kérdés* (Budapest: Grill Károly, 1912), 485–94. Translated by P. F. Sugar.

it, the ruling clique's cries of protecting the state against treason only protects the momentary class interests of the feudal-bureaucratic element.

The unavoidable result of forced assimilation is that it demoralizes the politically active segment of the ruling nation while it strengthens the healthy segment of the oppressed people and develops it mentally and morally... In the national struggle, I came across only two vocal elements of the ruling nation's protagonists: the honest, but narrow-minded noisy patriot and the shady businessman incapable of looking into your eyes... It is impossible to shoot constantly at a badly equipped or defenseless people from well-financed and protected positions without becoming morally degraded and acquiring the attitude of a paid gladiator. On the other hand, those who fight facing constant danger not for their own advantage, but for a distant future will develop a better critical sense... This is why in our country the Slovak and Romanian middle class is ahead of the Hungarian in intelligence and willingness to sacrifice...

Forced assimilation produces a fight for a minimal cultural existence and in its fight against the oppressor eliminates all differences be they ideological, religious or that of class... The same struggle is the reason why the struggling nation is more bigoted, religious and backward. This nation judges everything from the angle of its nationality problem and finds protection in its long-standing and religious organizations... The oppressed nation is almost incapable of seeing problems other than its struggle...

Where economic and other means do not support the work of schools, the linguistic result of forced assimilation will be minimal and lead to the decline of intellectual values. We know very well the reasons for this neglect. Yet, it is not unnecessary to point out that where forced assimilation brings linguistic results, its serves the interests of the oppressed nation because it creates a bilingual social stratum...

We cannot be surprised by the failure of forced assimilation, especially in the case of Hungary. If this policy would, indeed, be a rational argument aiming at the common good, we could easily show the unacceptability of our nationality policy by the following reasoning:

Let us look abroad. In spite of their military and economic might, 52 million Germans were incapable of forcibly assimilating 3 million Poles, 210,000 Frenchmen, 160,000 Danes; 42 million Englishmen, in spite of being a world power, could not subjugate 3 million Celts and long ago adopted a policy of broad liberalism and willingness to cooperate in dealing with them; the colossus of 84 million Russians is incapable of dealing with 7 million Poles, 3 million Germans, with the same number of Armenians, and not even with 5 million Jews who are "born renegades." Who is either naive or stupid enough to believe that 9 million Hungarians are capable of assimilating the other half of the country? There are this many Hungarians only according to census figures, but in fact their ranks are saturated with only halfway or minimally assimilated elements and they must deal with colonizing Austria without any military of their own. What is involved is not a small number of people in the diaspora. About the same number of Germans, Slovaks and Romanians live in Hungary as the total population of Denmark, Alsace-Lorraine, Greece, Norway or Serbia. Is not every million a waste of money we spend to magyarize our nationalities when we earn only their hate and distrust in place of our aim?...

Feudalism, the militaristic rule based on the large agrarian estates, can still maintain itself for a while. In multinational states it even plays the role of defending the fatherland. Its days are, nevertheless, limited in our country. Because it can maintain itself only with force, corruption or extraordinary legal measures and because it can live only in an atmosphere that lacks culture and thrives on superstition, it will, sooner or later, come into conflict with all productive elements of society... The old feudal locks cannot control any longer the giant energy of the flood created by popular culture and capitalism. That these newly developing energies explode as national struggles in areas with mixed populations is not the fault of the industrial tidal wave, but that of the useless old locks... The inevitability which forced the industrial states, beginning with England and Belgium, to take the liberal road and which will soon give Ireland her home rule, will continue to move from West to East... The same forces will also change the direction of Hungary's nationality policy... The half state [that of nationalities] is as yet weaker than the Hungarian, but it is already strong enough to demand important compromises... These compromises have become unavoidable... We need a democratic popular parliament a thousand times more than we need the forcible assimilation of the children of the nationalities. We need a liberal law of association a thousand times more than the singing of our national anthem in Balázsfalva. We need a thousand times more a land reform than we need a notary public speaking Hungarian in Trencsény. For a developing Hungarian industry we would gladly dispense with single-language shop names in the miserable Romanian or Slovak villages.

Document 2

from Count Kunó Klebelsberg, "Hungarian Neonationalism" (1928).[2]

The individual—and the nation as well—not only suffers, but also profits when he passes through a crisis. His soul, which is transported into a new world, is reborn. For us Hungarians, the tragedy of losing the World War was turned into a double tragedy by the fact that *the revolution as well as the counterrevolution proved to be sterile for the soul.*[3] They did not bring a single new idea, a single new thought that could have led to a fresh national life. The nation has simply rejected the revolution of Mihály Károlyi and Béla Kún. When, during the winter of 1919–1920, the public was voting for the first time in a general secret election, *it almost unanimously turned against the political movements of 1918–1919.* The best proof that the movement of Károlyi and Kún was merely an uprising and not a revolution *is its rejection by the nation itself.* A rejected revolution is something quite unique in history. *But the counterrevolution was no luckier.* Recently, searching for our intellectual history, I leafed through the records of our first national assembly looking for new ideals or at least new ideas or formulations. We can find speeches which were interrupted with great applause after almost every sentence. Yet when we ask, "Who was the speaker?" we find that we cannot remember one or the other and *do not know that he lived.* Even if we go through the speeches of better known individuals, we find nothing but the *echo of what was said at the constitutional convention at Weimar or the Austrian Parliament.* The order of the day was mutual recrimination and the drastic rejection of the dualist period without the presentation of any equally useful positive solution. Consequently, it was the task of the Bethlen cabinet *to liquidate the revolution and counterrevolution and bring back normal life.* It is noteworthy that *not a single achievement of either the revolution or the counterrevolution was retained...*

---

2 Count Kunó Klebelsberg, *"A magyar neonacionalizmus," Pesti Napló* (1 January 1928), reprinted in Count Kunó Klebelsberg, *Neonacionalizmus* (Budapest: Athenaeum, 1928), 120–26; and in *Tudomány, kultúra, politika. Gróf Klebelsberg Kunó válogatott beszédei és irásai (1917-1932)* ("Scholarship, Culture, Politics. Select Speeches and Writings by Count Kunó Klebelsberg, 1917-1932"), Ferenc Glatz, ed. (Budapest: Europa Könyvkiadó, 1990), 434–39. The above translation is by P. F. Sugar.

3 Note: emphasis in original throughout.

This is a great misfortune because in those days the soul of the nation liquified in the hellfire of the catastrophes and could have been reshaped with ease. We must melt down the old bell before we can cast a new one in a new shape. If a statesman of genius would have led either the revolution or the counterrevolution, *he could have truly reshaped the Hungarian general attitude,* because everything in this country was in transition. By today the fire of catastrophes is extinguished, the political atmosphere cooled down, everything became more rigid, more difficult to shape. At the end of 1919 and the beginning of 1920 everything was as malleable as wax which was easy to shape. Today, everything is as hard as marble, which can be shaped only with steel chisels and hammers.

If we ask, "What is the most important talent a head of state can have?" we will find that nothing is more important than is the ability to select good prime ministers. When we wish to understand what the reason was for France's greatness in the seventeenth century, it was the appointment of Richelieu by Louis XIII, the selection of Mazarin by his widow, Anne of Austria, and that of Colbert by Louis XIV. In the nineteenth century Queen Victoria's selection of a succession of great statesmen accounts for the greatness of her empire. William I achieved the same result by selecting Roon, Moltke, and Bismarck. An objective student of our history will find that *Francis Joseph I was one of our greatest kings, but was not the most perspicacious in selecting his army commanders and statesmen.* The lasting merit of Hungary's regent was giving the nation a true political leader by selecting Count István Bethlen, who calmly waited for the right moments *to solve the unresolved problems that had to be eliminated before one could even talk about consolidation.*

Helped by the political vision of Count István Bethlen we reached a point where *defeated small stump Hungary in many respects presents a better consolidated picture than do the so-called victors.* István Bethlen built a solid platform on which the nation can work with confidence. Almost without notice, a new country emerged from the ruins, standing on the old foundation but with new strength. A certain *new public spirit is emerging* which is still not quite conscious, but is already at work. This new public spirit retains very little from the counterrevolution, nothing from the revolution, nothing from the world's revolutionary suffering, but it is not yet clearly formulated. *The most noble task of Hungarian publicists and journalists would be to bring this subconscious public spirit from the nation's soul to the conscious surface and act as its leaders and directors.*

I am trying to bring two supreme concepts to the nation through the school system: *a nationalism resting on a moral basis and the idea of economic productivity.* I must call the national feeling and concept which I try to cultivate with the help of Hungarian schools *"neonationalism."* It is neonationalism in spite of the fact that we, Hungarians, are nationalists longer than any other nation living in Europe.... In this sense, nationalism is not new but very old, but its content is new. What was the content of Hungarian nationalism for the last four centuries? In the first place it was a struggle in the face of Austrian centralism and germanization. This question became moot when we separated from Austria. Then it was the struggle of Hungarian nationalism to inculcate the Hungarian state concept into the souls of those nations that became numerous in our fatherland during the years in which Turks and Germans ravaged the country. This attempt also became moot because the Treaty of Trianon tore our nationalities away from us. Thus Hungarian nationalism lost its most important features. As a result, *we must find new aims for old feelings...* [As a minister] I can speak only about two goals: we want to be an *educated and well off* nation, in other words a racially more important nation, than are the people living around us.

From the point of view of nationalism the *European situation* is also of great interest. Those countries in which the various forms of socialism gained strong positions and in which, as a result, anti-nationalism became strong *lost their great power position.* Bolshevism has excluded Russia from the community of nations for all practical purposes. How different from it is on the other hand the steadily growing strength of Italy. Right after the war, anti-nationalism became strong in Italy also, preventing its government from reaping the fruit of its sacrifices and victory at the peace negotiations. It is no wonder that Italian patriots are troubled by a feeling that *during the peace negotiations they were the least successful of the victors.* Worse than the failure of foreign policy was the domestic situation. *Communism became more and more bold,* and an endless wave of strikes brought the Italian economy to a practical standstill. In this tragic situation *Mussolini* appeared...awakening Italian nationalism, defeating the various types of anti-nationalism...making the nation aware of the fact that they were victors. From this lately acquired elevating feeling of victory stemmed the strength for those great achievements which even those must admit who travel in Italy with hostile eyes and hearts.

When I ask, "What is the inner content of fascism?" I can find it only in this Italian nationalism, which also has new aims. These are the colonizing of the empty lands in Campagna and Sardinia; the drying up and making into arable land the malarial sea coast; the acquiring of colonies where Italy's surplus population can find a home on Italian soil; the creation of an army, navy and air force allowing Italy to take on the role once played by Venice in the Eastern Mediterranean, the Balkans and the Levant; and, after completing the resorgimento, the creation of new goals and ideals in the name of a nationalism created by fascism.

The motto paralleling fascism in Italy is always: *we want to be rich.* The goal is the renewing of what the rich Italian states, Venice, Genoa and Florence, had in the late Middle Ages. In contrast, it is typical of the general

Hungarian thinking that it still sees as heroes the happy-go-lucky cardplayers who, in the middle of the last century, lost their entire fortune in one night. A *truly romantic image of prodigality and risk taking lives in our country,* and our economic history does not mention those who were successful in producing tangible goods. Even disregarding the important creators of tangible goods, a magnificent process is taking place before our eyes: the creation of small farms on the Alföld [the central Hungarian plain]. This is nothing else but the purchase or renting of land outside of the villages' inner land belt, of lands devastated and left empty since the days of Turkish rule. This is not only a movement of repopulation, but is also the *acquisition of wealth,* the most fruitful work a Hungarian can perform. Now we follow the people bringing elementary schools to their new habitats and take to them the religious and national ideals, the ideals of Hungarian neonationalism.

We do not want to sit always in the half-shade; we do not want always to suffer, be needy, die or live hand-to-mouth. *With the might of morals and knowledge we want to raise to the square the fruitfulness of Hungarian labor.* As a result of this fruitful labor, we want to become better off, more independent, and above all, we want to be more *devotedly and consciously Hungarians.* This is the healthy aim of Hungarian neonationalism.

Document 3

from Erik Molnár, "The National Question" (1969).[4]

All of us remember the October days of 1956 and the slogan of the counter-revolution: whoever is a Hungarian is on our side. This slogan tried to mobilize the national sentiment and the communality of the national being of the Hungarians against the proletarian national community. Several people could be fooled by this slogan. Are Hungarians not united by language, culture, customs and a common fate, in short by everything that bourgeois science used to call the nation's communality? Does the individual not share the good or bad fortune of the nation? Does it not follow from it that we must consider the nation's interest the supreme measure of individual action?

History formulates the crucial questions differently. At the deciding moment of history the question is: on whose side are we? The true question

---

4 In Erik Molnár, *Válogatott Tanulmányok* (Select Studies) (Budapest: Akadémiai Kiadó, 1969), 383–85, 392–400. Translated by P. F. Sugar.

in October 1956 was again: shall we be on the side of those who wanted to correct their mistakes and continue to develop socialism further or on the side of those who knowingly or unknowingly were working for the reestablishment of capitalism?

History poses its own basic questions from the angle of class war and that of the national question. This is the position of Marxism. Here, nevertheless, Marxism encounters the bourgeois-national ideology which states that the nation is an eternal category. Even if it admits that it originated in historical development, it looks at it as an eternal category, the basic category of communal life. Superficially it might appear that this bourgeois explanation can find arguments even in Marxism. They can truly argue that Marxism considers the nation the fruit of historical development. But, does Marxism—even if only with some reservations—not speak about the feudal nation that predates the bourgeois nation, and is the feudal nation not a historical reality? Does the socialist nation not follow the bourgeois nation according to Marxism? Is it not also true that according to Marxism during the years of development the essence of the nation remains unchanged and it is only the social form that is changing?

The above argument is typical of the bourgeois-metaphysical reasoning which sees permanence as the essence of history. The historical approach demands that we learn to see the changing content behind the seemingly unchanging forms. During historical development the slave society was followed by the feudal and this by the bourgeois and this again by the socialist society. The specific mechanism and communal ideology corresponds to any given class structure. It remains specific even if it should be clothed in the garb of a previous social order. This is something that the bourgeois view of history does not accept because of its specific class essence. In this question the basic assumptions of Marxist and bourgeois historical approaches clash. These differences cannot be eliminated, just as the interest of the bourgeoisie and the proletariat cannot be brought to a common denominator.

Marxism sees in the nation a peculiar fruit of bourgeois development. Accordingly Stalin defined the concept of nationalism as follows: "The nation is the historically developed community of people which was based on the spiritual essence found in the communality of language, territory, economic life and culture." ...Territorial unity can take two forms. The first which, according to Lenin, is typical and normal, is the one in which a given nation's territory corresponds to a political unit limited to its members; this is the nation-state. The second form is the multinational state in which each nation's living space is incorporated in a common state structure. In this case the common market develops within the framework of the common state under the leadership of one nation which oppresses the others...

It happens that those whom Marxist criticism excludes from the bourgeois fortress of a nation that moved beyond the historical and class development turn to the concept of the fatherland. Yet the concept of fatherland and nation are seen, even by bourgeois ideologists, as the manifestation of the same essence. In this they are right....

Marxist historiography had and has a direction which separates the concept of fatherland from that of nation. It sees in the latter the fruit of bourgeois development and in the fatherland a force that determined the behavior of the people even prior to the development of the bourgeoisie. I have in mind those historical studies which see, in the common struggle of the people, in essence the feudal peasantry, with the lords against foreign conquerors the expression of the love of the homeland. Yet the feudal order is a class order in which the exploited peasantry is separated by the sharpest and most naked hostility from the lords. The feudal state is a class state which does not serve the common interests of the exploiters and the exploited. It is the collective power tool which the lordly class used against the peasantry. This is such a basic assumption of historical materialism that its correctness cannot be questioned by a Marxist unless he wants to take the road to revisionism. The correctness of this assumption is also proven by the long series of jacqueries[5]...

The antipathy which societies on a low level of development feel for those speaking a foreign language or practicing different customs cannot be classified as parts of national feeling or national consciousness.... The antipathy felt for things foreign which is joined by the bragging based on a given society's group characteristics is, by itself, not a motif of political action, but only the ideological expression of the political and economic conflicts of interests that act as a true motivating force when those involved belong to different ethnic groups. In the Hungarian Middle Ages the hatred of everything German was simply the ideological expression of that struggle which the Hungarian lords fought with those of German origin for their share of power and wealth. Modern nationalism is not choosy and uses this primitive antipathy in the service of its class interests....

The *Communist Manifesto* unveiled the error perpetrated by the bourgeoisie with the national spirit when it stated that in bourgeois society "there is no place for workers." To this it promptly added that "the proletariat must transform itself into a nation," meaning that it has to create the fatherland of the workers and all other working people in place of the bourgeois fatherland. In what follows, we will try to show, using Hungarian history as an example, how the socialist nation developed....

---

[5] Note: peasant revolts.

We can state that in Hungary subsistence agriculture remained dominant until the end of the thirteenth century. While urban development began in the fourteenth century, production for the market did not create a unified country even as late as the eighteenth century. The feudal class-society was shaped in the eleventh and twelfth centuries. It was at that time that Hungarian workers lost their freedom and sank into serfdom.... The feudal state organization, which kept the serfs in their place, also divided Hungary into large, estates-based mini-states. In the fourteenth century, a lord of a large estate had his own army and acted as administrator and judge of his serfs without any limits [on his power]....

In the eleventh and twelfth centuries the members of the ruling feudal class were tied to each other and the king only by the personal loyalty they owed to the latter. This tie was by nature very brittle. The lordly factions fighting for power had no qualms in using German or Byzantine help, disregarding the fact that this endangered the independence of the country. Even more questionable were the forced loyalties of the serfs tying them to their lords. When, in the thirteenth century, the Czechs invaded the country, the serfs did not fight the Czechs, but used this opportunity to liberate themselves.

...As a result of the alliance of the king and the nobility, the noble[-dominated] county came into being in the thirteenth century, and in the fourteenth the estate-based Diet, representing the nobility, was established.... Thus, between the thirteenth and fifteenth centuries the estate-based monarchy came into existence with the king exercising little or—under king Matthias—greater power. Paralleling this development, the feeling of communality changed as early as in the thirteenth century.... A royal document from the mid-fourteenth century refers to "the Hungarian national state." Obviously, the feudal estates-state was not the state of the peasantry but that of the nobility and [this document] refers to the nobility when mentioning the nation.... The peasant had no honor, no glory, no reputation. These were reserved for the military nobility....

The ruling class—the social unit that was the Hungarian nation since the thirteenth and fourteenth centuries—was of mixed origin when we speak of the nobility. When the state was established, this group was made up of Hungarians, Slavic and German elements which were later joined by those of Croat origin. During the Middle Ages further additions were made. These came either from those who immigrated or from domestic elements, Slovaks and Romanians, who were able to improve their status. What united the ruling class was not ethnic origin and characteristics, but common class privileges. The feudal "Hungarian nation" was as multi-national as were the working people of the country and, consequently, very different from the single-language national state. It should be noted that the majority of the Hungarian nobility was ethnically and linguistically Hungarian....

We have no information telling us that Hungarian, Slovak, Romanian and peasants of the other nationalities fought among themselves. But we know that the Romanian serfs fought together with the Hungarians against the Romanian and Hungarian members of the nobility in 1437 and 1514....

After the battle of Mohács [1526] the political situation changed. Facing the Turkish danger, Hungary was forced to rely on the protection of a foreign power, the realm of the Habsburgs. Soon, the Hungarian nobility came face-to-face with the absolutist attempts of the Habsburgs. This double pressure did not prevent the nobility, protected by Habsburg power, from increasing the exploitation of the serfs. This exploitation grew to previously unknown magnitude especially in the sixteenth and seventeenth centuries. Under these circumstances, the weight of the absolutist state, taxes and the misdeed of the imperial professional soldiers rested heavier and heavier on the shoulders of the serfs. This explains why the serfs not only joined the estate-based revolts against Habsburg absolutism, but they even started the last one of these which was led by Francis Rákoczi....

The nobility never acknowledged the right of the serfs to a fatherland, and continued to hold on to the concepts of the nobilitarian nation. The Peace of Szatmár, with which the nobility protected its privileges, was a compromise with absolutism, but gave nothing to the peasantry. With the end of the noble-peasant cooperation, the patriotic element disappeared from the peasantry's ideology. By the second half of the eighteenth century, the peasantry already looked to the Habsburgs, not without some results, to have its load lightened....

At the end of the eighteenth and the beginning decades of the nineteenth centuries industrial shops appeared in Hungary. The nobility turned gradually to market-oriented agriculture. The major outlines of the country's market began to emerge. The bourgeois element remained weak. The politically ruling element remained the nobility. The nobility's attempt to develop a market-oriented agriculture was hindered by the feudal structure and by the colonial position of the country in the Habsburg Empire. This also made industrial development difficult. This situation and the fear that the Habsburgs might take advantage of the peasantry's hatred against them, pushed the nobility to take the road of bourgeois reform—of emancipation and the demand for independence. It wanted to achieve this double goal by maintaining its own rule.... The struggle to achieve the program of the nobility was paralleled by the transformation of the concept of nation into a bourgeois definition. This national program had to be promulgated in a multi-national state....

After the failure of the 1848 revolution and the defeat of the war of independence, the 1867 Compromise realized the nobility's program of the bourgeois nation based on another compromise as far as independence was concerned. Thus, the bourgeois nation of Hungary was only a misshapen form when compared to its classic French model. The reason for this was not the limited independence of the nation. According to Lenin, when the Hungarians tried to safeguard the unity of Austria-Hungary after 1867, "they did this in the interest of national independence" which "could be totally eliminated by the rapacious and strong neighbors." ...Engels also believed, as becomes obvious from a letter he wrote to Kautsky, that the Compromise of 1867 sufficiently guaranteed Hungary's national independence to open the road leading to internal class war. The Hungarian national state was not misshapen because it was a multi-national state. The Hungarian nation ruled the other nationalities. The concept of the nation-state is compatible with the oppression of other nationalities in one or another form. The Hungarian bourgeois nation was misbegotten and remained misbegotten during its entire existence because it was not established by the bourgeoisie, by a revolutionary destruction of the feudals, but was established by the feudals themselves who accepted into the feudal nation protected by "the defenses of the constitution" the peasants and the bourgeoisie.... The leading political class of the bourgeois Hungarian nation, the one representing the large landowners and large capitalists, during and even after the years of Dualism...remained the feudal class which claimed this role as the "historical class" of the state. Consequently, bourgeois Hungary did not know the bourgeois institution of equality before the law when the rights of workers, especially agricultural workers, was involved.... It is certain that the many hundred thousands who emigrated from Hungary before the First World War did not leave as proud patriots....

In the second half of the 1930s the safeguarding of national independence, endangered by German fascism, became the cornerstone of the politics of the Hungarian Communist Party. The aim of the communists was to unite all progressive forces in a united national front for the protection of independence. Did this attempt contradict that statement in the *Communist Manifesto* that stated that the workers have no fatherland in the bourgeois order? Not in the least. The extension to Hungary of German fascism which destroyed all freedoms would have made the struggle for democratic rights and socialism much more difficult.... The partially realized national unity front during the war years was organized by the Communist Party; it was built around the core of the working class and working people filled its ranks. If we disregard its small bourgeois component, it was the germ of the burgeoning socialist nation, which was the task assigned to the working class by the Communist Party....

The nation, a real community formed by history, does not disappear when the proletariat takes political power into its hands. As a linguistic, political and economic unit the nation remains in existence and serves as the framework for the building of socialism.... The socialist national self-awareness has two components that are inseparable and influence each other completely. One of these is proletarian patriotism. Its source is the love of the progressive social order of the socialist fatherland. It expresses the willingness to defend the socialist homeland against the attacks of the imperialist bourgeois states....

The second component of socialist national self-awareness is the growing proletarian internationalism.... Beyond national unity, the bourgeoisie of each state is at war with that of all other states. In contrast, the interrelatedness of international considerations force the proletariat to embrace internationalism which is the framework within which each nation's working class fights its own bourgeoisie and its bourgeois-national ideology. Subsequently, socialist nations develop facing bourgeois nations. The class war between the proletariat and the bourgeoisie is by now a war between states, and in this war the proletarian nations cooperate as closely as possible. Proletarian internationalism is the ideological expression of this cooperation and is inseparably linked in socialist national self-awareness with socialist patriotism.

Document 4

from Sándor Csoóri, "What Is the Hungarian, Today?" (1989).[6]

What is the Hungarian now? This light and shadowed Janus-face? The "Yes" and the "No" together? The minority that found itself in politics and the masses that stay away from politics? The intellectuals on the one side, and everybody else on the other? A long time ago, Catholics opposed Protestants, anti-Habsburg faced pro-Habsburg, revolutionary 48-er hated the compromising 67 generation—and now comes this? No, no. The borders cross more mysterious forests. I sit on the streetcar, facing a purple-faced, sad man. I have known him for years, though we have never spoken. I know he drinks. From

6 In Sándor Csoóri, *Nappali hold* (Budapest: Püski, 1991), 146–54. Translated by T. Frank.

my briefcase I take the third number of the journal *Világosság* to read György Konrád's thoughts on Central Europe. We run through Margaret bridge when my fellow traveller starts speaking, as if to himself: "*Világosság?* [i.e., "light" in Hungarian] That's what we'd need here, too. For years, everybody spoke only of Marx and his younger brothers, Lenin, Brezhnev, Kádár. Now they speak of the Americans. There is the money of course. The dollar! I would like to live long enough to see someone turn to the Greek in this rotten country. Light? That's great, that could be their notion. To drink the poisonous glass at noon, not only when the candle is gone... I am just a poor furnace stoker in Bimbó Street, a nobody, but my father was a teacher of Latin and Greek and he always said: in the olden days they were few in number but of higher quality. Why are they not our examples? Furthermore, they lived on their islands spread out in the same way as we live in the world.... Kaposvár, Kolozsvár [Cluj-Napoca in Transylvania, Romania], San Francisco..., but their brain kept them together. But show me a Hungarian genius here at home! Whoever might have achieved something under Socialism—his head would have rolled."

I listen, nodding, to this unexpected monologue. Where does this voice come from, from what depth? I can only suspect that Life itself has been directly threatened in this disturbed man. Life, the natural impulse which was about to do something also for him, only to be drowned into coal dust and brandy....

How many of our lost compatriots warn us everywhere that we who want to reorganize this country in terms of public and national law have to rehabilitate legally not just our martyred dead but also threatened Life itself. The hurt impulses that reveal more about us than any word....

László Németh said in an article on the post–1848/49 period...: "Hungarians between 1850 and 1880 aged not just thirty years, but three hundred. They became older—more complex and evil. They turned the reforms of [István] Széchenyi into reality and got rid of his spirit."

We couldn't write any more gently about the period after 1956 either. The [János] Kádár régime, due to a guilty conscience or to the very logic of things, tried to make a lot of the ambitions of the revolution a reality, but wiped out of this nation the lofty spirit of the revolution which saved us morally in October [1956] in front of the world and of ourselves.

This political sterilization brought about a whole series of divisions. Contrary to the general practice of socialism worldwide, the system undoubtedly gave space to private life, to family life, and to the limited realization of the self, but it stretched freedom in these "private spheres" while narrowing life itself. The only one remaining biological life. Private persons could only become citizens through a one-sided compromise, out of actual politics, and undertaking the burdens of a mishandled economy. The overwork. The surplus problems. The "second economy" quickly became a real "labor front." An internal war with a double effect creating both successes and victims. Due to overwork, the mortality and disability rate of men of working age became threateningly high. The number of alcoholics, the ones shocked by "battlefield neurosis" rose equally high. And as we witnessed day after day, there is no one in a family or a community who did not also hurt others while hurting himself. There was no inventory needed to assess the amount of disruption heaped up in society through individuals giving up themselves, their friends, or trying to accommodate something which they deeply despised, just to secure their own separate freedoms.

By throwing its almost individually weakened citizens into a state of division, the state sinned against the very spirit of the nation. Yes, against the nation, which, ever since [the battle of] Mohács, is not identical with the state. The state, particularly ours, is first and foremost an economic and political structure, with drawn borders, while the nation is a spiritual, linguistic, historical formation, with traditions reaching beyond the borders, and common patterns. The nation cannot be directed by the poor tools of the state administration.

No wonder that the cause of the nation was handled by the [János] Kádár–[György] Aczél administration with mythological suspicion. They saw the seven-headed dragon of nationalism materialize in any life-sign of the Hungarian nation. Whenever the tragic decline of the population was mentioned, or when the protection of the Hungarians across the borders was urged....

There is no nation without its stubborn nationalists. Hungary too has its own. But it is not this manageable minority which I find dangerous but the majority which lives without consciousness and strength. As Imre Kovács said: "the people" means passivity, "the nation" is readiness. What were the Hungarians for decades? Threatening readiness? On the contrary. "Nationalism" was still a governmental stick over the head....

Eternally-losing Hungary had only one victorious moment since 1848, and that was 1956. And this again in a moral sense only. And we had to wait for its adequate recognition for thirty-three years! [Hungary] would have been satisfied during all those years to win at least the truth from the losers. But even that was beyond its spiritual strength.

In the 1960s when, as a not-quite-starting author, I began to survey the troubles that destroyed the body of the nation, starting as a titular nationalist, soon I became a dangerous one. My very ambition was enough for this "promotion." Yet I always liked the kind of Hungarians like [Ferenc] Kölcsey, [István] Széchenyi, [Zsigmond] Kemény, [Gyula] Illyés, [István] Bibó. The ones who considered and admitted everything, who doubted even themselves. Those who, if necessary, kept the nation alive with words about the death of the nation, as if our very existence would be not so much a historical, as an esthetic or moral existence.

This was, however, impossible. Among other reasons, because complete freedom would have made it necessary to confess everything or to doubt ourselves. Where one truth is forbidden, so is the other.

However astonishing or funny, for a long time I could only be a Hungarian in Hungary as if I had been invited to a masked ball. When I tried to work on the rebirth of the folk art, the folk-dance tradition, in other words popular culture, and the ill-famed critic of [the party paper] *Népszabadság* made fun of me—alleging that I wanted to carry Hungarians into a new Reform Age by teaching them the [old Hungarian folk dance] *csürdöngölö*—few people realized that through popular culture I wanted actually to lay down the foundations of a missing Hungarian consciousness. The revitalization of shared emotions, of a shared language, of a basically shared tradition that might have survived though in countless varieties. I thought if I could speak directly about who I was in a denationalizing system, I would do it indirectly. And if we cannot speak even a tiny bit about the Hungarians of Transylvania [in Romania], the [former Hungarian] Uplands [in Slovakia], the Voivodina [in former Yugoslavia], we have to turn to their songs again. Because the folksong from the *Mezőség* region [in Transylvania, Romania] is also Hungarian, and so is the one from around *Nyitra* [Nitra, in Slovakia], the *Kalotaszeg* area [in Transylvania, Romania], and *Beregszász* [Beregovo, in Ukraine]....

I do hope that once the history of the post–1956 opposition is written in Hungary, the objective historians of the period will not forget about the cultural opposition which appeared before the small though very significant radical opposition and which wanted to start changing the system not by mending the social structures or by reforming the Party, but by restoring the intellectual-spiritual self-consciousness of the Hungarians, by regalvanizing the weakened moral forces. As it appeared in the mask of popular culture, this group thought that it is more difficult to transform man than society, the system, so it is with him that the work of exploding must start. And, also, the darkest dangers of Hungarian history have never come from being beaten, but from having lost ourselves.

Out of this somewhat romantic though active idea, built around the study of the fatherland, through visiting Transylvania, frequenting dance-houses and organizing folk-camps, grew the crowd of the new populists or new nationalists, sometime around the turn of the 1960s or 1970s. Later the meeting at Lakitelek [1987] and, finally, the Hungarian Democratic Forum....

Let us consider now the first of our concerns, loaded with fear and tragic boredom. According to this, the Hungarians are a people like Hamlet, repeating since [the battle of] Mohács [1526] the monologue of "to be or not to be," starting from the Protestant preachers through [Miklós] Zrínyi, [Ferenc] Kölcsey, [István] Széchenyi to [Endre] Ady, László Németh, and Gyula Illyés. And I wouldn't mind if it was a mere fixed idea. But it is an experience written into our impulses. And this impulse keeps repeating all over again that we have to go down, to collapse, since we can only start something if thinking that way. And this is not the entire problem: even rising periods like the Age of Reform [1825–1848] or the intellectual achievement of the interwar era did not bring us any reward. By the time the crop was ready to be harvested, the hailstorm of world history smashed it.

The fear is therefore justified: if this was always the case in the past, why would it not happen in the future? Particularly when we are threatened by tragic contradictions. Here it is immediately the most devastating: we are liberated intellectually and spiritually, just when the material concerns drag us down deeper and deeper. That was the pattern at all the turning points in our life: our liberations brought, by the same token, yet another occupation. The Habsburgs after the Ottomans, the Soviets after the Germans. Let me continue the threats: the decrease of our population is alarming, series of epidemics destroy the people; we are spread out and dissolved in the world; and those of us beyond our borders, together with us in the mother country, are weakened daily by a "war in peace." As long as our neighbors tore away only parts of our land, the phantom pain could keep the nation somehow together, but even our own well-being in the world is attacked since the Hungarians of Kolozsvár [Cluj-Napoca in Romania], Kassa [Košice in Slovakia], or Léva [Levice in Slovakia] are deprived of their birthplace of 10–20 square meters, as well as their language.

Isn't the danger bigger than our actual political success? It would never occur to a Frenchman, an Englishman, an Italian, or a Russian that his nation could be broken by the next day. But it could occur to us! We are haunted by our own statistics just like terrorist groups are.

....Slowly, every Hungarian has to understand that this country has already lost everything in this century that was there to be lost, however unhappy or guilty the process was. There is not even a bit of land to be broken off by anybody. But our losses are just as unmeasurable within. How many treacheries in the last half a century alone. How many revenges, directed trials, what hate of Hungarians, of Jews, how much robbery of the soul! We have no other alternative but to say farewell to our losses and head toward another direction. Where? Which way? Into ourselves! I think this way because to be a Hungarian is no longer a physical force. It can only be spiritual. Conquer we can by our example only. And particularly through the conquest of ourselves; by the establishment of a Hungarian universality. It is a general experience, that a person sure of himself will be sure of his relationships. This can be extended to the nation as a whole.

We can never start a war again to defend our national minorities over the border. Just like a new work of art, an unknown masterpiece, only a rebuilt, reformed Hungarian nation can exert an incredible influence, both in the Carpathian basin and in a united Europe just now in the making.

Introduction

There is perhaps nothing more central and essential to the understanding of modern Hungarian history than *changes in the meaning of nation, national minority, and nationalism in the Danubian basin.* Over the past 100 or 150 years, the meaning of nationalism in Hungary has undergone repeated and very significant changes, both semantic and political. The second part of the nineteenth century saw the gradual transformation of Hungarian nationalism from an originally anti-Habsburg, basically defensive, "reconstructive" movement geared at national self-determination, into an offensive, anti-minority, imperialist venture.[7]

Magyarization at the Turn of the Century

While under the Austro-Hungarian Monarchy (1867–1918), Hungary made a continuous and desperate effort to change the ethnic composition of the country where, quite until the very end of the nineteenth century, ethnic

---

7 For some bibliographical references on, and a general overview of, the nineteenth century, consult Robert A. Kann, *A History of the Habsburg Empire 1526-1918* (Berkeley: University of California Press, 2nd printing, 1980), 579–80. For the double nature of Hungarian nationalism during much of the nineteenth century, including the revolution of 1848–49, see the pioneeing articles of Endre Arató, *"A magyar nacionalizmus kettös arculata a feudalizmusból a kapitalizmusba való átmenet és a polgári forradalom időszakában, 1790–1849"* (Two Faces of Hungarian Nationalism during the Transition from Feudalism to Capitalism and the Bourgeois Revolution, 1790–1849), and György Szabad, *"Nacionalizmus és patriotizmus konfliktusa az abszolutizmus korában"* (The Conflict of Nationalism and Patriotism in the Absolutist Era), both in the otherwise painfully dated *A magyar nacionalizmus kialakulása és története* (Budapest: Kossuth Könyvkiadó, 1964), 79–142 and 143–64.

Hungarians (usually meaning those who spoke Hungarian as their mother tongue) constituted a minority. Statistics based upon the official census showed 40.7 percent ethnic Hungarians in Hungary in 1851, shortly after the great revolution and war of national independence in 1848–49; 46.9 percent in 1869, right after the Austro-Hungarian Compromise of 1867; and 48.5 percent in 1890. In only the last two prewar censuses were Hungarians a cautious majority: 51.4 percent in 1900 and 54.5 percent in 1910.[8] Language use, of course, was a somewhat deceptive tool for determining the ethnic status of the people in the Carpathian/Danubian Basin, where hundreds of thousands if not millions lived in bilingual or multilingual zones, or in language frontiers where people in their childhood almost automatically acquired two or more languages at roughly the same level. Statistics based upon the notion of a single mother tongue concealed the delicate interplay of both natural and artificial forces that were increasingly at work. One such force was the internal migration of various groups and the growing number of Hungarian speakers in the big cities such as Budapest, particularly after the 1867 Compromise and the unification of the Hungarian capital in 1873. Most major cities became Hungarian even if they were surrounded by villages where Slovak, Romanian, or German was spoken by the majority.

Nevertheless, the ruling Hungarian oligarchy at the turn of the century was less and less satisfied with natural social developments and was ready even to revert to force while envisaging a "greater Hungarian empire." Forced "magyarization" became the order of the day under subsequent Hungarian governments, particularly that of Prime Minister Baron Dezső Bánffy (1895–1899), who employed literally any means in an effort to Hungarianize artificially the bulk of the population. Typically, turn-of-the-century Hungarian chauvinists legislated to magyarize the names of cities and villages, and exerted severe pressure on people as well to magyarize their often Slavic, often German names.[9] The influential author and journalist Jenő Rákosi (1842–1929) widely publicized his dream of an empire of "30 million Hungarians" in his popular *Budapesti Hírlap*, in which he called for a forced magyarization of the various national minority groups.

Though the press and several subsequent governments pursued this idea of bringing about an "ethnically pure" Hungarian state, the plan found some

---

8 Zoltán Dávid, "Statistics: The Hungarians and Their Neighbors 1851-2000," in *The Hungarians: A Divided Nation,* Stephen Borsody, ed. (New Haven, CT: Yale Center for International and Area Studies, 1988), 343.

9 Géza Jeszenszky, "Hungary through World War I and the End of the Dual Monarchy," in *A History of Hungary,* Peter F. Sugar, Péter Hanák, and Tibor Frank, eds. (Bloomington: Indiana University Press, 1990), 269–70.

very influential critics. The great modernist poet Endre Ady (1877–1919), who also wrote very powerful pieces of journalism, reflected on some official statistics in 1907 and noted:

> Shhh, now we should keep silent for some time. We should cast our eyes on a book. On a cruel, official statistical book. The fools of the Hungarian empire and of the thirty million Hungarians should be mute.... What happened? Nothing happened, nothing new. Simply some figures stood up in front of us. Close to eleven million people don't know Hungarian in this country. And in this same country close to eleven million people are illiterate. Why should we beat each other, when we are so terribly beaten anyway?[10]

Ady's poetry, so emphatically critical of the barren nationalism and empty officialdom of contemporary Hungary, made him a constant scapegoat for Hungarian conservatives who doubted his very patriotism while reading some of his best pieces, such as "The Magyar Fallow":

> I walk on meadows run to weed,
> on field of burdock and of mallow.
> I know this rank and ancient ground—
> this is the Magyar fallow.
>
> I bow down to the sacred soil;
> this virgin ground is gnawed I fear.
> You skyward groping seedy weeds,
> are there no flowers here?
>
> While I look at the slumbering earth,
> the twisting vines encircle me,
> and scent of long dead flowers steep
> my senses amorously.

[10] Endre Ady, *"Jegyzetek a napról, II: A Kegyetlen statisztika"* ("Notes on the Day, II: Cruel Statistics"), in *Ady Endre összes prózai művei* (Collected Prose), VIII kötet (Budapest: Akadémiai Kiadó, 1968), 263.

Silence. I am dragged down and roofed
and lulled in burdock and in mallow.
A mocking wind goes whisking by
above the mighty fallow.[11]

Critical attacks on the state of Hungary and the empty nationalism of the early part of this century did not come from poets alone, though Ady's voice became by far the most far-reaching and effective between 1906 and the revolutions of 1918–19. Some of the best scholarly minds of Ady's generation gave a great deal of critical attention to the problem of nation and nationalism, making it one of the central issues of opposition politics and the social sciences. The social and political scientist Oszkár Jászi (1875–1957), who was best known in the United States perhaps for his 1929 book on *The Dissolution of the Habsburg Monarchy,* published a voluminous treatise in 1912 on "The Emergence of Nation States and the Nationality Question."[12] By that time, Jászi had produced a whole series of articles on the nationality question for the radical daily *Világ* and the social science journal *Huszadik Század*, and was considered perhaps the best Hungarian expert on this issue. Jászi came from an assimilated Jewish-Hungarian family and, like Endre Ady, from multilingual and multicultural Transylvania, and he married into a family with a similarly diverse ethnic background. Therefore, facing the problems of nation, national minority, and nationalism was natural for Jászi, who was also an intimate of Ady. As early as 1902, young Jászi presented his views to his close friend, the future law professor Károly Szladits in unusually succinct terms. In an unpublished letter Jászi wrote:

> From the highest considerations, striving at the happiness of *humankind,* it is our duty to do everything conceivable to lift up our own country: as human solidarity is only possible with educated nations. True, in our particular conditions at home the national very frequently hurts the higher sentiments of the generally human. And this is most tragic. If we do not succeed in bridging this difference, this is going to be the end of Hungarians. Because it is impossible to make

---

[11] Endre Ady, "The Magyar Fallow" *("A magyar Ugaron"),* in *Poems of Endre Ady,* Anton N. Nyerges, translator (Buffalo, NY: Hungarian Cultural Foundation, 1969), 78.

[12] Oszkár Jászi, *A nemzeti államok kialakulása és a nemzetiségi kérdés* (Budapest: Grill Károly, 1912). On Jászi's "Danubian patriotism," see Péter Hanák's excellent *Jászi Oszkár dunai patriotizmusa* (Budapest: Magvető, 1985).

> politics constantly *against* the universal human development. In other words, it is impossible to create a clever, educated, wealthy Hungarian next to an oppressed, stupid, poor, usurped Slovak, Romanian, Ruthenian, etc. I consider this dilemma to be the most astonishing question of our national existence.[13]

Characteristically, in the decade that elapsed between this letter and the publication of his 1912 chef d'oeuvre, Jászi's views got very close to those of the best-known foreign critics of the virulent Hungarian nationalism of the early twentieth century. In the prewar years, Jászi entered into a then extremely courageous correspondence and personal relationship with the British scholar and journalist R. W. Seton-Watson,[14] whose tough criticism of the nationalism and minority politics of the Hungarian ruling elite he shared, though not without reservations. Just before World War I, Jászi (originally in French) stated explicitly to an evermore anti-Hungarian Seton-Watson:

> I participate in that sort of literary propaganda only which, though [it] points out the grave vices committed by the Hungarian oligarchy against the language and culture of the national minorities, respects, however, at the same time, the ideals and the rightful self-esteem of the Hungarian nation, which tries to achieve a creative harmony among all national minorities within the historical borders of our state.[15]

---

[13] Oszkár Jászi to Károly Szladits, Budapest (14 May 1902). I am indebted to my friend András Szőllősy-Sebestyén in Budapest for allowing me to copy this letter from his private collection.

[14] [Scotus Viator], *Racial Problems in Hungary* (London, 1908); [Viator], *Political Persecution in Hungary. An Appeal to British Public Opinion* (London, 1908); and [Viator], *Corruption and Reform in Hungary. A Study of Electoral Practice* (London, 1911).

[15] Oszkár Jászi to R. W. Seton-Watson (27 April 1914), translated from French. Published in Géza Jeszensky, "The Correspondence of Oszkár Jászi and R. W. Seton-Watson before World War I," *Acta Historica Academiae Scientiarum Hungaricae* 26 (1980), 452–53. Quoted also in Jeszensky, *Az elveszett presztízs. Magyarország megítélésének megváltozása Nagy-Britanniában 1894-1918* ("The Lost Prestige: The Changing Image of Hungary in Great Britain 1894-1918") (Budapest: Magvető, 1986), 309.

Seton-Watson's books and pamphlets, together with some influential work by *The Times* (London) Vienna correspondent Harry Wickham Steed and Paris Peace Conference historian H. V. W. Temperley, played a crucial role in changing public opinion in Great Britain and turning the British political elite against Hungary, just at the critical junction immediately before and during the years of World War I.[16] Jászi and his book, in part through his approving references to Seton-Watson's works[17] made a significant contribution to, and had to take full responsibility for exposing, on the eve of World War I, the nature of Hungarian nationalism and the chauvinism of the Hungarian oligarchy which he bitterly opposed and fearlessly attacked.

Document 1 is an important chapter from Jászi's book that describes the potential results of forced magyarization in highly critical, comparative terms. Drawing on examples of Anglo-Irish, Polish-German, and Danish-German national coexistence, Jászi points out some of the most typical consequences of forced assimilation: strengthening of the national identity and moral leadership in the minority group, spiriting away of class differences within the oppressed minority group, general lowering of educational standards through forced linguistic assimilation and chauvinistic pedagogical principles. *Forced* assimilation makes *real* assimilation impossible, Jászi concludes, and he urges democracy and equality instead of the declared linguistic supremacy of the Hungarian nation.[18]

The Treaty of Trianon and the Interwar Years

As a result of World War I and the ensuing peace treaties, Hungary was transformed from being half of a huge, multinational empire into a small nation-state. The Peace Treaty of Trianon (4 June 1920) took some three-fifths of Hungary's total population, including 28 percent of the Hungarian speakers, and transferred a total of over 3 million ethnic Hungarians into neighboring states, including a vastly aggrandized Romania, the newly established Czechoslovakia, and Yugoslavia (then "the Kingdom of the Serbs, Croats and Slovenes"). Only about 7.5 million people remained in the country

---

[16] Jeszensky, *Az elveszett presztízs.*

[17] Jászi, *A nemzeti államok kialakulása és a nemzetiségi kérdés,* 463.

[18] Jászi, *A nemzeti államok kialakulása és a nemzetiségi kérdés,* 490, 494–95.

out of the prewar population of close to 21 million.[19] Overnight, the treaty, signed in one of the fun-palaces of Louis XIV in the royal gardens of Versailles, made the word "Trianon" a symbol and a household word for subsequent generations of Hungarians. "Trianon" brought about probably the second biggest European diaspora after that of Jewry—that of Hungarians—and created the single biggest ethnic minority in Europe—that of Transylvanian Hungarians in Romania, which remains so today. Territorial changes and the corresponding fundamental transformation of the ethnic composition of post–World War I Central Europe drastically changed the course of Hungarian politics, both foreign and domestic, and altered the options for the national economy as well as the patterns of social development. More important, the strange and painful journey of Hungarians from the Austro-Hungarian monarchy to a new Hungary and a new Central Europe based on the Treaty of Trianon left an unparalleled imprint on the mind of every Hungarian generation since World War I, in and out of Hungary's current political borders.[20] Millions of Hungarians had to accept a new identity as citizens of different states, typically hostile to what was left of the Kingdom of Hungary after 1920. To make the new situation even more difficult for Hungarians and Hungary, a political alliance of Romania, Czechoslovakia, and (what was to become) Yugoslavia was brought about mainly as a barrier against Hungary.[21] A tool of French foreign policy, the Little Entente was destined to consolidate the new borders of Hungary by

---

[19] Tibor Hajdú and Zsuzsa L. Nagy, "Revolution, Counterrevolution, Consolidation," in *A History of Hungary,* Peter F. Sugar, Péter Hanák, and Tibor Frank, eds. (Bloomington: Indiana University Press, 1990), 314; Henry Bogdan, *From Warsaw to Sofia. A History of Eastern Europe* (Santa Fe, NM: Pro Libertate Publishing, 1989), 179; and Gyula Szekfű, *Három nemzedék és ami utána következik* ("Three Generations and What Follows") (Budapest: Királyi Magyar Egyetemi Nyomda, 1934), 384.

[20] For a brief, factual survey of the Hungarian national minorities in Eastern Europe in 1919–80, see Martin L. Kovacs, "National Minorities in Hungary, 1919-1980," in *Eastern European National Minorities 1919-1980,* Stephen M. Horak, ed. (Littleton, CO: Libraries Unlimited, 1985), 160–74; and N. F. Dreisziger and A. Ludanyi, eds., "Forgotten Minorities: The Hungarians of East Central Europe," *Hungarian Studies Review* XVI: 1-2 (Spring-Fall 1989), a valuable collection of essays focusing primarily on the more recent period.

[21] Piotr Wandycz, "The Little Entente: Sixty Years After," *The Slavonic and East European Review* 59:4 (October 1981), 548–64.

providing international control and supervision of Hungary's potential political ambitions.

The Treaty of Trianon is not only one of the most crucial turning points in modern Hungarian history but certainly a watershed in the history of Hungarian nationalism. The only reaction postwar Hungarians could possibly give to Trianon was "No, no, never," the semi-official slogan all children in Hungarian schools were brought up reciting during the entire interwar period. For these generations, "Mutilated Hungary was no country, while the whole of [original] Hungary was Heaven," was deeply ingrained into the public mind, particularly in schools, by a widely quoted propaganda verse, or Mrs. Elemér Papp-Váry's popular "Magyar Hiszekegy" (Hungarian Credo). Trianon became the pivot and rationale of politics and thinking in interwar Hungary, and a new kind of nationalism was born.

After the shock of World War I and the series of major social and political "aftershakes" in 1918 and 1919, Trianon gave birth to a defensive, protective interpretation of nationhood. Now the country appeared to have been "misjudged," as one of the many Hungarian pamphlets declared, in eloquent English, in 1920:

> Come here and ask the nationalities themselves (not only their fallacious misleaders) whether the races of Hungary really wish to separate from Hungary? If this search for the truth is carried out without any pressure being brought to bear on the people, I am convinced that with the honest application of Wilson's principles the majority of the nationalities will remain loyal to old Hungary...[22]

Based on this assumption, Hungarian foreign policy throughout the entire period between the wars was based upon the philosophy and political strategy of revisionism. All political parties and factions (even Béla Kún in 1919) accepted the notion that the stipulations of the treaty were unacceptable and forced upon Hungary only by the overwhelming military and political power of the Paris Peace Conference. Consequently, the treaty had to be reversed, and virtually any means or tool seemed suitable to achieve this purpose. "Treaty revision" became the official Hungarian government policy, the utmost in national ambition, particularly in the late 1920s, which resulted in a treaty with Mussolini's fascist Italy in 1927 and in extremely early contacts at the highest levels with Hitler's Nazi Germany in the summer of 1933.

---

[22] Professor Dr. Béla Krécsy, *Misjudged Hungary: An Appeal* (Budapest: American-Hungarian Association, 1920), 7.

Relations with Hitler and Mussolini became instrumental in the two "Vienna Awards" (1938 and 1940) which returned significant portions of former Hungarian territories, first in Slovakia and later in Transylvania (Romania). The harsh logic of Hungary's revisionism paved her way to a fateful role in and after World War II.

The lost war, the dismemberment of the country, and the social upheavals of 1918 and 1919 lent Hungarian nationalism an anti-Semitic tinge. Anti-Jewish sentiment was particularly strong in 1919–20 after the catastrophic failure of the Republic of Councils, which was engineered, to a large extent, by Communists and Social Democrats with Jewish backgrounds. As a result, Jews as a social group were made indiscriminately responsible for the Communist coup, and severe measures were introduced to curtail radically their role in Hungarian society where they previously enjoyed a great measure of freedom and equality. An early example of pre-Nazi, indigenous Hungarian racism was Act 1920/XXV, which limited the number of Jewish students at the universities to a certain fraction of the student body.

The Great Depression hit Hungary particularly hard and, as early as 1931, gave rise to several extremist parties on the radical right whose "nationalism" incorporated and helped to strengthen the anti-Jewish sentiment. Official Hungary also went further to the right: from Gyula Gömbös (1932–36) to Béla Imrédy (1938–39), the Hungarian prime ministers of the 1930s became loyal supporters of the rising Hitler and started to discriminate actively against the then-large Jewish population. In 1938–39 anti-Jewish legislation was enacted in Hungary, first on a religious and a year later on an explicitly racist basis. Increasingly, the conservative Horthy regime looked upon Nazi Germany as the only possible major patron that could help achieve revision of the Treaty of Trianon and Hungary's territorial claims. The various Hungarian national socialist parties established even stronger links with Hitler's Germany. National/nationalist aspirations ultimately pushed the country irrevocably into Hitler's camp.

Hungarian nationalism in the post–World War I setting needed a new, official philosophy, which emerged ultimately from the capable pen of a conservative aristocrat who dominated the field of culture and education throughout the 1920s and very early 1930s. Count Kunó Klebelsberg (1875–1932) was an ingenious and productive minister of religion and education for almost a decade (1922–31) in Prime Minister Count István Bethlen's government. Count Klebelsberg tried to build up a Hungarian cultural and educational system superior to that of the neighboring countries and to convince the world of Trianon's injustice through Hungary's "cultural superiority." In a series of articles and lectures, Count Klebelsberg also tried to construct the philosophy of "neonationalism," a new set of ideas destined to serve as a philosophical underpinning of the new political situation after the war, the revolutions of 1918–19, and the counterrevolution of Adm. Miklós Horthy in 1919–20. Count Klebelsberg admitted that he found even the latter completely "unproductive." As illustrated by Document 2, his 1928 New Year's Day article on "Hungarian Neonationalism," he fully and clearly realized the obvious and inevitable differences between pre- and postwar Hungarian nationalism. Unlike during the previous 400 years, Hungary no longer had to fight against Austria, and with most of the minorities gone, there also was no need to fight for their magyarization. "Hungarian nationalism thus lost its main content, and we have to define new ambitions for the old sentiment."[23] This new ambition, the minister continued, should be cultural superiority over the neighboring peoples. He presented the example of Mussolini's Italy, where fascist "neonationalism" started to produce a viable economy—just as Hungarian "neonationalism" should do "by multiplying the productivity of Hungarian labor through the power of ethics and knowledge."[24]

Count Klebelsberg found his new term "neonationalism" so relevant that he used it as the title of an entire collection of articles he published the same year. He devoted a good deal of his energy to explaining the significance of neonationalism, which he described in the *Nemzeti Ujság* a little later as a "people-friendly nationalism." He was anxious that it "win over the Hungarian masses to the national thought and the national sentiment," because "if it continues to be an ideal of a relatively smaller social class only, it will undoubtedly be overwhelmed by internationalization that considers the globe one single ball."[25]

Perhaps the most powerful way to rebuild national self-confidence and restore self-esteem was writing history. The single most influential history book of the interwar period, *Magyar Történet* ("Hungarian History") by Bálint Hóman and Gyula Szekfű, provided a basic framework for conceptualizing the past and documenting historical arguments against the injustices of Trianon. The popular "Hóman-Szekfű" had two editions before World War II and generated a widely shared historical philosophy across the Hungarian middle class. In an introduction to the second edition, the authors emphatically related their multivolume effort to the renewed interest toward the nationality

---

[23] From Klebelsberg, *"A magyar neonacionalizmus,"* in Glatz, *Tudomány, kultúra, politika,* 434–39. The translation here and at the next note is by T. Frank.

[24] Glatz, *Tudomány, kultúra, politika,* 439.

[25] Count Kunó Klebelsberg, *"Népbarát nacionalizmus"* ("People-Friendly Nationalism"), in Glatz, *Tudomány, kultúra, politika,* 455; cp. Klebelsberg, *"A magyar neonacionalizmus,"* 185–88.

question, providing a link between Trianon and the need for a "new" history of Hungary:

> The Hungary of the millennium...was hardly interested in the nationality composition of the country's population. Her historians, educated on the Romantic theory of the twenty million Hungarians, had little understanding of the nationality question. Today, in this age of country-mutilation carried out under the excuse of the nationality principle, we have no more burning problem than the coexistence of the Hungarian race with the other nationalities, in the frame of the Hungarian state. Tested by the squalor of Trianon, our eyes look for nothing so keenly as for the historical antecedents of the nationality question.[26]

The success of R. W. Seton-Watson's *A History of the Roumanians*[27] convinced former Hungarian Prime Minister Count István Bethlen, a champion of Hungarian propaganda efforts in the Western countries, that the publication of a shortened English and French version of *Magyar Történet* would be the right scholarly and political answer to Romanian historico-political claims and that it should serve more general Hungarian interests as well. Count Bethlen considered such "a great historical handbook...the standard theoretical work on our international political struggles."[28] The former prime minister succeeded in raising some 100,000 Pengős from governmental and private sources to launch the English translation project of "Hóman-Szekfű" as well as the publication of *The Hungarian Quarterly*, the first major quality journal in English from Hungary (1936–1944).[29] Throughout the preparations of the English manuscript, Count Bethlen pointed out the links between the history book and Hungarian politics and suggested that "Those aspects of Hungarian history should be given more prominence which

---

26 [Bálint Hóman and Gyula Szekfű], *"A szerzők előszava"* ("Introduction by the authors"), in *Magyar történet* ("Hungarian History"), vol. 1, 2nd ed. (Budapest, 1935), 8.

27 Cambridge, England: Cambridge University Press, 1934.

28 Tibor Frank, "Luring the English-Speaking World: *Hungarian History* Diverted," *The Slavonic and East European Review* 69:1 (January 1991), 60.

29 Tibor Frank, "Literature Exported: Aspects of *The Hungarian Quarterly* (1936–1944)," in *Studies in English and American*, vol. 4 (Budapest: Eötvös University, 1978), 255–82.

are essential from the point of view of the Treaty of Trianon. (The nationality question, its development and roots to be discussed as widely as possible.)"[30]

In a separate, though equally successful history book that turned out to be a powerful political statement, Professor Gyula Szekfű presented a gloomy picture of Hungary's gradual decay over *Three Generations*. The book was finished immediately after Trianon, in July 1920, and had three editions before World War II. Written by perhaps the country's most celebrated authority on history and a dominant figure in Hungarian intellectual life, the book was probably the most popular and certainly the best known academic product of the entire interwar period. In a third edition of 1934, Szekfű added a new chapter on post-Trianon Hungary and, somewhat in the spirit of Count Klebelsberg, suggested "building national self-consciousness" as a substantial means of recreating "a more Hungarian Hungarianness."[31] His nationalism sought its roots in the people of Hungary as well as in tradition and in spiritual history. Szekfű pointed to the collection, preservation, and use of folk songs in classical music by Béla Bartók and Zoltán Kodály as the prime example of reaching out for the folk tradition in a pioneering way, often to the chagrin of "neo-baroque" Hungarian officialdom. In the world of letters, he referred to literature professor János Horváth as a remarkably similar example of digging for the spiritual roots of the nation.[32]

Out of what the radical Imre Csécsy once called "the single most unpopular issue" in pre–World War I Hungary,[33] the nationality question became the primary focus, the central tenet of interwar Hungarian politics and thought. What "splendid books, countless articles, speeches and the astonishing visions of [the poet Endre] Ady could not achieve by alerting the feudal Hungarian public opinion to the detrimental significance of this question"[34] was now achieved by the shocks and aftershakes of Trianon.

---

[30] Frank, "Literature Exported," 67. It is a strange fact that with all the financial and political backing of a significant portion of the Hungarian ruling elite, the "Hóman-Szekfű" translation and publication project was never fully completed. The finished part of the final English manuscript was burned during the siege of Budapest without ever becoming a printed book.

[31] Szekfű Gyula, *Három nemzedék és ami utána következik*, 474.

[32] Szekfű Gyula, *Három nemzedék és ami utána következik*, 492–97.

[33] Imre Csécsy, *"Régi és mai radikalizmus," Huszadik Század*, no. 6 (1948), reprinted in Imre Csécsy, *Radikalizmus és demokrácia*, Tibor Valuch, ed. (Szeged, 1988), 295.

[34] Csécsy, *"Régi és mai radikalizmus,"* 296.

Nationalism under Postwar Communism

Largely because of its desperate attempts to regain its severed territories, Hungary joined Germany and Italy in World War II. Although Hungary did regain some of Slovakia and Transylvania through German and Italian arbitration (Vienna 1938 and 1940), it went as far as declaring war also on the Soviet Union almost immediately after the German attack in 1941, hoping to receive more from Germany. Hitler's perception of this "unwilling satellite,"[35] however, was adequately demonstrated by the German occupation of Hungary in the last year of the war, which made Hungary part of a vast battleground where the Red Army was chasing the German troops out of the Soviet Union and back into Germany proper, quite until the final surrender in May 1945. With the Soviet armed forces already in Hungary in late 1944, the country almost immediately became part of the region that Stalin claimed as part of a Soviet-dominated Eastern Europe, the region where the Iron Curtain went down right after the war. Hungary thus became part of the Soviet orbit for forty-five years.

The Soviet military takeover helped the Hungarian Communist Party to establish and consolidate rule relatively quickly and smoothly. As a result of the controversial nature of Hungary's role in the war—its very disputable relations to Germany and the Soviet Union and the protracted, and often armed, conflicts with practically all her neighbors—the new regime faced major political and ideological difficulties when defining a position on the national and the national minority question. The coalition governments of the transition period (1945–48) tried to contribute to a reassessment of Hungarian nationality policies vis-à-vis the Slovaks and the other minorities of Hungary in order to thereby provide an encouraging example to the neighboring countries. Schooling and education were the focus, though by 1948 it was "Stalin's constitution for the nationalities" that was to serve as a "gigantic example for Eastern Europe."[36]

There were a few important statements made in this relatively brief period, the most valuable of which was written by the political scientist and social philosopher István Bibó (1911–1979). His essay on "Distorted

---

35 Cp. John Flournoy Montgomery, *Hungary: The Unwilling Satellite* (New York: Devin-Adair, 1947). Montgomery was the last prewar U.S. minister to Budapest.

36 Gyula Ortutay, *"A szlovák iskolaügy Magyarországon"* ("Slovak Schooling in Hungary") (4 November 1948), in Gyula Ortutay, *Művelődés és politika* (Budapest: Hungária, 1949), 313–19, quote on p. 313.

Hungarian Character, Dead-Ended Hungarian History" made "the distortion of the Hungarian character" responsible for all the catastrophes of the last hundred years and for all the persistently manifest unhealthy features of Hungarian social values and intellectual development.[37] It was not just Bibó's own tragedy but that of his entire generation that his work could hardly influence public thinking and the political agenda outside the short period of 1945–48.

As soon as the Communist Party completed its takeover by around 1947–48, it appropriated a special segment of the national past and disavowed most of the heated issues of Hungarian history. The fate of the Hungarian diaspora and the Treaty of Trianon itself became anathema, while the plebeian traditions of the national past, the underdogs of former "class struggles," heroes and heroism of anti-Habsburg freedom fights were all grouped together into a new and extremely narrowminded pantheon of national glory. The Party accepted "the purposes of Kossuth, Petőfi, Táncsics," as Hungary's Stalin, Mátyás Rákosi, declared in 1948, and added the names of the poets Endre Ady and Attila József a few months later.[38] Sándor Petőfi became almost the "official poet" of the Party,[39] and his name and poetry became a "banner." "Four hundred years"[40] of anti-Habsburg freedom fights were celebrated in an attempt to suggest a revolutionary continuity from historical heroes through the current leaders of the Communist Party. At the same time, however, what the regime used was a highly narrowminded, exclusionary, and all-too-suspicious approach to anything genuinely national. Typical was the harsh and threatening judgment of József Révai in September 1948: "It is time for us to unveil and smash once and for all the pseudo-populist, ill-spirited Hungarian *narodn'ik* ideology, so hostile to the working

---

[37] István Bibó, *"Eltorzult magyar alkat, zsákutcás magyar történelem,"* in István Bibó, *Válogatott tanulmányok* (Select Papers), vol. 2, 1945–1949 (Budapest: Magvető, 1986), 571.

[38] Mátyás Rákosi, *"A Magyar Dolgozók Pártjával erős, virágzó Magyarországért"* ("For a Strong, Flourishing Hungary with the Hungarian Workers' Party") (13–14 June 1948), and *"Harmincéves a Magyar Kommunista Párt"* ("Thirty Years of the Hungarian Communist Party") (20 November 1948), both in Mátyás Rákosi, *Válogatott beszédek és cikkek* ("Select Speeches and Articles") (Budapest: Szikra, 1950), 323, 350.

[39] Cp. Márton Horváth, *Lobogónk: Petőfi* (Budapest: Szikra, 1950).

[40] Aladár Mód, *400 év küzdelem az önálló Magyarországért* ("400 Years of Struggles for an Independent Hungary"), 7th ed. (Budapest: Szikra, 1954 [1943]).

class."[41] Révai, then Rákosi's ideological deputy, went as far as describing (populist) ideology "as a likely tool of imperialist anti-communism in Hungary."[42]

To make Trianon taboo in a country where practically every third family had relations across the border, and to make populist thinking an ideological threat where close to 60 percent of the population made their living still in, and off, the land, proved to be fatal mistakes. Symbolic references such as statues and street signs remembering Kossuth and Petőfi everywhere across the country were but makeshift facades in a land that was just about to lose its national consciousness. Unbelievably repressive measures, such as putting about one-tenth of the total population (an estimated 1 million people) into jail or concentration or detention camps, executing them, or at least driving them out of Budapest, certainly did not help. It is justified to argue that the systematic campaign of the Rákosi regime against the national spirit and the fatal treatment of the Hungarian minority issue across the borders were equally instrumental in bringing about the revolution of 1956.

It is characteristic that the short-lived Hungarian national movement of 1956 immediately brought back some of the long-denied national symbols such as the old (pre-Soviet) Hungarian coat of arms and the national flag with the Stalinist coat of arms visibly cut out. The movement declared Hungary's national independence just before it was crushed. Nineteen-fifty-six was essentially a major demonstration of the continued, independent existence of the idea of the Hungarian nation, as embodied in the fierce resistance to the Soviet Union and the unwillingness to accept the internationalist, dogmatic, pseudo-Marxist political philosophy that was forced upon the Hungarian mind between 1948 and 1956. Hungary was the first country in Soviet Eastern Europe that openly rebelled against the oppressive, imperialist spirit of the Soviet Union and of the Yalta conference of 1945, where the much distorted national question made a fundamental contribution to the outbreak of national/nationalist sentiments.[43]

One of the lessons the postrevolutionary regime of János Kádár (1956–88) had to learn from the national tragedy of 1956 was to address the

---

41 József Révai, *Marxizmus, népiesség, magyarság* ("Marxism, Populism Hungarianness") (Budapest. Szikra, 1949), introduction to the 3rd ed., 6.

42 Révai, *Marxizmus, népiesség, magyarság,* 6.

43 There is more literature on 1956 in major languages than on any other aspect of Hungarian history, perhaps even combined. For a good introduction in English, see Bill Lomax, *Hungary 1956* (London: Allison and Busby, 1976).

problem of nation, national minority, and nationalism, so fatefully intertwined in the case of Hungarians. A great deal of this was done, or was allowed to be done, in literature, history, and film. Also, in contrast to the early 1950s, it was done in a spirit of slowly increasing openness, particularly in the 1970s and early 1980s. In the long run, these efforts exerted some influence on, though could not fundamentally change, Hungarian politics.

The first major effort to discuss the evolution of "socialist"—that is, politically correct—patriotism came from the influential Marxist historian and philosopher, Erik Molnár (1894–1966). In what was to become a series of articles on "the national question," Molnár started a major ideological discussion on nationalism in the 1960–64 period, motivated partly by his own experiences in and after 1956 and partly by a decree of the Hungarian Socialist Workers' Party in 1959 calling for a fight against nationalism in Hungarian culture and ideology. Document 3 is therefore a typical product of post-Stalinist, post–1956 official Hungarian thinking, trying to reconcile newly invented socialist patriotism and Soviet-sponsored proletarian internationalism, acknowledging thereby the right at least to a new "socialist" attachment to the fatherland. The combination of "socialist patriotism" and "proletarian internationalism" Molnár defined as "socialist national self-consciousness."

Molnár had a versatile and erudite mind. He built up his concept of the rise of a Hungarian nation by comparing it to developments in France. He rightly argued that the medieval notion of *natio* in Hungary did not include any other people but members of the feudal nobility and thus, throughout much of its history, the Hungarian nation was expropriated by one particular social class alone. Molnár, however, also tried to argue that "when the working class comes to power, the social content of the national community drastically changes," and "the nation becomes the community of the workers under the leadership of the working class." "Socialist nations" now cooperate in the big international class struggle between the bourgeoisie and the proletariat, which is now waged also as a war among states, he argued.[44] Thus, the Stalinist reinterpretation of a Marxian tenet survived all the national and international calamities of the 1950s, and the empty and incoherent idea of a "socialist national self-consciousness" through "proletarian internationalism" entered the official mind of even the early and mid–1960s.

The international political climate of the next two decades (1965–85) provided more opportunity for Hungarian authors, scholars, and artists to do

---

44 Erik Molnár, *"A nemzeti kérdés"* ("The National Question"), *Magyar Tudomány* 5:10 (1960), 571–87; reprinted in Molnár, *Válogatott Tanulmányok,* 383–400, quotes from p. 399.

a lot of the work of recreating a generally acceptable agenda on the national question. The poetry and prose of Gyula Illyés, the novels of Tibor Cseres, the drama of András Sütő, and films by Zoltán Fábri, András Kovács, or Miklós Jancsó tried to grasp some of the essential turning points of Hungary's national evolution and provided increasingly attractive and persuasive visions of the national past. Just as in the nineteenth century, authors continuously played a leading role in shaping the climate of opinion, with Gyula Illyés (1902–1983) as their leading spirit through most of the last three decades of his life. The "Hungarian national agenda," even if it was not directly nationalist, was generally considered far too sensitive because of its potential or actual anti-Soviet stance and its threat to disrupt the makeshift "socialist" peace between Hungary and its neighboring countries that had large Hungarian minorities.[45] Characteristically, the Kádár regime increasingly resorted to what the sociologist Sándor Szalai called "fragmented liberty of speech" and delegated the right to address the "existential problems of the nation" to a group of authors. Authors and poets like Sándor Csoóri, Mihály Czine, Gyula Fekete, László Nagy, or Ferenc Sánta openly hinted at the moral decay of the nation during the long decades of Soviet domination which Csoóri considered "both liberation and occupation at the same time."[46] Semi-public debates in the Writers' Union (especially a fierce one in 1974), the clandestine publication of an István Bibó *Festschrift*, a major meeting at Monor, as well as the secret support given to the Hungarians of the neighboring countries in terms of food, books, and basic commodities coming from "mainland" Hungary—all marked the gradual success of this populist group, which was often considered nationalist by officialdom.

This group of Hungarian intellectuals was deeply rooted in the Hungarian populist tradition of the interwar period and after, represented at the highest level by Zsigmond Móricz, Gyula Illyés, László Németh, and Péter Veres. The populist tradition looked back to rural Hungary, the village culture, folk art, and the peasant mind for spiritual inspiration and moral initiative, particularly as they formed, for a very long time, the predominant part of the civilization of a largely agricultural country, where industrialization and urbanization came much later. Just as in many other East European countries, this "city culture" had been looked upon as alien or foreign rather than indigenous or genuinely native. Post–1956 populists, who were still often together with the best representatives of the "urban" "democratic" political opposition, were particularly concerned about the population decrease in the

---

[45] Dreisziger and Ludanyi, *Forgotten Minorities,* particularly the editors' introduction (pp. 7–21).

[46] Sándor Csoóri, *"Nappali hold,"* in Csoóri, *Nappali hold,* 289.

country and the threatening signs of a social and moral crisis including growing alcoholism, a high suicide rate, astonishing patterns of divorce and the disintegration of the family, and growing poverty, as well as the failure of the government to reach out for and provide at least moral support to the Hungarian population of the neighboring countries.

The 1980s

Throughout the latter part of the Kádár era the government preferred raising and maintaining living standards at all costs to demanding any kind of ideological commitments. By contrast to other East European countries, Hungary could boast of a much more relaxed atmosphere, comparatively better living conditions, and a relatively liberal political, almost depoliticized climate. These differences were particularly noticeable compared to Ceauşescu's Romania, Husák's Czechoslovakia, or Honecker's East Germany. As a result of this generally more tolerant climate in Hungarian politics in the 1980s, changes in the treatment of national and national minority issues started earlier than perhaps anywhere else in Eastern Europe. As a good example, well before the revolutions or pseudo-revolutions that broke out in the wake of Soviet *glasnost* and *perestroika,* a major three-volume history of Transylvania was published by the Hungarian Academy at the end of 1986, edited by the then minister of culture and education, the reputable historian and literary scholar Béla Köpeczi.[47] The book became a huge popular success and a characteristic symbol of unexpected openness in Hungary, directly challenging official Romanian positions on the issues of Transylvanian political and social history and on the interpretation of centuries of coexistence and conflict among the nations of Transylvania. Hungarian journals also started to publish previously unimaginable pieces of poetry and prose in the mid–1980s, one even on the executed prime minister of 1956, Imre Nagy. It was a natural that Illyés's role as spiritual leader and "national guru" was increasingly taken over by the politically sensitive, outspoken, and morally critical populist poet and author of the younger generation, Sándor Csoóri (1930–). The poet was courageous enough to go as far as openly declaring his support for the Hungarians of Slovakia in a widely publicized introduction to the U.S. edition of a book by "Czechoslovak"-born Hungarian Miklós Duray in 1982.

---

[47] Béla Köpeczi, ed., *Erdély története* ("The History of Transylvania"), vols. 1–3 (Budapest: Adakémiai Kiadó, 1986).

Major changes in the Soviet Union under Mikhail Gorbachev and the dissolution of Soviet power in and out of Eastern Europe brought about a series of radical transformations in practically all former Socialist countries. Changes in Hungary started in 1988 and climaxed in 1989–90, first perhaps by allowing East Germans to cross Hungary for West Germany, and leading ultimately to a multiparty system (for the first time since the Communist takeover forty years before), free elections, a parliamentary democracy, the withdrawal of all remaining Soviet troops, the deconstruction of the Iron Curtain system, and the dismantling of the Warsaw Pact. These were revolutionary changes by any standard, and yet their essentially peaceful, nonviolent execution, again by contrast to Romania or, later, Yugoslavia, made them—perhaps even more so than in Czechoslovakia—into a "velvet revolution."

One of the fundamental issues that would divide the never-quite-unified opposition to the Kádár regime was in fact the national issue. Nationhood and nationalism, just as almost everywhere else in Eastern Europe and the former Soviet territories, came to dominate and divide the Hungarian agenda. "Urban" intellectuals soon found themselves in a different political party from that of the "populists." The latter came to be organized in the fall of 1987, at a meeting in Lakitelek in the east of Hungary, where even Imre Pozsgay, a cooperating member of the government, was invited to consult about Hungary's impending doom, which was presented and discussed by most participants as an immediate threat and was focused particularly on the fate of Hungarians in the neighboring countries and the diminishing Hungarian ethnic stock. How very far these concerns were from the idle illusions of Jenő Rákosi's "30 million Hungarians," and how much closer to the tragic vision of the great nineteenth-century poet Mihály Vörösmarty (1800–1855), who dreaded the eventual death of his nation as early as 1836, in his patriotic act of faith, "Szózat" (Oration).

Emotions were particularly triggered by the fact that the Kádár administration habitually handled issues like these with considerable suspicion and neglect, immediately associating any question on the nation's fate with nationalism. This gave the newly launched, strongly national party of the Hungarian Democratic Forum a slight majority in the first free general elections of 1990, while the "urban"-oriented, "cosmopolitan" Alliance of Free Democrats, with a comparatively thin national agenda, had to settle for the role of the biggest opposition party. Sadly enough, the adjective "populist" had acquired over the years not only a nationalist, but often a somewhat anti-Semitic tinge, with urban, cosmopolitan intellectuals casually considered to be Jewish. None of these labels, of course, have been fully accurate, though there is a measure of truth to these widely shared public judgments.

Document 4 is a powerful, brief description of some of these issues by one of Hungary's leading poets today, Sándor Csoóri.[48] Csoóri's question, "What Is the Hungarian, Today?" is a reference to a famous pre–World War II anthology *(Mi a magyar?)*, in which illustrious intellectual leaders such as the poet Mihály Babits, the composer Zoltán Kodály, or Calvinist Bishop László Ravasz addressed some of the basic questions of the nation on the very eve of World War II.[49] Csoóri's essay also may have referred to a somewhat similar but earlier collection of left-wing essays, *Mi a magyar most?* most probably from 1937.[50] Csoóri sensed, in 1989, a national calamity of comparable proportions and called for a spiritual renewal, as well as for a readiness to deal with fundamental national issues. His essay was also the best brief critical summary of what the Kádár era considered "nationalism" and showed the previous thirty years in a new light. Some of his work also was intended as part of a "national" program or agenda, frequently accused by his opponents as nationalist and, even, anti-Semitic.

Unfortunately, growing nationalism in the East European and former Soviet area left Hungarian thought and politics less and less intact. Considered previously by Csoóri and his friends to be an abyss, almost a national cataclysm, Hungary's contemporary history urged a lot of people to unveil publicly those responsible for the past forty-five pro-Soviet, anti-national years. Some right-wing politicians and authors, however, went further than that and started to demand, once again, "treaty revision," a renewed fight against the legacy of Trianon, and what the playwright István Csurka described as a new Hungarian *Lebensraum*. This new, radical wave of right-wing, extremist, and abusive nationalism, triggered by international economic depression, growing unemployment, and pauperization, is no longer the genuine national pride of responsible men like Sándor Csoóri. It tragically divides the country at a time when Hungary's relations to her neighbors already are strained and jeopardizes the political stability, often the very existence, of the Hungarian minorities in neighboring countries. Although Hungarian national leaders of the Hungarian communities in neighboring countries, such as Calvinist Bishop László Tőkés in Transylvania, Romania, or

---

48 Sándor Csoóri, *"Mi a magyar, ma?"* ("What Is the Hungarian, Today?"), in Csoóri, *Nappali hold,* 143–54.

49 Gyula Szekfű, ed., *Mi a magyar?* ("What Is the Hungarian?") (Budapest: Magyar Szemle Társaság, 1939).

50 *Mi a magyar most? Tanulmányok a jelen legfontosabb kérdéseiről* ("What Is the Hungarian Now? Essays of the Most Important Issues of Our Time") (Budapest: Pantheon, n.d. 1937?).

Miklós Duray in Slovakia, are usually moderate and calm, the early 1990s seem to have created a situation, in and out of Hungary, when a long dormant, but by now virulent, nationalism might recall the spirit of "No, no, never" with all the devastating international consequences Hungary experienced during and after World War II. One can only hope that today's bigger and stronger Hungarian middle class, a functioning parliamentary democracy, and a more favorable international climate in and out of Europe can act as stabilizing factors capable of keeping the situation under control.

7

The Poles and the Search for a National Homeland

by Anita Shelton

Document 1

from Roman Dmowski, *Thoughts of a Modern Pole* (1902).[1]

The Purpose and Subject of Politics

Politics, as a sphere of activity, affecting collective organizations of social life, must recognize as its main purpose the good of the social whole—that is, the nation—as well as the maintenance and favorable development of the organization of its collective life—the state. Any other politics, having more limited purposes, either stems from the above, or is its complement, or places itself in conflict with it and then becomes immoral, inimical to the good of the nation, and must be combatted—without regard to whether it is personal politics; the politics of material interest; the doctrine of individualism; or aristocratism, traditional or class based. The nation above all as a whole must thrive and develop, equally for the sake of the good of all, made up of both individuals and groups, as well as for the sake of the national moral imperative, which is to leave unshaken for coming generations the foundation for

1 Roman Dmowski, *Thoughts of a Modern Pole (Myśli Nowoczesnego Polaka)*, 4th enlarged ed. (Warsaw: Skład Główny "Gazeta Warszawska," 1933), 250–56; 258–66. Translated by Anita Shelton.

continuing national survival, itself an inheritance from past generations. National politics, through the means of law, must fight against and appropriately limit all particular aspirations which have as their goal the benefit of any individual or group at the cost of the rest of the nation, or undermine in any way the foundations upon which rests the ages old national existence.

From precisely this general standpoint, that is, keeping in mind the good of the whole, politics can be broken down into the following subdivisions: 1) state administration, in the broadest understanding of the word, that is, including holding vigil over basic national organizations, maintaining law and order, and, finally, forming national economic policy; 2) defense of the interests of the state on the outside, that is, foreign policy; 3) the adaptation of political structures, laws, and the economic system to the changing needs of the nation, that is, reform, initiating change—the essence of political creativity.

In discussing politics, too often we forget about the first of the above-mentioned categories, state administration, which is the main and most difficult task of politics. In order to be able to work for national progress domestically or to defend its interest on the outside, one must first of all protect the very existence of the state, by ensuring that it has a solid basis for survival. One must ensure that the inheritance from the past, which determines the basic identity of the nation, as well as its viability and strength, will be passed down to future generations. About this task, which healthy people recognize instinctively, but which is very difficult to understand completely without deeply immersing oneself in the essence of the nation's collective life, the wider spheres of society generally forget. This is because they do not have the means to assess it, and because they rely upon the state administration to protect it. Nevertheless, the healthier, more vital, and more mature a nation is, the more involved it is with the state in all aspects of social collectivity.

A nation in our situation, which does not have its own state or administration, and which lies at the mercy of foreign administrations which undermine its national traditions, exploit it economically, and maintain order through mechanical and repressive means—such a nation must work 100 times as intensively to foster within its politics this dedication to the survival of the nation. The position of a political nation deprived of its independent existence as a state is so difficult and so complicated that even with the greatest effort it is hard to comprehend it in its entirety. At the same time, where the possibilities for pragmatic action are curtailed, thinking becomes lazy, loses its ability to measure itself against real life, and contents itself with a superficial mimicking of what it observes elsewhere. From this derive two phenomena which are unhealthy and even dangerous for our political life.

Broad spheres within our society without thinking equate their own relationship to politics and the state administration with the relationship which exists within independent nation-states. Despising their own state administration as foreign, they search for political inspiration and models to follow among those other nations that have a strong tradition of opposition, or even revolutionism. The result of this superficial imitation is a warped and one-sided understanding of politics: exclusively as the reforming of the society, of its overturning in all its aspects, without comprehending the need first to preserve the very existence of the society as a nation, by protecting the essence that is bound up in its most basic traditions. Then and only then can long-lasting and viable improvement be pursued. This sort of ultra-radical political approach fails to consider whether or not there will be anything left to reform, or whether, having lost the moral foundations of its national existence, the society, atomized, reduced to dust, might not become the helpless prey of others. In such a condition it would be so utterly debased anyway, in fact, that for its own sake, as well as for the sake of humankind as a whole, it might be better for it to perish and serve as a raw material in the growth of some more enduring political organism. Because the fate of a nation that does not preserve its domestic cohesion is the same as that of a centuries-old castle which, when the roof caves in, deteriorates under the effects of wind and rain until nearby residents come to cart away what remains of the bricks and stone to use in their houses and barns.

On the other hand, those who understand that a society cannot easily survive the destruction of basic order and stability, who from their social perspective have a horror of radicalism, are often too lazy, and too tied to their material possessions and privileges, to oppose in any way the regime. They want to make of the rule that exists a protectorate over the social status quo, at the expense of all the most important national traditions, which are by definition inimical to the foreign rulers. This produces a moral degeneration within the nation, rendering it helpless before the physical might of the foreign rulers. They seek to help—and do help—in the transformation of their compatriots into the mere subjects of a foreign people.

Both one and the other way of thinking, radical or excessively conservative, push from the realm of political action autonomous activity on the part of the nation in the maintenance of its traditions, protection of internal order, and the development of domestic policy, economic or ideological. One ignores the fundamentally preservative nature of politics, while the other gives it away to a foreign regime, and even goes further and asks that the foreign rulers destroy our most sacred inheritance from the past, our moral inheritance, that which makes of us a nation. One acts consciously or unconsciously as if without national identity, as a cosmopolitan; the other is, in the final result, antinational.

In the meantime, the nation, which is prevented from creating its own government, whether in an independent state or in an autonomous partition within a foreign state, or even, in the absence of the other two, as an organized moral presence within the nation, is entirely excluded from the political process. Where there is no established, sacred, generally recognized tradition to establish order within the nation, where no collective authority asserts itself in defense of the nation, there is nothing to reform, and reforming activity will be an empty exercise, a shouting of slogans into the wind, as our would-be reformers demonstrate, or a fruitless inciting of passions which will produce only anarchy, as the socialists now are proving. Where there is no national organization for domestic order, there can be no foreign policy....

Beginnings of National Politics

National politics for such a nation as ours, finding itself in such circumstances as ours, cannot be an imitation of the politics of other nations, whether those that have independent states or those that have never had independent states and are just now for the first time building a sense of national identity on the basis of linguistic difference. The first type do not have to concern themselves with saving or restoring the bases of their nationhood, because the existence of an independent nation-state ensures their survival. The second type represent a sociological category with which we have nothing in common; they have different moral foundations and different aspirations. In any event, they are fated sooner or later to be assimilated and absorbed into the national organism represented by the state and regime in power.

We must have our own autonomous national politics, with roots in a deep feeling for and understanding of our own peculiar circumstances, as well as a clear vision of our national goals.

If our politics are to be national in more than just name, if they are to be more than just an imitation of political functions without any real substance, if they are not to serve foreign interests, if they are not to contribute to the rape and pillage of the national heritage, they must be consciously developed on a basis of real strength.

The result of overwhelming foreign influence, stemming primarily from our partition and occupation by foreign powers, but also from the presence of foreign elements living in our midst, themselves the by-product of certain long-term economic developments including the growth of industry and commerce which depend upon foreign sponsorship to a large degree, and the result of surrendering new generations to the continuing destruction of national tradition, thus rendering them morally degenerate, can only be the serious erosion of the national base upon which we hope to rebuild our national politics. This is especially true of certain groups within the society that have been especially weakened.

As a result of this fact, we must recognize our first priority to be the strengthening of the foundations of our nation. The main elements involved in this undertaking are as follows:

1) The reinforcement and stabilization of the national ethic, which requires fighting the impulse to apply standards of individual morality to national affairs.

2) The crystallization of a national identity that is firmly wedded to the existence of a state, that is, not settling for the twilight existence that would result from accepting an exclusively linguistic and cultural definition.

3) The inculcation of the proper understanding of the subject and priorities of politics, which must above all be concerned with the maintenance of a durable social order, without which national politics are not possible.

These are the main political-educational tasks with which any truly national politics, rooted in moral impulses and an authentic understanding of the national essence...must concern itself if the nation is not to degenerate and ultimately perish...

It is possible for a nation living without a state of its own to conceive its own national regime in several ways: One can create a revolutionary organization, establishing authority in the society by means of terror, and organizing it around a self-appointed small group of "notables" claiming the exclusive right to define and enforce the national interest. However, for such an organization to have real authority it must truly reflect, and be the generally recognized embodiment of, a strong, clear, and conscious sense of national identity. It must have the certainty that behind it stands all that is Polish in thought and feeling, and only then will it have the will and ability to defend the national interest against elements working against it within the society.

This is why, if we want to have a national politics, we must work hard to organize a strong, united, national public opinion regarding criteria for behavior, as well as a sort of penal code to protect it. We must achieve a unanimity of opinion and a firm resolve where the national interest is concerned. This cannot be achieved if we are willing to make compromises on critical issues. One cannot in the name of social solidarity compromise with elements hostile to the very idea of the nation.

We must not tolerate an ethic that does not recognize the nation as a whole or does not regard it as the supreme good. We cannot accept within our ranks whole elements that reject the very idea of Polishness, or that would be content without independence or political statehood. We will not tolerate any doctrinairism that would delude the nation with barren fictions about the universal brotherhood of man. We must not grant the rights of citizenship to those who would reject the very idea of order within the society or of national discipline, who work to disarm the nation within to render it vulnerable to the outside.

It is impossible to achieve true unity through compromise of conflicting interests, the attempt to join fire with water. Rather, it is achieved through organization in the ranks of those who stand firm by a single idea, and the subordination by force of those who will not recognize it voluntarily. Only then can a nation truly become the master of its fate when it not only has many good sons, but also the power to hold the bad ones in check.

Never perhaps since the fall of the Polish state [in the partitions] have we been in a situation so demanding of self-discipline and of national discipline. As long as those states that partitioned Poland were themselves cohesive and strong, our position seemed hopeless, but stable. We as a nation did not feel a great need to curb our actions since we were anyhow held on such a short rein that moving forward was impossible. From time to time we were able momentarily to break free, but only grievously to shake our chains before being dragged back into the powerlessness that gripped entire generations.

But history does not stand still. It produces new powers and drives to destruction old ones. Austria, defeated several times in war and disintegrating from within, became the battleground for the most diverse and conflicting interests, in the midst of which even we could have played a great role had we been better organized, more united, and led by elements that understood with both hearts and minds the larger issues confronting a truly national politics. Today [1902] we are witnessing the historic breakdown of Russia both as a world power and as a state. This breakdown surely will produce a profound change in the circumstances facing a large portion of our population, an opportunity for greater self-reliance and ultimately for wider spheres of activity.

Weak souls, who look at all changes in the nation's circumstances to see whether their own private fates will be easier or harder, predict either that the fall of Russia will produce for Poles perfect conditions for autonomy, after which very little will need to be done, or that for one reason or another not much will change, and our fate will be as hard as ever. We disagree with both, insisting that we must be prepared to take on responsibility for our own fate and, in fact, be prepared ourselves to shape it.

According to our convictions, a period is opening before us neither of comfortable rest nor of renewed oppression. We are entering a period of extreme disorder and profound change, in which we must not lose our way, but to the contrary, from which we must emerge as a nation victorious. Our ship of state will be launched on treacherous seas—and so we must be sure that she is seaworthy and that her rudder is held by a strong hand. We must create a clear and strong order within our society and see to it that it is obeyed.

Document 2

from the Program of the Popular National Union passed at the first postwar congress (11–12 May 1919).[2]

As a result of the world war, which brought about the collapse of all three partitioning powers, Poland was freed from enslavement. The period of our hundred years of struggle for independence has ended. Now we face the task of consolidating the regained independent existence of the state by our own strength. The tasks of Polish policy have increased and broadened, [and] the older political programs and organizations, created in times of slavery, no longer suffice....

All-Polish principles, the principles of national unity without distinction of sections and states, of subordinating class interests to the general good of the nation, of basing the strength of Poland on national consciousness and a sense of duty to the Fatherland of the broadest strata of people are equally binding in independent Poland, just as they bound us in times of slavery. And it has not ceased to be true that the nation must rest its future primarily on its own strengths, and the first condition for the independence of the nation is its internal cohesion, resistance to foreign influence, and economic independence. It remains equally true that the most dangerous enemy of Poland is Germany and that only by uniting in one state entity all the lands on which the Polish population, by its numbers or its cultural work, has pressed the stamp of Polishness, will Poland establish her place among her neighboring states and nation....

But now the nation is laying the foundations not only for its statehood. The building of the whole state system of the Republic has begun. An

---

2 Program of the Popular National Union (Związek Ludowo-Narodowy), written by Stanisław Grabski. Halina Janowska and Tadeusz Jędruszczak, eds., *Powstanie II Rzezcypospolitej: Wybór Dokumentów 1866-1925* (Warsaw: Ludowa Spółdzielnia Wydawnicza, 1981), 517–23. Translated by Richard G. Seitz.

indispensable need of the nation is a clear definition of the tasks of independent Poland comprising a program, so that the organization of the state does not take place haphazardly, and the borders of the Republic, the Constitution of the state, social arrangements and reforms, and the direction of Poland's foreign policy are not changing, accidental struggles of divergent class and party interests or, worse, of foreign influences.

For the political program to be realized in life, it must penetrate into the depths of national consciousness. The whole construction of the Polish state cannot be turned over to the Sejm and government, because the Sejm is only a reflection of the aspirations and currents existing in the nation. We will build a strong and lasting edifice of the republic only through close cooperation of the State organs, the Sejm and government, with self-governing organizations and vital civil activity....

The Power of Poland

The primary goal of the Popular-National Union is the power of the Polish nation and state....

The Borders of Poland

The Popular-National Union directs all its energy toward enabling Poland's borders to embrace all lands on which the Polish population dominates by its numbers or by civilization, and towards enabling Poland to have a secure foothold on the sea. The renunciation of any of these lands to other nations in order to gain their friendship is inadmissible.

The Popular-National Union emphatically opposes the recreation of the historic Grand Duchy of Lithuania, joined with Poland only by personal union, and giving up to it any lands liberated by Polish blood and the strength of Polish arms. These lands, in accordance with the will of their population which clearly demands complete union with Poland, must enter the Polish state as an inseparable part....

Strong Government

Simultaneous with the establishment and securing by force of arms of the borders, the internal peace and order of the Republic must be established and secured. Efforts toward revolution and violent social upheavals, striking at the foundations of statehood, must be opposed equally with the threats of external enemies.

The Popular-National Union demands a strong government that will insure the strict observance and execution of law as well as the respect of authority....

Relation of the State to the Nation: The Least Possible State Coercion, The Most Possible Civil Action

While it demands a strong government, the Popular-National Union opposes the overextension of the tasks of the state and the subordination of the whole cultural, social, and economic life of the nation to the state's control.

Poland cannot be a police state on the model of Prussia and Russia. In the Republic any licence must be curbed, but the civic freedom must not be restrained.

The power of Poland demands the fullest possible development of all the creative/productive powers of the nation. But they will develop only in an atmosphere of freedom.

The leading principle of internal policy must be: the least possible state coercion, the greatest possible civil action. The state ought to move above all toward its own goals, assisting and encouraging those aspirations of the citizens and strata of the population that are advantageous for the good of everyone, and to apply compulsory prohibitions and orders and its direct control only where necessary....

Homogeneity of Nation-State

The Republic must strive for the greatest possible nation-state homogeneity. The century-long governments of the partitioning powers forced into the Polish organism many foreign and hostile elements, especially in the *kresy* [eastern borderlands with Russia]. The control of nearly all commerce and industry by Jews, who have no connection with the nation, has obstructed the proper development of a Polish middle class, impeded the unity and mutual understanding of the educated strata of the nation and the peasant strata, and excessively inflamed all social clashes. While condemning all pressure and any exceptional laws directed against anyone by reason of his nationality and faith, while granting to all citizens of the Republic full freedom to cultivate and develop their own nationality, the Popular-National Union will work persistently so that the Republic as a whole will have a clearly Polish character, that all vital forces of social, economic, and cultural life of the nation be in Polish hands, that the marks of foreign control be erased as quickly as possible, [and] that both the borderlands and the cities be Polish not only by possession but in spirit and national culture....

The Moral Strength of the Nation: Religious, National, and Civil Social-Education

The development of the cities, of native trades, industry, and commerce; a strong, native Polish middle class; numerous and prosperous peasant farms; the prosperity of the working classes—all these create the material basis for

Polish strength. The moral strength necessary so that Poland will consolidate her independence must be given by the education of society in a religious and national spirit, in a feeling of equality of citizens before the law and of state responsibilities.

The elements of this education are: Church, school, family, and state authority....

Church

Basing the moral education of the nation on religion and recognizing the Church as the director of its moral life, the Popular-National Union demands for the Church full independence and a proper position in the state.

All creeds ought to enjoy full freedom of faith and rites in Poland. The Protestant population, which despite a century-long separation from Poland and persistent Germanization has preserved its ardent love of the fatherland, must be assured warm protection in the Republic. But since the tremendous majority of the Polish nation is Catholic, the Popular-National Union reserves the leading position for the Catholic Church.

Document 3

from an Address by the First Secretary of the Polish United Workers Party, Władysław Gomułka, before a Citizens' Rally in Warsaw (24 October 1956).[3]

COMRADES! CITIZENS! Working People of the Capital!

I greet you in the name of the Central Committee of the Polish United Workers Party which at its last plenary session turned over the helm of the Party to a new leadership.

A great deal of evil, injustice, and many painful disappointments have accumulated in the life of Poland during the past years. The ideas of socialism, imbued with the spirit of the freedom of man and respect for the rights of a

---

[3] Paul E. Zinner, ed., *National Communism and Popular Revolt in Eastern Europe* (New York: Columbia University Press, 1956), 270–77. Reprinted with permission of the publisher.

citizen, have been greatly distorted in practice. The words were not borne out by reality. The heavy toil of the working class and of the entire nation did not yield the expected fruits.

I deeply believe that these years belong to an irrevocable past.

The Eighth Plenum of the CC of our Party executed a historic turn. It created a new period in our work, a new period in the history of socialist construction in Poland, in the history of the nation...

The leadership of the Party does not want and will not give empty promises to the nation. We turn with full confidence to our class, the working class, to the intelligentsia, to the peasants....

Workers and employees of all sectors of national economy! Help the Party and the Government in the great work of improving the socialist economy of People's Poland!

Develop the economic initiative of your crews, search, together with us, for the best forms of participation of the working class in the management of enterprises. Raise labor productivity, combat waste, and lower the cost of production. Take advantage of all opportunities of increasing industrial and agricultural output in order best to fulfill the growing needs of the masses.

The Party is telling the unvarnished truth to the working class.

The increase in the earnings of millions of people during the past months will be a lasting one only when the increased purchasing power of the population is balanced by an increased volume of goods on the market. At the present we cannot afford further wage increases because the string has already become so tight that it threatens to break.

Further wage raises will be possible only if there is increase of goods of mass consumption and if there is a decrease in production costs. To produce more, better, and more cheaply is the only road leading to a higher standard of living of the working class and of the entire nation.

Comrades! The Eighth Plenum, by selecting a new leadership, has declared a determined struggle against all that hindered and strangled the socialist democratization of life in the country until now.

The Party will demand of its workers full responsibility for carrying out the tasks entrusted to them. Persons who compromised themselves because of their inefficiency or serious mistakes cannot remain in responsible posts. *{Ovation.}*

Only by following consistently the path of democratization and uprooting all the evil of the past period, shall we achieve the creation of the best model of socialism corresponding to the needs of our nation. *{Applause.}*

A decisive role on this road must be played, above all, by a broadening of our workers' democracy, by increasing the direct participation of working crews in the management of enterprises, by increased participation of the working masses of the city and the countryside in the government of the people's state.

We will not permit anyone to take advantage of the cause of regeneration and of the peoples' freedom for purposes alien to socialism....

The mutual relations between the parties and states of the socialist camp, welded together by an identity of aims and interests, should not cause any misunderstandings. Of this consists one of the main features of socialism. These relations should develop on the basis of the international solidarity of the workers, of mutual trust and complete equality of rights, of granting mutual aid, of mutual and friendly criticism, should there be a need for it, on reasonable solution of all controversial problems, a solution stemming from a spirit of friendship and from a spirit of socialism.

Within a framework of such relations every country should have full independence and sovereignty, and each nation's right to sovereign government in an independent country should be fully and mutually respected.

Independent nations and sovereign states, which are building a system of social justice, a socialist system, and which are cemented from within by a strong and unbreakable will of achieving this purpose in a manner most suitable to each country, must act together and in unity in the world arena in order to strengthen, by mutual effort and determined attitude, the invincible ideas of peace—ideas which embrace all mankind—and the striving for peaceful coexistence of all nations of the world....

I can assure you that these principles are finding an ever fuller understanding, and that these principles are shared not only by our Party, but by the Communist Party of the Soviet Union as well.

(Our last meeting with the delegation of the CPSU allowed the Soviet comrades to orient themselves better in the political situation in Poland.)

Recently, we received assurances from the First Secretary of the CC of the CPSU, Comrade Khrushchev, to the effect that he does not see any obstacles to the development of our mutual Party and state relations on the basis of the principles outlined by the Eighth Plenum of the CC of our Party. *{Prolonged ovation.}*

All concrete matters pertaining to our internal affairs will be solved in accordance with the estimate of the Party and the Government. The question whether we need Soviet specialists and military advisers, and for how long we need their aid, will depend on our decision alone. *{Prolonged ovation.}*

At the same time, we received assurance from Comrade Khrushchev that within two days Soviet troops in Polish territory will return to their locations, in which they are stationed on the basis of international treaties, within the framework of the Warsaw Pact. *{Ovation.}*...

Comrades! The Eighth Plenum of the CC of our Party has received a warm welcome from the working class and the widest masses of the people.

At thousands of meetings throughout the entire country, workers, the intelligentsia, students, soldiers, and all the toiling people had expressed their approval and support, and their trust in the new leadership.

Nothing is more important for us, for the Party, for its leadership, than this trust and support. There is nothing more important for the nation, for the realization of its desires and aspirations, than unity between the Party and of the people, a unity stronger than ever before.

In the name of the Central Committee, I am expressing warmest thanks to the workers of many industrial enterprises who, in a noble upsurge, expressed their readiness to work overtime, and even to float a state loan, although there is no need for it at the present moment, and for voluntary deductions from their earnings in order to help the people's authority and the new leadership of the Party. I thank the students of the Polish universities who demonstrated in these days so much enthusiasm for and trust in the Party. I thank the soldiers and officers of the Polish Army who demonstrated their loyalty to the Party and to the Government and their support for the results of the Eighth Plenum.

The nation can completely trust its army and the command of the army *{ovation}*, which, in our country, as everywhere in the world, is completely and entirely subordinated to the government of its country. *{Applause.}*

Comrades! The tremendous wave of the political activity of the masses brought about by the Eighth Plenum here and there has encountered forces hostile to socialism, opposed to the Polish-Soviet alliance, inimical to the people's authority, forces which would like to distort, hinder, and retard socialist democratization.

Comrades! Let us not allow reactionary troublemakers and various hooligans to obstruct our way. Let them keep away from the pure current of the struggle of socialist and patriotic forces of the nation! Drive away the provocateurs and reactionary loud mouths! The state authority will not tolerate for a moment any action directed against the Polish state interests and against our state system.

Comrades! Time is pressing. The Party must embark on the solution of daily, difficult problems of our economy and state life. How can you help the Party and the Government today? Above all, every one of you should stand at your workbench, at your post, and demonstrate your loyalty and devotion to our cause by intensified work or study.

Today we turn to the working people of Warsaw and of the entire country with an appeal: enough meetings and demonstrations! Time has come to embark on daily work—full of faith and consciousness that the Party united with the working class and with the nation will lead Poland on the new road to socialism.

Long live the unbreakable bond of the Party with the working class and with the entire toiling people!

Long live socialism!

Long live People's Poland! *(Ovation.)*

Document 4

from Marcin Król, "National Homeland" (1992).[4]

Not Any Poland Will Do

I myself naturally know very well what my national homeland means to me. Nevertheless, it is the homeland of my imagination, and the most private world of imagination at that, one that is impossible for others to enter without my express invitation—and even then very rarely will I allow anyone permanent residency. No one can deprive me of such a homeland. There is also another national homeland, that I would like to—and perhaps must—share with others, whom, for this very reason, we call our compatriots. With our compatriots we carry on conversations deep into the night, have interests in common, similar points of view, and similar public and private mores. Compatriots share the same homeland. But does our national homeland in fact continue to exist?

Theoretically, but only theoretically, Poland consists of all of its inhabitants or citizens, the land and culture, the economy and customs. And yet I do not sense a closeness among all its people, nor a unity among its lands. Everyone chooses, consciously or maybe even more often unconsciously, what he or she likes. Perhaps it would be most helpful to begin with a closer look at some of the conscious choices people have been making.

In our modern history, many have turned to a nationhood of exclusion. For extreme conservatives of the nineteenth century, this meant excluding peasants; for the Endecja, it meant Jews and other ethnic minorities; for the Communists, it meant exploiters and the bourgeoisie. Lately, some have sought to divide the nation into two or more distinct nations...but my nation is not like that. My nation endured and grew always as a result of a reverse process—that of inclusion and cooptation.

---

4 Marcin Król, "National Homeland" (Ojczyzna), *Tygodnik Powszechny* (Universal Weekly) (9 February 1992). Translated by Anita Shelton.

...Zygmunt Krasiński wrote many times that Poland will not be worthy of the name nation if certain moral rules are not observed, and many among the Polish emigration after World War II would only acknowledge their ties to the homeland under the condition that basic freedom and democracy be implemented. As a matter of fact, many among those of us who lived for forty years under the postwar reality, could only partly recognize this as their homeland. I also impose my conditions, and therefore I think it worthwhile to pause and consider what those conditions are.

If for me (and it is probably the same for others) my homeland, my nation, must live up to certain standards in order to be accepted as my own, that seems to indicate that love of country is neither a natural nor a simple emotion. When at the start of the last great war George Orwell wrote his famous essay "England, My England," many among his friends on the left criticized him for expressing an attachment to a nation that had thrived on social inequality and capitalist exploitation. Orwell, despite his own strong leftist convictions, still asserted that there are times and circumstances when one must adjust one's priorities: in first place, the nation, and only in second position the question, what kind of nation? ...Still, while we acknowledge that there are moments of extreme danger when it would be inappropriate to dwell on these kinds of distinctions, for the most part, life is not composed of such extreme situations.

...There is also no requirement that one must recognize Poland as one's own nation at all. Many among those Poles who left this country after World War II after some time abandoned their attachment to Poland as their homeland as well. No one can criticize them for this. If we are free at all, then we are free to choose whether or not to acknowledge membership in a nation, and cannot be sentenced to belong to any nation. If I did not myself choose this course of action, then it was for many reasons, the least among them being the difficulties associated with emigration. I can after all choose to be only partly a member of my nation. Moreover, I have the right to refuse membership in the larger nation and to exist merely within my own small, private, friendly one. One fragment of the landscape, a few people, a selection of literature, I accept into my nation—as for the rest, forget it. I can just as well divide Poland into two unequal halves, and place in one sack everything that appeals to me, and in the other (and this would for most of us be the larger sack) put in everything that I no longer want to see. Or I can do battle with everybody and everything that together conspires to make me feel excluded from my nation. I can attempt, if only for my own sense of self-respect, to participate in the rebuilding of my nation. I do not have to subject myself to ways of thinking and being that surround me. The freedom that Poland has now regained for the first time in a very long time affords me the opportunity to criticize whatever I please in public life, without having to express my own rather conservative attitude toward issues of nationalism between the lines of some other text.

National Reconstruction

When the Church recently attempted to indicate to us how we should vote, it spoke of Christian values, which, if not completely clear, were strongly identified with the need to "preserve our national identity." We were to vote for those parties that placed a priority on preserving that identity. This demand seemed to me to be incomprehensible, on two grounds. To begin with, it assumes that there are groups who are opposed to preserving the national identity. And second, it does not explain what really is meant by national identity. After all, it is more than just a language or certain cultural elements (Mickiewicz, Sienkiewicz) held in common, because everyone without exception is ready to embrace these, but something else. What? I do not know, if I discard the suspicions that I do not even dare to harbor against the Church hierarchy.

If we are to address this issue of preserving the national identity seriously and pragmatically, questions remain which I am unable to answer. To begin with, is it the same as honoring one's fatherland, and, if so, which? And second, what use is a national identity? What use is a fatherland? Is it really worth speaking about a fatherland if behind our words lurks only a banality?

Here we approach one of the most basic questions. Do we need a national fatherland as such, or one that has little to do with nationalism, but is more of a common spiritual homeland? I do not intend to get caught up in a semantical dispute that can lead to no substantive resolution, so I will remain with my intuitive sense that one can speak of a spiritual homeland, even if it is difficult to define and not dependent upon the continued physical existence of the nation. So what role is there in my imagination for ties to the existing material world, so to speak...?

Put simply, without my homeland I cannot understand my own spiritual self. One can, of course, imagine oneself as a member of the world community, and, especially for the intelligentsia, there do exist important contacts and friends beyond Poland's borders. But for anyone for whom feelings and instincts are as important as intellectual curiosity, it is impossible to live fully outside of the borders of familiar landscapes and traditions. This is not exclusive of feeling oneself a citizen of Europe, but I cannot be fully European unless I am fully a member of my own community first.

National Allergies

I have in mind two types of allergies. Some react to the very word "nation," everywhere seeing threats to the nation's survival, while others perceive the nation everywhere and in everything and do not comprehend that the national community in today's Poland is among the weakest of human communities. It is obvious that historically and sociologically the nation represents a rather primitive form of community. Every people passes through this phase in one way or another, but Poles already have this phase behind them and do not have to concern themselves with questions of national or historical legitimacy in the same way that other newly emerging nations in Eastern Europe must....

There are those, however, who worry that in Poland there is too little true national feeling. These have to be divided into two groups. To the first belong the descendants of the National Front *(Stronnictwo Narodowe)* and related groups, or put simply, the Endecja. I have no intention of here weighing the achievements and sins of the Endecja during the interwar years. Suffice to say that the ideology of Roman Dmowski and his followers is today not only dangerous but deeply anachronistic. This is the case because although the Endecja always placed a great emphasis on modernization, their prescriptions are all now badly out of date (for example, their obsessive criticism of gentry romanticism, their focus on civic responsibility, or their aggressive foreign policy), while the pure nationalists are morally at variance with Christian principles, in addition to being superfluous from a practical point of view. Denationalization does not threaten Poles today.

The inheritors of the Endecja's brand of politics simply exploit sentimental traditions of martyrdom to gain an advantage with the electorate. To some extent this sort of ploy still works, but there can be no doubt that the Endecja tradition is slowly dying. One might simply point out that in no Western European country is there a viable political party representing a continuation of the views of interwar nationalists, who, after all, once thrived everywhere. This is the result in part of the nationalists' record of wartime collaboration, and in part simply from an intellectual bankruptcy. In Poland, things were slightly different, since there was no possibility of wartime collaboration, while Communist totalitarianism prevented intellectual discourse after the war. Today the time is past for discussions, but rather there is a need to be very clear that in my country such attitudes are simply not acceptable. Any sort of anti-Semitism or xenophobia, no matter how subtle, is simply a scandal, which should find its resolution in the courts, and not be allowed to dominate the political debate. In my country, there was and is no room for manure, even if it is wrapped in colored paper and tied with a pink ribbon.

And yet, self-styled (if anachronistic) ideological nationalists form a large part of that group that likes to look at all issues through the prism of nationalism. These are people who lost their way intellectually after the fall of communism. Before that, they had a fairly easy way to orient themselves in the sphere of public morality. This was through a mix of patriotism with elements of Christian morality. However, when communism fell, or rather when it began to totter—that is, in 1980–81—a second fairly simple orientation within public morality emerged—Solidarity. Solidarity's appeal was irresistible, because in addition to patriotism and Christian values, it provided a means for public activism. And yet, even Solidarity ultimately failed. In post-Solidarity, allegedly liberal Poland, there are no simple answers.

One cannot accept, after all, that establishing a free market and the possibility of making money provides any real answers, as some thoughtless liberals would seem to suggest. After all, most Poles realize that for the foreseeable future they will not be part of the rising middle class. They also realize, if only dimly, that the aforementioned mixture of patriotism and religion, with its later addition of Solidarity, somehow altogether defined for them their sense of nationhood, of a Poland that was dear to their hearts. And then suddenly, in the space of two years, all of that seemed to have been forgotten, or cast aside as no longer relevant, not European, not universal enough. Polish society in the main lived through the postwar years in a world that was totally anachronistic; yet it was a warm world. Now the time has come for normalization and modernization, but their world has become much colder.

People are therefore seeking warmth, without comprehending that its source is poisoned. Afraid of national spiritual disintegration, they attempt to accomplish a sort of artificial reconstruction, but the only way to do this is through a kind of inbreeding, no longer patriotism, but xenophobia, no longer Christian universalism, but Polish-Catholic particularism, no longer the naive but noble notion of fighting for freedom, above all yours, and only afterward ours, but a convulsive grasping onto whatever is within reach, closing the borders to the goods, money, and ideas of other countries. This is undoubtedly a harsh and offensive portrait, but let us consider whether or not we have really done much to save the ideal of national spirit and make it relevant and useful to ourselves and to those who, let's face it, sorely need it.

My first impulse is to push away from myself the reality that is taking hold in this country, where boorishness is gaining the upper hand, and money and the battle over access to it, decide everything. The country has been stripped of the charm it had for us—let's not delude ourselves—during Communist times. And so if some look to replace it in somewhat primitive ways, then in my view we should not seek to condemn or deride them, but simply to separate ourselves from them, reject their solutions, and seek a more authentic way of rebuilding the nation in which ultimately even they may feel at home. If we lose, there will be no satisfaction in apportioning blame.

Polish Pride and Polish Memory

Much has been done in recent years to deprive us of our pride. Let's enumerate some of the examples: First, the Communist powers tried to deprive us of the most elementary and spontaneous joy at the election of a Polish pope; then the relentless repetition of the formula "Pole-Pope" by the Church authorities drove us to the edge of indifference. First we rejoiced at the extraordinary spectacle that Solidarity staged in front of the entire world; then the Communist powers reminded us (with little effect, to be sure) that there's no use in tilting at windmills; finally, the leader of Solidarity himself shattered what remained of its image, assisted in this work by his aides and allies. First, we thrilled at our regained independence; then thrice we had elections and the new style of politics turned many away from participating in free public discourse. First, we rejoiced at gaining a free market and access to material wealth; then, we were reminded that capitalism is, in fact, a dirty business and capitalists are really no better than thieves. And so in what should we rejoice now? About what should we feel pride?

For myself, I will reply somewhat shamelessly. I am proud that despite all of the above pressure we never allowed ourselves to be manipulated or forced into any role desired by any of the various political lines represented in all of this. We have become neither xenophobic nor closed-minded; we do not, in the majority, support punishing legislation, even in the case of the most basic moral issues; we nurse hatred neither toward the Russians, nor toward the Germans, nor toward the Ukrainians, nor, for that matter, toward any particular group, at least not to a degree that would justify rehashing old issues. Our vision of politics and politicians is remarkably clearsighted, as was reflected in the failure of nearly 60 percent of the electorate to vote in the last elections, despite all the campaigning and cajoling with which they were bombarded. We understand—and I continue here to speak of that vast majority of Poles who are enlightened and rational—the commonsense value of maintaining certain restrictions on economic activity, and we perceive quite well how and where reforms could be moved along more quickly.

Are these not reasons enough for pride? And to this we might also add that we are the only country from the former [Soviet] bloc which is not experiencing a witch-hunt, that is, of former collaborators with the secret police....

We have indeed many reasons to be proud, and yet pride can serve as the foundation upon which to rebuild our homeland only if it is supported by memory. One cannot feel pride without memory because without the latter there is no real sense of identity. But true memory also should not be confused with mere reminiscence.

We happily celebrate our national holidays (although even they are slowly losing the particular sweetness of forbidden fruit). On the other hand, we remember our past only grudgingly. In Poland we have to contend not only with anti-Semitism (to a moderate degree), but, as Alexander Smolar has pointed out, even more importantly with a dearth of memory about the Jews, who dwelt among us and were murdered in our country. Those Poles who now live in the so-called redeemed lands of the west, appear to have forgotten utterly that 100 years ago Germans dwelled there, and apparently have no curiosity about who they were, their history or their culture. Finally, Poles do not want to remember even themselves from just a few years ago. The fact that we are now living in the Third Republic is testimony to the haste with which we would like to forget that we used to live in the People's Republic. Beyond anti-Communist sallies, there is no interest in remembering this past, even though the vast majority of us grew up and spent our entire adult lives in it.

We do not need to be ashamed of the entire postwar era. I don't mean this in any political sense, but only in the sense of ordinary human lives and decisions. If we want to reconstruct our common spiritual homeland, then we should not forget all of this. We will surely fail, on the other hand, if we do not come to grips with our own heritage: How successfully did we coexist with the Jews? To what extent did the intelligentsia feel and fulfill social obligations? Did the massive and very rapid modernization of our peasantry succeed in producing new citizens, or rather only self-interested materialists?

One could go on and on. But there is no doubt that the reconstruction of our homeland must begin on the bases of both pride and memory. This is a task for us all, but most particularly for the intelligentsia, that strange and seemingly anachronistic group who nevertheless still are so necessary to us. The idea of the homeland was always its particular terrain for exploration, but if it allows itself to be displaced by the middle class or intimidated by the new god of materialism, it will forfeit its last opportunity. It already has compromised itself quite severely by becoming involved in politics, not as the conscience of the nation, but in an effort to assume leadership. Now, thank God, the intelligentsia again has been removed from politics and can return to more important matters. It can begin the task of reconstructing the nation, without which our life in this new, postmodern world not only will not make sense, but will be dangerously barren. I say "dangerously," because nature abhors a vacuum, and if we allow a spiritual vacuum to exist we may soon find it filled with some alien and, to us, inhospitable, content.

And so I return to my original questions about our nation, and now answer them decidedly and emphatically. My nation is in need and in danger.

Nothing threatens us from the outside. We are threatened by all those who, for a variety of different reasons, would like to use the opportunity afforded by the recent political and social revolutions, to try to impose altogether new and alien designs on us. We are threatened by those who feel shame at their Polishness, together with all the historical baggage that term implies....

I have two outs. I can give up and retreat into my own world. But I can also refuse to give up my toys. And as long as I have any strength left—I won't give them up. Anyhow, my strength derives only from the certainty that I am not alone in my feelings, but that I have allies and sympathizers in my quest to defy normalization, amnesia, and primitive liberalism. I am convinced that there are legions of such people in Poland. We won our independence; now let's make use of it. Let's not allow our country to drift in the margins of European culture. My homeland is before me, and it demands of me not defeatism, but courage; not flight, but engagement; not political partisanship, but spiritual profundity. If we succeed in genuinely engaging ourselves in this struggle, then we will not be condemned to spend the foreseeable decades in mediocrity and anomie.

Introduction

Like other East European nationalisms, like nationalism in general when it feels itself to be on the defensive, Polish nationalism can appear endlessly and even mindlessly repetitive and self-referential. Combative chauvinism, furtive or open xenophobia, feelings of insecurity masquerading as superiority—all of these attitudes and behaviors are familiar to the students of East European nationalism. In the Polish case, one can add to this generic East European list a number of other factors. Among these are the geopolitical preoccupations of a people caught on an open plain between the *Drang Nach Osten* of the Germans on one side and the seemingly obsessive expansionism of the Russians on the other; and the troubling legacy of the *Rzeczpospolita (Res Publica)*, at once the Poles' greatest historical achievement and their most lamentable and tragic failure (ending in the partition and extinction of the nation of over a hundred years). There is also a profound confusion, and also contradiction, between Poland's pre-partition, multi-ethnic, multilinguistic, multireligious identity and its twentieth-century incarnations, which have been progressively more homogeneous; a persistent and symptomatic anti-Semitism (even into her virtually *judenfrei* present); and polarized political traditions, ricocheting sometimes wildly between, for example, democracy and dictatorship, or romantic insurrectionism and pragmatic "organic work" traditions, depending upon the context of the moment. All of this, indeed all of Poland's dramatic and troubled history since the late eighteenth century, adds up to two not easily reconcilable realities: a powerful and emotional sense of attachment to and pride in national identity, and a very fundamental uncertainty regarding that identity—What *does* it mean to be a Pole? The documents that have been reproduced and excerpted here to represent evolving Polish nationalism over the course of the twentieth century all speak eloquently, if inconclusively, to the persistence of this very question.

The Partitions

It is impossible to speak about twentieth-century Polish nationalism without referring back, as the Poles themselves do in three of the essays here, to their loss of statehood in the partitions of the eighteenth century.[5] The implications of this for Polish national identity are enormous. Some Poles had a certain degree of "self-government" in several "states" during the long years of partition, but do not consider them interruptions of their stateless existence.[6] Between 1795 and 1918 they concentrated their efforts on following Jean-Jacques Rousseau's advice: "If you cannot prevent your enemies from swallowing you whole, at least you must also do what you can to prevent them from digesting you."[7] Basically, this is what they did again during the Nazi German occupation (1939–45) and the Soviet domination (1945–89).

To begin with, the Polish nation prior to the partitions was defined largely in terms of its large gentry class, the *szlachta,* whose ethnic roots mingled Polish, Ukrainian, and Lithuanian blood, and whose corporate status gave them a monopoly on the political life of the Polish state. Their management of state affairs was widely interpreted in the nineteenth century (and

---

5 For the years of partition, see Piotr S. Wandycz, *The Lands of Partitioned Poland, 1795-1918,* vol. 7 of *A History of East Central Europe,* Peter F. Sugar and Donald W. Treadgold, eds. (Seattle: University of Washington Press, 1974).

6 These "states" were the Duchy of Warsaw (1807–15), the Grand Duchy of Posen (1815–49), the Kingdom of Galicia and Lodomeria (1772–1918), the Kongress Kingdom of Poland (1815–74), and the Republic of Krakow (1815–46).

7 Quoted from *Considerations sur le gouvernment de la Pologne* (1772) in Norman Davies, *God's Playground: A History of Poland,* vol. 2 (New York: Columbia University Press, 1982), I/369.

afterward) as a tragic *mis*management, if not indeed squandering, of the state's resources and ability to defend itself. This discrediting of the *szlachta,* reflected in Dmowski's *Thoughts of a Modern Pole* (1902), for example, brought the very tradition of the democracy of the *Res Publica* into disrepute in the minds of many. In other words, because Poland's proud experience as a "historic nation" contained within it also the seeds of its long extinction, someone had to be responsible, and that someone seemed to be the natural leadership elite in the political context of democracy. Interestingly, Dmowski's preoccupation with the inadequacies of Poland's political elite on the eve of Poland's regaining of independent statehood at the turn of the last century is echoed in the discussion of Marcin Król as Poland struggled to emerge from the decades of Soviet-era bondage. It is merely a historical accident that in each case there seemed quickly to develop a popular urge to turn to a single charismatic leader (Józef Piłsudski in 1926 and Lech Wałęsa in the 1990s) who could "rise above" the messiness and uncertainty of democratic give-and-take. However, despite the striking similarities in circumstances (the collapse of a Russian imperial state providing in each case the opportunity for regained independence, for example), Poles in the 1980s reflecting back on their national historical experience could reach radically different conclusions from "modern" Poles of the 1890s.

Another very important repercussion of the partitions is that they "froze" the Polish national identity in time at a crucial moment in the history of European nationalism: on the eve of the Napoleonic experience and the victory of the nation-state idea in Europe in the nineteenth century. In the nineteenth century Poles reacted in various ways not only to their statelessness, but also to this drastic change. The basically literary romantic approach to nationalism represented by men such as Adam Mickiewicz and Stanisław Staszic became political, which led first to the various armed uprisings of that century and later to populism and socialism by its end. Realism/positivism was another attempt to face the new situation. This approach, according to Peter Brock, included the "advocates of organic work and triple loyalty, whether under Russia, Prussia, or Austria, and whatever differences in detail among them" turning them into "essentially cultural nationalist."[8] Realpolitik was the next and final step.

One can readily see the same struggle to bring Poland's by then very dated national traditions (class-based and multi-ethnic) into the modern European context (class-free and ethnically homogeneous) in Dmowski's

---

[8] Peter Brock, "Polish Nationalism," in *Nationalism in Eastern Europe,* Peter F. Sugar and Ivo J. Lederer, eds. (Seattle: University of Washington Press, 1969), 334.

Thoughts. To point out another parallel: Król also struggles at the end of the Soviet period to fit a Poland once again emerging from servitude into a changed European context (but one that is obviously very different from that at the end of the nineteenth century). Now, emphasis on national homogeneity and concepts of state morality ("modern" to Dmowski) seem decidedly dated and clearly at odds with broader currents within the "European Community." In a sense Gomułka also speaks at a moment of "liberation," this time from total dependence on Moscow. While he uses general terms when he states that "each nation's right to sovereign government in an independent country should be fully and mutually respected," he clearly claims full sovereignty and independence for Poland.

Twentieth-Century Nationalism

The documents here representing Polish nationalism over the course of the century must be read and comprehended in historical context. To begin with, two of these documents (Dmowski and Król) were written when Poland was on the eve of or just after regaining independence. The first was originally published in 1902, when Poles, like many other submerged nationalities, were hoping for and preparing to take advantage of a "universal war for the freedom of nations" (in the words of the nineteenth-century poet Adam Mickiewicz) that might provide an opportunity for national liberation. Król wrote his essay in 1992 after the regime of Wojciech Jaruzelski and the Soviet Union had collapsed and Solidarity—which must be seen not least as a movement for national liberation—had splintered. In each case, there is a palpable sense of new opportunities for the nation in the prospect of the impending or effected collapse of a Russian Empire (tsarist or bolshevik). Yet, Król's musings also reflect his uneasiness with a "common national identity" and suggest "a homeland of the 'spirit.' "

The other two documents are representative of opinions voiced once national independence had in fact been regained, but already had managed in some way to disappoint. The 1919 Program of the Popular National Union (Związek Ludowo-Narodowy), the single largest vote-getter in the national elections of that year, was passed at that movement's first postwar congress in the face of a reality that was developing along lines decidedly different from those advocated by the followers of Roman Dmowski. Finally, Gomułka's speech, received with enthusiasm by a huge audience, marked the birth of "national communism" after its traditional Leninist-Stalinist form was rejected even in the Soviet Union. It reasserted the national identity of the Poles in

1956, albeit in a Communist framework at a time when this was already anything but popular.

Roman Dmowski was the personification of modern Polish nationalism from the turn of the century until his death on the eve of World War II. The preoccupation of contemporaries such as Król with his ideas and movement (the *Endecja* or National Democratic Party) a good many decades after his death speaks to the strength of his impact on twentieth-century Polish national consciousness. Dmowski was a typical exponent of his times in Europe. He stated, "The nation is the product of the state's existence."[9] His emphasis on the state as the only legitimate vessel to contain, shape, and preserve national identity is completely consistent with the "Prussian" ideas about nation-states that prevailed among that most dynamic of European peoples, and the Poles' immediate neighbors to the west, the Germans. In fact, Dmowski's ideas were shaped to a large extent in reaction to the Germans. He admired their combative nationalism and saw in it a praiseworthy model for the Poles, but he also saw them as the greatest threat to Polish prospects. Born in the town of Poznań (Posen), a German town in a mixed Polish-German area, Dmowski was committed to the idea of creating a Poland that would be smaller; nationally, linguistically, and religiously more homogeneous; and geographically more western than the pre-partition Poland had been. He despised the democratic traditions of the Polish *szlachta* and categorically rejected their suitability for a new Polish nation-state. His small book, *Thoughts of a Modern Pole,* was a best-seller when it first appeared in 1902, and it went through numerous editions during Dmowski's life and gained a renewed popularity and topicality during the 1980s, as the Polish nation came together in Solidarity. Outside of Poland, and dating back at least (and most notably) to his representation of Polish interests in Paris at the end of World War I, Dmowski is known for his national chauvinism and visceral anti-Semitism. He made no apology for either, regarding tolerance as a sign of national weakness that could lead only to eventual national extinction. Like many apologists for the German state writing in the Hegelian tradition that there must exist a different standard of morality for the state than for private individuals, Dmowski placed the "national interest," as he saw it, above all else. His personal intransigence on this point was chillingly demonstrated by the plaster cast of an assassin's hand that he reportedly kept on his desk until his death; it was the hand that had killed Poland's first president, Gabriel Narutowicz, whose election to the presidency had been decided by Poland's minority voters.

---

9 Brock, "Polish Nationalism," 343.

One of the tragedies of interwar Poland lies in the bitter and destructive division of opinion on the national question that was evinced in the personal rivalry of Dmowski with Józef Piłsudski. Narutowicz had been elected president only because neither of the other two could prevail against his rival. Piłsudski represented the antithesis to Dmowski in virtually every way. Born in the eastern territories, in Vilnius, of aristocratic blood, and committed both to the democratic traditions of the *Res Publica* and to the multinational tradition of the Polish-Lithuanian Commonwealth, Piłsudski envisioned a large, geographically more eastern, heterogeneous, federally organized, and nationally tolerant state. Where Dmowski feared German national dynamism and the *Drang Nach Osten* of modern times, Piłsudski was convinced that the greater threat lay to the east, in Russia, particularly in the context of the new Bolshevik expansionism. Because Piłsudski, as the creator of the Polish army and unrivalled leader of its fight for independence during World War I, was de facto leader of the state in 1918, Poland's postwar borders more closely resembled Piłsudski's vision than Dmowski's (despite the latter's presence in Paris). The two could agree on one thing in the early 1920s, however: the new Polish republic was in danger of self-destructing under the fragmented and quarrelsome leadership of the many political parties that vied with each other for power within its democracy. In disgust, Piłsudski carried out a coup d'état in May 1926, imposing his own fairly benevolent dictatorship "above" the fray. To Dmowski and his followers, the only thing worse than the national confusion of the early 1920s was Piłsudski's version of order. The polarization of the two camps continued to dominate Polish politics throughout the interwar period. The 1919 Program of the Popular National Union reflects the influence of Dmowski's vision of the Polish nation, even as the Poland being forged by Piłsudski on the Russian front and by the diplomats of the Great Powers in Paris took on a very different shape.

Adam Michnik's "Conversation in the Citadel,"[10] written while Michnik was interned during martial law, is above all a conversation with Dmowski. While Michnik cannot claim to be Dmowski's counterpart for his own age (Dmowski's personal influence and prestige was far greater), he is surely among the best known and most eloquent spokesmen for Solidarity, that great national movement of the 1980s. Michnik's personal history, moreover, is inextricably bound up with the history of his nation. Although he was in his early youth a committed, if reforming, Communist (raised in a Communist household), Michnik quickly came to the conclusion that communism was antithetical to the interests of the Polish nation. Expelled from the University

---

10 in *Letters from Prison and Other Essays* (Berkeley: University of California Press, 1985).

of Warsaw in 1968 for his involvement in student demonstrations, Michnik devoted himself to activities in opposition to the state and in support of a renaissance of the Polish nation. His was a leading voice in the "dialogue" between Polish intellectuals and Polish Catholics in the search for a renewed identity. He also was one of the founders of KOR (Committee for the Defense of Workers) after the brutal repression of striking workers by the police in Radom in 1976. Here, again, his interest lay in seeking a consensus for a common ground among polarized segments of the population. Fittingly, Michnik became one of the key representatives of the intellectual community within Solidarity. His has remained a respected voice within the debate over national issues into the present time.

Władysław Gomułka, like Michnik a Communist from an early age, never gave up his allegiance to communism, yet, in a sense, he never became a true internationalist. He was probably too much of a Pole for this.[11] He served the Party (under whatever its name was at any given time) all his life. He was arrested for his political activities first in 1932 and subsequently in 1936. M. K. Dziewanowski pointed out that Gomułka's second arrest probably saved his life, because he was in a Polish prison while Stalin liquidated practically the entire leadership of the Party during his well-known purges at the end of the 1930s.[12] It is not clear what Gomułka knew about the fate of his comrades, but he remained in occupied Poland when the outbreak of World War II freed him from prison. He made his way in the Communist resistance and became Secretary-General of the Polish Workers' Party in 1943. Yet, this lifelong Communist was something of an old-fashioned, romantic Polish nationalist. In 1945 he wrote, "There exist two reasons why Poland cannot become a Soviet republic. First, the Polish nation does not want it; second, the Soviet Union does not want it"; he indicated that his Party stood "for Poland's sovereignty and independence."[13] When the Soviets insisted in 1948 on a somewhat more subtle but just as strict a subordination by pointing out that the Communist Party of the Soviet Union (CPSU) "serves as an example of all fraternal Communist parties" and demanded total subservience, Gomułka pointed out that while he was a thoroughly convinced Communist and ready to build a Communist Poland,

---

[11] The literature on Gomułka is extensive. An excellent thumbnail sketch of his career can be found in Adam Bromke, *Poland's Politics* (Cambridge, MA: Harvard University Press, 1967), 57–58n.

[12] M. K. Dziewanowski, *Poland in the 20th Century* (New York: Columbia University Press, 1977), 97.

[13] Bromke, *Poland's Politics,* 59.

"he was a Pole not a Russian puppet."[14] He lost his position and was even expelled from the Party. It should, therefore, not have come as a surprise to Moscow that in the wake of de-Stalinization and the success of Tito, the Poles saw in Gomułka a "national" leader. It was in this capacity that he made the speech offered as Document 3.

Marcin Król is one of the best-known Catholic intellectuals in Poland. He is the author of many works on topics of political philosophy, and also has served as the editor of several very influential Polish journals of liberal or liberal-Catholic opinion (for example, *Tygodnik Powszechny* and *Res Publica*). In the excerpts here from "National Homeland," Król poses the questions: Is it possible to define a national tradition that can provide for cohesiveness, a sense of the comfort of being "home," without necessarily and crudely excluding those whose vision is different? Is it moral to do so? And, is it worthwhile? Almost in spite of himself, Król seems to answer "yes" to all of these questions. And yet, his idea of a cohesive and moral Polish nation is surely a far cry from that described by Dmowski or in the Program of the Popular National Union. In his ambivalence about the search for an answer, he certainly has nothing in common with Gomułka.

Conclusion

In tracing the evolution of Polish nationalism through the four documents here, one is first struck by the elements of continuity. In particular, it is the continuing preoccupation with the ideas and legacy of Roman Dmowski, who never even held a position in the independent Polish state between the world wars, that links the different documents and eras. Dmowski did indeed create an image of the "modern Pole" (or at least what Dmowski thought that should be), which, for better or worse, has taken hold of the Polish national imagination. Somewhat ironically, one of the more important characteristics Dmowski ascribes to this modern Pole is a reverence for the past traditions of the nation. This historical mindset also is reflected in all of the documents, even in Gomułka, regardless of the time period or point of view of the particular author. Even Marcin Król concedes that a spiritual homeland without historical tradition is a barren homeland indeed. Which traditions are to be gladly embraced and which are to be only regretfully acknowledged are questions answered differently by each of the authors, but all rummage through the historical grab bag in search of treasures.

---

[14] Bromke, *Poland's Politics,* 62.

At least as important as these elements of continuity, however, is the undeniable change that manifests itself between the two earlier documents and the two later. This is a change both in substance and in tone. Where Dmowski can write with supreme confidence, and often arrogance, of what or who a Pole is or ought to be (and who, by extension, is not a Pole, or does not deserve the name of Pole), Gomułka speaks of the people in the sense and manner of a Marxist, but his people are Poles and he considers it the duty of the state and the Party to serve them and their state. Król is much more circumspect to define a nation in which national solidarity is the main theme, but in which the individual nonetheless can freely breathe, while he is both insistent on reminding Poles of their weaknesses and pointing out dangers, and more fearful for the individual in the context of the new Poland in 1992. Dmowski confidently speaks *for* all Poles. Król somewhat more tentatively speaks *of* them, hardly able to speak for himself. Yet all are searching, insistently and yearningly, for the elusive national homeland.

8

Romanian Nationalism: An Ideology of Integration and Mobilization

by James P. Niessen[1]

Document 1

from Nicolae Iorga, "What Is Nationalism?" (1908).[2]

There are many who call themselves nationalists without realizing that nationalism is a doctrine that, once understood, cannot be abandoned, for there are no arguments that can destroy it. There are many who do not imagine that nationalism is also a special way to understand and judge all current problems of our life—political, economic, and cultural—which, given our conditions at this moment—the need to transform all things on the basis

---

1 This study was written with support from the Europa Institute, Budapest, and an IREX travel grant. It benefited from the comments on an earlier draft by fellow scholars at the Europa Institute and by Stephen Fischer-Galati, and the comments on a later draft by Andrei Pippidi. In extending my grateful appreciation for their advice, I wish to stress that I am solely responsible for the views expressed. Limitations of space permit me to indicate only a few of the secondary works that proved valuable.

2 Nicolae Iorga, *"Ce este naționalismul?" Neamul românesc* 3:61–63 (23, 25, and 28 May 1908), 951, 953 (introduction and conclusion). Translated by James P. Niessen.

of a reality which must be our own and must reflect our own being—is therefore, at the same time, also a moral note.

This nationalism cannot be compared to those other political "nuances," that is, those market signs or old historical rubrics that one can still read where our people congregate, allegedly to make policy, but in fact to satisfy, to the greatest degree possible, their particular material interests...

True nationalists are a group of people with understanding, conscience, diligence, and character, who realize that a people is an organic being, *a living fact of the world,* which can be or not be, come into being or die, but cannot be remade into another organic creation. And, since it is so, it is called to nothing else than *the perfection of its being in the interest of universal civilization,* which spreads light and happiness. And those who, through happy circumstances, are in a position to conduct it, must be able to fulfill, through virtue and patriotism, the higher function of *serving natural, national goals.* Their power is not, and cannot be, something proceeding from political metaphysics, but, in agreement with a simple but powerful political *physics,* proceeds from the number and significance of roots planted in that national soil, *that furrow of the people* that alone can give the needed energy.

Formerly, the power of duty to the father earth, repeatedly confirmed in its fight with the enemy, was self-evident. But we will *never* abandon it, nor permit the dragon-like evil spirits to find accommodation in us. We are *here;* we think, speak, and work for the spirits that are *here,* which we know better, yet also study more insistently.

We advance in keeping with this faith, conquering a terrain that prepares our organic reality in its natural course, and we have, for our friends, only the passing smile of the soldier for his comrade as he goes on the attack; for the enemy, clean weapons; for false friends, disdain; and for the traitor who tosses his cap away and passes over to the other side, the most absolute indifference.

Document 2

from Nichifor Crainic, "Program of the Ethnocratic State" (1938).[3]

Romania has been, and must be, the ethnic state of the Romanians.

---

[3] Nichifor Crainic, *"Programul statului etnocratic,"* in Nichifor Crainic, *Ortodoxie și etnocratie* (Bucharest: Cugetarea, 1938), 283–84, 310–11. Translated by James P. Niessen.

The state is the dynamic organization of the nation through the will and power of native Romanians. The people's will for life is expressed through the political organization of the ethnocratic state.

Our state is monarchical throughout its entire history. The monarchy is the principle of its continuity. The crown of the Romanian King symbolizes the glory of the people and the permanence of Romanian consciousness.

Created through our power and will, the state can only survive by our power and will. The sole guarantee of its durability is ethnocracy.

A nationalist state is an ethnocratic state, that is a state that exists through the will and power of our people.

The ethnocratic state differs profoundly from the democratic state. The democratic state is based on the number of population, without racial or religious distinction. The foundation of the ethnocratic state is the Romanian soil and people.

The democratic state is more of a registration office.

The ethnocratic state is the will for power and the increase of the Romanian people. Its principal factors are: soil, blood, soul, and faith.

The soil of the Romanian people has today inhabitants of other races and faiths, as well. They came here through invasion (like the Hungarians), colonization (like the Germans), through crafty infiltration (like the Jews). Every one of them, fonder of its own people than ours, presents no guarantees of security for the official organism of the state.

The Jews are a permanent danger for every national state.

The experience of other states teaches us that any unassimilated member of a minority, active in the organism of the state, is an element of dissolution and ruin. It follows from these judgments that it is a vital necessity for Romania to be an exclusively ethnocratic state. Only native Romanians, who have created it through their sacrifice, guarantee the durability of the state...

Contemporary Romania has been unable to progress in culture and civilization due to the lack of a reliable orientation for the state, and due to the discontinuity of the matters begun.

This evil cannot be cured except through the creation of a great plan of construction, whose systematic execution must be supervised by the supreme authority of the state.

This plan of nationalizing natural wealth, of culturalizing the Romanian soul, and civilizing material life and the Romanian soil, containing work of vast proportions, long in term and epochal in significance, will be supported by a special state bank.

Popularized and accepted by the entire nation, executed by government teams selected from the elites of the professions and controlled by parliament, it will supervised by His Majesty the King.

In the ethnocratic state, the King is the dynamic factor of the entire work of Romanian creation.

The corporatist regime culminates in royal authority.

The great plan of reconstruction of the ethnocratic state engages the entire nation, through the professions, in the work of creation, under the tutelage and authority of His Majesty the King.

Document 3

from a speech by Nicolae Ceauşescu (1974).[4]

Dear Comrades,

I would like to start by conveying to you, the participants in this big rally, to all the working people in the Argeş and Sibiu counties, a warm salute on behalf of the Central Committee and of the government, and on my own behalf.

This gathering here, on this mountain top, is dedicated to the inauguration of the newly built national road across the Făgăraş Range—the "Transfăgărăşan"—the highest in this country, built at more than 2,000 meters, linking Muntenia with Transylvania. The construction of this roadway is a brilliant feat of the working people in this country, showing the force and creative power of a free people, master of its destinies, a people that is building its future according to its wishes.

Thousands of people have worked at the construction of this national road. First, the soldiers of our army, the engineers' corps, who have demonstrated their skill and working power, their firmness and resolution to overcome any difficulties. That is why I want to congratulate warmly all the military who have cooperated in building this road and wish them fresh success in their activity....

Crossing this road, beholding the high summits soaring on every side, we can better build up in our mind the image of the impact they always have

---

4 Nicolae Ceauşescu, "Speech at the Great Popular Rally on the Inauguration of the Trans-Făgăraş National Road, On the Occasion of the Working Visit to Sibiu County" (20 September 1974). Reprinted in *Romania on the Way of Building Up the Multilaterally Developed Socialist Society,* vol. 10 (Bucharest: Meridiane, 1976), 703–706. Translated from the original edition by James P. Niessen.

had on our people, acting from time immemorial and in the hardest circumstances, as a compelling force to keep alive the national feeling and defend this sacred soil by hard struggles. This is our fathers' and forefathers' earth, this is the home of the Romanians! The people living in these stretches have always sought liberty—like the deer on the crests and the birds in the sky—and have cherished the feeling of freedom to have their own country, and master their own destinies....

As I have already mentioned, the military made a decisive contribution to the building of the Transfăgărăşan road. This allows us to entrust it with more tasks in the future. In this way, parallel with military and political training, with the raising of our defense capacity in order to be always ready to defend the revolutionary conquests and the country's independence, the military will have a share in the actual building of the multilaterally developed socialist society, in the building of communism in Romania. After all, the real defensive capacity of any country resides in its economic and political force, in the unshakable unity of the entire people around the Party. And, there is no force in the world able to quell a people desiring to live freely, to build communism in their own country....

Document 4

from the "Platform of the Greater Romania Party" (1991).[5]

Romania, less than two years after the events of December 1989, is experiencing a dramatic situation, a profound crisis on all levels: political, economic, social, and spiritual. In the general European context, contradictory, strained, accentuating disequilibrium, destroying the totalitarian Communist system,

---

5 *"Platforma-Program a Partidului România Mare," România Mare* 2:54 (21 June 1991), 8 (introduction). Translated by James P. Niessen, and published with the consent of Corneliu Vadim Tudor.

The words for "the people" merit a few observations. *Neam,* appearing in the first two documents, was common in the first half of the century. It roughly corresponds to the German *Volk,* with its racial or tribal connotation. Subsequently, writers such as the author of Document 3, preferred *popor,* a word of Latin origin that corresponds directly to the English term. Document 4 uses *etnie,* meaning ethnic group.

occult, extremist, antidemocratic forces exist in our land which, maintained and manipulated from abroad, provoke a state of chaos—the continual disorganization of the national economy, of education, science, and culture. Similarly, values of the national patrimony, of the land's wealth in general, created through much work and sacrifice of the Romanian people, are worn down and alienated. We are witnessing an incredible diminution of the country's capacity to defend itself due to an organized campaign by others to denigrate the wearers of military uniforms.

Deliberately, in a veiled fashion, or at times openly, conflicts are being provoked between ethnic and religious groups and between generations. Hostile ideas are raised with territorial pretensions, pursuing step by step, by an entire arsenal of means, the dismemberment of Romania.

Faced with this situation, the creation of the Greater Romania Party—the declared continuator of the traditions of struggle of the National Party in the last century—becomes an immediate necessity and represents the response and patriotic engagement of all those who consider themselves citizens in thought and deed, with love for the glorious historical past and the ancestral soil, for the progress of all of Romanian society, of all those who desire that Romanians should feel themselves rulers in their own home.

The Greater Romania Party, as a party of the center-left, assumes the task of national reconciliation, of the unification of all democratic and progressive forces of the land, for the realization of an open, pluralistic, and democratic political system, for the real separation of powers in a state of law. We advocate the respect of political, philosophical, and religious convictions and options guaranteed by law, the guarantee of a dignified, civilized life through the realization of an efficient system of social protection that is valid for all socio-professional categories in Romania. We will persistently pursue the application of moral and ethical norms in the promotion of the entire hierarchy of state and politics with respect to the freedom of organization and association.

The Greater Romania Party proposes, through its program and statute, the defense at any price of the integrity and sovereignty of the land, of the national and unitary character of the Romanian state, the restoration of the dignity of our people, one of the oldest and most noble peoples of Europe.

All these things will be realized through the revitalization of the entire Romanian people, springing from two overwhelming realities: first of all, through the Christian faith, which through the vale of tears of history has formed our people, and, second, through the unparalleled genius, energy, and resistance of our people, which has survived, by a miracle, all the hostilities of the ages. This is why our slogan is the famous adage of the Voevode Petru Rareş: "We will be again what we were, and even more!"

Introduction

—— In your opinion, do the Legionary Movement or the ideas promoted by this Movement have a future?

—— There is no need for it, because it did not invent nationalism, and another form than [that of] Eminescu is impossible.

—Petre Ţuţea (1901–1991) in an interview (December 1990)[6]

It is possible to accept Ţuţea's hypothesis on three levels. Romania's greatest poet, Mihail Eminescu (1850–1889) presented an idealized view of a Romania beset by enemies; Eminescu the journalist raised xenophobia to a philosophical principle; Eminescu the martyr inspired generations of disciples. The lives of Iorga, Crainic, Codreanu, and even Ceauşescu and Tudor reflect some of these themes. This study of Romanian nationalism examines the contributions of these nationalists to an ideology serving territorial and political consolidation in the twentieth century. Paradoxically, while territorial unification was largely achieved, political integration remains elusive. This accounts for the continuing appeal of national ideology.

Nicolae Iorga and Populist Nationalism

Nicolae Iorga (1871–1940) was the leader of a new generation of Romanians who advocated, during the first thirty years of this century, a more selfless and democratic style of politics. He was unrivaled for the sheer volume as well as the lasting influence of both his historical scholarship and his nationalist propaganda. The separation of these spheres is difficult: although he was a tireless investigator of sources, taught at the University of Bucharest from 1893, and was member of the Academy since 1910, he stood out even more for his ability to synthesize and his capacity, even compulsion, to popularize his views through brilliant prose and public activity. His journal, *Neamul românesc* ("The Romanian People"), published between 1906 and 1940, became the principal organ of this public activity, most of it written by Iorga

---

6 Petre Ţuţea, *Intre Dumnezeu şi neamul meu* (Bucharest: Arta Grafică, 1992), 294.

himself. The journal, and Iorga's Democratic Nationalist Party, which was formally constituted in 1910, propagated a more populist and aggressive brand of nationalism. *Neamul românesc* focused in particular on three themes of Iorga's "organic nationalism" that are observable in Document 1: the corrupt and self-serving comportment of Romanian politicians, the peasant question, and the life of Romanians living outside the Kingdom of Romania.

Iorga's attack on politicians reflected the traditional lack of sympathy between rulers and ruled in Romania. An influential contemporary book by Constantin Rădulescu-Motru[7] condemned the country's politicians as a cynical and manipulative clique who were too eager to imitate Western culture. The notion that the country's rulers served foreign interests was deeply rooted. Voevodes of the Danubian Principalities, who fought Hungarian and Turkish domination, were succeeded by others who maintained direct control of the government at the expense of tribute payments recovered through the exploitation of their subjects. This form of indirect rule became more blatant between 1711 and 1821, when Greeks from the Phanar district of Constantinople controlled the Voevodal throne and dominated the boiars and the Orthodox Church. Romanians secured the end of Phanariot rule, the unification of the Principalities, and the creation of the independent kingdom between 1821 and 1881 through a skillful exploitation of Russian and French support. Critics of political gamesmanship deplored the rulers' clever compromises with foreigners and saw foreign influence as the root of corruption.

Two targets of popular xenophobia were the Phanariot agents of the Turkish sultan and, increasingly, the Jews. Ballads recounted the struggle of peasant bands against Greeks and Turks; proverbs made hostile reference to Turks, Tatars, Russians, Hungarians, or foreigners in general who "always harm and torment you" and whose tracks "should be burned with nine cartfuls of wood."[8] As Greeks (like Iorga's ancestors) assimilated, the Jews supplanted them as the ideal enemy. Eminescu's Moldavia was the site of the most dramatic growth in the Jewish population of Romania in the course of the nineteenth century. Three-fourths of Romania's 270,000 Jews lived there in 1900. Barred from ownership of land and marginalized by the animosity of the Orthodox Church, a portion of the Jews gained a dominant position, alongside foreign concerns, in the fitful beginnings of Romanian capitalism.

---

[7] *Cultura română si politicianism* ("Romanian Culture and Politicianism") (Bucharest, 1904).

[8] Al. Stănciulescu-Bîrda, "Elements of National History Reflected in Romanian Proverbs," *East European Quarterly* 24:4 (January 1991), 513–28.

The Moldavian capital, Iaşi, and its university became the center of both the intellectual movement *Junimea* (Youth) and of Romanian anti-Semitism. *Junimea* began in 1868 as a conservative critique of Western cultural influences, denouncing the francophilia of the liberal patriots in Bucharest, from an organicist, not a strictly nationalist, perspective. Two graduates of the university in Iaşi, A. C. Cuza and Iorga, provided the synthesis of Eminescu's xenophobia and the nativism of *Junimea.* As professor of economics at the university, Cuza demanded "the creation...of a *national middle class* through the elimination of foreigners, who impede its formation, [and] the formation of a *purely Romanian culture*."[9] For Cuza and many contemporaries, "foreign" meant Jewish, as is suggested by the somewhat exaggerated remark of the French ambassador in 1900: "Anti-semitism is more than just an idea, it is a passion common to politicians of all parties, the Orthodox church, and one could also add, to all the peasants, both Wallachian and Moldavian."[10]

Iorga not only applauded Cuza's treatise, but showed how to apply it. In 1906 he launched an attack on the ruling elite, and launched himself into national politics, by a dramatic condemnation of the exaggerated role of French culture in boiar circles. French had long been the language of polite society in Bucharest, indeed the vehicle of liberalism. But Iorga protested when a group of prominent public figures sponsored a series of charity performances in French. Following speeches by Iorga on "the rights of the national language in the modern state" and "the national danger that results from the alienation of the leading classes," students and others blocked the entrance of the theater; 102 were wounded when the police attacked. The students went on strike, closing the university.[11] The success of this protest emboldened Iorga and Cuza to organize "The Brotherhood of Good Romanians" "to support under all circumstances the language, literature, and

---

9 A. C. Cuza, *Naţionalitate în arta. Principii, fapte, concluzii. Introducerea la doctrina naţionalistă-creştină,* 3rd ed. (Bucharest: Editura "Cartea Românească," 1927), 294–95 (from the preface to the first, serialized edition of 1905). Emphasis in original.

10 Quoted in Leon Volovici, *Nationalist Ideology and Antisemitism. The Case of Romanian Intellectuals in the 1930s* (New York: Pergamon Press, 1991), 16. The author provides an impressive catalog of anti-Semitic intellectuals.

11 On this and other episodes of Iorga's political career, see Petre Ţurlea, *Nicolae Iorga în viaţa politică a României* (Bucharest: Editura enciclopedică, 1991). Iorga's brief notice on Cuza's work appeared in *Sămănătorul* (4 December 1905); see Nicolae Iorga, *O luptă literară,* vol. 2 (Bucharest: Minerva, 1979), 250.

highest interests of the Romanian people." In May 1906 he used the proceeds of a lecture tour organized by the Brotherhood to found *Neamul românesc.* The public response to the journal encouraged Iorga also to run for parliament. Supported by Cuza's circle in Iaşi, he was elected in 1907.

Iorga owed his political notoriety in 1907 as much to his view on rural questions as to his views on the Jews and the national language. The peasant uprising of 1888 emphasized the failure of the parliament, elected by 20 percent of the adult population, to address the poverty, ignorance, and hopelessness of the peasantry. One new group, the *ţărănişti* (peasantists) concentrated on socioeconomic issues and collaborated with the Liberal Party, while another, the literary populists, viewed the problem more paternalistically. At the turn of the century, the literary populists' journal *Sămănătorul* ("The Sower") emerged as an influential forum for fiction and essays dealing with peasant life. Iorga became the editor of the journal in 1903, taking it in a more nationalistic direction and increasing its popularity. Iorga brought these concerns also into *Neamul românesc,* addressing rural questions so forcefully, and to such a large readership, that after the peasant revolt of 1907 he received threats from landowners who considered him to be a leading instigator of the revolt.

Radical activists and writers among the peasantists actually encouraged revolt, and the authorities involved with rural affairs sinned through omission and commission. They bear more responsibility than Iorga for the events, but Iorga's linkage of exploitation with the Jews was explosive. He wrote in *Sămănătorul,* for instance, that "...however high the dirty wave of profit-seekers, the soil is ours. And one day the wind will blow away the scum it has brought, and we shall remain."[12] Jewish tenants of absentee landlords, Jewish moneylenders and innkeepers—these were standard figures in *Neamul românesc* and the targets of racially motivated peasant violence. The Orthodox clergy's campaign against peasant alcoholism had targeted Jewish innkeepers, and priests participated in the revolt itself and were among the 10,000 killed in the subsequent crackdown. *Neamul românesc* could thus argue that the revolt was not merely a consequence of oppression and neglect by landlords and politicians, but an act of righteous retribution by the peasants against enemies of the people.

Rural issues formed the core of Iorga's first legislative activity and also of the political program he and Cuza presented a year later. The "Democratic Nationalist Program"[13] focused on three areas: peasant agriculture, public

---

[12] Quoted in Volovici, *Nationalist Ideology and Antisemitism,* 32.

[13] *"Declaraţie de program naţionalist-democrat," Neamul românesc* 3:13 (30 January 1908), 193–94.

education, and administration. Many points favored the villagers, including the autonomous organization of the clergy; others demanded the exclusion of Jews and foreigners from industrial employment, land ownership, innkeeping, and military service. The program proposed a democratic system serving the interests of ethnic Romanians. The introduction of a professional civil service and universal suffrage, finally, was to make officials accountable to the people rather than to party bosses. Xenophobic and demagogic themes complemented others that were progressive and anti-elitist.

Iorga's "What Is Nationalism?" (Document 1) illuminates the ideas behind the Democratic Nationalist Program. The organicism of the article, like that of literary populism, evokes the continuity and strength of peasant agriculturalists, who, for the good of the nation, ought to be educated and given rights, while alien interlopers should be removed like weeds. The references to merchants, evil spirits, and dragons are conventional metaphors for the Jews in contemporary religious language. Iorga was not particularly religious, but he concurred with Rădulescu-Motru and others who saw the Orthodox Church as a central national institution.

Both the program and the article lack any reference to the one-third of Romanians who lived outside the kingdom. The call to work for the people *here* might even suggest a renunciation of irredentism. The image of the people as an organic being, of the cultivation of the furrow of the people, however, points to a biological definition of the people and the need to raise its consciousness. Romanians living abroad had a prominent place in Iorga's activities outside parliament. *Sămănătorul* and *Neamul românesc* gave extensive treatment to the life of Romanians abroad. As director after 1908 of *Liga culturală* (an irredentist organization founded in 1890), Iorga intensified his propaganda and used it to question Romania's alliance with Austria-Hungary. In 1908, too, Iorga initiated the summer school at Vălenii de Munte, in the Carpathians close to the Transylvanian frontier. For the next six years, the courses on Romanian culture and history, taught also to students from neighboring countries, would prove to be a source of inspiration for selected Romanians of Hungary and of exasperation for Hungarian authorities who sought to prevent attendance by their subjects. Iorga dedicated many of his scholarly works in these years to Transylvania.[14]

Prince Carol, the future king, visited Vălenii de Munte, an act that displeased King Carol and the Crown Prince Ferdinand because the king's

---

14 The most important of these was *Istoria românilor din Ardeal si Ungaria,* based on his lectures, which appeared in Romanian and French versions in 1915–16 and was recently reissued as *Istoria românilor din Ardeal si Ungaria* (Bucharest: Editura ştiintifică şi Enciclopedică, 1989).

alliance with Austria-Hungary precluded official claims by Bucharest on Hungarian territory. Similarly, Transylvanian[15] Romanian politicians avoided open demands for unification that could be construed as treason against the state where they lived. In the eighteenth century, a group of Uniate (Greek Catholic) clergy and scholars had formulated the theory of Daco-Romanian continuity to legitimize their church's tie to Rome and to secure political rights (on grounds of historical priority) for all Romanians within Transylvania. The propagation of the theory through church schools created the first nationally conscious intelligentsia in the first half of the nineteenth century. An ideology originally designed for ethno-religious and provincial motives soon transcended confessional and territorial bounds.[16] The political champion of this ideology in Transylvania, the Romanian National Party, never openly demanded unification. The party's leaders, albeit militant nationalists, were too cautious to espouse a strategy that transcended Hungary.

The evolution of the "eastern question" favored the increasing influence of Iorga's sympathizers in both Hungary and Romania. While the Liberal Party in Romania moved under the leadership of Ionel Brătianu toward serious political reform, Iorga's platform of 1910 made foreign policy its first priority, insisting upon ethnic solidarity and unity. A young Transylvanian, Onisifor Ghibu, had the impression in 1910 that people in Romania were little interested in "the great national issues," i.e., irredentism and unification. But King Carol warned the Austro-Hungarian ambassador in 1912 that a planned Hungarian measure affecting the Romanian minority would cause an increase in Romania of "religious and nationalist fanaticism, that He and His government would be powerless to oppose...placing a weapon in the hands

---

15 The term "Transylvania" is used broadly here to refer to the regions in which Romanians predominated—Transylvania, Maramureş, Crişana, and Banat—and which passed from Hungarian to Romanian rule in 1918.

16 For more detail on the role of the Uniates in Romanian nationalism during this century, see James Niessen, "The Greek Catholic Church and the Romanian Nation in Transylvania," in *Religious Compromise, Political Salvation: The Greek Catholic Church and Nationbuilding in Eastern Europe,* Carl Beck Papers No. 1003 (Pittsburgh: University of Pittsburgh Press, forthcoming), 17–68; Niessen, *"Relaţiile interconfesionale şi procesul formării naţiune romane în Transilvania," Anuarul Institutului de Istorie Cluj-Napoca* 31 (1992), 79–92; and Niessen, "Romanians and Hungarians in Habsburg and Vatican Diplomany: The Diocese of Hajdudorog, 1912," *The Catholic Historical Review* 79:2 (1994).

of enemies of His foreign policy."[17] The radicals' influence was growing. Ghibu was one of several Transylvanian admirers of Iorga who were becoming impatient with the moderation of the National Party's leadership. He had been one of the student leaders in the demonstrations in 1906 in Bucharest. Two others in the group were the poet Octavian Goga and the historian Ioan Lupaş. These so-called youth of steel resembled Iorga's Democratic Nationalists in their populism, Orthodox Christianity, anti-Semitism, and militancy, as expressed in two journals that were visibly modelled upon *Sămănătorul* and *Neamul românesc.*[18]

After King Carol failed to gain the support of his Crown Council for war on the side of the Central Powers in 1914, Goga and Ghibu, now in Bucharest, and Iorga led the militants who rejected the alliance and applauded the decision to invade Transylvania in 1916. Facing a grim military prospect in the short term, Prime Minister Brătiănu told King Ferdinand: "See today's responsibilities in the perspective of this people's destiny and its future, and advance decisively on the path which national consciousness indicates."[19]

The Interwar Period and World War II

Romania faced repeated defeat in World War I and suffered enemy occupation and a separate, punitive peace in 1918. Therefore, the rapid reversal of fortunes and the unification of Transylvania with Austria's Bucovina and Russia's Bessarabia struck many as a miracle. Lupaş's popular history wrote of the Calvary of King Ferdinand and the nation in 1916–18 and their resurrection at the end of the war.[20] As satisfying as the victory was and

---

17 Onisifor Ghibu, *Oameni între oameni* (Bucharest: Editura Eminescu, 1990), 252. Fürstenberg to Berchtold, Bucharest (26 February 1912), in Hungarian National Archives, Budapest, K26 (The Prime Minister's Office), 1915-XXV-1042.

18 Ţurlea, *Nicolae Iorga în viaţa politică a României,* 20–28; Ghibu, *Oameni între oameni,* 224–29. The journals were *Luceafărul* ("Morning Star," after a poem by Eminescu) and *Ţara noastră* ("Our Land").

19 Quoted in Sterie Diamandi, *Galeria oamenilor politici* (Bucharest: Editura Gesa, 1991 [1935]), 76.

20 Lupaş, *Istoria unirii românilor* (Bucharest: Fundaţia culturală regală "Principele Carol," 1937).

comforting as the impression of divine favor may have been, Romanians were unprepared for the sudden achievement of a united state. The radically altered context of their lives inspired anxious hypersensitivity to the superior economic status of Romania's largest minorities, the Hungarians, Germans, and Jews. Romanians were surrounded by other peoples, outside and inside the frontiers, who seemed poised to take the prize away.[21] Hence the dominant preoccupations of interwar nationalists, illustrated by Crainic's program (Document 2): the need for the political unity of Greater Romania, Orthodox Christianity as a source of spiritual unity, and the advocacy of measures to redress the superior economic status of ethnic minorities.

Romania's territory and population more than doubled between 1912 and 1920, and ethnic minorities increased from 10 percent to 28 percent of the population. Bulgarian, Russian, and Hungarian blocs at the extremities of the state were unfriendly to the central authority, but so were the more numerous Romanians in these provinces who applauded unification but whose political traditions were different and often more democratic than those of the old kingdom. The granting of universal suffrage and a radical land reform accentuated these problems. The minorities gained a new grievance, the Conservative Party ceased to be a major force, and the Liberals were further isolated.

During the 1920s, politicians seeking to fashion a nationwide constituency devised two rival strategies, once centralist and the other populist. Liberals inherited the confidence of the dynasty and the kingdom's strongest political machine, and they sought to counteract what they saw as dangerous centrifugal tendencies by establishing direct administrative control over the new provinces. Their economic doctrine of *prin noi înșine* ("through ourselves" or "do it yourself") advocated trade protectionism and government investment in Romanian industries. The population was generally appalled by the Liberals' violation of democratic principles and their terrorization of the electorate, particularly in the Transylvanian and Bessarabian strongholds of the National and Peasant parties. These parties denounced the corruption and "colonialism" of the central government and in 1922 boycotted the coronation of King Ferdinand in the Transylvanian town of Alba Julia—an act celebrating the dynasty's achievement of Greater Romania. They fused in 1926 as the National Peasant Party and demanded decentralization, free trade, and a genuine democracy that would unite Romanians against foreign enemies. The

---

[21] Zeev Barbu, "Psycho-Historical and Sociological Perspectives on the Iron Guard, the Fascist Movement of Romania," in *Who Were the Fascists? Social Roots of European Fascism* (Bergen: Universitetsforlaget, 1980), 382.

Liberals and National Peasants alternated in power for much of the interwar period and succeeded by the 1930s in creating nationwide constituencies.[22]

The existential anxiety that underlay these rival strategies had a real basis in the territorial revisionism of neighboring Hungary and the Soviet Union and, for many, in resentment of the concession in 1923 of citizenship for Romania's Jews, made in response to pressure from the League of Nations. By the logic of this anxiety, Hungarians, Russians, Communists, and Jews were hostile to Greater Romania's survival. The two major parties' dedication to liberal democracy was sufficient to moderate this resentment. Iorga himself, though a member of neither party, abandoned anti-Semitic politics after 1920.

An observer calculated in the mid–1930s that 36 percent of the Liberals' and National Peasants' parliamentary deputies were former members of Iorga's Democratic Nationalists. For the younger generation of his disciples, Crainic would write: "Iorga could no longer give us direction...fulfilled prophecy consumed the prophet in him, leaving the historian and chief of a small political grouping."[23] Another disciple was Octavian Goga, the poet turned politician and founder of the Agrarian Party. He became increasingly critical of democracy because it tolerated urban Jewish and Hungarian influences in the city that he felt corrupted traditional Romanian culture. The new generation's blend of resentment and fervent Orthodox Christianity lent the new nationalism, or neonationalism, its characteristic note.[24]

The new nationalism had ecclesiastic, intellectual, and populist components. The centrality of Orthodox Christianity was not strictly dependent upon religious faith, but became an axiom for the new nationalists. Traditional Orthodox hostility to other churches reinforced the rejection of the

---

22 Henry L. Roberts, *Rumania, Political Problems of an Agrarian State* (New Haven, CT: Yale University Press, 1951); Paul A. Schapiro, "Romania's Past as Challenge for the Future: A Developmental Approach to Interwar Politics," in *Romania in the 1980s,* Daniel N. Nelson, ed. (Boulder, CO: Westview Press, 1981), 29–37.

23 Ţurlea, *Nicolae Iorga în viaţa politică a României,* 36. Nichifor Crainic, *Zile albe, zile negre, Memorii, I* (Bucharest: Casa Editorială "Gândirea," 1991), 148. This is the first edition of the memoirs that Crainic wrote while a fugitive in 1944–47.

24 Octavian Goga, *Mustul care fierbe* (Bucharest: Editura Scripta, 1992 [1927]). The term "neonationalism" is from Armin Heinen, *Die Legion "Erzengel Michael" in Rumänien. Soziale Bewegung und politische Organisation* (Munich: R. Oldenbourg, 1986), which is a thorough and insightful account of this generation.

non-Orthodox ethnic minorities. Nationalists therefore applauded the decision to streamline the church and strengthen its ties to the state. The establishment of a uniform church statute and an Orthodox Patriarchate in 1925 coordinated the dioceses of the new provinces with those of the old kingdom. The Orthodox opposed the conclusion of a Concordat with the Holy See, which the government and Uniates desired in order to bring diocesan borders in line with those of the state. Opponents argued that it gave the Catholic minority a degree of freedom not enjoyed by the "national church" and that it facilitated Hungarian influence. Nicolae Bălan, Metropolitan of Transylvania, and Onisifor Ghibu, now a university professor, led the unsuccessful opposition. Ghibu's break in 1932 with his longtime friend Iorga, then prime minister, over this issue symbolizes the separation of the old and new nationalists.

The intellectual component of the new nationalism, as in the case of Iorga's earlier movement, was popularized at first by a single writer and his journal: the poet-philosopher Nichifor Crainic (1889–1972) and *Gândirea,* published between 1921 and 1944 and directed by Crainic from 1926. Crainic followed Russian theological writers in characterizing Orthodox peoples as more collectivist and unselfish than people in the West. For Romanians, as for Russians, all that was valuable in national culture had been created by divine intervention and through the church.[25] Lucian Blaga and Nae Ionescu were other influential theorists of the new nationalism. For Blaga, the Romanian character was a synthesis of Orthodoxy with the ancestral religion of the Dacians and the migratory experience of mountain shepherds, while Ionescu asserted that Romanians' Orthodoxy was innate and independent of individual will. The Orthodox theologian Dumitru Stăniloaie denounced Ionescu's denial of personal responsibility as amoral, but he, too, saw nationalism as divinely ordained.[26]

These ecclesiastic and intellectual tendencies became more significant with the rise of the Legion of the Archangel Michael, or Iron Guard. Crainic and Ionescu both were members of the National Peasant Party in the 1920s; later, their enthusiastic support for the Legion in their newspapers, along with

---

[25] See Keith Hitchins, "*Gândirea:* Nationalism in a Spiritual Guise," in *Social Change in Romania, 1860-1940,* K. Jowitt, ed. (Berkeley: University of California, Institute of International Studies, 1978), 140–73. It also appeared in Hitchins, *Studies on Romanian National Consciousness* (Pelham, NY: Nagard, 1983), 231–58.

[26] Nae Ionescu, *Roza vînturilor, 1926-1933* (Bucharest: Editura "Roza Vînturilor," 1990 [1937]); and Dumitru Stăniloaie, *Ortodoxie şi românism* (Sibiu: Tiparul tipografiei Archidiecezane, 1939).

Ionescu's joining with the movement in 1933, inspired many intellectuals. The Orthodox evangelical movement "Lord's Army" supported by Stăniloaie and Metropolitan Bălan also had contributed to the growth of the Legion. These, however, were not the movement's founders.

The Legion had its origin in the League of National Christian Defense (LNCD), founded by A. C. Cuza in 1923. His younger associates, Corneliu Zelia Codreanu and Ion Moţa, moved in 1927 to form the Legion. Codreanu (1899–1938) was not content to campaign for electoral support on the basis of a platform: with the zeal of a missionary, he proclaimed, "Today the country is going to ruin not for lack of programs, but for lack of men...the Rumanian people need today a great teacher and leader, who will overcome the powers of darkness and destroy the brood of Hell."[27] Unlike Cuza, Codreanu and Moţa were truly religious and charismatic individuals. Codreanu had attended a military academy and sought to inculcate a spirit that was both ascetic and combative. Moţa was the descendant of Orthodox priests from Transylvania. Adopting the practice of villagers in the restless *moţ* region of Transylvania, he formed members into Brotherhoods of the Cross which were sealed in their own blood. The Legionary mystique evoked Christian themes but also the methods of the haiduke, touring villages to assist the poor against the rulers and exploiters and undertaking periodic violent assaults on officials and Jews.

The Legion's fanatical anti-Semitism did not distinguish it from Cuza's LNCD, Goga's Agrarians, or Cuza's and Goga's National Christian Party (founded in 1935). Even Patriarch Christea made hostile remarks about the Jews and justified the Romanians' need to "defend themselves." It was the Legion's acts of violence that distinguished them from these others. The violence was condemned by the Orthodox hierarchy, but economic hardship lessened the public's abhorrence of them. Romanian students' resentment of Jews in their ranks and of the competition for scarce intellectual employment accounted for the strong appeal of anti-Semitic extremism among the students, a great many of whom were of rural origin. Intellectual unemployment, hence resentment of Jewish rivals, increased during the Depression. The Orthodox episcopate applauded the social welfare and church-building activities of the Legion. Its demand for Christianization of national politics and society, in two declarations written by Bălan in 1937, revealed a totalitarian view of public morality.[28]

---

[27] Roberts, *Rumania,* 230. The citation is from Codreanu's *Pentru legionari* (1936).

[28] Cited by István Juhász, *Az új értelmű román nacionalizmus* (Cluj: Tipografia "Gloria," 1937), 4–7.

Under the impact of the Depression, nationalists associated "Christianization" with attacks on the superior wealth of many members of the Jewish and Hungarian minorities. Leaders advocating the redress of minorities' economic advantages through state policy emerged from the established parties. Mihail Manoilescu adapted industrial protectionism to a corporative model of society, while Alexandru Vaida-Voevod, a member of National Peasant governments, maintained good relations with the Legionaries and proposed harsh restrictions on minority employment—the "numerus Valachicus," which his own party refused to accept. Both formed splinter parties, the National Corporatist League and the Romanian Front, that advocated ethnic quotas in the economy and in university admissions. National concentration and defense against foreigners were increasingly stressed by the larger Romanian parties as well, and punitive measures against industrial and commercial concerns owned by the minorities were put into effect.[29] Crainic himself became an admirer of corporatism, announcing that its Romanian variant would ensure for true Romanians their rightful place in the state and in economic development. He later asserted that his "Program of the Ethnocratic State" (Document 2) "had none of the chaotic violence of Legionarism and Cuzist absurdities...[and] addressed itself to all nationalities, offering a positive basis for an understanding."[30]

Neonationalists demonstrated a partiality for autocratic rule that was both philosophical and opportunistic. The image of Codreanu was a combination of Orthodox sainthood and *Führerprinzip.* The careers of both Crainic and Ionescu benefited from their early support for the return of Carol II from exile in 1930. As one of the king's closest advisers until 1934, Ionescu was "the philosopher of monarchic mysticism" and prophet of "inevitable political transformations" in which Carol would be the savior.[31] The neonationalist right attained its greatest electoral success in 1937, officially gaining over a quarter of the vote. The short-lived National Christian government led by Goga and Cuza enacted anti-Semitic measures that survived its own brief tenure, but its incompetence proved a convenient pretext for Carol to

---

[29] Elemér Illyés, *National Minorities in Romania, Change in Romania* (Boulder, CO: East European Quarterly, and New York: Columbia University Press, 1982), 92–93; and *Politics and Political Parties in Roumania* (London: International Reference Library Publishing Co., 1936), 129–305.

[30] Crainic, *Zile albe, zile negre,* 283.

[31] These phrases are from another member of Carol's inner circle, Grigore Gafencu, *Insemnări politice 1929-1939,* 1st ed. (Bucharest: Humanitas, 1991), 121, 172, 251–52.

establish a royal dictatorship with the Patriarch as titular prime minister. Carol created an umbrella party, the Party of National Rebirth, in 1938 (later renamed the Party of National Unity, then the Party of the Nation) and erected a corporative regime. He also decimated the Legion itself through arrests and executions, including of Codreanu. Crainic's glorification of royal power had been timely.

The loss of Bessarabia and northern Bucovina to the Soviet Union and of northern Transylvania to Hungary in 1940, the latter known to Romanians as the Vienna Diktat, thoroughly discredited King Carol and helped bring the Legion and General Antonescu, a hero of World War I, to power in September 1940. During a four-month reign of terror, the Legion conducted a pogrom in Bucharest and a massacre of its critics, including Nicolae Iorga—an act of patricide against the father of modern nationalism. Romania's intellectuals applauded Antonescu's subsequent suppression of the Legion, as did the Orthodox Church, but they tolerated his continued persecution of the Jews and, at least in its initial phase, supported the crusade against the Soviet Union beginning in 1941. Crainic served the royal dictatorship, then Antonescu, as minister of propaganda. Roughly half of Romania's Jews perished between 1940 and 1944, including most of those living under Hungarian rule in northern Transylvania and others in Moldavia, Bessarabia, and areas of the Soviet Union under Romanian military occupation after 1941.

Postwar Communism

After 1945, an ostensibly internationalist regime took power, executing, imprisoning, or exiling the neonationalists and outlawing their works. Nationalism therefore manifested itself in the impotent, often extremist voice of the emigration and in the gradual invention by the Communists of a new, ideologically acceptable variant. Nicolae Ceaușescu's speech from 1974 (Document 3) represents an example of the three-part message of Romanian national communism: the priority of building a country that would be strong enough economically to ensure both well-being and independence, the achievement of integration and assimilation through growth, and, finally, the selective appeal to prewar nationalism to support these themes.

The unfolding of the national Communist strategy had to overcome the low patriotic standing of the Romanian Communist Party. The Comintern's position that Romania's acquisition of Transylvania and Bessarabia were imperialist annexations had kept popular support for the party to a minimum, and only one of the party's leaders between 1922 and 1944 was an ethnic

Romanian. While Stalin ordained the return of northern Transylvania to Romania, he required special treatment for the Hungarians and retained Bessarabia. Party membership rose from less than 1,000 in mid–1944 to 717,480 two years later, and many of the new recruits were Hungarians and Romanians who desired immunity from prosecution for minor war crimes or right-wing extremism. Really prominent nationalities, several hundred thousand members of the political parties, religious leaders, and others were imprisoned.

The regime provided the Hungarian minority with a Stalinist education in its native language and a nominally autonomous Hungarian region. The Jews also received visible favors, associated in the mind of the public with the presence of a few Jews in the leadership, notably the powerful Ana Pauker. Iorga had accused a political adversary in 1908 of relying upon the money and connections of "Fischers and...Rappoports and...Honigmanns and a legion of insects called Wechsler, Kaufmann, and Pauker."[32] Forty years later, Gheorghiu-Dej and Pauker led a takeover by Stalin's "insects" and facilitated large-scale emigration to the newly created state of Israel. Then, they combined to oust the "nationalist" Lucreţiu Pătrăşcanu, who had denounced chauvinism and anti-Semitism but had insisted upon communism's patriotic character: "We will tie the national idea to the idea of the masses, realizing the national idea in truth by raising the masses to a conscious life. Between our political faith as communists and the national idea thus understood there is no contradiction."[33]

"The national idea thus understood" created its own contradictions and odd alliances. Only months after Pătrăşcanu's ouster, the party's "Resolution on the National Question" launched a campaign against Zionism with anti-Semitic overtones. Like Stalin, the Communists also endorsed the neo-nationalists' abhorrence of the Catholic Church as a hostile foreign agency by abrogating the Concordat, strictly regulating foreign contacts by the churches, and reuniting the 1.5 million-strong Uniate Church with the Orthodox. Orthodox bishops such as Metropolitan Bălan assisted in the long-desired union, accepting the arrest of the recalcitrant bishops and thousands of priests—methods, Onisifor Ghibu wrote, "that not even the most persistent

---

32 Nicolae Iorga, "Naţionalism şi tachism," *Neamul românesc* 3:21 (1908), 321–22.

33 Lucreţiu Pătrăşcanu, *Poziţia Partidului Comunist faţa de intelectuali* (Bucharest: Editura P.C.R., 1946), 14. Cited in Katherine Verdery, *National Ideology under Socialism: Identity and Cultural Politics in Ceauşescu's Romania* (Berkeley: University of California Press, 1991), 54.

enemies of our nation would have dared apply."[34] Stalinist rejection of Western democracy echoed that of the neonationalists, but with a very different emphasis. Some historical and linguistic works of the 1950s denied the Dacian and Roman origins of the Romanians and exaggerated their links to Slavic culture. Ana Pauker reportedly stated, "All that is known of the Romanian language is that it consists of a very large number of Slav elements."[35]

The strident anticommunism of Romanian culture in exile provided a strong motive for the Communists to isolate the country from the West. Romanian research institutes in Paris and Freiburg sponsored scholarly journals after their founding in 1949, while Italy and Spain were centers of both the Legionnaire and Greek Catholic emigration. The Legionaries and Catholics enjoyed disproportionate influence in emigré politics: the surviving leaders of the Legion had been interned in Germany since 1941 and hence escaped to the West more easily than moderate opponents of the Romanian Communists, while Catholics benefited from the support of the Holy See and its nonrecognition of their suppression in 1948. Among the Orthodox, the former youth leader of the Legion, Viorel Trifa, became bishop of coreligionists in the United States.

The Stalinist model of state-sponsored industrialization was an unlikely basis for the doctrine of state independence that evolved after Stalin's death, accompanied as it was by extreme Soviet exploitation. Large segments of the population were probably aware of this exploitation and resented it, hence the leadership could rely upon their support when it began to resist the Soviets. De-Stalinization in the Soviet Union after 1956 and the first difficulties between the Soviet Union and China provided the opportunity. Gheorghiu-Dej, like Khrushchev's adversaries in Moscow, sought to preserve a high rate of industrial investment and opposed liberalization in the areas of culture and agriculture. He took advantage of the emerging Sino-Soviet conflict to increase Romanian independence by echoing Chinese slogans of autonomous development.

---

[34] Mircea Păcurariu, *Pages from the History of the Romanian Church (The Uniatism in Transylvania)* (Bucharest: Romanian Orthodox Church Bible and Mission Institute Publishing House, 1991), 64–69; and Onisifor Ghibu, letter to Prime Minister Petru Groza (March 1949), in Ghibu, *Chemare la judecata istoriei,* vol. 1 (Bucharest: Editura Albatros, 1992), 113.

[35] George Schöpflin, "Rumanian Nationalism," *Survey* 20:2/3 (1974), 84–89; and Trond Gilberg, *Nationalism and Communism in Romania: The Rise and Fall of Ceaușescu's Personal Dictatorship* (Boulder, CO: Westview Press, 1990), 43; Verdery, *National Ideology under Socialism,* 47–51.

The more significant break with the Soviet Union occurred in 1963. Romanian determination to continue Stalinist industrialization policies conflicted with Khrushchev's proposal to assign Romania a primarily agricultural role within the Council for Mutual Economic Assistance (or CMEA), restricting large industrial projects. Gheorghiu-Dej rejected this plan and built a mammoth steel mill with Western support. The party's April Theses of 1964 asserted, "The planned management of the national economy is one of the fundamental, essential and inalienable attributes of sovereignty of the socialist state." Romania also rejected a plan for international cooperation put forward by the Soviet economist E. B. Valev which sketched an "interstate economic complex" on the lower Danube. According to the response of a Romanian economist, the project sought to "theorize about a process of dismemberment of the national economies and of the national territories of certain socialist states."[36] Stalinist orthodoxy provided the ideological basis for the defense of territorial integrity.

Nicolae Ceauşescu (1918–1989) continued the policy of industrial independence of Gheorghiu-Dej after 1965. The new leader used nationalist themes even more, but like Gheorghiu-Dej he subordinated cultural policy and rural society to industrialization. Nonsocialist countries soon gained a large share of Romanian foreign trade, and their loans became a part of the Romanian investment strategy, without alteration of the centralized model of the economy. A logical extension of the independent industrial course was the blueprint for the "multilaterally developed socialist society" in the party program of 1974, which proposed maximal autarky with the simultaneous development of all branches of production in order to minimize dependence on imports. The program took the interwar principle of *prin noi înşine* ("do it yourself") to the extreme, leading to disaster when oil for the Romanian petrochemical industry had to be imported at prohibitive prices.

The economic strategy inspired not only a policy of state independence, but also an aggressive attack on the problem of the economic inequality of Romania's ethnic groups through urbanization and administrative measures in Transylvania. During the interwar period, industrialization, the preferential placement of Romanians in the civil service, and their wider access to education began to offset the dominance of the minorities in the urban population. The Communists' construction of factories in towns traditionally dominated by minorities attracted Romanians in large numbers, while regulations concerning the settlement and employment of new graduates helped to break up concentrations of minorities. Between 1910 and 1977, the concentration of Hungarians in eight major Transylvanian towns declined

---

[36] Schöpflin, "Rumanian Nationalism," 79–81.

from as high as 95 percent to an average of 40 percent. The recruitment of Romanian workers for Transylvania accelerated after 1975.[37] The program of 1974 stated that "equal rights are first of all reflected in the growing degree of economic and social development of the whole country," which would be made possible by "locating most rationally the productive forces on the territory of the homeland." Similar arguments were used to justify the elimination of special minority status in the Hungarian Autonomous Region (dissolved in 1968) and educational institutions.[38] Despite theoretical differences, this practice bears a resemblance to Crainic's ethnocratic state. Future historians may determine whether it was a coincidence that in 1970 Ceauşescu began his association with the ultranationalist Romanian-Italian millionaire Josif Constantin Drăgan, who had written his dissertation on corporatism in Rome in 1940.[39]

In defense of the economic course, Gheorghiu-Dej loosened the reins on historians. Some interwar historians began to write again, Daco-Romanian continuity became a central theme in archaeology, and the first Romanian synthesis of Transylvanian history was published in 1960. The patriotic initiatives were received enthusiastically by intellectuals and students. Ceauşescu proved even more willing to raise historical themes. In 1966 he sought to demonstrate his succession within the national pantheon by staging events in which he was greeted by actors portraying his predecessors, Voevodes Stephen the Great and Michael the Brave.[40] National unity was palpable in the genuine enthusiasm for Ceauşescu's public defiance of a threatened Soviet invasion of Romania in 1968. This response helped

---

[37] Illyés, *National Minorities in Romania,* 55–69; and *Report on the Situation of the Hungarian Minority in Rumania. Prepared for the Hungarian Democratic Forum* (Budapest, 1988), 18–41.

[38] *Programme of the Romanian Communist Party for the Building of the Multilaterally Developed Socialist Society and Romania's Advance toward Communism* (Bucharest: Agerpres, 1975), 153–54; and Gilberg, *Nationalism and Communism in Romania,* 163–73.

[39] Nicolae Balta, "Iosif Constantin Dragan—From the Career of a Collaborationist," *22* (11 January 1991), from *JPRS*-EER-91-019 (12 February 1991), 27–28; and Traian Filip, *Munţii văzuţi din Câmpie. Dialog cu Josif Constantin Drăgan* (Supplement to *Europa şi neamul românesc*) (Roma: Nagard, 1991).

[40] Michael Shafir, "The Men of the Archangel Revisited: Anti-Semitic Formations among Communist Romania's Intellectuals," *Studies in Comparative Communism* 16:3 (1983), 228.

Ceauşescu to improve his position in the party and to become the sole arbiter, by 1974, of the national course.

In classical Stalinist style, Ceauşescu sought to motivate producers through ideology rather than material incentives. Party resolutions of 1971, instituting a "little cultural revolution" following Ceauşescu's visit to China, and 1974, assigning special importance to historians and other cultural producers in the revolutionary transformation of society, signaled the end of the cultural thaw born of the power struggle. "Multilateral development" was easier to justify in terms of national ideology than economic rationality. Historical scholarship on continuity, independence, and unification received preferential support after the 1974 Party Congress. Many Romanian writings of the interwar period came back into currency, although not the overtly fascist ones.[41]

Historical anniversaries were a characteristic manifestation of the new directives. The customary national celebrations of independence and unification in 1918 no longer sufficed. The "2030th anniversary of the establishment of the first centralized unitary state on the territory of Romania" in 1980, in which Drăgan also participated, demonstrated the regime's special fascination with myths about the origins of the people. Emil Cioran had written in 1935, referring to the "crimes" of the Jews: "The myths of a nation are its vital truths. They might not coincide with *the truth;* this is not of importance." As recently noted in another context, a myth about origins may be a comforting "ego massage," but its implicit racism makes it susceptible to divisive and illiberal ends.[42]

Circles outside the party and academic establishment provided the framework for the most nationalistic writing. Books produced by the military and ecclesiastic presses glorified national tradition, even as the Romanian demands for the deportation of Bishop Viorel Trifa from the United States as a war criminal were crowned with success. The rallies of poet-journalist Adrian Păunescu gained a large following, combining music and the personality cult with fervent patriotism. Overtly anti-Semitic and anti-Hungarian voices were heard beginning in 1980 through the poems and articles of Corneliu Vadim Tudor and in Ion Lăncrănjan's *A Word on*

---

[41] My argument on the link between economic policy and nationalist propaganda follows that of Verdery, *National Ideology under Socialism.*

[42] The citation from Cioran is in Volovici, *Nationalist Ideology and Antisemitism,* 187; see also Molly Myerowicz Levine, "The Use and Abuse of Black Athena," *American Historical Review* 97:2 (April 1992), 450–53.

Transylvania, a poetic invocation of Transylvania that branded rival Hungarian views as revisionist and fascist.[43]

In the years of "high Ceauşescuism," the appeal to patriotism and resistance to foreign enemies successfully mobilized people for economic growth and for huge projects like the Transfăgărăşan Highway and the Danube–Black Sea Canal. Ceauşescu revived construction of the canal, finally completing it in 1984. Both projects displayed Stalinist gigantomania, the conquest of nature at great human cost, and the deployment of military engineers to defeat a putative external threat: the loss of Transylvania, or the closing of the mouth of the Danube by the Soviet Union. Ceauşescu's imagery of the Carpathians is oddly reminiscent of its symbolic role in the interwar works of the recently rehabilitated Lucian Blaga. (By an ironic coincidence, the Transfăgărăşan Highway passed not far from the mountain village of Plătiniş; in 1974 Blaga's contemporary, the philosopher Constantin Noica (1909–1987), editor of the chief Legionary newspaper in 1940, took up his residence there and became an admired figure of the anticommunist intelligentsia during the 1980s.)

After the Fall of Communism

Economic hardship and political disarray since 1989 have fostered the revival of open ethnic conflict and nationalist extremism. The revival is accentuated by the collapse of federal states to the southwest and north, events that have fascinated Romanian patriots who are fearful of the Hungarian threat, but eager to reunite with Romania the lands lost to the Soviet Union since 1940. Ceauşescu's cultivation of Romanian anxieties concerning the Hungarians guaranteed the continuing popularity of this theme and encouraged his successors to exploit it.

As in earlier periods, the government and nationalist opposition have frequently seen eye to eye on the Hungarian question, and religious and military themes have regained their traditional prominence. The opportunism of the chauvinist press and the official sponsorship it sometimes enjoyed contributed to the success of former national Communists in the new era. The

---

43 Antonie Plămădeală (Metropolitan of Transulvania), *The Role of the Orthodox Clergy: The Founders of the Romanian Language and Culture* (Bucharest, 1977); Ion Lăncrănjan, *Cuvînt despre Transilvania* (Bucharest: Editura Sport-Turism, 1982); and Ilie Ceauşescu, *Transylvania: An Ancient Romanian Land* (Bucharest: Military Pubishing House, 1984).

Platform of the Greater Romania Party (Document 4) is characteristic with its emphasis on Orthodoxy, territorial integrity, and militarism.

Deterioration of the Romanian living standard accelerated after 1982, when Ceauşescu decided to drastically increase exports in order to retire the foreign debt. Resentment of this policy was strong among educated members of the minorities, for whom the relative well-being and freedom of Hungarians and Germans beyond the borders intensified antipathy for Romanian culture. The government tacitly encouraged emigration, not only for the Jews, but also for Germans, in exchange for payment in hard currency. For Hungarians, this meant even greater isolation and vulnerability. Ceauşescu asserted at the Party Congress in 1984 that to criticize Romania's treatment of its Hungarian minority "would be to blow the horn of reactionary imperialist circles."[44] Criticism of nationality policy and the economic debacle were invariably classed as "interference in Romania's internal affairs."

The importance of inter-ethnic solidarity in the outbreak of the revolution has been a problem for the nationalists. The resistance of Romanians as well as Hungarians to pastor László Tőkés's transfer was crucial in the events of 17 December 1991 in Timişoara. Ceauşescu's frenzied denunciation on 21–22 December of "chauvinist-irredentist" demonstrations "reminiscent of the dark days that preceded the Vienna Diktat" failed to impress crowds in either Bucharest or the towns of Transylvania. Citizens of all ethnic groups rejoiced when the violent crackdown failed and the Ceauşescus were executed on Christmas Day.

The leadership of the National Salvation Front (NSF) has used its substantial influence over the media to manipulate nationalist symbols. Yet nationalist revival also builds on widely held traditional attitudes and an intolerance inculcated by the fallen regime. Even the relatively liberal minister of culture, Andrei Pleşu, a former dissident, presented the varied but often chauvinistic intellectual life of the interwar period as a model to be emulated.[45] The dramatic increase in publishing activity included reprints and memoirs of many of the prominent neonationalists discussed in this study. Alongside the moderate and oppositional press, many nationalist papers appeared with possible official sponsorship. Two of the most popular were scandal sheets edited by the former "court poets" of national communism: *România Mare* ("Greater Romania") of Corneliu Vadim Tudor, and *Totusi iubirea* ("Love Nonetheless") of Adrian Păunescu.

---

44 Brigitte Mihok, *"Die rumänische Nationalitätenpolitik seit 1945," Südosteuropa* 39:3/4 (1990), 221.

45 Andrei Pleşu is paraphrased in an interview with Petre Ţuţea in January 1990 in Ţuţea, *Intre Dumnezeu şi neamul meu,* 294.

The effusive religiosity of the nationalist press strikes a pose that was employed by these authors under Ceauşescu, but it is truly responsive to popular sentiment. While the NSF never promised salvation in the religious sense *(salvarea* literally means rescue), it associated the new leaders Ion Iliescu and Petre Roman with the Orthodox liturgy and hierarchy and with the complex claims to historical legitimacy this entailed. These actions and the religious quotations, themes, and metaphors employed in statements and publications of the NSF were a response to the deliverance from a traumatic period in the history of the nation that struck many people as genuine and timely.[46] The canonization by the Orthodox Church in July 1992 of Stephen the Great, a sixteenth-century voevode known primarily for his victories over the Turks, drew an overwhelmingly positive response from Romanians.

The Orthodox bishops' quest for nationalist legitimacy is hampered by their record of collaboration with the Communists and their contest for souls with the long-persecuted Uniates. Following their legalization (in a declaration on 8 January 1990), the Uniate bishops emphasized that their church was a "national institution" speaking with "a European and universal spirit."[47] Orthodox leaders have responded to the violent dispute over repossession of the Greek Catholics' former churches by criticizing this "universal spirit." Greek Catholic Metropolitan Alexandru Todea and several colleagues had shared prison cells with Hungarian bishops and had collaborated with the Hungarian bishops in the first unified Catholic episcopate in Romanian history. The Orthodox accuse them of excessive friendliness with the Hungarians.

The divisive potential of Orthodox xenophobia is suggested by reports that Orthodox clergy incited the attack on Hungarians in Tîrgu Mureş by Romanian villagers in March 1990. Undeniably, this clash was essentially ethnic rather than religious and was fought over secular political issues. At the core of these was the reemergence of Hungarian ethnic politics and the anxiety it inspired among some Transylvanian Romanians. The first alarm for Romanians was the outbreak of ethnically selective violence against Romanian policemen in the days of the revolution. The Hungarian call for separate Hungarian-language schools (misleadingly labelled "separatism" by Iliescu himself) also disturbed many. Finally, the Hungarian Democratic Federation

---

46 Matei Călinescu and Vladimir Tismăneanu in "Epilogue: The 1989 Revolution and the Collapse of Communism in Romania," in Vlad Georgescu, *The Romanians: A History* (Columbus: Ohio State University Press, 1991), 279, 319.

47 Excerpted in *Kirche und Glaube in Rumänien* (Munich: Kirche in Not/Ostpriesterhilfe, 1990), 124–26.

of Romania (HDFR) mobilized the support of most Hungarians in local politics, posing a threat to the authorities. To counter this threat, Romanians in Tîrgu Mureş and other Transylvanian towns organized an ostensibly cultural organization, the Romanian Hearth [or Cradle] Federation (RHF), *Uniunea Vatra Românească*. The confrontation of these political forces fuelled the violent events in Tîrgu Mureş.[48]

The RHF describes itself as "an organization of Romanian spirituality in Transylvania," rejecting "all territorial and administrative separatism and the creation of cultural enclaves," and demanding that Romanian be the only official language on Romanian territory.[49] The abhorrence of separatism has historical, psychological, and international roots. The loss of northern Transylvania in 1940 and the special status of the Hungarian districts in the 1950s strengthened the insistence upon Romania's unitary and centralized character. Due to the popularity of federalism among Hungarians, according to one writer, Romanians are "haunted by the ghost of federalism." The allusion to the Communist Manifesto ridicules both the international appeal of the idea and the psychology of the Romanian response.[50] The dissolution of Yugoslavia prompts many to wonder whether Romania might be next. *România Mare* asserted that there is a Hungarian strategy for territorial revision in the region, and dubbed 1991 "the international year of struggle against Hungarian imperialism."

Two controversies in the fall of 1991 demonstrated the powerful fear of separatism: a Polish plan for regional cooperation, and a proposal for a referendum on Hungarian autonomy. Because the Polish plan included Transylvania but not the rest of Romania, President Iliescu accused Poland of interfering in Romania's internal affairs. He drew a parallel to the Valev plan

---

48 The most thorough account of the events, including reports of the Orthodox clergy's role, is Előd Kincses, *Marosvásárhely fekete Márciusa* (Budapest: Püski, 1990); the Romanian edition is *Marţie negru la Tîrgu-Mureş* (Sfîntu Gheorghe: Editura "Háromszék," 1991). Compare the account in Valentin Borda, *Uniunea "Vatra Românească." Pretext: doi ani de la înfiinţare* (Tîrgu-Mureş: Casa de editură "Petru Maior," 1992). Vlad Socor and Michael Shafir, in *Report on Eastern Europe* 1:15 (13 April 1990), 36–47, place most of the responsibility on the side of the RHF and the government.

49 Rompres, 21 February 1990, in Foreign Broadcast Information Services (hereafter FBIS)–Eastern Europe, *Daily Report* (22 February 1990), 77.

50 Victor Ivanovici, *"O stafie bîntuie Europa: Stafia federalismului," 22* 2:46 (22–29 November 1991), 9; and a hostile response by Marian Ţuţui, *"Stafia federalismului"* in revista "22," *Europa* (December 1991), 7.

of 1964: "This plan is conceived with the logic of the CMEA. It ignores state structures...Transylvania must not be separated from the ethnicity of the Romanian national state."[51] The HDFR quickly denounced the proposal for a referendum, but parliament dedicated two full days to the reading of reports about the alleged terrorization by the Hungarians of Romanians living in the Székely region. The event revealed the unwillingness of most politicians to resist the wild assertions of the chauvinists.

The government appears to appreciate and support the resistance of the RHF and its political wing, the Party of Romanian National Unity (PRNU) to the HDFR and the democratic opposition in Transylvania. In July 1990, the official press agency praised the efforts of the RHF "to educate and develop civic consciousness, to surmount some negative phenomena connected to the complex conditions of the democratization and national rebirth process, to protect and promote national interests.[52] Because the HDFR and Romanian opposition have allied in many electoral districts in 1990 and 1992, the PRNU denounced "the ever more obvious general process of so-called civic and antitotalitarian forums and alliances, the activity of which proves to be antidemocratic, antistatal, and antinational."[53]

In addition to territorial unity, military traditions have been an important theme. Drăgan and the historian Mircea Muşat have worked hard to rehabilitate Antonescu, with the support of war veterans and the Ministry of National Defense.[54] There is much popular interest in Antonescu because his recovery of Bessarabia from the Soviet Union, his attempts to extricate Romania from the war without a Soviet alliance, and his execution in 1946 were proscribed topics under the Communists. The nationalists' attacks on the Jews derive only partly from this historical association. They blame Jews for foreign trade dependency and Communist oppression in the past, use innuendo to imply a Judeo-Hungarian conspiracy, and remind readers of the Jewish origins of Prime Minister Roman before his fall in 1991. The diatribes of Tudor in *România Mare* and the serial republication of the *Protocols of the Elders of Zion* have gained international attention. But only 15,000 Jews,

---

[51] Interview with Iliescu in *Népszabadság* (Budapest) (21 September 1991), 1, 6–7.

[52] Rompres, 18 July 1990, in FBIS–Eastern Europe, Daily Report (19 July 1990), 48.

[53] Rompres, 10 December 1990, in FBIS–Eastern Europe, Daily Report (11 December 1990), 30.

[54] Dan Ionescu, "Marshal Ion Antonescu Honored by Old and New Admirers," Radio Free Europe, *Report on Eastern Europe* 1:34 (24 August 1990), 35–40.

mostly elderly, remain in the country, and the popular appeal of anti-Semitism appears to be limited, perhaps because it is harmful to Romanian prestige and the negative image of the still-illegal Legion.

Interest in World War II naturally relates to the Romanian lands of the former Soviet Union. The nationalists' demand for the return of occupied territories is shared by all major Romanian parties. Of the 3.5 million Romanians recorded in the last Soviet census, nearly 3 million live in Moldova, and more than half of the remainder live within the present borders of Ukraine. Romanian papers of every orientation have applauded the national revival in Moldova. In both Romania and Moldova, the voices favoring reunification have been strongest outside the government. Cooler heads in both the NSF and the opposition have pointed out that Romania is far less prepared than Germany to restore the economy of an impoverished branch of the nation. The military conflict in the Transnistrian region of Moldova has aroused massive Romanian sympathy for Moldova, but the danger of war with Russia causes even the nationalists to address the issue more circumspectly.

In May 1991, *România Mare* announced the organization of the Greater Romania Party (GRP). The forty-point program gives heavy attention to economic planning and social safety nets, clearly appealing for support from officials and ex-Communists and demanding the elimination of dangers to "the Independence, Sovereignty, and Integrity of the Romanian state."[55] The economic program hedges the demand for a free market in many key areas. The Orthodox Church is identified as "an historical factor of unity, culture, and stability," and the army praised as a "factor of stability, social equilibrium, and guarantor of territorial integrity" whose political role should be strengthened.

While the RHF and PRNU arose as movements of Transylvanian Romanians in response to local conditions, the GRP had a nucleus of individuals who became known for their militant nationalism already before 1989, then gained more notoriety through their new weekly in 1990. The comprised Tudor, Eugen Barbu, Muşat, Radu Theodoru, and Theodor Paraschiv—two writers, a historian, and two retired military officers. The call for a militarization of politics was a response to recurrent social disorders that threatened the government and its reputation. Four times in 1990 and 1991, miners descended upon the capital to wreak havoc upon the opponents of the NSF, and the army did nothing. Officers resentful of the armed forces' abuse by Ceauşescu have proven unreliable as the nomenclatura fought for power, but the GRP sees an ally in the reformist officers' hardline opponents.

---

[55] *"Platforma-program a Partidului România Mare," România Mare* 2:54 (21 June 1991), 9–11.

Similarly, the commander of the army in Transylvania is sympathetic to the PRNU and RHF and has welcomed their activity in his ranks.

Romanian nationalism has proved to be an ally of those elements in the NSF, Orthodox Church, and army that seek to preserve a centralized, authoritarian state. The results of the elections of 1992 appear to confirm this. While the opposition made gains in local and national elections, it was defeated in many localities by a de facto or open coalition of the NSF, PRNU, GRP, and the Socialist Labor Party (SLP), a reconstituted Communist Party. Gheorghe Funar of the PRNU became mayor of Cluj, Transylvania's largest city, with the support of workers settled by Ceauşescu in its newer districts, and enacted various measures unfavorable to the Hungarian minority. In the weeks before the general election in September, the NSF and state television repeatedly called attention to the opposition's electoral alliance with the HDFR. The PRNU, GRP, and SLP, all advocates of conservative economic policies, together gained 16 percent of parliamentary seats, and the GRP and SLP announced the formation of a National Bloc *(Partida Naţională)* in the senate led by Adrian Păunescu. Following the election, the U.S. House of Representatives voted overwhelmingly to continue to deny Most-Favored-Nation status to Romania. Representative Tom Lantos asserted on the floor of the House, with some hyperbole, that "both the previous Communist power structure and the newly emerging Fascist power structure are likely to take over that country." Romania has continuously made progress toward a freer society, but the weakened position of the NSF, now enjoying a mere plurality, makes it likely it will rely more on the ultranationalists.[56]

National Communists have taken advantage of the country's worsening economic and diplomatic position "between the two wars" in Yugoslavia and Moldova. As nostalgia for Ceauşescu increases, the low-key SLP has become more viable, and efforts to present Ceauşescu as the latest martyr in the national pantheon have emerged. The nomenclatura's influence on nationalism also is suggested by the relatively small attention given to Romania's Gypsy problem and the political weakness of the emerging Legionary movement. The politically inchoate Gypsies may be Romania's largest minority. Popular dislike for them is very widespread, yet despite verbal violence in the nationalist press and sporadic assaults on Gypsy villages, the major parties seem content to ignore them. Neonationalist writers are

---

[56] Michael Shafir, "Romania's Elections: More than Meets the Eye," *RFE/RL Research Report* 1:44 (6 November 1992), 1–8; Tom Gallagher, "Electoral Breakthrough for Romanian Nationalists," *RFE/RL Research Report* 1:45 (13 November 1992). *Congressional Record* 138:130, part 1 (22 September 1992), H8851.

popular, but a party openly modeled on the Legion emerged only at the end of 1991. Marian Munteanu's Movement for Romania, like the Legion in its early years, as yet enjoys significant influence only among the students.[57] The combination of fervent nationalism and anticommunism appears, at the end of 1992, to have only limited popular appeal.

57 Helsinki Watch, *Destroying Ethnic Identity: The Persecution of Gypsies in Romania* (New York: Human Rights Watch, 1991); and Michael Shafir, "The Revival of the Political Right in Post-Communist Romania," in *The Reemergence of the Political Right in Post-Communist Eastern Europe*, Joseph Held, ed. (forthcoming).

9

The Yugoslav Peoples

by Dennison Rusinow

Document 1

Letter from R. W. Seton-Watson to Prince Regent Alexander of Serbia, London (17 September 1915).[1]

Sir,

For several weeks and indeed even months the political situation has been changing with such kaleidoscopic rapidity that I have more than once hesitated to send Your Royal Highness any kind of report or memorandum; for I always feared that such a report might lose its actuality or even give a false impression before it could reach Niš. It seemed to me more useful to concentrate all my efforts here in London to act upon those who have the power to take decisions on the subject of the Yugoslav problem.

We have at last arrived at the decisive stage in the negotiations, and I feel it my duty—without inflicting on Your Royal Highness long descriptions concerning tendencies and development that must already be well known—to summarize as briefly as possible the dangers of the situation as friends of Serbia in London believe they understand them.

---

1 Hugh Seton-Watson et al., eds., *R. W. Seton-Watson and the Yugoslavs: Correspondencce 1906–1941*, vol. 1 (London/Zagreb: Graficki zavod Hrvatske, 1976), 237–40. Original in French, translation by Dennison Rusinow.

One cannot sufficiently emphasize the fact that in certain diplomatic circles (happily not British) there is a very marked tendency to induce (or even constrain) Serbia to substitute for its solemnly proclaimed program of liberation and unity another program of conquest and annexation. If Serbia should concede in a moment of weakness and indecision, this would be the ruin of the Yugoslav idea. Serbia holds a true solution of the problem in her hands. In holding strictly to the tradition of Vittorio Emanuele and Cavour, she will show herself worthy of the proud name of "the New Piedmont." The policy of these two great statesmen had a dual purpose, the cession of Nice and Savoy as means and Italian unity as supreme goal. Today Serbia has the possibility to copy the celebrated *coup de main* of Cavour, who in corresponding circumstances won the alliance of the Western powers through Piedmontese military aid in the Crimea. As compensation for the sacrifices demanded of her to the south of her territory [presumably a reference to renouncing the promised acquisition of Salonika], Serbia has not only the right—even the honor and interest—to demand to be admitted into the alliance on an equal footing, and not only as Serbia, but as the representative and spokesman of all the Yugoslav race, of the Croats and the Slovenes as well as the Serbs, and as protagonist of that national principle that the allied nations have adopted in their war goals.

If Cavour had consented to negotiate on the basis of the territorial expansion of Piedmont, instead of identifying the local interests of his province and the Savoyard dynasty with "the Italian idea" in the largest sense of the word, he would without doubt have gravely compromised the development of Italian unity. To the same degree, Serbia today, if she should consent to bargain with whatever Entente Power or the central group on the basis of territorial compensations, would for the first time in her history accept the obsolete methods of Metternich and that eighteenth-century diplomacy which, by treating living nations as pawns in their game, made themselves responsible for crimes such as the Polish partition. Above all, in acting thus she would fatally compromise herself in the eyes of her conationals on the other side of the western frontier and would undermine the moral position, so far inviolate, that the heroism of her soldiers and the honesty and good faith of her responsible statesmen have won for her.

Serbia should hold at all costs and in all circumstances to the Yugoslav program. She should never justify the fatal insinuation that it would suffice to enlarge Serbia with as many provinces as possible and to disinterest herself in the rest of the race. But one should not only adhere to this program; one should proclaim it to the entire world through the voice of the Regent of Serbia and his government, as the indispensable price of the concessions that the Entente is demanding. Western public opinion would accept such a gesture, which would have its enthusiastic moral support, with great sympathy.

For Serbia it is a matter of always presenting herself at the negotiations as the true representative of Croatia as well, as the protector of the traditions and constitutional rights of the ancient Triune Kingdom, and in consequence vigorously to oppose every design that might menace the territorial integrity of that kingdom. The *entire* Triune Kingdom ought to be united with Serbia. For it would certainly be unnecessary to point out to Your Royal Highness that if Croatia became an independent state alongside Serbia, the situation of the latter would be still less favorable than before the war; for in that case, the two sister nations would be enemies; in place of the idea of the national unity of all Serbs, Croats, and Slovenes in a single state, we would have an acute conflict between two opposing Slav programs; and in view of the impossibility of drawing any territorial line of separation between Serbs and Croats, each of the two states—the new Serbia as well as the new Croatia—would be torn apart from one end to the other by two rival irredentisms—the Catholics and Muslims of enlarged Serbia looking to Zagreb, and the Orthodox of Dalmatia looking to Belgrade. I do not need to emphasize the extreme danger of such a situation, from a political, economic, military, and above all dynastic point of view. It would be very easy to demonstrate that the vital interests of the Serb national dynasty require the strictest loyalty to the Yugoslav program even more than the interests of a race paralyzed by disaccord requires it. It is *precisely to create such dangers* that certain diplomats would like to tempt Serbia by offering her Slavonia or the southern part of Dalmatia, regions that are truly "scattered limbs, cut from the living body of the Triune Kingdom."

Italian intrigues to impede Yugoslav unity have found support among some individuals of great influence in Russia, who have allowed themselves to be carried away by prejudices—half confessional, half political—and who are myopic enough to believe that national unity and expansion toward the west would "emancipate" [Serbia] from Russia and from the Orthodox Church of the Serb nation. They would view very happily Serbia's assimilation of the purely Orthodox population of Bosnia, Dalmatia, Slavonia, and the Banat, but they would like to abandon the Croats and Slovenes. (It goes without saying that they would indignantly deny these ideas, if they were openly attributed to them; but their attitude and policy permits no other explanation.) In their naïveté they forget that the acquisition of Bosnia-Herzegovina would inevitably give Serbia a population of nearly 500,000 Catholics; that for geographic reasons one cannot annex the Orthodox population of Dalmatia without including 400,000 Catholics; and that even in Slavonia (if one wished to take it without Croatia!) there are at least 350,000–380,000 Catholics. Thus this miserable intrigue, the goal of which is the creation of a *greater Serbia,* which is still insufficient and incomplete ("unsaturiert" is the appropriate term of Aehrenthal [Austro-Hungarian Foreign Minister at the time of the Bosnian Crisis of 1908 and First Balkan War]), would only result in the destruction of the purely Orthodox character of the Serb state!

Serbia would risk too much in being a party to such secret plans. It is necessary to choose between two contradictory conceptions: the one Byzantine, medieval, reactionary—presuming the idea of confessional uniformity (under the aegis of the Eastern church) as the cornerstone of true citizen[ship?]; the other modern and progressive, on which the British Empire and its political institutions are based—the idea that religion is only a private affair of the citizen, and that a Catholic *as* Catholic is as good a citizen as a Protestant or an Orthodox. Were Serbia to become a slave to such prejudices, she would only be assisting Italy's political game. In opposing propositions that are inspired by such secret tendencies, Serbia would not place herself in opposition to the true Russia, to that Russian nation to whom she owed her very political existence last year, to that future Russia that we too wish for our ally. Thus Serbia will only be opposed to a little clique of reactionaries who rather belong to the Middle Ages and whose influence should be destroyed at any cost.

On this occasion permit me to remind Your Royal Highness of a phrase which You used in our last conversation at Kragujevac in January—that Serbia, while eternally maintaining the most intense gratitude to Russia, would never become a vassal or client. The moment has come to put this worthy sentiment into practice; for today the entire future of the Serb race and the Yugoslav idea depends on the political foresight of Your Royal Highness and his counselors.

Finally, permit me to emphasize to Your Royal Highness that Yugoslav and British interests are today entirely identical and equal. British policy requires, in my view, that the new Yugoslavia be as complete as possible from the national point of view, as self-sufficient as possible from the economic point of view, as independent as possible from the geographic point of view—in other words, that the unity of the South Slavs be realized in the broadest sense of the word. Our statesmen have been slow enough in recognizing these truths, but finally they are beginning to be fully appreciated.

If one would like to summarize the problem from our point of view, one might say, "Leave Croatia outside of the Union as a separate political body, and in a few years it will be a German province, and perhaps lost forever to its Serb brothers."

For Serbia, the Union would mean that she would become a real force in Europe, a force so considerable as to be able to speak with all its European neighbors on the basis of equality and to follow a policy of her own. The realization of the program of *Greater Serbia* instead of that of *Yugoslavia* would on the contrary signify the permanence of the old situation in which Serbia would be the toy of the Great Powers and the endless victim of foreign intrigues.

It is possible that public opinion in Serbia is not completely aware even now of all that could be lost. But the task of princes and that of Your Royal Highness is to place themselves at the head of their nations, to be ahead of their times, to follow the great traditions of Vittorio Emanuele II, not that of Carlo Alberto!

I have written with absolute frankness: for if I may not say all that I think, I have nothing to say. Furthermore, I write as a son of Scotland, which after two centuries of union with England has lost none of its national identity. Perhaps for this reason it is easier for me to appreciate the desires of the Croats, that their relations with their Serb brothers should be regulated according to the same principles as the relations of the English and the Scots two centuries ago.

Mr. Steed, of the *Times* [Wickham Steed, another influential British friend of the South Slavs], fully associates himself with the ideas that I am permitting myself to express to Your Royal Highness.

Please deign, Sir, to accept the respectful greetings of Your very humble and devoted

R.W. S.W.

Document 2

Article by Josip Broz Tito, "The National Question in Yugoslavia in the Light of the National Liberation Struggle" (1942).[2]

I should like this article, addressed to the people at large, to contribute to a better grasp of the tremendous significance for all the nations of Yugoslavia of the great and just struggle in which the best sons of our nations have been engaged for the past nineteen months. I should like all those who fear for their fate, who are anxious about the future, to realize that there is only one

2 Translated by Dennison Rusinow on the basis of Josip Broz Tito, *Military Thoughts and Works: Selected Writings (1936–1979)* (Belgrade: Vojnoizdavacki zavod, 1982), 151-57, from Tito, *Sabrana djela,* vol. 13 (Belgrade: Komunist, 1982), 95–101. Footnotes deleted. The article was first published in *Proleter* 16 (December 1942).

possible but thorny road to a better future, to liberty and equality; that road is participation in the National Liberation Struggle, in the ranks of the National Liberation Army and Partisan Detachments of Yugoslavia. No one today need feel isolated, or fear the manifold threats being uttered by those who have committed so many crimes against our nations and our whole country that they have lost all right to speak in anyone's name. The brotherhood and military unity being cemented, in the arduous liberation struggle, by the blood of the finest sons of our peoples offer us a clear prospect that our nations will win true freedom and independence and there must be no more national oppression and social exploitation in Yugoslavia.

It appears that what is now perfectly clear to the progressive person—the anti-fascist and the patriot, not only in our own country but in all the countries of the world fighting the Axis fascist invaders—is not at all clear to the exiled Yugoslav rulers in London. They simply cannot grasp:

- First, that this war is not like the last world imperialist war, that it is a patriotic liberation war—a just war;
- Second, that in practically all the subjugated countries, and particularly in Yugoslavia, war against the invaders is not being fought by generals and ministers, and so on, but by the people themselves against the will of those generals, officers, and the rest of those treacherous gentlemen;
- Third, that the Soviet Union is participating in this liberation war, that it bears 90 percent of the burden of the war on its shoulders and that it will not permit the fruits of its gigantic struggle to be plucked by various traitors and reactionaries who would again oppress other nations and lay plans for new wars;
- Fourth, that it was precisely the national oppression and inequality in many countries that enabled the fascist invaders to enslave the countries in question so easily;
- Fifth, that the Atlantic Charter does not signify extension of the borders of one nation at the expense of others, does not mean the enslavement and oppression of one nation by another, but should rather mean self-determination for nations because the charter states that nations will be able to determine their own future after the victory over the fascist invaders.

The Atlantic Charter is the result of bitter experience with the Versailles Peace Treaty, the consequences of which were catastrophic particularly for the peoples of Yugoslavia. This treaty paved the way for this fascist-imperialist war of invasion, the most frightful war in mankind's history.

This is what the gentlemen in exile in London do not want to understand, and that is why Draža Mihailović and his Chetnik cohorts are collaborating with the occupiers—which is why they have never uttered a word about the need to solve the national question in Yugoslavia but, on the contrary, openly threaten other nations, devise plans to extend their borders and dream of Greater Serbian hegemony. Draža Mihailović's present treatment of the Muslims, the Croats, and so on clearly reveals what these plans are.

Born in Corfu, in London, and in Paris, Yugoslavia as created by the Versailles Treaty became the most typical case of national oppression in Europe. The Croats, Slovenes, and the Montenegrins were subjugated peoples, unequal citizens of Yugoslavia. Macedonians, Albanians, and others were in bondage, exposed to extermination. Muslims and German and Hungarian national minorities were used as bargaining cards in the struggle against the Croats and other nations of Yugoslavia.

A numerically insignificant minority of Greater Serbian hegemonists, headed by the King and insatiable in its greed for riches, ruled Yugoslavia for twenty-two years by creating a regime of gendarmes, of dungeons, of social and national injustice. The reply of these gentlemen to every justified demand for equality put forward by the oppressed nations of Yugoslavia was, "We were the ones who fought at the Salonika Front," "We were the ones who liberated the country," "We were the ones who shed our blood at Kajmakčalan!" This brazen lie served the private ends of these ruthless gentlemen, speculators of all sorts, war profiteers and corruptionists, who desecrated thereby the hallowed graves of the true Serbian heroes—peasants who died in the deep belief that they were giving their lives for the freedom and better future of the Serbian people. On the other hand, various Frankists, the present-day ustashis and their ilk have put the blame for the criminal deeds of the Greater Serbian hegemonistic clique upon the entire Serbian nation, thus generating hatred among the Croatian and other nations toward the fraternal Serbian nation. Not only did the Serbian people have nothing in common with the felonious national policy pursued by those gentlemen, but it has itself been equally exploited and subjected to the same gendarme-supported oppression as the other nations of Yugoslavia. Moreover, it realizes that it has been deceived and that the tremendous sacrifices made in the past war were in vain, that the fruits of its struggle have been appropriated by those who sat the war out in French, London, and Swiss cafes, Rivieras. It has been a source of pain for the Serbian nation to be insulted and accused unjustly of being an accomplice of those traitors in the national oppression of the other nations of Yugoslavia.

The national policy of the Greater Serbian hegemonistic clique was:

1) corruption of the most reactionary elements among the Croats, Slovenes, Muslims, etc., utilizing them to disrupt from within the nations fighting for equality;

2) bribing the top people in the Slovene, Muslim, and [Macedonian Muslim] Dzemiat parties and with their help, to keep the Croatian nation in subjugation. In other words, one nation was exploited against another in a systematic implementation of the policy of causing division among the nations of Yugoslavia, of sowing hatred and broadening the gulf between the fraternal nations of this country. This was disunification rather than unification of the nations of Yugoslavia into a fraternal, equal state community.

The persistent and stupid babbling of this hegemonistic clique that the Serbs, Croats and Slovenes were only various tribes of one and the same nation was aimed at the Serbization of the Croats and Slovenes. Yugoslavia was simply a cover for that Serbization, a mask that was torn off during the period of the "January 6 Dictatorship" of King Alexander and Pero Živković [the first prime minister under the dictatorship].

The Croats, as the most powerful individual nation among the oppressed nations of Yugoslavia, offered the fiercest resistance to this kind of Greater Serbian national policy. It is understandable, however, that this resistance could not yield the results the Croatian nation expected. First of all, because the gentlemen heading the Croatian Peasant Party regarded the solution of the Croatian national question from the standpoint of a division of power between themselves and the Greater-Serbian gentlemen, a division into spheres of interest. Second, because these same Croatian gentlemen channeled the struggle of the Croatian nation against the entire Serbian nation, not just against the Greater Serbian hegemonists, sowing hatred of the Croatian nation. Third, because the gentlemen in executive positions in the Croatian Peasant Party were indifferent to the solution of the national question of other nations such as the Slovenes, Macedonians, etc. In this manner, the struggle of the Croatian nation remained isolated not only from the Serbian nation but also from the other nations of Yugoslavia. The other oppressed nations of Yugoslavia were justified in considering the aspirations of the Croats as a Greater Croatian tendency, a tendency to oppress other nations in the same manner as the Greater Serbian hegemonistic clique. And finally, because the Greater Serbians and the gentlemen from the Croatian Peasant Party thought they could simply strike a bargain [the Cvetković-Maček agreement creating a Croatian Banovina in 1939] dividing power among themselves and thereby removing from the agenda the national question of all the nations of Yugoslavia.

What was the outcome of the rulers' pursuit of such a national policy in Yugoslavia? The clearest answer to this question is the catastrophe Yugoslavia experienced in April 1941 when the country was enslaved by the Axis fascist invaders.

During twenty-two years in power, the Greater Serbian hegemonistic clique derived support for its anti-popular policy from those who had been godfathers at the birth of the Yugoslav state created by the Versailles Treaty, mainly from French and British reactionaries. As soon as the rotten system set up by the Versailles Treaty in Europe had made it possible to alter the balance among the imperialist European powers in favor of the Axis fascist states, the Greater Serbian reactionary hegemonistic clique oriented itself toward the Rome-Berlin Axis, in order to maintain its hegemony and to keep the other nations of Yugoslavia in subjugation. The cases of [Prime Ministers] Stojadinović, Jeftić, Cvetković, and others provide the best proof of this.

It would, however, be incorrect to accuse only these reactionaries of such an anti-popular policy. The same policy was pursued by the reactionary Slovene gentlemen, headed by Korošec, Natlačen, Krek, and others; the same policy was pursued by the gentlemen-reactionaries in the leadership of the Croatian Peasant Party, headed by Maček, Krnjević, Pernar, and others; the same policy was pursued by the leaderships of various parties of the other nations of Yugoslavia.

Faithful to its principle that each nation has the right to decide its own future, the Communist Party struggled without ceasing, during the entire existence of prewar Yugoslavia, against the national policy followed by the Greater Serbian hegemonists. The Communist Party of Yugoslavia made a most determined stand against the oppression of the Croats, Slovenes, Macedonians, Montenegrins, Albanians, and others. It was precisely for this reason that the Greater Serbian hegemonists vented their fury on our Communist Party. That is the reason why for twenty-two years Yugoslav jails were filled to overflowing with the best Communists, why the gentlemen in exile in London and their agents in the country hate us so, because they know that national liberty and equality in Yugoslavia are the greatest obstacles to their selfish aims, to their freedom to plunder and exploit.

The German and Italian fascist invaders knew well how to take full advantage of the national antagonisms in each country, including Yugoslavia. In Czechoslovakia, they worked with all their might to stir up hatred between Czechs and Slovaks, by fanning among the Slovak reactionaries the desire for alleged independence and secession. Thus did the German fascists succeed in dividing up Czechoslovakia and enslaving it without a struggle.

In Yugoslavia, the German and Italian fascists juggled things about in the most incredible ways in order to exploit national antagonisms and weaken the country. On the one hand, they took Pavelić and his small gang of ustaše under their protection, supporting them for years and enabling them to organize attacks on trains and so on in Yugoslavia, while on the other hand praising Stojadinović and his heirs to the skies, in their newspapers and at banquets, for their great statesmanlike "wisdom" and "wise and determined internal and foreign policy." They alternately praised the Serbs for their strong-arm policy and refusal to yield and urged the Croats not to yield, telling them that their demands were justified, and so on. Their purpose was to disrupt and weaken the country from the inside at all costs and then to subjugate it. And in this the fascist invaders succeeded. Their work was facilitated by their having found a sufficient number of traitors to support them among each nation in Yugoslavia. The fascist solution to the national question is: to find one or a number of quislings in each country, depending on the number of nations it consists of; to set up a puppet government; to subjugate completely the country economically and politically; and then to proclaim it "free" and an ally within the so-called new order in Europe.

What do Pavelić and his ustaše gang represent in Croatia today? They are nothing but ordinary agents in occupied, enslaved Croatia. What do Nedić [the Germans' "Quisling" ruler of occupied Serbia] and company represent in Serbia today? Nothing but agents of the invaders in occupied, enslaved Serbia. What do Draža Mihailović and his chetniks represent in Yugoslavia today? Nothing but agents and allies of the invaders in the struggle against the people. All these bandits serve not only as agents but as vicious hangmen in the service of the occupiers, with whose help the latter are endeavoring to keep the peoples of Yugoslavia in bondage.

It is apparent from all this that fascism is the greatest and cruelest enemy of the freedom and equality of each nation. It follows that a fight for life or death must be fought against all who aid Axis fascism.

Today's National Liberation Struggle and the national question in Yugoslavia are inextricably bound up with each other. Our National Liberation Struggle would not be so staunch nor so successful did the Yugoslav nations not feel that, in addition to triumphing over fascism, it would put an end to the state of affairs existing during past regimes, and would bring victory over those who have oppressed and wish to continue oppressing the nations of Yugoslavia. The slogan "National Liberation Struggle" would be a mere phrase, or even a deception, were it not in addition to the liberation of Yugoslavia also to signify the liberation of the Croats, Slovenes, Serbs, Macedonians, Albanians, Muslims, etc., or were it not genuinely imbued with the aim of bringing freedom, equality, and fraternity to all the nations of Yugoslavia. In this lies the essence of the National Liberation Struggle.

The present National Liberation Struggle could not terminate in victory over the invaders and their henchmen if it were not for the unity of the people in that struggle, if it were not for participation in the ranks of the National Liberation Army and Partisan Detachments of Yugoslavia by Serbs, Croats, Slovenes, Montenegrins, Macedonians, and Muslims. The full-fledged liberation of each separate nation could not be achieved if each one did not now take up arms and fight for a common victory by all the nations of Yugoslavia over all the enemies of the people....

Macedonians, Albanians, Croats, Muslims, and others ask in fear, what will happen to us if the former regime returns? The Government-in-exile in London is already threatening; the Chetniks, with the help of the occupiers, are already massacring wherever they can and sharpening their knives for even more frightful slaughters—that is what all the peoples fear. But we call out to all of them not to fear; salvation is possible but only if they all take up arms now, immediately, without hesitation, and join the dedicated struggle our heroic National Liberation Army is waging against the invaders to ensure freedom and equality to all the nations of Yugoslavia. That is the only road of salvation, the road that all the nations of Yugoslavia should take.

I must stress the fact that Serbs have comprised the great majority of our National Liberation Army and Partisan detachments of Yugoslavia since the very beginning, instead of the opposite being the case. Serbian, Montenegrin, Bosnian, and Lika Partisans and brigades composed exclusively of Serbs have been fighting and are fighting a relentless war not only against the invaders but also against Mihailović's Chetniks and other enemies of the oppressed nationalities. What does this prove? It proves that all the nations of Yugoslavia, who have been oppressed by the Greater Serbian hegemonists in the past, have their best and staunchest ally in the Serbian nation. The Serbian nation has made and is still making the greatest contribution in blood to the fight against the invaders and their traitorous hirelings—not only Pavelić, Nedić, and Pećanac, but also Draža Mihailović and his Chetniks—for full freedom and independence for all the nations of Yugoslavia. The Serb people no more desire a return to the old [system] than the Croats, Slovenes, Macedonians, Montenegrins, and Muslims. The Serb people know very well the cause of the national tragedy, and the identity of the chief culprit; that is why they are fighting so courageously and why they detest the local traitors. It is therefore the sacred duty of all the other nations of Yugoslavia to participate, at least to the same extent as the Serbian nation if not more, in this great liberation war against the invader and all his henchmen.

The banner of the National Liberation Struggle against the occupiers, raised by the Communist Party of Yugoslavia in 1941, is at the same time the banner of struggle for national freedom and equality among all the individual nations. It is the same banner that has been kept aloft unsullied by the Communist Party ever since the creation of Yugoslavia, as it fought uncompromisingly for national freedom and equality. Never has the Communist Party renounced, nor shall it ever renounce, the principle formulated by our great teachers, Marx, Engels and Lenin, the principle that each nation has a right to self-determination, including secession. At the same time, however, the Communist Party of Yugoslavia rejects and will fight against exploitation of this right by enemies of the people who, instead of bringing the people freedom and independence, mete out medieval bigotry and colonial slavery, as is the case with Pavelić's "independent" Croatia.

The Communist Party of Yugoslavia will continue to fight for a fraternal, free, and equal community of all nations in Yugoslavia. It will fight equally against the Greater Serbian hegemonists, who aspire to subjugate the other nationalities of Yugoslavia once again, and against those who would attempt to sow dissension and to obstruct fraternal concord among the peoples for the benefit of any enemy power whatsoever.

The question of Macedonia, of Kosovo and Metohija, of Montenegro, of Croatia, of Slovenia, of Bosnia and Herzegovina will easily be solved to the general satisfaction only if the peoples themselves solve them, and each nation is acquiring the right to do so, with arms in its hands, in the present National Liberation Struggle.

(Bosanski Petrovac, December 1942)

Document 3

from the Program of the League of Yugoslav Communists (LCY) (1958).[3]

The Federation and Relations among the Peoples of Yugoslavia

Self-Determination and Equality of Peoples

One of the fundamental antagonisms which rent the social-political life of bourgeois Yugoslavia was the unsolved nationality question.

The Communist Party of Yugoslavia in its political action followed a nationality policy whose basic principle was recognition of the individuality, equality and right of self-determination of all Yugoslav peoples—Serbs, Croats, Slovenes, Macedonians and Montenegrins—and their unity on the basis of a federal organization of the state. This policy and a persistent struggle for its application were among the chief reasons why the Communist Party earned the confidence of the masses of all the peoples of Yugoslavia and succeeded in rallying them around its program and taking them into the common battle for liberation and creation of new Yugoslavia.

---

3 Translated by Stoyan Pribechevich [sic] as *Yugoslavia's Way—Program of the League of Yugoslav Communists* (New York: All Nations' Press, 1958), 188–97.

In the course of the National Liberation War, in the common struggle for liberation, the desire grew among the peoples of Yugoslavia for union in a common state of equal peoples, in a new, people's democratic and socialist Yugoslavia, on the basis of a full application of the rights of self-determination.

Unity of Yugoslavia is possible only on the basis of free national developments and full equality of the Serbs, Croats, Slovenes, Macedonians and Montenegrins, as well as national minorities. For this reason, socialist Yugoslavia was born as a federal state of equal and sovereign peoples. It could not have been created otherwise.

Rights guaranteeing equality and free material and cultural developments to all peoples of Yugoslavia are determined by the Constitution and ensured by the status of the People's Republics and by other institutions of the federal state. These rights are respected and actually practiced in all internal relations of the Yugoslav community—relations among citizens as well as among nationalities.

The League of the Communists of Yugoslavia will also in the future take vigilant care that these achievements of the Socialist Revolution and socialist construction are respected, consolidated and further developed.

Material Foundations of National Equality

The independence and equality of the peoples of Yugoslavia are not reflected in equal political and cultural rights alone. They must necessarily rest on a material foundation.

This foundation consists, in the first place, in the unity of social-economic relations based on social ownership of the means of production, in the unity of the economic system, in the unity of the Yugoslav market, and in equality of rights and obligations of the basic economic units (economic organizations and Communes). From these relations originates the system of broad self-management of the working people in the fields of production and material relations. In this sense the material foundation of the quality of the peoples of Yugoslavia consists especially in management of the means of production by the working collectives and in their participation in the distribution of the social product, in the self-government of the Communes, and in social management of the funds of the Communes, the Districts and the People's Republics. The aim of our policy of nationalities is also served by equal participation of representatives of all peoples of Yugoslavia, through the political system of federation, in the management and disposition of the resources of the Federation either by drawing up the budget and social plan or by direct management of the various economic and budget funds.

People's Republics take part, under equal general conditions, in the distribution of the income realized in the production and work in their territories and utilize credits from federal funds, available to all under equal conditions. On this foundation, the Republics independently establish programs of their own economic development within the general proportions of the economic plan of the Federation.

Constant Care for Rapid Economic Development of Underdeveloped Regions

This equality, however, would mean only a formal equality for certain parts of Yugoslavia if the socialist community did not take into account the fact that, for specific historic reasons, they have been retarded in economic development. The urgent need for a balanced economic development of the whole country and the indispensable condition of brotherhood and unity of the Yugoslav peoples demand that their political and legal equality be gradually supplemented by their economic equality.

For these reasons, an essential element of the economic policy must be continuous care for an accelerated economic development of the backward regions. Material investments in this field should be used primarily for development of the forces of production which will create an independent material base in these areas. Only after this should budget grants be used to ensure a certain equal level of social services and social welfare.

The economic prosperity of Yugoslavia and a healthy development of her economy are possible only through an increase of the common wealth of the whole country, through a steady rise in the productivity of labor of each working man. A more rapid economic development of underdeveloped regions means that a greater contribution on their part of the Yugoslav community and an improvement of the material welfare of all peoples and all working men of Yugoslavia. Therefore the concern of the community in the solution of this question is not an end in itself but an interest of the material progress of the whole country and an economic need of all peoples of Yugoslavia.

The problem of stimulating the development of under-developed provinces must be solved within the frame of the common Yugoslav economic policy and in harmony with the interests of the Yugoslav economy as a whole. Therefore accomplishment of this task must not harm the necessary and normal development of the production forces of other regions of the country or the optimum possibilities of the Yugoslav economy as a whole.

A different policy would in the end reduce the material possibilities for solving the problem of the underdeveloped sections of the country. Only a co-ordinated economic development of all People's Republics and all regions of Yugoslavia, reflected in the best possible result of the whole Yugoslav economy, offers a solid foundation for carrying out the true socialist policy in the question of nationalities.

Brotherhood and Unity of the Peoples of Yugoslavia

Just as equality of our peoples does not rest merely on formal rights but is made certain primarily through a material basis, social-economic relations and the socialist system itself, so unity of the peoples of Yugoslavia is not only the national-political interest of each nationality but the social and material interest of each working man. This unity derives from the fact that the means of production are social property and can be used to the maximum for the benefit of all peoples of Yugoslavia only through their common effort and cooperation. In this way, unity of the peoples of Yugoslavia acquires its full meaning and a solid social-economic foundation only in socialism.

Because the means of production belong to society and because the principle of workers' and social self-managements is actually being carried out, a system of social relations is now under construction which offers wide opportunities to every individual producer and every economic organization and Commune for a fuller satisfaction of their own immediate material, moral and other interests, satisfying at the same time the general interests of the socialist community. The individual producer, wherever employed, enters the same and equal relations as do other producers. This right to equal participation in all organs of workers' and social self-management is guaranteed. All this represents the new link which inter-connects all citizens of Yugoslavia on a solid socialist economic foundation.

Thus elementary interests of social development and of the material progress of the working class and working men of all peoples of Yugoslavia require a universal interlinking of these peoples. Common administering of a host of economic and social functions is indispensable. The League of the Communists of Yugoslavia encourages and supports the processes of socialist unification, because they increase the strength and independence of the Yugoslav socialist community of peoples and correspond to the progressive search of contemporary humanity for rapprochement of nations.

Yugoslav Socialist Patriotism

The common interest is increasingly manifest in the general social and cultural consciousness of the working masses. On this basis grows Yugoslav socialist consciousness, Yugoslav socialist patriotism, which is not contrary to democratic national consciousness but is its necessary internationalist supplement in a socialist community of peoples. This is not a question of creating a new "Yugoslav nation" to replace the existing nationalities but of organic growth and strengthening of the socialist community of producers or working men of all nationalities of Yugoslavia: assertion of their common interests on the basis of socialist relations. Such Yugoslavism does not stand in the way of national languages and cultures. It presupposes them.

In this sense, socialist Yugoslavism as a form of socialist internationalism and democratic national consciousness which is permeated by the spirit of internationalism are not two different things but two sides of the same process. Trying to make one or the other absolute would necessarily result in veering off either toward reactionary nationalism and chauvinism or toward equally reactionary super-state hegemony and denial of the principle of self-determination and equality of peoples.

Rights of National Minorities

Within the community of Yugoslav peoples, national minorities also have their place. In a socialist and democratic state, members of national minorities enjoy all the political and economic rights that the community guarantees to all citizens. On this basis they are assured free development of their national cultures and character.

The Revolution fundamentally altered the situation of the minorities and gave them a place and role in a socialist construction. The number of members of the working class and intelligentsia from the ranks of the minorities increased suddenly. Their participation in all organs of social self-management is quite substantial; their socialist consciousness has grown—consciousness of the community of their own and all Yugoslav peoples' interests in the struggle for socialism. All this ensures equal participation of national minorities in Yugoslav socialist construction, as well as further progress of their national socialist cultures.

In postwar socialist construction of Yugoslavia, such relations with national minorities have at no stage of development depended on inter-state relations between Yugoslavia and neighboring countries. This was particularly evident after 1948 [when the breach occurred between Tito and Stalin], which again showed what results a consistent application of socialist principles can produce. The policies have made still firmer the alliance and unity of national minorities with all peoples of Yugoslavia.

The Tasks of the Communists in the Field of the Policy of Nationalities

In Yugoslavia today the question of nationalities does not exist as a problem of national hegemony and oppression of peoples. The guarantee for this is the entire political and social system, which assures equality to all peoples and national minorities of Yugoslavia, and to each people the right to decide its fate.

Negative Manifestations in Relations among Nationalities

However all this does not mean that all factors which can negatively affect relations among the peoples of Yugoslavia have disappeared.

In the first place, political and ideological remnants of bourgeois nationalism are active. In the present conditions, they have found new encouragement in bureaucratism, which is always locally patriotic toward the center of the country and centralistic toward those below. In our conditions, local nationalism appears either as a cover for anti-socialist tendencies and selfish and local patriotic interests; or as an expression of the unbalanced economic development of certain parts of the country.

Bourgeois nationalism in our situation pulls back, is reactionary and of extreme harm to the development of socialist relations. It is capable of undermining many results of the National Liberation Struggle and of the Revolution, befogs the socialist perspective, weakens the imperative unity of action in socialist construction, becomes an assembly point of all possible anti-socialist tendencies and thus has a harmful effect on further socialist development.

Tendencies of bureaucratic centralism and its ideological political manifestations, super-state hegemony, are the second factor which can negatively affect relations among the peoples of Yugoslavia.

Consolidation of such tendencies could undermine the democratic achievements of the Socialist Revolution, distort relations among the peoples, endanger their equality, open the door to local nationalist hegemony, and, as a result of all this, substantially obstruct and deform the development of socialist relations.

Differences in the degree of economic development of the various parts of Yugoslavia also affect the development of relations among the Yugoslav peoples. Out of these differences grow contradictions which under certain conditions also may take the form of local nationalism, weakening the unity of the peoples of Yugoslavia and even slowing down the development of socialism. Therefore, a steady effort to liquidate gradually the material sources of these contradictions is an imperative task of the socialist forces, in order to secure both a real equality of the peoples of Yugoslavia and unimpeded further development of socialist relations in the country.

Strengthening of the Spirit of Socialist Internationalism

The Communists of Yugoslavia will struggle in everyday practice, with all ideological and political means, against all sources and manifestations of local nationalism, chauvinism and egoism, as well as against tendencies of bureaucratic centralism and super-state hegemony.

They will actively oppose all attempts to exploit material contradictions inherited from the past in order to inflame local nationalism, chauvinism and egoism. They will cultivate in the masses the spirit of fellowship, mutual understanding and assistance among the peoples of Yugoslavia, the idea of brotherhood and unity, the idea of proletarian internationalism, rapprochement and friendship among nations in general; and will oppose everything that causes hatred among peoples, national and racial prejudices or policies of national privilege.

Following Lenin's well-known principle, the Communists above all will cultivate within individual People's Republics the idea of unity and brotherhood of the peoples of Yugoslavia and the idea of a socialist internationalism. From the center they will first of all and vigilantly guard the constitutional, political, ideological and economic factors ensuring equality and free development of all peoples of the federal social community. And they will combat every appearance of hegemony that could threaten the unity of the peoples of Yugoslavia. In other words, the Communists will conduct a continuous struggle against all that is narrow-mindedly nationalistic within a nationality and also against all that handicaps free development of any nationality.

Document 4

from Franjo Tudjman, "The Sources, Changes and Essence of the National Question in the Socialist Federal Republic of Yugoslavia" (1981).[4]

The victory of the anti-fascist partisan movement in Yugoslavia in the 1941–45 war was achieved primarily as a result of the program for solving the national question. Even the revolutionary change of power, and the collapse of the bourgeois socio-political system, which lent this movement the characteristics of a socialist revolution, was explained by the need to destroy all the preconditions for the return of a monarchist Yugoslavia, hated as a prison of the people by all the non-Serbian nations.

The formation of a federal (socialist) Yugoslavia meant, therefore...the collapse of all those socio-political forces and tendencies which aspired towards

---

4 Franjo Tudjman, "The Sources, Changes and Essence of the National Question in the Socialist Federal Republic of Yugoslavia," part III of *Nationalism in Contemporary Europe* (Boulder, CO: East European Monographs, 1981), 103–89 passim.

either the renewal of the old kingdom, with its greater-Serbian hegemony and unitarian centralism, or national separation and irredentism....

The greatest number of new intra-national controversies arose over the various criteria used to determine both the status and the boundaries of various lands and provinces and in the application of non-uniform principles in the demarcations between various federal states (republics).

In the construction of the federal system within the context of the National Liberation Movement and after the war the CPY [League of Communists of Yugoslavia] leadership proceeded largely from its pre-war program and from the real situation and practical needs dictated by its leadership of the Partisan movement, that is, it sought the least painful solutions of the extremely exacerbated national question. However, it is still not known on what assumptions the CPY leadership reached its various decisions during and after the war, for there are virtually no written sources, public discussion of this was never held and the population itself never had the opportunity of expressing its feelings in a referendum....

Several reasons could be given in favor of the decision to unite Vojvodina with Serbia. The two areas had strong historical, national, economic and cultural ties, and their union was also in the interest of the state community as a whole. The fixing of the boundaries for Vojvodina and Serbia is a different question and will be discussed later. However, there are many indications that the same logical criteria were not applied in the case of Bosnia and Hercegovina, which according to the same yardstick should have been made a part of the Croatian federal unit. Bosnia and Hercegovina was declared a separate federal republic within the borders established during the Turkish occupation. But large parts of Croatia had been incorporated into Bosnia by the Turks. Furthermore Bosnia and Hercegovina were historically linked with Croatia and they together comprise an indivisible geographic and economic entity. Bosnia and Hercegovina occupy the central part of this whole, separating southern (Dalmatian) from northern (Pannonian) Croatia. The creation of a separate Bosnia and Hercegovina makes the territorial and geographical position of Croatia extremely unnatural in the economic sense and, therefore, in the broadest national-political sense, very unfavorable for life and development and in the narrower administrative sense unsuitable and disadvantageous....

There is little doubt that the main reasons for declaring Bosnia and Hercegovina a separate federal state was the mixed composition of its population and the fact that since the last century the greatest controversy between Croatian and Serbian political leaders concerned the ownership of Bosnia and Hercegovina. The decision, therefore, to make Bosnia and Hercegovina a separate federal unit was purportedly taken as an unbiased standpoint. Croatia laid claim to Bosnia and Hercegovina on the basis of a common history and the fact that they constituted a geo-political whole. Serbia's claim was based on "natural right" as the Serbian, Orthodox population constituted a plurality (about 44 percent) while the Croatian, Catholic made up about 23 percent of the population and the Moslems 33 percent. Though the Orthodox population was in the minority as compared with the ethnically largely identical Catholic and Moslem population, which together comprised a majority of 56 percent (which has now grown to 62 percent) the Serbian side overly stressed the "right of the sword" since Serbia had entered World War I because of Bosnia and Hercegovina and had been a victor in the conflict.

An objective examination of the numerical composition of the population of Bosnia and Hercegovina cannot ignore that the majority of the Moslems is in its ethnic character and speech incontrovertibly of Croatian origin. Despite religious and cultural distinctions created by history, the vast majority of Moslems declared themselves Croats whenever an opportunity arose.... On the basis of these facts we arrive at the conclusion that a majority of the population of Bosnia and Hercegovina is Croatian. On the other hand the geoeconomic connection of Bosnia with the other Croatian lands is such that neither Croatia in its present boundaries nor the separate Bosnia and Hercegovina possess the conditions for a separate, normal development.

Moreover, as regards the unification of Serbia and Vojvodina, the national, political and economic factors were considered despite the greater diversity of population. Historical factors were respected in the inclusion into Serbia of Kosovo, though the Serbs and Montenegrins are in the minority compared with the far more numerous Albanians. Secular historical consideration dictated division of Sandzak, where the majority is Moslem. If applied to Bosnia and Hercegovina all these reasons testified with equal force to the fact that the union would be in the interests of not only Croatia but also Bosnia and Hercegovina. Such a union would be in the interest of Croatia, Bosnia and Hercegovina and all of Yugoslavia and would create more favorable conditions for internal Yugoslav harmony and its political, cultural and economic development....

If we add to all this that Boka Kotorska, which was formerly (up until 1918) part of Croatia, has been incorporated into Montenegro and that Srijem [Syrmia], which also belonged to Croatia historically (up until the unification in 1918), was made part of Vojvodina and Serbia and that the border is much less favorable to Croatia in that area than were the boundaries of the Banovina of Croatia (1939), and that northern Bačka, even though predominantly Croatian in population, was left to Vojvodina, then the question arises as to why in all these cases of determining the status of various lands the *historical* and *natural rights* criteria were applied to the advantage of Serbia and Montenegro and to the detriment of Croatia!

The answers may lie in the fact that the Serbian members of the CPY leadership made not only these but also other demands, such as, for example, that Bosnia and Hercegovina should be united with Serbia as an autonomous province and that the areas of Lika, Kordun and Banija in Croatia, where the population consists of both Croats and Serbs, should become an autonomous province of the Croat republic. According to Djilas, the Bosnian leadership's views prevailed regarding Bosnia and Hercegovina. They believed that it would be better for Bosnia and Hercegovina to be an independent federal unit. The proposal regarding a Serbian autonomous province in Croatia was dismissed because its boundaries would have a strange "intestine-like" shape and it could not embrace the Serbian population in Slavonia. If it did, too many Croats would have been included in the autonomous region. In making these demands the Serbian Communists were continuing the traditions of Serbian bourgeois politics. They felt that Serbia was entitled to these gains because of its "suffering," the "guilt of the NDH" [i.e., the Independent State of Croatia, during World War II] and the proportionally greater part the Serbian population in Croatia and Bosnia and Hercegovina played in the national liberation struggle. They conveniently forgot that the policy of the NDH and the fratricidal Ustasha-Chetnik war resulted from the greater-Serbian tyranny in the Kingdom of Yugoslavia. Tito, Kardelj and Bakarić probably viewed the territorial and other concessions made Serbia in the organization of the federation as secondary tactical questions compared to the consolidation of revolutionary power. They paid their price to win over Serbia, which almost to the very end of the war was largely under the influence of Draža Mihailović's Chetnik movement. There was great dissatisfaction in Serbia over both the abolition of the monarchy and deposition of the Serbian dynasty and the new establishment of a federal structure of government....

The adopted solutions regarding organization of the federal order caused as much dissatisfaction and mistrust on the part of those who opposed them as satisfaction of those who favored them. This was, after all, becoming clear even before the end of the war and immediately afterwards when the first constitution was being promulgated. At that time all of these questions were raised by the Croatian Communist leaders. It became especially clear later as national relations worsened in the context of other questions affecting all spheres of economic, cultural and political life....

The granting of federal status to Bosnia and Hercegovina meant the continuation of the endeavour, dating from Turkish and Austro-Hungarian times, to create an artificial Bosnian statehood. In spite of the constitutionally proclaimed equality of the Serbian, Croatian and Moslem population, authority was in fact for a long time after the war in the hands of the Serbs since the Croatians (Catholics and Moslems) had been compromised by collaborating with the NDH to such an extent that any manifestation of

Croatian feeling (right up to the fall of Ranković in 1966) was equated with Ustashi. For this reason the Socialist Republic of Hercegovina was at that time more a source of conflict than of conciliation between the Serb and Croatian population....

In reality, the constitutionally proclaimed federal order remained insufficiently effective. It was at odds with the fundamental social and political aims of the CPY, which imposed on the country its one-party system in keeping with its doctrinaire principles and the Soviet model.... Also in the immediate post-war period (1945–50) the basic question for the CPY was the construction of a planned socialist society, in Yugoslavia. In the name of an allegedly inevitable and necessary ***revolutionary etatism*** was built a political system of ***greater-state centralism,*** which in reality made impossible the implementation of a federal state structure making it merely into a facade behind which stood the centralized monopolistic power of the CPY. The federal structure was meant to satisfy and give expression to the nations, which according to the Marxist interpretation were the product and residue of a bourgeois society. This, however, was only of incidental, secondary importance: most important was that revolutionary etatism (due to the doctrine and structure of the ruling communist party) necessarily took on the form of greater-state centralism.... This meant that revolutionary etatism was an instrument for imposing the socialist order throughout Yugoslavia on all the social sectors which did not accept it on class or ideological grounds and also an instrument for imposing the federal order on those republics in which the revolution and federal order did not enjoy firm support because the majority felt that through it they had lost too much (Serbia) or gained too little (Croatia)....

In order to understand the essence of the "resolved," yet "unresolved," national question in Yugoslavia and the mystery of the permanent controversy over its international position, one must proceed from certain important and undeniable historical facts.

The Yugoslav state was established in 1918, after the end of World War I.... In the new, South-Slav state, the Kingdom of the Slovenes, Croats and Serbs, nations came together which were admittedly akin as regards their languages but very different as regards their historical tradition and the level of their general and cultural development. The intra-national contradictions which rent apart this state from the very outset, as greater-Serbian hegemony had been imposed by force in it, took on the characteristics of a Serbo-Croatian quarrel and clash. Even though other non-Serbian nations were also oppressed and subjected to a policy of denationalization, the firmest stand against this policy was taken by the national movement of the Croatian nation, which was the largest of the non-Serbian nations and historically the most developed. For this reason it could not reconcile itself to having in the new joint state less rights than in Austro-Hungary or to losing all those marks of national and state independence which it had retained throughout the whole of its history. The unitarian and centralist policy, which was bent on building up Yugoslavia as an expanded Serbia, was opposed by the Croatian national movement as early as the beginning of the 1920s in the programme: *either confederation or separation.*

Relying on their armed (military and police) forces and on aid from the allied states, the champions of hegemonism attempted with the most brutal methods to wipe out the national movements of both the Croatian and other nations. The struggle between Croatian federalism and greater-Serbian centralism deepened to the extreme the contradictions, gulf and controversies between the two nations which were great because it was due to the differences in their historical development. The Croatian nation largely belonged to the western European culture and the Roman Catholic Church, and partly also to the Moslem and Arab culture of the Islamic faith, while the Serbian nation belonged to the eastern Byzantine civilization and Orthodoxy, which refuted both the Roman and Islamic faiths with equal virulence.

As a result of the unresolved *Croatian question,* which arose in both the political and state-legal senses (the national question of the other nations arose in the sense of recognition for the Slovene, Macedonian and Montenegrin nations, [but] was eclipsed by the Croato-Serbian conflict and depended on its outcome), the Yugoslav state constantly experienced state political crises in the period between the two wars and the Croatian question also became the subject of international politics as part of the demand for the revision of the Versailles order made by Germany, Italy, Hungary and Bulgaria. It thereby became one of the crisis spots threatening peace in Europe....

The solution of the complex multi-national question through the restoration of Yugoslavia on a federal basis contained at first sight a puzzling contradiction: The new Yugoslavia was to be a "federal state community of nations equal in rights," based on socialist order and the power of the working class led by the CPY. As far as the Communist leaders were concerned, this was to be the *definitive* solution of the national question....

However, despite the fact that it has been pushed into second place by problems and theories concerning the "essential" "class" issues of internal socio-political development and the international position of "nonaligned" Yugoslavia, the national question has been emerging more and more in the internal life of Yugoslavia, manifesting itself again, and primarily, as a question of Serbo-Croatian relations on which both the internal and international stability of the Yugoslav state community primarily depend.

In what consists the essence, and mystery, of the re-emerging national question, "definitively" solved by the revolution and the constitution, and now taking on ever new, all-embracing and severe forms?

Even though governed by federal, socialist and self-government determinants, it is clear that the example of the Yugoslav multi-national community has demonstrated the historical law that in every multi-national state one, usually the largest, nation nearly always retains or gains a leading and privileged position over the other nations, which in itself inevitably gives rise to national contradictions, conflicts and disputes.

In the SFRY [Socialist Federal Republic of Yugoslavia] the Serbs admittedly lost the hegemonistic position, in the ideological, political and state-legal sense, of the ruling and only state-founding nation which they had in monarchistic Yugoslavia, but in reality, because of the continuation of these traditions in some form or other, because they are the largest nation and because the center of the federation is in Belgrade, the capital of Serbia, they nevertheless succeeded, more than any other nation, in identifying the interests and state policy of the federation with their own national interest.

Even following World War II Serbia was quick to retain in the federal, socialist Yugoslavia essentially the same position regrading economic and political power as it had in the monarchistic-centralistic and capitalist Yugoslavia after World War I, even though the conditions for this were quite different in each case. While Serbia could impose its domination after World War I in the newly created Kingdom of the Slovenes, Croats and Serbs as the victorious state and in the name of "liberation and unification" under the leadership of Serbian politics and the Serbian dynasty, at the end of World War II traditional Serbian policies suffered collapse. The abolition of the centralistic monarchy also meant the downfall of the Serbian hegemony, and the victorious Tito drew his main support from the non-Serbian nations. Croatia, Slovenia, Macedonia and Montenegro were already declared federal states when Serbia was still to be liberated from the occupying forces and the Chetnik movement, which would certainly have been much more difficult politically (and militarily) if the National Liberation Movement had not already carried off victory in the ranks of the non-Serbian nations and if such a large number of Serbs, living outside Serbia (from Bosnia and Hercegovina and also Croatia) had not taken part in Tito's partisan movement.

Merely a few facts suffice to illustrate how relations changed quickly in the post-war period in the federal socialist order and on what questions contradictions between Belgrade and the non-Serbian nations, and primarily Serbo-Croatian contradictions, began to develop.

In multi-national countries under communist rule the very membership of the communist parties reflects the intra-national relations, or their part in the ruling structures. Immediately after the war in 1946 the membership of the League of Communists (CPC) in Croatia accounted for 30.7 percent of the entire membership of the League of Communists of Yugoslavia (CPY). This was about eight percent more than the percentage of population and a reflection of the proportionately greater part played by the Croatian population in the National Liberation Movement, and the greater force of the party organizations in Croatia, than was the case in certain other republics, and in particular Serbia. Gradually this proportion was to decrease year by year with the result that as early as the 1950s it fell below the percentage of the population... In 1975 this figure fell to 18.3 percent and in 1978 a mere 17 percent.... This picture becomes even blacker when one takes into account the fact that the League of Communists of Croatia membership has included a proportionately larger number of Serbs than their number in Croatia and that, particularly in Ranković's time and after Karadjordjevo, they have made up almost a ruling stratum within the ruling system: in the organs of the League of Communists, state security, foreign trade and even in the administrative positions in the economy of Croatia....

The consequences of these relationships are, of course, multiple in nature: there is not one sphere of material or spiritual life in which they are not manifested.

The consequences of this policy reflect negatively on the psyche of the Croatian nation and on its attitude towards the community, especially as in everyday life and in all spheres—from economics to culture, from state administration to sport—evident facts exist to speak of the constant restriction and deprivation of Croatia. The dissatisfaction over this has been enhanced by the feeling that Croatia entered the joint state at a much higher level of development than all the other areas in Yugoslavia (with the exception of Slovenia) and that its relative lagging behind the others, or the extraction of its surplus of labor for their development, has gone on just as persistently in the post-war federal socialist period, and sometimes in even more pronounced forms, than between the two wars in centralistic capitalist Yugoslavia. This conviction has taken root in the soul of the Croatian nation as a result of their personal and common experience in everyday life, which is growing with each generation. However, at issue here is not only dissatisfaction over various forms of material (economic) deprivation and neglect, which has created in the consciousness of the Croatian people the justified but also sometimes exaggerated, impression of incessant and all-round exploitation and the unnecessary paying of tribute, but also the bitterness they feel over the continual injury done to their national sentiments and human dignity at every juncture in life....

[Note: Thirteen pages of evidence of intellectual and political deprivation, economic neglect, demographic (national) diminution, and repression in the 1970s that follow here are omitted.—Ed.]

And so today the circumstances are almost the same as one or more decades ago. Instead of sober and reasonable solutions being found for the removal of the reasons causing this situation, which by necessity maintains the dissatisfaction and inevitably gives rise to sporadic crisis situations in which this dissatisfaction can be seen, efforts are made to perpetuate the mental derangement deriving from not only the guilt associated with the "nationalist" and "counter-revolutionary" sins of those Croatian representatives which recently sought, in the interests of both Croatia and the SFRY, the "settling of accounts" and changes in relations about which Bakarić also spoke, but also from the exceptionally great historical guilt of the Croatian nation in the collapse of the Kingdom of Yugoslavia and, in particular, the Ustasha crimes in the war. It is certainly not a case here of establishing historical truth and, on the basis of it, deriving the necessary historical experience, no matter how painful it might be, but rather of a particular and more far-reaching goal: that of imposing on the Croatian nation the feeling that it does not have any right to protest but only atonement, regardless of the things which have happened to it. This follows from the fact that the Ustasha crimes, in themselves horrible enough, like the Chetnik and all other crimes, have been manifoldly exaggerated, even as much as *12 or so times*. Year after year for decades now the assertion has been rammed into the heads of the Yugoslav and world public almost every day and on all kinds of occasions, by means of the media (press, TV and radio), that during the NDH, in just one camp at Jasenovac, there were at least *700,000* men, women and children killed and that they were mostly Serbs. Conceived once upon a time in some clearly Chetnik hegemonistic rhetoric, with the obvious aim of making the Croatian nation odious in the eyes of the world and itself, because of co-responsibility for what were relatively speaking the greatest crimes in World War II, and thereby shutting it up, this erroneous figure (with variations from 600,000 to 800,000) is persistently repeated in order to create the myth of a new battle of Kosovo in spite of the fact that as far back as the time of Ranković in 1965 (as Director of the Institute for the History of the Workers' Movement of Croatia) I placed proof before the most responsible people in the political leadership of Croatia to the effect that this figure was historically inaccurate, absurd in its size and morally and politically harmful for future Croato-Serbian relations. They agreed with my arguments but so far nothing has been done to put an end to these ominous machinations with victims of history. On the contrary, those who made a stand for reason and truth in this matter have been shut up. Claims that about 700,000 were killed in Jasenovac alone are completely arbitrary, for it is a historical fact that in the war, in all camps and prisons, about 60,000 people from the territory of Croatia perished, and they were of all nationalities: Croatian anti-fascists, Serbs, Jews, Gypsies and others.

In order to see how absurd the claim is that in the Jasenovac camp alone 600,000–800,000 people were killed, we need only recall that in all probability the number of all the victims in the whole of Yugoslavia in World War II (all the population on all warring sides) does not exceed this number!

In this terrifying exaggeration of the Ustasha crimes during the NDH not only is the fact forgotten that the historical causes of the Ustasha thinking lay in the hegemonistic violence done to the Croatian nation in monarchistic Yugoslavia and that the Chetniks were no less dangerous for the Croatian population in the war than the Ustashas were for the Serbs, but also that on these falsified foundations it is impossible to create the preconditions for the harmonious co-existence of Serbs and Croats in one state community. People who lack the courage to look historical truth in the eyes usually also lack honorable intentions regarding the future. Moreover, the dissemination of the theory of the enormous historical guilt of the Croatian nation also serves to cover up the truth that in World War II Croatia was not only on the side of the Axis Powers but was also one of the firmest footholds of the anti-fascist movement, giving not a smaller but larger contribution in blood to the victory of the democratic forces over fascism than the other Yugoslav nations....

Just as there can be no doubt that the introduction of the federal socialist order meant a great step in the solving of the national question for all nations in Yugoslavia, and particularly for the Slovenes and Macedonians, who for the first time in history were constituted politically and in the state-legal sense as nations, so it is equally incontrovertible that the unitarian-integralistic tendencies, particularly in the periods of great-state etatism and centralistic hegemony, were felt with special severity on Croatian soil. As they were manifested, except in the political administrative and economic spheres, in even more severe forms in everyday life, in the spheres of language, culture and sport, the Croatian question again became the main national question, as had been the case in monarchistic Yugoslavia, and the normalization of Serbo-Croatian relations was again the central question of stability and the federal state community. Croato-Serbian relations are particularly hampered by the problem of Bosnia and Hercegovina, which geographically comprise such an economic whole with southern and north-western Croatia that even a layman can conclude this from a brief glance at the map. They are also largely linked to Croatia through both historic and ethnic and linguistic identity, but greater-Serbian hegemonism, ever since the formation of a joint state, has done everything to reduce and debilitate these natural connections, and even those which link these areas more to Belgrade, as far as possible. It has never achieved lasting results in this, especially in the most recent period of federal development....

In contrast to this, the contemporary Serbian question in Yugoslavia appeared with the collapse of the hegemonistic position of the ruling nation, brought about by the very establishment of the federal order, and became more palpable the more the federal system strengthened by degrees, albeit largely in the political-legal sense, particularly following the first serious show-down with centralistic hegemonism in 1966 and the last constitutional reform of 1970–74. In a similar way in which formerly, in capitalist Yugoslavia, the policy of the Serbian bourgeois parties and trends was almost without exception directed against any kind of federalization and towards the maintenance of centralism at all costs, and regardless of the manner employed (either through parliamentary majority, open dictatorship, or a programme of general democratization and local self-government), so in the most recent past in the socialist community the champions of unitarian and liberal-centralistic views have emerged largely from the ranks of the Serbian communist movement....

All this leads us to the conclusion that the real political relations in the Yugoslav federation are such that, on the one hand, the Serbs have not the predominance to impose their domination lastingly and effectively, even though they are the most numerous and hold the greatest part of the federal bureaucracy and power in their hands, and on the other, the other nations cannot realize, in the effective self-management sense, the AVNOJ [Anti-fascist Council for the National Liberation of Yugoslavia] idea of a community of nations with equal rights. This is the case largely because the Croats, who are the most important counterweight to the centralistic impediment of the federation, and traditionally the most resolute champions of its transformation into a community (confederation) with truly equal rights, meet with merely partial support from the other republics, which either because of their particular position or their individual interests are satisfied with minor compromises and temporary concessions....

Document 5

from "Memorandum of the Serbian Academy of Science and Arts" (1986).[5]

[5] "Memorandum SANU" as pubished in *Nase teme,* Zagreb, 33:1–2 (1989), 147–63 passim. Translated by Dennison Rusinow and Aleksandar and Sarah Nikolić. The first part of the Memorandum (pp. 128–47), omitted here, discusses "the crisis of the Yugoslav economy and society" in terms widely accepted throughout Yugoslavia by 1986. The more "Serbo-centric" portions of that first part are generally repeated in the second sections translated here.

The Situation of Serbia and the Serb Nation

6. Many of the misfortunes suffered by the Serb nation originate in circumstances that are common to all the Yugoslav nations. However, other calamities also burden the Serb nation. The long-term lagging behind of the economy of Serbia, undefined state and legal relations with Yugoslavia and the provinces [Kosovo and Vojvodina], and also genocide in Kosovo have appeared on the political scene with a combined force that has created a tense if not explosive situation. The crucial nature of these three tortured questions, which derive from a long-term policy toward Serbia, threaten not only the Serb nation but also the stability of Yugoslavia as a whole. They must therefore be given central attention.

Extensive knowledge and data are not required to confirm the longstanding lagging-behind of the Serbian economy....Throughout the postwar period the Serbian economy suffered from lopsided terms of trade. A primary example is the low price for electrical energy, which is supplied in large quantities to other republics. Economic instruments and measures taken in credit, monetary policies, and especially the contribution to the federal fund for the economic development of inadequately developed regions, have lately been the most important factors in its relatively slow growth. Along with the fact that the most developed republics, because of Serbia's lack of capital, have penetrated its economy (agriculture, the food-processing industry, commerce, and banking) with their capital, the picture is one of a subordinated and neglected economy within Yugoslavia.

Consistent discrimination against the Serbian economy in the postwar period cannot be fully explained without taking into consideration the nature of inter-nationality relations during the interwar period as these were seen and evaluated by the Communist Party of Yugoslavia. The decisive influence in shaping these views was the authoritative Comintern, which in its efforts to achieve its strategic and tactical international goals sought the disintegration of Yugoslavia. Finding its ideological justification in the opposition between a Serb "oppressor" nation and other "oppressed" peoples, this policy is a drastic example of the retreat of Marxist teaching about every nation's class divisions in the face of political pragmatism, which pushed classic internationalism into the background in an effort to exploit international tensions. That at least partly explains why the CPY [League of Yugoslav Communists] did not attempt to arrive at the real truth about the economic nature of inter-nationality relations by means of its own investigation. Its view of these relations, reduced to the conclusion that the political hegemony of the Serbian bourgeoisie was accompanied by corresponding Serbian economic domination, was in fact taken over from bourgeois parties with separatist orientations....

Postwar policy toward the Serbian economy, very clearly described in commentaries on the first Five Year Plan, was based on this prewar judgment.

In that plan Serbia was unjustifiably assigned the slowest tempo of industrialization, after Slovenia. In practice, that policy began with the transfer to other republics of industries for the production of aircraft, trucks, and armaments, and continued with compulsory purchase [of agricultural products from peasants] at price scissors to the disadvantage of raw materials and agricultural products; per capita investment lower than the Yugoslav average; and [Serbian] contributions to the development of underdeveloped regions. Nothing more clearly indicates the subordinate position of Serbia than the fact that it did not take the initiative in a single crucial question concerning the political and economic system. The position of Serbia can therefore appropriately be examined in the context of the political and economic domination of Slovenia and Croatia, which proposed all changes in the systems until now.

Slovenia and Croatia started at the highest level of development and enjoyed the fastest growth. With the improvement of their relative positions, the gulf between them and the other parts of Yugoslavia drastically deepened. Such a process, which deviated from the proclaimed policy of equal development, would not have been possible if the economic system had not been biased, if those two republics had not been in a position to impose solutions that corresponded to their economic interests. Processing industries, relatively more important in their economic structures, enjoyed more advantageous conditions, especially in terms of price ratios but also in tariff protection, throughout the postwar period. Greater emphasis on the market in the 1960s was more beneficial to developed regions. Suspension of the 1961–65 Five Year Plan, which gave priority to developing the production of raw materials and energy, can be interpreted as an evasion by the republics to invest in less developed regions that are relatively rich in raw materials. From that time development in Yugoslavia was based more on the composition of production of the two developed republics than that of the rest of the country. The labor force therefore did not receive adequate attention in the orientation of development, from which Serbia and underdeveloped regions suffered.

The economic subordination of Serbia cannot be fully understood without its politically inferior position, which also determined all relations. For the CPY the economic hegemony of the Serbian nation between the wars was not disputable, although the industrialization of Serbia was slower than the Yugoslav average. Thinking and behavior with a dominant influence on later political events and inter-nationality relations were formed on the basis of that ideological platform. Slovenes and Croats created their national Communist parties before the war and achieved decisive influence in the CC [Central Committee] of the CPY. Their political leaders became the arbiters of all political questions during and after the war. These two neighboring republics shared a similar history, had the same religion and desire for ever-greater independence, and as the most developed had common economic interests, all of which supplied sufficient reason for a permanent coalition in an attempt to realize political domination. This coalition was solidified by the long lasting co-operation of Tito and Kardelj [respectively, a Croat and a Slovene], the two most prominent personalities of post-war Yugoslavia, who enjoyed unlimited authority in centers of power. A cadre monopoly allowed them essential influence over the composition of the political apex of Yugoslavia and all the republics and provinces. The exceptionally great contribution of Edvard Kardelj in preparing and carrying out the decisions of AVNOJ and of all post-war constitutions is well known to all. He was in a position to build his personal views, which could not realistically be opposed, into the foundation of the social order. The determination with which Slovenia and Croatia today oppose any constitutional change shows how much the Constitution of 1974 suits them. Views concerning the social order had no chance of being accepted if they were different from the conceptions of [those] two political authorities, and it was not possible to do anything even after their deaths,given that the Constitution insured against any such change by granting the possibility of a veto. In view of all of this, it is indisputable that Slovenia and Croatia established a political and economic domination through which to realize their national programs and economic aspirations.

In such circumstances and subject to continuous accusations that it is an "oppressive," "unitaristic," "centralistic," and "gendarme" nation, the Serb nation could not achieve equality in Yugoslavia, for whose creation it had made the greatest sacrifices. A policy of revenge against the Serbs began even before the war, in the view that a Communist party need not be given to an "oppressor" nation. Serbs were relatively under-represented on the CC CPY, and some of them, probably so that they could stay there, declared themselves as members of other nations. During the war, Serbia was not in a position to participate in full equality in adopting decisions which prejudiced future inter-nationality relations and Yugoslavia's social order. The Anti-Fascist Council of Serbia was founded in the second half of 1944, later than in the other republics, and the Communist Party of Serbia only after the end of the war. Delegates to the Second AVNOJ Congress were elected from Serb military units and members of the Supreme Command who happened to be on the territory of Bosnia and Hercegovina, in contrast to delegates of some other republics, who came to the meeting from their territories and who had behind them national political organization with developed positions and programs.

These historic facts demonstrate that during the war Serbia was not formally, and certainly not actually, in an equal position when decisions of long-term significance for the future state order were adopted. That does not mean that Serbs would not have voluntarily decided in favor of federalism as the most suitable order for a multi-national community, but only to note that they found themselves in the situation of accepting—in war conditions and without proper preparation and the support of their own political organizations—solutions which created wide possibilities for their fragmentation. The position of the Serbs should have been considered and regulated from the standpoint of their national integrity and undisturbed cultural development and in good time, and not that this exceptional question, which concerns the vital interests of the Serb nation, should remain open....

[Note: Five paragraphs on the "capitulation" of postwar Serbian Communist leaders in the face of this situation that follow here are omitted. —Ed.]

7. The attitude toward the economic lagging behind of Serbia demonstrates that a revanchist policy toward her did not weaken over time. On the contrary, nourished by its own success, it became ever stronger until it finally expressed itself also in genocide. It is a politically unacceptable discrimination that citizens of Serbia, because of equal representation by the republics, have less access than others to positions as federal functionaries and delegates to the federal parliament, and that the votes of voters from Serbia are worth less than those of any other republic or province. In this light Yugoslavia does not appear as a community of equal citizens or equal nations and nationalities, but as a community of eight equal territories. However, even this equality does not hold for Serbia because of its special legal-political situation, which supports a tendency to keep the Serb nation under constant control. The dominant idea of such a policy has been "a weak Serbia, a strong Yugoslavia," advanced under the influence of the view that if the Serbs, as the most numerous nation, were permitted rapid economic development, that would represent a danger for the other nations. From this stems the exploitation of every possibility to limit its economic development and political consolidation in ever greater measure. One of these very acute limitations is the present constitutional position of Serbia, which is undefined and full of internal contradictions.

Serbia is in fact divided in three parts by the Constitution of 1974. The autonomous provinces are equivalent to republics in everything except that they are not defined as states and do not have the same number of representatives in some federal organs. They compensate for this deficiency through their ability to intervene in the internal affairs of Narrow Serbia [i.e., Serbia without the two autonomous provinces] through a common republican parliament, while their own parliaments are totally autonomous. The political-legal situation of Narrow Serbia is completely undefined, it is neither a republic nor a province. Relations in the Serbian republic are confused. The Executive Council [Government], which is an organ of the Republican Parliament, is in reality the Executive Council of Narrow Serbia. That is not the only illogicality and restriction of competence. The excessively wide and institutionally firmly anchored autonomy of the provinces creates two new cleavages in the Serb people. The truth is that autonomous and separatist forces insisted on a widening of autonomy, but this would have been difficult to realize if they had not received moral and political support from republics in which separatist tendencies have never disappeared.

Enlarged autonomy was justified by assurances that it would lead to greater equality among the nations and better performance of public functions. Events in Kosovo at the end of the 1960s were a warning of all that could happen if autonomy were enlarged. There was absolutely no reason for greater autonomy of Vojvodina. Its enlargement gave a powerful support to bureaucratic autonomist tendencies, to serious expressions of a separatism that had never previously existed, to closing of the economy, to political voluntarism. The influence grew of those outside the province and in Vojvodina who sought, by spreading disinformation, to divide the Serb people into "Serbians" and "*prečani* Serbs." With the enthusiastic help of others, the provinces became "a constitutive element of the federation," which gave them inducement to feel and behave like federal units, ignoring the fact that they are a component part of the Republic of Serbia....

Relations between Serbia and the provinces are not only and not primarily a matter of formalistic-legal interpretation of two constitutions. It is primarily a question of the Serb nation and its state. A nation which after a long and bloody battle again achieved its own state, which itself opted also for bourgeois democracy, and which in the last two wars lost 2.5 million co-nationals, has had the experience of an arbitrarily constituted party commission established that, after four decades in the new Yugoslavia, is the one that does not have its state. A worse historical defeat in peace cannot be imagined.

8. The exile of the Serbian people from Kosovo is a spectacular testament to its historic defeat. In the spring of 1981, the Serbian people received a declaration of a special but also open and total war, which had been prepared during different periods of administrative, political and judicial-state changes. This war was waged with the skillful application of various methods and tactics, with not only passive but very active and not so tacit support from various political centers in the country. This support was even more fatal than that coming from neighboring countries. This unconcealed war, which we have yet to face clearly or call by its true name, has been going on for almost five years. It has thus lasted much longer than this country's entire war of liberation—from April 6, 1941, to May 1945. The rebellion of the Balisti in Kosovo and Metohija at the very end of the war, begun with the help of Nazi units, was militarily crushed between 1944 and 1945, but it was not politically beaten. Its present form, disguised in a new context, has been developing more successfully and has been approaching a victorious outcome.

Therefore a true reckoning with neofascist aggression never occurred. All measures taken to date have only hidden it from view, and in fact have strengthened its irrevocable goals, which are motivated by racism and which must be achieved by all means regardless of cost. Even the intentionally drastic sentences given to young offenders were pronounced in order to provoke and deepen inter-ethnic hatred.

The five-year Albanian war in Kosovo has convinced its organizers and supporters that they are even stronger than they thought, that in the various power centers of the country they enjoy immensely greater support than the support the Kosovo Serbs have from the Republic of Serbia or than Serbia itself has from the rest of the country. Their aggression has been encouraged to such an extent that even the highest officials of the province as well as its scientists have become not only arrogant, but also cynical, when they proclaim slanders to be truths and blackmail to be their inalienable right. The organized political powers of our country, who carried out the revolution under almost impossible conditions, fighting the most powerful enemy of our century, suddenly appear to be not only inefficient and unfree, but almost uninterested in responding to this unconcealed war in the only possible way: by a determined defense of their people and their territory. Once the aggression is defeated, political reckonings cannot be carried out through more arrests, "differentiations," or false oaths of loyalty, but must be carried out through true revolutionary strife, open confrontations, freedom of expression, and even the voicing of opposing opinions.

The physical, political, legal and cultural genocide of the Serbian population in Kosovo and Metohija is the worst defeat in the Serbian-led battles of liberation from Orašac in 1804 to the 1941 uprising. Responsibility for this defeat falls primarily on the Comintern heritage present in the policy of the Communist Party of Yugoslavia and the loyalty of the Serbian communists to this policy, to the extremely costly ideological and political delusions, ignorance, immaturity, or already incorrigible opportunism of the generation of Serbian politicians who arose after the war, who are always defensive and always care more about what other people think of them and their timid "postings" of Serbia's status than about the objective facts which determine the future of the people they govern.

Egalitarian national relations, for which Serbian soldiers in Kosovo and Metohija fought more than anybody else, have been turned upside down—through a very clearly defined policy carried out "developmentally," with planned steps and with a clear goal—by Albanian nationalists in the political leadership of Kosovo. The autonomous region, in a convenient moment, obtained the status of an autonomous province, and thereafter the status of a "constitutional part of the federation"—with greater prerogatives than the rest of the republic to which it only formally belonged. This next step in the "escalation," which appeared together with the Albanization of Kosovo and Metohija, had therefore been prepared in a very legal manner. In the same way, the unification of the literary language, national name, flag and schoolbooks—according to instructions from Tirana—was completely open as well as was the border itself between the two state territories (Albania and Yugoslavia). Conspiracies, which are usually organized secretly, were created in Kosovo not only in an obvious manner but with arrogance. That is why the popular unrest of 1981 appeared to many more like an act of consummation than like a new phenomenon that could be dangerous to the whole country, just as later every bit of truth about the exile of the Serbs from Kosovo was considered "digging through the Albanians' guts." That is why the writings of the Belgrade press were considered a greater offense than the arsons, murders, rapes and sacrileges that actually took place—many of which to this day remain politically and judicially unidentified....

The Serbs of Kosovo and Metohija have not only their past, personified in precious cultural-historic monuments, but also living spiritual, cultural and moral values: they have the motherland of their historic existence. The violence which has, over the centuries, thinned out the Serbian population in Kosovo and Metohija is—in this our time—entering its relentless endgame. The emigration of Serbs from Kosovo and Metohija in socialist Yugoslavia exceeds in numbers and in character all former phases of this great exile of the Serbian people. Jovan Cvijić in his time estimated that in all migrations, beginning with the great one under Arsenije Crnojević in 1690 to the first years of our century, more than 500,000 Serbs had been exiled; of that number between 1876 and 1912 about 150,000 Serbs had to leave their hearths under the ruthless terror of the local and privileged Albanian "basibazuks" [local confederates of the Ottomans]. In the course of the last war, over 60,000 Serbian colonists and natives were exiled, but after the war this wave of emigration really reached its crest: in the last 20 or so years, 200,000 Serbs left Kosovo and Metohija. The remaining Serbian people are not only leaving their land at an undiminished pace, but, being persecuted by oppression and physical, moral and psychological terror, they are preparing for their final exodus, according to all sources of information. In less than the next ten years, if the situation does not change considerably, there will no longer be any Serbs in Kosovo, and an "ethnically clean" Kosovo—that unequivocally expressed goal of the "Greater-Albanian" racists established in the programs and actions of the "Prizren League" as early as 1878–1881—will be completely fulfilled.

The petition of 2016 Serbs from Kosovo Polje, submitted to the Federal Assembly and other political institutions in the country, is the lawful consequence of the above-described state of affairs. There are no formal assessments that can dispute the right of the Serbian people to defend itself from violence and destruction by all legal means. If it cannot exercise this protection in the Province, the people can and must look for protection in the Republic and the Federation. The visit of the citizens of the Province to the Federal Assembly is an expression of civil consciousness about this right. Only an autonomous-separatist and chauvinist viewpoint could judge the actions undertaken by the citizens as unacceptable and hostile.

The destiny of today's Kosovo is no longer "complex," nor can it still be reduced to empty self-assessments, evasions, illegible resolutions, and overgeneralized platforms—it is simply a question of Yugoslav consequences. Between provincial segregation, which is becoming more and more exclusive, and federal arbitration, which only paralyzes every correct and often also unpostponable measure, the interplay of unresolved situations becomes a closed circle of the unresolvable. If this question is not resolved through the only just outcome of the imposed war; if true security and unequivocable equality for all peoples who live in Kosovo and Metohija are not established; if objective and lasting conditions for the return of the exiled people are not created, then that part of the Republic of Serbia and of Yugoslavia will become a European question as well with very serious, unpredictable consequences. Kosovo represents one of the most important points in the inner Balkans. Ethnic variety on many Balkan territories is congruent with the ethnic profile of the whole Balkan peninsula. Therefore, the demand for an ethnically-pure Kosovo, which is being acted upon, is not only a direct and serious threat to the peoples who have found themselves in the minority in this region, but will (if this demand is fully realized) begin a wave of expansion which will represent a real and constant threat to all Yugoslav peoples.

Kosovo is not the only region in which the Serbian people has found itself under the pressures of discrimination. Not only the relative but the absolute decline in the numbers of Serbs in Croatia is evidence enough for the above claim. According to the census of 1948, there were 543,795 Serbs in Croatia, that is, 14.48 percent of the Croatian population. According to the 1981 census, these numbers had diminished to 531,502 which was 11.5 percent of the entire population of Croatia. During the 33 years of peace, the number of Serbs in Croatia had declined even in relation to the immediate postwar period, when the first census was carried out, and when the consequences of World War II on the number of Serbs were well known.

Lika, Kordun and Banija have remained the least developed regions in Croatia, which greatly motivated Croatian Serbs to migrate to Serbia as well as to other regions of Croatia, where Serbs, as a minority group of newcomers and a socially inferior people, were extremely susceptible to assimilation. The Serbian people have been, in general, exposed to a sophisticated and efficient assimilation policy. A consistent part of this policy is a ban of all Serbian societies and cultural institutions in Croatia. They were part of a rich cultural tradition during the reign of the Austro-Hungarian Empire and the Kingdom of Yugoslavia between the wars. This policy also includes the imposition of an official language, which is named after another people (Croatian), thus signifying national inequality. That language was, through a constitutional act, made obligatory for all Serbs in Croatia. Also, nationalistically inclined Croatian language experts, through systematic and extremely well-organized action, have been distancing that language from the language spoken in other republics where Serbo-Croatian is the mother-tongue. This action contributes to the weakening of connections between Serbs in Croatia and other Serbs. In order to achieve this goal, the Croats are ready to sacrifice the continuity of their own language and lose from it international terms necessary for communication with other cultures, especially in the fields of science and technology. Moreover, the Serbian people in Croatia are not only culturally cut off from the mainstream of the Motherland, but the Motherland has no possibility of informing itself—to nearly the extent that other nations who live in Yugoslavia are connected with their fellow peoples—about the Serbian people's economic and cultural position in Croatia. The question of the integrity of the Serbian people and their culture in all of Yugoslavia is a fateful one for their survival and progress.

The fate of Serb constitutions created during and immediately after the war are also part of this picture....

Except for the period of the existence of the NDH [the Independent State of Croatia], Serbs in Croatia were never so endangered as they are today. The solution of their national position imposes itself as a first priority political question. Unless a solution is found, the consequences can be damaging in many ways, not only for the situation in Croatia but for all of Yugoslavia.

What gives important weight to the question of the position of the Serbian people is the fact that outside the Republic of Serbia, and particularly outside the geographic region of Serbia proper, there live a great number of Serbs, a number greater than the total number of people of any other one nationality. According to the 1981 census, 24 percent of all Serbs live outside the territory of the Socialist Republic of Serbia—that is, 1,958,000 people, which is a greater number than the number of Slovenians, Albanians, and Macedonians in Yugoslavia respectively, and almost as many people as there are Muslims in Yugoslavia. Outside the region of Serbia proper, there are 3,285,000 Serbs, or 40.3 percent of the total number of Serbs. In the general disintegrative process that is affecting all of Yugoslavia, the Serbs are more affected than anyone else. The present trend in our society in Yugoslavia is in total contrast to that of decades and centuries before the creation of a common fatherland. This process aims to destroy completely the national unity of the Serbian people. The best illustration that this process was dedicated to such a goal is today's Vojvodina, with its autonomy.

Vojvodina was given autonomy, among other reasons, because the Serbian people in the Habsburg monarchy aspired to it since the end of the 17th century. The Serbs in Austria and later Austria-Hungary sought the creation of an autonomous region (a despotate or dukedom [vojvodina], which they called Serbia) in order to preserve their national identity and their Orthodox faith even while surrounded by more numerous and more powerful Germans and Hungarians. By creating a separate autonomous region in another state's territory, Serbs worked to weaken that state with the goal of having a better chance, in a convenient moment, to separate from it and unite with their brethren south of the Sava and Danube.

That is how Serbian Vojvodina came to be, for the creation of which Serbs from Serbia also shed their blood in 1848–49. Today this development has been stood on its head. The political leadership of the Autonomous Province of Vojvodina does not work for closer relationships and unity, but for ever greater independence and separation from the Socialist Republic of Serbia. But however much this process seems unnatural, contradicting the logic of history, it yields obvious results, powerfully contributing to the disintegration of the Serbian people.

9. Carrying upon itself for more than half a century the brand and the burden that it was the warden of the other Yugoslav peoples, the Serbian people was incapable of finding support in its own history. In many of its aspects, that very history was brought into question. The democratic civil tradition for which Serbia fought and won in the 19th century had remained, until recently, completely in the shadow of the Serbian socialist and workers' movements because of the narrow-mindedness and bias of official historiography. Thus the historical picture of the true judicial, cultural and political contributions of Serbia to civil society was so impoverished, reduced and warped that it could serve no one as spiritual and moral support or as a basis for the preservation and restoration of historic self-awareness. A similar fate befell the righteous and brave efforts of Serbs from Bosnia and Hercegovina and all Yugoslav youth, of which Young Bosnia was a part. They were all pushed out of their place in history by a class ideology whose carriers and creators were Austro-Marxists, renowned enemies of national liberation movements.

Under the influence of the ruling ideology, the cultural heritage of the Serbian people is being alienated, usurped, invalidated, neglected, or wasted; their language is being suppressed and the Cyrillic alphabet is vanishing. The field of literature in this sense serves as a main arena for arbitrariness and lawlessness. No other Yugoslav nation has been so rudely denied its cultural and spiritual integrity as the Serbian people. No literary and artistic heritage has been so routed, pillaged and plundered as the Serbian one. The political maxims of the ruling ideology are being imposed on Serbian culture as more valuable and stronger than scientific and historic ones. While Slovenian, Croatian, Macedonian and Montenegrian culture and literature are today being integrated, Serbian culture and literature alone are being systematically disintegrated. It is ideologically legitimate and in the spirit of self-management to divide and disperse freely the Serbian literary heritage and attribute it to authors from Vojvodina, Montenegro or Bosnia and Hercegovina. Serbia's best authors and most significant literary works are being torn from the Serbian literary canon so that new regional literatures can be artificially established. The usurpation and fragmentation of the Serbian cultural heritage goes so far that children in schools learn that Njegos is not a Serbian author, that Laza Kostić and Veljko Petrović were from Vojvodina, and that Petar Koćič and Jovan Dučić are from Bosnia-Hercegovina. As only yesterday Mesi Selimović was not allowed to declare himself a Serbian author, even today his wish to be classified as a Serbian author is still not respected. Serbian culture has more politically incorrect, banned, unmentioned or undesirable authors and intellectual creators than any other Yugoslav literature; many of them have moreover been erased from literary memory.

Reputable Serbian authors are the only ones who are blacklisted by all Yugoslav mass media. In compulsory school texts, Serbian literature has been severely harmed, since it has been mechanically submitted to the administrative doctrine of republican-provincial reciprocity, and not represented according to quantity and value. In the school curricula of certain republics and provinces the historical past of the Serbian people has not only been rudely ideologically reduced but has been laid open to chauvinist interpretations. Thus the Serbian cultural and spiritual heritage seems less significant than it actually is, and the Serbian people is losing an important base of moral and historic self-awareness....

[Note: Six paragraphs of criticism of Yugoslav educational reforms of the 1970s that follow here are omitted.—Ed.]

10. After the dramatic inter-ethnic conflicts of the Second World War it seemed that nationalism suddenly deflated, that it was about to perish. This impression proved fallacious. It was not long before nationalism began its ascent as the institutional preconditions for its flourishing grew with every constitutional change. Nationalism was created from above; its chief initiators were politicians. The basic cause of our multi-dimensional crisis lies in the ideological defeat that nationalism delivered to socialism. Disintegrational processes of all kinds, which have brought the Yugoslav community to the brink of disaster, are, together with the demise of our value-system, the consequences of this defeat.

Its roots can be found in the ideology of the Comintern and the national policy of the Communist Party of Yugoslavia before World War II. This policy included revanchism toward the Serbian people as an oppressor-nation.

It had far-reaching consequences for international relations, domestic politics, the economy and the fate of moral and cultural values after World War II. A feeling of historic guilt was imposed on the Serbian people, although only they did not solve their national question, or receive their own state like other nations did. Thus, our first and basic objective is to remove the mortgage of this historical guilt from the Serbian people, to refute officially claims that they had an economically privileged position between the two world wars, and to ensure that the denial of their liberating history and contribution in the creation of Yugoslavia end.

The Serbian people have a historic and democratic right to establish full national and cultural integrity independently, regardless of the republic or province in which they live. The acquisition of equality and independent development have a deeper historic meaning for the Serbian people. In less than 50 years, within two consecutive generations, twice exposed to physical annihilation, forceful assimilation, religious conversion, cultural genocide, ideological indoctrination, invalidation, and denunciation of their own tradition under the imposed complex of guilt, intellectually and politically disarmed, the Serbian people were exposed to temptations that were too great not to leave deep scars on their spirit. We cannot allow ourselves to forget these facts at the end of this century of great technological achievements of the human mind. If the Serbian people see their future in the family of cultured and civilized nations of the world, they must find themselves anew and become a historical subject; they must once again acquire a consciousness of their historic and cultural being; they must put forth a modern societal and national program, which will inspire contemporary and future generations.

The existing feelings of depression among the Serbian people, accompanied by the growing fierceness of chauvinistic and Serbo-phobic displays, are fertile ground for the revival and increasingly more dramatic displays of the national sensitivity of the Serbian people, and for reactions that can be contagious, and even dangerous. It is our duty not to oversee and underestimate these dangers for a single moment, whatever form they might take. But in the course of this principled fight against Serbian nationalism we must not accept the pervading ideological and political symmetry of historic guilts. Denouncing this symmetry—which is spiritually and morally fatal—along with denouncing cliches of injustices and untruths, is a prerequisite for the mobility and efficacy of a democratic, Yugoslav, humanistic consciousness in contemporary Serbian culture.

The fact that citizens and the working class are not represented in the Federal Assembly in appropriate numbers cannot be attributed only to priority for the national [units], but also to an aspiration to bring Serbia into an unequal position and thus weaken her political influence. However, the greatest misfortune for the Serbian people is that they do not have a state like all other nations. It is true that the first article of the Constitution of the Socialist Republic of Serbia includes the declaration that Serbia is a state, but it must be asked what kind of a state it is that is proclaimed to lack competence over its own territory, and that does not have the means to introduce order to one part of its territory, to provide personal and material security to its citizens, to stop the genocide in Kosovo and the migration of Serbs from their ancient hearths? Such a position demonstrates political discrimination against Serbia, especially taking into consideration the fact that the Constitution of the SFRY imposed upon her an internal federalization as a continuous source of conflicts between Serbia proper and the provinces. Aggressive Albanian nationalism in Kosovo cannot be suppressed if Serbia does not stop being the only republic whose internal relations are regulated by others.

The equality of all republics, formally affirmed by the Constitution of the SFRY, was in reality invalidated when the Republic of Serbia was forced to give up a good part of her rights and authority in favor of the autonomous provinces whose status is for the most part regulated by the Federal Constitution. Serbia must openly state that this system was imposed upon her. This [imposition] especially pertains to the position of the provinces, in reality promoted into republics, which think of themselves much more as constituent elements of the Federation than a part of the Republic of Serbia. In addition to ignoring the state[hood] of the Serbian people, the Constitution of the SFRY also created insuperable barriers to its constitution. A revision of this constitution is unavoidable in order to satisfy Serbia's legitimate interests. The autonomous regions must become genuine constituent parts of the Republic of Serbia, giving them a level of autonomy which does not hamper the integrity of the republic and which provides for the realization of the general interests of the broader community.

The unsolved question of Serbia's statehood is not the only defect which ought to be removed through constitutional changes. Through the Constitution of 1974, Yugoslavia became a very loose state community in which consideration is given to alternatives even to Yugoslavia. This is evident from recent statements by Slovenian public officials and earlier positions taken by Macedonian politicians. Such thinking and basically completed disintegration lead one to believe that Yugoslavia is in danger of further fragmentation. The Serbian people cannot calmly wait for its future in such uncertainty. That is why a possibility must be created for all nations in Yugoslavia to declare their aspirations and intentions. In that case, Serbia herself could define her national interests and commit herself to them. Such a discussion and agreement would have to precede the re-examination of the [Federal] Constitution. Naturally, in that case, Serbia must not allow herself a passive attitude, merely awaiting the others' statements, as she has done so frequently to date.

Espousing AVNOJ's tenets, Serbia must also realize that this espousal does not depend only on her, that others might have different alternatives. This is why her task is clearly to assess her economic and national interests lest she be surprised by future events. By insisting on a federal system, Serbia would contribute not only to the equality of all nations in Yugoslavia but also to the solution of the political and economic crisis.

The egalitarian position which Serbia must insist on also presupposes her taking the initiative in solving key political and economic questions to the same extent that others take such initiative. Four decades of Serbia's passive position have proven wrong for all of Yugoslavia which was deprived of the ideas and criticism of a region with a long-standing tradition of statehood and an acute sense of national independence and rich experience in fighting domestic usurpers of political freedoms. Without the equal participation of the Serbian people of Serbia in the entire process of creating and carrying out all vital decisions, Yugoslavia cannot be strong. Her very existence as a democratic and socialistic community would be in question.

One epoch in the development of the Yugoslav community and of Serbia is obviously ending with a historically exhausted ideology, global stagnation and ever greater regressions in the economic, political, moral, cultural and civil spheres. Such a state of affairs urgently calls for basic, carefully considered, scientifically-based and decisively executed reforms of the whole state structure and social organization of the Yugoslav community of nations, and in the sphere of democratic socialism also a quicker and more fruitful inclusion into contemporary civilization. Societal reforms also must activate, to the greatest extent, the country's human resources in order for us to become a productive, enlightened and democratic society capable of living off its own labor and creations, capable of offering its own contribution to the world community.

The first condition of our metamorphosis and rebirth is democratic mobilization of all the creative and moral powers of the people, but not only to carry out decisions made in political forums, but to create programs and a blueprint for the future in a democratic manner. By this means, for the first time in recent history, a task engaging the whole of society will unite experience and knowledge, courage and consciousness, imagination and responsibility on the basis of a long-term program.

On this, as on other occasions, the Serbian Academy of Sciences and Arts expresses its readiness to apply itself wholeheartedly and with all its means to the fateful and historic tasks of our generation.

Introduction

Yugoslavia, twice born and now twice dead, has gone to its second grave in a storm of inter-communal warfare, vicious mutual atrocities, and brutal "ethnic cleansing" to fortify "national" claims most frequently by Serbs but also by Slavic Muslims and Croats in districts and towns where two or all three of these had lived together, usually in peace if not harmony, for centuries. As the storm engulfed Croatia and then Bosnia-Hercegovina in 1991–92, the magnitude of the violence and the bestiality of the massacres, mutilations, and genocidal "ethnic cleansing" that created more than two million refugees—"an evil not seen in Europe for fifty years"[6]—shocked the world. This was shocking even to those who had accurately forecast that disintegration of the South Slav state could not be consummated without violence and that a civil war in Bosnia-Hercegovina would be far more ferocious than one in Croatia.

In this "tide of hatred"[7] and paroxysm of death, destruction, and deportations, the nationalisms *couchantes* of the Tito era became nationalisms *rampantes* with a fury and vengeance exceeding their most pessimistic anticipations.[8] The only period of comparable inter-communal violence in the

---

6 Tim Judah, "Thousands flee evil of 'ethnic cleansing,'" in *The Times* (London) (25 July 1992), 1. Sifted for exaggerated and false reports, the record of authenticated atrocities by all sides justifies this and numerous similar descriptions in the media.

7 Adam Roberts on the BBC World Service, 2100 GMT, 7 August 1992.

8 Basic works in English on the Yugoslav national question in the Tito era and before include Paul Shoup, *Communism and the Yugoslav National Question* (New York: Columbia University Press, 1968); Ivo J. Lederer, "Nationalism and the Yugoslavs," in *Nationalism in Eastern Europe,* Peter F. Sugar and Ivo J. Lederer, eds. (Seattle: University of Washington, 1969); Dennison Rusinow, *The Yugoslav Experiment, 1948–1974* (Berkeley: University of California, 1977); Ivo Banac, *The National Question in Yugoslavia* (Ithaca, NY: Cornell University Press, 1984), which covers up to 1921; Steven L. Burg, *Conflict and Cohesion in Socialist Yugoslavia* (Princeton, NJ: Princeton University Press, 1984); Pedro Ramet, *Nationalism and Federalism in Yugoslavia* (Bloomington: Indiana University Press, 1984); Aleksa Djilas, *The Contested Country: Yugoslav Unity and the Communist Revolution, 1919–1953* (Cambridge, MA: Harvard University Press, 1991), which is broader in scope than its title indicates; and the chapters by Banac, Geert van Dartel, and Shoup in Martin van den

pre-national and nationalist history of the South Slavs[9] was during their triune war of resistance to foreign occupation, civil war, and social revolution during World War II, which occurred in exceptional circumstances and with external (Axis) provocation.

The demise of communism and one-party Communist regimes at the end of the 1980s has been accompanied in all of the societies examined in this book by a resurgence of nationalist passions, programs, and parties that were prominent and usually dominant in these societies during the pre-Communist and even nineteenth-century periods. As in nature, so in politics: when a thaw finally and abruptly comes to long-frozen ground, the first things to sprout or send out new shoots are often old plants and trees that appeared to have been killed. When their roots are in fact dead or hopelessly damaged, and the new growth therefore is supported only by thawing sap in the trunk and stems, it soon withers again. Where the roots have survived and again find appropriate nourishment, such sturdy old plants may have important comparative advantages over younger and more fragile competitors. In the thaw after four decades of Communist frost in East-Central and Eastern Europe, revived pre-Communist peasant and liberal parties seem to be examples of the first, withering type. Nationalism, both as a set of ideas and sentiments and as embodied in political parties and movements, clearly belongs to the second type.

Nowhere has the resurgence of nationalism and "the national question" been as dramatic, and its consequences as traumatic and tragic, as in the lands that were Yugoslavia. The exceptionality of this phenomenon, the possibility that the trauma and tragedy will be replicated in other multinational ex-Communist states and regions, and the continuing worldwide importance of nationalism as both promise and threat combine to make an examination of the how and why of Yugoslavia's violent demise more significant.

Other developments in the 1980s also were involved in Yugoslavia's ultimately unavoidable disintegration: deepening economic and consequently social crisis, Albanian unrest in Kosovo and Serb reactions to it, and the

---

Heuvel and Jan G. Siccama, eds., *The Disintegration of Yugoslavia* (Atlanta, GA: Rodopi, 1992).

9 In this chapter, "nationalism" and "nationalist" follow Hugh Seton-Watson, *Nations and States* (London: Methuen, 1977), 3. They have "two basic meanings...One...is a doctrine about character, interests, rights and duties of nations. The second...is an organized political movement, designed to further alleged aims and interests of nations." "South Slav" denotes the southern Slavic peoples of "Yugoslavia" and thus does not include the Bulgarians.

transparent incapacity of both federal and regional-national political elites and institutions. The consequences of all of these was the step-by-step "de-legitimation" of leaderships, the regime, "the system" and its federal (or quasi-confederal) and "self-management socialist" principles, and finally the state itself. However, all these factors were part of a vicious circle of cause and effect centered around the national question and embodied in diverse and divergent national interests, perceptions, prejudices, and programs, and in regional and national(ist) political and economic elites as their exponents, aggravators, and exploiters.[10]

Although the nationalisms of the Yugoslav peoples are thus the root of all the evils currently besetting them,[11] the specificity and intractability of the national question in ex-Yugoslavia and the magnitude and brutality of the violence accompanying its latest phase are not explained by the content of its national ideologies and its national diversity per se. South Slav nationalisms are no more exclusivist, no more prone to irredentism and competing territorial and cultural claims, and no more or less defensive in origin and offensive in action than other nationalisms in Eastern Europe's ethnic, religious, and cultural shatterbelt. Almost all other states in the region are also multinational, if in lesser magnitude, and therefore also are subject to the tension caused by modern nationalism's insistence on the exclusive-inclusive nature of the nation-state.

Nor is there anything particularly new and more vicious about the contemporary rhetoric and programs of Serb, Croat, and other South Slav nationalists and their followers, which—along with the histories, grievances, and aspirations that they partly remember and partly imagine—closely resemble their pre-Communist and even pre-Yugoslav antecedents. Thus the section of the 1986 memorandum of the Serbian Academy of Science and Art excerpted here (Document 5), which was widely regarded as the charter of contemporary Serb nationalism, also can be read as a codicil to Ilija Garašanin's *"Nacertanije"* of 1844, which was similarly regarded as the "bible"

---

[10] Non-Yugoslav analyses include van den Heuvel and Siccama, *The Disintegration of Yugoslavia;* Ivo Banac, "The Fearful Asymmetry of War: The Causes and Consequences of Yugoslavia's Demise," *Daedalus* (Spring 1992); Steven L. Burg, "Nationalism and Democratization in Yugoslavia," *Wilson Quarterly* (Autumn 1991); Dennison Rusinow, "To Be or Not To Be? Yugoslavia as Hamlet," *Field Staff Reports* 18 (1991); Rusinow, ed., *Yugoslavia: A Fractured Federalism* (Washington, DC: Woodrow Wilson Center Press, 1988); and Mojmir Krizan, "Nationalismen in Jugoslawien," *Osteuropa* 2 (1992).

[11] Except the Slovenes, who escaped the storm of war and forced migrations, after a few skirmishes, virtually unscathed in the summer of 1991.

of nineteenth-century Serb national-irredentism. It incorporates the same concepts of the Serb nation, its place in history and the map, and its frustrated aspirations. The concept of the Croat nation, its "state right," and its national program as embodied in the writings of Franjo Tudjman (such as the excerpts in Document 4), ex-Communist historian and president of Croatia at the time of its secession in 1991, bear a similarly close resemblance to those of Ante Starčević, the pioneer of integralist Croat nationalism in the nineteenth century. Except for some significant shifts in priority and emphasis (examined in detail below), the experience and consequences of forty-five years of "Titoist" communism, and the social and economic transformations and "answers" to the national question that it either encouraged or inhibited, have had more influence on the economic and social aspects of post-Tito nationalist programs (and on the vocabulary even of those who were never Marxists)[12] than on perceptions of and answers to strictly national issues.

It is the *number* and *distribution* of ex-Yugoslavia's "nationally conscious" peoples and nationalist leaders and programs, in a territory the size of Wyoming or Minnesota, that provides an essential first key to any understanding of the specificity and violent denouement of its national question.

Tables 1 and 2 provide a very oversimplified summary of the distribution of these communities. Their intermingling in many areas and large diasporas outside their core homelands (defined for the eight most numerous by the six republics and two autonomous provinces of the postwar Yugoslav federation) always have been the strongest pragmatic argument for some kind of common state. The Slovenes are the only community with no significant diaspora outside or national minorities inside their home territory. In the census of 1991, taken when conditions surrounding the run-up to Yugoslavia's disintegration and civil war affected the reliability of some (but probably not Slovene) data, 99 percent of the 1.76 million persons who were registered as Slovenes lived in Slovenia, their "matrix" republic, where they constituted 87.6 percent of the total population.[13] The other extreme, and the central

---

[12] The first part of the Serbian Academy's memorandum, which focuses on economic and social issues (and is not included in Document 5), provides a good example. However, it can be argued that the infiltration of Marxist terminology and categories into the vocabulary of anti-, non-, and post-Marxists significantly affects vocabulary-dependent modes of thought.

[13] The Macedonians, 95.7 percent of whom lived in Macedonia, came close to the Slovenes in their degree of concentration in their "matrix" republic, but constituted only 65 percent of its very heterogeneous (and 21 percent Albanian) population. Data on nationality from the 1991 census are usefully analyzed, with due acknowledgment for "its considerable limitations" because of the circumstances

issue in any attempt to create and draw boundaries for even largely mononational nation-states in this region, is represented by former Yugoslavia's three most numerous nations: Serbs, Croats, and Muslims, all of whom speak variants or dialects of what is variously called Serbo-Croatian, Croato-Serbian, Serbian, or Croatian.

More than a quarter (25.6 percent) of Yugoslavia's 8.5 million Serbs reportedly lived outside Serbia in 1991, most of them in Bosnia-Hercegovina (1.37 million, comprising 31.4 percent of the total population) and Croatia (581,000 or 12.2 percent). Of the 4.6 million who declared themselves to be Croats, 20 percent lived outside Croatia, mostly in Bosnia-Hercegovina (756,000 and 17.3 percent of the total population) and Serbia (131,000, mostly in Vojvodina). Of the 2.35 million Slavic Muslims, 19 percent lived outside Bosnia-Hercegovina, the republic they officially shared as a "homeland" with Serbs and Croats; their largest diaspora was in the Sandjak of Novi Pazar, a territory divided between Serbia and Montenegro since 1912 and in 1991 the home of most of Serbia's 237,000 and Montenegro's 90,000 Muslims-as-nation.[14]

These statistics—that is, knowing that the population of Bosnia-Hercegovina was 43.7 percent Muslim, 31.4 percent Serb, and 17.3 percent Croat before "ethnic cleansing" began in 1992—constitute an inadequate introduction to the complexity of the situation at the local level. An appropriate example of the role played by local ethnic complexities in the prologue to and civil war that began in 1990 is provided by the ethnic demography of the former Habsburg Military Frontier *(Vojna krajina)* in Croatia—a largely mountainous, poor, and sparsely inhabited territory where Serbs were settled as free warrior-peasants who pledged to drop their ploughs and seize their guns to confront Turkish incursions—and in adjacent parts of Slavonia. In western Krajina, Serbs are a majority in six *općine* (counties) in the sparsely inhabited Knin region, where 89,551 Serbs were 77 percent of the population in the 1991 census, and in six *općine* in nearby Banija and Kordun, where 73,481 Serbs accounted for 65 percent of the 1991 population. In Slavonia, which is far more fertile and densely populated, 83,558 Serbs constituted sizeable minorities (more than 25 percent) in six *općine,* four in central Slavonia and two on the Serbian border in eastern Slavonia, but

in which the survey was carried out, in Ruza Petrovic, "The National Composition of Yugoslavia's Population, 1991," *Yugoslav Survey* 33:1 (1992), 3–24.

14 In percentage terms, the Montenegrins have the largest diaspora of all (nearly 30 percent live outside Montenegro) and comprise only 62 percent of the population of their own republic, but the total numbers are in both cases small (of 539,000 "declared" Montenegrins, 380,000 are in Montenegro).

Table 1. Estimated Population by Nationality (1991)

	Bosnia-Hercegovina		Croatia		Macedonia		Montenegro		Serbia		Slovenia	
	000s	%	000s	%	000s	%	000s	%	000s	%	000s	%
Albanians					427	21.0	41	6.6	1,687	17.2		
Croats	756	17.3	3,708	77.9					131	1.3	54	2.7
Hungarians									345	3.5		
Macedonians					1,314	64.6						
Montenegrins							380	61.8	140	1.4		
Muslims	1,906	43.7	48	1.0			90	14.6	237	2.4	27	1.4
Romanies					56	2.7			137	1.4		
Serbs	1,369	31.4	581	12.2	44	2.2	57	9.3	6,428	65.8	47	2.4
Slovenes											1,718	87.6
Turks					97	4.8						
Yugoslavs	240	5.5	105	2.2			26	4.0	318	3.2		
Total	4,365	100.0	4,760	100.0	2,034	100.0	615	100.0	9,791	100.0	1,963	100.0

Groups with under 1.0 percent are not listed.

Source: Ruza Petrovic, "The National Composition of Yugoslavia's Population, 1991," *Yugoslav Survey* 33:1 (1992), 3–24.

Table 2. Diaspora of the Six Nations and Albanians as of 1991 (000s)

	Albanians	Croats	Macedonians	Muslims	Montenegrins	Serbs	Slovenes
Number in:							
Bosnia-Hercegovina	4[a]	756	2[a]	1,906	14[a]	1,369	3[a]
Croatia	14	3,708	5[a]	48	10	581	24
Macedonia	427	3[a]	1,314	40[a]	4[a]	44	>1
Montenegro	41	7[a]	>1[a]	90	380	57	>1[a]
Serbia	1,687[b]	130	47	237	140	6,428	12[a]
Slovenia	3	54	4	47	4	54	1,718
Total Population	2,178	4,637	1,372	2,353	539	8,527	1,760
Number in "own" region	1,686[c]	3,708	1,314	1,906[d]	380	6,428	1,718
% in "own" region	77.4[c]	80.0	95.7	81.0[d]	70.6	74.4	99.3

a. 1981 census figures b. 76,000 outside Kosovo per 1981 census c. Kosovo d. Bosnia-Hercegovina

Source: Ruza Petrovic, "The National Composition of Yugoslavia's Population, 1991," *Yugoslav Survey* 33:1 (1992), 3–24.

outnumbered Croats only in central Slavonian Pakrac. Furthermore, all of the Serbs of the eighteen Croatian *općine* where they were a majority or a large minority accounted for only 42 percent (or with the rest of Slavonia 62 percent) of Croatia's 581,000 Serbs recorded in 1991, many of them in Zagreb and other major cities.[15]

The cohabitation imposed by this patchwork of peoples was a frequent source of strife, although inter-communal cooperation seems to have been as common as conflict, over matters such as the ownership or use of fields, woods, grazing rights, and chattels like cattle and women. However, it was only with the advent and widening acceptance of the ideas and aspirations of modern nationalism that the differences between Serbs, Croats, and Muslims assumed broader and deeper meaning.

Like the "Yugoslav idea" that purported to offer a solution in the form of some kind of single state for the South Slavs, their national question was born of a conflict between, on the one hand, historical and anthropological realities as "givens" and, on the other, political ideals. The realities consisted of the cultural (ethnic, linguistic, religious, and political) shatterbelt of Southeastern Europe and the more recent spread of "proto-national" if not yet national consciousness—i.e., consciousness of shared membership in a distinctive community and destiny—among those who had always known or were now learning to call themselves Serbs, Croats, Slovenes, etc. The ideas that conflicted with these "givens" concerned the rights and proper definitions of nations and the nation-state as these had evolved and had been "adapted" to Central and Eastern Europe by the late nineteenth century; that is, as Mazzinian "rights of nations" (every nation a state and only one state for the entire nation), with a "nation" defined by "stressing the linguistic and cultural community, which was a nineteenth-century innovation."[16] The conflict became acute when these rather abstract ideas were translated into idioms and

---

15 As analyzed by Adolf Karger, *"Die serbischen Siedlungsräume in Kroatien," Osteuropa* 42:2 (February 1992), 141–46.

16 Eric Hobsbawm, *Nations and Nationalism Since 1780* (Cambridge, England: Cambridge University Press, 1990), 101, quoting "Austro-Marxist" Karl Renner's influential *Staat und Nation* (p. 89), as "a representative statement of that 'principle of nationality'": "Once a certain degree of European development has been reached, the linguistic and cultural communities of peoples, having silently matured throughout the centuries, emerge from the world of passive existence as peoples *(passive Volkheit)*. They become conscious of themselves as a force with a historical destiny. They demand control over the state, as the highest available instrument of power, and strive for their political self-determination."

"answers" to existential problems as well as traditional grievances and aspirations. Translating these ideas was the function, and the goal, of the nationalists and nationalist parties that surfaced among the South Slavs one by one in the century before World War I.[17]

Although Yugoslavia is usually described as a multinational and/or polyethnic state,[18] just how many nations and/or ethnic communities (sometimes awkwardly called "ethnicities" or "ethnies") there are is highly controversial. The passions and prejudices often displayed in these controversies are reminders of the question's centrality in determining who does or does not have a "right" to a state or a special status, as a community, in modern theories of nations and nation-states.[19] In any case, none of former Yugoslavia's putative South Slav nations fulfills Hugh Seton-Watson's criteria for designation as an "old, continuous nation."[20] Some, however, are older (measured by the date when "national consciousness" can be identified among a significant number of the community's members) and more continuous (if continuity is defined by uninterrupted memory of and identification with a state that was once "their own") than others. Three of the originally five and later six South Slav "nations" that were designated as such in the ideology and constitutions of the second Yugoslavia are in this sense "older"—and have a better claim to the label "continuous"—than the others, whose entitlement to call themselves separate nations is still disputed.

By the beginning of the twentieth century, the three South Slav peoples that would comprise the Kingdom of the Serbs, Croats, and Slovenes in 1918 were each and separately possessed of a widely distributed national consciousness and fully formed national ideology. The content of this consciousness and ideology (i.e., the packages of ideas, values, and emotions they represented) and the greater or lesser importance ascribed to individual parts of these packages by those (always initially few in number) who ascribed to them were in each case strongly marked by differences in the political and social histories

---

17 See Banac, *The National Question in Yugoslavia;* A. Djilas, *The Contested Country;* and Lederer, "Nationalism and the Yugoslavs."

18 The latter term is preferred by Anthony Smith in *State and Nation in the Third World* (Brighton, England, 1983), 123.

19 As an alternative answer, in *The Contested Country,* Aleksa Djilas suggests provocatively that "the whole of Yugoslavia could be defined as a mono-ethnic state with three closely related languages (Macedonian, Slovenian, and Croato-Serbian or Serbo-Croatian) and many different national political consciousnesses...and state loyalties" (pp. 181f).

20 Seton-Watson, *Nations and States,* chapter 1 and passim.

and political cultures of these peoples. The basic set of such differences, often emphasized to the point of exaggeration and abuse in cultural stereotyping, was between Balkan (Ottoman) and Central European (Habsburg) political and cultural worlds and worldviews. However, differences *within* each of these—like those between the Habsburgs' Austrian, Hungarian, and ex-Venetian possessions and even subdivisions of these—could be almost as significant. Serbs, Croats, and even Slovenes all had lived and had taken shape as cultural and proto-national communities in several such environments. The national consciousness and ideology of these communities therefore differed *territorially* as well as ethno-culturally—both within and among them.

The formative experience of the Serbs and for Serb nationalism under Ottoman rule and later in autonomous/independent Serbia (thus the distinction "Serbians" [*Srbijanci*] as a subcategory of Serbs [*Srbi*] as a nation or people) differed significantly from those of the Serbs of the Habsburg Empire. Among the latter the formative experiences and outlook of the free warrior-peasants of the (largely karstic and poor) Habsburg Military Frontier, with their proud rough-and-ready martial traditions,[21] differed from those of the *"prečani"* Serbs of (fertile) Vojvodina, whose growing merchant and cultural elites were the pioneers of Serb cultural and national renaissance in the eighteenth and nineteenth centuries. Croats in Austrian Dalmatia (formerly Venetian) and Dubrovnik (formerly and proudly independent) were made uncomfortable and were threatened by their Serb neighbors and by the influences of Italian culture. These Croats viewed and felt about their community and membership in it differently than the Croats in Hungarian Croatia-Slavonia, who faced a different mix of neighbors, social and political conditions, and associated challenges and opportunities. Relatively few Slovenes lived under Hungarian rule before 1918 (in Prekomurje), but even today their descendants often are reputed to have a different attitude to national (and other) questions, which is attributed to their Prekomurje background. The development, timing, spread, and content (hierarchy of values) of national consciousness and sentiment among the far more numerous Slovenes of the Austrian half of the empire, where each Crownland had a distinct historical-communal identity and considerable political autonomy, was

---

21 See Lederer, "Nationalism and the Yugoslavs," 404: "In the military frontier the Serbs came to number about one third of the population and came to play a vital military role in the Habsburg defense system. In return they received special privileges from Austrian emperors, legal ownership of land, and important economic advantages. They served the Austrian court against feudal magnates and rebelling peasants alike, all in efforts to protect their special privileges."

affected by whether they lived as local and largely rural majorities or minorities in predominantly German Styria and Carinthia; as regional but non-urban majorities in Italian-dominated Küstenland (Primorje); or in almost solidly Slovene Carniola.

The Serbians

The *Serbians* possessed an expanding autonomous principality and later fully sovereign kingdom after the first quarter of the nineteenth century. Unlike the Croats and Slovenes, and the "unredeemed" Serbs of Croatia and Bosnia, their state and their "national awakening" developed together. Both drew inspiration and legitimacy from preexisting "popular proto-nationalism"[22] vested in communal memories of and identification with medieval Serb statehood and grandeur, transmitted to successive generations through epic poems and the institution, art, and liturgy of their (discontinuously autocephalous) Serbian Orthodox church. Enjoying the protection of a state of their own, which was a mono-ethnic Serb nation-state until the addition of Kosovo and large parts of Macedonia and the Sandjak in 1912, the Serbians had no reason to fear for their survival as a people, a culture, a nation—again, unlike the Croats, Slovenes, and Serb communities outside Serbia. On the other hand, they also had no experience of competitive coexistence in a multinational situation. By seeking from the outset to include other Serbs (and putative Serbs) that remained outside their initially diminutive state, they were irredentists—before the concept was invented as part of an Italian national program (which Serbian political elites later saw as a model and legitimation for their own aspiration to unite all Serbs in a single state). In any case, Serbian nationalists and nationalism were basically outward-looking, expansionist, and self-confident.

The *Serbs of the Habsburg Empire* (after 1878 de facto and in 1908 de jure including Bosnia-Hercegovina) were in this same period experiencing Austrian and Hungarian variants of the empire's increasingly dominant national question, competitive coexistence with members of other nations, and the challenge of both Croat nationalist and Yugoslav ideas and programs. The reactions of those whose views we know something about—as always usually meaning people with at least secondary education—were varied, in contrast to the singleminded irredentism of Serbian nationalism until World War I. Many were increasingly drawn toward Serbia as their "Piedmont," but in two

---

22 The term is from Hobsbawm, *Nations and Nationalism Since 1780,* chapter 2, "Popular Proto-nationalism."

quite different understandings of what this meant. The first looked forward to a Greater Serbia in which all Serbs, but in principle *only* Serbs, would ultimately be included. This goal was identical to that of the dominant prewar current in Serbian nationalism. It either ignored the existence and significance of the Croats and others among whom the diaspora Serbs lived (as minorities except locally and in Vojvodina), or it defined these others out of existence (as discussed below). The second looked to Serbia as the core, by virtue of population and its "state-creating" role, of a united state of the Serbs, Croats, and Slovenes as separate and in principle equal peoples. This was nearly identical to those versions of "the Yugoslav idea" whose chief inventors and advocates were Croats—the important exception being the special role and status it assigned to Serbia as the Yugoslav Piedmont. Including Serbia in a totally independent future South Slav state implied the dismemberment of the Habsburg realm. Shying away from this last prospect or with different perceptions of the problems and opportunities arising from cohabitation with Croats, some were attracted to either or both of two less radical and largely compatible solutions. The first and more limited was binational political collaboration against common enemies (who could be partly different in different regions) and in pursuit of common interests. This tendency produced the Croato-Serb Coalition, founded by a group of leading Croat and Serb political leaders in 1905 and the dominant party in Croatia in the following decade. The second, an alternative version of the Yugoslav idea, was Yugoslavia as an autonomous South Slav entity within the Habsburg Empire (Austro-Hungaro-Yugoslav "trialism" in place of Austro-Hungarian "dualism"). This implied either the exclusion of Serbia or its incorporation into the Habsburg realm, neither of which was a prospect likely to warm many Serb nationalists' hearts.

The Croats

Like the Serbs of the Habsburg Empire, the Croats developed a number of national ideologies, programs, and parties, with differences ranging from contradictory to subtle variations, in largely sequential responses to (perceived) changes in the nature or priority of challenges emanating from Budapest, Vienna, and Serb nationalism(s).[23] Most but not all had two themes

[23] Banac, in *The National Question in Yugoslavia,* 70–115 passim, provides a concise, clear, and balanced survey of these from Renaissance precursors of the "Illyrianist awakeners" to World War I. See also Lederer, "Nationalism and the Yugoslavs,"

in common, although they assumed varying importance. The first was Croatia's "historic state right," intact since the founding of the medieval Croatian Kingdom and unsullied by "personal" union with the Hungarian and then Habsburg crowns since 1102. The territory envisioned as subject to this right frequently included Bosnia and Hercegovina (or more) as well as all three parts of the "triune Kingdom" as these were delineated and ultimately divided in the Habsburg Empire after 1815 (Croatia and Slavonia to Hungary and Dalmatia and Istria to Austria). The second was the Croat nation's need to be larger, in a world of competing nations and legal and territorial claims, by including or coopting in the definition of "Croat" various peoples with another or no national consciousness—for which some protagonists of Croat national programs were willing to use another name if it seemed helpful to the cause.

The earliest such ideology and program, as formulated by "Illyrianist awakeners" in the first third of the nineteenth century, was based on the premise that all South Slavs were descended from the ancient Illyrians (conveniently, a term already widely used as a synonym for Croats or sometimes all South Slavs), that they spoke variants of basically the same language, and that they were therefore actually or potentially a single people or nation. Officially suppressed in 1843, demoralized by failure to win many Serbian supporters, and with the discrediting of the idea that all South Slavs descend from the Illyrians, the Illyrianists and Illyrianism faded in the 1840s and vanished after 1849, when their (and other Croats') faith in the house of Habsburg to defend Croatian interests against the Magyars seemed cruelly betrayed. Their legacy would endure in the linguistic field (see below) and in Illyrianism's later revival as the Yugoslav idea.

The following decades brought two conflicting national ideas and programs onto the Croatian stage. Ivo Banac describes the first, which was associated with the names of Ante Starčević and Eugen Kvaternik and the Party of Right *(Stranka prava)* that they eventually founded as "an integral Croat national ideology that negated Illyrianism in almost every respect."[24] He provides an equally succinct description of the other, known as "Yugoslavism" *(jugoslavjenstvo),* which together with the National Party *(Narodna stranka),* the creation of Bishop Josip Juraj Strossmayer of Djakovo and Canon Franjo Rački, he characterizes as "a sort of modified revival " of Illyrianism, which sought

---

409–23, 427; Charles Jelavich and Bogdan Krizman, "Croatians in the Habsburg Monarchy in the Nineteenth Century," *Austrian History Yearbook,* vol. III, part 2 (1967), 83–158; and Croatian sources cited by all of these.

24 Banac, *The National Question in Yugoslavia,* 85–91 passim.

> a spiritual unification of the South Slavs, founded on a common culture and literary language.... [Strossmayer and Rački's] ultimate goal—about which they were understandably furtive—was a federal South Slavic state, built on the ruins of [the] Habsburg Monarchy and embracing Serbia and Montenegro.

Starčević disdained Serbs as an inferior and barbaric people—"Slavoserbs," whose name he derived from the Latin *servus* (servant). His ideology, in Banac's interpretation, vested Croatia's state right in the Croat "political people" (not, as traditionally, the Croatian nobility), but also held that "there could be only one political people in a given state, and the Croats, as the bearers of the indivisible Croat state right, were the sole political people on the territory of Starčević's Great Croatia." Furthermore, there could be "no Slovene or Serb people in Croatia because their existence could only be expressed in the right to a separate political territory." They were therefore respectively "mountain Croats" and "Orthodox Croats." In contrast, Strossmayer and other proponents of the Yugoslav idea, like the Illyrianists, recognized separate Serb (and Slovene) "genetic nationhoods"; they regarded Serbs who lived in Croatia as part of the Croatian political nation, and those who lived in Serbia as the Serbian political nation.

By the early years of the twentieth century these two basic approaches to the national question—the one "Croatian integralist," the other Croat "Yugoslavist"—had spawned a proliferating number of mutants and combinations. Josip Frank and his followers, the *frankovci* (Frankists) and Pure Party of Right were a more radical offshoot of the Party of Right and were characterized by their focus on Budapest as the principal challenge to Croatia's state right (and therefore advocacy of accommodation with Vienna); by their emotional anti-Serbism; and by their concomitant accusations that Croatian Serbs were guilty of high treason because of their allegedly consistent identification with Serbia. In 1908 the *frankovci* split and one faction formed a "Starčevicist Party of Right" that claimed to have returned to the founder's original principles. It, in turn, gave birth to a youth group, Young Croatia *(Mlada Hrvatska)*, some of whose members eventually assumed a "unitarist" Yugoslav position.

Meanwhile, in Dalmatia (with its distinct history, problems, and perspectives), a tendency to seek solutions through Croat-Serb cooperation had found its spokesmen in Ante Trumbić of Split and Frano Supilo of Dubrovnik, later the leading personalities in the Yugoslav Committee that would lobby the Entente Powers on behalf of the Yugoslav idea during World War I. In 1905 the initiatives of these two and others created the Croato-Serb Coalition, "an alliance of Croatia's Serb parties, the fused Strossmayerites and anti-Frank Starčevicists, and an independent group of Progressive Youth."[25] The Coalition, advocating Croat-Serb "national oneness" *(narodno jedinstvo,* also translatable as national "unity" or "concord"), won a solid majority in elections to the Croatian Sabor in 1906 and became the ruling party in Croatia-Slavonia. Two years earlier, Stjepan Radić, who had made his first appearance on the political scene by leading an anti-Magyar student demonstration in Zagreb in 1895, had founded the Croat People's Peasant Party, which he would lead and dominate (under various names and with changing national programs) until his assassination in 1928. At this stage, and until the collapse of the monarchy in 1918, he advocated a genuinely autonomous Kingdom of Croatia as a federal unit, bound to the rest of the monarchy in personal union under the emperor-king, in which the Habsburg Croats, Serbs, and Slovenes would organize their own affairs on the basis of *narodno jedinstvo*—a formula that Banac calls belated Austro-Slavism.

With all of these and other ideas and parties in play, Croat nationalists and nationally conscious Croats entered World War I, and then in 1918 the Kingdom of Serbs, Croats, and Slovenes, with a variety of views and programs concerning their future place in either the Habsburg Empire or an independent state, and whether as Greater Croatia or in a broader South Slav (Yugoslav) unit. In each of these geopolitical contexts some were "Croat integralist," some "integral Yugoslavist," and others Yugoslav federalist.

The Slovenes

If the Slovenes had no state tradition like that of Serbs and Croats, they had a strong tradition of cultivating their language and culture.[26] Their nationalist historiography traced this back to a translation of the Bible into Slovenian

---

25 Banac, *The National Question in Yugoslavia,* 98, and see pp. 94–114 for more details on the range of parties and programs summarized here. See also Mirjana Gross, *Vladavina Hrvatsko-srpske koalicije 1906–1907* (Belgrade: Institut drustvenih nauka, 1960); and *Povijest pravaske ideologije* (Zagreb: Institut za hrvatski povijest, 1973).

26 See Lederer, "Nationalism and the Yugoslavs," 417f, 422–24; and Banac, *The National Question in Yugoslavia,* 112–14. Both utilize the works of Fran Zwitter, the best-known modern Slovene historian of the period, including (in English) "The Slovenes and the Habsburg Monarchy," *Austrian History Yearbook,* vol. III, part 2 (1967), 159–88.

during the Reformation, or even further. The nineteenth-century Slovene linguistic and cultural "renaissance" was inhibited by a combination of specific political and social problems. These initially included the lack of a standardized literary language for a people who spoke a number of mutually almost incomprehensible dialects and who wrote (when they knew how) in the languages of their dominant neighbors (German-Austrians and Italians) or in Latin. In the first quarter of the century this was overcome through the combined efforts and influence of linguistic reformer Jernej Kopitar (also the mentor of Vuk Karadžić, the Serbs' great linguistic reformer) and the great poet France Prešeren, whose widely read work confirmed and disseminated a unified Slovene literary standard. But they remained a largely rural, peasant, and illiterate people in lands where the literate upper and urban classes were German and Italian, or germanized and italianized, and the language of administration and education also was German or Italian. Moreover, these lands were several—Carniola, Gorizia and the Austrian Küstenland, parts of Styria and Carinthia, and Hungarian Prekomurje—and quasi-autonomous in the decentralized Austrian system. This was not only a further inhibition to Slovene cultural and political unification; it also increased their vulnerability to germanization, italianization (and the challenge of Italian irredentism after 1866), or magyarization in all of these provinces and Prekomurje except almost solidly Slovene Carniola.

In these circumstances, the primary focus of nineteenth-century Slovene nationalists and other still proto-nationalist promoters of Slovene culture was on the acceptance of (standardized) Slovene as a language of education and administration (and thereby a vehicle for rural-urban and upward social mobility), wherever Slovenes constituted a majority or considerable minority of the population. Their geopolitical division provided a secondary but increasingly important focus expressed in demands, or at least hopes, for administrative-territorial changes that would bring most of them under a single provincial government and regime based on their Carniola heartland and Ljubljana as its capital.

The struggle for Slovene schools and Slovene as a language of education and administration in mixed districts (often fought town by town as rural-urban migration and resistance to germanization and/or italianization created Slovene majorities and town councils) had by the end of the century produced a rare phenomenon: a still largely peasant people almost entirely literate, in their own language. The people were thereby both nationally conscious and ready for (or already participant in) the momentous economic and social changes sometimes called "modernization." In the political sphere, however, they were still divided, increasingly frustrated with what Vienna had offered or might still offer to help them counter German cultural counteroffensives and Italian cultural and political irredentism, and increasingly drawn to "trialism" in alliance with the monarchy's Croats and Serbs—or to a broader Yugoslavism under Serbian leadership as the South Slav Piedmont. In the process, Slovene political life and the national movement also underwent a change unique among the South Slavs: from leadership by (national) liberals in their founding in the revolutionary movement of the 1840s, to leadership by (Catholic) clerics in the 1880s and after. In this, as in many other respects, they were more "Austrian" than "Balkan." From 1898 on, the dominant Slovene clerics lent their support to the essentially Croat concept of trialism—as propounded by the Party of Right and sometimes believed to have the support of Habsburg Archduke and Heir-apparent Franz Ferdinand—to unite the monarchy's South Slavs and end both German-Austrian and Magyar domination.

The Language Problem and Nationhood

All three nationalist ideologies implicitly accepted late nineteenth-century Central European definitions of the nation that focused, like Herder, on a distinctive language as the primary and even necessary criterion of nationhood. This was not a problem for the Slovenes, who had a language of their very own (although it initially had a variety of dialects that required "standardization" to become a national literary language). It was a problem for Serbs, Croats, and later the Slavic Muslims, who (with the Montenegrins) spoke dialects and wrote in variants of what could be considered a single language (although this language was usually called "Serbian" by Serbs and "Croatian" by Croats). The problem was complicated by the fact that those who felt in some measure that they were Croats spoke three quite distinct dialects: Čakavian, Kajkavian, and Štokavian, the last of these also spoken by almost all Serbs.[27] National ideologies could deal with this problem in one of two ways. If what these people spoke was in fact or could be developed into a single language, they were or should be one nation. If they (or their nationally conscious elites) "knew" they were separate peoples, then they must be speaking separate languages. The dispute over this issue lasted through and beyond the Tito era. The most dramatic moment in that era came when a regime-sponsored agreement, which had been signed at Novi Sad in 1954 and

---

[27] Banac, in *The National Question in Yugoslavia,* 46–49, 76–81, maps the history and distribution of these dialects and variants and describes the attempts of early nationalists like Vuk Karadžić, the great Serb linguistic reformer, to make nationalist sense of the confusion.

had defined a common language with two variants, called Serbo-Croatian or Croato-Serbian but also known as Serbian or Croatian, was repudiated in a "Declaration on the Croatian Language" endorsed by all important Croatian cultural organizations in 1967. Serb intellectuals responded with a "Proposition for Discussion" arguing that in this case Serb children in Croatia should be educated in their own Serb language.[28]

In their nineteenth-century evolution, both Greater Serbian and Greater Croatian nationalists sought to cope with the "counter-fact" of the ethnic shatterbelt and the language problem in a variety of ways. One was to define the other(s) out of existence. This could be done by asserting that a religious difference had been misconstrued as a national distinction. Accordingly, Croats were "really" Roman Catholic Serbs, or Serbs were "really" Orthodox Croats, and Slavic Muslims were either Islamicized Serbs or Islamicized Croats. It could also be done by asserting or devising a common language. If that common language was "Serbian" in a variant also spoken by many Croats, that would redefine Štokavian-speaking Croats as Serbs (the task the great Serb "linguistic nationalist" Vuk Karadžić set for himself). If the language was "Croatian," that would exclude those who used another alphabet or vocabulary from membership in the Croatian political nation.

In its later evolution—when "Illyrianism" had become "Yugoslavism"—advocates of the Yugoslav idea sought to cope with the problem in one of two ways. The first, which has been called "integral Yugoslavism" or "Yugoslavist unitarism,"[29] was to deny the separate nationhood of Serbs, Croats, and Slovenes alike, or to seek to supersede it by positing the existence of a single "Yugoslav nation" (subdivided into ethno-linguistic and perhaps other historically formed "tribes" or merely "names") or by creating one ("nation-building"). The second, found in all phases of the "Titoist answer" to the national question except its drift toward integral Yugoslavism around 1953–62, was to recognize separate nationhoods and to seek constitutional and other formulae for a multinational state of related peoples with shared interests and aspirations.

---

[28] The Croatian "Declaration" was first published in *Telegram,* a Zagreb intellectual weekly (17 March 1967). Shoup, *Communism and the Yugoslav National Question,* 195, 215, describes the incident and the uproar it produced.

[29] The latter by Banac, in *The National Question in Yugoslavia,* and in "Post-Communism as Post-Yugoslavism: The Yugoslav Non-Revolutions of 1989–1990," in *Eastern Europe in Revolution,* Ivo Banac, ed. (Ithaca, NY: Cornell University Press, 1992), 168–87.

Macedonians, Montenegrins, and Muslims

The national consciousness and aspirations of the other South Slav peoples who also would be accorded the name of "nation" in the second Yugoslav state—the Macedonians and Montenegrins at its founding in 1943 and the Muslims in a gradual process completed in 1968—were still in the process of formation and were ambivalent and changeable at the beginning of the twentieth century. The perception that one does or should belong to a *national* community came later to these peoples. The persistence of the ambivalence between belonging to a separate or to a neighboring nation is reflected in the solemn declaration of a native of Skopje (with Italian and Montenegrin grandparents) to this writer in 1968: "I am a Macedonian, but my brother is Bulgarian." Many and very possibly most Montenegrins—the precise number is uncertain—consistently or sometimes agree with the almost universal Serb view that they are merely part (if in their own eyes the best part) of the Serb nation. Slavic-speaking Muslims are claimed by Croat nationalists as part of the Croat nation and also by Serb nationalists as part of the Serb nation. Most Serb, Bulgarian, and Greek nationalists competitively claim the Slavs of Macedonia (whom Greek nationalists call "Slavophone Greeks") for their respective nations.

Many outsiders join these rival claimants in regarding the idea of a Macedonian and a Muslim nation as purely and simply "Tito's inventions"—although they may admit that many Macedonian and Muslim Slavs subsequently have been persuaded or found it in their self-interest to believe that they are indeed nations. Such views deny or disregard the evidence of cultural anthropologists and other scholars (as well as in some inventive Macedonian and Muslim nationalist historiography) of a longer history, during which some sense of distinctive communal identity gradually became (Hobsbawm's) "popular proto-nationalism," which then ripened into an undeniably national consciousness and program. They do, however, focus attention on the pragmatic rationale underlying the Yugoslav Communist regime's "affirmation" (as they preferred to call it) of a Macedonian and a Muslim nation as part of the "Titoist solution" to the national question. Even if it were true that a Macedonian nation did not (yet) exist, it was arguably necessary to invent one, because once Slavic Macedonians were neither Bulgars nor Serbs, but Macedonians, the ground presumably would be cut out from under the rival Bulgarian and Serbian irredentisms that had sowed violence and war since 1878 in the geographic region called Macedonia. Recognition of a Macedonian nation with regional autonomy within a federal Yugoslavia and promotion of Macedonian national consciousness therefore were designed to provide a definitive solution to the "Macedonian question," liquidating a classic "powder keg of Europe" and taming the "Greater Serbian" and "Greater Bulgarian" nationalists who had made life unpleasant for so many people for more than a half-century.

The same logic applied (with more gradual effect, consummated only in 1968) to the Slavic Muslims of Bosnia-Hercegovina, claimed by both Serb and Croat nationalists. If, however, the Muslims comprise a separate nation, then Bosnia-Hercegovina is neither Serb nor Croat but rather, as Yugoslavia's new rulers would claim at Jajce in 1943 and in postwar constitutions, the common homeland of its Serb, Croat, and Muslim peoples—none of whom were a majority of the population.

In 1991–92, as the disintegration of the state and the second death of the Yugoslav idea plunged Yugoslavia into civil war, new challenges simultaneously validated and overran the pragmatic rationale for these "validations" of Muslim and Macedonian nations. In Bosnia-Hercegovina the Titoist solution was negated by Serb and Croat claims, which were backed by forceful seizure and which left the Muslims with little more than a Balkan Gaza Strip, and by Muslim reflexive and belated claims to predominance over the whole or at least a commensurate part. Each claim implied "ethnic cleansing" of whatever parts could be held or occupied, which duly ensued. In Macedonia a desperate, *faute de mieux* declaration of independence was bolstered by good credentials as a state (control of territory within clearly defined borders, etc.) and by guarantees that minority rights would be respected, which the European Community's Badinter Commission proclaimed adequate for recognition. However, the infant state's consolidation and security were frustrated by a Greek veto on EC recognition (on the ground that infringement of a 2,400–year-old Greek copyright on the name "Macedonia" would bring the fall of the government or worse); by Bulgarian recognition of the Macedonian state but not the Macedonian nation (a reprise of pre–1914 Bulgarian nationalist support for Macedonian autonomy as a prelude to annexation?); and by the potential this situation seemed to offer to competing or collaborating Serb, Greek, and Albanian irredentism.

In the apologetic of its "ethno-genesis" written by Bosnian Muslim historians and social scientists and seconded by others,[30] the Slavic Muslim

[30] The Bosnians, who differ about highly significant matters such as the weighting of Islam and other factors in "making" a Muslim nation and the extent and content of this achievement, include Salim Cerić (author of *Muslimani srpskohrvatskog jezika,* 1968), Atif Purivatra (*Nacionalni i politički razvitak Muslimana,* 1969), and Muhamed Hadžijahić (*Od tradicije do identiteta: geneza nacionalnog pitanja bosanskih Muslimana,* 1974), all published in Sarajevo (by Svjetlost) after full official recognition of the Muslim nation in 1968.

nation in Yugoslavia is a modern and essentially secular nation—*Muslimani* as a national community, distinguished by a capital "M" from *muslimani* as a religious community. Its national specificity and consciousness are said to be products of a combination of factors. The impact of Islam as culture and ethos as well as religion is one of the most important of these, but so is the fact that the impacted culture was a distinct (Bosnian) one before Ottoman rule and influence led to the conversion of most Bosnian nobles and many peasants to Islam after the Ottoman conquest of Bosnia in 1463. The role of Islam was to add new dimensions to a process of differentiation and individualization that was already underway in the medieval Bosnian state, as in the medieval Croatian and Serbian states, and was capable of developing into a separate *national* culture and identity. The product of this dynamic synthesis of Islamic and Bosnian Slav cultural elements was a society distinct from other Slav and other Muslim communities—a culture sui generis, which is one way of defining a proto-nation. The growth and penetration of this distinctiveness was enhanced by the growing and fiercely defended local authority and autonomy of the Bosnian Muslim nobility (the only "native" and Slavic aristocracy in the Ottoman Balkans), who ruled over Christian and Muslim *raya* alike and with such power that they were long able to prevent the sultan's official representative from residing in Sarajevo.

The emergence of a national or even proto-national consciousness appropriate to this unique culture was delayed, however. The Slavic Muslim nobility, despite its own "Bosnianism," closely identified with the Ottoman Empire as protector of the Islamic faith and embodiment of the antinational or at least nonnational concept of a universal Islamic community *(umma islamiyya)* and Islam as both state and religion *(Islam din wa dawla)*. In this context, the Ottoman *millet* system, which tended to encourage a transition "from millets to modern nations" among Orthodox Balkan peoples with their own "national" churches,[31] may have had the opposite effect among Slav

---

Dennison I. Rusinow, *Yugoslavia's Muslim Nation,* UFSI Reports no. 8 (1982), and Steven L. Burg, *The Political Integration of Yugoslavia's Muslims: Determinants of Success and Failure* (Pittsburgh: Carl Beck Papers in Russian and East European Studies no. 203, University of Pittsburgh Press, 1983), make extensive use of these and other Bosnian sources, including interviews, and provide the basis for the following. See also Banac, *The National Question in Yugoslavia,* 359–77.

31 As persuasively argued by Kemal Karpat, *An Inquiry into the Social Foundations of Nationalism in the Ottoman State: From Social Estates to Classes, From Millets to Nations* (Princeton, NJ: Center of International Studies, 1973).

Muslims. It is indicative that until the twentieth century most of them continued to call themselves *"Turcini"* (Turks), a term they understood to mean "adherents of Islam" rather than "ethnic" Turks, whom they called *"Turkusi"* (Turkics?) or "Osmanli."

Equally important were the consequences of Bosnia-Hercegovina's proximity to the European "West," its geographic marginality to the rest of the Muslim world, and the fact that (Central) European concepts of nation and nation-state came to Bosnia primarily from Austria-Hungary and Serbia and primarily in Starčević's Croatian "integralist" and Karadžić's Serb linguistic-nationalist versions. With a nation defined as a specific kind of linguistic, ethnic or racial, and territorial community, the Slav Muslims, speaking the same Štokavian dialect as their Orthodox and Catholic neighbors (although with more Turkish and Arabic loan-words) and sharing the same origins (or myths of origin), must be either Serbs or Croats. And that, of course, was what they were hearing from both Serb and Croat nationalists. For the relatively few Bosnians drawn into this argument in the first two decades of Austro-Hungarian occupation—when the great majority were still isolated, illiterate, and preoccupied by a simple struggle for survival and freedom from oppression (still primarily by Muslim fellow-Slavs, since the new Catholic Christian regime surprised the Bosnians by not tampering with the existing social order)—the only alternative was the idea of a multi-religious "Bosnian nation" promoted by Benjámin von Kállay (Austro-Hungarian governor of Bosnia-Hercegovina from 1882 to 1903) as a counter to both Serb and Croat nationalist proselytism.

A number of Muslim intellectuals responded to the political program of Serb nationalists and the Serbian government, who also (but for different reasons) supported the maintenance of nominal Ottoman sovereignty in the Habsburg-occupied province, by identifying themselves as "Serbs of Muslim faith." An apparently larger number, attracted by Croat cultural flattery (e.g., in a "Turcophilic" and pro-Islamic literary vogue) and educated in an expanding network of schools largely staffed by Habsburg Croats and Zagreb-educated Muslims, similarly called themselves Croats. However, "all sources agree that the identification of Bosnian Muslims with either the Serbian or the Croatian *nation* remained limited."[32] Kállay's promotion of a tri-communal Bosnian national identity attracted the support of some Muslim intellectuals but could not really compete with already widespread Serb and Croat national consciousness or most Muslims' still fundamentally religious self-identification and Ottomanist nostalgia.

---

[32] Burg, *The Political Integration of Yugoslavia's Muslims,* 11. See also Banac, *The National Question in Yugoslavia,* 364–66.

Meanwhile, other developments under Habsburg rule were contributing to the wider penetration and secularization of Bosnian Muslim communal identity, and then its translation into what looked increasingly like a national identity. These included the dramatic expansion of secular primary and secondary education and of Muslim cultural societies, reading clubs, and economic and political organizations—the same developments that had provided a basis for the earlier spread of Slovene national and nationalist consciousness, but simultaneously also led to a secularization of the foundations of Muslim identity. Especially revealing in this regard are descriptions of members of the first post-1878 generation of "westernized" Muslim intellectuals, living in fin de siècle Vienna, calling themselves *"Muslimani"* rather than *"Turcini,"* and seeking to develop a secular but distinctive Bosnian-Muslim literature in their native (like their Serb and Croat neighbors Štokavian) dialect/language, which they initially wrote in (Islamic) Arabic and later in ("European") Latin script.

With these new "secular, cultural-educational bases of the Bosnian Muslim community," Steven Burg concludes,

> Bosnia became, in large part, a "divided society": Serbs, Croats, and Muslims each could live their lives wholly within the framework of Serb, Croat and Muslim organizations. There can be no doubt that the development of such parallel organizations hastened the transformation of the meaning of self-identification as a "Muslim" from the narrowly religious to the national.[33]

The Slavs and other peoples of the geographic region historically known as Macedonia do not seem to have felt a need for even proto-national identity until it was demanded of them by their neighbors after the treaties of San Stefano and Berlin opened "the Macedonian question" in 1878.[34] By the end of the century, Macedonia's Greeks and Albanians were increasingly conscious of being Greeks and Albanians, but the Slavs remained uncertain or divided over the question of whether they were Bulgarians, Serbs, or "something in between" called Macedonians. People of all three persuasions can be identified

---

33 Burg, *The Political Integration of Yugoslavia's Muslims,* 12.

34 The list of studies of the Macedonian question (even in English) is too large to include here. The following is based largely on Banac, *The National Question in Yugoslavia*, 307–28, and Dennison Rusinow, *The Macedonian Question Never Dies,* American Universities Field Staff (AUFS) Reports, Southeast Europe Series, vol. 15, no. 3 (1968).

among members of the notorious Internal Macedonian Revolutionary Organization (IMRO) of the 1890s and later years and among participants in the Ilenden (St. Elias Day) uprising of 1903. As a further complication, among those who have been counted in national(ist) Macedonian historiography as proto-nationalist or nationalist Macedonians because of their support for Macedonian "autonomy"—a status that had been a way-station on the road to full independence for Serbia and Bulgaria in the nineteenth century—many or most either clearly or putatively regarded autonomy as a necessary first step toward union with Bulgaria rather than as a goal in itself. Furthermore, many would change their sentiment as well as their declared support for nationality several times as the wind of pressure and/or advantage veered repeatedly from east to north and back again.

In the first phase of Bulgaro-Serb competition for the allegiance of the Macedonian Slavs, from the 1870s until 1912, when Macedonia was still Ottoman, the contest was waged with the weapons of rival schools, churches, reading rooms, and cultural societies. In the Ottoman Balkans, however, the struggle also characteristically assumed more violent irredentist and social-revolutionary organizational forms, with a dynamic confusion of names and shifting memberships. IMRO and its kin, founded in the 1890s to foment terrorism and eventually an armed uprising, became the most famous and ideologically variegated of these.

The partitioning of Macedonia as a result of the Balkan wars of 1912–13 altered the parameters of the contest by creating Serbian, Bulgarian, and Greek cultural and religious as well as political monopolies in their respective shares: "Vardar," "Pirin," and "Aegean" Macedonia. In Vardar Macedonia, or "south Serbia"—Kosovo, also "redeemed" in the Balkan wars, became "Old Serbia"—Serbian colonization and cultural policies designed to Serbianize the natives led to a widespread readiness to welcome the Bulgarians as liberators in the First (and again in the Second) World War. This was a welcome that Bulgarian policies and behavior would betray on both occasions. On each occasion the winner would be that something-in-between and initially weakest third national idea: the strengthening and spread of the sense of being neither Serb nor Bulgarian, but Macedonian.

World War I

The situation circa 1914, just before World War I, can be summarized as follows. The Serbians possessed a widespread (but still far from ubiquitous) national consciousness armed with a clear and fundamentally irredentist national program in two substantively identical variants: Greater-Serbianism and a Yugoslavism in which the concept of Yugoslavia was hardly distinguishable from the first variant's vision of Greater Serbia. The Croats and diaspora Serbs in Croatia and Bosnia-Hercegovina possessed similarly widespread national consciousnesses, which were less prevalent in isolated and usually illiterate peasant and village environments, with a greater variety than the Serbians' of national programs and corresponding political parties. Some of these envisioned Croato-Serb cooperation as some kind of Habsburg or independent South Slav state, with or without the Slovenes and Serbia; others saw an exclusivist Greater-Croatia or Greater-Serbia. The Slovenes had achieved nearly universal literacy and national consciousness, except where the language and culture of primary schools was not Slovene, as in Carinthia. However, the national aspirations of most Slovenes, including the nationalists, were still exclusively or primarily cultural or culturo-political rather than political in the sense of seeking an independent or autonomous state. The national and social programs of other peoples who would later become part of Yugoslavia were still under formation, limited to relatively few members of these groups and usually ambivalent and/or changeable.[35]

In September 1915, with the war in its second year, Professor R. W. Seton-Watson, the influential Scottish historian and champion of the Slavic and other small nations of East Central Europe, wrote to Serbian Prince-Regent Aleksandar Karadjordjević, then with his government in Niš, to urge him and Prime Minister Nikola Pašić not to deviate from "the Yugoslav program" for a united Kingdom of Serbs, Croats, and Slovenes (which they had lately adopted in principle) or to adopt the formation of "Greater Serbia" as their country's war aim (see Document 1). Seton-Watson's letter was written at a critical moment for Serbia on the battlefield and vis-à-vis its Entente allies.[36] It was a prophetic warning that might very appropriately have been readdressed, seventy-five years later and with contextual updating, to Slobodan Milošević, president of the Socialist Republic of Serbia, whose corresponding deviation was about to plunge an existing Yugoslavia into civil war. If Croatia were to become an independent state alongside a Greater Serbia, as Seton-Watson considered likely in such a case,

---

[35] The exceptions were indeterminate numbers of Italians, Albanians, and Bulgarophil Macedonian Slavs mobilized as nationally conscious irredente of their respective and neighboring nation-states.

[36] For details, including Entente offers to Serbia of parts of the Croatian "Triune Kingdom" (Syrmia and parts of Slavonia and Dalmatia), see Ivo Lederer, *Yugoslavia at the Paris Peace Conference* (New Haven, CT: Yale University Press, 1963), 14-20; and Dragovan Sepić, *Italija, savveznici i jugoslavensko pitanje 1914–18* (Zagreb: Skolska knjiga, 1970), 147–88.

> the two sister nations would be enemies...and in view of the impossibility of drawing any territorial line of separation between Serbs and Croats, each of the two states—the new Serbia as well as the new Croatia—would be torn apart from one end to the other by two rival irredentisms—the Catholics and Muslims of enlarged Serbia looking to Zagreb, and the Orthodox of Dalmatia looking to Belgrade.

The prince, Pašić, and the government did in the end continue to espouse the cause of Yugoslav unification, but with doubtful enthusiasm. Their concept of "Yugoslavia" differed sharply and ominously from that of the Yugoslav Committee (of exile Habsburg South Slavs) in London, primarily because the further course of the war and Entente disposition left them with little choice.[37]

The Kingdom of the Serbs, Croats, and Slovenia

The history of the birth in 1918 and brief, stormy life of the Kingdom of the Serbs, Croats, and Slovenes (renamed Yugoslavia in 1929) is too well known in general and studied in detail[38] to require or justify retelling here. Some brief comments on aspects of that history that are particularly relevant to the subject of this chapter will suffice.

---

37 Lederer, "Nationalism and the Yugoslavs," 428–32, provides an excellent brief summary of wartime developments and the creation of Yugoslavia (and of the national question between the wars; see pp. 432–36). The following is largely a condensation and paraphrase of that summary.

38 Primarily in monographs on specific aspects or periods, including several cited herein. For example, Lederer, "Nationalism and the Yugoslavs," 428–36, surveys the national question in the birth and life of the kingdom briefly but very well. The best detailed studies of its first and last years are Lederer, *Yugoslavia at the Paris Peace Conference;* and J. B. Hoptner, *Yugoslavia in Crisis 1934–1941* (New York: Columbia University Press, 1962). The best general surveys are Stevan K. Pavlowitch, *The Improbable Survivor—Yugoslavia and Its Problems 1918–1988* (Columbus: Ohio State University Press, 1988); and Pavlowitch, *Yugoslavia* (New York: Praeger, 1970), which is longer.

Contrary to the view of "revisionists" and Communists within Yugoslavia and abroad, and of many who supported the disintegration of the second Yugoslavia seventy years later, the Kingdom of Yugoslavia was not "a creation of Versailles," i.e., of the Entente powers as victors and peacemakers, although their blessing at critical stages was essential. It was a fait accompli among Serbs, Croats, and Slovenes before peacemaking began. On 29 October 1918—six days before the Austrian surrender at Padua on 3 November—a revolutionary Croato-Serbo-Slovene government *(Narodno vijeće)* was established in Zagreb; it declared independence on behalf of all of the Serbs, Croats, and Slovenes of the Habsburg Empire and called for union with Serbia and Montenegro. The *Narodno vijeće* was recognized by Emperor Charles two days later; acts of accession by provincial assemblies in Bosnia-Hercegovina and Vojvodina soon followed. In Belgrade on 1 December—more than a month before the peacemakers assembled in Paris—Prince Regent Aleksandar acceded to an urgent request of a delegation from the *Narodno vijeće,* which was alarmed by pre-emptive Italian occupation of Habsburg lands that had been promised to Italy in the 1915 Treaty of London but which were predominantly South Slav in population. The prince formally proclaimed "the union of Serbia and the lands of the independent state of the Serbs, Croats, and Slovenes into the united Kingdom of Serbs, Croats, and Slovenes."[39] On 26 November the Montenegrin parliament had already adopted a resolution proclaiming the union of Montenegro with Serbia and the other Yugoslav lands. As Lederer notes:

> World War I, in sum, created the first real opportunity for a unified Yugoslav state. Had Serbs, Croats, and Slovenes not wanted it, no doubt the Entente would not have imposed it. But given Entente victory, most Yugoslavs assumed it and that premise involved relegating, at least temporarily, pure Croatianism and Serbianism to an uncertain second place. It was not long, however, before these currents re-emerged.[40]

Although it was thus their joint creation, the new kingdom was not the Yugoslavia desired by the political elites of two of its three titular and cofounder nations, the Croats and Slovenes. Except for "unitarist Yugoslav" Serbs, all the other parties to unification from the disintegrating Habsburg Empire apparently would have preferred a federal state to the unitary one that

---

[39] Cited by Lederer, *Yugoslavia at the Paris Peace Conference,* 52.

[40] Lederer, "Nationalism and the Yugoslavs," 432.

was in fact created, on the French pattern, and which gave Belgrade and the Serbs effective control of central apparatus of government—the army and police and national finance.[41] Serb predominance in this unitary state, Croat and other non-Serb resentment and resistance, and the consequent growth of Serb-Croat tensions into political confrontation throughout the system became the principal themes of interwar Yugoslavia. These also became major themes of reciprocal national recriminations when the second Yugoslavia began to unravel in the 1980s, as shown in the contrasting Croat and Serb views of Franjo Tudjman and the Serbian Academy (Documents 4 and 5).

One consequence of non-Serb and especially Croat disenchantment with what they perceived as a Serb-dominated Yugoslavia and, later, an attempt at Serbianization by the royal dictatorship created in 1929 was the "delegitimation" of the Yugoslav idea among most Croats and other non-Serbs who had either actively or passively accepted it in 1918 or earlier. At the same time, however, it was being "legitimated" as never before for Serb political elites and other Serbs, who were pleased to have achieved Serb unity in a single, unitary state which in their perceptions was still basically Serb but was larger and economically and internationally stronger than Greater Serbia would have been. They could be genuine and fervent Yugoslavs without being less Serb. The prewar and pre-unification situation, in which Yugoslavism was primarily a Croat sentiment that was rejected by most Serb elites as a movement for Croatian national expansion, was thus reversed. As Aleksa Djilas puts it:

> Many [Serbs] did not consciously pursue hegemony but were simply unable to see Yugoslavia as anything but an extension of Serbia. Some were even ready to give up the Serbian name and part of Serbia's identity and traditions for the greater concept. Yet their failure to see the difference between Serbia and Yugoslavia and their effort to impose the Serbian concept of the state on Yugoslavia inevitably meant that non-Serbian nations, Croats in particular, perceived their Yugoslavism as Serbian hegemony in disguise.[42]

---

[41] Banac, *The National Question in Yugoslavia,* part V and passim, is the standard and most detailed study of how this happened; Lederer, *Yugoslavia at the Paris Peace Conference,* chapter 2, also describes the haste with which the Croat and Slovene leaderships agreed to union without federal preconditions.

[42] A. Djilas, *The Contested Country,* 193 n38.

On the other hand, the survival of the state never was seriously threatened by inter-nationality conflicts and delegitimation of the Yugoslav idea among non-Serbs, although its external vulnerability invited exploitation for domestic political reasons. As Lederer points out, for the Croats

> except for lunatic fringes, singularly the Ustašas who were maintained in exile and manipulated by Mussolini—there were limits beyond which even the aggrieved and disgruntled Croatian Peasant Party would not venture in exploiting the international vulnerability of the state. In fact, when the Yugoslav state as such faced dire crisis, its bitterest critics, among them the Croatian Peasant Party leader Vladko Maček, elected to save the state rather than to destroy it.[43]

There is thus a striking difference between the demise of the first Yugoslav state and that of the second, although delegitimation of the Yugoslav idea played a key role in both instances. The disintegration of the second Yugoslavia came entirely from within and against the overt wishes of all interested foreign powers; the first Yugoslavia, however, was destroyed by Axis invasion. Whether it might otherwise have survived, despite losing or never gaining the loyalty of many and perhaps most of its non-Serb citizens, is possible but unknowable.

The position of the Slovenes in the new kingdom was special and tended to make them the most satisfied of the non-Serbs. They were largely protected from Belgrade and from serious pressures for Serbianization by geographic distance and by their greater linguistic and cultural distance as well as Serb recognition of that distance. At the same time, Yugoslavia, and the Serbs as its defenders, provided some protection against possible further Italian inroads on Slovene territory and culture and provided some (in fact ineffectual) protection of the Slovene irredente in Italy, where the Slovene minority was subjected to enormous assimilative pressures after the advent of fascism, and in Carinthia, where such pressures were endemic. Furthermore, the dominant Slovene Popular Party under Monsignor Antun Korošec, who served briefly in 1928 as the only non-Serb prime minister of the first Yugoslavia, proved adept at striking deals with the central government to its own and the Slovenes' benefit. Despite their cultural disdain of "Balkan" Serbs and their resentment of what they regarded as economic exploitation by the rest of the country which was less developed, they often preferred Serbs to Croats and probably entered World War II as the most Yugoslavist of non-Serbs.

---

[43] Lederer, "Nationalism and the Yugoslavs," 433.

Macedonian and Muslim Slavs, as well as Montenegrins, were all classified by Yugoslavia's rulers as Serbs (and after 1929 as part of the Serb "tribe" of the "three-named Yugoslav nation"). They were treated accordingly. Some Montenegrins considered themselves to be a separate nation, and others (possibly more) at least sometimes nurtured a nostalgia for their separate state. The Slavic Macedonians, or "south Serbs," continued to be ambivalent or divided about their national identity. As during the brief period between the Balkan wars and World War I, they had more reason to resent Serb domination, assimilative policies, and colonization than to resent Bulgarian rule, which most apparently welcomed in 1915 and then learned to dislike. As for the Bosnian Muslims, they found themselves in the position of underdogs, subject to some religious and social discrimination for the first time since their conversion to Islam. But they also had a political party of their own, the Yugoslav Muslim Organization (founded in 1919), to make deals with Belgrade in the fashion of the Slovenes' Popular Party and to further the penetration and secularization of an emerging and at this point still largely confessional nationalism.

With all the political parties of significance being basically mononational in membership and nationalist in program (except for the Communist Party, which was outlawed in 1921 and reduced to a few thousand members and a leadership in exile by the early 1930s), political life centered on the national question. Its first prominent victim was Stjepan Radić, founder and leader of the national-populist Croat Peasant Party that dominated the interwar Croatian political scene. The political crisis precipitated by Radić's fatal wounding on the floor of parliament in June 1928, by a Montenegrin deputy and member of the Serb Radical Party, led to the imposition in January 1929 of a royal dictatorship and King Aleksandar's proclamation of a single "three-named" Yugoslav nation. As part of his nation-building project, the king reorganized the state into *banovine* (governorships), named for natural features like rivers and with boundaries that largely ignored both historical and ethnic ones. The second prominent victim was the king himself, whose assassination in Marseille in October 1934 was a combined operation of the Croatian fascist and separatist Ustaše and the Macedonian terrorist and (at this stage) separatist IMRO.

The state survived these and other blows. But as war clouds gathered to the north and the *Anschluss* made Hitler's Germany an immediate neighbor, the Yugoslav government (now under a regency headed by Prince Paul, young King Peter II's uncle) found it expedient to seek an accommodation with the restive Croats and Radić's successor as head of the Croat Peasant Party, Vladko Maček. In August 1939, only weeks before the German army invaded Poland to start World War II, Prime Minister Dragoslav Cvetković and Maček signed the agreement *(Sporazum)* that created a large and autonomous Croatian *banovina*. In addition to including the historic Triune Kingdom (Croatia, Slavonia, and Dalmatia) and Dubrovnik, the *banovina* included adjacent districts in Hercegovina and Bosnia that had Croat majorities or pluralities—less than the whole of that disputed land, still claimed in principle by Croat nationalists forty years later (see Document 4), but roughly the same portions that Tudjman, as president of independent Croatia, would treat as Croatia's share in 1992. Many Croats regarded the *Sporazum* as too little and too late. On the other hand, most Serbs (who had no promise of a similar *banovina* nor any guarantees about the Serbs within the boundaries of the Croatian *banovina)* regarded it as too much and too soon. It was certainly too late, since war was on its way by then and would only be briefly deterred by desperate attempts to maintain neutrality.[44]

Axis invasion would accomplish what domestic national disputes and nationalisms had not. The invasion began on 6 April 1941, with a savage German bombing of Belgrade, and ended eleven days later with an armistice that was in effect an unconditional surrender. King Peter II and his government, both newly installed on 27 March by the military coup d'état and anti-Axis demonstrations that precipitated Hitler's decision to attack, was already en route to form a government-in-exile in London and later in Cairo. The collapse was more than a military defeat, which was inevitable considering the overwhelming military supremacy of the Axis powers. It was, as one chronicler describes it, "the total disintegration of a ruling system, a disintegration after which it looked as if the Yugoslav state as a unified political entity would never recover."[45]

Yugoslavia in fact had ceased to exist. In Zagreb an "Independent State of Croatia" (known as NDH after its frequently used Croatian initials) already had been proclaimed, with the fanatically nationalist and fascist Ustaše under *Poglavnik* (Leader) Ante Pavelić. It included Bosnia and Hercegovina, fulfilling an older and later dream of Greater Croatian nationalists, but excluded a large part of Dalmatia and its islands, which were annexed by Italy as *terre irredente* that had been promised at London in 1915 and then (except for Zadar-Zara) stolen for Yugoslavia by Woodrow Wilson at Paris in 1919. The Ustaša regime took as its first task the ethnic cleansing of their domains, which meant the extermination of Serbs through expulsion, voluntary or forced conversion

---

[44] Hoptner, *Yugoslavia in Crisis,* provides a detailed and balanced account of these efforts and of the period in general.

[45] Jozo Tomasevich, "Yugoslavia during the Second World War," in *Contemporary Yugoslavia,* Wayne S. Vucinich, ed. (Berkeley: University of California Press, 1969), 74. See also Rusinow, *The Yugoslav Experiment,* 1f, on this topic and that covered in the following paragraph.

to Roman Catholicism (which thereby erased their Serbness), and massacre. They were most successful with the latter, although this was disputed by later Croat nationalists (as described in Document 4). Slovenia disappeared, with the southern two-thirds annexed by Italy and the rest by Germany. Montenegro was declared a kingdom once again, its crown united with that of its Italian occupiers. Kosovo, with its Albanian majority, became part of Albania, which since 1939 had been under direct Italian rule. The Bulgarians occupied and anticipated annexing Vardar Macedonia, and the Hungarians annexed Prekomurje and Medjumurje, Baranja, and the Bačka. The Banat was administered directly by the Germans, largely through its large German minority. The rump of Serbia, which approximated the Principality of 1878, was occupied by the Germans and administered by local collaborators under their strict tutelage.

But Yugoslavia, like the legendary phoenix and in some views a phoenix too frequent, would rise from the ashes of this total disintegration even before the war and Axis occupation were over.

The Second Yugoslavia and World War II

The first Yugoslavia was not the creation of Woodrow Wilson or the peace process of 1919–20, although these facilitated and consummated its creation. Likewise, the second Yugoslavia was not solely the recreation of Tito and his Communist-led National Liberation Struggle, although these were essential to its restoration. Both states were created by South Slavs for whom "the Yugoslav idea" at least momentarily took precedence over the national identity and over exclusive national interests that they also highly valued. In 1941–45 and later, this group included Communists who honestly imagined that they had "risen above" such parochial and "bourgeois" identities and interests.[46]

The regeneration and triumph of the Yugoslav idea, now called "brotherhood and unity," during a fratricidal war that at times and in places assumed the dimensions of reciprocal genocide is difficult to explain and seems almost incredible.

---

[46] In an article written shortly before his fall and in many of his later books, Milovan Djilas bears witness to the sentiments of Communists, like himself, who came to "breathe, think, and feel Yugoslav" ("Yugoslavia," *Borba,* 18 October 1953, cited by his son Aleksa Djilas in *The Contested Country*, 179).

World War II, in what had been Yugoslavia until 1941, was three wars in one. It was simultaneously a guerrilla war of liberation against foreign occupiers and the domestic forces aligned with them, an intercommunal civil war, and a social (or socialist) revolution.[47] The three dimensions were intermixed in crosscutting patterns of participation by ideologically and ethno-nationally disparate groups with various and often incompatible goals. These groups and their goals were sometimes national-exclusivist and sometimes one or another variant of Yugoslavism. Some sought to restore the old social order and its class and national division of labor and power. More demanded or hoped for radical change, as befit a poor and largely peasant society in which the disadvantaged greatly outnumbered the advantaged, although there were disparate visions of what these changes should encompass. Meanwhile, and with only one exception of significant size and importance, each of the three sides was composed entirely or overwhelmingly of members of one national community.

In this complex triple war, more death and human tragedy, which were enormous for all of these communities,[48] were inflicted by other Yugoslavs,

---

[47] This was denied by the postwar regime and in publishable (i.e., regime-tolerated) domestic historiography until the late 1960s. Until then the "official" view, which lingered on in popular and some supposedly more serious studies and texts, held that there was only one war: a "national liberation struggle" waged between patriotic, anti-fascist, and "progressive" forces (i.e., the Communist-led Partisans) on one side, and foreign occupiers and their "domestic quislings" (i.e., Ustaše, Četniks, Domobrans, etc.) on the other. This is evidence of the failure to "come to grips with the past," which had such dire consequences in the 1980s and is discussed below.

[48] Recent studies generally concur that the total number of Yugoslav war losses was far less than 1.7 million (15 percent of the population), the figure claimed by the postwar regime as early as 1946 and generally accepted for thirty-five years. The most persuasive of these, in methodology and objectivity, are Bogoljub Kočović, *Žrtve Drugog svetskog rata u Jugoslaviji* (London, 1985), and Vladimir Žerjavić, *Gubici stanovništva Jugoslavije u drugom svjetskom ratu* (Zagreb, 1989), who come to very similar conclusions: 1,014,000 and 1,027,000, respectively. See also Ljubo Boban, "Jasenovac and the Manipulation of History," *EEPS (East European Politics and Societies)* 4:5 (Fall 1990), 580–82, and the questions raised by Robert M. Hayden in "Balancing the Discussion of Jasenovac and the Manipulation of History," *EEPS (East European Politics and Societies)* 6:2 (Spring 1992), 207–12, and in "Recounting the Dead: The Rediscovery and Redefinition of Wartime Massacres in Late and Post-

usually from other national communities, than by the Axis occupiers. It was true that members of some communities participated (in resistance or collaboration) and/or suffered more in absolute or proportionate numbers, and for sometimes different reasons. However, this fact became divisive, a further burden on wartime and postwar intercommunal relations, and a matter of dispute. Because the postwar regime was concerned about the divisiveness of this and other issues involving the national question during the war, frank discussion of them was suppressed or aired only cautiously in small-circulation scholarly journals. The result was a dangerous legacy of failed *Vergangenheitsbewaltigung* ("coming to grips with the past"),[49] which exploded in the 1980s and played a significant role in the violent disintegration of the second Yugoslavia. The magnitude of wartime Serb losses in the NDH and especially at Jasenovac—the most notorious Ustaše concentration camp and for Serbs subsequently "a metonym for that [genocidal Ustaša] machine"[50] became a symbolic central issue. Serb historians such as Vladimir Dedijer and Milan Bulajić claimed that 700,000 Serbs died at Jasenovac alone.[51] Meanwhile, Croat historian and later President Franjo Tudjman called it "a historical fact that in the war, in all camps and prisons, about 60,000 people from the territory of Croatia [the whole NDH?] perished, and they were of all nationalities: Croatian anti-fascists, Serbs, Jews, Gypsies and others" (see Document 4). The actual number is almost certainly closer to Bogoljub Kočović's estimate of Serb losses in Croatia of 125,000, or 17.4 percent of their population there, and of 209,000 in Bosnia-Hercegovina, or 16.7

Communist Yugoslavia," a paper for a seminar on "Secret Histories: The Politics of Memory under Socialism," Santa Fe (October 1991).

49 Paul Shoup also sees this as a "major failing of the Titoist system." See Shoup, "Titoism and the National Question: A Reassessment," in van den Heuvel and Siccama, *The Disintegration of Yugoslavia,* 61.

50 Hayden, "Balancing the Discussion of Jasenovac and the Manipulation of History," 209.

51 Dedijer in *Vatikan i Jasenovac: Dokumenti* (Belgrade, 1987) and Bulajić in *Ustaski zlocini genocida i sudjenje Andriji Artukovicu,* 2 vols. (Belgrade, 1988). For a further sample of these polemics and games with numbers, see the exchange between Boban, "Jasenovac and the Manipulation of History," and Hayden, "Balancing the Discussion of Jasenovac and the Manipulation of History," and the sources they cite.

percent.[52] In any case, it seems clear that the Serbs of the NDH, who were subjected to the Ustaša regime's *deliberate* attempt at genocide through a combination of expulsion, conversion, and extermination (grimly repeated in "ethnic cleansing" in these same regions in 1991–92, this time primarily by Serbs), both suffered and participated the most in that principal battle zone for all three parts of the triune war.

In these circumstances and with "the tide of hate" that would flood the land again fifty years later, the restoration of any kind of Yugoslavia seemed highly unlikely. However, precisely because the horrifying magnitude and brutality of the multiple holocaust bore grim and persuasive witness to what unbridled nationalism and competing nationalist programs could do in such an environment, it encouraged a predilection to try again among people who were not yet overwhelmed by the tide or who were still struggling against it. Increasing numbers of both active and passive participants and victims seem to have come to the conclusion that, to adapt Ben Franklin's warning at the signing of the American Declaration of Independence: if the Yugoslav peoples did not indeed all hang together, they would most assuredly all hang one another.

This precarious basis for "a reconsecration of Yugoslavism"[53] found a focus and mobilizer, and a captor, in the guerrilla force and later "National Liberation Army" generally known as the Partisans. Organized, led, and usually firmly controlled by the minuscule Communist Party of Yugoslavia (about 12,000 members in 1941) and its Politburo Under General-Secretary Josip Broz Tito—after 1943 Marshal of Yugoslavia—the Partisan movement was the only domestic participant in the triune war to include members of all, or in significant numbers more than one, of Yugoslavia's national communities. Its leadership, basically identical with that of the party, was ostentatiously representative of all groups from whom appropriately qualified cadres (i.e., both Communist and reasonably capable) could be recruited. Its national program was Yugoslavism—in contrast with the interwar years when the CPY and Comintern had advocated the dissolution of Yugoslavia—the brotherhood and unity of the South Slav nations. To the prewar "official" three nations now were added the Macedonians and Montenegrins, plus the Muslims as an ambiguously separate community. These redefinitions increased the appeal of the movement among these peoples but narrowed it among

---

52 Kočović, *Žrtve Drugog svetskog rata u Jugoslaviji.* These are the calculations preferred also by Aleksa Djilas in his balanced assessment of conflicting estimates of "the scope of Ustasha terror" in *The Contested Country,* 125–27, 212 fn58f.

53 The phrase is Lederer's, from "Nationalism and the Yugoslavs," 436.

others, particularly Serbs, who passionately considered these groups to constitute their own nations. Equally or perhaps more important, simultaneous pursuit of both national liberation from foreign occupation (with the Partisans as the most constantly and militantly active and eventually most numerous resistance force) and radical social change contributed to a powerful amalgamation of (Yugoslav) patriotism and desire for social change that benefited both the CPY/Partisan efforts to seize power and Yugoslavism. (It should be noted that the extent of the CPY's radicalism—namely its advocacy of a Communist dictatorship and a Soviet-type socioeconomic system—was not advertised and was even denied.)

Tito himself summarized the CPY/Partisan vision of the past and future of the national question, along with his revision of its history and that of CPY policies on the subject, in a widely distributed 1942 article, "The National Question in Yugoslavia in the Light of the National Liberation Struggle" (Document 2). His basic argument was that "national oppression" of non-Serbs and aggravation of the national question in the prewar kingdom were the work of "a numerically insignificant minority of Greater Serbian hegemonists" (but explicitly not "the Serbian nation," which also suffered) and other "reactionary gentlemen" in the leading parties of other nations, who were aided and abetted by those who made Yugoslavia at "Versailles" and then by the machinations of fascist powers. It followed that the question now could and should be solved through unity and struggle in the National Liberation Struggle—in which "the slogan 'National Liberation Struggle' would be a mere phrase, or even a deception, were they not...also to signify the liberation of the Croats, Slovenes, Serbs, Macedonians, Albanians, Muslims, etc., or...not genuinely imbued with the aim of bringing freedom, equality and fraternity to all the nations of Yugoslavia."

Tito's article was written immediately after the end of a first congress of the Antifascist Council of the People's Liberation of Yugoslavia (AVNOJ), an ostensibly multiparty "Partisan parliament" organized by the (Communist) high command of the National Liberation Struggle (NOB), convened at Bihać, on temporarily "liberated" territory in Bosnia, in November 1942. At Bihać, AVNOJ declared itself the legitimate representative of the Yugoslav peoples. At its second congress at Jajce on 29–30 November 1943—subsequently celebrated as the birthday of the second, "AVNOJ" Yugoslavia—the Partisan parliament took a further step (against Stalin's explicit advice and in the presence of British and U.S. liaison officers to Partisan headquarters) by proclaiming itself the provisional government of a new and federal Yugoslav state. The new state was to consist of five republics (federal units) as homelands of the Slovenes, Croats, Serbs, Macedonians, and Montenegrins and a sixth, Bosnia-Hercegovina, for that "historical" rather than national entity's three (Serb, Croat, and Muslim) peoples. The Jajce congress further endorsed declarations already adopted by the formally autonomous national liberation movements of Croatia (the Regional Antifascist Council of the People's Liberation of Croatia; ZAVNOH) and Slovenia (the Liberation Front; OF) annexing territories with Croat or Slovene majorities that had been claimed by the Kingdom of the Serbs, Croats, and Slovenes but awarded to Italy at the end of World War I: the Julian March (Julijska krajina or Venezia Giulia), Rijeka (Fiume), Zadar (Zara), and some Adriatic islands. The Communist Party of Yugoslavia and AVNOJ, as well as their respective Slovene and Croatian branches, thereby coopted a further and important part of the prewar national aspirations and programs of these two peoples.

Aleksa Djilas summarizes the views of a significant portion of Croats, Yugoslavia's second most numerous nation:

> Many Croats accepted the solution to the national question proposed by AVNOJ and ZAVNOH. Great-Croatian solutions had been completely compromised by the Ustasha movement, and those attempted by the Chetniks and the Yugoslav government in London inspired mistrust and fear among Croats, since both were seen as representing great-Serbian ideology. ZAVNOH demonstrated to the Croats that the Communists were responding to their demands for national autonomy. Its activities and proclamations gave the Partisan movement in Croatia an aura of Croatian patriotism, and the Partisans were increasingly perceived as a mass movement at the same time Yugoslav and Croatian.[54]

Slovenes and others, to whom the Partisans and AVNOJ offered recognition as nations and republics "of their own," appear to have reacted similarly. "Brotherhood and unity," which by the late 1980s was widely despised as a Communist propaganda slogan with no content, then seemed a reality in the making, or at least a highly appealing possibility.

However, at least some had different ideas, even in the ranks of the NOB. "Autonomist," if not separatist, preferences persisted among Croatian, Dalmatian, Slovene, and some other Communists throughout the war.[55] The most prominent and controversial case focused on Andrija Hebrang, head of the quasi-autonomous Communist Party of Croatia (CPC) after the autumn of 1942. Hebrang, a party member since 1919 and a veteran of both Royal

---

[54] A. Djilas, *The Contested Country,* 159.

[55] Shoup, *Communism and the Yugoslav National Question,* chapter 2, passim.

and Ustaša prisons (from 1928 to 1941 and the summer of 1942, respectively), was accused of having become a German and Ustaša agent in 1942 and a postwar Stalinist agent as well as a Croatian separatist and died as an alleged suicide in a prison of the new regime in 1949. His growing problems with Tito and other members of the leadership in 1943–44 ultimately led Tito to move him from leadership of the CPC to the federal government in the autumn of 1944, after having accused him in a letter of "entering with all your might into separatism." The basic issue, according to a recent review of earlier and new evidence by an American scholar, was a conflict over how best to construct a new Yugoslav state between "Hebrang's efforts to increase the autonomy of regional party and political organizations" (i.e., the CPC and ZAVNOH) and Tito's "efforts to gain recognition from the Allies and to centralize the [National Liberation] movement," with Hebrang's strategy to attract more Croats to the NOB, at the risk of alienating Croatian Serb Partisans, as a subsidiary issue.[56] By 1990, Hebrang, the Stalinist villain and traitor, had become a Croat national hero, with a major Zagreb street renamed in his honor by the new anti-Communist Croatian regime.

Largely ignored and suppressed until the 1980s is the fact that development during the war years disregarded the Serbians' national and special aspirations. The CPY/Partisan vision for a future Yugoslavia offended the Serbians' general if qualified satisfaction with the old political and social order, which they dominated as the leading nation and as a society of smallholders and a relatively prospering bourgeoisie. Until late 1944, when the wind was unmistakably blowing in another direction, toward a Communist-Partisan takeover of Serbia with the help of the Red Army, most Serbians appear to have preferred the Četniks, who sought to restore that old order (in some cases with increased Serb hegemony), over the Partisans and their Communist masters. Although the Communist-Partisan uprising against Axis occupation had begun in Serbia alongside that of the Četniks, Partisan activity in Serbia and Serbian participation in the Partisans remained relatively minor from the time of the suppression of the "Užicka Republic" in late 1941 until the Partisans and the Red Army converged on Belgrade in October 1944. Just as Croats and Croat national aspirations suffered from the "collective guilt" for the Ustaša regime and its crimes, so open expression of Serb sentiments and interests were later inhibited by reminders of Serbian (in contrast to diaspora Serb) absenteeism in the NOB as well as their "hegemony" in the first

---

[56] Jill A. Irvine, "Tito, Hebrang, and the Croat Question, 1943–44," *EEPS (East European Politics and Societies)* 5:2 (Spring 1991), 306–40. Tito's September 1944 letter to Hebrang, which charged him with "entering into separatism," is quoted from a Croatian archive (p. 333).

Yugoslavia. There also would be more tangible and local forms of distinction and reward or punishment. A British man who had been liaison officer to the Partisans in 1943 revisited in the late 1960s places he had known then and could quickly reidentify what had been Partisan versus Četnik or Ustaša villages by their relative prosperity and the number of new buildings.[57]

Albanians in the new Yugoslavia bore the corresponding incubus of the preference for Albania that many of them manifested, whether as Partisan-Communists or as anti-Communists during the war and in early postwar rebellion. Added to Slavic and especially Serb prejudices that they were inferior, fecund, and congenitally irredentist, this would reinforce and be used to justify the discrimination and oppression they suffered until 1966—and after 1981.

Slavic Muslims also paid a price, in the form of ambiguous attitudes on the part of the regime toward and delayed recognition of their separate nationhood, which were the result of existing prejudice that had been reinforced and new suspicion that had been engendered by the wartime behavior of a significant number of them. The Ustaše, despite their militant Catholicism and in accordance with more mainstream Croat nationalist concepts, had declared that their Muslim subjects were brother Croats and that Croatia was a nation with two recognized religions, Catholicism and Islam. Thus wooed and also stimulated to see in Hitler's Germans (and Hitler's Austrians, who staffed many key German offices in the NDH) a return of the Habsburg rule they now remembered as having been benevolent and pro-Islamic, more members of the Muslim community initially contributed their sympathies and arms to the German and Ustaše cause than to that of the Communist-led Partisans. Only in 1943 did Muslims begin to flock to the Partisan standard in significant numbers. By then the Germans and the Ustaše, whose slaughter of Serbs had brought brutal reprisals by Serbian royalist Četniks against Muslim as well as Croat villagers, looked increasingly like losers, and Jajce had brought the promise of Muslim equality a tri-communal Bosnia-Hercegovina.

These wartime developments established a contradictory framework for the subsequent evolution of the status, the self-image, and the other Yugoslavs' view of the Muslim community. On the one hand, it emerged from the war tarred with the brush of having been collaborators of the "Nazi-fascist" occupiers, enemies of the Communists who now ruled the country (an image enhanced by a surge of anti-Communist feeling and activity among the Muslim clergy and middle class in 1946–47), and parochial chauvinists in

---

[57] F. W. Deakin, *The Embattled Mountain* (London: Oxford University Press, 1971), epilogue.

their own right. On the other hand, the pledges made to them were genuinely and sincerely rooted in the CPY's ideological and strategic view of the national question, the dangers inherent (and lately so dramatically demonstrated) in the Serb-Croat dispute over Bosnia-Hercegovina, and the vital role of the nationality of the Muslims—Serb, Croat, or other—in that dispute.[58]

The stage was thus set for the further development of Yugoslavia's multiple nationalisms in the postwar period. The nationalities were suppressed and at other times deliberately or incidentally encouraged by the CPY/Partisan regime's experiments for solving the national question and other policies.

The "Titoist" Solution to the National Question

The second Yugoslav state, also known as "AVNOJ Yugoslavia" or "Tito's Yugoslavia"[59] existed for not quite fifty years—from 1943 or 1945 to 1991 or 1992, depending on which events are chosen to define its birth and death—and outlived Tito, its founder and chief sustainer, by a little more than a decade. In that period the "Titoist solution" to the national question passed through five phases, four during Tito's long reign (1943–80). The post-Tito fifth phase brought a grim harvest of disintegration, war, and reciprocal atrocities. During this phase, the "national Communists" and their nationalist, nationalist ex-Communist, and pseudo-ex-Communist nationalist successors incited and exploited the communal and national(ist) fears and hopes of their constituents to attain and maintain power and to destroy the state either purposefully or accidentally.

---

[58] Rusinow, *Yugoslavia's Muslim Nation,* 3f.

[59] Its successive official names were Democratic Federal Yugoslavia (March–November 1945), Federal People's Republic of Yugoslavia (1945–63), and Socialist Federal Republic of Yugoslavia (1963–92). On the question of whether the "second" Yugoslavia was a new state or a continuation of the prewar kingdom, see Frits W. Hondius, *The Yugoslav Community of Nations* (The Hague: Mouton, 1968), 130f.

The first four phases have been described and analyzed in numerous studies that are in most cases easily available.[60] Therefore, this review focuses on aspects and issues of particular importance for the fifth phase and its violent denouement.

The First Phase

The first phase, like other aspects of the early postwar system, closely adhered to Soviet theoretical, constitutional, and policy precedents.[61] It brought full recognition of five separate Yugoslav nations (something the *ancien regime* had latterly sought to deny even to Serbs, Croats, and Slovenes) and the institutionalization of this recognition in a federation of six republics. Each of these, except explicitly trinational Bosnia-Hercegovina, "was considered a nation-state in the sense that it served as a rough equivalent of the homeland of the dominant nationality within its boundaries," and was "to serve as a lightning rod for national emotions, without limiting the power of the Party or the jurisdiction the centralized administration."[62]

These symbolic and formal arrangements and a considerable degree of genuine cultural autonomy and recognition of cultural differences (for example in folklore, education systems, and languages) were counterbalanced by a highly centralized but carefully multinational one-party dictatorship, security apparatus, and centrally planned "command" economy. Added to popular revulsion against divisive nationalisms after the horrors of civil war, the fact and psychological impact of recognition of their separate national identities and cultures, the creation of republics as nation-states of "their

---

60 See Shoup, *Communism and the Yugoslav National Question;* Lederer, "Nationalism and the Yugoslavs"; Rusinow, *The Yugoslav Experiment;* Banac, *The National Question in Yugoslavia;* Bung, *Conflict and Cohesion in Socialist Yugoslavia;* Ramet, *Nationalism and Federalism in Yugoslavia;* A. Djilas, *The Contested Country;* and van den Heuvel and Siccama, *The Disintegration of Yugoslavia.* The following summary is an expanded adaptation of pp. 133–39 of Dennison Rusinow, "Nationalities Policy and the 'National Question,'" in *Yugoslavia in the 1980s,* Pedro Ramet, ed. (Boulder, CO: Westview Press, 1985), 131–61.

61 Edvard Kardelj, the ideological guiding spirit behind all postwar Yugoslav constitutions, wrote: "For us the model was the Soviet Constitution, since the Soviet federation is the most positive example of the solution of relations between peoples in the history of Mankind." Quoted in Hondius, *The Yugoslav Community of Nations*, 137.

62 Shoup, *Communism and the Yugoslav National Question,* 115, 113.

own," and multinational in place of Serb-dominated ruling apparatus acted to pacify intercommunal tensions and grievances, at least temporarily. Where this was not enough, the regime and its police ruthlessly suppressed any display of what they chose to define as "nationalist" rather than acceptable "national" sentiments. In the ensuing quiet,[63] it was momentarily possible to imagine that the national question really had been solved, as the regime claimed, or was at least on its way to a happy and peaceful solution.

Looking back from the perspective of the disintegration of Yugoslavia in the 1980s and the civil war of the 1990s, three issues that were contentious when the federation was being established, but that seemed relatively unimportant in the following three decades, merit special mention.

Serbia and Its Provinces

Again following Soviet precedents, the constitution that confirmed the federation of six republics promised at Jajce also created two autonomous regions in districts with large or majority non-Serb populations that were to be included in Serbia, the largest republic: the Autonomous Province of Vojvodina and the Autonomous Region of Kosovo-Metohija (Kosmet, which would be elevated to the "higher" status of Autonomous Province in 1963 and renamed simply "Kosovo"—a concession to Albanian dislike of "Metohija" as a Serb coinage—in 1968. Non-Serbs of many nationalities, including a half-million Magyars, comprised nearly half the population of Vojvodina, which was composed of the Banat and Bačka districts of prewar Yugoslavia which had been part of Hungary before 1918 and most of Syrmia, which had belonged to Croatia-Slavonia before 1918 and to the "Independent State of Croatia" during the war. Kosovo-Metohija had an Albanian majority (initially about 65 percent but an estimated 90 percent by 1990), but was of enormous symbolic importance for Serbs as the "cradle" of their culture and state, a historic but no longer demographically Serb *terra irredenta* lost in 1389 and redeemed in 1912, and then lost and redeemed again during World War II. There was also, however, an additional but hidden reason for establishing these two autonomous regions. As a foreign commentator on postwar Yugoslav constitutional history noted as early as 1968: "It was, fundamentally, a correction of the federal formula, a counterweight thrown onto the scales of the Federation in order to prevent the predominance of one of the

---

63 For a meticulously researched survey of early postwar nationalist disturbances (the most serious and durable by Albanians in Kosovo-Metohija) and their supression, see Shoup, *Communism and the Yugoslav National Question,* chapter 3.

People's Republics"[64]—namely Serbia. Kosovo in particular later became a fatally difficult double minority problem, and after 1968, when autonomy was transformed into reality and Serb domination ended, it also became a double irredentist problem—for Albanians as a minority in Yugoslavia, and for Serbs and Montenegrins as a minority in Kosovo.

Other candidates for autonomous status also had been proposed and considered during and shortly after the war but were rejected before the Constituent Assembly met in November 1945. One was Sandžak of Novi Pazar, where there was a large Slavic Muslim population, and which also had been "redeemed" from the "Turkish yoke" and divided between Serbia and Montenegro during the Balkan wars of 1912–13. Another was Dalmatia, with its distinctive history and culture, long separation from the rest of the Triune Croatian Kingdom, and widespread wartime animosity to the Ustaša regime and participation in the Partisan struggle. A third comprised Lika, Banija, and Kordun, parts of the former Habsburg Military Frontier in Croatia that had local Serb majorities.[65] Except for the Sandžak, which in the end was simply redivided between Serbia and Montenegro (apparently in defiance of local party and popular sentiment),[66] autonomy for any of these would have diminished Croatia, not Serbia. The decision not to create additional autonomous regions therefore could be construed by Serbs—as it would be by Serb politicians and media in the 1980s (and by the Serbian Academy in Document 5)—as further evidence of consistent anti-Serb prejudices and

64 Hondius, *The Yugoslav Community of Nations*, 159.

65 A. Djilas, *The Contested Country,* 171f. Sandžak and Dalmatia (but not Kosovo!) appeared in an early Partisan high command listing of "all regions of Yugoslavia—Serbia, Croatia, Slovenia, Montenegro, Bosnia and Herzegovina, Macedonia, Vojvodina, Sandzak and Dalmatia." From "the first instructions to Partisans on the higher goals of the struggle [issued by Partisan headquarters] in its Bulletin of 10th August 1941," quoted in Hondius, *The Yugoslav Community of Nations*, 122. More significant, the creation of a regional National Liberation Committee for the Sandžak in November 1943, corresponding to those created in the same year for Slovenia, Croatia, and Bosnia-Hercegovina (but not Serbia!), "gave the impression that the area was being prepared for autonomous status after the war." Shoup, *Communism and the Yugoslav National Question,* 118.

66 A special commission, headed by Mose Pijade, was sent to "explain the move to the local Communists" before the Sandžak assembly gave its approval to the division in March 1946. Shoup, *Communism and the Yugoslav National Question,* 118.

efforts "to weaken Serbia" by Tito, Edvard Kardelj, and other architects of "AVNOJ" Yugoslavia.

Secession

The Soviet constitution of 1936 explicitly recognized the right of union republics to secede from the Soviet Union. The Yugoslav constitutions of 1946, 1963, and 1974 did not. Their single, prefatory references to the subject declared that the Yugoslav nations (or peoples), who indeed had a right to separation or union, had already exercised it during the war, which was explicitly construed by one of the 1946 constitution's authors, Mose Pijade, as a rejection of any future right to secede.[67] Thus the first article of the 1946 constitution defined the Yugoslav state as "a federal people's state, republican in form, a *community of peoples* [nations] equal in rights who, on the basis of the right of self-determination, *including the right of separation, have expressed* their will to live together in a federative state."[68] The sense of the key phrases in this formulation was repeated in the first "Basic Principles" articles of the constitutions of 1963 and 1974 as follows: "The *nations [peoples] of Yugoslavia,* proceeding from the right of every nation to self-determination, including the *right to secession,* on the basis of their will freely expressed in the common struggle of all nations and nationalities in the National Liberation War and Socialist Revolution, and in conformity with their historic aspirations, aware that further consolidation of their brotherhood and unity is in the common interest, *have...united* in a federal republic..."[69] Despite the authors'

---

[67] In a letter, published in 1950 as an apparent indication that it was considered authoritative, Pijade wrote: "Our Constitution contains no clauses which would give the republics the right of secession in the same sense as expressed for example by Article 17 of the Constitution of the USSR... We do not wish to include such a provision into our Constitution for it would be insincere, as it is in fact in the Soviet Union." Quoted in Hondius, *The Yugoslav Community of Nations*, 142, from Pijade's exchange of letters with Vlado Strugar as published in *Vojno-političko glasnik* 10 (1950). Aleksa Djilas calls Pijade "probably the most persistent defender of what might be called a 'once and for all' interpretation of the unification of Yugoslav nations" *(The Contested Country,* 167).

[68] From the official English translation, *Constitution of the Federative People's Republic of Yugoslavia* (Belgrade, 1946). Italics and alternative translation of *narod,* meaning either "people" or "nation," added here and below.

[69] The authorized English translation (by Marko Pavičić), *The Constitution of the Socialist Federal Republic of Yugoslavia* (Belgrade, 1974), 53. Except for the

apparent intentions, the ambiguities in these formulations encouraged conflicting interpretations. Had the right to self-determination really been exercised once and for all in the (alleged) wartime expression of will to abjure separation and live together, as Pijade and other claimed, or could it be exercised again? If the latter, how and by whom? Successive constitutions stipulated "nations" (or "peoples"), not republics, as bearers of the right to unite or to separate. But were the republics not the incarnation of nations in nation-states and thereby articulators of the national will? Was that national will therefore to be exercised by all members of a nation or people, wherever they might live, and by plebescite, or by (through) their elected representatives at the republican level or in mixed districts at the local level? The issue was further complicated by another legal and conceptual ambiguity: was a Serb living in and a citizen of Croatia (for example) a member of the Croatian nation/people, of the Serb nation/people, or of the Croatian people and the Serb nation?[70]

Such questions were moot until the late 1980s, when they—and the nationalities of those who favored contradictory answers to them—became matters of great importance.

Republican Borders

Questions concerning the borders between the republics—who drew them, the criteria used, and whether they should be considered as state borders that were protected under international law or merely as "administrative" borders—also took on great importance at the end of the 1980s. At their establishment, however, the borders

> aroused only minor disagreements among the Communists and no great excitement among the general population, with the exception of Croatian and Serbian nationalists. But they did not dare to express dissatisfaction, since it would have been immediately identified with "Ustaša ideology" or Četnik ideology."[71]

---

placement of a reference to "nationalities" (minorities), omitted here, the wording in the 1963 constitution was identical.

70 See A. Djilas's discussion of this last point in *The Contested Country,* 162 and notes.

71 A. Djilas, *The Contested Country,* 171.

The task of setting borders—and apparently of resolving disagreements over them—was entrusted to a border commission appointed by the Party leadership that was formally confirmed by the National Assembly and was headed by Milovan Djilas.[72] Djilas wrote much later that he was appointed "probably"

> because I was thought to have a feel for nationality problems. On the commission were Serbs, Croats, and others. We held to the principle of ethnicity: that there be as little "foreign" population as possible in either Serbia or Croatia, that we disturb the national fabric as little as possible.[73]

As at the Paris peace conference of 1919, of course, it was not as simple as that. Historical as well as ethnic criteria were used in almost every case. Some "historic boundary" was chosen (usually nineteenth- or early twentieth-century borders but occasionally older) and then sometimes was locally amended for economic as often as ethnic reasons. It could hardly be otherwise—Tudjman calls it "the least painful solution" (in Document 4)—to avoid endless disputes in an ethnic patchwork and especially for Bosnia-Hercegovina, which had to be a "historic" rather than ethnic entity if it were to exist at all. The principal disagreements, apart from those over minor local issues,[74] seem to have been over Syrmia, historically a part of Croatia-Slavonia but predominantly Serb in population, and Boka Kotorska, which Montenegrin and Serb nationalists claimed for Montenegro on ethnic grounds but which Croatian nationalists claimed for Croatia as part of Austrian and

---

72 Discussion of the subject and primary sources on it were until recently scarce, and most recent discussion (and sources) are too tendentious to be useful without careful examination. See A. Djilas, *The Contested Country,* 170–74, on Croatia's borders, and Shoup, *Communism and the Yugoslav National Question,* 117f, which together provide the best but tantalizingly brief and scantily documented references to disputes available in English. See also Vladimir Dedijer, *Novi prilozi za biografiju Josipa Broza Tita* (Belgrade: Rad, 1984), III, 170–72 and passim.

73 Milovan Djilas, *Rise and Fall* (New York: Harcourt Brace Jovanovich, 1985), 99.

74 Many of these and later minor inter-republican border adjustments are described by Miodrag Zecević and Bogdan Lekić, in *Frontiers and Internal Territorial Division in Yugoslavia* (Belgrade: Ministry of Information of the Republic of Serbia, 1991).

earlier Venetian Dalmatia. Boka Kotorska was ultimately assigned to Montenegro, and most of Syrmia to Vojvodina (Serbia), with the Syrmian border between Croatia and Vojvodina "established solely on the basis of nationality: its meandering path between villages reflected whether a majority of Croats or of Serbs lived in each place."[75] Further north, some mixed but predominantly Croat districts in Bačka were left to Vojvodina, partly on historical grounds but also apparently to bolster the province's Slav population against its large Magyar minority.

In summary, most of the borders of the new Yugoslavia's republics had a stronger historical legitimacy (if history grants legitimacy to borders) than Serb nationalists would admit when disintegration loomed forty-five years later. However, these Serbs could still argue that, as internal borders, they did not enjoy the sanctity of state borders under international law or under the Final Document of the Conference on Security and Cooperation in Europe of 1976.[76]

In addition to these issues, which were basically constitutional in nature, the enduring legacy of this first period for intercommunal relations and the content of national(ist) programs included two related aspects, which concerned the victorious Partisans' primary wartime locus (the Dinaric mountain ranges of the "Independent State of Croatia" and Montenegro) and the national composition of these areas (primarily Serb and Montenegrin). Both had more to do with the Partisan victory as a triumph of highlanders over lowlanders—the latest in a long series of conquests of fertile Balkan plains by fecund Balkan mountaineers—than with nations and national considerations per se.[77]

The first such consequence was proportional overrepresentation of Serbs and Montenegrins in the postwar Communist Party and its *nomenklatura* dependencies, which was initially a consequence of their relative preponderance in the wartime Partisans and often a reward for service in same. These included the army, the security services and other state apparatus at the federal level and in republics where Serbs constituted numerically significant minorities (Croatia and Bosnia-Hercegovina), and state-owned enterprises in

---

[75] A. Djilas, *The Contested Country,* 171.

[76] The Serb argument would be that Yugoslavia's external borders, arbitrarily changed by Slovene, Croatian, and Macedonian "secessionists," did enjoy this sanctity.

[77] An interpretation argued by Ernst Halperin in *The Triumphant Heretic* (London: Heinemann, 1958).

nationally mixed districts.[78] The maintenance of this overrepresentation in later years, when post-Partisan generations began to enter the labor market, was partly a function of familial and patron-client "old boy" networks established by the Partisan generation, which favored friends, relatives, and hometown youngsters. It also was partly a result of the fact that in Yugoslavia, as in other societies, economically backward regions offering few other escapes from agriculture and the village tend to send higher proportions of their sons and daughters into military and government service, which also are regarded as prestigious. It was easy, however, for members of other nations—whether competing for jobs without the benefit of such patronage networks or merely confronting a disproportionate number of Serb/ Montenegrin police, bureaucrats, and work-place supervisors—to attribute the disproportions to national and deliberate rather than socioeconomic motivations and calculations.

A related but more broadly demographic consequence of the locus and national composition of the National Liberation Struggle was the predominance of "highlanders," particularly Partisan veterans and their families, in the rural-urban and rural-rural migrations that followed the end of the war. Such families, who had been previously landless or in possession of largely infertile and usually minuscule holdings in Karstic uplands, were delighted to be endowed with the fertile farmlands and decent houses that had belonged to expelled Germans or had been expropriated from "collaborators" and with large estates in Vojvodina and other lowlands. Others, such as the Montenegrin family of Bosnian Serb leader during the civil war of 1992, Radovan Karadžić, were similarly delighted to move to and take advantage of the greater opportunities in urban areas such as Sarajevo—where they found that they were not really "accepted" by the older, more cosmopolitan, and often clannish society of such cities.[79] These transplants, still unassimilated or insecure in their new environments by the 1980s, often proved to be prime recruits for nationalist programs and propaganda.

The Second Phase

The second phase of the "Titoist" solution to the national question began after Yugoslavia's break with Stalin in 1948 and with Stalinism after 1950. The

[78] Shoup, *Communism and the Yugoslav National Question,* chapters 3, 5, 6, and appendices B and D, provides a careful source of data and analysis on the national composition of these "cadres."

[79] As noted in a profile by Maggie O'Kane in *The Guardian Weekly* (23 August 1992).

regime's first modest steps in the direction of political and economic decentralization reopened the national question in a new postwar form: competition among regions and localities, and therefore among national communities, over the means of economic development. Power and incentives to take economic initiatives such as building or expanding factories and supporting and protecting local economic interests and clienteles devolved to the republics and communes *(opstine/općine)* and their "self-managed" enterprises. At the same time, however, control over most investment funds, fiscal instruments, and foreign currency and trade remained centralized at the federal level. In this contradictory situation, interregional competition over the allocation of scarce, important, and centrally allocated resources inevitably came to be regarded as competition among the Yugoslav nations, although the issue was argued in terms of Marxist or market economic principles. Questions about the location and priority to be given to basic or processing industries, or about which resource, port, railroad, or highway should be developed first, were again and by 1963 openly interpreted as national questions by those involved and the public at large.[80] Political leaders defending regional and local interests were increasingly regarded (and saw themselves) as national leaders defending vital national interests. The more relaxed cultural environment of the early 1950s also brought what the regime nervously regarded as a corresponding revival of nationalist themes and prejudices in literature, theater and films, and other cultural media.

The first reaction to such new evidence that divisive and potentially disintegrative nationalisms were alive and incarnate among Communist officials as well as among "reactionary bourgeois nationalists" was a short-lived campaign for "Yugoslavism," defined as a pan-Yugoslav patriotism, culture, and economy that would function as a supranational and unifying umbrella over the country's diverse national identities, cultures, and economies.[81] The "Constitutional Law" adopted by the Federal Assembly in January 1953—not formally a new constitution, although it replaced most provisions of the constitution of 1946, rendering it obsolete—was a harbinger of the campaign. The party leadership's obsession with more extreme forms of decentralization (to the level of communes and enterprises), their euphoric belief that the national question really had been solved in favor of growing "Yugoslav

---

80 An early case study is Dennison Rusinow, *Ports and Politics in Yugoslavia*, American Universities Field Staff Reports, Southeast Europe Series, vol. 11, no. 3 (April 1964), 24ff.

81 Shoup, *Communism and the Yugoslav National Question,* 190–211, remains the best brief description and analysis of the rise and fall of the "Yugoslavism campaign" of the 1950s.

socialist consciousness," and a tendency to ignore a republican autonomy that had been little more than a legal fiction combined to bring a formal downgrading of the status of the republics. Reference to the Yugoslav nations' right to secede was deleted, and the republics were no longer defined as "sovereign" (which gave rise to a portentous debate between Serbian and Croatian constitutional lawyers).[82] The Chamber of Nationalities in the Federal Assembly, in which the republics and provinces were directly represented and which was a primary aspect of federalism, was absorbed into the Federal Chamber as a curious, semi-autonomous body with few separate areas of jurisdiction.[83]

In 1958, at the high point of the campaign, Yugoslavism found a place and a kind of codification in the program adopted in Ljubljana at its Seventh Congress by the ruling party—renamed after 1952 the League of Communists of Yugoslavia (LCY)—to replace the long obsolete "Stalinist" Program of 1948. After repeating familiar themes about "the individuality, equality and right to self-determination of all Yugoslav peoples," the ten pages (out of 263 pages) devoted to the national question (Document 3) struck a a new note. The future of national relations, it said, lay in the development of socialist relations and of "a socialist, Yugoslav consciousness, in the conditions of a socialist community of peoples," leading eventually to a "Yugoslav culture." Although the campaign carefully and repeatedly stated that there was no intention of creating a Yugoslav nation to replace the existing ones, the concept of "Yugoslav culture" inevitably involved more specific questions—for example, about the language or variant in which "Yugoslav literature" would be written—that were bound to stir unpleasant memories and grave suspicions in non-Serbs.

The later years of the Yugoslavism campaign coincided with efforts by conservative elements in the party and security services to halt or reverse a new wave of economic liberalization and political decentralization that was drawing its principal support from Slovenia and Croatia, which were economically more developed and, according to their political and economic elites, demonstrably the losers in competition for central funds and favors. For

---

82 Described in Hondius, *The Yugoslav Community of Nations*, 194–98; and Shoup, *Communism and the Yugoslav National Question,* 191f; as well as Rusinow, *The Yugoslav Experiment,* 71.

83 The second chamber in the Federal Assembly and the chambers of the federal units became a Chamber of Producers, an extension from the local to the republican and federal levels of Edvard Kardelj's concept of functional or corporativist representation and a "hierarchy of supreme workers' councils" culminating in the federation.

a number of reasons only partly connected with national prejudices and preferences, the most visible protagonists of the conservative and recentralizing camp happened to be Serbs in federal party and state apparatus, including the state security service, where Serbs were disproportionately and in some views dangerously overrepresented. "Yugoslavism" and the centralizers were linked in the perceptions of most non-Serbs and were seen as an ominous attempt to repeat King Aleksandar's efforts to decree a "Yugoslav nation" that would be the self-image of the Serb nation and a device for Serb domination and Serbianization. The combined opposition of non-Serb regional leaders and proponents of economic and/or political liberalization, which finally enlisted Tito's vital support, brought down the centralizers. A purge of the latter and the security service in 1966 ended the second phase.

The Third Phase

If nationalism and national disputes were not to be suppressed by a centralized and (by implication) ultimately Serb-dominated dictatorship, killing divisive nationalisms with kindness might be an alternative solution. The third phase brought, in effect, such an effort. It was done in the name of "self-management" and by a political coalition forged in the struggle against centralism by ideological and economic liberals or "reform-Communists" (the term had not yet been invented) and regional party barons whose motivations were sometimes liberal-reformist, sometimes localist and nationalist, and sometimes all of these. The beneficiaries of the resulting expansion in political participation, liberty, and autonomy included a broad range of social and interest groups as well as national communities per se. It is the primacy of regional (national) political barons in the power equation that made these changes possible. These barons, and the importance of regional and national interests and prejudices in their reasons for playing this role, justify the contention that Yugoslavia's multinationality and multiple nationalisms, more often blamed than praised, were the principal and essential driving force behind this broad-ranging liberalization.

A major reform of the economic system was proclaimed in 1965 that was to introduce a genuine (socialist) market economy and enhance the powers of "self-managed" enterprises through a withering away of the state's economic role, a process called "de-etatization" *(de-etatizacija),* at all levels. The reform did eliminate almost all central planning and control over investment funds, which were turned over to banks and enterprises, and virtually completed the liquidation of federal economic powers. However, it later became apparent that de-etatization had stopped with the destruction of the federal citadel, leaving other "etatisms" intact and correspondingly strengthened. With most enterprises and banks limiting their activities to the territory of a single federal or smaller unit and with most enterprises too inefficient and financially weak to forswear turning to the state and party for help, tendencies to regional autarky persisted. "Politicization" of the economy thus was enhanced at the regional and local levels. The result was an increasingly powerful symbiosis between regional and therefore national political elites and regional (regarded as national) economies, each dependent on the other and both legitimizing and legitimized by national(ist) sentiment.

The same period brought the definition of the Muslims as a separate nation and genuine autonomy for Kosovo (under Kosovo-Albanian Communist leadership), both in 1968. It also brought regime-directed consummation of the emancipation of the Orthodox Church in Macedonia into an autocephalous church, which in Ottoman fashion certified the separateness of the Macedonian nation.

A series of constitutional amendments and then a new constitution (in 1974) converted the Yugoslav Federation into a quasi-confederation. The powers of the federal center were limited to foreign policy, defense, and a minimum of economic instruments, with decision-making even in these spheres (except foreign policy, Tito's private domain) to be the product of consensus among representatives of the federal units. The number of these units also was effectively enlarged from six to eight as Vojvodina and Kosovo, although still formally autonomous provinces within Serbia, acquired most of the attributes of separate republics. The two provinces henceforth would be directly represented and accordingly empowered at two state and party levels: the Serbian and the Federal, a double representation (and power to block decision-making on subjects where consensus was required) that led to republican-provincial confrontations on the issue in 1977 and more publicly in 1981 and 1984.[84]

Of equal and lasting importance, appointments to federal administrative and elective bodies, including party ones, passed into the hands of republican and provincial party and state leaderships. "Republican and ethnic keys" were rigidly applied in apportioning and rotating senior and many middle-level jobs at the federal level. These frequently were based on producing equal numbers from each republic regardless of population, and they provided smaller federal units and nationalities with further guarantees that their interests and cadres would be well represented. However, the system also had negative effects on both the quality of federal personnel and sentiments of "brotherhood and unity" in those individuals who were passed over because it was some other

---

[84] See the Belgrade newsmagazine *NIN* (17 May 1981; 3 January 1982; and 11 November 1984) and its Zagreb counterpart *Danas* (20 November 1984; 4 December 1984) for overviews of the 1981 and 1984 phases and "revelations" about the earlier, 1977 one.

republic's turn for a desirable post or promotion. Meanwhile, "federalization" of cadre selection meant that those with political ambitions, knowing that their careers were dependent on the approval of the republican or provincial apparatus that sent them to Belgrade, and to whose ranks they would return, would tend to be highly responsive to their home constituencies and more "national" than "Yugoslav" in their attitudes and activities.

While these arrangements were evolving in the later 1960s and in 1970–71, they were subjected to a severe test that produced the most serious political crisis of the Tito era. The growing autonomy of the republics and provinces and debates about how much further the process should go generated a surge of nationalist sentiment almost everywhere. It was particularly intense in Kosovo, where a series of Albanian nationalist demonstrations and the reactions of the Slavic minority, largely in the form of emigration, were a mild taste of what would come in 1981. It was also intense in Croatia, where young, popular, and self-confident leaders (themselves more liberal reform-Communist than nationalist) accepted the political help and growing influence of non-Communist and nationalist elements to push demands for fuller autonomy, with symbols of sovereignty. Under the aegis of this coalition of Communists and nationalists, a Croatian "national euphoria" became a popular-nationalist "Mass Movement" *(MasPok* in its Croatian acronym).

Late in the autumn of 1971, after the leadership of the Croatian party had split over the *MasPok* question, these developments alarmed Tito enough to take drastic action. Threatening to use the army if necessary, he summarily brought about the removal of the Croatian leadership in an expanding purge of "nationalists" and "liberals" that later extended to Serbia, Vojvodina, Slovenia, and Macedonia. The *MasPok* collapsed in a matter of days, and the "normalization" of Croatia began (to borrow a term from Czechoslovakia after the "Prague Spring"). Denouncing any "federalization" of the LCY, Tito also moved to reassert central party discipline and authority, which had been in steep decline since 1967.[85]

---

[85] Recent contributions to the now extensive literature (much of which is polemical and/or tendentious) on the "Croatian Spring" of 1971 and related events in other republics include memoirs like Miko Tripalo, *Hrvatsko prolece* (Zagreb: Globus, 1989); and Jure Bilić, *'71 Koja je to godina* (Zagreb: Centar za informacije i publicitet, 1990). My 1972 attempt to tell the tale is based on my resident observations and contemporary press and other sources: Dennison Rusinow, *Crisis in Croatia,* a four-part series in American Universities Field Staff Reports, Southeast Europe Series, vol. 19, nos. 4–7.

The Fourth Phase

Tito's coups of 1971–72 ushered in a fourth phase in the "Titoist" solution. It did not change as much as many feared or hoped. The quasi-confederal structure of the state was maintained and indeed reconfirmed in the 1974 constitution. "Cadre selection" in federal and republican state and party organs was not really recentralized, although the LCY in Tito's last years, which was "returning to Lenin" with renewed emphasis on "democratic centralism," was again a somewhat more centralized, disciplined, and authoritarian agency than in the third phase (although less so than Tito apparently intended). In part this merely reflected Tito's reassertion of his own unchallengeable authority. In part it was because new republican/provincial party leaderships—although they were potentially as localist and therefore national(ist) as their deposed predecessors—were usually lackluster people without the inherent or accumulated personal stature or the political base and following to assert or expose themselves in this way.

This last was particularly true of the new Croatian leadership, widely regarded as Tito's dutiful hatchet-bearers. These leaders apparently internalized the lessons of 1971 so well that the formerly notoriously liberal Croatian party became one of the most conservative, especially in suppressing dissent. More broadly, the impact of the 1971 crisis and its denouement was greatest, both in intensity and in reach, for the Croats: they experienced the bitterness of euphoria disappointed, underwent extensive purges and arrests, witnessed the inglorious collapse of the Croatian "mass movement" at a shove from Tito, were disappointed over the character of the new republican leadership, and were surprised at the survival and even extension of decentralizing reforms. Besides, the 1970s were again economically and socially good years for most Yugoslavs of all nationalities, including Croats, which made it easier to reduce the priority of national grievances and disappointments. "Silent Croatia," a rare phenomenon in Yugoslav history, endured well into the 1980s, permitting the fulcrum of the national question as it was revived in that decade to lie elsewhere until almost the end.

The Fifth Phase: Disintegration

In the decade following Tito's death in May 1980, the "will to live together" allegedly expressed by the Yugoslav nations in their National Liberation Struggle, and actively or passively conceded by almost all for forty years, gradually dissolved for a large enough number of Slovenes, Croats, and Serbs to render separation in some form and degree increasingly inevitable.A "large enough number" does not mean a majority of any of the three communities.

Indeed, it is reasonable to guess that a country-wide plebescite as late as 1990 would have found a majority of these peoples, and of Yugoslavia's other nations and nationalities (apart from the Albanians), still in favor of some form of "living together," even if they were unable to agree on the particulars.[86] "A large enough number" does mean that a critical mass (among the political elites and in the politically mobilized portions of their constituencies) preferred the disintegration of Yugoslavia when the chips were down, and at the risk of civil war, over abandoning or compromising national goals which were by that time quite clearly incompatible with preservation of the federation within its current boundaries.

None of these goals was new to the national programs of the nationalist participants, but the dynamics of the post-Tito era accentuated and gave primacy to certain particulars: the desire of the Serbs to unite all Serbs in one state; the Croats' assertion of their "historic state right" to a unitary Croatian state; and the Slovenes' desire to preserve the integrity and "European-ness" of Slovene national culture in (or outside) a changing Yugoslavia. Corresponding priorities emerged for other communities caught up *nolens volens* in the confrontation between these first three: the desire of Muslims to preserve Islamic cultural integrity and the right of the South Slavic Muslim nation to a state; the assertion by the Macedonian Slavs of a separate identity; and the ambivalence both of Montenegrins over the expression of their identity (a separate nation or the best Serbs?), and of Yugoslavia's Albanians (union with Enver Hoxha's Albania or quasi-sovereignty in a second and better Albania within a Yugoslav federation or confederation?).

The precise point of no return on the road to disintegration and civil war is debatable and largely a function of differing views about how individual and communal shares of responsibility for disintegration and civil war should be allocated. Benchmarks along the way and the factors in play at each stage are easier to identify, and there is already an extensive and sometimes balanced literature on the subject, which provides the basis for the following summary.[87]

---

[86] See note 100 below for the Slovenes at this point.

[87] These include van den Heuvel and Siccama, *The Disintegration of Yugoslavia;* Banac, "The Fearful Asymmetry of War"; Burg, "Nationalism and Democratization in Yugoslavia"; and Krizman, "Nationalismen in Jugoslawien"; as well was my own contributions, which the following paragraphs partly repeat: Rusinow, "Yugoslavia: Balkan Breakup?" *Foreign Policy* 83 (Summer 1991); Rusinow, "To Be or Not To Be?"; Rusinow, "The Avoidable Catastrophe," in *After Yugoslavia,* Sabrina P. Ramet, ed. (Boulder, CO: Westview Press, 1995).

The chronology of the second demise of the Yugoslav idea and state does not begin with Tito's death in May 1980, although that event did remove the system's ultimate arbiter and linchpin. In defiance of widespread media expectations at the time, there was no immediate sign of disaffection and disintegration, nor did the Red Army attend Tito's funeral to secure the reincorporation of at least part of Yugoslavia into the Soviet bloc. Instead, the transition was initially smooth to his collective, rotating multinational and multi-regional successors, who were granted a kind of honeymoon of transposed legitimacy that they and the institutions they inherited proved incapable of exploiting. Their inability to consolidate power, which was a combined function of their personal inadequacies and those of the system they inherited, the intransigence of both economic problems and the unresolved national question, and external and other factors, would in fact be extraordinarily delayed by the remarkable patience of most Yugoslavs.

The first benchmarks of the fifth, disintegrative postwar phase of the national question are the mass demonstrations in April 1981 by Albanians in Priština and other Kosovo cities and the violent but only temporarily successful suppression of them. The demonstrators' central demand was Kosovo's promotion from an Autonomous Province (since 1968–74 almost a de facto republic) to full de jure republican status, which was widely regarded (in a curious misreading or non-reading of the constitution) to include a right to secede. In the following years, a simmering Albanian rebellion—abetted by repeatedly purged but still recalcitrant Kosovar Albanian party and government leaders and cultural elites—was periodically repressed but never suppressed by police and other measures. These measures led to massive violations of the Kosovar Albanians' individual rights and brought new funds for development, but there was little economic improvement and less law and order in Yugoslavia's poorest region. A further exodus by Kosovo's remaining Serbs and Montenegrins, whose numbers had already been reduced from 20.8 percent of the population in the 1971 census to 14.9 percent in 1981, accompanied demonstrably exaggerated (when not wholly invented) tales of Albanian intimidation, including allegedly widespread and nationalist-motivated rapes of Slav women, which Serbian media portrayed as an organized attempt to create an "ethnically pure" Albanian Kosovo. By the late 1980s the province's Slav communities were reduced to an estimated 10 percent or less of the population.

As early as May 1968 two members of the Serbian Party's Central Committee had warned a plenary session that Albanian "nationalism and irredentism" were being openly promoted in Kosovo and that systematic discrimination was forcing numbers of Serbs and Montenegrins to emigrate.[88] Accused of being "nationalistic" and "opposed to self-management," both men were dropped from the committee. One of them was Dobrica Ćošić, widely regarded as Serbia's outstanding living writer, who was later named president of the "third" or "rump" Yugoslavia proclaimed by Serbia and Montenegro in March 1992.

Until 1987 the reaction of most other Serbs to dramatic media portrayals of the plight of fellow Serbs and of Albanian pretensions in the Kosovo cradle of their culture, church, and statehood—"the Serb Jerusalem"—was remarkably mute, often reduced to an angry but fatalistic "Kosovo is lost!"[89] However, the reaction of a significant portion of the Serbian cultural elite[90] was a harbinger of a more activist approach and program. It also seized upon and accentuated a subtheme found in earlier Serbian and Croatian (and other small-nations') national consciousness and ideology:[91] the Serbs as a victimized and diminishing nation, whose sacrifices and victories on the battlefield and on behalf of others as well as themselves were perennially betrayed by the egoism and deviousness of those others. This is the origin of the "Memorandum" drafted by Dobrica Ćošić and others for the Serbian Academy in the spring of 1986 (extracted in Document 5) and initially denounced by the Serbian party leadership as an unacceptable nationalist manifesto. After Serbia's greater sacrifices and leading role in creating both Yugoslav states, its impoverishment while more developed republics grew richer, its division into three parts and deprivation of the kind of statehood enjoyed by all other republics, "genocide" in Kosovo and discrimination against diaspora Serbs and their culture, the distortion and suppression of

88 Described in greater detail in Rusinow, *The Yugoslav Experiment,* 246.

89 A conclusion I often heard in Belgrade as late as 1986.

90 This included Marxist critics of Marxism who had incurred the wrath of Tito and the Communist establishment in the 1960s and 1970s, but who were now discovering that the threat was to their nation as well as (more than?) to their democratic socialist ideals.

91 See, for example, Aleksa Djilas's observations on "Croatian nationalists' almost paranoid belief, in the nineteenth and twentieth centuries, that it was the fate of Croatia to become ever smaller until it disappeared altogether. Since the nineteenth century many Croatian and Serbian intellectuals and political figures have viewed their nations in an exaggerated, romantic way, as border nations doomed to devastation by foreign armies, situated on the periphery of Europe, and never fully benefiting from European civilization." *The Contested Country,* 8.

Serbian history, etc.—all were fruits of the ingratitude and machinations, motivated by "chauvinism and Serbophobia" in alliance with "Comintern ideology," of people for whom Serbia had done so much. Remedies were long overdue: "Restoration of the full national and cultural integrity of the Serb people, whatever republic or province it finds itself in, is its historic and democratic right."

With equal passion and appropriate modifications of subtexts to suit their different circumstances, the same basic themes of victimization and right to remedy were being articulated by and for Slovenes and Croats as well, as in Tudjman's writings (e.g., Document 4), which could still bring prosecution for "verbal crimes" in the early 1980s. It was not long, however, before the mass media grew less and less inhibited by the party's and prosecutors' fading vigilance against forms of "coming to grips with the past" that were considered nationalist and damaging to brotherhood and unity. The mass media began eagerly to transmit the most polemical and inflammatory contributions to equally eager mass audiences. "De-mystification" (and re-mystification) of history joined forces with "de-Titoization" in the wider context of Eastern Europe's accelerating rejection of anything "Communist" to create a propensity to reject everything the old regime and system had said was good, including brotherhood and unity. Conversely, what the regime had damned as evil and nationalist and had used to discredit Serb, Croat, or other national pride and aspirations—such as the NDH, Ustaše, and Četniks—must ipso facto merit rehabilitation.[92]

One year after the Academy's memorandum was leaked to the media and formally denounced by the Serbian party, the search for a mobilizer of Serb anger and resentment was finally rewarded, on an April night in 1987, during a demonstration by Kosovar Serbs at Kosovo polje, site of the epic battle of 1389. When local police began beating the demonstrators, Slobodan Milošević, recently elevated to the presidency of the League of Communists of Serbia and previously little noticed, found his voice ("No one will ever beat you again!") and learned how to ride the tiger of aroused Serb national passion to a new Battle of Kosovo and beyond.[93]

---

[92] This point is made by Ivan Zvonimir Cičak, *"Bauk fasizma kruzi Evropom i Hrvatskom," Slobodna Dalmacija* (13 April 1992), in explanation of why Croats "are idealizing the NDH as a state creation" and thereby ignoring its fascist ideology and crimes.

[93] Milošević's dramatic mise-en-scène at Kosovo polje may not have been as spontaneous and unrehearsed as his supporters believed or indicated. For a discussion of his alleged careful preparations to take power in Serbia, including infiltration of party, state, and economic apparatus with largely provincial

In the name of unity to save the beleaguered Serbs of Kosovo and an "anti-bureaucratic revolution" to rid Serbia (and then, ominously, the rest of the country) of opponents defined as "bureaucratic forces," Milošević skillfully purged the Serbian party and mass media of dissenting voices. He then embarked on a campaign to "re-unify" Serbia by reducing its two autonomous provinces, Vojvodina and Kosovo, to autonomy in name only, and to install a pro-Serbian client regime in Montenegro, his own ancestral homeland. The means included d'Annunzian-style mass meetings to incite frenzied support (in Serbia and by Serbs in other republics) and to depose "autonomist" government and party officials in Vojvodina; procedurally and constitutionally dubious amendments to the Serbian constitution; and finally (in July 1990) simply closing down Kosovo's parliament, government, and principal Albanian-language media. In January 1989 the political leadership in Montenegro was replaced, in a coup resembling the one in Vojvodina, by Milošević supporters. Meanwhile, his claim to be the protector of Serbs and Serbdom in "reunited" Serbia was being extended to diaspora Serbs elsewhere in the country. In the process and in consonance with historical Serb preferences, as the largest nation with the largest diaspora, for a centralized ("unitarist") Yugoslav state in which Serbs would play the leading role and could better protect that diaspora, he also launched a campaign for a strengthened federal center, in both government and the League of Communists.

The alarm engendered in non-Serbs by this apparent strategy for a Serb- and therefore Milošević-dominated Yugoslavia first became widespread and acute in Slovenia. Even before Milošević appeared on the scene, police brutality in Kosovo and the recidivist nationalism apparent in Serb reactions to events there had led some "dissident" Slovene intellectuals to entertain second thoughts about the present form and the future direction of Slovenia's association with such culturally different (perhaps not really "European") and apparently dangerous people. In 1986, at almost precisely the same time Serbian academicians were completing the draft of their memorandum,[94] the Slovenes ruminations and program for Slovenia—in effect an equivalent

---

loyalists beholden to his patronage for their jobs or advancement, see Slavoljub Djukić (an anti-Milošević journalist), *Kako se dogodio vodja* (Belgrade: Filip Visnjić, 1992), and Dragiša Pavlović (one of the Serbian leaders Milošević deposed), *Olako obecana bržina* (Zagreb: Globus, 1988).

94 In a society endemically prone to conspiracy theories and in view of the close and frequent contacts between Slovene and Serb intellectuals (particularly "dissidents"), it has been suggested that this simultaneity was not coincidental.

Slovene "national manifesto"—were published in *Nova Revija,* then the most widely read and influential dissident journal. In an intellectually and politically incestuous relationship (which often characterizes small relatively homogenous communities and capital cities, where government and opposition may be literal as well as educational and career siblings), "reform-Communists" and other members of the Slovenian political establishment played catch-up through a combination of competition and convergence.

The Slovenes' traditional pro-Yugoslavism was based largely on perceptions of Austrian and Italian threats to their national identity or territory, with Yugoslavia (and the Serbs as its largest and "state-building" people) as their protector. If the threat to their small nation and its culture were instead to come from within Yugoslavia, which more and more of them now perceived in the form of Milošević's apparent bid for Serb political (and then cultural?) domination, they would prefer to be out. Besides, "Europe" in the form of the European Community appeared to be beckoning but seemed to be restrained by violations of European-standard human rights in Kosovo. Slovene calls multiplied for a loose confederation of "sovereign" states or outright secession, and by 1989 conflict between Slovenia and Serbia, escalating from mutual accusations and threats to boycotts, temporarily took over from Serb-Croat issues as the centerpiece of the national question.

As Milošević extended his claim to be the anointed defender of the Serbs in Croatia and Bosnia-Hercegovina, the Croats of Croatia and the Muslims and Croats of Bosnia-Hercegovina were increasingly prone to similar fears. So were "nationally conscious" Macedonians, mindful of their definition as "South Serbs" and their Serbianization during the prewar period, as were those Montenegrins who believed they comprised a Montenegrin nation rather than merely the tallest, fiercest Serbs.

Perhaps the primary reason why conflicting interests and values and other "nationalist/historical/religious/cultural strains"[95] among Yugoslavia's diverse peoples had never before threatened the survival of the post–1945 Yugoslav state is that few members of any of the major national communities, however much each considered itself disadvantaged or exploited, felt that their existence *as a national community* actually was endangered, either in their "own" republic (for the six South Slav "state nations") or autonomous province (for the Albanians of Kosovo) or as a numerically significant minority in another republic (e.g., the Serbs of Croatia). This had been the minimalist achievement of the "Titoist solution," which was being undone in a vicious

---

95 Former U.S. Ambassador to Yugoslavia David Anderson, "Yugoslavia in the 1990s: A Very Uncertain Future," unpublished paper, Aspen Institute, Berlin, 22 May 1991.

circle of economic free-fall, political paralysis, delegitimation of the regime and system, and the cause-and-effect of competing nationalist sentiments and ambitions. Kosovo was in this sense a time-bomb that detonated a chain of explosions in which growing numbers of first Serbs and then Albanians, Slovenes, Croats, and others came to believe that part or all of their nation indeed was faced with extinction as a national community—that is, as a community living in a place or places where history and modern doctrines of national sovereignty and self-determination gave it a right to live and to determine its government.[96]

With such fears refracted from group to group, and with individual identity and interests identified with those of the nation reified as a collective individual, the national question was again an existential question. For Slovenes, Croats, and Albanians, this implied a right to secede in order to ensure survival; for Serbs, an identically motivated right, wherever they might live, to the protection of unity in Yugoslavia—or, failing that, in an enlarged Serbia. Emotional expressions of hypertrophied national sentiments mounted almost everywhere. Defied by first one and then most of the republics, the writ of federal authorities, highly limited in content since 1974, ceased to run in almost all matters. All of this was compounded by an apparently irreconcilable contradiction between joint Slovene-Croatian proposals for a loose confederation, which Serbian and other Serb leaders found totally unacceptable, and a Serbian-inspired proposal for a "modern federation" (more centralized than Yugoslavia had been since the 1950s), which was equally unacceptable to Slovenes and Croats. The combination provided further benchmarks on the road to disintegration and violence.

Nineteen-ninety began with the self-destruction of the League of Communists (formerly the Communist Party) of Yugoslavia, together with the legacy of Tito as the creator and sustainer of the second Yugoslav state. It disintegrated when the Slovene delegation, thwarted in its efforts to convert the LCY into a loosely associated "League of Leagues" by Milošević's bloc of four delegations,[97] walked out of an all-Yugoslav Party Congress in January, and the rest of the delegates, except for the minority controlled by the Serb leader, voted to adjourn *sine die*. In the following months the LCY evaporated almost unnoticed. By the end of the year, its republican remnants one by one accepted multiparty elections and their consequences, which had taken place

---

96 This argument is more fully developed in Rusinow, "Yugoslavia: Balkan Breakup?"; Rusinow, "To Be or Not To Be?"; and Rusinow, "The Avoidable Catastrophe."

97 From the still formally separate LCs of Vojvodina and Kosovo as well as Serbia as a whole and Montenegro.

in all six republics: in Slovenia and Croatia in April–May, in Macedonia and Bosnia-Hercegovina in November, and in Serbia and Montenegro in December.[98]

Four of the six produced non-Communist majorities and governments, although the latter invariably contained some current and/or ex-Communists (including all new republican presidents except Alija Izetbegović, president of the tri-national collective presidency of Bosnia-Hercegovina, who had been in prison as an Islamic nationalist). There were Communist victories in Serbia (where the party was renamed Socialist in July) and Montenegro. In every case, the winner was the party or electoral alliance that had been first or most effective in appropriating the national(ist) symbols and programs of its republic's nominative and dominant nation. The exception was Bosnia-Hercegovina, where the votes won by Muslim, Serb, and Croat national parties were proportionate and nearly equal to the three communities' respective shares in the adult population.

In Serbia (where Kosovo's Albanians boycotted the elections) and in Montenegro, the Communists profited from Milošević's early and dramatic capture of the Serb national flag and other advantages[99] to win handily over the combined opposition, including parties and personalities whose even more radical nationalist rhetoric and programs represented a vain attempt to take that flag from him. With this renewed and now formally democratic mandate—and with his apparent strategy for a more centralized, Serb-dominated Yugoslavia in tatters since the demise of the LCY—Milošević shifted to his putative alternative strategy for keeping all Serbs in one state, the creation of a Greater Serbia. If Croats might exercise their right to self-determination by secession or by insisting on constitutional arrangements that would reduce Croatian Serbs to a minority, he was now saying, the same right must permit Serbs and the places they lived to secede from Croatia. His actions also suggested that he was now more eager to see Slovenia out of Yugoslavia than to keep it in.

In Slovenia the former League of Communists, renamed the Party of Democratic Renewal, campaigned in large part on its own and the outgoing

[98] The following is based on my more detailed analysis of the elections in Rusinow, "To Be or Not To Be?" 6–9.

[99] Including control of mass media (especially television) and ubiquitous patronage networks; a populist and socialist platform promising avoidance of unemployment and other miseries plaguing other East European countries and Yugoslav regions in transition to market economies; and the legal and illegal advantages that people and parties in power usually enjoy over the opposition at election time.

government's record in defending Slovene autonomy and national interests against Serbian pretensions. It achieved mixed results. Milan Kučan, a popular national- and reform-Communist who had led the party's walk-out at the LCY Congress in January, won the presidency of the republic, and his Party of Democratic Renewal won the most votes for any single party in parallel parliamentary elections. However, the real winner, with a cumulative 53.8 percent of the vote and 126 of 240 seats, was an electoral and subsequently governing alliance, called Demos, of seven anti-Communist but otherwise heterogeneous small parties.

Some Demos leaders, particularly in the national-liberal Democratic Party (9.5 percent of the vote), were already overt or covert advocates of secession under any circumstances, with a strategy for its achievement in their pockets. In the following months, outmaneuvering waverers and opponents in Demos's ranks and the parliamentary opposition, they and others of like-mind mobilized coalition and mass support for its implementation. In a referendum on 23 December 1990, 89 percent of the electorate (of the 94 percent who participated) voted for "an independent and sovereign Slovenia."[100] The independent state was to be delivered at the end of six months (i.e., in June 1991) if the other republics had not by that time agreed, as at least Serbia surely would not, to a loose confederation of sovereign states. Methodical legal and other preparations began for the process of "disassociation," a deliberately ambiguous Slovenian and Croatian euphemism for secession and term for such a confederation—where they were not already underway.

In Croatia, the winner (assisted by a new electoral law that converted a plurality of the votes into a solid absolute majority in parliament) was the Croatian Democratic Union (HDZ in its Croatian abbreviation) and its leader, Franjo Tudjman, who duly became president of Croatia. Tudjman had been a wartime partisan, Communist, and Yugoslav army general before becoming a military historian and anti-Communist who was imprisoned in the 1970s for his allegedly "nationalist-separatist" activities in the Croatian "Mass Movement." (Document 4 contains a representative sample of his views on the Croatian and more general national question.)

The new regime, pledged to restore Croatia's historical state right (although not yet necessarily outside Yugoslavia) and apparently intoxicated with Croatian national symbols, was soon committing acts of omission and

---

[100] This contrasts with the results of an in-depth poll taken early the same year, which found a majority of Slovenes still in favor of belonging to a looser and preferably "confederal" Yugoslavia. Cited in Rusinow,"To Be or Not To Be?" 7.

commission that demonstrated extraordinary insensitivity to the concerns of Croatian Serbs who still had vivid memories of attempted genocide by the Ustaše during World War II. Tudjman and the HDZ came to power already burdened, in the eyes of all Serbs and some Croats, by a failure to condemn the Ustaše "Independent State of Croatia" as a misbegotten and evil realization of Croatian statehood, although they had occasionally criticized the most heinous acts of the Ustaše. The national symbols they now chose to replace those of communism on flags, coats of arms, and uniforms were identical or very similar to those used by the Ustaša regime. After some early conciliatory gestures, Tudjman refused to moderate his regime's commitment to eliminating overrepresentation of Serbs in the police and other government services and in employment more generally, or to consider even cultural autonomy for the Serb-majority districts in Lika, Kordun, and Banija.

By August 1990 the Serbs of these districts, which they called Krajina, were in a state of insurrection. It began with a confrontation between Croatia's new paramilitary "special" police and armed Serbs that was provoked in part by a locally organized "plebescite" on Krajina's autonomy which the Croatian government vainly attempted to prevent. The writ of the Croatian Republic soon ceased to run in most of the region, and the rail line and most roads from inner Croatia to Dalmatia were permanently or periodically blocked by the rebels. On 16 March 1991, Krajina's repeated declarations of autonomy became a declaration of separation from Croatia, followed two weeks later by a declaration of union with Serbia (to which the Serbian government did not respond). On 2 May tensions and episodic confrontations in other parts of Croatia that had significant Serb minorities turned into serious violence at Borovo selo, a Serb village near the Danube border between Slavonia and Vojvodina (with the participation of Serb irregulars who infiltrated from Serbia and called themselves Četniks). Borovo selo can be said to mark the beginning of Yugoslavia's civil war, seven weeks before Croatia's and Slovenia's declarations of independence.

The Macedonian elections produced such a fragmented parliament that it could not elect a president of the republic until January (when Kiro Gligorov, a reform-Communist was elected) or form a government until March 1991. The largest party in the new, unicameral National Assembly, with 37 of its 120 seats, borrowed the name and nationalist sentiments of the Internal Macedonian Revolutionary Organization (IMRO), which in its first incarnation was notorious for its terrorist activities against Ottoman and then Serbian rulers of Vardar Macedonia. But the new government and its policies remained anxiously pro-Yugoslav until Yugoslavia was reduced by other secessions to a Serbo-Montenegrin rump. Only then, when the alternative seemed to be a return to Macedonia's prewar status as "South Serbia," was independence declared.

In Bosnia-Hercegovina President Izetbegović cobbled together a fragile tri-national(ist) government including his own Muslim and the Bosnian Serb and Croat parties. He and others imagined or pretended that their "Yugoslavia-in-miniature" could if necessary survive as an independent "Balkan Switzerland," somehow and improbably immune to the same nationalist passions, competitive irredentisms, and intolerance of national minorities that would break up the greater Yugoslavia. With the only alternative clearly being a civil war of horrendous proportions, given the patchwork ethnic map of Bosnia-Hercegovina's cities and countryside and its tradition of extremism and violence, this hope may have been necessary and was certainly worthy. But that is beside the point. The tri-national government, stressed to the breaking point from the beginning, did not survive the beginning of the breakup of the larger Yugoslavia. As Aleksa Djilas describes the process:

> [I]t was soon obvious that the three national parties not only had mutually exclusive programs, but that they actually represented incompatible national ideologies that could not be modified through political compromises. It was only a matter of time before irreconcilable differences in the government would be transformed into civil war.
>
> Muslims imagined Bosnia as an independent state in which they should predominate....
>
> The Serbs, for their part, wanted Bosnia to stay inside Yugoslavia and increasingly demanded a Yugoslavia dominated by Serbs.... When the Muslims demanded Bosnia's independence, the Serbs demanded "cantonization" of Bosnia. But their views about the size of this Serbian canton.... were megalomaniacal....
>
> The Croatian maximal fantasy was to incorporate the whole of Bosnia.... More realistically, Croats planned to take those territories of Bosnia with a Croatian majority and integrate them into Croatia.[101]

The stage was now set for the end-game of secession and civil and inter-state war that began with declarations of independence by the Croatian and Slovenian governments on 25 June 1991, followed by skirmishes in Slovenia, Serb-Croat and Serbo-Croatian war in Croatia, tri-national war in Bosnia-Hercegovina, and the special brutality and inhumanity of "ethnic cleansing." Yugoslavia's national question was to be given another and grim answer.

---

[101] Aleksa Djilas, "The Nation That Wasn't," *The New Republic* (21 September 1992), 31.

10

Nationalism, The Victorious Ideology

by Peter F. Sugar

Eastern Europe is an integral part of the continent and has shared with the rest of Europe the three dominant ideologies of the twentieth century: nationalism, communism/Bolshevism, and fascism/national socialism. The periods during which each of these basic ideologies dominated the thinking of people differed drastically from one region of the old continent to another, especially in the lands west of those in which Bolshevism/Stalinism triumphed in the form of Leninism in 1917 and remained dominant until 1990.

In the West, communism had numerous followers, especially in Germany, France, and Spain, but was nowhere successful enough to become dominant—although it came close in Germany after the end of World War I. Communists in these and in other Western states compromised their ideology and program in the 1930s when they joined or supported "national fronts" or "coalition governments" at Moscow's bidding. In East Central and Southeastern Europe, Communists had more success in initially establishing a short-lived Republic of Soviets in Hungary in 1919; winning the first city council elections after 1918 in several countries; and representing enough of a danger to the established ruling elements to be outlawed everywhere except in Czechoslovakia.

Stalinist governments were established everywhere in Eastern Europe except in Greece after World War II. This development did not occur as the result of local preferences, but because the Soviet Union was in a position to dictate the type of "friendly governments" it wanted to see established in its "security zone." Let us not forget that Yugoslavia was considered to be "the model satellite" prior to the break between Stalin and Marshal Tito in 1947. For forty-five years—a considerable segment of the present century—the people of Eastern Europe lived in "People's" or "Socialist" republics, although their governments gradually moved away from their original commitments and practices to become "National Communists" and, after 1989, "Social Democrats." While these changes reflected to some extent developments taking place in the Soviet Union, they were also the result of domestic factors. The violent, peaceful, and practical/economic manifestations of popular discontent made the Communist masters of the various states realize that, like governments everywhere, they also needed community support to be "legitimate" and to be able to govern. They strove to acquire this legitimacy by moving closer and closer to identifying themselves with the old "national" goals, using "national" slogans and emblems and demanding less and less conformity. János Kádár's oft-repeated dictum, "those who are not against us are for us," which turned Marx's statement around, illustrates this change as clearly as does Alexander Dubček's "socialism with a human face." When local developments, combined with Mikhail Gorbachev's reforms in the Soviet Union, brought about the final collapse of what was left of Communist governments in Southeastern and East Central Europe, the leaders of the various ruling parties suddenly discovered that they were, after all, good nationalists.

What had failed was not the Marxist ideal of a classless society in which economic and social equality reigned. As a matter of fact, the ideal of equality was more or less accepted by the masses who showed hostility to those who began the first "capitalist" enterprises once these became legal again. What had failed—besides one-party dictatorship—was internationalism, which had forced people to relearn their national histories and to make sacrifices for such "brothers" as the Cubans or Vietnamese who also were fighting to achieve "socialism." This attempt to denationalize entire nations and to remold them into "socialist men" demanded from the various people of the region a renunciation of their past, and this made them value their national identity even more.

Fascism/national socialism was much less successful in Eastern than in Western Europe. Mussolini was in power from 1922 to 1943; Hitler ruled Germany from 1933 to 1945; Salazar was master of Portugal from 1933 to 1968; and Franco ran Spain from 1939 to 1975. With the exception of the short-lived (forty-four days) Goga-Cuza government in Romania from December 1938 to February 1939, no extreme right-wing party came to power anywhere in Eastern Europe prior to the outbreak of World War II, when Hitler was able to force on his allies and on defeated nations leaders of his choice for shorter or longer periods. This is somewhat surprising because the interwar years brought some of the clearest expressions of extreme nationalism—be they status quo or revisionist—in Southeastern and East Central Europe and because the same extremist slogans were used by both the

Fascists and the National Socialists to gain popular support. When examined more closely, however, these movements appear in their true, antinationalist light.

Mussolini's fascism subordinated the individual and the nation and to the state. In *The Philosophy of Fascism* (1936), Mario Palmieri wrote:

> Without the State there is no Nation. These words reverse the commonly accepted principle of modern political science that without Nation there is no State.[1]

Mussolini himself wrote in 1932:

> Against individualism, the Fascist conception is for the state; and it is for the individual insofar as he coincides with the State... Fascism reaffirms the State as the true reality of the individual... Fascism is for liberty. And for the only liberty which can be a real thing, the liberty of the State... Therefore, for a Fascist everything is in the State, and nothing human and spiritual exists, much less has value, outside the state.[2]

What the classless, proletarian-dominated international order was to Marxism (in whatever form it may take), the state was to the fascists. Both subordinated the nation, and within it the individual, to a supreme good with which they were supposed to identify.

National socialism presented an ideology that was even harder to swallow than was fascism for the people of Eastern Europe. It was easy to make anti-Semitism into a virtue and equally easy to feel superior to the minorities living in any given nation-state or to the usually hated majorities in neighboring countries. The trouble was that in the racist world created by Hitler, there was room for only one master race. As it happened, not even the master race lived up to the Hitler's expectations. This is clearly evident from the much-quoted lines in Albert Speer's memoirs. When Hitler ordered the application of the scorched-earth policy in Germany, he said:

---

1 Quoted in Carl Cohen, ed., *Communism, Fascism, Democracy: The Theoretical Foundations* (New York: Random House, 1962), 377.

2 Benito Mussolini, "The Doctrine of Fascism," in *Encyclopedia Italiana* (1932), quoted in Cohen, *Communism, Fascism, Democracy*, 351–52.

> If the war is lost, the nation will also perish. This fate is inevitable. There is no need to consider the basis even of the most primitive existence any longer. On the contrary, it is better to destroy even that, and to destroy it ourselves. The nation has proven itself weak... Besides those who remain after the battle are of little value; for the good have fallen.[3]

What went wrong with the Aryan "superman"? Hitler explained:

> In regard to the preparation of our morale...it [the war] came far too soon. I had not yet had time to shape the people to the measure of my policies.[4]

Hitler also made clear what his policies were. Talking to some members of his inner circle during the night of 21–22 October 1941, he stated: "If I try to gauge my work, I must consider, first of all, that it contributed, in a world that had forgotten the notion, to the triumph of the idea of the primacy of the race."[5]

These quotations prove that neither fascism nor national socialism were "nationalist" policies. The first subordinated the nation to the state, and the second subordinated the nation to race. Even the Germans, the supposed master race, did not learn from Hitler what their destiny was and have proven themselves "weak," failing to transform the world into a racially—not nationally—organized universe. Nationalism survived Bolshevism/Stalinism, fascism, and national socialism although as a clearly formulated ideology it did not predate Jean-Jacques Rousseau (1712–1778) and Johann Gottfried von Herder (1744–1803). In Eastern Europe nationalism had existed for roughly 200 years before its position was challenged by newer and supposedly stronger theories propagated by the mass media of modern life. Why, then, did it survive to dominate the political landscape at the end of this century just as at its beginning?

---

3 Quoted in Alan Bullock, *Hitler, A Study in Tyranny* (New York: Harper & Row, 1962), 774–75.

4 Quoted from *Le testament politique de Hitler. Notes recueilles par Martin Borman* (Paris, 1959), in Joachim C. Fest, *Hitler* (New York: Harcourt, Brace, Jovanovich, 1973), 742.

5 *Hitler's Secret Conversations, 1941–1944,* with an introductory essay on "The Mind of Adolf Hitler" by H. R. Trevor-Roper (New York: Farrar, Straus and Young, 1953), 67.

It is my contention that by the beginning of the twentieth century, the nationalism of all nations of Eastern Europe was "integral," demanding the unquestioning absolute loyalty of every individual belonging to any given nation. Going beyond this statement, it is not difficult to find additional common features in the nationalistic feelings of the Eastern Europeans that differentiate them from those living in the western part of the continent. In an essay, "What Is the Hungarian, Today?" by Sándor Csoóri, a good example of contemporary Hungarian nationalism, we find the following statement: "It would never occur to a Frenchman, an Englishman, an Italian, or a Russian that his nation could be broken by the next day."[6] The fear that this could happen bothered Hungarians ever since Herder predicted their disappearance.[7] The Hungarians were not the only nation afraid of the future. Bernd Fischer described the nationalism of the Albanians as "siege nationalism." Maria Todorova used the same words to describe Bulgarian nationalism that were used by Gerasimos Augustinos for the Greeks: "defensive nationalism." The Czechs suffered and suffer from the "Munich syndrome," and the Slovaks feared that extreme magyarization might end their existence prior to World War I. The Poles and Hungarians stressed their historic role as "defenders of the West" and bemoaned the fact that this was not recognized and rewarded by those whom they protected from the dangers coming from the "East." This feeling of being treated unjustly is also the cause of the traditional martyr complex of the Serbs.

This rather pessimistic nationalism produced national holidays or historical benchmarks tied to military or political defeats: the Battle of Kosovo (1389) for the Serbs, the Battle of Mohács (1526) for the Hungarians, the Battle on the White Mountain (1620) for the Czechs, the three partitions (1772, 1793, 1795) for the Poles, and the Treaty of Berlin (1878) for the Bulgarians.

---

6 Quoted by Tibor Frank in chapter 6, "Nation, National Minorities, and Nationalism in Twentieth-Century Hungary."

7 Herder wrote: *"Da sind sie [the Hungarians] jetzt unter Slawen, Deutschen, Wlachen und andern Völkern der geringere Teil der Landeseinwohner, und nach Jahrhunderten wird man vielleicht ihre Sprache kaum finden."* ("Here they are—the Hungarians—living among Slavs, Germans, Vlachs and other people the smaller portion of those living in their land, and after centuries one could, possibly, hardly find their language.") Johann Gottfried von Herder, *Ideen zur Philosophie der Geschichte der Menschen,* Part IV, Book XVI (n.d. [1791]), chapter 2, 660f., in Eugen Kunsmann, ed., *Deutsche National-Literatur, Historisch-kritische Ausgabe* (Stuttgart, n.d.).

Another important feature of Eastern European nationalism was the search for self-identification, something not found in the Western world. In Great Britain one could be and was English, Scottish, or Welsh, but this did not prevent anybody from being British. In Germany one could be and was Bavarian, Saxon, Prussian, etc. without feeling that this belonging prevented anybody from being a patriotic German. Similar situations are true for the citizens of France, Switzerland, Belgium, and even Spain. In contrast, practically every nation in Eastern Europe felt the need to discover its identity and turned to one or another form of populism to find "its specific roots." When the Grimm brothers began collecting folk and fairy tales, they might have had some nationalistic motives, alongside their primarily scientific ones, but they were certainly not trying to find out what it meant to be a German.

The drastic economic and social changes that created the modern world in Western Europe were developments that occurred there gradually and were part of the various people's regional-national history. These changes were "imported" into East Central and Southeastern Europe, transformed urban life on the Western European model, and increased the differences between the cities and the practically unchanged villages. Did the Westernization of city life "de-nationalize" those who lived in the major population centers? Were the city dwellers still members of any given nation, or were they too "cosmopolitan" for membership in any of them? To be a cosmopolitan citizen of the world without a clearly defined homeland was something only very few individuals could accept. This is the reason why populism and the exploration of life in the villages became important. Some of those who explored and chronicled rural life might and did have goals resembling those of the Grimm brothers, but the majority searched for the specific features of their nations among the peasantry, which was uncorrupted by foreign ways of thinking and living. The peasantry still was easily found in all of Eastern Europe's states.[8] Hugh Seton-Watson contrasted, correctly, the image of the peasantry created by the populists for the city-dwellers with the true life in the villages. Seen by those who never set foot into the countryside,

> ...the peasants lead almost idyllic lives, tilling the soil they mystically love, dancing their ancient national dances, clad

---

[8] In 1918 the number of people living from agriculture was 78 percent in Romania; 80 percent in Bulgaria; 75 percent in Yugoslavia; 63 percent in Poland; 55 percent in Hungary; and 34 percent in Czechoslovakia. Figures from Hugh Seton-Watson, *Eastern Europe between the Wars, 1918–1941* (Hamden, CT: Archon Books, 1962), 75.

> in their picturesque national costumes and singing...their soulful national songs.

The truth differed sharply from the above impression created by the populists. The peasants were living in

> mud hovels, adorned by no rugs or pottery, housing families of seven or eight.... returning from their work in tattered rags...and look fearfully at the officials who examine their labor permits.[9]

The fake happy peasant, who supposedly embodied the undiluted national spirit, helped the city-dweller to feel that he belonged to a unique and lovely nation. That this happy peasant was a myth made no difference. The Romanian Emil Cioran wrote in 1935, "The myths of a nation are its vital truths. They might not coincide with *the truth;* this is not of importance..."[10]

Besides its defensive character and populist myths, the nationalism of the people of Eastern Europe had one more feature that differentiated it from those of the Western nations. This was the lack of coinciding ethnic, ethno-nationalistic, linguistic, and political borders. Besides the centuries-old problem of Alsace-Lorraine, no major border was in constant dispute in Western Europe. In contrast, there were hardly any undisputed borders in East Central and Southeastern Europe. The *Megale Idea* of the Greeks clashed with the demand for Great Serbia and with Bulgaria's desire to regain the San Stefano borders. The two Balkan wars resulted from this clash, bringing some satisfaction to Greece, Serbia, and Romania and creating a new state, Albania; moving Bulgaria, the major loser, even further from the borders it desired; but failing to fully satisfy even the winners. Only the Ottoman Empire, whose new European borders were recognized as just by its heir, the Turkish Republic, had no complaints. The maximal demands for national borders based on memories of long-lost or mythical "empires" were still contradictory desiderata.

North of the Danube-Sava line the situation was even more complex. Hungarians were satisfied with their borders but fearful that these would be challenged not only by the irredenta of Romania and Serbia, but also by the growing national movements of the Slovaks and Croats. The latter had a double trialist program demanding equality with Germans and Hungarians

---

9 Seton-Watson, *Eastern Europe between the Wars,* 76.

10 Cited by James Niessen in chapter 8, "Romanian Nationalism: An Ideology of Integration and Mobilization."

in the Habsburg realm for their reunited "Triune Kingdom." The Croats also could opt for an alternative solution, the Yugoslav idea, provided they and the Serbs could agree on the form their common state was to take. This, as is well known, was something on which these two nations could never agree. While the Czechs were not certain of what their aim was—equality in the lands of the Habsburgs with "ruling" nations or an independent state—there was no doubt about the goal of the Poles: reunification of their partitioned lands into an independent state. Yet there was disagreement among the Poles on what this state's borders should be. To make the future of Austria-Hungary even more questionable, and therefore the planning of the various "nationalities" living within its borders more difficult, was the growing number of those Germans who were dreaming a *Grossdeutsch* dream as the only secure answer to the problem created by the restless "nationalities."

The peace treaties that ended World War I drastically altered the borders in Eastern Europe but failed to eliminate the tensions and hostilities of conflicting nationalisms. The victors were only less unhappy than the losers. Old roles were played by new actors. Hungarians and Bulgarians were the irredentists, although now they were called "revisionists." The nationalisms of the victors were now defensive, although the new label for them was "status quo nationalism." Greece, while on the winning side of the great conflict, lost in her attempt to win Ionia and had to give up the *Megale Idea.* The Hungarians and Greeks realized that they could not expect to regain the momentum of their national aspirations by using force. Independently of each other, they turned to the same solution. In Greece it was first Trikoupis and later G. Papandreou who saw in economic and cultural activities the new form of the *Megale Idea.*[11] The minister of cults and education of Hungary for ten years, Count Kunó Klebelsberg, developed a massive educational program which had as its goal to produce

> "The Hungarian cultural superiority" as the basis on which revision of the Trianon treaty was justified,...and hoped that the cultural policy would attract not only Hungarians, but even the non-Hungarians living in the lost territories...[12]

Several years later, the same idea reemerged in the closing statement of the Sándor Csoóri essay quoted above:

---

[11] See chapter 5, "Hellenism and the Modern Greeks," by Gerasimos Augostinos.

[12] Peter F. Sugar, Péter Hanák, and Tibor Frank, eds., *A History of Hungary* (Bloomington: Indiana University Press, 1990), 325.

> We can never start a war again to defend our national minorities over the border. Just like a new work of art...only a rebuilt, reformed Hungarian nation can exert an incredible influence...[13]

The interwar years, the period of the "long armistice," continued to be the years of insecurity for the various nations of East Central and Southeastern Europe. Czechoslovakia, Romania, and Yugoslavia were not content with their Little Entente and sought added security in alliances with France. Poland did the same, while Greece remained a client of Great Britain. The losers of the war naturally turned to the dissatisfied victorious power, Italy, for help and protection. As the years went by and the great Western powers appeared more and more reluctant to stand up to fascism and national socialism, reliance on them appeared to be useless. The Poles signed a Non-Aggression Pact with the Soviet Union in 1932 and with Germany in 1934. Yugoslavia signed a Political Agreement with Italy in 1937. Even Bulgaria and Hungary moved gradually from the Italian into the German camp. The success of fascism (prior to the Ethiopian campaign) and especially of national socialism, to which Great Britain and France seemed to acquiesce, appeared as models of systems that could overcome defeat, economic depression, and massive unemployment. While the parties of the strict imitators of these models did not manage to gain power, they forced the old established parties to move further and further to the right. This push to the right was not only the result of the successful populist-nationalist propaganda emanating mainly from Germany, but also of a steadily growing dependence on trade with Hitler's Germany, which helped the states east and south of the Reich to rebuild their Depression-ravaged economies.

There also was a growing dissatisfaction with "politics as usual," a wish to find a new way to change drastically the "old social order." The failure of communism in Germany, Hungary, and Bulgaria, coupled with the "illegal" status of the various Communist parties made moving to the left impractical for those who wanted drastic change. There was only one "master race," the German, but racism allowed the chauvinists everywhere to preach their superiority over all minorities in their midst and over their hated neighbors. It also justified the anti-Semitism, which was present, to a lesser or greater degree, everywhere. Romanian Nichifor Crainic wrote in 1938, "The Jews are a permanent danger for every national state,"[14] but this could have come from

---

13 Quoted in Frank, chapter 6.

14 Quoted in Niessen, chapter 8.

the pen of a great many people living in any one of the states in Eastern Europe. The supernationalists everywhere needed a moral code to buttress their arguments and turned to religious bigotry, which had the added usefulness of excluding Jews from their nations. Hungarians followed a "Christian-national" path; nobody could be a good Romanian who was not Orthodox; a good Pole had to be Catholic; and the Greeks followed a "Helleno-Christian civilization." This supposedly religious morality also justified the hostility towards atheistic Marxism-communism.[15]

The interwar years were also the test period for the viability of the new states, Czechoslovakia and Yugoslavia. The problems that led to the breakup of these states recently were visible and vexing already during the years of the "long armistice." On 28 October 1918, those members of the National Committee who were still in Prague proclaimed that the independent Czechoslovak state had come into being. "The several territories incorporated within the new Czechoslovakia's frontiers had never before been united as a sovereign state or even as a distinct administrative entity within another state.[16] Fusing the new states into a manageable unit depended on the success or failure of creating unified Czechoslovak and Yugoslav nations. The fusion of Czechs and Slovaks would have produced a "majority" or 66.9 percent in this new multiethnic state; the Czechs alone would have been a minority of 44.89 percent in the new republic. The largest minority group, the Germans of the Sudetenland, and the "Zipps" in Slovakia, were more numerous than

---

15 For details on the Eastern European extreme right during the interwar years, see Peter F. Sugar, ed., *Native Fascism in the Successor States, 1918–1945* (Santa Barbara: ABC-Clio, 1971); and the chapters on Hungary and Romania in Hans Rogger and Eugene Webber, eds., *The European Right: A Historical Profile* (Berkeley: University of California Press, 1966); and in Eugene Webber, ed., *Varieties of Fascism* (New York: Van Nostrand, 1964). S. J. Woolf, ed., *European Fascism* (New York: Vintage Books, 1969), has chapters on the same two states and also on Poland. Alan Cassel, *Fascism* (New York: Thomas Y. Crowell, 1975), covers Hungary and Romania (pp. 209-25). These two countries also are covered in F. L. Carsten, *The Rise of Fascism* (Berkeley: University of California Press, 1967), 169–93. Finally, Walter Laqueur and George L. Mosse, eds., *International Fascism, 1920–1945* (New York: Harper & Row, 1966), has a chapter on Romania.

16 Joseph Rothschild, *East Central Europe between the Two World Wars*, vol. 9 of *A History of East Central Europe*, Peter F. Sugar and Donald W. Treadgold, eds. (Seattle: University of Washington Press, 1974), 86.

the Slovaks.[17] The creation of a Czechoslovak nation had to fail because the economic and educational differences between the Czech and Slovak lands were too big. The percentage of illiterates in Slovakia was seven times that in the Czech lands. The number of Slovaks trained to perform judicial or civil service jobs was totally inadequate to replace the departing Hungarian functionaries. "In 1910, for example, there were only 184 Slovak speakers out of 3,683 judicial functionaries in Slovak-populated counties of northern Hungary, and only 164 Slovaks out of the other 6,185 civil servants."[18] To staff these and other offices as well as to supply the needed number of teachers, Czechs had to move into Slovakia. They looked down at the less well educated, unsophisticated, and economically backward Slovaks who, in turn, resented the replacement of Magyars by a new "foreign nation," the Czechs.

"Nation-making" failed in Yugoslavia also. R. W. Seton-Watson's statement in a letter of 17 September 1915 to Prince-Regent Alexander has a prophetic ring today:

> ...if Croatia became an independent state alongside Serbia, the situation of the latter would be still less favorable than before the war; for in that case, the two sister nations would be enemies...[19]

Once again, two documents written much later could easily have been produced in the interwar years. In 1981 Franjo Tudjman wrote the following in discussing the drawing of borders in post–World War II Yugoslavia:

> Bosnia and Hercegovina was declared a separate federal republic within the borders established during the Turkish occupation. But large parts of Croatia had been incorporated into Bosnia by the Turks...Bosnia and Hercegovina occupy the central part of this whole [Croatia], separating southern (Dalmatian) from northern (Pannonian) Croatia.[20]

---

17 See Rothschild, *East Central Europe between the Two World Wars,* 89; and Kurt Glaser, *Czech-Slovakia: A Critical History* (Caldwell, ID: Caxton Printers, 1961), 6.

18 Rothschild, *East Central Europe between the Two World Wars,* 82.

19 Quoted by Rusinow in chapter 9.

20 Quoted by Rusinow in chapter 9.

Seen from Belgrade, the situation was different. It was explained at great length by the well-known "Memorandum of the Serbian Academy of Arts and Sciences" of 1986, of which I will quote only one typical sentence:

> ...subject to continuous accusations that it is an "oppressive," "unitaristic," "centralistic," and "gendarme" nation, the Serb nation could not achieve equality in Yugoslavia, for whose creation it had made the greatest sacrifices.[21]

Sentiments like these were voiced from the very beginning. When Nikola Pašić, the prime minister of Serbia, and Ante Trumbić, president of the Yugoslav Committee, signed the Corfu Agreement on 20 July 1917,

> the delegates could not agree on the crucial issue of the internal political system, on adopting the federal principle sought by Trumbić and his associates or on the Serb-oriented centralized system demanded by Pašić. On this subject the document was left deliberately vague.[22]

When, at the end of World War I, the Serb army marched into Croatia-Slovenia, Dalamatia, Slovenia, and Bosnia-Hercegovina, Pašić and his Serb colleagues were in a position to prevail. The 28 June 1921 (Vidovan) Constitution created a highly centralized Serb-dominated government for the new state. Trumbić reacted bitterly:

> A centralist system is pushed through under the guise of unity...This constitution will sharpen the tribal [sic] conflict all the more...they are today acerbated more than under Austria-Hungary.[23]

The Serb form of government gained a pyrrhic victory, but the Serbs also gained the numerous uncomplimentary labels which the writers of the Serb Academy's memorandum resented seventy-five years later.

---

[21] Quoted by Rusinow in chapter 9.

[22] Ivo J. Lederer, *Yugoslavia at the Paris Peace Conference: A Study in Frontiermaking* (New Haven, CT: Yale University Press, 1984), 26.

[23] Ivo Banac, *The National Question in Yugoslavia: Origins, History, Politics* (Ithaca, NY: Cornell University Press, 1984), 402.

The creation of a Czechoslovak nation failed because the Czechs had to supply the Slovak lands with administrators, judges, and teachers—many of whom, unfortunately, did not hide their contempt for what they found when entering their new posts—and thus appeared to be the "conquerors" of the Slovaks. The "nation-building" experiment in the Kingdom of Serbs, Croats, and Slovenes failed because the Serbs acted like conquerors. The impressions created by the Czechs and Serbs in the interwar years carried over to the present.

Maria Todorova writes:

> The hegemony of the classical Marxist doctrine in the immediate post–World War II period...in Eastern Europe...was only a brief, and certainly not uncontested, caesura that was quickly replaced by the practice of state communism and which left its mark only on the articulation of the national idea.[24]

This statement is correct in indicating that the supremacy of the Marxist ideology was short-lived. It also is correct in stating that the various versions of "state communism" moved gradually away from Marxism and to a greater or lesser extent became versions of the "national idea" of the various people living in "People's" or "Socialist" republics.

What I would add is that while some of the early leaders of these republics might have been good theoretical Marxists, their practices were local adaptations of Stalinism. As far as nations and nationalism were concerned, Stalinist policy produced a contradiction. On the one hand, it made it quite clear that national antagonisms were wrong, a thing of the past, and that the only true and valid difference was the one separating classes. Yet, at the same time, it stressed the rights of minorities, forcing the Romanians to establish the Hungarian Autonomous Region in 1952 (it was abolished in 1967) and the Yugoslavs to create the Autonomous Province of the Vojvodina and the Autonomous Region of Kosovo-Metohija in 1946 (both were abolished in 1990).[25]

Following Stalin's death in 1953 and for the next three years—often labeled the period of de-Stalinization—there was a gradual move away from

---

[24] From chapter 3 of this volume, "The Course and Discourses of Bulgarian Nationalism."

[25] A good study dealing with the problems of minorities in post–World War II Eastern Europe is Robert R. King, *Minorities under Communism* (Cambridge, MA: Harvard University Press, 1973).

the strict enforcement of whatever passed for Marxism toward national communism. This trend could not be reversed after April 1956, when Khrushchev condemned Stalin's practices. The success of the Polish October, which brought the moderate wing of the party with Władisław Gomułka to power, and the Revolution of October-November of the same year in Hungary, signaled the birth of national communism, which had previously only been attempted in Yugoslavia.[26] Now Marxism and nationalism had to be reconciled.

"The Program of the League of the Yugoslav Communists" presented its views on national communism in 1958, without explaining them. The relevant statements read: "Yugoslav socialist patriotism...is not contrary to democratic national consciousness but is its necessary internationalist supplement." The statement continued: "...Socialist internationalism and democratic national consciousness...are not two different things but two sides of the same process."[27] The trouble with these pronouncements is that they explain nothing, although they try to bridge the ideological gap between nationalism and internationalism.

The Hungarian historian/philosopher Erik Molnár gave the required explanations in his essay on "The National Question." Proletarian patriotism,

---

[26] On the "Polish October," see M. K. Dziewanowski, *Poland in the 20th Century* (New York: Columbia University Press, 1977), 173–209; Hans Roos, *A History of Modern Poland,* J. R. Foster, translator (New York: Alfred A. Knopf, 1966), 252–89; Adam Bromke, *Poland's Politics* (Cambridge, MA: Harvard University Press, 1967), 86–121. The Hungarian Revolution produced an extensive literature. Some of the volumes produced are: United Nations, *Report of the Special Committee on the Problem of Hungary* (New York, 1957); László Beke, *A Student's Diary: Budapest, Oct. 16–Nov. 1, 1956* (New York: Viking Press, 1957); Tamás Aczél and Tibor Méray, *The Revolt of the Mind* (New York: Praeger, 1959); Tibor Méray, *Thirteen Days That Shook the Kremlin: Imre Nagy and the Hungarian Revolution* (New York: Praeger, 1959); *La Revolution Hongroise vue par les Parties Communistes de l'Europe de l'Est* (Paris: Centre d'Études Avancées du Collège de l'Europe Libre, 1957); Paul E. Zinner, *Revolution in Hungary* (New York: Columbia University Press, 1962); Richard Lettis and William E. Morris, *The Hungarian Revolt* (New York: Charles Scribner & Sons, 1961); Melvin J. Laski, ed., *A White Book: The Hungarian Revolution* (New York: Praeger, 1957); B. K. Király and Paul Jonás, eds., *The Hungarian Revolution of 1956 in Retrospect* (Boulder, CO: East European Monographs, 1978).

[27] Quoted in Rusinow, chapter 9.

the first of the two components comprising "socialist national self-awareness," was based on the "love of the progressive social order of the socialist fatherland." It was an expression of the "patriot's" willingness to defend his "socialist homeland against the attacks of the imperialist bourgeois states." Here is an attempt to redefine patriotism, a self-identifier void of the ethnically loaded term "nationalism," in a way that subordinates it to the primary loyalty due to the Marxist ideology. The second component of "socialist national self-awareness"—according to Molnár—was "proletarian internationalism." In nonsocialist states the bourgeoisie of one state fights that of all other states and also the socialist states. Within proletarian internationalism the proletariat fights the bourgeoisie of its own state and helps the proletariat of all other states to fight their bourgeoisie for their states. The result of this is that "the class war between the proletariat and the bourgeoisie" becomes "a war between states."[28] In this manner, patriotism and internationalism are reconciled. These definitions of patriotism and internationalism permitted Enver Hoxha—who was, according to Bernd Fischer, first a nationalist, second a Stalinist, and third an intellectual—to replace Albanian tribalism with a "national society."[29]

Definitions are one thing; feelings and convictions are another. In spite of the Communist regimes' emphasis on "fraternal" cooperation among "socialist" states, the old preferences and dislikes of the people did not change. Ethnic and racial biases were not eradicated. I am certain that all Western scholars, businesspeople, and other frequent visitors to the countries behind the "Iron Curtain" shared my experience: after repeated visits, when I had established a "friendly" relationship with colleague X, it was not unusual for this good "national" contact to point out that colleague Y was, after all, only a Jew or a member of a given minority. This remark never went beyond this simple labeling, but it was certainly intended as a warning. It is this concern that was expressed by the Romanian Nichifor Crainic in his "Program of the Ethnocratic State":

> A nationalist state is an ethnocratic state, that is a state that exists through the will and power of our people.

---

28 Quoted in Frank, chapter 6.

29 See Bernd J. Fischer, "Albanian Nationalism in the Twentieth Century," chapter 2 in this volume.

> The ethnocratic state differs profoundly from the democratic state...based on the number of population.... The democratic state is...a registration office.[30]

These lines were written in 1938, but could have easily come from a speech of Gheorghe Funar, the present-day (1993) mayor of Cluj or from a page of *România Mare*. What is more, it could have been written in any other country of East Central or Southeastern Europe in the 1930s or even today. The prejudice and bias expressed in these lines were directed against minorities, but it could easily have been aimed at one or another of any given country's "fraternal" neighbors. In Yugoslavia and Czechoslovakia some of the most pronounced hostile feelings were those that concerned fellow members of the "majority," as has amply been shown by the events of the last two to three years. What happened was that since 1945 expressing these feelings was simply forbidden. When the ban was lifted, the pent-up and suppressed hostilities exploded and signaled the collapse of the Yugoslav and the Czechoslovak states. They also made living with neighbors more difficult.

The peaceful separation of Slovakia from what is today the Czech Republic is certainly preferable to the civil war that has wracked what was Yugoslavia, but life in Slovakia also will become more difficult than it was before independence and this downturn will be blamed on minorities. While politicians of all countries realize that revisionist or irredentist wars (although not civil wars) are things of the past, they watch their minorities very carefully and try to defend their conationals across their borders with all other means at their disposal. While Western Europe was slowly but surely building the European Union and trying to lessen national differences, which were at least as old and bitter as those in the eastern part of the continent, development there was different. The Communists in the East also attacked the old nationalistic hostilities, but did not offer anything tangible in their place. Western unity was built on a better way of life which was made possible by the move toward unity. The Eastern governments had very little to offer besides socialist brotherhood. The West moved gradually and carefully; the East tried to change everything overnight by fiat. The people of East Central and Southeastern Europe did not enjoy being under the tutelage of the Soviet Union, resented being converted by force to a new denationalizing ideology, and as soon as they could, they began to push their governments more and more to the right with the help of national communism. This trip to the right ended in 1989–90 with the feeling that their national fight against foreign masters and ideology brought victory.

---

[30] Quoted in Niessen, chapter 8.

The ideology that made the defeat of communism possible (besides the changes occurring in the Soviet Union) was nationalism. Nationalism is still the dominant consideration in both Greece and the ex-Communist countries in the middle of the 1990s although officially all governments in East Central and Southeastern Europe proclaim that they are democratic and as such should be admitted to the European Union and NATO.

Democracy and nationalism can coexist provided that the former is dominant and the latter is a moderate, patriotic variety. This, unfortunately, is not characteristic of the 1990s in the countries surveyed in this volume. It was nationalism of an intolerant, integral variety that destroyed Czechoslovakia and Yugoslavia, that created minority problems in practically every state, and that produces propaganda statements that often lack a basis in fact and are hostile in tone directed against its neighbors by practically every nation. In spite of several agreements signed by the various governments, their policies toward each other are often hostile or at least based on suspicion of the others' intentions. Even the dream of economic self-sufficiency has resurfaced because it would guarantee independence from the good will of neighbors whom they do not like or trust. All this clearly contradicts the expressed belief in democracy and the desire to be included in a common European market.

Nationalism was the victorious ideology in 1989–90 and is still the dominant force in our region. It is the same nationalism that was responsible for the Balkan wars and World War I, that made the states emerging from the latter conflict too weak to resist first German and subsequently Soviet domination. It is this extreme form of nationalism that makes it very difficult for these states to be accepted as integral parts of a united European community. It is its extreme form that makes the victory of nationalism in East Central and Southeastern Europe a pyrrhic victory. Writing at the end of the twentieth century, one can only express the hope that by the end of the next century the nations of the area will have adopted a more constructive ideology and, as a result, will find themselves in a better position to play a normal role in European affairs.

Index

Page references to specific people and states in this index do not include those in chapters devoted specifically to them. For these, please see the Table of Contents. Titles of books, articles, and newspapers are italicized in this index; foreign words and phrases are not italicized.

Two or more capital letters refer to abbreviations for organizations or political parties. Their full names, in English or the original language, are also noted unless they are generally known (e.g., NATO, USA).

One capital letter or one capital letter followed by a lowercase letter identify nations as follows: A—Albanian; B—Bulgarian; Bo—Bosnian; C—Czech or Czechoslovak; Cr—Croatian; G—Greek; H—Hungarian; P—Polish; R—Romanian; S—Slovak; Sl—Slovene; Sr—Serb; and Y—Yugoslav.

Editor and Contributors

Peter F. Sugar is Professor Emeritus of History and International Studies at the University of Washington. He specialized in Ottoman, Southeast European, and East Central European histories. Among his works are *Industrialization of Bosnia-Hercegovina, 1878–1918;* and *Southeastern Europe under Ottoman Rule, 1354–1804.* He is also editor or co-editor of a dozen volumes dealing with Eastern Europe, including *Nationalism in Eastern Europe.*

Gerasimos Augustinos is Professor of History at the University of South Carolina. He teaches courses on Eastern Europe and comparative nationalism. His works include *The Greeks of Asia Minor: Confession, Community and Ethnicity in the 19th Century; Diverse Paths to Modernity in Eastern Europe; Consciousness and History;* and *Nationalist Critics of Greek Society.*

Bernd J. Fischer is Assistant Professor of History at Indiana-Purdue University in Fort Wayne. In addition to several articles, he has published *King Zog and His Struggle for Stability in Albania. Albania at War, 1939–1945* is in preparation.

Tibor Frank is Associate Professor at the Eötvös Loránd University in Budapest. He was Visiting Professor at the University of California in Santa Barbara and at the University of Nevada-Reno. His works include *The British Image of Hungary, 1865–1870; Marx és Kossuth;* and *Egy emigráns alakváltásai* (also available in Japanese). *Culture and Society in Early 20th Century Hungary* is the latest of several edited volumes.

Carol Skalnik Leff is Assistant Professor of Political Science at the University of Illinois, Urbana-Champaign. She specializes in Eastern European communism and politics. In addition to several articles, she has published *National Conflict in Czechoslovakia, 1918–1987.*

James P. Niessen is Subject Librarian for the Humanities at Texas Tech University. He earned his Ph.D. in East European history at Indiana University. He has published several articles and has edited *Religious Compromise, Politics of Salvation: The Greek Catholic Church and Nation-Building in Eastern Europe.* He is co-moderator of the HABSBURG electronic discussion group.

Dennison Rusinow worked for the American Universities Field Staff from 1963 until his appointment in 1988 as Research Professor and Adjunct Professor of History at the University of Pittsburgh. He has published over sixty *Field Staff Reports* and articles, mainly on Yugoslavia. His books include *The Yugoslav Experiment,* and *Yugoslavia: A Fractured Federalism.*

Anita Shelton is Associate Professor of History at Eastern Illinois University, where she teaches Russian and Eastern European history. She was Book Review Editor for three years for *Nationalities Papers.* She has published several articles on Polish history as well as *The Democratic Idea in Polish History and Historiography.*

Maria Todorova was Professor of Balkan history at the University of Sofia (Bulgaria) until 1988, when she came to the United States as a Woodrow Wilson Center Fellow. Subsequently, she taught at the University of Maryland, University of California at Irvine, and Rice University. Since 1992 she has been Associate Professor of History at the University of Florida. She has also done work at St. Anthony's College (Oxford), the Institutes for Balkan Studies in Moscow and Leningrad, and in Paris and Cambridge. Her works include *England, Russia and the Tanzimat* (also available in Russian); *British Travellers' Accounts of the Balkans, 16th–18th Centuries;* and *Balkan Family History and the European Pattern.*